OXFORD EUROPEAN COMMUNITY LAW SERIES

General Editor: F.G. Jacobs
Advocate General, The Court of Justice
of the European Communities

The External Relations of the European Communities

OXFORD EUROPEAN COMMUNITY LAW SERIES

The aim of this series is to publish important and original studies of the various branches of European Community Law. Each work will provide a clear, concise, and critical exposition of the law in its social, economic, and political context, at a level which will interest the advanced student, the practitioner, the academic, and government and Community officials.

Other Titles in this Series

The European Internal Market and International Trade: A Legal Analysis
P. Eeckhout

The Law of Money and Financial Services in the European Community
J.A. Usher

Legal Aspects of Agriculture in the European Community
J.A. Usher

European Community Sex Equality Law
Evelyn Ellis

European Community Competition Law
Second Edition
Dan Goyder

EC Tax Law
Paul Farmer and Richard Lyal

European Community Company Law
Vanessa Edwards (forthcoming)

Directives in European Community Law: A Study of Directives and their Enforcement in National Courts
Sacha Prechal

The External Relations of the European Communities

A Manual of Law and Practice

I. MACLEOD

Assistant Legal Adviser,
Foreign and Commonwealth Office, London

I. D. HENDRY

Legal Counsellor,
Foreign and Commonwealth Office, London

STEPHEN HYETT

Solicitor with the Department of Trade and Industry,
London

CLARENDON PRESS · OXFORD
1996

Oxford University Press, Walton Street, Oxford OX2 6DP
Oxford New York
Athens Auckland Bangkok Bombay
Calcutta Cape Town Dar es Salaam Delhi
Florence Hong Kong Istanbul Karachi
Kuala Lumpur Madras Madrid Melbourne
Mexico City Nairobi Paris Singapore
Taipei Tokyo Toronto
and associated companies in
Berlin Ibadan

Oxford is a trade mark of Oxford University Press

Published in the United States
by Oxford University Press Inc., New York

British Library Cataloguing in Publication Data
Data available

Library of Congress Cataloging in Publication Data
Data available
ISBN 0–19–825929–8
ISBN 0–19–825930–1 (Pbk)

1 3 5 7 9 10 8 6 4 2

Typeset by Hope Services (Abingdon) Ltd.
Printed in Great Britain
on acid-free paper by
Bookcraft Ltd.
Midsomer Norton, Bath

Les traités, voyez vous, sont comme les jeunes filles et comme les roses:
ça dure ce que ça dure.

(Treaties, you see, are like girls and roses: they last while they last.)

de Gaulle

General Editor's Foreword

The European Community (and in some respects now the European Union) is a unique entity in the international arena. The Community has wide treaty-making powers. It participates in many international organizations. It establishes diplomatic relations. Its position is far from symbolic; in many fields of international activity, not only in world trade but in many other areas, it has common policies which supplement, and sometimes wholly replace, those of its Member States. Yet the Community is not a State or an entity of a kind with which the international community has customarily had to deal.

Thus the European Community has powers, policies and programmes in the international arena which raise a wide range of wholly novel issues, both in Community law and in international law. Those issues are expertly and systematically examined in this highly original book.

Part I of the book starts from the basic features of the external relations of the European Community (where appropriate, also the ECSC and Euratom) and of the European Union. It deals with fundamental issues of principle: after explaining the legal structures of the Community and of the European Union, and their various decision-making procedures, it examines, among other matters, the international legal personality of the Community, its powers, express and implied, the issues of exclusive Community competence and shared competence, and the procedures by which each Community enters into international commitments. It discusses in depth the legal effects, both in international law and in Community law, of agreements concluded by the Community.

Where an international agreement covers matters in which Member States and the Community share competence (and competence may be shared in a number of different ways), the Community and the Member States together will normally become parties to the agreement. As the authors observe, these 'mixed agreements' are one of the most distinctive features of the external relations law and practice of the Communities, as well as one of the most difficult. The acknowledged difficulty does not preclude the authors from providing a detailed and lucid analysis of the problems attendant upon mixed agreements and their negotiation, conclusion and implementation.

Other subjects expertly dealt with in this Part include the Community's participation in international organizations – both those of which the Community is a member and those in which it has the status of an observer – and the diplomatic relations of the Community, covering relations with Member States, with third States and with international organizations.

On every topic, the authors combine legal analysis with an examination of the practice, an examination often based on first-hand experience. This combination makes their work both a textbook and an invaluable repository of practice and the evolution of the subject.

Part II, dealing with the Community's powers in practice, describes the main external powers of the Community and summarizes the activities of the Community in exercising these powers. It deals first with fisheries and transport since these are the areas where the Community's implied powers are most firmly established. It covers the common commercial policy, setting out the main features of the Community's regime for trade with the rest of the world, with the emphasis on the Community's practice in implementing the common commercial policy. But it goes beyond the traditional fields: it has chapters on education, on culture, on public health, on research and technology, on environment and on development and aid policies. It deals with economic sanctions, again setting out recent practice. It has a chapter on Association Agreements, up to and including the 'Europe Agreements' with Central and Eastern Europe. The three final chapters in this Part deal with non-nuclear energy, with Euratom and with the ECSC.

Thus the authors examine in this Part, systematically and comprehensively, the very wide range of the Community's international activities.

Part III of the work is devoted to the European Union's Common Foreign and Security Policy which, although outside the scope of the Community Treaties, is often closely related to the conduct of the Community's external relations. The Member States of the Community, which had for many years cooperated, on a primarily intergovernmental basis, in the sphere of foreign policy, introduced in the Treaty on European Union a Title V entitled 'Provisions on a common foreign and security policy'. Part III examines the Treaty structure, explains the scope of the policy, discusses the methodology and analyses the institutional framework. While the Common Foreign and Security Policy in its new Treaty format must still be regarded as embryonic, this Part is a necessary complement to the Community policies investigated in the rest of the work. It also emphasizes even more strongly the unique character of the Community/Union structure as a novel enterprise in international relations.

This remarkable work will be of interest not only to lawyers (Community and international lawyers alike) but to all those concerned with international relations in general and with the new configuration of Europe in particular.

Francis G. Jacobs
October 1995

Preface

The aim of this book is to state briefly the laws and practices which govern the conduct of the external relations of the European Communities. The focus is on what the law is. We have not attempted to give an historical account of the development of the law, nor to say what we think the law ought to be. Both are interesting and important subjects in their own right, but to treat them fully would have required more time and opportunity for research than were available to us.

There are several reasons for trying to write a book like this now. The Union created by the Maastricht Treaty is important for relations between the Member States and the outside world, and is founded on the European Communities: a summary of the law on the external relations of the Communities is therefore timely. Furthermore, the last few years have seen many dramatic developments in this area of Community law. The fourth enlargement of the Communities has just occurred; the European Community became a full member of a UN Specialised Agency for the first time when it acceded to the FAO in December 1991; relations with the rest of Europe are being transformed by a range of association and co-operation agreements; and the European Community became a member of the WTO in December 1994. The Court of Justice has also been active: more Opinions were delivered under Article 228 EC in the last four years than were delivered in the previous history of the Communities. Two further important Opinions are awaited, and many other recent cases have dealt with questions about the Communities' external powers.

But the main reason for writing this book was that, to our knowledge, there has been no recent statement of the rules and practices which govern the external relations of the Communities. As a result, important and interesting areas of Community and international law have been largely ignored. This book is an attempt to begin to fill that huge gap: we hope it will encourage others to explore the field in more depth.

We owe an immense debt of gratitude to many colleagues in Whitehall and in Brussels. Several took the time to read over parts of the manuscript: their comments and suggestions always improved the text. Others contributed unwittingly to the book over the years by their requests for advice. Special mention should be made of Claire Bury, now of the Commission Legal Service, who was a co-author for most of the period of writing. Without her encouragement and enthusiasm the book would not have been begun, and Chapters 7, 8, 12, 17, 18 and 19 in particular owe much to her. But none of these colleagues is responsible for the final shape or content of the book: its errors and blemishes are our responsibility.

We are very grateful too to our publishers, Oxford University Press, for their assistance and advice throughout. Above all, however, our deepest thanks go to our families, in particular Alison MacLeod, Annabel Hendry and Robin Legard, without whose patience, understanding and constant encouragement our efforts would have been abandoned long ago.

The opinions expressed in what follows are our own, and should not be taken as an expression of official government policy. The writing of this book has not been subsidised by any public or private source.

We have tried to state the law as at 8 May 1995, but it has been possible to take account of some developments after that date.

IM
IDH
ASH

Short Table of Contents

Part III

Table of Contents

Part III

Table of Abbreviations

ACP	African, Caribbean, and Pacific States
AG	Advocate-General
AETR	See discussion of Case 22/70 *Commission* v. *Council*
AFDI	*Annuaire français de droit international*
AJIL	*American Journal of International Law*
Bull. EC	Bulletin of the European Communities (monthly)
BYIL	*British Yearbook of International Law*
CCP	Common commercial policy
CCT	Common Customs Tariff
CDE	*Cahiers de droit européen*
CFI	Court of First Instance
CFSP	Common foreign and security policy
CLP	*Current Legal Problems*
CMLR	Common Market Law Reports
CMLRev.	*Common Market Law Review*
Cm/Cmnd./Cmd.	United Kingdom Command Paper
COREPER	Committee of Permanent Representatives
EAEC	European Atomic Energy Community (Euratom)
EBRD	European Bank for Reconstruction and Development
EC	European Community
ECB	European Central Bank
ECJ	European Court of Justice
ECR	European Court Reports
ECSC	European Coal and Steel Community
EDF	European Development Fund
EEA	European Economic Area
EEC	European Economic Community
EFTA	European Free Trade Association
EJIL	*European Journal of International Law*
ELRev.	*European Law Review*
EP	European Parliament
EPC	European Political Co-operation
ERTA	See discussion of Case 22/70 *Commission* v. *Council*
EU	European Union
Euratom	European Atomic Energy Community
FAO	Food and Agriculture Organization
FSU	Former Soviet Union
GATS	General Agreement on Trade in Services

GATT	General Agreement on Tariffs and Trade
General Report	Commission's General Report on the activities of the European Community/Union (annual)
Germ.YBIL	*German Yearbook of International Law*
Hague Recueil	*Recueil des cours de l'Académie de droit international*
HL	House of Lords
ICJ	International Court of Justice
ICLQ	*International and Comparative Law Quarterly*
ILC	International Law Commission
ILO	International Labour Organization
JCMS	*Journal of Common Market Studies*
JDI	*Journal de Droit International*
JO	Journal Officiel (French version of the OJ)
JWTL	*Journal of World Trade Law*
LIEI	*Legal Issues of European Integration*
NATO	North Atlantic Treaty Organization
Neth. YBIL	*Netherlands Yearbook of International Law*
OCT	Overseas Countries and Territories
OECD	Organization for Economic Co-operation and Development
OJ	Official Journal of the European Communities
PCIJ	Permanent Court of International Justice
REIO	regional economic integration organization
RGDIP	*Revue Générale de droit international public*
RMC	*Revue du Marché Commun*
RTDE	*Revue Trimestrielle de Droit Européen*
SEA	Single European Act
TEU	Treaty on European Union
UKTS	United Kingdom Treaty Series
UNCLOS	United Nations Convention on the Law of the Sea
UNCTAD	United Nations Conference on Trade and Development
UNJY	*United Nations Juridical Yearbook*
UNTS	United Nations Treaty Series
VCLT	Vienna Convention on the Law of Treaties
VCLTIO	Vienna Convention on the Law of Treaties between States and International Organizations or between International Organizations
WEU	Western European Union
WIPO	World Intellectual Property Organization
WTO	World Trade Organization
YBEL	*Yearbook of European Law*

Table of Cases

Table of Treaties establishing the European Communities and the European Union

Table of Secondary Measures

Table of Agreements

List of Frequently Cited Works

Brownlie	I. Brownlie, *Principles of Public International Law* (4th edn., Clarendon Press, Oxford, 1990)
General Report	*General Report on the Activities of the European Communities* (annually) (Commission, Brussels and Luxembourg). (Since 1994, the *General Report* is entitled *General Report on the Activities of the European Union*).
Groux and Manin	J. Groux and P. Manin, *The European Communities in the International Order* (European Perspectives, Brussels and Luxembourg, 1985)
Halsbury's Laws	*Halsbury's Laws of England* (4th edn., Butterworths, London, 1986), li and lii
Hartley	T. C. Hartley, *The Foundations of European Community Law* (3rd edn., Clarendon Press, Oxford, 1994)
Kapteyn and VerLoren van Themaat	P. J. G. Kapteyn and P. VerLoren van Themaat, *Introduction to the Law of the European Communities* (2nd edn by Gormley, Kluwer, Deventer, 1989)
Lasok and Bridge	D. Lasok and J. W. Bridge, *Law and Institutions of the European Union* (6th edn., Butterworths, London, 1994)
Mégret	J. Mégret *et al.*, *Le droit de la Communauté Européenne*, vol. 12: *Relations Extérieures* by J. V. Louis and P. Bruckner (Brussels 1980)
Oppenheim	Oppenheim, *International Law* (9th edn. by Sir R. Y. Jennings and Sir A. D. Watts, Longman, London, 1992), i (Peace)
Relations	*Relations between the European Community and International Organizations* (Commission, Brussels and Luxembourg, 1989)
Satow	Satow, *Guide to Diplomatic Practice* (5th edn., by Lord Gore-Booth, Longman, London, 1979)
Sinclair	Sir I. Sinclair, *The Vienna Convention on the Law of Treaties* (2nd edn., Manchester University Press, Manchester, 1984)
Smit and Herzog	H. Smit and P. Herzog, *The Law of the European Community* (New York, 1976)
Wyatt and Dashwood	D. Wyatt and A. A. Dashwood, *European Community Law* (3rd edn., Sweet and Maxwell, London, 1993)

PART I

The External Relations of the Communities: General Aspects

This Part summarizes the rules of law and practice which govern the exercise of the external competence of the Communities.

Chapter 1 outlines the legal structures of the Communities and the Union under the Treaties, and the procedures for decision-making within these structures. Chapter 2 considers the international legal personality of the Communities, and some of the implications of that personality. Chapter 3 describes the sources, extent, and nature of the legal powers conferred on the Communities under the Treaties.

Chapter 4 sets out the procedures by which each Community undertakes international commitments. Chapter 5 is about the legal effect of agreements concluded by the Communities in international and Community law. Chapter 6 examines the meaning and consequences of the concept of the 'mixed agreement'.

Chapter 7 outlines the legal rules governing the Communities' participation in international organizations, and summarizes the practice to date. Chapter 8 considers the extent to which the Communities may be said to conduct diplomatic relations.

Chapter 9 examines some of the ways in which the powers of the Communities interact with those of the Member States.

1

The European Communities and the European Union:
The Basic Legal Structure

In law there are three European Communities: the European Coal and Steel Community (ECSC), the European Community (EC)—which was originally called the European Economic Community (EEC), and the European Atomic Energy Community (Euratom). They are distinct legal entities established by separate treaties. There is also the European Union, which was also established by treaty but which has no legal personality. This introductory chapter describes the basic legal structure of the Communities and the Union.[1]

THE EUROPEAN COMMUNITIES

The Community Treaties

The ECSC Treaty[2] was signed in Paris on 18 April 1951 and entered into force on 25 July 1952. It is sometimes called the Treaty of Paris. The contracting parties were the original six Member States: Belgium, France, Germany, Italy, Luxembourg, and the Netherlands. The duration of the Treaty is fifty years. By the Treaty the Member States established the ECSC, 'founded upon a common market, common objectives and common institutions', as a separate entity with international legal personality. The Treaty set up four institutions of the ECSC: a High Authority, which was given supranational legislative and executive powers to control the production and distribution of coal and steel; a Common Assembly representing the peoples of the Member States, with supervisory powers; a Special Council of Ministers, consisting of Ministers representing the Member States, with legislative and consultative powers; and a Court of Justice,

---

[1] Within the confines of this book, it can only be a summary. For greater detail, see such standard works as Hartley, *The Foundations of European Community Law* (3rd edn., Clarendon, 1994); Wyatt and Dashwood, *European Community Law* (3rd edn., Sweet & Maxwell, 1993); Vaughan (ed.), *Law of the European Communities* (Butterworths, 1986); D. A. O. Edward and R. C. Lane, *European Community Law* (Butterworths, 1991); Mégret *et al.* (eds.), *Le Droit de la Communauté Économique Européenne* (Université de Bruxelles, 1991–3); Kapteyn and VerLoren van Themaat, *Introduction to the Law of the European Communities* (2nd edn., Gormley (ed.), Kluwer, 1990); Lasok and Bridge, *Law and Institutions of the European Union* (6th edn., Butterworths, 1992). See also J. C. Piris, *After Maastricht, are the Community Institutions More Efficacious, More Democratic and More Transparent?* (1994) 19 *ELRev.* 449; A. A. Dashwood, *Community Legislative Procedures in the Era of the Treaty on European Union* (1994) 19 *ELRev.* 343.

[2] UKTS 2 (1973); Cmnd. 5189.

with the responsibility to ensure that in the interpretation and application of the Treaty the law was observed. In short, the Member States agreed to share and surrender part of their sovereignty within the new Community for limited purposes.

The EEC Treaty[3] and the Euratom Treaty[4] were signed at Rome on 25 March 1957 and entered into force on 1 January 1958. The contracting parties were the six Member States of the ECSC. The Treaties were concluded for an unlimited period. Each established a distinct entity with international legal personality. The task of Euratom was to create the conditions necessary for the speedy establishment and growth of nuclear industries. The scope of the EEC Treaty, sometimes called the Treaty of Rome, was much broader; it aimed to establish a common market for all forms of economic activity outside the scope of the ECSC and Euratom Treaties. Like the ECSC Treaty, the EEC and Euratom Treaties each established four autonomous institutions with supranational powers: an Assembly, a Council of Ministers, a Commission (equivalent to the ECSC High Authority, but with less legislative power), and a Court of Justice. These Treaties made the Council the main legislative organ, acting almost exclusively on proposals by the Commission, with the Assembly having a consultative role.

By virtue of the Convention on Certain Institutions Common to the European Communities,[5] which entered into force on the same day as the EEC and Euratom Treaties, the three Communities shared a single Assembly and a single Court of Justice. But each Community had a separate Council, the EEC and Euratom had separate Commissions, and the ECSC had its High Authority. This continued until 1 July 1967, when the Treaty establishing a Single Council and a Single Commission of the European Communities[6] entered into force. This Treaty (often called 'the Merger Treaty') established a single Council for the three Communities and merged the ECSC High Authority and the EEC and Euratom Commissions into a single Commission for the three Communities.

In 1970 the Community Treaties were amended to give the Assembly greater powers in relation to the budget of the Communities.[7] At the same time the system of financing the budget by contributions from the Member States was replaced by the 'own resources' system.[8] The Assembly's powers in respect of the budget were further enhanced by treaty amendments in 1975.[9] The Treaties

---

[3] UKTS 1 (1973)—Pt. II; Cmnd. 5179–II.   [4] UKTS 1 (1973)—Pt. II; Cmnd. 5179–II.

[5] UKTS 1 (1973)—Pt. II; Cmnd. 5179–II.

[6] UKTS 1 (1973)—Pt. II; Cmnd. 5179–II; [1967] OJ 152.

[7] Treaty amending Certain Budgetary Provisions ('the First Budgetary Treaty'), Luxembourg, 22 Apr. 1970: [1971] OJ L2/1.

[8] See Council Dec. 70/243 of 21 Apr. 1970 ([1970] OJ L94/19), since repealed. At the time of writing, the current Own Resources Decision is Council Dec. 94/728 of 31 Oct. 1994 ([1994] OJ L293/9). The relevant treaty Arts. are now Arts. 201 EC, 173 Euratom, and 49–50 ECSC.

[9] Treaty amending Certain Financial Provisions ('the Second Budgetary Treaty'), Brussels, 22 July 1975 ([1977] OJ L359/1).

were amended and supplemented in 1976 to provide for direct elections to the Assembly.[10] Meanwhile the membership of the three Communities was enlarged, and the Treaties were amended and supplemented to deal with this. The first enlargement saw the accession of the United Kingdom, Denmark, and Ireland on 1 January 1973.[11] Greece joined the Communities on 1 January 1981,[12] and Spain and Portugal acceded on 1 January 1986.[13] In 1985 Greenland, which was part of the Communities by virtue of its dependence on Denmark, withdrew following a referendum in the territory in 1982.[14]

Substantial amendments to the Community Treaties were made by a treaty called the Single European Act,[15] which was signed by the twelve Member States at Luxembourg on 17 February 1986 and at The Hague on 28 February 1986. It came into force on 1 July 1987. Its main effect was to provide the necessary decision-making processes to enable the Community internal market to be completed, by the removal of the remaining barriers to trade within the Community, before a target date of 31 December 1992. To this end it increased the scope for legislative decisions to be taken by majority voting in the Council. It also enhanced the powers of the Assembly in the legislative process, and formally renamed the Assembly 'the European Parliament'. It clarified the scope for the Council to delegate to the Commission the power to adopt measures to implement Community legislation. In addition, it expanded the substantive scope for action under the EEC Treaty, particularly in the fields of economic and monetary policy, social policy, economic and social cohesion, research and technological development, and the environment.

Further important amendments to the Community Treaties were made by Titles II, III, and IV of the Treaty on European Union (TEU),[16] which was signed by the twelve Member States at Maastricht on 7 February 1992 and came into force on 1 November 1993. The EEC became the 'European Community' (EC), and the EEC Treaty (as amended) became the Treaty establishing the European Community (the EC Treaty).[17] This change reflected the progressive expansion in the scope of the EC Treaty since 1957. The TEU

---

[10] Council Dec. 76/787 and Act concerning the Election of the Representatives of the Assembly by Direct Universal Suffrage, 20 Sept. 1976 ([1976] OJ L278/5).

[11] Treaty concerning the Accession of the Kingdom of Denmark, Ireland, the Kingdom of Norway, and the United Kingdom of Great Britain and Northern Ireland to the European Economic Community and the European Atomic Energy Community, Brussels, 22 Jan. 1972 (UKTS 18 (1979); Cmnd. 7463; [1972] OJ L73/5), and Dec. of Accession to the European Coal and Steel Community (*ibid.*). Following a referendum, Norway did not ratify and the instruments of accession were amended accordingly: see Council Dec. of 1 Jan. 1973 ([1973] OJ L2/1).

[12] Treaty of Accession 1979 (EC 18 (1979); Cmnd.7650; [1979] OJ L291/9).

[13] Treaty of Accession 1985 (EC 27 (1985); Cmnd. 9634; [1985] OJ L302/9).

[14] Treaty amending, with regard to Greenland, the Treaties establishing the European Communities, Brussels, 13 Mar. 1984 (EC 19 (1985); Cmnd. 9490; [1985] OJ L29/1).

[15] EC 12 (1986); Cmnd. 9758; [1987] OJ L169/1.

[16] UKTS 12 (1994); Cm. 2485; [1992] OJ C191/1.   [17] Art. G(1) TEU.

contributed to this by increasing and rationalizing the EC's objectives and tasks and the policy areas for Community action, above all with the aim of gradually achieving economic and monetary union. It enhanced the powers of the European Parliament, especially in the legislative process, where in many areas the Parliament acquired the power of 'co-decision' with the Council. It increased the subjects on which legislative decisions could be taken by majority voting in the Council. It introduced subsidiarity as a principle of general application. It enhanced the status of the Court of Auditors, making it an institution of the three Communities alongside the Parliament, the Council, the Commission, and the Court of Justice. It gave the Court of Justice new powers to impose fines on Member States which fail to comply with its judgments.

Other treaties and agreements have since modified or supplemented the Community Treaties. The composition of the European Parliament has been increased to take account of German unification[18] (which had been substantially accommodated in 1990 without the need for treaty amendment). Two inter-governmental Decisions were agreed in December 1992: one settled long-standing arguments about the seats of the Communities' institutions;[19] the other dealt with certain Danish concerns about the TEU and eased the way for Danish ratification.[20] A new budgetary 'own resources' Decision was adopted in 1994.[21] Finally, the Community Treaties were modified and supplemented to take account of the accession, with effect from 1 January 1995, of Austria, Finland, and Sweden.[22]

Accordingly, the Community Treaties have undergone many changes, and there are several related treaties and other instruments. Together they comprise the constitutional instruments of the Communities. Collectively they are some-times described as 'the Treaties establishing the European Communities and the subsequent Treaties and Acts modifying and supplementing them'.[23]

The French text of the ECSC Treaty is the sole authentic text. Otherwise the texts of the Community Treaties in the following languages are equally authen-tic: Danish, Dutch, English, Finnish, French, German, Greek, Irish, Italian, Portuguese, Spanish, and Swedish. Council Regulation 1 of 15 April 1958,[24] as

---

[18] Council Dec. of 1 Feb. 1993 amending the Act of 20 Sept. 1976 ([1993] OJ L33/15).

[19] Dec. taken by common agreement between the Representatives of the Governments of the Member States on the location of the seats of the institutions and of certain bodies and departments of the European Communities, Edinburgh, 12 Dec. 1992 ([1992] OJ C341/1). See also the Dec. of 8 Apr. 1965 ([1967] OJ 152/18).

[20] Edinburgh European Council, 11 and 12 Dec. 1992, Conclusions of the Presidency, Pt. B ([1992]OJ C348/1).

[21] Council Dec. 94/728 of 31 Oct. 1994 ([1994] OJ L293/9).

[22] Treaty of Accession concerning the accession of the Kingdom of Norway, the Republic of Austria, the Republic of Finland and the Kingdom of Sweden to the European Union (EC 7 (1994); Cm. 2606; [1994] OJ C241/1). Following a referendum, Norway did not ratify and the Treaty was amended accordingly: see Council Dec. of 1 Jan. 1995 ([1995] OJ L1/1).

[23] See e.g. Arts. E and M TEU.

[24] [1958] OJ 17/385 (as amended by each Act of Accession).

amended, provides that the official languages and the working languages of the Community institutions are Danish, Dutch, English, Finnish, French, German, Greek, Italian, Portuguese, Spanish, and Swedish. Community legislation is adopted and published in all eleven official languages. There is provision for the use of Irish, in addition to these eleven languages, at the Court of Justice in accordance with the Court's Rules of Procedure (although in practice the use of Irish is rare).

The Aims and Objectives of the Communities

From the beginning the Communities were conceived as having long-term political aims, to be achieved through economic means. The Schuman Declaration, which led to the ECSC Treaty, spoke of 'common foundations of economic development as a first step towards a European Federation'.[25] In the preamble to the ECSC Treaty the original six resolved 'to substitute for age-old rivalries the merging of their essential interests' and 'to create, by establishing an economic community, the basis for a broader and deeper community among peoples long divided by bloody conflicts'. In the preamble to the EEC Treaty they expressed their determination 'to lay the foundations for an ever closer union among the peoples of Europe'. The twelve Member States expressed their will, in the preamble to the Single European Act, to continue the work undertaken on the basis of the Community Treaties and 'to transform relations as a whole among their States into a European Union'. The meaning of this aspiration to political union was, and remains, highly controversial. The Treaty on European Union established a 'European Union', but this did not constitute a single, federal State subsuming the individual Member States. The Member States agreed to pool their sovereignty to a greater degree than hitherto, but they remain independent sovereign States. The preamble to the Treaty notes their resolve 'to mark a new stage in the process of European integration undertaken with the establishment of the European Communities' and 'to continue the process of creating an ever closer union among the peoples of Europe, in which decisions are taken as closely as possible to the citizen in accordance with the principle of subsidiarity'. So the way to further political integration was left open, should the Member States choose to take it.

Against the background of these political aims, the objectives of the Community Treaties are set out in their opening Articles. The task of the ECSC is 'to contribute, in harmony with the general economy of the Member States and through the establishment of a common market as provided in Article 4, to economic expansion, growth of employment and a rising standard of living'.[26] The means of achieving this are then described in greater detail. The

---

[25] Documents on International Affairs (1949–50), 315 (in French): 22 Department of State Bull., 936 (English translation).
[26] Art. 2 ECSC.

task of Euratom is 'to contribute to the raising of the standard of living in the Member States and to the development of relations with other countries by creating the conditions necessary for the speedy establishment and growth of nuclear industries'.[27] Again, the means of achieving this aim are then spelt out.

The EC has broader objectives. Article 2 of the EC Treaty provides:

> The Community shall have as its task, by establishing a common market and an economic and monetary union and by implementing the common policies or activities referred to in Articles 3 and 3a, to promote throughout the Community a harmonious and balanced development of economic activities, sustainable and non-inflationary growth respecting the environment, a high degree of convergence of economic performance, a high level of employment and of social protection, the raising of the standard of living and quality of life, and economic and social cohesion and solidarity among Member States.

Articles 3 and 3a then describe at some length the activities of the Community 'for the purposes set out in Article 2'. These are elaborated in Part Three of the Treaty, under the heading 'Community policies', in a series of 'Titles' covering: free movement of goods; agriculture (including fisheries); free movement of persons, services, and capital; transport; common rules on competition, taxation, and approximation of laws; economic and monetary policy; common commercial policy; social policy, education, vocational training, and youth; culture; public health; consumer protection; trans-European networks; industry; economic and social cohesion; research and technological development; environment; and development co-operation. Part Four of the Treaty deals with the association of certain overseas countries and territories having special relations with some of the Member States.

The bulk of each of the Community Treaties sets out a detailed framework for action by the institutions to achieve its prescribed objectives, though the Treaties also contain several substantive provisions. The action envisaged by the Treaties is both internal and external. The Communities and their institutions may only act within the limits of the powers (or 'competence') conferred upon them by the Treaties[28] and in accordance with the applicable procedures prescribed by the Treaties. But it is vital to keep in mind the aims and objectives of each Community, in particular by reference to the opening Treaty Articles and the preambles, since they are regarded, most importantly by the Court of Justice, as an essential yardstick for determining the extent and scope of the powers of the Communities and their institutions.

---

[27] Art. 1 Euratom.

[28] Arts. 4 EC, 3 Euratom, 3 ECSC. See further pp. 17–18 below. The nature of competence is discussed in detail in Ch. 3.

The Institutions of the Communities

The Community Treaties accord the status of 'institution' to five bodies: the European Parliament, the Council, the Commission, the Court of Justice, and the Court of Auditors.[29] The Treaties also establish a number of other bodies which do not have the status of institution, such as the Economic and Social Committee[30] and the Committee of the Regions,[31] which have an advisory function, and the European Investment Bank.[32]

The Treaty on European Union formally reconstitutes the European Council, composed of the Heads of State or Government of the Member States and the President of the Commission.[33] While the European Council, which meets at least twice a year, plays a leading role in providing political direction, it is not a Community institution and has no powers in the formal legislative process. In particular, it should not be confused with the Council.

The European Parliament

The Parliament consists of representatives of the peoples of the States brought together in the Community.[34] Its members, often called MEPs, are elected by direct universal suffrage for a term of five years.[35] It has 626 members, who are elected from the Member States in numbers very roughly proportionate to their respective populations.[36]

The Parliament has varying powers in relation to legislation. Under the ECSC and Euratom Treaties, and in some areas of policy under the EC Treaty, the Council must consult the Parliament before adopting a legislative act. This is known as the 'consultation procedure'. The opinion of the Parliament is advisory, and does not bind the Council. But the EC Treaty gives the Parliament greater powers in several important fields of policy. In some cases, the 'co-operation procedure' applies: this gives the Parliament two separate readings, the first on the Commission's proposal and the second after the Council has reached a 'common position'.[37] The procedure is complex, and the effect is to give the Parliament greater influence but ultimately no decisive power. In other fields of activity, the Parliament has a power of 'co-decision' with the Council in the adoption of legislation.[38] The procedure is even more complex, and can involve a formal conciliation process between the Parliament and the Council; in the last resort the Parliament can veto the proposed legislation (hence the procedure is sometimes called the 'negative assent procedure'). In a few cases,

---

[29] Arts. 4 EC, 3 Euratom, 7 ECSC.
[30] Arts. 193–198 EC, 165–170 Euratom.
[31] Arts. 198a–198c EC.
[32] Arts. 4b, 198d, and 198e EC.
[33] Art. D TEU. Art. 2 SEA first provided a treaty basis for the European Council; it was repealed by Art. P(2) TEU.
[34] Arts. 137 EC, 107 Euratom, 20 ECSC.
[35] Arts. 1 and 3, Act of 20 Sept. 1976.
[36] Art. 2, Act of 20 Sept. 1976, as amended.
[37] Art. 189c EC.
[38] Art. 189b EC. See Dashwood, n. 1 above.

the (positive) assent of the Parliament is required before an act can be adopted.[39] To determine which procedure is applicable in a particular case, it is necessary to examine the Treaty Article under which the proposed action is to be taken. It is obviously important to proceed on the basis of the correct Article (known as the 'legal basis'), and if this is not done the act is liable to be annulled by the Court of Justice.[40]

The role of the Parliament in the process of concluding international agreements varies as between the three Community Treaties.[41] It is most extensive in the EC Treaty, which provides that, as a rule, the Parliament must be consulted before the Community can conclude an agreement.[42] In these cases the Parliament's opinion is advisory. But some important types of agreement may not be concluded until the assent of the Parliament has been obtained.[43]

In practice, the Council and the Commission often consult the Parliament voluntarily about a proposal for action, even in cases where the Treaties do not require it.

The Parliament has considerable powers in relation to the Community budget. The Treaties prescribe a complex balance of powers between the Parliament, the Council, and the Commission in the budgetary procedure.[44] The Parliament may in the last resort reject the budget outright, and it has exercised this power.[45] The Parliament also has important powers in relation to the Commission, which must answer questions put to it by the Parliament or its Members.[46] The Parliament's approval is required before a new Commission can be appointed;[47] and if the Parliament passes a motion of censure on the Commission, the members of the Commission must resign as a body.[48] Among its other powers, the Parliament may establish committees of inquiry,[49] hear petitions,[50] and appoint an Ombudsman.[51]

The Council

The Council consists of 'a representative of each Member State at ministerial level, authorised to commit the government of that Member State'. Each

[39] See Arts. 8a and 228(3)(2nd subpara.) EC.
[40] See e.g. Case C–300/89 *Commission* v. *Council (Titanium Dioxide)* [1991] ECR 2867.
[41] See Ch. 4.
[42] Art. 228(3) (1st subpara.) EC. See also Art. 206 Euratom. There is no equivalent provision in the ECSC Treaty.
[43] Art. 228(3) (2nd subpara.) EC.
[44] Arts. 199–209 EC, 171–180b Euratom, 78–78g ECSC.
[45] Art. 203(8) EC. The Parliament rejected the draft budget in 1980, 1982, 1986, and 1988.
[46] Arts. 140 EC, 110 Euratom, 23 ECSC.
[47] Arts. 158(2) EC, 127(2) Euratom, 10 ECSC.
[48] Arts. 144 EC, 114 Euratom, 24 ECSC.
[49] Arts. 138c EC, 107b Euratom, 20b ECSC.
[50] Arts. 138d EC, 107c Euratom, 20c ECSC.
[51] Arts. 138e EC, 107d Euratom, 20d ECSC.

Member State takes it in turn to hold the office of President, according to a prescribed order. The term of each Presidency is six months.[52]

In practice the Council meets in various formats, according to the subjects for discussion. So, for example, for agriculture matters the Council is composed of national ministers for agriculture, and for economic and financial questions it is composed of finance ministers; and the Council is then called the Agriculture Council or the Economic and Finance Council (or Ecofin), as appropriate. A supervisory, co-ordinating role is assumed by the General Affairs Council, composed of Foreign Ministers (hence often called the Foreign Affairs Council), which is also responsible for institutional questions. But constitutionally the Council is one and indivisible, and so its powers can be exercised at a meeting of the Council in any format, irrespective of the subject matter. The Council can also take urgent decisions without meeting, according to a written procedure.[53]

Under the ECSC Treaty the Council has a largely supervisory role; the Commission has most legislative power, subject to the assent of the Council in certain cases. By contrast, the Council is the pre-eminent legislative authority under the EC and Euratom Treaties. The Treaty Article forming the legal basis for the proposed action specifies the procedure and often the form of legislative instrument. With few exceptions, the Council must act 'on a proposal from the Commission', which means a text drawn up by the Commission and formally submitted to the Council as the Commission's proposal; and, again with few exceptions, the Council may only amend a Commission proposal (against the Commission's will) by unanimous vote.[54] As noted above in the discussion of the Parliament, the Council is often required to follow a procedure involving the Parliament before it can act; and under the co-decision procedure legislative acts are adopted jointly by the Council and the Parliament.[55] Various Treaty Articles also require the Council to consult other bodies, such as the Economic and Social Committee and the Committee of the Regions. The Council shares power with the Parliament in the adoption of the Community budget.[56]

In the external field, the Council has the principal responsibility for the conclusion of agreements, which are negotiated by the Commission subject to the Council's authorization and in accordance with directives issued by the Council.[57]

---

[52] Arts. 146 EC, 116 Euratom, 27 ECSC. From 1 Jan. 1995 the Presidency is to be held in the following order: France, Spain, Italy, Ireland, Netherlands, Luxembourg, United Kingdom, Austria, Germany, Finland, Portugal, France, Sweden, Belgium, Spain, Denmark, Greece (see Council Dec. 95/2 of 1 Jan. 1995: [1995] OJ L1/220).
[53] Art. 8 Council Rules of Procedure (Council Dec. of 6 Dec. 1993: [1993] OJ L304/1). On the consequences of failing to follow the written procedure, see Case 68/86 *United Kingdom* v. *Council* [1988] ECR 855.
[54] Arts. 189a(1) EC, 119 Euratom.   [55] See Arts. 190 and 191 EC.   [56] See n. 44 above.
[57] Arts. 228 EC, 206 Euratom. See Ch. 4. The powers of the Commission are greater under the ECSC Treaty: see Ch. 23.

Decision-making in the Council is either by unanimity, qualified majority, or simple majority. A simple majority (meaning a majority of the Member States) suffices save where the Treaty provides otherwise.[58] In fact few substantive decisions may be taken by simple majority since a different rule is most often specified, but it is the general rule for procedural questions. Where unanimity is required by the Treaty, abstentions are not counted.[59] Where, as in most cases, a qualified majority is required, the votes of the Member States are weighted very roughly according to their respective populations.[60] For the Council to act by qualified majority, sixty-two votes in favour are required out of a total of eighty-seven; and in some cases at least ten Member States must also have voted in favour.[61] According to the so-called 'Luxembourg Compromise',[62] some Member States maintain that a decision which may be taken by majority vote must be postponed while discussion continues, if necessary indefinitely (which would amount to a veto) or until unanimous agreement is reached, if a Member State considers that it would affect its 'very important interests'. The compromise has been invoked rarely and not always successfully, and some Member States deny it any validity. It is not mentioned in the Treaties.

The Council is assisted by a Committee consisting of the Permanent Representatives of the Member States (known by its French acronym COREPER[63]). COREPER is responsible 'for preparing the work of the Council and for carrying out the tasks assigned to it by the Council'.[64] In practice the workload is such that COREPER meets in two formats, or 'parts': part I consists of the Deputy Permanent Representatives, and part II consists of the Permanent Representatives (Ambassadors).[65] Each part meets weekly for at least a day, and in a real sense represents continuity in the negotiating process. COREPER seeks to resolve as many issues as possible, and where it reaches

---

[58] Arts. 148(1) EC, 118(1) Euratom, 28 ECSC (but there the rule is qualified).

[59] Arts. 148(3) EC, 118(3) Euratom, 28 ECSC (where the rule is qualified).

[60] The votes are weighted as follows: Germany, France, Italy, and the UK each has 10 votes; Spain has 8 votes; Belgium, Greece, Netherlands, and Portugal each has 5 votes; Austria and Sweden each has 4 votes; Denmark, Finland, and Ireland each has 3 votes; and Luxembourg has 2 votes.

[61] Arts. 148(2) EC, 118(2) Euratom, 28 ECSC. Under the 'Ioannina Agreement', if members of the Council representing a total of 23 to 25 votes indicate their intention to oppose adoption of a decision by qualified majority, the Council is required to do all in its power to reach a solution that could be adopted by at least 65 votes: see Council Dec. of 29 March 1994 ([1994] OJ C105/1) as amended by Council Dec. of 1 Jan. 1995 ([1995] OJ C1/1).

[62] The full text of the Luxembourg Compromise is published in the EC Bull., Mar. 1966, 8.

[63] COmité des REprésentants PERmanents. See Noel, '*The Committee of Permanent Representatives*'(1966) 5 JCMS 219.

[64] Arts. 151(1) EC, 121(1) Euratom, 30(1) ECSC. See also Art. 19 Council Rules of Procedure. By informal understanding, COREPER operates in French, English, and German only.

[65] The allocation of subjects to each part of COREPER is varied from time to time according to relative workload. At the time of writing, Deputies prepare Budget, Education, Environment, Fish, Health, Internal Market, Social Affairs, Transport, Research, Energy, and Telecommunications Councils; Ambassadors prepare Foreign Affairs, Economic and Finance, Development, Industry, and Justice and Home Affairs Councils.

agreement the Council adopts the relevant decision without discussion.[66] Where COREPER cannot reach agreement, it seeks to minimize the unresolved points and present them clearly for discussion and decision by the Council. The work of COREPER is in turn prepared, according to a similar process, by several specialist committees and working groups consisting of officials from the Member States.[67]

The Council is served by a General Secretariat[68] (often called the Council Secretariat), headed by a Secretary-General and including a Legal Service. Apart from providing the necessary translation, interpretation, and documentary services, the Secretariat and its Legal Service often provide helpful independent advice and mediation skills, and are represented at meetings of the Council, COREPER, and the other committees and working groups.

The Commission

The Commission consists of twenty members 'who shall be chosen on the grounds of their general competence and whose independence is beyond doubt'. Only nationals of the Member States may be members of the Commission; it must include at least one national of each Member State, but may not include more than two members having the nationality of the same State.[69] By convention, the membership includes two nationals of each of the five largest Member States (France, Germany, Italy, Spain, and the United Kingdom) and one national of each of the other Member States. The Commissioners must be 'completely independent in the performance of their duties' and 'neither seek nor take instructions from any Government or from any other body'. The Member States are obliged 'not to seek to influence the members of the Commission in the performance of their tasks'.[70]

The Commission is therefore an autonomous institution, with interests, tasks, and policies independent of the Member States. Its members are often experienced politicians who have held high ministerial office. It takes decisions by a majority of its members,[71] but it acts as a 'college' and maintains the principle of collective responsibility. It is served by a staff organized into several Directorates-General, each responsible for a given area of policy, with a coordinating Secretariat-General, and a Legal Service. Each Commissioner is personally assisted by a small group of officials known as a 'cabinet'.

---

[66] These are known as 'A' points on the Council agenda; points for discussion are 'B' points: see Art. 2 Council Rules of Procedure.

[67] See Art. 19 Council Rules of Procedure. Meetings of COREPER (Ambassadors) are informally prepared by the 'Antici Group', consisting of the Ambassadors' political counsellors. Meetings of COREPER (Deputies) are prepared by the 'Mertens Group', consisting of advisers to the Deputies.

[68] Arts. 151(2) EC, 121(2) Euratom, 30(2) ECSC. See also Art. 21 Council Rules of Procedure.

[69] Arts. 157(1) EC, 126(1) Euratom, 9(1) ECSC.

[70] Arts. 157(2) EC, 126(2) Euratom, 9(2) ECSC.

[71] Arts. 163 EC, 132 Euratom, 13 ECSC.

Under the ECSC Treaty, the Commission is the main legislative authority.[72] Under the EC and Euratom Treaties,[73] its powers in relation to legislation are more limited but still considerable. In general it has the exclusive 'right of initiative', since the vast majority of Treaty Articles empowering the enactment of legislation require the Council to act 'on a proposal from the Commission'; and while the Commission is usually free to amend or withdraw its proposal before enactment,[74] the Council can only amend it by unanimity.[75] The Commission also has extensive powers, delegated to it by the Council in Community legislation, to take legally binding implementing measures.[76] These can be either legislative or executive in character. The Commission is often required to exercise these powers with the involvement of a committee composed of the Member States. There are various complex procedures for the operation of these committees (known in Community jargon as 'comitology'), the choice of which in the parent act determines the degree of control over the Commission. In 1987 the Council adopted a Decision setting out the framework for these procedures.[77]

The Commission makes proposals for the annual Community budget and plays an influential role in its adoption. Subject to control by the Parliament and the Council, the Commission is responsible for implementing the budget once adopted.[78]

The Commission has significant administrative powers, derived from the Treaties and from Community legislation, especially in the competition field,[79] including the power to impose fines and other penalties. It also has the duty under the EC Treaty to 'ensure that the provisions of this Treaty and the measures taken by the institutions pursuant thereto are applied'.[80] It has the power to bring Member States before the Court of Justice for failing to fulfil their obligations under the Treaty,[81] a power it exercises regularly. In the exercise of these functions the Commission is sometimes referred to as the guardian of the Treaties.

In the external field the Commission negotiates, under the authority of the Council, agreements with non-Member States and international organizations.[82] Its powers to conclude agreements are limited.[83] In matters falling within the exclusive competence of the Communities, the Commission takes the

---

[72] Art. 14 ECSC.
[73] Arts. 155 EC and 124 Euratom set out the Commission's powers in general terms, but these are supplemented by many other treaty Arts. and provisions of Community legislation.
[74] Arts. 189a(2) EC, 119 Euratom.   [75] Arts. 189a(1) EC, 119 Euratom.
[76] Arts. 145 EC, 124 Euratom.
[77] Council Dec. of 13 July 1987 ('the Comitology Dec.'): [1987] OJ L197/33.
[78] Arts. 203–206 EC, 179–180b Euratom, 78c–78g ESCS.
[79] See e.g. Arts. 85–94 and EEC Reg. 17 [1959–62] OJ Spec. Ed. 87; Arts. 91, 92, and 95 ECSC.
[80] Art. 155 EC; see also Art. 124 Euratom.   [81] Arts. 169 EC, 141 Euratom.
[82] Arts. 113 and 228 EC. See Ch. 4.
[83] See Ch. 4. But the Commission has greater powers under the ECSC Treaty: see Ch. 23.

lead in speaking for the Communities in international conferences and organizations.[84]

The Court of Justice

The Court of Justice consists of fifteen Judges[85] assisted by nine Advocates-General.[86] They must be chosen from persons whose independence is beyond doubt and who possess the qualifications required for appointment to the highest judicial offices in their respective countries or who are jurisconsults of recognized competence. They are appointed by common accord of the Governments of the Member States, for a (renewable) term of six years.[87] In practice each Member State nominates one Judge. Each of the five larger Member States nominates one Advocate-General (and for an interim period until October 2000 there is a second Italian Advocate-General); the other three Advocates-General are nominated by the ten smaller Member States in rotation. The Advocates-General are as much members of the Court as are the Judges.

The Court hears cases either in plenary session (for which the quorum is nine Judges) or in chambers of three, five, or seven Judges.[88] Its judgments are published as judgments of the Court; there are no dissenting opinions. An Advocate-General is assigned to each case, with the function 'acting with complete impartiality and independence, to make, in open court, reasoned submissions . . . in order to assist the Court'.[89] The opinion of the Advocate-General is not binding on the Court, but it is often very influential.

Attached to the Court of Justice is the Court of First Instance, which was established by the Council pursuant to amendments to the Community Treaties made by the Single European Act.[90] It consists of fifteen Judges, one from each Member State; it has no Advocates-General. The Court of First Instance has jurisdiction over all direct actions brought by natural or legal persons, and as such serves to share the considerable overall workload of the Court. A right of appeal lies from the Court of First Instance to the Court of Justice on points of law only.

According to each of the Community Treaties the function of the Court of Justice is to 'ensure that in the interpretation and application of this Treaty the law is observed'.[91] The Treaties prescribe the type and extent of the Court's jurisdiction, with supplementary details set out in the Statutes of the Court and

---

[84] See Ch. 3.   [85] Arts. 165 EC, 137 Euratom, 32 ECSC.

[86] Arts. 166 EC, 138 Euratom, 32a ECSC. The 9th A.G. is appointed only until 6 Oct. 2000.

[87] Arts. 167 EC, 139 Euratom, 32b ECSC.

[88] Arts. 165 EC, 137 Euratom, 32 ECSC.

[89] Arts. 166 EC, 138 Euratom, 32a ECSC.

[90] Arts. 168a EC, 140a Euratom, 32d ECSC. See Council Dec. 88/591 ([1988] OJ L319/1), as amended by Council Dec. 93/350 ([1993] OJ L144/21).

[91] Arts. 164 EC, 136 Euratom, 31 ECSC.

its Rules of Procedure.[92] The main categories of jurisdiction are direct actions, references for preliminary rulings, and opinions.

There are several forms of direct action. The first is the action against a Member State for failure to fulfil an obligation under Community law. This may be brought against a Member State by the Commission[93] or by another Member State.[94] If the Court finds that the Member State has failed to fulfil an obligation, the State is required to take the necessary measures to comply with the Court's judgment. The Court has power to fine a Member State which fails to do so.[95] The second type of direct action is the action for annulment of an act of a Community institution. This may be brought by a Member State, the Council, the Commission, in limited circumstances by the Parliament, and, subject to strict rules as to their *locus standi*, by affected natural or legal persons. The grounds of action are lack of competence, infringement of an essential procedural requirement, infringement of the Treaty or any rule of law relating to its application, and misuse of powers.[96] If the Court annuls an act on any of these grounds the institution which enacted it is obliged to take all necessary measures to comply with the Court's judgment.[97] The third form of direct action is the action for failure to act. This seeks to compel the Council, the Commission, or the Parliament to take action which it is bound under the Treaty to take. Such action may be brought by one of the institutions or by a Member State,[98] and, if successful, the defendant institution must comply with the Court's judgment.[99] The other forms of direct action are those for damages for non-contractual liability of the Community,[100] and disputes between the Community institutions and their staff.[101]

The other main area of the Court's jurisdiction is references from national courts for preliminary rulings.[102] The purpose is to provide national courts with an authoritative ruling on a matter of Community law, and thus to ensure its uniform application in the Member States. Any court or tribunal in a Member State may, and a court or tribunal from which no appeal lies must, refer to the Court any question on the interpretation of Community law or the validity of an act of a Community institution which arises in a case before it. The ruling of the Court is sent back to the national court, which is bound by the ruling in deciding the case. Many important developments in Community law have

---

[92] The Statutes of the Court are set out in a Protocol to each Treaty. The Rules of Procedure are published in [1991] OJ L176/7 (with amendments at [1995] OJ L44/61).

[93] Arts. 169 EC, 141 Euratom. Art. 88 ECSC provides for a different procedure.

[94] Arts. 170 EC, 142 Euratom, 89 ECSC.   [95] Arts. 171 EC, 143 Euratom.

[96] Arts. 173 EC, 146 Euratom. Arts. 33 and 38 ECSC are similar.

[97] Arts. 176 EC, 149 Euratom, 34 ECSC.

[98] And in certain circumstances natural or legal persons: Arts. 175 EC, 148 Euratom. Arts. 35 and 37 ECSC are similar.

[99] Arts. 176 EC, 149 Euratom.

[100] Arts. 178 and 215 EC, 151 and 188 Euratom. See also Art. 40 ECSC.

[101] Arts. 179 EC, 152 Euratom, 40 ECSC.

[102] Arts. 177 EC, 150 Euratom, 41 ECSC.

resulted from the case law of the Court in the exercise of this form of jurisdiction.[103]

Although its exercise has not been frequent, the Court's jurisdiction to give opinions has produced important case law in the field of external relations.[104] It derives from Article 228(6) of the EC Treaty, under which the Council, the Commission, or a Member State may obtain from the Court an opinion on the compatibility with the Treaty of a proposed agreement between the Community and one or more States or international organizations. If the Court gives an adverse opinion, the agreement may enter into force only after the Treaty has been amended. The Court has a similar jurisdiction to give 'rulings' under Article 103 of the Euratom Treaty.

The Court of Auditors

The Court of Auditors consists of fifteen members, appointed for a term of six years by the Council, acting unanimously after consulting the Parliament. Its members are obliged to be completely independent in the performance of their duties.[105] The function of the Court of Auditors is to 'examine the accounts of all revenue and expenditure of the Community', and to 'examine whether all revenue has been received and all expenditure incurred in a lawful and regular manner and whether the financial management has been sound'. The other institutions and the national audit bodies or departments are obliged to forward to the Court, at its request, any document or information necessary to carry out its task. It publishes annual reports in the Official Journal, and is required to assist the Parliament and the Council in exercising their powers of control over the implementation of the budget.[106]

The Scope and Exercise of Powers: Competence and Subsidiarity

The Communities and their institutions have only the powers, or 'competence', which the Member States have conferred upon them in the Treaties. The Communities therefore operate on the principle of the attribution of powers.

As regards the EC, this principle is expressed in the first sentence of Article 3b of the EC Treaty: 'The Community shall act within the limits of the powers conferred upon it by this Treaty and of the objectives assigned to it therein.' As regards the institutions, Article 4(1) of the EC Treaty provides: 'The tasks entrusted to the Community shall be carried out by the following institutions: a

---

[103] See, e.g., the cases concerning direct effect and the supremacy of Community law referred to at pp. 22–3 below.

[104] See e.g. *Opinions 1/75* [1975] ECR 1355; *1/76* [1977] ECR 741; *1/91* [1991] ECR 6079; *2/91* [1993] CMLR 800; *1/94* [1995] 1 CMLR 205. Pursuant to a similar procedure under the Euratom Treaty, see, e.g., *Ruling 1/78* [1978] ECR 2151. On this jurisdiction see further Ch. 4.

[105] Arts. 188b EC, 160b Euratom, 45b ECSC.

[106] Arts. 188c EC, 160c Euratom, 45c ECSC.

European Parliament; a Council; a Commission; a Court of Justice; a Court of Auditors. Each institution shall act within the limits of the powers conferred upon it by this Treaty.'[107]

The actual empowering provisions are then to be found scattered throughout the Treaty. It is often difficult to determine the precise scope of the powers, and the ultimate authority for this is the Court of Justice. The Court has tended to adopt a purposive, rather than a literal, approach.[108] In general, provisions conferring powers have tended to be interpreted widely (and exceptions, limitations, and derogations have been interpreted restrictively). The Court very soon held that the existence of a given power implies also the existence of any other power which is reasonably necessary for the exercise of the former.[109] More recently it has gone further, holding that the existence of a given objective or task implies the existence of any powers which are necessary to carry it out.[110] The Court's general method is to consider the broad context and to pay particular attention to purposes and objectives. For example, it has said that 'every provision of Community law must be placed in its context and interpreted in the light of the provisions of Community law as a whole, regard being had to the objectives thereof and to its state of evolution at the date on which the provision in question is to be applied'.[111]

A further difficulty is that many Treaty provisions confer powers in very broad and general terms.[112] Exceptions and limitations are often imprecise and capable of differing interpretations.[113] Moreover, Community law is in a constant state of evolution. It is often difficult at any given time to determine the limits of Community competence, or of the institutions' powers, especially in areas where there is no clear case law of the Court of Justice. The boundaries are continuously being tested, in negotiation during the legislative process and, ultimately, in litigation before the Court.

A separate but related issue is the principle of subsidiarity. This was introduced into the EC Treaty[114] as a fundamental principle of general application by the Treaty on European Union.[115] Article 3b reads:

The Community shall act within the limits of the powers conferred upon it by this Treaty and of the objectives assigned to it therein.

In areas which do not fall within its exclusive competence, the Community shall take

---

[107] cf. Arts. 3(1) Euratom and 3 ECSC.

[108] In doing so it accords with the basic rule of international law regarding the interpretation of treaties: 'A treaty shall be interpreted in good faith in accordance with the ordinary meaning to be given to the terms of the treaty in their context and in the light of its object and purpose' (see Art. 31, Vienna Convention on the Law of Treaties).

[109] Case 8/55 *Fédération Charbonnière de Belgique* v. *High Authority* [1956] ECR 245.

[110] Cases 281, 283–5, 287/85 *Germany and Others* v. *Commission* [1987] ECR 3203.

[111] Case 283/81 *CILFIT Srl* v. *Ministry of Health* [1982] ECR 3415.

[112] See, e.g., Arts. 100a and 235 EC.   [113] See, e.g., Art. 100a(2) EC.

[114] In Art. 3b. The principle had been partially reflected in the environmental field in Art. 130r(4) EEC, inserted by the SEA.

[115] The application of the principle is extended to the Union by Art. B TEU: see p. 27 below.

action, in accordance with the principle of subsidiarity, only if and in so far as the objectives of the proposed action cannot be sufficiently achieved by the Member States and can therefore, by reason of the scale or effects of the proposed action, be better achieved by the Community.

Any action by the Community shall not go beyond what is necessary to achieve the objectives of this Treaty.

The principle of subsidiarity does not affect the existence of the Community's powers; it is concerned rather with the question whether in a given case it is appropriate for the Community (and hence its institutions) to exercise those powers, in areas where competence is shared between the Community and the Member States. This is essentially a political question, but the inclusion of Article 3b in the Treaty gives it a legal and constitutional form. At the time of writing the Court of Justice had not had occasion to interpret Article 3b. But in its case law the Court, even before the appearance of Article 3b, has often applied some of its concepts;[116] in particular, the last sentence of Article 3b closely resembles the principle of proportionality developed by the Court.[117] It should be noted that the requirement in the last sentence of Article 3b applies even in areas of exclusive Community competence.

Forms of Community Acts

Article 14 of the ECSC Treaty lists three kinds of act which may be adopted by the Commission in accordance with the Treaty: 'decisions', 'recommendations', and 'opinions'. It goes on to specify the characteristics of each type of act. *Decisions* are 'binding in their entirety'. *Recommendations* are 'binding as to the aims to be pursued but shall leave the choice of the appropriate methods for achieving these aims to those to whom the recommendations are addressed'. *Opinions* 'shall have no binding force'.

Article 189 of the EC Treaty and Article 161 of the Euratom Treaty list, in identical terms, five kinds of act which may be adopted by the appropriate legislative authority[118] in accordance with the Treaty: 'regulations', 'directives', 'decisions', 'recommendations', and 'opinions'. Their characteristics are defined as follows. A *regulation* 'shall have general application' and 'shall be binding in its entirety and directly applicable in all Member States'. A *directive* is 'binding,

---

[116] See, e.g., Case 120/78 '*Cassis de Dijon*' (*Rewe-Zentral AG* v. *Bundesmonopolverwaltung für Branntwein*) [1979] ECR 649; Case C–2/90 *Commission* v. *Belgium* [1993] 1 CMLR 365; Cases C–312/89 '*Conforama*' (*Union Departementale des Syndicats CGT de l'Aisne* v. *SIDEF Conforama*) and C–332/89 *State (Belgium)* v. '*Marchandise*' [1993] 3 CMLR 746. As for the Council's view, Pt. A of the Presidency Conclusions of the Edinburgh European Council of 11/12 Dec. 1992 sets out the 'overall approach to the application by the Council of the subsidiarity principle and Art. 3b': see Bull. EC No. 12 of 1992, 12.

[117] See p. 25 below.

[118] For the EC, according to the relevant empowering treaty Art. (or parent legislation), this may be the Parliament and the Council (acting by co-decision), the Council or the Commission, and for Euratom the Council or the Commission.

as to the result to be achieved, upon each Member State to which it is addressed, but shall leave to the national authorities the choice of form and method'. A *decision* is 'binding in its entirety upon those to whom it is addressed'. *Recommendations* and *opinions* 'shall have no binding force'.

Accordingly, *decisions* under the ECSC Treaty broadly correspond to *regulations* and, in some circumstances,[119] *decisions* under the EC and Euratom Treaties. ECSC *recommendations* are equivalent to EC and Euratom *directives* (although, unlike directives, they need not be addressed to Member States). Unlike ECSC recommendations, EC and Euratom *recommendations* are not binding. Nor are *opinions* under each of the Treaties.

The Treaties envisage that ECSC decisions, and EC and Euratom regulations and decisions, are to have immediate legal effect. By contrast, ECSC recommendations and EC and Euratom directives require further implementing measures. Accordingly, the requirement that an EC regulation is 'directly applicable' and needs no further implementing measures means that Member States are not allowed to enact legislation which might limit or alter its effects. It has effect and must be enforced in the national legal system as it stands.[120] On the other hand, Member States are obliged to adopt the necessary measures to implement a directive, within a time limit specified in the directive. If they fail to do so, they may be brought before the Court of Justice. Moreover, the provisions of the directive may be found to have direct effect and be directly enforceable in the national courts; this will be so where the provisions impose on Member States a clear, precise, and unconditional obligation but a Member State has failed to implement the directive, or failed to do so correctly, within the prescribed time limit.[121] In such circumstances the directive can only be directly enforced against the defaulting Member State (or an emanation of the State[122]), known as 'vertical direct effect', and not against another private party[123] ('horizontal direct effect'). Failure to implement a directive on time can also, in certain defined circumstances, result in the Member State incurring liability to compensate an injured party.[124]

EC regulations, directives, and decisions must state the reasons on which they are based and refer to any proposals or opinions which were required to be obtained pursuant to the Treaty. Failure to fulfil these requirements may result in the annulment of the act by the Court of Justice.[125]

---

[119] In particular when addressed to natural or legal persons, although some EC decs. are of more general application.

[120] See, e.g., Case 93/71 *Leonesio* v. *Italian Ministry of Agriculture and Forestry* [1972] ECR 287.

[121] See, e.g., Case 41/74 *Van Duyn* v. *Home Office* [1974] ECR 1337; and pp. 22–3 below.

[122] See, e.g., Case C–188/89 *Foster* v. *British Gas plc* [1990] 2 CMLR 833.

[123] Case 152/84 *Marshall* v. *Southampton and South-West Hampshire Area Health Authority (Teaching)* [1986] ECR 723; Case C–91/92 *Faccini Dori* v. *Recreb Srl* [1994] ECR I–3325.

[124] Cases C–6/90 and C–9/90 *Francovich* v. *Italy* and *Bonifaci* v. *Italy* [1991] ECR I–5357.

[125] See Art. 190 EC, and Case 24/62 *Germany* v. *Commission* [1963] ECR 63. This rule does not necessarily apply to Council decs. *sui generis:* see Case 22/70 *Commission* v. *Council (ERTA case)* [1971] ECR 263, at paras. 97–8.

EC regulations, directives and decisions adopted jointly by the Parliament and the Council are published in the Official Journal. So are EC regulations of the Council and the Commission, as well as directives of those institutions which are addressed to all Member States. Other EC directives and decisions must be notified to those to whom they are addressed, and in practice are often published too.[126]

The lists of acts in Article 14 of the ECSC Treaty, Article 189 of the EC Treaty, and Article 161 of the Euratom Treaty are not exhaustive. Acts may be, and are, adopted by the Community institutions which do not fall into any of these categories. Some may be intended to be legally binding, others not. Various forms of instrument have been used, but the form is less important than the substance in determining their legal status and effects. A commonly used form is a Council decision *sui generis*. This is not a decision in the sense of Article 189 of the EC Treaty. It is sometimes called a 'Beschluß', a German word for 'decision' which conveniently distinguishes this form from an Article 189 decision, which is rendered in German as 'Entscheidung'. Decisions *sui generis* are usually intended to be legally binding and to take effect in the operation of, and sometimes in relations between, the Community institutions.[127] Some such decisions are published with the formal title 'Decision'; and some are of great constitutional importance.[128] Others are more transient, and may be contained in the published conclusions of a particular Council meeting. Others, such as mandates to the Commission for the purposes of negotiating international agreements, are not usually published at all. The Council also frequently adopts 'resolutions', which are normally not intended to be legally binding; and the same applies to many of the 'conclusions' agreed by the Council. All acts (whatever their form or title) adopted by Community institutions and intended to have legal effects are capable of judicial review by the Court of Justice.[129]

Acts of the Council should be distinguished from intergovernmental instruments agreed by the Member States. Sometimes Ministers meeting within the Council adopt a resolution, agreement, or decision on a matter falling within national competence, which applies as between the Member States. These acts may be legally binding and thus similar in nature to international agreements. The constitutional requirements of each Member State will determine whether they require implementation in national law. Alternatively, they may be non-binding arrangements of a political character. The position is often complicated because the subject matter of a resolution falls partly within and partly outside Community competence; in that case the practice is to adopt a 'mixed'

---

[126] Art. 191 EC. See also Art. 18 Council Rules of Procedure.

[127] On the use of the dec. *sui generis* in the conclusion of international agreements, see further Ch. 4.

[128] e.g. Council Dec. ('Comitology') of 13 July 1987, see n. 77 above; Council Dec. 94/728 (Own Resources) of 31 Oct. 1994, see n. 8 above; Council Decs. ('Ioannina Agreement') of 29 Mar. 1994 and 1 Jan. 1995, see n. 61 above.

[129] Case 22/70, n. 125 above; Case C–316/91 *Parliament* v. *Council* [1993] ECR I–625.

resolution, that is to say a 'Resolution of the Council and of the representatives of the Governments of the Member States meeting within the Council'.[130] Finally, the Treaties require certain decisions to be taken by agreement between all the Member States (by 'common accord'); these are usually matters of constitutional importance or political sensitivity, such as the appointment of members of the Commission, the Court of Justice, and the Court of First Instance, and the determination of the seats of the Community institutions.[131]

Community law

Sources

The main sources of Community law can be described as follows:

(a) the Treaties establishing the Communities and the subsequent Treaties and Acts modifying or supplementing them;

(b) legislative acts and other legally binding decisions of the Community institutions acting in accordance with the powers conferred on them by the Treaties;

(c) international agreements to which any of the Communities is a party, and certain decisions adopted by bodies established pursuant to such agreements;

(d) the case law of the Court of Justice;

(e) general principles of law derived from the constitutions and laws of the Member States or from international agreements binding the Member States, such as the European Convention on Human Rights.[132]

Nature

Community law owes its existence to international law, as do the Communities themselves. But Community law, as it has been developed in the case law of the Court of Justice, has long been an autonomous system of law. It has special features which derive from the supranational quality of the Communities and their institutions.

One fundamental feature is the doctrine of 'direct effect'. This was established in an early case, in which the Court denied that the EEC Treaty conferred rights and duties only on the Member States and that it did not confer enforceable rights on individuals. The Court said that:

the Community constitutes a new legal order of international law, for the benefit of which the States have limited their sovereign rights, albeit within limited fields, and the subjects of which comprise not only Member States but also their nationals.

---

[130] See, e.g., the Res. of 13 Nov. 1991 published at [1991] OJ C328/1.
[131] See Arts. 158(2), 167, 168a(3), and 216 EC respectively.
[132] UKTS 71 (1953); Cmd. 8969.

Independently of the legislation of Member States, Community law therefore not only imposes obligations on individuals but is also intended to confer upon them rights which become part of their legal heritage.[133]

As developed by the Court, the doctrine of direct effect applies where a provision of the Treaty or of Community legislation (a) is clear and precise, (b) is unconditional and unqualified and is not subject to the taking of further measures on the part of the Member States or of the Community, and (c) leaves no substantial discretion to the Member States or the Community institutions.[134] Where these conditions are fulfilled and the provision in question creates rights or obligations, it is said to have direct effect and may be enforced before a national court. The Court has held that several Treaty Articles have direct effect,[135] as well as a vast number of provisions of Community legislation, including, in certain circumstances, provisions of directives.[136]

The doctrine of 'direct effect' should not be confused with the requirement that EC (and Euratom) regulations are 'directly applicable'. That a regulation is 'directly applicable' means that it has legislative effect in the Member States without national implementing legislation or other action. Whether or not a provision of a regulation has 'direct effect' depends on whether or not it satisfies the conditions described in the previous paragraph.

A further cardinal feature of Community law is its supremacy over the national law of the Member States. This is really an application of the fundamental principle of international law that *pacta sunt servanda*.[137] The principle of the supremacy of Community law was established by the Court of Justice in 1964, when it rejected the argument that a national court was obliged to apply national legislation adopted later than, and inconsistent with, the EEC Treaty.[138] The principle is very clearly stated in a 1978 case by the Court of Justice as follows:

[I]n accordance with the principle of the precedence of Community law, the relationship between the provisions of the Treaty and directly applicable measures of the institutions on the one hand and the national law of the Member States on the other is such that those provisions and measures . . . render automatically inapplicable any conflicting provisions of current national law . . . [and] preclude the valid adoption of new national legislative measures to the extent to which they would be incompatible with Community provisions . . . [E]very national court must, in a case within its jurisdiction, apply Community law in its entirety and protect rights which the latter confers on individuals and must accordingly set aside any provision of national law which may conflict with it, whether prior or subsequent to the Community rule.[139]

---

[133] Case 26/62 *NV Algemene Transport- en Expeditie Onderneming Van Gend en Loos* v. *Nederlandse Administratie der Belastingen* [1963] ECR 1.

[134] See, e.g., Case 148/78 *Pubblico Ministero* v. *Ratti* [1979] ECR 1629.

[135] e.g. Art. 119 EC.   [136] See p. 20 above.

[137] This principle is codified in Art. 26, Vienna Convention on the Law of Treaties.

[138] Case 6/64 *Costa* v. *ENEL* [1964] ECR 585.

[139] Case 106/77 *Amministrazione delle Finanze dello Stato* v. *Simmenthal SpA* [1978] ECR 629.

Among the consequences is that, in the enforcement of Community law in national courts, no rule of national law—including a rule as fundamental as that the national court cannot set aside primary national legislation—can be invoked to prevent the grant of a remedy for the effective protection of a Community right;[140] and in criminal proceedings it is a successful defence that the national law creating the offence is contrary to Community law.[141]

General Principles of Law

The Court of Justice has developed certain general legal principles in interpreting and applying Community law. These have largely been inspired by the basic legal principles of constitutional and administrative law of the Member States, and of natural justice, as well as by important treaties binding the Member States, above all the European Convention on Human Rights.

The Court has held that *respect for fundamental human rights* 'forms an integral part of the general principles of law protected by the Court of Justice'.[142] The sources of such rights are 'the constitutional traditions common to the Member States' and 'international treaties for the protection of human rights on which the Member States have collaborated or of which they are signatories'.[143] The most important such treaty is the European Convention on Human Rights, to which all the Member States (but not the Communities themselves) are parties. Respect for fundamental rights was expressly referred to in the preamble to the Single European Act, and is reiterated in the preamble and Article F of the Treaty on European Union.

The Court has also developed the principle of *legal certainty*. The application of the law to a particular situation must be predictable.[144] There are various related principles. They include respect for acquired rights, so that a legal right, once acquired, ought not to be withdrawn;[145] the principle of legitimate expectation, by which a person is entitled to act in the reasonable expectation that the law as it exists will continue to apply;[146] the principle of non-retroactivity, so that a rule of law should not be applied to acts or transactions completed before the rule was promulgated;[147] and prescription, according to which an act cannot be declared unlawful, a penalty exacted, or performance of an obligation required after an excessive lapse of time.[148]

---

[140] Case C–213/89 *R. v. Secretary of State for Transport, ex parte Factortame Ltd* [1990] 3 CMLR 1.
[141] Case 269/80 *R. v. Tymen* [1981] ECR 3079.
[142] Case 11/70 *Internationale Handelsgesellschaft mbH* v. *Einfuhr- und Vorratsstelle für Getreide und Futtermittel* [1970] ECR 1125.
[143] Case 11/70, n. 142 above; Case 4/73 *Nold, Kohlen- und Baustoffgroßhandlung* v. *Commission* [1974] ECR 491.
[144] See, e.g., Case 43/75 *Defrenne* v. *SABENA* [1976] ECR 455.
[145] See, e.g., Case 1/73 *Westzucker GmbH* v. *Einfuhr- und Vorratsstelle für Zucker* [1973] ECR 723.
[146] See, e.g., Case 112/77 *Töpfer & Co. GmbH* v. *Commission* [1978] ECR 1019.
[147] See, e.g., Case 1/73 n. 145 above.
[148] See, e.g., Case 48/69 *ICI Ltd.* v. *Commission* [1972] ECR 619.

The principle of *proportionality*, as developed by the Court, requires that the action taken or means used must be proportionate to the objective to be achieved. Accordingly, penalties should be proportionate to the gravity of the offence, and burdens should not be imposed on a person which are clearly out of proportion to the end in view.[149]

The principle of *equality*, or non-discrimination, requires that similar situations should not be treated differently unless there is an objective justification for doing so. The principle is expressed in the EC Treaty in Article 6, which prohibits any discrimination on grounds of nationality within the scope of application of the Treaty, and in Article 119, which provides for men and women to receive equal pay for equal work. The Court of Justice has gone further, however, and held that there is a general principle of non-discrimination in Community law.[150]

THE EUROPEAN UNION

Article A of the Treaty on European Union begins:

By this Treaty, the High Contracting Parties establish among themselves a European Union, hereinafter called 'the Union'.

This Treaty marks a new stage in the process of creating an ever closer union among the peoples of Europe, in which decisions are taken as closely as possible to the citizen.

The precise nature of the Union is unclear. The concept appears to be a political rather than a legal one. The Treaty does not give the Union legal personality; and the Articles in the three Community Treaties which give each of the Communities legal personality are unaffected.[151] There is evidently no intention to create an international legal person separate from, or in substitution for, the three Communities.[152] Accordingly the Union, as such, has no treaty-making power and cannot undertake international legal obligations. It can only act through its component parts, the Communites and the Member States.

The Union appears, rather, to represent a political aspiration, and a staging post along the road to an 'ever closer union among the peoples of Europe'. That language had been used in the preamble to the EEC Treaty in 1957; and in the preamble to the Single European Act in 1986 the signatories expressed their

---

[149] See, e.g., Case 5/73 *Balkan-Import-Export GmbH* v. *Hauptzollamt Berlin-Packhof* [1973] ECR 1091.
[150] Case 1/72 *Frilli* v. *Belgium* [1972] ECR 457; Case 152/73 *Sotgiu* v. *Deutsche Bundespost* [1974] ECR 153.
[151] Arts. 210 EC, 184 Euratom, 6 ECSC. See further Ch. 2.
[152] And in changing its name from 'Council of the European Communities' to 'Council of the European Union', the Council declared that this change in no way affected the current legal position that the European Union does not enjoy legal personality: see *Agence Europe*, 9 Nov. 1993.

will to 'transform relations as a whole among their States into a European Union'. The Union established by Article A of the Treaty might be described as a loose association between the Member States within the framework of which they have agreed to carry on certain activities in common.

The structure of the Union has sometimes been likened to that of a Greek temple facade, with three pillars and an overarching pediment. The Treaty reflects this structure.

The first pillar is the three Communities: the EC, the ECSC, and Euratom. Titles II, III, and IV of the Treaty respectively set out a series of amendments to the three Treaties establishing these Communities.

The second pillar is the common foreign and security policy, provision for which is made in Title V of the Treaty. This activity is to take place intergovernmentally, outside the Community Treaties, and according to its own special procedures. The common foreign and security policy is considered in more detail in Chapter 24.

The third pillar is co-operation between the Member States in the fields of justice and home affairs, as provided for in Title VI of the Treaty. This activity is also to take place intergovernmentally, outside the Community Treaties, and according to its own special procedures.[153]

Overarching these three pillars is the European Council, which according to Article D 'shall provide the Union with the necessary impetus for its development and shall define the general political guidelines thereof'. The European Council, as before, is composed of the Heads of State or Government of the Member States and the President of the Commission, and is assisted by the Ministers for Foreign Affairs of the Member States and by a Member of the Commission.[154] The provisions relating to the Union and the European Council are mostly contained in Title I of the Treaty. Like the provisions in Titles V and VI, they are clearly separated from the provisions dealing with the three Communities in Titles II, III, and IV. So is Title VII, which sets out the final provisions of the Treaty. At the same time, provisions in both Title I and Title VII relate to all three pillars, and this explains why in the Treaty structure they are distinct from the five Titles they span.

This structure of the Union finds prosaic expression in the third paragraph of Article A as follows:

> The Union shall be founded on the European Communities, supplemented by the policies and forms of cooperation established by this Treaty. Its task shall be to organise, in a manner demonstrating consistency and solidarity, relations between the Member States and between their peoples.

---

[153] See Hendry, 'The Third Pillar of Maastricht: Cooperation in the Fields of Justice and Home Affairs' (1993) 36 *German Yearbook of International Law* 295; Monar and Morgan (eds.), *The Third Pillar of the European Union* (European Inter-University Press, 1994).

[154] The European Council was given a treaty basis, with the same composition, by Art. 2 SEA, which was repealed by Art. P(2) TEU.

Article B describes a number of objectives of the Union, three of which correspond broadly to the three pillars of the Union: to promote economic and social progress, to assert its identity on the international scene, and to develop close co-operation on justice and home affairs. In addition, it is to strengthen the protection of the rights and interests of the nationals of the Member States through the introduction of a citizenship of the Union. Provision for citizenship of the Union was made in a new Part Two of the EC Treaty. Finally, the Union is to maintain and build on the *acquis communautaire*, which means the achievements of the Communities and the state of Community law at any given time. Article B concludes that the Union's objectives are to be 'achieved as provided in this Treaty and in accordance with the conditions and the timetable set out therein while respecting the principle of subsidiarity as defined in Article 3b' of the EC Treaty.

Article C provides that the Union shall be served by a 'single institutional framework', which is to 'ensure the consistency and the continuity of the activities carried out in order to attain its objectives while respecting and building upon the *acquis communautaire*'. The single institutional framework is explained in Article E, which provides:

> The European Parliament, the Council, the Commission and the Court of Justice shall exercise their powers under the conditions and for the purposes provided for, on the one hand, by the provisions of the Treaties establishing the European Communities and of the subsequent Treaties and Acts modifying and supplementing them and, on the other hand, by the other provisions of this Treaty.

Accordingly, these Community institutions are envisaged as the organs through or in connection with which activities are to be carried out under the umbrella of the Union. But Article E draws a careful and deliberate distinction between the exercise of their powers under the Community Treaties as modified and supplemented, on the one hand, and under 'the other provisions of this Treaty' (that is, the TEU), on the other. These 'other provisions' refer chiefly to Titles V and VI, which concern the second and third pillars. The powers of these institutions under Titles V and VI differ significantly from the supranational powers conferred upon them by the Community Treaties.[155] In particular, there is no power to adopt Community legislation, and decision-making is by unanimity. In addition, Article L of the Treaty excludes from the jurisdiction of the Court of Justice the whole of Title V; and in respect of Title VI it envisages the Court having only such jurisdiction as may be expressly provided for in separate conventions concluded under that Title.

The last Article in Title I of the Treaty, Article F, obliges the Union to respect the national identities of its Member States, and to respect fundamental rights as guaranteed by the European Human Rights Convention 'and as they result from the constitutional traditions common to the Member States, as general

---

[155] See Ch. 24.

principles of Community law'. This reflects the practice of the Court of Justice, as noted above;[156] and the Court might be expected to have regard to these provisions even though, by virtue of Article L, the provisions of Title I are in principle outside the Court's jurisdiction.

Article M of the Treaty provides that, subject to the provisions amending the Community Treaties, and to the final provisions (Articles L to S), 'nothing in this Treaty shall affect the Treaties establishing the European Communities or the subsequent Treaties and Acts modifying or supplementing them'. This has the effect of preserving the Communities, and the powers of their institutions under the Community Treaties, from encroachment as a result of activities carried out under the common foreign and security policy or justice and home affairs co-operation. So the second and third pillars cannot undermine the first.

Article O of the Treaty provides that 'any European State' may apply to become a member of the Union. The conditions of admission and the adjustments to the treaties on which the Union is founded which such admission entails are to be the subject of an agreement between the Member States and the applicant State, which must be submitted for ratification by all the contracting parties. The Community institutions also have an important role in the process: before the Council can finally decide on an application for admission (and its decision is by unanimity), it must receive an opinion from the Commission and the assent of the European Parliament (by an absolute majority of all its members). The effect of Article O is that a State can only join the Union, and not just the Communities; and if it joins the Union it thereby joins all the Communities. The provisions of each of the Community Treaties which dealt with accession to the Communities were repealed by the TEU.[157] Austria, Finland, and Sweden were the first countries to join the Union pursuant to Article O.[158]

Finally, by virtue of Article Q, the Treaty on European Union was concluded 'for an unlimited period'. An intergovernmental conference of the Member States is to be held in 1996, pursuant to Article N(2), to review certain provisions (at least) of the Treaty; and a conference to consider proposed amendments to the Treaty can be held at any time under Article N(1) provided there is a simple majority in the Council in favour of convening one. The agreement of all the Member States is required for any amendment to the Treaty; and 'the amendments shall enter into force after being ratified by all the Member States in accordance with their respective constitutional requirements'.[159]

---

[156] See p. 24 above.

[157] Art. 237 EEC, repealed by Art. G(83) TEU; Art. 205 Euratom, repealed by Art. I(28) TEU; Art. 98 ECSC, repealed by Art. H(21) TEU.

[158] See Booss and Forman, 'Enlargement: Legal and Procedural Aspects' (1995) 32 *CMLRev.* 95.

[159] Art. N(1) TEU. The procedure prescribed in Art. N TEU is the means for making amendments to any of the Community Treaties; the Arts. of each Treaty providing for its own amendment were repealed by the TEU (Art. 236 EEC, repealed by Art. G(83) TEU; Art. 204 Euratom, repealed by Art. I(28) TEU; Art. 96 ECSC, repealed by Art. H(21) TEU).

2

Legal Personality of the Communities

Each of the Community Treaties expressly confers legal personality on the Community it establishes. Article 210 of the EC Treaty provides: 'The Community shall have legal personality.' Article 184 of the Euratom Treaty is in identical terms, as is the first sentence of Article 6 of the ECSC Treaty.

Each Treaty goes on to provide for the legal capacity of the Community in each of the Member States. Article 211 of the EC Treaty provides:

In each of the Member States, the Community shall enjoy the most extensive legal capacity accorded to legal persons under their laws; it may, in particular, acquire or dispose of movable and immovable property and may be a party to legal proceedings. To this end, the Community shall be represented by the Commission.

Article 185 of the Euratom Treaty is in identical terms. Article 6 of the ECSC Treaty is very similar, but it provides for the ECSC to be represented by its institutions (not just by the Commission), each within the limits of its powers. It also provides that in international relations, the ECSC shall enjoy the legal capacity it requires to perform its functions and attain its objectives. There is no equivalent provision in the EC and Euratom Treaties.

Article 28 of the Treaty establishing a Single Council and a Single Commission of the European Communities ('the Merger Treaty') provides that the Communities shall enjoy in the territories of the Member States such privileges and immunities as are necessary for the performance of their tasks, under the conditions laid down in the Protocol annexed to that Treaty.[1] The Protocol on the Privileges and Immunities of the European Communities, which is annexed to the Merger Treaty, makes provision regarding the property, funds, assets, and operations of the Communities; communications and *laissez-passer*; the privileges and immunities of Members of the European Parliament, the Commission, and the Court, of representatives of Member States taking part in the work of the Community institutions, of officials and other servants of the Communities, and of missions of third countries accredited to the Communities. It also deals with the position of the European Investment Bank and, by virtue of an amending Protocol, that of the European Central Bank and the European Monetary Institute.[2]

[1] Art. 28 of the Merger Treaty also repealed the Arts. in the founding Treaties dealing with privileges and immunities (Arts. 218 EEC, 191 Euratom, and 76 ECSC) as well as the Protocols on Privileges and Immunities originally annexed to those Treaties. On privileges and immunities, see further Ch. 8 and p. 35 below.

[2] The Protocol annexed to the Merger Treaty was signed at Brussels on 8 Apr. 1965 ([1967] OJ 152). The amending Protocol was annexed to the EC Treaty as amended by the TEU.

It is perhaps useful to consider the legal personality of the Communities[3] from the point of view of international law, in Community law, and within the legal systems of the Member States.

INTERNATIONAL LAW

The leading authority on the international legal status of organizations composed of States is the Advisory Opinion of the International Court of Justice in the *Reparations Case*.[4] The Court was asked for an opinion on the capacity of the United Nations, as an international organization, to bring an international claim in respect of injuries suffered by its employees in circumstances involving the responsibility of a State. The United Nations Charter does not expressly confer legal personality on the United Nations Organization. But the Court examined the Charter as a whole and concluded that the United Nations was an international person capable of possessing international rights and duties, and capable of maintaining its rights by bringing international claims. The Court noted that the Charter equipped the Organization with organs and gave it special tasks. The Charter defined the position of the members in relation to the Organization by requiring them to give it every assistance in any action undertaken by it, and to accept and carry out the decisions of the Security Council; by authorizing the General Assembly to make recommendations to the members; by giving the Organization legal capacity and privileges and immunities in the territory of each of its members; and by providing for the conclusion of agreements between the Organization and its members.[5] The Court noted that practice, in particular the conclusion of conventions to which the Organization was a party, had confirmed that the Organization occupied a position in certain respects in detachment from its members. The Organization was a political body, charged with political tasks of an important character, covering a wide field; and in dealing with its members it employed political means.

---

[3] On international organizations generally, see H. G. Schermers, *International Institutional Law* (2nd edn. 1980), especially paras. 1377–1488 (on the status of international organizations in international law) and paras. 1660–4 (on the capacity to bring claims); D. W. Bowett, *The Law of International Institutions* (4th edn. 1982); Brownlie, *Principles* (4th edn., Clarendon, 1990) ch. XXX; Hague Academy of International Law, *A Handbook on International Organizations* (Dupuy (ed.), 1988); P. Pescatore, 'Les Relations Extérieures de la Communauté européenne' (1961) II *Hague Receuil* 103; W. J. Ganshof van der Meersch, 'L'ordre juridique des Communautés européennes et le droit international' (1975) V *Hague Receuil* 148; J. Boulois, 'Le droit des Communautés européennes dans ses rapports avec le droit international général' (1992) IV *Hague Receuil* 235; Groux and Manin, *The European Communities in the International Order*, European Perspectives (European Perspectives, 1985). On recognition of and by the European Communities, see Groux and Manin, 19–28.

[4] *Reparations for Injuries Suffered in the Service of the United Nations* [1949] ICJ Rep. 174.

[5] The Court drew attention to the Convention on the Privileges and Immunities of the UN, noted that it created rights and duties between each of the signatories and the UN, and remarked that it was difficult to see how such a convention could operate except on the international plane and as between Parties possessing international personality: *ibid.* 179.

From this the Court concluded that the Organization was intended to enjoy, and was in fact exercising and enjoying, functions and rights which could 'only be explained on the basis of the possession of a large measure of international personality and the capacity to operate on an international plane'.[6] The members of the United Nations, by entrusting certain functions to the Organization, with the attendant duties and responsibilities, had clothed it with the competence required to enable those functions to be effectively discharged. The Court went on:

Accordingly, the Court has come to the conclusion that the Organization is an international person. That is not the same thing as saying that it is a State, which it certainly is not, or that its legal personality and rights and duties are the same as those of a State ... Whereas a State possesses the totality of international rights and duties recognized by international law, the rights and duties of an entity such as the Organization must depend upon its purposes and functions as specified or implied in its constituent documents and developed in practice.[7]

There can be no doubt that each of the Communities, given the supranational powers conferred on them and their institutions by their constituent treaties,[8] satisfies the criteria for international legal personality established in the *Reparations Case*. Moreover, unlike the Charter, each Community Treaty expressly confers legal personality on the organization it creates,[9] thus plainly demonstrating the intention of the Member States to establish a legal entity separate from themselves. Furthermore, each Treaty confers powers on the Community to act on the international plane by concluding international agreements, and sets out procedures for that purpose.[10] There is a wealth of practice in the exercise of these powers,[11] including its exercise in developing the Communities' participation in other international organizations.[12] This provides firm evidence of the recognition accorded by the international community to the legal capacity of the Communities under international law. So is the widespread acknowledgement of the Communities and their representatives as being entitled to possess certain rights and duties corresponding to the rights and duties of States and their representatives: what might be seen as the exercise by the Communities of something akin to a right of legation.[13]

The rights and duties of the Communities as international legal persons depend, as the International Court said, upon their respective purposes and functions as specified or implied in their constituent documents and developed in practice; and they have the competence required to enable their functions effectively to be discharged. Subject to these qualifications, the Communities have potentially broad international legal capacity. Their international rights and duties are not limited to the treaty-making sphere. They could, for

---

[6] *Ibid.* 179.   [7] *Ibid.* 179–80.   [8] See Ch. 1.
[9] Arts. 210 EC, 184 Euratom, 6 ECSC.
[10] See in particular Art. 228 EC, and Chs. 3 and 4.   [11] See Chs. 10–23.
[12] See Ch. 7.   [13] See Ch. 8.

example, exercise the right of protection of their employees acting in the course of their duties and bring international claims in respect of injuries done to them by States. They could bring international claims in respect of the unlawful expropriation of their property; and by the same token they could incur international responsibility towards a State, if, for example, Community legislation unlawfully expropriated the property of that State or its nationals. The Communities could, of course, be liable under international law for the breach of treaties by which they were bound.[14] The Court of Justice has recognized that the Communities are subject to, and must exercise their powers in accordance with, the rules of customary international law.[15]

The Communities could, by agreement, submit disputes with other international persons to compulsory forms of settlement, such as arbitration.[16] They could not, however, avail themselves of the International Court of Justice, the contentious jurisdiction of which is limited to States.[17] Nor are they subject to the jurisdiction of the European Court of Human Rights, since the Communities are not themselves parties to the European Convention on Human Rights.[18]

The classification of the Communities in multilateral treaty practice has not been uniform. In some instances they have been treated in the same way as other international organizations.[19] In other cases the Communities have succeeded in obtaining acknowledgement of their particular status in a special clause covering 'regional economic integration organizations' (REIO).[20] The definition of REIO involves two elements: the grouping of States of a particular region for common purposes connected with their shared geographical location; and a 'transfer of competences' from the members of the REIO to the organization. It is common for the extent of this transfer to be described in a declaration of competence deposited at the time of conclusion of the treaty in question by the REIO. The term REIO is usually understood to refer only to the European Communities.

[14] See Case C-327/91 *France* v. *Commission* [1994] ECR I-3641, at para. 25.

[15] See, e.g., Case C-286/90 *Anklagemyndigheden* v. *Poulsen and Diva Navigation* [1992] ECR 6019; Case C-432/92 *R.* v. *Ministry of Agriculture, Fisheries and Food, ex parte Anastasiou* [1994] ECR I-3087. See also van der Meersch, n. 3 above, 44–6 and 181–95.

[16] The ECJ has held that if an international agreement to which the Community is a party provides for an international tribunal to settle disputes between the Community and third countries, the decisions of that tribunal would bind the ECJ when called upon to rule on the interpretation of that agreement as part of the Community legal order: *Opinion 1/91 (the first EEA Opinion)* [1991] ECR 6079, at paras. 39 and 40. For an example of a multilateral dispute settlement mechanism available to the Community, see the discussion in Ch. 12 of the dispute settlement provisions of the Agreement establishing the World Trade Organization.

[17] See Art. 34 of the ICJ Statute.

[18] At the time of writing the question whether accession of the Communities to the Convention would be compatible with the Community Treaties was before the ECJ (*Opinion 2/94*).

[19] The EC is dealt with as an 'international organization' for the purposes of participation in the 1982 Convention on the Law of the Sea: see Art. 305(1)(f) and Annex IX.

[20] This has occurred most often in multilateral environmental agreements; see, e.g., the agreements cited in Ch. 17, n. 32.

The Communities act internationally through their institutions, in particular the Council and the Commission. But it must be emphasized that it is the Communities, not the institutions, which have international legal personality. As the Court of Justice has said: 'it is the Community alone, having legal personality pursuant to Article 210 of the Treaty, which has the capacity to bind itself by concluding agreements with a non-member country or an international organization'.[21] The Commission as such has no capacity to enter into agreements binding upon it under international law; and the same must apply to the Council and the Parliament. The Commission has been given specific powers to establish relations and forms of co-operation with various international organizations.[22] The Commission may be given further specific powers under secondary legislation which enable it to enter into international agreements, for example in order to carry out obligations undertaken in an agreement concluded by the Community. But in exercising any of these powers the Commission can only be acting on behalf of the Community, and not on its own account. Even where the Commission had been found to have exceeded its powers in purporting to conclude an international agreement with the authorities of a non-Member State, the Court of Justice held that the resulting agreement was binding on the Community; the Commission could not conclude an international agreement in its own behalf.[23]

COMMUNITY LAW

The Treaty provisions cited at the beginning of this Chapter[24] mean that in Community law each of the Communities has legal personality separate from that of the Member States. The Communities act through their institutions, but in the Community legal order the institutions have defined powers and separate standing before the Court of Justice. Under the EC and Euratom Treaties, the Court has jurisdiction 'to give judgment pursuant to any arbitration clause contained in a contract concluded by or on behalf of the Community, whether that contract be governed by public or private law'.[25] Otherwise, actions before the Court of Justice involve the institutions of the Communities, or the Member States, rather than the Communities as such.

The legal personality and nature of the Communities have however been considered by the Court of Justice. The following characteristics of the legal order established by the Community Treaties have been emphasized by the Court. By contrast with ordinary international treaties, the EEC Treaty created

---

[21] Case C–327/91 *France* v. *Commission* [1994] ECR I–3641, at para. 24.
[22] Arts. 229, 230, and 231 EC; 199, 200, and 201 Euratom; 93 and 94 ECSC. See Ch. 7.
[23] Case C–327/91, n. 21 above.
[24] Arts. 210 and 211 EC, 184 and 185 Euratom, 6 ECSC.
[25] Arts. 181 EC, 153 Euratom.

its own legal system which became an integral part of the legal systems of the Member States.[26] By creating a Community of unlimited duration, having its own institutions, its own legal capacity and capacity of representation on the international plane, and real powers stemming from a limitation of sovereignty or a transfer of powers from the States to the Community, the Member States have limited their sovereign rights.[27] This limitation of Member States' sovereignty is permanent.[28] The EC Treaty, albeit concluded in the form of an international agreement, nonetheless amounts to the constitutional charter of a Community based on the rule of law,[29] of which the Court sees itself as the supreme constitutional court.[30]

NATIONAL LAWS OF THE MEMBER STATES

The Treaties provide that, in each of the Member States, the Communities shall enjoy the most extensive legal capacity accorded to legal persons under their laws; and that they may, in particular, acquire and dispose of movable and immovable property and may be party to legal proceedings.[31] They also provide for the Communities to enjoy in the territories of the Member States considerable privileges and immunities.[32]

The status of the Communities in the laws of the Member States derives from these provisions. But their precise status and powers within the Member States' legal systems depend on the law of each Member State. Thus, for example, the Tribunale di Torino has refused to accord to the ECSC a status in Italian bankruptcy proceedings superior to that of a private corporation.[33] In English law, the status of the EEC was recently considered in the litigation concerning the International Tin Council.[34] The conclusions which can be drawn from those

---

[26] Case 6/64 *Costa* v. *ENEL* [1964] ECR 585, at 593.   [27] *Ibid.*

[28] *Ibid.* at 594. It is an interesting question whether the powers conferred on the Communities by the Treaties can be returned to the Member States, and, if so, how. If the Member States were to choose to amend the Treaties so as to transfer back to themselves powers now vested in the Communities and their institutions, it is difficult to see what could stop them; and ultimately they could, by agreement, terminate the Treaties and all the institutions they created. Equally, if a Member State were determined to leave the Communities, that would in practice require negotiation and, if possible, agreement (as in fact happened when the territory of Greenland seceded). In answer to a question in the HL, Baroness Chalker of Wallasey said: 'It remains open to Parliament to repeal the European Communities Act 1972 and for the United Kingdom to withdraw from the European Union. The terms of that withdrawal would have to be negotiated with the other Member States. The Government believe that the future prosperity and security of the United Kingdom depends on our membership of the European Union' (Hansard, HL, 22 Mar. 1995, WA 76).

[29] *Opinion 1/91 (The First EEA Opinion)* [1991] ECR 6079, at para. 21.

[30] Cf. the views of Lagrange AG in Case 8/55 *Fédération Charbonnière de Belgique* v. *High Authority* [1956] ECR 245.

[31] Arts. 211 EC, 185 Euratom, 6 ECSC.

[32] Art. 28 Merger Treaty and the Protocol on Privileges and Immunities annexed thereto.

[33] *High Authority* v. *Concordato Officine Elettromeccaniche Merlini* [1964] CMLR 184.

[34] *J. H. Rayner (Mincing Lane) Ltd.* v. *Department of Trade and Industry* [1989] 1 Ch. 72.

cases are that the English courts do not regard themselves as bound at common law to accord to the Community the same immunity as they are bound to accord to a foreign State; and that no legislative source in the United Kingdom conferred any such status, nor was it to be inferred from the Treaties themselves or from the developments in the powers and status of the Community in Community law. It would therefore seem that the position of the Communities in the law of the United Kingdom approximates to that of a statutory corporation rather than to that of a foreign State, although the Communities do, of course, enjoy the privileges and immunities provided for by the Treaties.[35]

Article 1 of the Protocol on Privileges and Immunities provides, *inter alia*, that 'the property and assets of the Communities shall not be the subject of any administrative or legal measure of constraint without the authorization of the Court of Justice'. This provision deals only with the immunity from execution of the Communities' assets. Immunity from suit is not dealt with specifically in the Protocol and seems to vary from one Member State to another. The ownership by the Communities of 'property and assets' is a matter to be determined by national law. The ECJ has taken a wide view of the purpose of Article 1 of the Protocol and has determined that it will not authorize any measure which would affect the independence and functioning of the Communities. It has consistently held that garnishee orders may, in certain circumstances, interfere with the independence and functioning of the Communities.[36] The Court has recently confirmed that the immunity granted by Article 1 of the Protocol is only waived where the Communities expressly renounce their rights to immunity or that immunity has been lifted by the Court itself.[37]

The Treaties make provision for the contractual and non-contractual liability of the EC and Euratom.[38] Actions for breach of contract and tort may be pursued before the national courts against these organizations. In any actions in national courts involving the EC or Euratom, or in any legal proceedings instituted by these Communities at the national level, the Communities are represented by the Commission.[39] The ECSC, on the other hand, is represented by its institutions, each within the limits of its powers.[40]

CONCLUSION

The Communities can be said to operate within three distinct legal orders: the international legal system, the Community legal system, and the national laws

---

[35] See n. 32 above.
[36] Case 1/87 SA *Universel Tankship Co. Inc.* v. *Commission* [1987] ECR 2807; Case 1/88 SA *Générale de Banque* v. *Commission* [1989] ECR 857.
[37] Case C-182/91 *Forafrique Burkinabe SA* v. *Commission* [1993] ECR I-2161.
[38] Arts. 215 EC, 188 Euratom.   [39] Arts. 211 EC, 185 Euratom.
[40] Art. 6 ECSC.

of the Member States. Depending on the viewpoint, the question of the nature and extent of the legal personality of the Communities can be answered in different ways. For present purposes, it is important to bear in mind that the view the Communities take of themselves is not determinative of, or necessarily the same as, the view others take of them, especially at the international level.

3

The Powers of the Communities

This Chapter sets out the principles and rules which determine the existence and extent of the Communities' powers in the external field. The exercise of these powers in practice in the principal areas of Community activity is considered in more detail in Part II.

The powers of the Communities derive from the Treaties. The Treaties determine the action which the Communities may take, and the procedures by which these powers may be exercised. Within the Community, the exercise of Community powers usually takes the form of legislation by the Council or the Commission, depending on the Community which is acting and the particular power being employed. In the external field, the exercise of Community powers usually involves the conclusion of agreements binding on the Communities in international law, but an assessment of the Communities' powers will also be relevant in determining whether the Communities may participate in international organizations, and whether the Communities should be held internationally responsible for a particular act or omission.[1] Although the law on the Communities' external competence has developed in the context of the making of agreements, the principles which determine the extent and nature[2] of Community competence are of general application, and apply in any context where questions about the Communities' powers arise.[3]

---

[1] See Ch. 2, pp. 31–2.

[2] i.e whether competence is exclusive to the Communities, or shared between the Communities and the Member States.

[3] Most of the cases relate to the exercise of competence by the EC under the Treaty of Rome, and some of the concepts which have developed may be less relevant to the activities of the other Communities. Nevertheless, the ECJ has been ready to look to principles developed in case law under one of the Treaties and to apply these to issues arising under another. It seems clear that the basic principles of the law in this area (e.g. the doctrines of the attribution of powers, of exclusive competence, and of the integration into the Community legal order of agreements concluded by the Communities) apply generally to all of the Communities. On the external competences of the Communities generally, see P. Pescatore, 'Les Relations Exterieures des Communautés Européennes', 103 *Hague Recueil* (1961, II); W. J. Ganshof Van der Meersch 'L'ordre juridique des Communautées européennes et le droit internationale' 148 *Hague Recueil* (1975 V); Leopold, 'External Relations Power of the EEC in Theory and Practice' (1977) 26 *ICLQ* 54; K. R. Simmonds, 'The Evolution of the External Relations Law of the European Economic Community' (1979) 28 *ICLQ* 644; C. W. A. Timmermans and E. L. M. Volker, *Division of Powers between the Eiuropean Communities and their Member States in the Field of External Relations* (Kluwer, 1981); Mégret, Vol. 12 *(Relations Exterieures)* (Brussels, 1980); Groux and Manin, *The European Communities in the International Order* (European Perspectives, 1985); J. Boulois 'Le droit des Communautées européennes dans ses rapports avec le droit international général' 235 *Hague Recueil* (1992 IV); HL Select Committee on the European Communities, 16th Rep. (1984–5), *External Competence of the European Communities*

In a recent summary of the law on external competence,[4] the Court implicitly distinguished between the source of the Communities' competence (whether competence arose from an express conferment under the Treaties or by implication), and the nature of that competence (whether it was exclusively for the Communities, or shared between the Communities and the Member States). The discussion in this Chapter broadly adopts that analysis. The first part of what follows considers (under the heading 'Sources of Community Competence') the powers expressly conferred on each of the Communities by the Treaties, and the powers which, according to the Court, arise from the Treaties by implication. The next part examines the nature of Community competence, in particular the distinction between 'exclusive' and 'shared' competence. The third part describes the geographical extent of Community competence. The last part looks at what is here for convenience called the 'temporal scope' of Community competence (the moment at which Community competence arises).

Before considering these matters in detail, it may be useful to recall briefly certain key concepts which are relevant to an understanding of the law.

'Competence': The powers of the Communities are often described as their 'competence'.[5] This expression has to be handled with care. It is commonly said that the Community 'has competence for' certain matters: agriculture, trade, and the environment are obvious and uncontroversial examples. This convenient shorthand is, however, inaccurate to the extent that it implies that the Community's powers are to be assessed by reference to areas, or subjects. It is true that, in certain areas of legislative and external activity, only the Community is competent to act: the Member States have lost their powers in these matters. But the extent of the Communities' powers is not measured by areas or subjects. The more accurate legal analysis is that the Communities are law-making structures to which the Member States have attributed certain powers for the attainment of stated objectives in accordance with the provisions conferring the powers in question. In relation to any given issue, therefore, the question is not really whether that issue arises in an area or subject 'within the Community's competence', but whether one of the objectives of the Treaties would be attained by the measures proposed, and whether adoption of such measures would be consistent with the procedures envisaged in the Treaty, in conformity with any conditions imposed by the Treaties on the exercise of the power in question and with other principles of Community law. Thus, it is true that the Euratom Community has competence 'for nuclear matters'; but the extent of that competence is to be determined by reference to the objectives and

---

(HL 236); *Halsbury's Laws*, ch. 4; Kapteyn and VerLoren van Themaat, *Introduction* (2nd edn. by Gormley, Kluwer, 1989), ch. XI; Hartley, *Foundations* (3rd edn., Clarendon Press, 1994), ch. 6.

[4] *Opinion 2/91 (Re ILO Convention 170)* [1993] ECR I–1061.

[5] From the French legal term *la compétence* (the jurisdiction, or proper domain, of a legal authority). The nearest UK domestic law equivalent to the doctrine of 'competence' as it applies to the external relations of the Communities is the doctrine of the *vires* of corporations.

powers in the Euratom Treaty, not by examining whether a particular issue relates in some way to nuclear energy. And it is true that the European Community has competence 'for education'; but its powers to adopt measures under Article 128 of the EC Treaty are carefully circumscribed. In assessing any action to be taken by one of the Communities, it is necessary to consider not just the subject matter involved, but also the precise powers conferred on the particular Community in that regard.[6]

Legislative discretion: the concept of competence (the legal power to act) must be distinguished from the political expediency of acting, which is a matter of the discretion of the Community legislator. Even where one of the Communities has powers which would enable it to adopt the measures proposed, it does not follow that the Community must act.[7] The Community legislator has a wide discretion in deciding whether action on a given matter would be the best or most appropriate course to take in the circumstances. The Council or Commission, faced with a particular problem, may decide that the prevailing political situation makes it inappropriate or impossible in practice for the Community to act.[8]

The competence of each of the Communities must also be distinguished from the competence of each institution within the scheme of each Treaty. An act may be within the competence of one of the Communities but outside the powers of the institution which purported to act, or outside the powers conferred on that institution by the Treaty under which the act in question was adopted.

Subsidiarity: *competence* must also be distinguished from *subsidiarity*. As has been noted, the concept of *competence* addresses the question whether the Community has legal power to act; the principle of *subsidiarity* addresses the question whether the Community should exercise its power to act, or whether action should be left to the Member States. The principle of subsidiarity is applicable to the exercise of Community powers externally as well as internally, and applies to the activities of all three Communities.[9]

SOURCES OF COMMUNITY COMPETENCE

The fundamental principle of Community law is the principle that the Communities' powers are attributed to the Communities by the Member States.[10] The Communities have no inherent sovereign powers in their own

---

[6] For the sake of convenience, throughout this Ch. and the rest of this book, the Community will often be described as having competence 'for' certain matters. The reader has however been warned of the essential inaccuracy of this phrase.

[7] Case 22/70 *Commission* v. *Council* [1970] ECR 263 at para. 95.

[8] But see Hartley, n. 3 above, ch. 13 for a discussion of situations in which the Community institutions may be obliged to act.   [9] See Art. B TEU.

[10] On this, see Kapteyn and VerLoren van Themaat, n. 3 above, ch. IV, 1.3. For discussion of the principle, see R. Barents, 'The Internal Market Unlimited: some observations on the legal basis of Community legislation' (1993) 30 *CMLRev*. 85.

right: they are creations of international law, owing their existence to the will
of the Member States expressed in the constitutive Treaties. This principle runs
through the Treaties: there is, for example, the recurrent theme that the
Communities are given 'tasks',[11] and powers to enable these tasks to be carried
out.[12] But the principle of the attribution of powers appears most clearly in
Article 3b EC, which provides that '[t]he Community shall act within the limits of the powers conferred upon it by this Treaty and of the objectives assigned
to it therein.' The Court has expressed the matter thus:

By creating a Community of unlimited duration, having its own institutions, its own personality, its own legal capacity, and capacity of representation on the international plane,
and more particularly, real powers stemming from a limitation of sovereignty or a transfer of powers from the States to the Community, the Member States have limited their
sovereign rights, albeit within limited fields, and have thus created a body of law which
binds both their nationals and themselves.[13]

The principle has also been formulated and elaborated by the European
Council in the conclusions of its Edinburgh meeting in 1992. Commenting on
Article 3b EC, the Heads of State and Government said '[t]he principle that
the Community can only act where given the power to do so—implying that
national powers are the rule and the Community's the exception—has always
been a basic feature of the Community legal order.'[14]

The principle of the attribution of powers does not mean that the Member
States are entitled unilaterally to take back the powers they have attributed to
the Community, by, for example, declaring that they intend themselves to act
in an area formerly the province of the Community. The Court commented in
Costa v. *ENEL* that '[t]he transfer by the States from their domestic legal system
to the Community legal system of the rights and obligations arising under the
Treaty carries with it a permanent limitation of their sovereign rights, against
which a subsequent unilateral act incompatible with the concept of the
Community cannot prevail.'[15]

Case law of the Court: the Treaties set out the objectives and tasks of each
Community, and indicate the way in which these are to be carried out. The
starting point, therefore, in any consideration of the nature and extent of the
Communities' powers is the text of the Treaties. In interpreting the text of the
Treaties, however, the Court of Justice has consistently looked not so much at

[11] Arts. 2 ECSC, 4 EC, 3 Euratom.
[12] Within the Community framework, the Treaties emphasize that the institutions are required
to act within the limits of the powers conferred upon them: see Arts. 3(1) ECSC, 4(2) EC, and 3(1)
Euratom.
[13] Case 6/64 *Costa* v. *ENEL* [1964] ECR 585 at 593 and 594.
[14] Edinburgh European Council, 11 and 12 Dec. 1992, Conclusions of the Presidency, Annex I
to Pt. A, Sect. I para. 2 (Bull. EC No. 12/1992, 12)
[15] Case 6/64, n. 13 above. As to the 'permanence' of the limitation of the Member States' powers, see Ch. 2, n. 28. On the situations in which the Member States may be called on to act for the
Community, see Ch. 9, pp. 236–7.

the literal meaning of the words of the Treaties, as at what it sees as the underlying purpose and objectives of the Treaties. A clear statement of the Court's view of the *raison d'être* of the Communities is in the *First EEA Agreement Opinion*,[16] where the Court said:

(16) [As] far as the Community is concerned, the rules on free trade and competition which the [EEA] agreement seeks to extend to the whole territory of the Contracting Parties have developed and form part of the Community legal order, the objectives of which go beyond that of the agreement.

(17) It follows *inter alia* from Articles 2, 8a and 102a of the EEC Treaty that that Treaty aims to achieve economic integration leading to the establishment of an internal market and economic and monetary union. Article 1 of the Single European Act makes it clear moreover that the objective of all the Community Treaties is to contribute together to making concrete progress towards European unity.

(18) It follows from the foregoing that the provisions of the EEC Treaty on free movement and competition, far from being an end in themselves, are only means for attaining those objectives.

. . .

(20) The EEA is to be established on the basis of an international treaty which, essentially, merely creates rights and obligations as between the contracting parties and provides for no transfer of sovereign rights to the intergovernmental institutions which it sets up.

(21) In contrast, the EEC Treaty, albeit concluded in the form of an international agreement, none the less constitutes the constitutional charter of a Community based on the rule of law. As the Court of Justice has consistently held, the Community Treaties established a new legal order for the benefit of which the States have limited their sovereign rights, in ever wider fields, and the subjects of which comprise not only the Member States but also their nationals. The essential characteristics of the Community legal order which has thus been established are in particular its primacy over the law of the Member States and the direct effect of a whole series of its provisions which are applicable to their nationals and to the Member States themselves.

In the area of the Communities' external relations, the Court has been particularly active and influential in shaping the law,[17] and a purposive approach has always informed the Court's analysis of the issues before it.

All three Communities[18] have powers to engage in international agreements, and to conduct activities on the international plane. The powers of each of the

---

[16] *Opinion 1/91 (Re the EEA Agreement)* [1991] ECR 6079 at para. 16.

[17] Fascinating though the subject is, no attempt will be made here to summarize the historical development by the ECJ of the principles governing the Communities' external competence. For accounts of the case law, see the sources referred to at n. 2 above, and P. Pescatore, 'External Relations in the Case Law of the ECJ' (1979) 16 *CMLRev.* 615; J. Groux, 'Le parallelisme des competences internes et externes de la CE' [1978] CDE 1; Kovar, 'Contribution de la Cour de Justice au développement de la condition internationale de la Communauté européenne' [1978] CDE 527; J. Boulois, 'La jurisprudence de la Cour de Justice des Communautés européennes relative aux relations exterieures des Communautés' (1978 II) 160 *Hague Recueil*, 333–93.

[18] The EU has no such powers: see Ch. 1, p. 25.

Communities are not the same, however: the position under each Treaty must be considered separately.

European Coal and Steel Community

Article 6 ECSC provides that 'in international relations, the Community shall enjoy the legal capacity it requires to perform its functions and attain its objectives'.[19] Although the Treaty establishing the ECSC does not in terms confer on that Community an express power to conclude agreements, most commentators hold that such a power exists, and that the ECSC may conclude agreements across the entire range of its activities.[20] The Community's practice bears this out. The ECSC has concluded agreements with many countries since 1953,[21] based generally on 'the Treaty establishing the European Coal and Steel Community', or on Article 95 ECSC, or occasionally on other Articles of the Treaty.

In addition, the ECSC Treaty provides that the Commission is to maintain all appropriate relations with the United Nations and the OEEC and is to keep these organizations regularly informed of the activities of the Community.[22] Furthermore, relations are to be maintained between the institutions of the Community and the Council of Europe as provided in the Protocol to the ECSC Treaty.[23]

Euratom

The parties to the Euratom Treaty wished to associate other countries with their work and to co-operate with international organizations concerned with the peaceful development of nuclear energy.[24] Chapter X of the Treaty deals expressly with the powers of the Community in the area of external relations. Article 101(1) Euratom provides[25] that '[t]he Community may, within the limits of its powers and jurisdiction, enter into obligations by concluding agreements or contracts with a third State, an international organization or a national of a third State.' The Treaty also provides that:

(a) in order to perform its task,[26] the Community is to 'establish with other

---

[19] Art. 6 (2) ECSC.

[20] The doctrine of parallelism applies in the case of the ECSC: see Hartley, n. 3 above, 179.

[21] The procedure for conclusion of agreements by the ECSC is considered in more detail in Ch. 4, and practice under the ECSC Treaty is examined in Ch. 23.

[22] Art. 93 ECSC: the continued reference to the 'OEEC' in this Art. appears to be an oversight. The corresponding provisions in the EC (Art. 231) and the Euratom (Art. 201) Treaties, which were amended by the TEU, refer to the 'OECD'.

[23] Art. 94 ECSC. As to relations between the Communities and international organizations, see Ch. 7.

[24] Preamble, para. 5.   [25] Art. 101 (1) Euratom.

[26] According to Art. 1(2) Euratom: 'It shall be the task of the Community to contribute to the raising of the standard of living in the Member States and to the development of relations with the other countries by creating the conditions necessary for the speedy establishment and growth of nuclear industries.'

countries and international organizations such relations as will foster progress in the peaceful uses of nuclear energy';[27]

(b) the Commission may, by contract, entrust the carrying out of certain parts of the Community research programme to Member States, persons, or undertakings, or to third countries, international organizations, or nationals of third countries;[28]

(c) where an agreement or contract for the exchange of scientific or industrial information in the nuclear field between a Member State, a person, or an undertaking on the one hand, and a third State, an international organization, or a national of a third State on the other, requires, on either part, the signature of a State acting in its sovereign capacity, it shall be concluded by the Commission. Subject to the provisions of Articles 103 and 104, the Commission may, however, on such conditions as it considers appropriate, authorize a Member State, a person, or an undertaking to conclude such agreements;[29]

(d) third States, international organizations, and nationals of third States may participate, on the basis of a Commission proposal agreed by the Council, in the financing or management of any Joint Undertaking established under Chapter V of the Euratom Treaty;[30]

(e) the Agency established by Article 52 Euratom has the exclusive right to conclude contracts relating to the supply of ores, source materials, and special fissile materials coming from inside the Community or from outside;[31]

(f) the Commission is to ensure the maintenance of all appropriate relations with the organs of the United Nations, of its specialized agencies, and of the General Agreement on Tariffs and Trade. The Commission is also to maintain such relations as are appropriate with all international organizations.[32] The Community is to establish all appropriate forms of co-operation with the Council of Europe,[33] and to establish close co-operation with the OECD, the details to be determined by common accord;[34]

(g) the Community may conclude with one or more States, or international organizations, agreements establishing an association involving reciprocal rights and obligations, common action, and special procedures.[35]

---

[27] Art. 2(h) Euratom.
[28] Art. 10 Euratom. On the meaning of 'contract', see Ch. 4, n. 142.
[29] Art. 29 Euratom.
[30] Art. 46(2)(e) Euratom: on the meaning of 'Joint Undertaking', see Art. 45 and the other provisions of ch. V Euratom.
[31] Art. 52(2)(b). On the powers of the Agency under the Treaty, see *Ruling 1/78 (Re the Draft Convention on the Physical Protection of Nuclear Materials, Facilities and Transports)*, [1978] ECR 2151 at paras. 13 ff. See, further, Ch. 22.
[32] Art. 199 Euratom. See, further, Ch. 7.   [33] Art. 200 Euratom.
[34] Art. 201 Euratom.
[35] Art. 206 Euratom. By contrast with the EC Treaty, association agreements under the Euratom Treaty do not require the Parliament's assent: see Art. 206(2). As to association agreements generally, see Ch. 20.

Practice under the Euratom Treaty, and the procedures for conclusion of agreements are examined elsewhere,[36] as are that Community's relations with international organizations.[37] The following points may be noted here. First, Article 101 of the Euratom Treaty is the clearest statement in all the Treaties of the doctrine of parallelism; that is, the doctrine that the Community's external competence operates across the entire range of the areas covered by its internal competences.[38] The powers conferred expressly on the Community are adequate for the conclusion of any agreement falling within the scope of the Community's competences under the Euratom Treaty: there is no need for the application of the doctrine of implied powers developed by the Court in the context of the European Community. Secondly, although the Treaty confers several powers in specific areas, in practice, the general power in Article 101 has been used as the basis for the conclusion of agreements by the Euratom Community. Finally, the Treaty confers power on the Community to conclude 'contracts' with third countries and international organizations, as well as 'agreements'. The meaning of these terms is considered further in the context of the conclusion of agreements by the Community.[39]

European Community

The external powers conferred on the European Community in the original Treaty of Rome were limited. There were provisions about co-operation with various international organizations,[40] and express powers to enter into agreements in only two areas. Article 113 provided for the conclusion of agreements relating to the common commercial policy, and Article 238 provided for the conclusion of a category of agreements which became known as association agreements.

There was argument for many years about whether the Community had power to conclude agreements in other areas. The controversy was settled by the Court's judgment in the *AETR*[41] case, in which the Court held that Article 210 of the Treaty (which confers legal personality on the Community) meant that in its external relations the Community enjoyed the *capacity* to establish contractual links with third countries over the whole field of the objectives defined in Part 1 of the Treaty. To determine the Community's *authority*, regard should be had to the whole scheme of the Treaty, no less than to its substantive provisions. Such powers arose from express conferment (such as Articles 113 and 238), but also from other provisions of the Treaty and measures adopted within

---

[36] On practice under the Euratom Treaty, see Ch. 22; on the procedures for conclusion of agreements, see Ch. 4.

[37] See Ch. 7.

[38] The doctrine of parallelism is sometimes encapsulated in the maxim *in foro interno, in foro externo*.

[39] See n. 142 in Ch. 4.   [40] Arts. 229, 230, and 231 EEC.

[41] Case 22/70 *Commission* v. *Council* [1971] ECR 263.

the framework of these provisions by the Community institutions. With regard to the implementation of the provisions of the Treaty, the system of internal Community measures could not be separated from that of external relations. In that particular case, the powers of the Community in the area of transport extended to the making of international agreements with third countries because of the provisions of Regulation 543/69 EEC on the harmonization of social legislation relating to road transport.

The Community's competence can therefore arise 'by express conferment' in a Treaty Article, or by implication from a Treaty Article. Competence deriving from the first source is usually described as the 'express' power of the Community. Competence based on the second source is described as the 'implied' power.[42] of the Community.

Express Powers

Express powers are powers conferred expressly in a provision of the Treaty. These competences, and the practice in the principal areas of the European Community's activities, will be considered in more detail in Part II. The important general point is that the scope of each of the 'express' external powers conferred on the Community in the Treaty has to be determined by interpreting the Article conferring the power in the light of the practice of the Council[43] and the case law of the Court. The measure of the scope of the Community's power in any such area is thus the Article in question. The powers expressly conferred on the European Community by the Treaty of Rome fall into three general categories.

A Power to Conclude Agreements

The Treaty expressly confers a power to conclude agreements in the following areas:

(a) where agreements concerning monetary or foreign exchange regime matters need to be negotiated by the Community with one or more States or international organizations;[44]

---

[42] 'Implied' powers are sometimes referred to as 'derived' powers. In theory, a distinction can be made between powers which exist by implication in the terms of a Treaty Art., and powers which 'derive' from a Treaty Art. by virtue of the adoption of measures under that Art. An example of the former might be the Community's powers in the area of fisheries: the power to regulate fisheries within the Community waters necessitates—according to the ECJ—a power to enter into international commitments on fisheries. The external power is therefore 'implicit' in the internal power. An example of the latter might be external competence arising from the adoption of common internal rules: the Community's powers 'derive' from the power in the Art. through the rules. However coherent this distinction may be, the Court has referred to both kinds of powers as powers which arise by 'implication' or 'implicitly'. For that reason, and to avoid complicating further an already complicated subject, this Ch. refers to 'implied' powers as encompassing both.

[43] The practice of the Council and the Commission is not, of course, determinative of the law: see, e.g., *Opinion 1/94 (Re WTO Agreement)* [1995] 1 CMLR 205 at para. 52.

[44] Art. 109(3) EC.

(b) where agreements relating to the common commercial policy need to be negotiated with one or more States or international organizations;[45]

(c) in implementing the multiannual framework programme to be adopted under Article 130i, the Community may make provision for co-operation in Community research, technological development, and demonstration with third countries or international organizations. The detailed arrangements for such co-operation may be the subject of agreements between the Community and the third parties concerned;[46]

(d) within its sphere of competence in environmental matters the Community is to co-operate with third countries and with the competent international organizations. The arrangements for Community co-operation may be the subject of agreements between the Community and the third parties concerned;[47]

(e) within its sphere of competence in development co-operation the Community is to co-operate with third countries and with the competent international organizations. The arrangements for Community co-operation may be the subject of agreements between the Community and the third parties concerned;[48]

(f) the Community may conclude with one or more States or international organizations agreements establishing an association involving reciprocal rights and obligations, common action, and special procedures.[49]

An 'agreement' for these purposes is any undertaking entered into by entities subject to international law which has binding force, whatever its formal designation.[50] The power to conclude agreements also appears to include the power to enter into unilateral obligations, and to make non-legally binding commitments.[51]

A Power to Foster Co-operation at the International Level

In the areas of education, vocational training and youth,[52] culture,[53] and public health[54] the Community and the Member States are to foster co-operation with third countries and the competent international organizations. The Council of Europe is mentioned specifically in the context of co-operation in the areas of education and culture. The Community may decide to co-operate

---

[45] Art. 113 EC. As to the common commercial policy, see Ch. 12.

[46] Art. 130m EC. On the Community's external competence on research and technological development, see Ch. 16.

[47] Art. 130r(4) EC. On the Community's external competence in the environment, see Ch. 17.

[48] Art. 130y EC. On the Community's external competence for development policy, see further Ch. 18.

[49] Usually known as 'association agreements': Art. 238 EC. See Ch. 20.

[50] See *Opinion 1/75 (Re OECD Local Costs Standard)* [1975] ECR 1355, and the discussion in Ch. 4, pp. 75–6.

[51] See Ch. 4.   [52] Arts 126(3) and 127(3) EC.

[53] Art. 128(3) EC.   [54] Art. 129(3) EC.

with third countries to promote projects of mutual interest and to ensure the inter-operability of the trans-European networks referred to in Title XII of the EC Treaty.[55]

The practice of the Council, though sparse to date, supports the view that the power 'to foster international co-operation' includes a power to enter into agreements.[56] But the Community cannot, by concluding international agreements, take action externally going beyond its powers to legislate or adopt measures internally. Thus, it is not open to the Community to attempt to harmonize by an international agreement the laws or regulations of the Member States on matters such as public health or education.[57] Any agreement entered into must fall within the particular objectives of the powers conferred on the Communities under the Articles in question. The power to foster co-operation no doubt extends to securing Community participation in international organizations and conferences (to the extent that the constitutions of such bodies allow).

A Power to Co-operate with International Organizations

Under the EC Treaty, the Commission is to ensure the maintenance of all appropriate relations with the organs of the United Nations, of its specialized agencies, and of the General Agreement on Tariffs and Trade. The Commission is also to maintain such relations as are appropriate with all international organizations.[58] The Community is to establish all appropriate forms of co-operation with the Council of Europe.[59] The Community is to establish close co-operation with the OECD, the details of which are to be determined by common accord.[60] These provisions mirror those of the other Community Treaties, and are considered elsewhere in this work.[61]

Implied Powers

The Euratom and ECSC Treaties confer on these Communities powers in relation to external activities which are co-extensive with their internal legislative powers.[62] Thus, for each of these Communities, provided that an agreement or other international act can be said to further one of the Community's

---

[55] Art. 129c(3) EC.

[56] The difference between the Community's power 'to enter into agreements' and the power 'to foster co-operation' is difficult to state precisely. The key point is probably that the areas in which the Community is given power 'to foster co-operation' (education, vocational training, youth, culture, and public health) are areas of particular sensitivity for the Member States. Strict limits are thus placed by the Treaty on the exercise of Community competence internally: harmonization of Member States' laws is prohibited, and so on. The external powers conferred on the Community likewise reflect the Member States' sensitivities. The Community is not given a general power to make agreements; but agreements may be made to the extent necessary to 'foster co-operation'.

[57] See Art. 126(4) (education) and Art. 129(4), 2nd indent (public health).

[58] Art. 229 EC.   [59] Art. 230 EC.   [60] Art. 231 EC.

[61] Ch. 7.   [62] See pp. 42–3 above.

objectives, the Community will have power to act externally. There is 'parallelism' between the Community's internal and external powers.

The position under the EC Treaty has always been more complicated. Originally, as has been seen, the Treaty only gave power to enter into agreements in two areas: the common commercial policy under Article 113 and association agreements under Article 238. The doctrine of implied powers developed in the jurisprudence of the Court ensured that the Community could enter into agreements in other areas within its internal competence: but the exact scope of the Community's implied powers, and the nature of the competence which arose from the operation of the principles developed by the Court were unclear and controversial. All the difficulties have not yet been resolved, but matters have been clarified by recent case law[63] and by the amendments made to the Treaty of Rome by the Maastricht Treaty. The former has resolved some of the contested points of legal theory in the doctrine of implied powers. The Maastricht Treaty has clarified matters by creating express powers to act externally in a range of areas where previously such powers were of uncertain scope, or arose only by implication. The extent and nature of the Community's powers in these areas is now in principle to be determined by reference to the Article conferring the express powers, rather than by application of the doctrine of implied powers.

As has been seen, the competence of the Community in the external field arises not only from express conferment by the Treaty, but may flow by implication from other provisions of the Treaty and the practice of the Community.[64] In *Opinion 2/91*,[65] the Court described the implied competence of the Community in the following terms:

[A]uthority to enter into international commitments may not only arise from an express attribution by the Treaty, but may also flow implicitly from its provisions. . . . [In] particular, . . . whenever Community law created for the institutions of the Community powers within its internal system for the purpose of attaining a specific objective, the Community had authority to enter into the international commitments necessary for the attainment of that objective even in the absence of an express provision in that connection. At paragraph [20] in its judgment in Joined Cases 3, 4 and 6/76 *Kramer and Others* [1976] ECR 1279, the Court had already pointed out that such authority could flow by implication from other measures adopted by the Community institutions within the framework of the Treaty provisions or the acts of accession.

Implied powers arise in broadly three situations. The commonest is where measures have been adopted by the institutions on the basis of an internal power.

---

[63] In particular, *Opinion 2/91 (Re ILO Convention 170)* [1993] ECR I–1061; *Opinion 1/94 (Re the WTO Agreement)*, n. 42 above; and *Opinion 2/92 (Re OECD National Treatment Instrument)*, 24 Mar. 1995, not yet reported.

[64] Joined Cases 3, 4, and 6/76 *Cornelis Kramer* [1976] ECR 1279 at 1308 paras. 19–20 of the judgment.

[65] N. 63 above.

But external powers may also arise from an internal power even where measures have not been adopted, either because external and internal competence must be exercised simultaneously, or because an external power is implicit in the scheme of the internal power. These situations will be considered in turn.

Where Measures have been Adopted by the Institutions

The leading case on this point is Case 22/70 *Commission* v. *Council* ('the *AETR* case') where the Court held that:

> 17. Each time the Community, with a view to implementing a common policy envisaged by the Treaty, adopts provisions laying down common rules, whatever form these may take, the Member States no longer have the right, acting individually or even collectively, to undertake obligations with third countries which affect those rules. . . .
>
> 18. As and when such common rules come into being, the Community alone is in a position to assume and carry out contractual obligations towards third countries affecting the whole sphere of application of the Community legal system. . . .
>
> 19. With regard to the implementation of the provisions of the Treaty the system of internal Community measures may not be separated from that of external relations.[66]

Thus, in principle, the adoption of internal measures by the Community can give rise by implication to a power to act externally in the area covered by the measures.

The most obvious example of an external power arising in this way is where an internal act expressly confers a power to negotiate and conclude international agreements. In the *AETR* case, the Court relied on the fact that Article 3 of Regulation 543/69 granted the Community the power 'to enter into any negotiations with third countries which may prove necessary for the purposes of implementing this regulation'.[67] And in its consideration in *Opinion 1/94* of the Community's powers in the area of services, the Court held that '[w]henever the Community has included in its internal legislative acts provisions relating to the treatment of nationals of non-member countries or expressly conferred on its institutions powers to negotiate with non-member countries, it acquires exclusive competence in the spheres covered by those acts.'[68]

A power to act externally can also arise, however, from measures which do not expressly provide for the conclusion of agreements. Where internal measures amount to 'common rules' or harmonization of internal legislation, the external Community competence created by the adoption of such measures is exclusive. But provisions of Community legislation which, though legally binding, do not set exhaustive or definitive standards[69] can also give rise to external competence.

---

[66] N. 7 above, paras. 17–19.   [67] *Ibid.*

[68] *Opinion 1/94*, n. 43 above, at para. 95. Examples of derived legal bases for external action in the area of services are cited in para. 94 of that *Opinion*.

[69] See *Opinion 2/91*, n. 63 above, discussed further below.

The *Kramer* Case provides an example of an external power arising in part from the adoption of internal measures. The question for the Court was whether the Community had authority to enter into international commitments on fisheries. It was accepted that no specific provisions of the Treaty authorized the Community to enter into such commitments. The Court accordingly turned to 'the general system of Community law in the sphere of the external relations of the Community'. Article 210 EC meant that the Community had capacity to enter into international commitments over the whole field of its objectives as defined in the EC Treaty.

To establish in a particular case whether the Community has authority to enter into international commitments, regard must be had to the whole scheme of Community law no less than to its substantive provisions. Such authority arises not only from an express conferment by the Treaty, but may equally flow implicitly from other provisions of the Treaty, from the Act of Accession, and from measures adopted, within the framework of those provisions, by the Community institutions.[70]

The Court examined Article 3(d) EEC (which provided that the adoption of a common agricultural policy was one of the objectives of the Community); Articles 39 to 43 (which dealt with the establishment of such a policy); Regulations 2141/70 and 2142/70 (setting up a fisheries policy); and Article 102 of the 1972 Act of Accession (which provided that the Council should determine conditions for fishing with a view to ensuring protection of the fisheries resources of the sea). The Court then said:[71]

It follows from these provisions taken as a whole that the Community has at its disposal, on the internal level, the power to take any measures for the conservation of the biological resources of the sea . . . It should be made clear that, although Article 5 of Regulation 2141/70 is applicable only to a geographically limited fishing area, it none the less follows from Article 102 of the Act of Accession, from Article 1 of the said regulation and moreover from the very nature of things that the rule-making authority of the Community *ratione materiae* also extends—insofar as the Member States have similar authority under public international law—to fishing on the high seas. The only way to ensure the conservation of the biological resources of the sea both effectively and equitably is through a system of rules binding on all the States concerned, including non-Member countries. In these circumstances it follows from the very duties and powers which Community law has established and assigned to the institutions of the Community on the internal level that the Community has authority to enter into international commitments for the conservation of the resources of the sea.[71]

Where Powers to Legislate Internally Exist but have not been Exercised

The Court of Justice has also held that the mere existence of an internal power can of itself give rise to a power to enter into agreements: it is not always nec-

---

[70] Joined Cases 3, 4, and 6/76, n. 64 above.   [71] *Ibid.*, paras. 30–33.

essary that the power should have been exercised. In the *Rhine Navigation* case,[72] the issue was the Community's participation in arrangements for the control of river traffic on the Rhine and the Moselle. It was within the Community's internal competence to regulate inland waterway traffic by means of its powers in the area of transport, but no such measures had been adopted. In the circumstances of the case, it was necessary to ensure that Switzerland, a non-Member State, also participated in the scheme under consideration. A regulation or other internal measure of Community law would clearly not suffice for this purpose, so the question arose whether the Community could conclude the agreement on the basis of its internal powers, without having first adopted internal legislation. In its *Opinion*, the Court reiterated the principle that external powers could flow by implication from measures adopted by the institutions as well as from express provisions in the Treaties,[73] and then said:[74]

This is particularly so in all cases in which internal power has already been used in order to adopt measures which come within the attainment of common policies. It is, however, not limited to that eventuality. Although the internal Community measures are only adopted when the international agreement is concluded and made enforceable, as is envisaged in the present case by the proposal for a regulation to be submitted to the Council by the Commission, the power to bind the Community *vis-à-vis* third countries nevertheless flows by implication from the provisions of the Treaty creating the internal power and in so far as the participation of the Community in the international agreement is, as here, necessary for the attainment of one of the objectives of the Community.

The scope of the principle thus enunciated by the Court remained however unclear. Until *Opinion 1/94*, most commentators[75] believed, on the basis of the Court's comments in the *Rhine Navigation* case, that the external competence of the EC could be regarded as co-extensive with its internal competence.

There was a certain logic in the view that the Community should be able to take action on the international stage in all the areas in which it had power to legislate for itself internally, but the Court, however, had not in terms said that the Community's internal and external competences were exactly co-extensive or parallel. In the *Rhine Navigation* case the Court based its conclusions on the fact that Community participation in the agreement was '*necessary for the attainment of one of the objectives of the Community*'.[76] Subsequent references by the Court to the principle in the *Rhine Navigation* case suggested, if anything, a more restrictive reading: in *Opinion 2/91*, the Court referred to 'powers within [the Community's] internal system *for the purpose of attaining a specific objective*'.[77]

---

[72] *Opinion 1/76 (Re the Draft Agreement for a Laying-up Fund for Inland Waterway Vessels)* [1977] ECR 741.

[73] i.e. the principle established in the *Kramer* case, n. 64 above.   [74] At para. 4.

[75] See e.g., Pescatore, n. 17 above, at 621; Kovar, n. 17 above, n 14; M. Hardy, *Opinion 1/76 of the Court of Justice* (1977) 14 *CMLRev.* 561 at 588; Hartley, n. 3 above, ch. 6, 178.

[76] *Opinion 1/76*, n. 71 above, at para. 4 (emphasis supplied).

[77] *Opinion 2/91*, n. 63 above, at para. 7 (emphasis supplied).

The question of the meaning of the *Rhine Navigation* case arose clearly in *Opinion 1/94 (Re the WTO Agreement)*.[78] The Commission argued that the Community's participation in the General Agreement on Trade in Services (GATS) was necessary to ensure the coherence of the internal market, and also because the Community could not allow itself to remain inactive on the international stage in matters of international trade. According to the Commission, whenever Community law conferred on the institutions internal powers for the purposes of attaining specific objectives, the international competence of the Community flowed implicitly from those provisions, if the Community's participation was necessary for the attainment of one of the objectives of the Community. Thus, the Commission argued, the Community, and the Community alone, should participate in the WTO Agreement even in respect of areas where no internal rules existed.

The Court rejected the Commission's interpretation of the *Rhine Navigation* case. That case, the Court said, related to an issue different from that arising in the *WTO Agreement* case. The issue in *Rhine Navigation* had been the rational use of the inland waterways in the Rhine basin, an objective which could not be achieved by the establishment of 'autonomous common rules' (internal Community legislation) because of the traditional participation of vessels from Switzerland in navigation on the waterways in question. The participation of those vessels meant that Switzerland had to be brought into the scheme envisaged by means of an international agreement. Similar considerations applied in the context of conservation of the resources of the seas. Internal legislative measures to control fishing by vessels of the Member States would not be effective if the same restrictions were not to apply to vessels flying the flag of a non-member country bordering on the same seas. It followed, according to the Court, that external powers could be exercised, and could thus become exclusive, without any internal legislation having first been adopted. This was not the case in the sphere of services: attainment of freedom of establishment and freedom to provide services for nationals of the Member States was not inextricably linked to the treatment afforded in the Community to nationals of non-member countries or in non-member countries to nationals of Member States of the Community. Thus the Commission's interpretation of the *Rhine Navigation* principle did not apply.

The Court offered further clarification of the law in *Opinion 2/92*:[79]

It is true that, as the Court stated in *Opinion 1/76*, the external competence based on the Community's internal powers may be exercised and may thus become exclusive, without any internal legislation having first been adopted. However, this relates to a situation where the conclusion of an international agreement is necessary in order to achieve Treaty objectives which cannot be attained by the adoption of autonomous rules (see *Opinion 1/94*, paragraph 85).

---

[78] [1994]ECR I–5267.   [79] N. 63 above.

It would therefore appear that the Community can only derive exclusive external competence on the basis of the *Rhine Navigation* principle where the participation of a third State in a particular measure or scheme is necessary to enable the Community to fulfil one of its objectives; that is to say, in matters where the Community's objectives cannot be achieved by a regulation or directive because third States also have to be bound by the measure in question. The scope of the principle has thus been narrowed to cases closely analogous to *Opinion 1/76*.

Certain points of difficulty remain, notably whether, and if so, to what extent, the *Rhine Navigation* principle can apply to services other than those which, under the Treaty, have a clear international element (such as transport services). But the practical consequences of this uncertainty are unlikely to be significant. In many areas of Community activity in which the doctrine of implied powers still operates, the adoption of internal measures has had the effect of creating extensive external competence. Furthermore, as has been noted, the TEU has provided express powers in many areas in which, formerly, external powers arose by implication.

Where a Power to Act is Implicit in an Article of the Treaty Conferring an Internal Power

Certain Articles of the Treaty which deal principally with matters internal to the Community nevertheless imply that the Community has a corresponding external power, even though no such power is expressly conferred, and no internal measures have been adopted. The Court seemed to say in the *Kramer* case[80] that the power to establish a common fisheries policy internally would have implied a power to enter into commitments even in the absence of internal measures, because the effective control of Community fishing stocks necessitated a power to conclude agreements. The same is probably true of the Community's powers to regulate competition:[81] the nature of the Community's internal power as regulator precludes the exercise of Member State competence externally on matters which fall within the Community's competition jurisdiction.[82]

Articles 95 ECSC, 235 EC and 203 Euratom

Each Treaty contains an Article[83] enabling the relevant Community to 'cope with any insufficiency in the powers conferred on it, expressly or by implication,

---

[80] At paras. 30–33.   [81] Arts. 85 ff. EC.

[82] The Community's powers to deal with state aids fall within the common commercial policy under Art. 113 EC. On the Community's powers to enter into agreements on competition matters, see *Opinion 1/92 (Second EEA Opinion)* [1992] ECR I–2821 at paras. 32–33. See also Ch. 12.

[83] Art. 95 ECSC provides that 'In all cases not provided for in this Treaty where it becomes apparent that a decision or recommendation of the High Authority is necessary to attain, within the common market in coal and steel . . . one of the objectives of the Community . . . the decision may be taken or the recommendation made with the unanimous assent of the Council and after the Consultative Committee has been consulted.' Art. 235 EC provides that 'If action by the Community should prove necessary to attain, in the course of the operation of the common market, one of the objectives of the Community and this Treaty has not provided the

for the achievement of its objectives'.[84] The terms of these Articles vary from Treaty to Treaty, but the essential conditions for the exercise of the powers thereby conferred are that (a) the adoption of a particular measure is 'necessary' for the attainment of one of the Community's objectives; and (b) the relevant Treaty has not conferred the necessary powers. The scope and legal nature of the competence thus conferred on the Communities are hard to determine, but for present purposes, several general points may be briefly noted.

First, the powers in the relevant Articles apply in the area of the Communities' external relations as well as in the adoption of internal measures.[85]

Secondly, whether the adoption of measures is 'necessary' is a matter within the discretion of the Community legislator. 'Although Article 235 EEC empowers the Council to take any "appropriate measures" equally in the sphere of external relations, it does not create an obligation, but confers on the Council an option, failure to exercise which cannot affect the validity of the proceedings.'[86] The same must be true of Articles 95 ECSC and 203 Euratom.

Thirdly, the discretion thus conferred on the Council, or in the case of the ECSC the Commission, is not unlimited. The measures adopted must be necessary to 'attain one of the objectives of the Community', a phrase which leaves scope for creativity, but sets the exercise of the power firmly within the legislative order of the Treaties: measures going beyond the objectives of the Treaties would have to be adopted by the Member States, or would have to be preceded by an amendment of the Treaties. The Court has frequently stressed that the powers in these Articles may only be relied on where no other provision of the Treaty gives the Community institutions the necessary powers.[87]

Furthermore, the powers in Articles 95 ECSC, 235 EC, and 203 Euratom must, like any other power conferred in the Treaties, be exercised in accordance with the basic principles of the Community legal order, such as the principles of subsidiarity and proportionality. Finally, it seems clear that these powers cannot be employed in contradiction of limitations imposed in other Articles of the Treaties. Thus, a prohibition on the adoption of measures of harmonization[88]

necessary powers, the Council shall, acting unanimously on a proposal from the Commission and after consulting the Parliament, take the appropriate measures.' Art. 203 Euratom provides that 'If action by the Community should prove necessary to attain one of the objectives of the Community and this Treaty has not provided the necessary powers, the Council shall, acting unanimously on a proposal from the Commission and after consulting the Parliament, take the appropriate measures.' For a discussion of these powers, see Hartley, n. 3 above, 111–19; Kapteyn and VerLoren van Themaat, n. 3 above, ch. IV, 1.3.1 and 1.3.2; Van der Meersch, n. 3 above, 148 *Hague Recueil* (1975 V), 54–72.

[84] *Opinion 1/94*, n. 43 above, at para. 89.
[85] See Case 22/70, n. 7 above, at para. 95; *Opinion 1/94*, n. 43 above, at paras. 89 ff.
[86] Case 22/70, n. 7 above, at para. 95.
[87] Case 56/88 *UK* v. *Council* [1989] ECR 1615; Case C–295/90 *Parliament* v. *Council* [1992] ECR I–4193; Joined Cases C–51/89, C–90/89, and C–94/89 *UK* v. *Council* [1991] ECR I–2757; *Opinion 2/92*, n. 63 above, para. 36.
[88] e.g. Art. 128(5) EC.

could not be evaded by the adoption of measures under Article 95 ECSC, 235 EC, or 203 Euratom.

External competence may arise under these Articles in two ways. If internal measures have been adopted, external competence will arise in accordance with the usual principles.[89] In addition, however, it has been the practice to use these Articles as the legal basis for the conclusion of agreements in areas in which a Community objective can be identified, but where internal measures have not been adopted. The clearest examples include the emergence of the European Economic Community's external action in the areas of the environment and development co-operation.[90] But *Opinion 1/94*[91] casts some doubt on the legitimacy of using Article 235 EC in this way. On one reading, the Court, in paragraph 90 of its *Opinion*, has confined the use of Article 235 in the external field to situations in which competence arises from the existence of common rules. On the other hand, the emphasis in that passage on 'exclusive' competence may leave open the possibility that non-exclusive external competence can arise even in the absence of internal rules.

The Communities' Powers in the Area of Diplomatic Relations

The 'diplomatic relations' of the Communities are examined in Chapter 8. Some general points relating to the Communities' powers in this area may be noted here.

The *Protocol on the Privileges and Immunities of the European Communities* provides that the Commission may conclude agreements with third countries for the recognition of the Community *laissez passer*[92] as a valid travel document.[93] This power is exercised for the benefit of all three Communities.

The Communities appear to have an inherent power to seek and maintain observer status at those international organizations which deal with matters within the competence of the Communities.[94] The Communities receive diplomatic representatives of third States,[95] but appear to have themselves no power to establish diplomatic relations with third States. The Commission's power to establish delegations in third countries is not an exercise of a competence of the Communities, but flows from the Commission's own powers to organize its services as seems most appropriate to it as an institution.[96] The Commission has a similar power to establish delegations at international organizations.

---

[89] See above, p. 49.   [90] See Chs. 17 and 18.
[91] N. 43 above. See also *Opinion 2/92*, n. 63 above, at para. 36.
[92] i.e., the *laissez passer* provided for in Art. 7 of the Protocol on the Privileges and Immunities of the European Communities.
[93] Art. 7 of the Protocol.   [94] Ch. 7.
[95] The Treaties expressly envisage this: see Art. 17 of the Protocol on the Privileges and Immunities of the European Communities.
[96] Ch. 8.

THE NATURE OF COMMUNITY COMPETENCE

Where competences have been attributed to the Communities by the Member States, the Member States' residual competence is subject to certain constraints deriving from their obligations under the Treaties. In some cases, competence over a particular matter has been transferred completely from the Member States to the Communities, and there is in theory no room for continuing Member State competence. The Communities' competence is 'exclusive'. In other areas, the Communities and the Member States retain powers to act; the Communities' powers in these areas are described as 'shared' with the Member States.

'Exclusive' Community competence

The Court has said that in respect of certain matters the Community's power to act leads to the exclusion of any Member State power to act in the same areas.[97] It is therefore important to know when the Community has such powers and what the consequences are for the Member States of the existence of such powers on the part of the Community. The rules which have been developed to determine when competence is exclusive have arisen mainly in the context of the EC Treaty, but appear to apply equally to the other Communities.

When is the Community's Competence Exclusive?

The Court recently summarized the law in its opinion in the *ILO* case[98] in the following terms:

The exclusive or non-exclusive nature of the Community's competence does not flow solely from the provisions of the Treaty but may also depend on the scope of the measures which have been adopted by the Community institutions for the application of those provisions and which are of such a kind as to deprive the Member States of an area of competence which they were able to exercise previously on a transitional basis.

The competence of the Communities may thus be said to be exclusive in the following cases.

Where that Consequence flows from the Treaty Provisions from which Competence derives
In the Treaty establishing the *European Community*, the Community's external competence is exclusive under the Articles establishing the common commercial policy and the common fisheries policy. The Articles on competition probably also give rise to an exclusive external competence.

---

[97] See the extracts quoted at n. 127 below. [98] *Opinion 2/91*, n. 63 above, at para. 9.

Common commercial policy: in relation to Article 113 EC, the Court has said[99] that the common commercial policy envisaged in that Article was conceived in the context of the operation of the Common Market, for the defence of the common interests of the Community. This conception of commonality of interests, the Court held, was incompatible with a freedom on the part of the Member States to act concurrently to secure their own interests. The provisions of Articles 113 and 114, concerning the conditions under which agreements on commercial policy had to be concluded, showed that exercise of concurrent powers by the Member States was impossible. Competence in relation to the common commercial policy under the EC Treaty[100] was therefore exclusive.[101]

Conservation of fisheries: the Court drew a similar conclusion from the terms of Article 102 of the United Kingdom/Ireland/Denmark Act of Accession in relation to the establishment of the common fisheries policy. The reasoning seems to have been that the Treaty gave the Community power to establish a common agricultural policy (which included a policy on fisheries), and internal legislation had been adopted to that end. In particular, the Community had power to take measures to ensure the conservation of the biological resources of the seas. Effective and equitable conservation measures could only be taken at the international level. So, 'since the expiration on 1 January 1979 of the transitional period laid down by Article 102 of the Act of Accession, power to adopt, as part of the common fisheries policy, measures relating to the conservation of the resources of the sea has belonged fully and definitively to the Community.'[102]

Competition: the Community's power to enter into commitments in the field of competition is probably exclusive in so far as these commitments fall within the scope of Articles 85 to 90 EC or the scope of measures adopted under these Articles.[103] The exclusive regulatory powers of the Community in these matters would seem to leave no room for the exercise of a concurrent external competence by the Member States.

According to the Court, *the Euratom Community* has exclusive competence[104] over the arrangements for the supply of ores, source materials, and special fissile materials;[105] the nuclear common market;[106] and the ownership of nuclear materials covered by the Treaty.[107]

---

[99] *Opinion 1/75* [1975] ECR 1355 at 1364.

[100] The same applies in relation to the Euratom Treaty (see n. 105 below); but not it seems in relation to the ECSC Treaty—Art. 71 ECSC.

[101] On the scope of the common commercial policy, see Ch. 12 below.

[102] See Case 804/79 *Commission* v. *UK* [1981] ECR 1045 at para. 17.

[103] See *Opinion 1/92* [1992] ECR I–2821 at paras. 32–33.

[104] But on the operation of these competences in practice, see Ch. 22.

[105] See *Ruling 1/78*, n. 31 above, at para. 14: 'These provisions [Arts. 52 to 76 Euratom] . . . show the care taken in the Treaty to define in a precise and binding manner the exclusive right exercised by the Community in the field of nuclear supply both internal and external.'

[106] *Ibid.*, at para. 18: 'the exclusive jurisdiction conferred on the Community with regard to nuclear supplies and its general responsibility for the normal functioning of the nuclear common market.'

[107] *Ibid.*, at para. 27: '. . . the right of ownership of fissile materials was concentrated by the

Where that Consequence follows from the Scope of Measures adopted by the Community Institutions

According to the Court of Justice, '[e]ach time the Community, with a view to implementing a common policy envisaged in the Treaty, adopts provisions laying down common rules, whatever form these may take, the Member States no longer have the right, acting individually or even collectively, to undertake obligations which affect those rules.'[108]

This principle, commonly known as 'the *AETR*[109] principle,' has been the subject of much argument since its enunciation. It is clearly based on good sense: the Community's internal legal order would be hopelessly compromised if the Member States were able to undermine Community rules by unilaterally entering into international agreements the content of which contradicted the Community rules. The principle that the existence of internal Community legislation has an effect on the external competence of the Member States and, by implication, of the Communities is therefore reasonable, and arguably no more than an application of the principle of the supremacy of Community law over national law.[110] The exact meaning of the rule in the *AETR* case has, however, been much debated. Although it cannot yet be said that the scope of the *AETR* principle is definitively settled, some of the uncertainties have been removed by recent case law.[111]

First, if internal Community rules have completely, or 'exhaustively', regulated a particular matter or area, so that further legislative action by the Member States is impossible as a matter of Community law,[112] the Community has exclusive external competence in respect of that matter or area. External action by the Member States, such as the conclusion of an agreement, would clearly 'affect' the Community rules (if only because their scope would have been altered by the Member State's agreement), and would accordingly be impermissible.

The *AETR* principle also applies, however, even where Community legislation is not complete or 'exhaustive'. In the *ILO* case, Part III of the Convention under consideration was concerned with an area 'which is already covered *to a large extent* by Community rules . . . adopted . . . with a view to achieving an

Treaty in the hands of a common public authority, namely the Community; therefore it is the Community and the Community alone which is in a position to ensure that in the management of nuclear materials the general needs of the public are safeguarded . . .'

[108] Case 22/70, n. 7 above, at para. 17.

[109] After the French initials of the agreement in issue. The principle is also referred to as the *ERTA* principle (from the initials of the agreement in English) .

[110] On which, see Case 106/77 *Amministrazione delle Finanze dello Stato* v. *Simmenthal SpA* [1978] ECR 629.

[111] Notably *Opinions 2/91*, n. 63 above, and *1/94*, n. 43 above.

[112] On the circumstances in which this may arise, see Temple Lang, 'The ERTA Judgment and the Court's Case Law on Competence and Conflict' [1987] *YBEL* 183 at 190 ff. and cases there cited.

ever greater degree of harmonization'.[113] The Court nevertheless concluded that the competence of the Community in respect of these matters was exclusive. The question in any given case will be whether the internal Community rules are intended to fix standards or establish common rules and, if so, whether the extent of the Community's legislative activity is such that independent action by the Member States would inevitably have the effect of undermining or affecting these rules or altering their scope. Clearly, the greater the amount of Community legislation on a matter, or the more extensively a matter is regulated at Community level, the less room there will be for the Member States to act unilaterally; the more likely, therefore, that the Community's competence will be exclusive.

On the other hand, the mere existence of Community legislation in a given area will not necessarily mean that Community competence in that area is exclusive. Even where internal measures have been adopted, there may still be room for the Member States to undertake commitments towards third countries. In *Opinion 1/94*,[114] the Court found this to be the case in relation to intellectual property. Furthermore, where Community legislation on a matter takes the form of 'minimum requirements'[115] the Member States are not precluded from concluding international agreements which establish higher standards. In its *Opinion* in the *ILO* case, the Court also said that the fact that it was not always possible to say with certainty whether the standards in the agreements were, in fact, higher than the Community standards did not mean that the Community's competence was exclusive.[116]

Secondly, the principle in the *AETR* case is not confined to the 'common policies' identified by that term in the EC Treaty,[117] but applies 'in all the areas corresponding to the objectives of the Treaty.'[118] It is, of course, true that the adoption of common rules is less likely to occur in some areas of Community activity than in others,[119] but the basic principle applies to all Community activities.

Thirdly, where common rules in the *AETR* sense exist, Member State competence would appear to be precluded even in the absence of a direct conflict between the terms of the agreement which the Member State proposed to conclude and the common rules. It is enough that the scope or effect of the Community rules could be altered by the conclusion of an agreement by a

---

[113] *Opinion 2/91*, n. 4 above, at para. 25 (emphasis added).

[114] N. 43 above.

[115] i.e. establishes a basic standard, but leaves it for the Member States to set higher or more rigorous standards if they wish. See also Case C–376/90 *Commission* v. *Belgium* [1992] ECR I–6153 on the meaning of 'uniform standards' in Art. 2(h) Euratom.

[116] *Opinion 2/91*, n. 4 above, at paras. 20 and 21.

[117] Art. 2 EC, paras. (b) (common commercial policy); (e) (common agricultural policy); (f) (common transport policy).

[118] *Opinion 2/91* at para. 10.

[119] Development policy and research are examples of areas where common rules may be less likely to occur.

Member State. In other words, the existence of exclusive competence in a given area on the basis of *AETR* principles has the same effect as exclusive competence based on Articles of the Treaties: it *ipso facto* excludes Member State competence.[120]

Although the *AETR* principle arose in the context of the European Community, there seems no reason to confine it to that Community. If, as has been suggested,[121] the *AETR* principle is in substance no more than the principle of the supremacy of Community law, as such it is equally applicable to the Communities established by the Euratom and ECSC Treaties.

Where External Competence arises from an Express Power in an Internal Act

Many measures adopted by the European Community, particularly in the area of financial services,[122] confer on the Community power to enter into agreements with third countries.[123] In *Opinion 1/94*, the Court said '[w]henever the Community has included in its internal legislative acts provisions relating to the treatment of nationals of non-member countries or expressly conferred on its institutions powers to negotiate with non-member countries, it acquires exclusive external competence in the spheres covered by those acts.'[124] The Court's dictum is in broad terms, but two qualifications may be noted. First, it is uncertain whether conferment of such a power in an internal act can remove the powers reserved to the Member States in Articles such as Articles 130r(4) and 130y(2) EC: probably it cannot. Secondly, the precise terms of the power conferred on the Community institutions must be examined to determine whether the Community's competence is exclusive or not. Just as it is open to the institutions to confer such a power, so it must be for them to set the limits of that power.

Where Internal Powers can only be Effectively Exercised at the Same Time as External Powers

In certain circumstances, the Community may have exclusive competence to act externally even where no internal rules have been adopted and where the power being exercised does not, in terms, give rise to an exclusive Community competence. The leading case is *Opinion 1/76*: in that case, it would not have been possible to achieve the Community's objective (rationalization of the inland waterways sector in the Rhine and Moselle basins) without involving a third country in the scheme envisaged. Thus, adoption of internal measures would not have sufficed: the conclusion of an international agreement was necessary instead. External powers could thus be exercised by the Community, and these

---

[120] This conclusion would seem to follow from *Opinion 2/91*, n. 4 above, at paras. 25 and 26. The ECJ did not base its conclusions on the existence of a contradiction between the common rules and the Convention, but on the existence of the common rules themselves .

[121] Text accompanying n. 110 above.

[122] The same is true of the legislation on public procurement.

[123] e.g. see *Opinion 1/94*, n. 43 above, at para. 94.   [124] *Ibid.*, at para. 95.

could become exclusive, without any internal legislation having first been adopted.[125] This principle, however, 'relates to a situation where the conclusion of an international agreement is necessary in order to achieve Treaty objectives which cannot be attained by the adoption of autonomous rules.'[126]

The Community therefore seems to acquire exclusive external competence in any situation in which its objectives cannot be achieved by internal measures because third countries also have to be bound by the measures envisaged. If, in such circumstances, the only available course is the adoption of an international agreement, the Community has exclusive competence to take such a step.

Consequences of the Existence of Exclusive Community Competence

The principal consequence of the existence of exclusive Community competence is that Member States may no longer act in the areas in which the Community has exclusive competence.[127] In legal theory, the powers of the Member States have been transferred completely to the Community, and the Member States may not enter into any international agreements which could affect measures adopted by the Community or alter the scope of these measures.[128] Nor may they adopt positions which differ from those which the Community intends to adopt in relations with third countries, or take other

---

[125] *Ibid.*, at para. 85. According to the ECJ, agreements relating to the conservation of the fishing resources of the seas are another example of the same principle. 'The restriction, by means of internal legislative measures, of fishing on the high seas by vessels flying the flag of a Member State would hardly be effective if the same restrictions were not to apply to vessels flying the flag of a non-member country bordering on the same seas' (*Opinion 1/94*, n. 43 above). The Court's reasoning on this point is not easy to follow. It is possible to see why Swiss participation in the Draft Laying Up Fund was necessary if the scheme was to succeed; and to have required that internal rules (i.e. a Laying Up Scheme binding the Member States only) should be adopted before external competence (i.e. an agreement with Switzerland) could be exercised would have been an unnecessarily roundabout way of achieving the overall objective. But the ECJ's comments on the Community's competence in relation to conservation of fisheries raise some difficulties. They explain adequately why the Community should have exclusive competence for agreements on conservation of fisheries with third countries geographically adjacent to the Community's waters. They do not, however, explain why the Community has exclusive competence for conservation of fisheries *generally*, even in waters distant from the Community: a proposition unchallenged in the practice of the institutions for over a decade. On the Community's exclusive competence in relation to fisheries, see Ch. 10.

[126] *Opinion 2/92*, n. 63 above, at para. 32.

[127] 'The exercise of concurrent powers by the Member States in this matter is impossible' (*Opinion 1/75*, n. 50 above) at 1364); 'The Member States no longer have the right, acting individually or even collectively, to undertake obligations with third countries' (Case 22/70, n. 7 above, at para. 17); 'The power to adopt measures . . . has belonged fully and definitively to the Community. Member States are therefore no longer entitled to exercise any power of their own in [these matters]. The adoption of . . . measures is a matter of Community law. The transfer to the Community of powers in this matter being total and definitive, . . . a failure [of the Council] to act could not in any case restore to the Member States the power and freedom to act unilaterally in this field' (Case 804/79, n. 102 above, at paras. 17, 18, and 20).

[128] See Case 22/70, n. 7 above, at para. 22.

action which would hinder the Community in the exercise of its tasks.[129] Nor may they adopt internal legislation which undermines, or contradicts, measures adopted, externally or internally, by the Community.

A second but related consequence is that the Community must be allowed to exercise its powers with unfettered freedom. 'The Member States whether acting individually or collectively, are no longer able to impose on the Community obligations which impose conditions on the exercise of prerogatives which thenceforth belong to the Community and which therefore no longer fall within the field of national sovereignty.'[130] Thus the Community may have to become party to international agreements which relate to areas of exclusive competence, in order to be in a position to comply with the obligations in the agreements in question,[131] and in order that the fulfilment of the tasks entrusted to the Communities by the Treaties is not put in jeopardy.[132] Furthermore, the Member States are under a duty to use all the political and legal means at their disposal in order to ensure the participation of the Community in such agreements.[133]

At least in respect of powers arising under a Treaty Article,[134] once it has been established that the Community's competence is exclusive, it retains that competence whether or not it exercises it: there is no question of Member State competence continuing, or being held in abeyance, only to re-emerge if the Community fails to act.[135] There is no authority on the effect on the Community's competence of revocation of common rules in a given area. On one view, the power to regulate the area concerned (including the power to leave it unregulated) remains with the Community, and accordingly a Member State cannot, by a unilateral act such as the conclusion of an agreement, limit the Community's future freedom of action in the area. But the alternative argument, that Member State competence revives to the extent that the common rules have been revoked, seems better and more consistent with underlying principles: non-existent rules can hardly be 'affected' by a Member State's acts or by conclusion of an agreement.

Unilateral action by a Member State in an area within the Community's exclusive competence would be a violation of the Member State's obligations under the Treaties;[136] procedures are available in the Treaties to enable the Commission,[137] or other Member States,[138] to bring the alleged violation before the Court of Justice.

---

[129] *Opinion 1/75*, n. 50 above, at 1364.

[130] *Ruling 1/78*, n. 31 above, at para. 32.

[131] *Ibid.*, para. 22.

[132] *Ibid.*, para. 33.

[133] Joined Cases 3, 4, and 6/76, n. 64 above, at paras. 44–45.

[134] Such as fisheries, common commercial policy, competition.

[135] Case 804/79, n. 102 above, at para. 20. In this case, the Community's exclusive competence derived from a Treaty Art. (Art. 102 of the 1972 Act of Accession).

[136] The Member State's act would not necessarily be void in international law, however: see Ch. 9, n. 36.

[137] Arts. 169 EC, 141 Euratom, 88 ECSC. For an example under the EC Treaty, see Case 804/79, n. 102 above.

[138] Arts. 170 EC, 142 Euratom, 89 ECSC.

However, although in principle the Member States have no power to act in areas of exclusive Community competence, in practice the Court has recognized that necessity can sometimes require the Member States to act in the interests of the Community. Any such action must, however, be taken in close consultation with the Commission, and must be limited to the minimum necessary to protect the interests of the Community. This principle was regarded by the Court as a justification for the enactment by the Member States of limited measures, in the absence of Community measures, to conserve fishing stocks.[139] Another example of this principle can be found in certain international organizations, where in practice Member States sometimes have to represent the interests of the Community because of the limited status it holds within the organizations in question.[140] The Court has based the Member States' power to act in such cases on the need to protect the interests of the Community and, more specifically, on the duty of co-operation set out in the Treaties.[141]

'Shared' Competence

Not all Community competence is 'exclusive'. The Court has on several occasions said that the Member States and the Community can 'share' competence in a particular area. The principal consequence of shared competence is that the Member States still have power to enter into agreements and to take action in the areas in question, subject to duties deriving from the Treaties. Although the concept of shared external competence is well established in Community law and practice, it has not always been possible to persuade third States to recognize that the legal powers and interests of the Community and the Member States co-exist.[142] Third States have tended to insist that either the Community or the Member States should accept legal responsibility for a given matter, and that both cannot be responsible, or exercise rights at the same time, on the same matters. The extent to which international law recognizes the concept of 'shared competence' is therefore open to debate.

When is competence shared?

'Shared' or 'joint' competence has been recognized to exist in five situations: where that consequence flows from the Treaty Article conferring power on the Community; where the Community has potential competence which it has not

---

[139] See Ch. 9, p. 236.

[140] It may be that the Member States will have to act for the Communities in international organizations, if the constitutions of the organizations in question do not allow formal Community participation. The ECJ appears to have recognized the legitimacy of this practice in *Opinion 2/91*, n. 4 above, at para. 5.

[141] Case 804/79, n. 102 above, at para. 28. See Arts. 86 ECSC, 5 EC, and 192 Euratom.

[142] This is particularly so in *fora* such as WIPO, and at conferences held under the auspices of the UN.

exercised; where an agreement includes provisions within Community competence and provisions within Member-State competence; where the Community's competence arises from the existence of internal 'minimum rules'; and in certain areas, such as intellectual property, where Community and Member State competence can co-exist without either displacing the other. There is, moreover, authority for the view that shared competence is the general rule, and exclusive Community competence the exception.[143]

Certain provisions of the Treaties expressly provide that the existence of Community competence does not prejudice the competence of the Member States to negotiate in international bodies and to conclude international agreements.[144] It can be inferred that the Community and the Member States share competence in respect of the matters covered by these Articles. This conclusion is supported by the judgment of the Court in the *Bangladesh* and *EDF* cases,[145] where it was noted that the Community's competence in relation to development co-operation policy under Article 130x was not exclusive: the Member States had competence to enter into agreements with third countries along with the Community, collectively or individually. The existence of shared competence in areas such as development policy and the environment does not, however, affect the principle that the adoption by the Community of common rules creates exclusive Community competence in respect of the matters covered by those rules.[146]

Secondly, the Court described[147] the Community's competence as 'shared' with the Member States where the Community has power to adopt common internal rules—and thus to acquire exclusive competence on the basis of the *AETR* principle—but has not yet done so. An example of such 'potential' competence arose in relation to the common fisheries policy, during the transitional period mentioned in Article 102 of the 1972 Act of Accession, at a stage when the Community had not taken action in pursuit of the common fisheries policy.[148] The Community's competence was potentially exclusive but had not been exercised, because the transitional period provided for in the Treaty had not then ended.[149] In these circumstances, the Court accepted that the Member

---

[143] See the Opinion of Jacobs A.G. in Case C–316/91 *Parliament* v. *Council* [1994] ECR I–625, at para. 40: 'With regard to development aid to the ACP States, there is nothing in the Treaty, or in provisions adopted by the Community institutions pursuant to the Treaty, which points to the conclusion that the Community's competence is exclusive. *In the absence of any indication to the contrary,* it can be accepted that the Community and the Member States share competence in that field' (emphasis added).

[144] See Arts. 109(5) EC, 130r(4) EC; and Art. 130y EC. See further Chs. 17 and 18 below.

[145] Joined Cases C–181 and C–248/91 *Parliament* v. *Commission and Council* [1993] ECR I–3685 and Case C–316/91, n. 143 above.

[146] See the Declarations on Arts. 109, 130r, and 130y EC contained in the Final Act of the TEU.

[147] See *Opinion 2/91* n. 4 above, at para. 7.

[148] Joined Cases 3, 4, and 6/76, n. 64 above, at para. 39. 'Shared' competence in this sense also exists in areas such as transport and services generally, where internal measures adopted by the Community are not exhaustive. See *Opinion 2/92*, n. 63 above, at paras. 29–36.

[149] By the time of the judgment in Case 804/79, n. 102 above, the transitional period had ended

States had a transitional power to act in the common Community interest. In so far as the Member States had any competence, it was transient and provisional.

The Court has also said that the Community and the Member States share competence where an agreement covers both matters within the exclusive competences of the Member States and matters within the exclusive competence of the Community. Examples of such shared competence arose in the *Natural Rubber* case[150] and the *Euratom* case.[151] The former related to Community participation in commodities agreements in pursuance of the common commercial policy. Although the essential policy of such agreements came within the Community's exclusive competence under Article 113 EC, the financing of such agreements—a central element of their operation—was still for the Member States.[152] That required their continued participation in the agreements: accordingly, competence was shared. The latter concerned the United Nations Convention on the Physical Protection of Nuclear Material, some parts of which fell within the competence of the Euratom Community and some parts of which were for the Member States. Again, the Court described the competence of the Community as shared with the Member States. In each of these cases, however, exclusive Community competence existed in respect of certain matters in the agreement before the Court, whereas in respect of other elements of the agreement, the competence of the Member States was exclusive. It would in theory have been possible to have separated the provisions of the Physical Protection of Nuclear Material Convention into two agreements, one containing all the elements of Community competence and one containing the elements which were for the Member States. The Community would have had competence to ratify the former and the Member States the latter. A similar task could have been performed—with more difficulty—in relation to the Natural Rubber Agreement. It seems inaccurate to describe this situation as involving 'shared competence': the competences involved were on each side exclusive, not shared. It is, of course, true that overall competence for the matters covered by these agreements was shared between the Community and the Member States, or that the agreements involved elements of both Community and Member State competence.

'Shared' competence also exists in cases where the Community's external competence derives from the existence of internal rules which set minimum standards. In *Opinion 2/91*,[153] the agreement in question (ILO Convention 170) contained matters where the Community's competence was exclusive, and

and Community competence had become exclusive: the scope for any Member State action had all but disappeared.

---

[150] *Opinion 1/78* [1979] ECR 2871.
[151] *Ruling 1/78*, n. 31 above.
[152] See *Opinion 1/78*, n. 150 above, at paras. 52–60. On the relevance of Member State financing of an agreement, see, however, *Opinion 1/94*, n. 43 above, at paras. 19 and 20, and Case C–316/91, n. 143 above, Opinion of Jacobs A.G., paras. 55–59.
[153] N. 4 above.

matters in respect of which certain Member States had exclusive competence.[154] Convention 170 therefore involved 'shared' competence in the way that the agreements in the *Natural Rubber* and *Euratom* cases did. But the Convention also covered areas where the Community's internal legislative competence consisted in a power to set 'minimum standards', and where the Member States were entitled to set higher standards in their national laws. The Court held that the Community and the Member States both had the competence to become parties to the Convention in respect of these areas, because Member States' participation would not 'affect' the scope of the relevant Community rules. If, on the one hand, the Community's rules were more stringent than those in the Convention, the Member States would be able to apply the Community rules; if, on the other hand, the Convention rules were more stringent than those adopted by the Community, nothing in Community law prevented the Member States from applying higher standards in these areas—whether by national legislation or by international agreement.[155] The Court made clear that this reasoning should be taken to apply to any areas where the Communities' competence consisted in the power to adopt minimum standards.[156]

Finally, a special example of 'shared' competence arises in certain limited areas such as intellectual property.[157] The creation of Community trade marks and other intellectual property rights does not displace any such rights in the legal systems of the Member States: the Community right and the rights of the Member States in a real sense exist in 'parallel'. There is, therefore, no reason of principle or logic why the Member States and the Community should not continue to exercise external competences each in relation to the protection of their own intellectual property rights. In practice, it has proved difficult to secure international recognition for the continuing parallel competences of the Community and the Member States in the area of intellectual property.

---

[154] e.g. for the dependent territories.   [155] *Opinion 2/91*, n. 4 above, at paras. 15–18.
[156] Such as measures adopted under Art. 100 EC: para. 21 of *Opinion 2/91*, n. 4 above.

[157] Schermers, *International Institutional Law* (2nd edn.) para. 1557, comments (of international organizations in general): 'The competence of international organizations to make agreements is related to the competence of their members to do so. Both may be competent at the same time. The best example is the case of a copyright convention to which an international organization accedes solely to protect its own publications. It then acts for the specific interests of the organization which are not at the same time covered by any legal provisions of the members.' This category of 'shared competence' may also extend to agreements establishing rules of international law, such as UNCLOS III or the Vienna Convention on the Law of Treaties between States and International Organizations and between International Organizations. The rules in such 'law-making' agreements should be equally applicable to the Member States and the Communities as subjects of international law; the competence of one does not displace or undermine the competence of the other. In theory, therefore, the Communities and the Member States should all be able to become parties to such agreements. The criteria for Community participation would seem to be (i) that the international agreement in question establishes general norms of international law binding on subjects of international law; and (ii) that the Community exercises powers which are affected by the norms thereby established.

Duties on the Member States when Competence is Shared

Where competence is shared between the Community and the Member States, the Court has said that there should be a 'close association between the institutions of the Community and the Member States both in the process of negotiation and conclusion and in the fulfilment of the obligations entered into. This duty of co-operation to which attention was drawn in the context of the EAEC Treaty, must also apply in the context of the EEC Treaty since it results from the requirement of unity in the international representation of the Community.'[158]

The practical implications of this duty, which applies to the Community institutions as well as the Member States, are considered further in discussion of mixed agreements[159] and the Communities' participation in international organizations.[160]

THE GEOGRAPHICAL EXTENT OF COMMUNITY COMPETENCE

The geographical extent of the Communities' competence is set by the provisions in each of the Community Treaties describing the territories to which that Treaty applies. These are Articles 79 ECSC, 227 EC, and 198 Euratom, supplemented by a series of special provisions, protocols, and declarations. The effect of this complicated web of legislation in respect of each Member State is probably as follows:[161]

> *Belgium, the Federal Republic of Germany,*[162] *Greece,*[163] *Ireland, Italy, Luxembourg, Austria, and Sweden*: the Treaties apply to the territories of these Member States.

---

[158] *Opinion 2/91*, n. 4 above, at para. 36. See also *Ruling 1/78*, n. 31 above, at paras. 34–36.
[159] Ch. 6.   [160] Ch. 7.
[161] For useful discussions of the effect of these provisions, see T. C. Hartley, *EEC Immigration Law* (European Studies in Law, 1978), chs. 2 and 3; R. R. Churchill, *EEC Fisheries Law* (Martinus Nijhoff, 1987), ch. 3; F. Burrows, *Free Movement in the European Community* (Clarendon, 1987), ch. IX; P. Oliver, *Free Movement of Goods in the EEC* (2nd edn., European Law Centre, 1988), ch. III; Groux, ' "Territorialité" et droit communautaire' [1987] *RTDE* 1. These accounts pre-date the TEU and the 1994 Accession Treaty. The law is complex: Oliver aptly comments, 'For those with a taste for the obscure a consideration of the territorial scope of the Treaty of Rome may afford a spree of intellectual satisfaction, involving as it does a glance at many a far flung corner of the globe, both in Europe and beyond.' Groux comments, 'On notera seulement que, . . . la notion de "territoire de la Communauté" est quelque peu simplificatrice, car la complexité, déjà signalée, du système d'application territoriale du droit communautaire est telle qu'il y a en réalité, autant de "territoires de la Communauté" qu'il y a d'éspaces dans lesquels les différents dispositions (matériellement territoriales) du droit communautaire, sont ou peuvent être d'application' (at 25).
[162] On the status of Berlin before unification of Germany, and the application of Community law there, see I. D. Hendry and M. C. Wood, *The Legal Status of Berlin* (Grotius, 1987), ch. 17; Groux and Manin, n. 3 above, at 133–4; Burrows, n. 161 above, 301–3.
[163] On the status of Mount Athos, see Joint Declaration concerning Mount Athos, in the Final Act of the Greek Accession Treaty.

Denmark: the Treaties apply to Denmark, but not to the Faeroes[164] or Greenland.[165] The provisions of Part Four of the EC Treaty (dealing with the association of overseas countries and territories) apply to Greenland.

Finland: the Treaties apply to Finland and, on certain conditions, to the Aaland Islands.[166]

France: the Treaties apply[167] to France and to the French overseas departments.[168] The French overseas territories[169] are within the scope of Part Four of the EC Treaty.[170] The Euratom Treaty applies.

Netherlands: the Treaties apply to the European territory of the Netherlands.[171] The overseas territories of the Kingdom of the Netherlands[172] are within the scope of Part Four of the EC Treaty.

Portugal: the Treaties apply to Portugal, and to the Azores and Madeira. They do not apply to Macao or East Timor, and neither benefits from the arrangements established by Part Four of the EC Treaty.[173]

Spain: the Treaties apply to Spain and, subject to certain conditions, to the Canary Islands and to Ceuta and Melilla.[174]

United Kingdom: the Treaties apply to the United Kingdom of Great Britain and Northern Ireland. The Treaties apply to the Channel Islands and the Isle of Man only to the extent necessary to ensure the implementation of the arrangements for those islands agreed on United

[164] Arts. 79(2)(a) ECSC, 227(5)(a) EC, 198(3)(a) Euratom.

[165] Until 1985, the Treaties applied to Greenland. By the Treaty amending, with regard to Greenland, the Treaties establishing the European Communities ([1985] OJ L29/1), Greenland withdrew from the Communities, and the Treaties were amended accordingly.

[166] The conditions in Prot. 2 to the 1994 Act of Accession. See Arts. 79(d)ECSC, 227(5)(d) EC, and 198(e) Euratom: the declaration mentioned in these Arts. was made on Finnish ratification of the Accession Treaty ([1995] OJ L75/18).

[167] Arts. 79(1) and (4) ECSC, 227(1) and (2) EC, and 198(1) Euratom.

[168] That is to say, Martinique, Guadeloupe, Réunion, Guiana, and St Pierre and Miquelon. On the application of the EEC Treaty to these territories, see Case 148/77 *Hansen & Balle* v. *Hauptzollamt Flensburg* [1978] ECR 1787.

[169] That is to say, Mayotte, New Caledonia and dependencies, French Polynesia, Wallis and Futuna Islands, and the French Southern and Antarctic territories.

[170] Art. 227(3) and Annex IV EC.

[171] Arts. 79(1) ECSC, 227(1) EC, and 198(1) Euratom. See also the Prot. on the application of the Treaty establishing the European Economic Community to the non-Community parts of the Kingdom of the Netherlands, the Declaration of intent on the association of Surinam and the Netherlands Antilles with the European Economic Community, and the Prot. on the application of the Treaty establishing the European Atomic Energy Community to the non-European parts of the Kingdom of the Netherlands. The effect of these was that the Treaties applied to the European territory of the Netherlands only.

[172] i.e. Aruba and the Netherlands Antilles (Bonaire, Curaçao, Saba, Sint Eustatius, and Sint Maarten).

[173] Macao and East Timor are, however, mentioned in Declaration (25) on the representation of the interests of the overseas countries and territories referred to in Art. 227(3) and (5)(a) and (b) of the Treaty establishing the European Community. There is a trade and co-operation agreement between the EEC and Macao: [1992] OJ L404/26.

[174] Art. 25 of and Prot. 2 to the Spanish/Portuguese Act of Accession. The common commercial policy, the common agricultural policy, and the common fisheries policy do not, as a rule, apply to the Canary Islands or to Ceuta or Melilla.

Kingdom accession.[175] By contrast, the Treaties in principle apply to Gibraltar, subject to certain important exceptions.[176] None of the Treaties applies to the Sovereign Base Areas in Cyprus.[177] All other British dependent territories[178] except Hong Kong are within the scope of Part Four of the EC Treaty, and the Euratom Treaty applies.

Several points may be noted. First, the Communities' powers are exercised primarily in, and in respect of, the territories to which the Treaties apply; and institutional acts adopted on the basis of the Treaties apply in principle to the same geographical area as the Treaties themselves.[179] 'Territory' for these purposes clearly includes the land territory and internal and territorial waters of the Member States, but the Communities' powers are not confined to these areas.

Maritime zones[180]: in maritime zones outside Member State sovereignty or

[175] Arts. 79(2)(c) ECSC, 227(5)(c) EC and 198(3)(c) Euratom, and Prot. 3 to the UK/Denmark /Ireland Act of Accession. In summary, the Channel Islands and the Isle of Man are part of the Communities for customs and trade purposes, but the provisions on free movement of workers, freedom to provide services, and freedom of establishment do not apply. On the application of the common fisheries policy to the Isle of Man, see Case 32/79 *Commission* v. *UK* [1980] ECR 2403.

[176] Art. 28 of the 1972 Act of Accession. Gibraltar is outside the common customs territory, and is treated as a third country for the purpose of the common regime for imports: thus the rules on free movement of goods do not apply. Gibraltar is not obliged to introduce VAT, nor to contribute to the Communities' own resources. The common agricultural policy and the common fisheries policy do not apply. The Commission (Written EPQ 1823/84 [1985] OJ C341/1) has said that 'On the basis of the 1972 Act of Accession, and in particular the exclusion of Gibraltar from the customs territory, the provisions of the EEC Treaty concerning the free movement of goods within the Community do not apply to Gibraltar and the territory is treated as a "third country" for the purposes of measures under the common commercial policy directly involving the import and export of goods.'

[177] Arts. 79(3)(b) ECSC, 227(b)EC, and 198(3)(c) Euratom.

[178] These are Anguilla, Bermuda, the Cayman Islands, the Falkland Islands, South Georgia and the South Sandwich Islands, Turks and Caicos Islands, British Virgin Islands, Montserrat, Pitcairn, St Helena and dependencies, British Indian Ocean Territory, and British Antarctic Territory.

[179] Case 61/77 *Commission* v. *Ireland* [1978] ECR 417.

[180] For discussion of the Community's competence in maritime zones and activities in these zones, see all the papers in (1992) 23 *Ocean Development and International Law*, 89–259, and especially D. Freestone, *Some Institutional Implications of the Establishment of Exclusive Economic Zones by EC Member States*, 97 at 103–7; R. R. Churchill, *EC Fisheries and an EZ—Easy!*, 145, at 146–9; P. Birnie, *An EC Exclusive Economic Zone: Marine Environment Aspects*, 193, at 200–6; A. H. A. Soons, *Regulation of Marine Scientific Research by the European Community and its Member States*, 259 at 262–7. The Commission considers that the EC Treaty 'applies to the Continental Shelf' (Commission Memorandum of Sept. 1970, SEC(70)3095, [1974] OJ C49/3). This view is supported by the fact that certain measures adopted by the Council (e.g. on the origin of goods) have a bearing on activities carried out on the Continental Shelf. But it is not shared by all the Member States; may be inconsistent with some provisions of the Treaty which expressly apply to the 'territory' of the Member States (see, e.g., Arts. 48 and 52); and may take insufficient account of the nature of Member States' rights over the Continental Shelf in international law. Probably the better analysis is that activities of the Member States on or in relation to the Continental Shelf can give rise to issues under the Treaties: in each case it is a matter of examining the facts in issue and the terms of the relevant Community legislation. Similarly, in deciding whether the Community or the Member States should exercise their competence in respect of an international agreement relating to the Continental Shelf, it is necessary to examine the objective of the agreement in the light of the powers conferred on the Communities by the Treaties.

jurisdiction, the Community has, in matters relating to the competences attributed to it, the same legislative powers as international law accords to the flag State, or State of registration of a vessel.[181] In particular, in respect of fisheries, the Community has competence to adopt measures which apply to activities within the exclusive economic zone, the territorial waters, internal waters, and ports of the Member States,[182] and, in so far as the Member Sates have similar authority under international law, to activities on the high seas.[183] The Communities' competences must be exercised in accordance with the applicable rules of international law.[184]

Airspace over the Member States: internal legislation of the Communities can apply to activities in the airspace over the Member States.[185]

'Extraterritorial' jurisdiction: the Communities appear to have competence to regulate the activities of nationals of the Member States (and, in certain cases, nationals of non-Member States) outside the territories of the Member States,[186] at least in respect of the enforcement of economic sanctions;[187] the application of Community rules on competition;[188] and the application of Community rules on fisheries.[189]

Secondly, when one of the Communities concludes an agreement, the provisions of that agreement apply throughout the 'territory of the Community'; in

---

[181] Case C–405/92, *Etablissement Armand Mondiet SA* v. *Armement Islais Sàrl* [1992] ECR I–6133, at para. 12.

[182] Case C–286/90, *Anklagemyndigheden* v. *Poulsen and Diva Navigation Corp.* [1992] ECR–6048 at para. 24.

[183] Joined Cases 3, 4, and 6/76, n. 64 above, at paras. 30–33; Case C–258/89 *Commission* v. *Spain* [1991] ECR I–3977.

[184] *Poulsen and Diva Navigation*, n. 182 above, at para. 9. For the ECJ's application of the rules of the law of the sea, see paras. 25 to 27 of that judgment.

[185] See, e.g., Dirs. 80/51 ([1980] OJ L18/26) and 89/629 ([1989] OJ L363/27) on the limitation of noise emissions from subsonic aircraft, and Reg. 3724/93 (applying economic sanctions in respect of Libya) ([1993] OJ L295/1), Art. 1 and Reg. 2471/94 (applying economic sanctions in respect of Bosnia-Herzegovina) ([1994] OJ L266/1), Art. 16. See also Art. 3(3) of Reg. 2913/92 establishing the Community Customs Code ([1992] OJ L302/1).

[186] On the 'personal jurisdiction' of the Communities, see Bleckmann 'Personal Jurisdiction' (1980) 17 *CMLRev.* 467. See also Churchill, n. 161 above, 73–75; Oliver, n. 161 above, ch. IV.

[187] See in particular, Reg. 2471/94, Art. 16, which provides that 'This Regulation shall apply . . . in any aircraft or on any vessel under the jurisdiction of a Member State and to any person elsewhere who is a national of a Member State and any body elsewhere which is incorporated or constituted under the law of a Member State.' The width of Community jurisdiction under this provision is doubtless partly because the Reg. was intended to give effect to a UN sanctions measure. As to sanctions generally, see Ch. 19.

[188] See Case 48/69 (*Dyestuffs*) [1972] ECR 619, paras. 125–146; Cases 89, 104, 114, 116, 117, 125 to 129/85 *Ahlström* v. *Commission (Woodpulp)* [1988] ECR 5193. The 'extraterritorial' jurisdiction of the Community in competition matters is obscure and, on some points, highly controversial: see D. G. Goyder, *EEC Competition Law* (Clarendon Press, 1988), 385–92; Wyatt and Dashwood, *European Community Law*, at 384–8; Vaughan Lowe 'International Law and the Effects Doctrine in the European Court of Justice' (1989) 48 *Camb.LJ* 9.

[189] *Poulsen and Diva Navigation*, n. 182 above. See also Churchill, n. 161 above, 75. On the position of Community nationals employed as crew of vessels flying the flag of a non-Member State, see *Poulsen and Diva Navigation*, at paras. 17–20.

other words throughout the entire territory to which the Treaty establishing that Community applies[190] in accordance with the terms of that Treaty. So where the Community's internal legislative competence is limited in respect of a certain geographical area, an agreement entered into by the Community will apply to that area only to the extent that its provisions relate to matters in which the Community is competent. The result is that not all provisions of an agreement entered into by the Community will necessarily apply uniformly throughout the territory to which the Treaty establishing the Community in question applies. In each case it is necessary to consider the terms of the agreement being entered into by the Community against the terms of the relevant Community Treaty.[191]

Thirdly, it is settled law[192] that the Member States retain competence in respect of the external relations of those of their dependent territories to which the Community Treaties do not apply. Thus, even where the subject matter of an agreement falls entirely within the exclusive competence of the Community in so far as a Member State's own metropolitan interest[193] is concerned, it may still be necessary for the Member State to become a party to the agreement in respect of the interests of its dependent territories.[194]

Finally, it will be noted that the customs territory of the Community is not coterminous with the territorial application of the Community Treaties. Article 3 of Regulation 2913/92[195] provides that the customs territory of the Community[196] shall comprise the territory of the Kingdom of Belgium; the territory of the Kingdom of Denmark, except the Faeroe Islands and Greenland; the territory of the Federal Republic of Germany, except the island of Heligoland and the territory of Busingen; the territory of the Kingdom of Spain, except Ceuta and Melilla; the territory of the French Republic, except the overseas territories and *collectivités territoriales*; the territory of the Hellenic Republic; the territory of Ireland; the territory of the Italian Republic, except the municipalities of Livigno and Campione d'Italia and the national waters of Lake Lugano which are between the bank and the political frontier of the area between Ponte Tresa and Porto Ceresio; the territory of the Grand Duchy of Luxembourg; the territory of the Kingdom of the Netherlands in Europe; the

---

[190] Cf Art. 29 Vienna Convention on the Law of Treaties. It should be noted too that this general presumption may be displaced by the terms of the particular agreement in question, or by other evidence of a contrary intention on the part of the contracting parties.

[191] For examples of territorial application clauses in Community agreements, see Ch. 5.

[192] See, e.g., *Opinion 1/78*, n. 150 above, at para. 62, *Opinion 2/91*, n. 4 above, at para. 35, and *Opinion 1/94*, n. 43 above, at paras. 15–18.

[193] Or, more accurately, the interest of those parts of the territory of the Member State to which the Treaties apply.

[194] The Member States may even enter into agreements with the Communities on behalf of their dependent territories: Denmark, on behalf of the Faeroes and Greenland, has concluded agreements with the Community on fisheries (see Ch. 10).

[195] Establishing the Community Customs Code, n. 185 above.

[196] The customs territory of the Community is the area within which Community customs rules (the common external tariff, the rules on free movement of goods etc) apply: Reg. 2913/92, n. 185 above, Art. 2(1).

territory of the Republic of Austria; the territory of the Portuguese Republic; the territory of the Republic of Finland, including the Aaland Islands; the territory of the Kingdom of Sweden; and the territory of the United Kingdom of Great Britain and Northern Ireland and of the Channel Islands and the Isle of Man.[197] The territories of the Principality of Monaco[198] and of the Republic of San Marino[199] are, taking the conventions and treaties applicable to them into account, considered to be part of the customs territory of the Community.[200] The customs territory of the Community includes the territorial waters, the inland maritime waters, and the airspace of the Member States and of Monaco and San Marino.[201] The Communities do not have external competence in respect of the customs territory as such, but in respect of the territories to which the Treaties apply.[202]

Accession of new Member States: the legal implications of accession to the Communities of new Member States are considered elsewhere.[203] Two points may be noted in this context. First, the consequence of accession is that the competences of the Communities are extended to the territories of the new Member States to which the Community Treaties apply. This may also involve an extension of the Communities' powers into new areas of activity.[204] Secondly, provision has to be made to regulate the effect of accession of new Member States on agreements entered into with third countries before accession by the Communities, and by the new Member States.

TEMPORAL SCOPE OF COMMUNITY COMPETENCE

The fundamental principle is easily stated: the Communities have competence from the moment that the Member States can be said to have attributed competence to them. Application of this principle in practice is more difficult.

Existence of Community Competence

Community competence began[205] with the entry into force of the Treaties in respect of the original Member States. In respect of States becoming Members

---

[197] It does not include Gibraltar or any other UK dependent territory.
[198] As defined in the Customs Convention signed in Paris on 18 May 1963.
[199] As defined in the Convention of 31 Mar. 1939.
[200] Reg. 2913/92, n. 185 above, Art. 3(2). [201] *Ibid.*, Art. 3(3).
[202] Thus, e.g., agreements concluded by the Community will not bind Monaco or San Marino. Indeed, an agreement on trade and customs union was concluded between the EEC and San Marino: see [1992] OJ L359/13.
[203] See Ch. 9.
[204] The provisions of the 1972 Act of Accession were important in the development of the Community's competence in respect of the common fisheries policy.
[205] On the possibility of Community competence ceasing, see p. 34, n. 28 and p. 62 above.

since the creation of the Communities, the Communities' competence took effect as from the date of their accession. Where amendment of the Treaties takes place—either on accession of new States, or as a result of an intergovernmental conference to amend the Treaties—any new competences thereby conferred take effect from the date of the entry into force of the Treaties as amended, or otherwise as provided by the Member States.[206] Where Community competence derives from the existence of Community measures, the Court has indicated that the Community has competence from the date of entry into force of the measures concerned.[207]

Exclusivity of Community Competence

Where, on the basis of the principles outlined elsewhere in this Chapter, the Community has exclusive competence in a given area by virtue of a Treaty Article, that competence must be regarded as exclusive from the entry into force of the Article.[208] Where the exclusivity arises from the adoption of internal measures, the Community's competence is exclusive from the date of entry into force of the relevant legislation.[209] Where Community competence arises from the simultaneous exercise of internal and external powers, that competence is exclusive from the moment when the powers are exercised.[210]

In certain circumstances, the submission of proposals to the Council by the Commission may place constraints on the exercise of Member State competence, even before the adoption of the proposals. Case 804/79 *Commission* v. *UK*[211] illustrates the point. In the area of fisheries, the Community had power to make legislation, but had not adopted any measures. The Court acknowledged that the Member States had a limited power to take measures to protect the common interest, but said that:

According to Article 5 of the Treaty Member States are required to take all appropriate measures to facilitate the achievement of the Community's task and to abstain from measures which might jeopardize the attainment of the objectives of the Treaty. This provision imposes on the Member States special duties of action and abstention in a situation in which the Commission, in order to meet urgent needs of conservation, has submitted

---

[206] Provision has commonly been made in the Treaties of Accession for transitional periods.

[207] See Case 22/70, n. 7 above, at paras. 17, 18, and 30: '*Each time the Community . . . adopts* provisions laying down common rules . . . the Member States no longer have the right . . . to undertake obligations with third countries . . . . *As and when such rules come into being*, the Community alone is in a position to assume and carry out contractual obligations towards third countries . . . Since the subject matter of the AETR falls within the scope of Regulation 543/69, the Community has been empowered to negotiate and conclude the agreement in question *since the entry into force of the said Regulation*' (emphasis added).

[208] Subject, of course, to the terms of the Art., and to any transitional periods laid down in it.

[209] The relevant legislation might be common rules on a particular matter, or legislation which had the effect of harmonizing or exhaustively regulating the law on a particular matter.

[210] See above, at p. 21, para. (d), commenting on *Opinion 1/94*, n. 43 above, at para. 85.

[211] Case 804/79, n. 102 above.

to the Council proposals, which, although they have not been adopted, represent the point of departure for concerted Community action.[212]

The facts of Case 804/79 are no doubt somewhat special: the Community had exclusive competence in the area concerned, and was attempting to exercise that competence even though it had not at that stage been able to do so. The 'duties of action and abstention' identified by the Court are probably less onerous in areas where the Community and the Member States share competence. And the Commission cannot, by the mere submission of a proposal to the Council, suddenly limit the powers of the Member States in areas which remain within the competence of the Member States. The essential point is probably that the Member States, in exercising such powers as they may retain, must act in good faith towards the Communities and the other Member States.

---

[212] Case 804/79, at para. 28. See also Case 325/85 *Ireland* v. *Commission* [1987] ECR 5041; Case 326/85 *Netherlands* v. *Commission* [1987] ECR 5091.

4

Acceptance of International Commitments

This Chapter summarizes the rules, practices and procedures involved in the exercise by the Communities of their powers to assume[1] international commitments. Such commitments usually take the form of international obligations contained in bilateral or multilateral agreements[2] negotiated with other subjects of international law. But the Communities may also accept international obligations unilaterally, and international commitments may be given in informal or non-binding arrangements.

AGREEMENTS

Meaning of 'Agreement'

The Treaties confer[3] on the Communities powers[4] to enter into 'agreements' with third States and international organizations. The meaning of the term 'agreement' was considered by the Court in its *Opinion* in the *OECD Local Costs Standard* case.[5] The Court had been requested to say whether a draft 'Understanding on a Local Cost Standard' was compatible with the Treaty of Rome, and whether the EEC could therefore validly participate in the Understanding. A preliminary question was whether such a request was admissible: that is to say, whether the Understanding constituted an 'agreement' for the purposes of Article 228 EEC. The Court held that the formal designation of an 'agreement envisaged under international law' was not decisive: the term 'agreement' in the Treaty should be interpreted 'in a general sense to indicate any undertaking entered into by entities subject to international law which has

---

[1] Subjects of international law may also become bound by international legal obligations involuntarily, where the law deems them to be under obligation, independently of agreement, as a result, for example, of conduct in breach of a legal duty. See Ch. 2, pp. 31–2.

[2] In international law, legally binding agreements between States are often generically known as 'treaties'. In the Community context, the term 'treaty' is almost invariably used to refer to one of the Treaties establishing the Communities. To avoid confusion, 'treaty' in this book has its Community meaning, and 'agreement' has been used generically to describe what the 1969 Vienna Convention on the Law of Treaties refers to as a 'treaty'.

[3] Explicitly in the case of the EC and Euratom (Arts. 228 EC, 101 Euratom respectively); implicitly in the case of the ECSC (Art. 6).

[4] On the powers of the Communities, see Ch. 3 above.

[5] *Opinion 1/75 (Re OECD Local Costs Standard)* [1975] ECR 1355.

binding force, whatever its formal designation'.[6] The Understanding before the Court fulfilled those conditions.

There would seem to be no reason to limit the Court's conclusion to the Community established by the EC Treaty: the same interpretation should be given to the word 'agreement' in the other two Treaties. The word 'agreement', in the context of the external relations of the Communities under the Treaties, therefore has the same meaning as the term 'treaty' in Article 2(1)(a) of the Vienna Convention on the Law of Treaties.[7]

In deciding whether a particular instrument is an 'agreement' for the purposes of the application of Community law and procedures, the most important point is to determine the intention of the parties. If it is to create a relationship governed by, and binding in, international law, the instrument should be regarded as an 'agreement'. It should be stressed that the formal designation of the instrument will often be an unsafe guide as to its true legal nature. 'From the standpoint of the obligatory character of international engagements, it is well known that such engagements may be taken in the form of treaties, conventions, declarations, agreements, protocols, or exchanges of notes.'[8] To this list Community practice might add: understandings, agreed minutes, decisions, and acts. 'The terminology used to describe treaty instruments has rightly been characterized as "confusing, often inconsistent, unscientific and in a perpetual state of flux".'[9]

Applicable Law

The rules in the Vienna Convention on the Law of Treaties apply in principle to agreements among States which are parties to that Convention,[10] and for the most part also codify the rules of the customary law of treaties between States. The rules applying to agreements involving international organizations are harder to determine with certainty, but are probably very similar to those applying to agreements between States. The 1986 Vienna Convention on the Law of Treaties between States and International Organizations or between International Organizations,[11] which contains a set of rules closely modelled on the 1969 Vienna Convention, had at the time of writing been ratified by 23 States but was not yet in force. None of the Communities is a party to the 1986

---

[6] *Opinion 1/75 (Re OECD Local Costs Standard)* [1975] ECR 1355, at para. 2; Case C–327/91 *France* v. *Commission* [1994] ECR I–3641 at paras. 23–26.

[7] UKTS 58 (1980), Cmnd. 7964; 1155 UNTS 331; (1969) 8 ILM 679. For an authoritative consideration of the Vienna Convention, see Sinclair, *The Vienna Convention on the Law of Treaties* (2nd edn., Manchester University Press, 1984).

[8] *Austro-German Customs Union* Case, Advisory Opinion (1931) PCIJ Reports, Series A/B, No 41.

[9] Satow, *Guide to Diplomatic Practice* (5th edn., Longman, 1979) at para. 29.5 (quoting the ILC).

[10] For agreements to which the VCLT does not apply, see VCLT, Arts. 2(1)(a), 3, and 4; and Sinclair, n. 7 above, 6–9.

[11] (1987) Misc. 11, Cm. 244; (1986) 25 ILM 543.

Convention, nor is there much likelihood of any of them becoming parties.[12] To the extent to which the Vienna Conventions embody customary international law, the rules they contain bind the Communities; but neither Convention can be said to apply in its entirety to agreements involving the Communities, and on some points the international law rules which govern the conclusion and implementation of agreements by the Communities are obscure.

International Practice

The manner and form in which agreements are negotiated and concluded is, in principle, governed by the intention of the parties, and international law is flexible as to the formal and procedural requirements.[13] Several stages are common to the process of negotiating and concluding most international agreements.

Negotiation

The process begins with the negotiation of the agreement. Negotiators may be required to produce evidence of their authority to enter into the discussions, and, during the negotiations, they will have to act within whatever mandate they have received from the authority they represent. Once the negotiators reach agreement, the authenticity of the text will be established, usually by initialling what has been agreed. Authority to negotiate is usually taken to include authority to establish the text. The legal significance of this step is that the authentic text is the only one to which appeal may be made to correct any inaccuracies of translation or reproduction.[14] Unless the parties agree otherwise, initialling implies no legal or political commitment on the part of the negotiators' authorities to the text which has been initialled.

Signature Subject to Approval

In classic international legal practice, signature subject to approval implied a political commitment to the agreement signed, and a willingness to recommend it to competent national authorities for eventual approval or ratification. In former times, the necessity for delay between signature and formal approval arose from the practical difficulty of speedy communication between the negotiator

---

[12] For a discussion of the VCLTIO, see G. Gaja, 'A "New" Vienna Convention on the Law of Treaties between States and International Organizations or between International Organizations: A Critical Commentary' (1987) LVII *BYIL* 253. For an explanation of why the Commission is doubtful about Community participation in the Convention, see P. Manin, 'The European Communities and the Vienna Convention on the Law of Treaties etc.' (1987) 24 *CMLRev.* 457.

[13] On modern treaty law and practice, see Oppenheim, *International Law* (9th edn., Longman, 1992), i Pt. 4, ch. 13; Sinclair, n. 7 above; Brownlie, *Principles*, (4th edn., Clarendon Press, 1990) ch. XXV; Satow, *Guide*, n. 9 above, chs. 28–33.

[14] VCLT, Art. 33.

and his capital. Although this particular difficulty no longer exists, the practice of signing agreements subject to approval persists, particularly if the agreement is important. The modern usefulness of signature subject to approval is probably that it provides an opportunity to stage a media event at which the political significance of the agreement reached can be celebrated. Signature subject to approval creates an obligation to refrain from acts which would defeat the object and purpose of the agreement.[15]

Provisional Application

Certain agreements provide for the 'provisional application' of some or all of their terms. According to an authoritative commentator, a distinction has to be made between 'mere application, which [is] a question of practice, and entry into force, which [is] a formal legal notion'.[16] The same commentator notes [17] that 'provisional application results from an accessory or secondary informal agreement among the parties to a treaty that the substantive provisions of the treaty, or certain selective substantive provisions should be applied pending the formal entry into force of the treaty'. The legal significance of such application has to be determined in the light of the agreement in question; but, as a general rule, provisional application appears to fall closer in legal effect to signature subject to approval than to final acceptance of the obligations in an agreement.

Expression of Consent to be Bound

The crucial consideration in determining when parties to an agreement become bound by its terms is their intention as expressed in the agreement. Consent to be bound may be expressed in several ways; for example, by initialling,[18] signature,[19] or by ratification, approval, or acceptance.[20] Once a party has indicated its consent to be bound, the agreement becomes binding on that party as soon as it enters into force in accordance with its terms.

Ratification and Accession

Strictly speaking, 'ratification' of an agreement is reserved to those States which participated in its negotiation and which have signed it. States which become parties without having signed an agreement (and sometimes without having participated in its negotiation) are said to 'accede' to it. *Acceptance* and *approval* are also used to describe a party's expression of consent to be bound, particularly in the case of the Communities.

---

[15] VCLT, Art. 18. See Sinclair, n. 7 above, 42 ff. [16] Sinclair, n. 7 above, 247.
[17] *Ibid.*, 247. [18] This is rare in practice. [19] Common.
[20] The classic form: still common, especially for important agreements.

Three further general points may be noted. First, not every agreement involves all the stages described above. It will always be necessary to signify that agreement has been reached on the text to which the parties wish to bind themselves, but this can be done in a variety of ways, not solely by 'initialling'.[21] Similarly, it will always be necessary to express consent to be bound by the terms of the agreement which has been reached. But again, such consent may be expressed in several ways: the classic route of signature followed by ratification is only one option. The conclusion of agreements by international organizations can in principle involve similar stages. Most agreements which allow for the participation of international organizations make special provision for such participation.

Secondly, the terms used to describe the steps in the process of the creation of an international agreement are not used consistently in practice. Thus, although 'initialling' usually means the step taken by negotiators to mark their agreement on the definitive text which they have negotiated, in other contexts, depending on the intention of the parties, 'initialling' may amount to acceptance of some or all of the obligations in an agreement. Similarly, 'signature' in classic international practice signifies a commitment to submit an agreement to the competent authorities for approval. Increasingly, however, international agreements become binding on signature, without the need for further approval. Accordingly, where questions arise about the significance of a particular step, or about the Community procedures required for the approval of that step on behalf of the Community, the first problem is to determine what in substance is involved: whether, for example, 'signature' in the instant case amounts to mere establishment of the text of the agreement, or whether it goes beyond that and amounts to acceptance of obligations. Once the legal significance of the proposed step has been ascertained, it will be possible to determine what is required from the Community institutions.

Finally, it is worth emphasizing that the process of acceptance of international agreements (whether by a State or an international organization) takes place at two levels. On the 'internal' level, a State or organization intending to accept international commitments must comply with whatever its own constitutional procedures require as a condition for the acceptance of such commitments: for example, the submission of the text of the proposed agreement to a domestic legislature for approval.[22] The procedures to be followed at the internal level are, of course, a question for the constitutional law of the intending party. Once that stage has been completed, and the necessary 'internal' steps have been taken, the intending party will be in a position to express to the other party or parties its formal consent to be bound. This is an 'external' step taken at the international level; and the procedures to be followed at this stage are a matter of international law, to be determined by reference to the agreement in

---

[21] VCLT, Art. 10; Sinclair, n. 7 above, 33 ff.
[22] In the case of the Communities, the procedures prescribed by each Treaty.

question and the law of treaties. This crucial distinction, although obvious, is easily neglected, not least because terms such as 'conclusion' and 'ratification' are used to refer to both 'levels' of procedure.

The first part of this section examines the 'internal' procedures by which each of the Communities decides whether to accept the commitments contained in an international agreement. The second part describes the jurisdiction of the Court of Justice in the scrutiny of agreements before conclusion.[23] There then follows a discussion of how the Communities express to the other parties to an agreement their consent to be bound. The last part mentions the main principles which apply on amendment and termination of agreements.

Conclusion of Agreements—The Communities' Internal Procedures

The internal procedures and practices by which each Community concludes agreements[24] are to be found in the Treaty establishing that Community. Although practice under the three Treaties has tended to converge, with similar forms of act and similar procedures being employed by each Community, it must be emphasized that, in law, each Community is a distinct entity, based on its own constituent Treaty. The procedures for conclusion of agreements established in each Treaty apply in principle for that Treaty only. Care must be taken in drawing analogies from the powers and procedures of one Community in determining what is required of one of the other Communities.[25] Before examining the procedures and practices developed under each of the Treaties, two general points may be noted.

Form of Council Acts

For most acts of the Council associated with the conclusion of an agreement, the decision *sui generis*[26] is employed. The negotiating mandate will always take that form, as will any directives[27] issued by the Council to guide the Commission in the negotiations, and any decision to sign an agreement subject to approval. In each of these cases, the Council's decision will usually be recorded as an entry in the Council's minutes, which will not usually be made

---

[23] The Court's role in adjudicating on agreements *after* conclusion is considered in Ch. 5.

[24] On conclusion of agreements by the Communities, see generally Mégret, *Le Droit de la Communauté européenne* (Brussels, 1990), vol. 12, *Les Relations Extérieures*; B. R. Bot, 'Negotiating Community Agreements: Procedure and Practice' (1970) 7 *CMLRev.* 286; Y. Quintin, 'Participation de l'Assemblée parlementaire européenne au déroulement de la procédure de négociation des accords commerciaux' [1975] *RTDE* 211; R. Kovar, 'La participation des Communautés européennes aux conventions multilatérales' [1975] *AFDI* 903.

[25] Opinion of Tesauro A.G. in Case C–327/91, n. 6 above, at para. 26.

[26] The distinction between the decision *sui generis* and the 'decision' referred to in Art. 189 EC is described in Ch. 1, p. 21.

[27] Not to be confused with 'directives' in the sense of Art. 189 EC: see p. 89 below.

public.[28] Exceptionally, a more formal, structured, style of decision is used.[29] Acts of the Council approving the conclusion of an agreement on behalf of the Community are usually either regulations or decisions *sui generis*, depending mainly on the content of the agreement to be concluded. If the agreement contains provisions which are capable of having direct effect, or which, if promulgated as internal legislation within the Community, would take the form of a regulation, the Council act concluding the agreement will often take the form of a regulation.[30] Otherwise, the decision *sui generis* is used.[31] Practice suggests that it is becoming common simply to use the decision *sui generis* even where the agreement in question is capable of having direct effect. Because conclusion of the agreement makes its provisions part of Community law and thus capable of applying directly,[32] the form of the act concluding the agreement is of little significance.

Where more than one of the Communities is participating in the same agreement, there is no objection to the use of a single act to authorize signature or conclusion of the agreement on behalf of all the Communities.[33]

Legal Basis

The Court has consistently held, in its review of the legality of internal acts, that the indication of the legal basis of a measure is an essential part of the reasoning necessary for its adoption.[34] Accordingly, unless the legal basis can

[28] e.g., a decision authorizing the Commission to negotiate an agreement will usually run as follows: 'The Council, on the recommendation of the Commission, has authorized the Commission to negotiate an agreement on . . . with State X.' The decision to sign the agreement subject to approval might simply state: 'The Council has decided to sign the agreement on . . . with State X subject to approval, and has authorized its President to sign the agreement on behalf of the Council of the European Communities.'

[29] e.g. Council Dec. 94/562 concerning the signing of the Agreement relating to the implementation of Part XI of the UNCLOS III ([1994] OJ L215/9).

[30] Examples of agreements concluded by regs. include the 1978 Co-operation Agreement with Egypt ([1978] OJ L266/1); the 1986 Agreement with Pakistan ([1986] OJ L108/1); and the Agreement establishing an International Science and Technology Centre ([1992] OJ L409/1). For comment on the Council's practice in choosing regs. or decs., see M. Waelbroek, 'Enforceability of the EEC-EFTA Free Trade Agreements: A Reply' (1978) 3 *ELRev.* 27; M. Maresceau, 'The Effect of Community Agreements in the United Kingdom under the European Communities Act 1972' (1979) 28 *ICLQ* 241 at 244.

[31] Where the dec. *sui generis* is the act expressing the Council's intention to approve the agreement, it will often take a more structured form.

[32] See the opinions of Rozès A.G. in Case 270/80 *Polydor Ltd.* v. *Harlequin Record Shops* [1982] ECR 329 and Case 104/81 *Hauptzollamt Mainz v Kupferberg* [1982] ECR 3641. On the effect of agreements concluded by the Communities, see Ch. 5.

[33] Thus, in the case of the Europe Agreement with Hungary, to which the EC, the ECSC, and Euratom were all to be parties, a single joint decision of the Council (for the EC) and the Commission (for the ECSC and Euratom) was adopted on the same day to approve conclusion (see [1993] OJ L347/1). The same was the case for the other Europe Agreements.

[34] See N. Emiliou 'Opening Pandora's Box: the Legal Basis of Community Measures before the Court of Justice' (1994) 19 ELRev. 488. For a discussion of the legal bases for internal market measures, see Wyatt and Dashwood, *European Community Law* (3rd edn., Sweet & Maxwell, 1993) 369–373.

be determined from other parts of the measure, its preamble must state precisely which legal basis has been chosen.[35] The choice of legal basis does not depend simply on an institution's conviction of the objective being pursued, but must be based on objective factors amenable to judicial review. These factors include, in particular, the aim and content of the measure in question.[36] Where a measure can be said to have more than one aim, or where its content spreads across several areas of Community activity, the legal basis will be the Article which most nearly corresponds to its principal purpose. Where a measure has more than one objective, and neither can easily be identified as the principal objective, it may be necessary to cite more than one legal basis.[37]

The application of these principles to the conclusion of agreements is not straightforward. The process of conclusion of an agreement by one of the Communities involves, at several stages, acts which have legal effects both internationally and within the Community legal order. The most significant step is, of course, the formal expression of the Community's consent to be bound, but decisions to authorize negotiations to begin, to sign the agreement subject to approval, or to apply it provisionally, all have legal effects. The practice of the Council is that legal bases are always cited in acts concluding agreements; but acts at earlier stages of the process tend not to cite the legal basis on which the Council is acting, often contain very little by way of preambular reasoning, and are sometimes not even published.

The authority for the Council's practice is Case 22/70 *Commission* v. *Council* (the *AETR* case).[38] In that case, the Commission challenged an act of the Council regarding the negotiation and conclusion of an agreement. The Council's act was clearly not a decision, directive, or regulation within the meaning of Article 189 EEC. However, the Court of Justice found that the act under challenge 'had definite legal effects both on the relations between the Community and the Member States and on the relationship between institutions' and was thus capable of judicial review under Article 173 EEC. In response to a Commission argument that the Council acts under challenge 'did not indicate the legal grounds on which they were based and provided no statement of reasons'[39] the Court said that the requirements in Article 190

---

[35] Case 45/86 *Commission* v. *Council* [1987] ECR 1493.

[36] The most recent and fullest exposition of the law on choice of legal basis was given in Case C–187/93 *Parliament* v. *Council* [1994] ECR I–2857.

[37] On the combination of two legal bases: see Case C–300/89 *Commission* v. *Council* [1991] ECR I–2867. The problem of combining a legal basis which requires the co-operation procedure with one which requires the Council to act by unanimity still exists in relation to the adoption of internal Community legislation. A welcome result of the new version of Art. 228 is that these problems will not arise in the adoption of acts relating to the conclusion of agreements: the co-decision and co-operation procedures will not be used for the adoption of such acts. As to the legal basis for an act amending an earlier act, see Case C–187/93, and below, 'Amendment and Termination'.

[38] [1971] ECR 213.   [39] *Ibid.*, para. 97.

EEC (to state the legal grounds on which a measure was based) were 'imposed by Article 190 in relation to regulations, directives and decisions and cannot be extended to measures of a special nature' such as the act of the Council under challenge in that case. The Court observed that 'the Commission's participation in the actual work of the Council afforded it all the legal safeguards which Article 190 was designed to ensure for third parties affected by the measures therein'.[40]

The position, therefore, seems to be that a legal basis need not be cited, and full reasoning need not be given, in Council acts relating to the process of conclusion of an agreement which only affect the relations of the institutions among themselves. If, however, a Council (or Commission) act affects the legal rights or duties of third parties, such as individuals or companies, adequate legal reasoning must be provided in support of the act, and the relevant legal basis must be cited. In practice, the rights of such third parties will probably only be affected by a Community act on provisional application or conclusion of the agreement: it is at these stages therefore that the institutions must take particular care to ensure that their acts set out clearly the legal grounds on which they are based, and provide an adequate statement of reasons.

European Community

Legal Basis

The basic framework for the conclusion of agreements by the EC has always been found in Article 228 of the EEC Treaty, but, before the amendments to that Treaty effected by the Maastricht Treaty, that Article was never itself cited as a legal basis. When the Community acted under an express power to make international agreements,[41] the Article conferring the express power was cited as the legal basis and the procedures in that Article were followed. When the Community's external competence derived from the existence of internal rules, it was assumed that the legal basis for the conclusion of an agreement relating to the area covered by the internal rules would be the same as the legal basis of the internal rules, and that the procedures required by that legal basis would apply in respect of the act concluding the agreement on behalf of the Community. Acts of the Council relating to the conclusion of agreements could thus require the Council to follow the co-operation procedure.[42]

The Maastricht Treaty consolidated in Article 228 the procedural provisions

---

[40] *Ibid.*, paras. 98 and 99.
[41] i.e. Arts. 113 and 238: see Ch. 3 above.
[42] See, e.g., the Council decision relating to the conclusion of the Framework Agreement on Science and Technology with Iceland ([1990] OJ L14/18).

relating to conclusion of agreements,[43] and deleted most[44] of the procedural provisions formerly contained in provisions such as Articles 113 and 238. Article 228 now sets out several possible procedures, and the exact procedure to be followed in any given case cannot be determined without reference to the substantive powers under which the Community is entitled to act in the area covered by the proposed agreement.[45] Thus, in order to determine in any given case whether a particular agreement is within the powers of the Community, and what the legal basis for conclusion should be, it is necessary to consider, first, whether the Treaty gives the Community competence in relation to the substance of the agreement and, secondly, which procedures should be followed in the light of the substantive legal basis read with Article 228. The result is that the conclusion of agreements by the Community now requires reference to two kinds of legal basis. Article 228 sets out the *procedural* steps to be followed in the conclusion of agreements involving the EC, and must accordingly be cited in any act adopted by the Council in connection with the conclusion of an agreement.[46] In addition, there must be cited the Article (or Articles) which most closely relates to the *substance* of the agreement in question.

Procedures for Negotiation and Conclusion of Agreements by the EC

Article 228 is of cardinal importance in the external relations of the EC, and needs detailed analysis. Although its provisions, as amended, are new in many

---

[43] There are two exceptions to this rule: agreements on an exchange rate mechanism for the ECU in relation to non-Community countries (Art. 109(1)) and agreements concerning monetary or foreign-exchange related matters (Art. 109(2)). Art. 109(3) envisages that the Council will establish arrangements for the conclusion of agreements concerning monetary or foreign-exchange matters. Such arrangements are to be decided on by the Council, acting by qualified majority on a recommendation from the Commission. The Council must consult the ECB. The arrangements made by the Council must ensure that the Community expresses a single position, and that the Commission is closely associated with the negotiations. But it would not seem to be necessary for the Commission to be the Community's negotiator: that task could be entrusted to the Presidency or the ECB. Once these arrangements have been established, agreements on exchange-rate systems for the ECU in relation to other foreign currencies may be concluded under Art. 109(1). The procedure for the conclusion of such agreements differs markedly from the usual procedures: the Council acts on a recommendation from the ECB or the Commission; after consulting the ECB; in accordance with the procedures established by the Council under Art. 109(3); and the Council's dec. is to be taken unanimously. Agreements concluded in accordance with Art. 109 are binding on the institutions of the Community, the Member States, and the ECB. See further, Dehousse and Gehmar 'Le traité de Maastricht et les relations extérieures de la Communauté européenne' (1994) 5 *EJIL* 151 at 154–8.

[44] Art. 113 EC still contains some procedural provisions; Art. 238, by contrast, contains none.

[45] In order to determine the majority needed in the Council, for example, and the extent of the Parliament's involvement in the process of conclusion.

[46] It is not sufficient to refer generally to Art. 228: the citation of the legal basis should specify exactly the procedure under which the act is being adopted. Thus if the Council acts unanimously, the legal basis should refer to 'the second sentence of para. 2 of Art. 228'; if the Parliament's assent is to be sought, there should be a reference to 'the second subpara. of para. 3 of Art. 228' and so on. For examples, see Council Dec. 94/13 on the conclusion of the UNRWA Convention ([1994] OJ L9/16) and Council Dec. 94/578 concerning the conclusion of the Co-operation Agreement with India ([1994] OJ L223/23).

respects, the procedures they describe are closely modelled on those of the pre-Maastricht EEC Treaty: practice under the old system is therefore still a relevant guide.

The Article is structured as follows. Paragraph 1 describes the procedure to be followed until the end of the *negotiation* of any agreement involving the Community. Paragraph 2 deals with the *conclusion* of the agreement by the Council: that is to say, the adoption by the Council of the legislative act authorizing the Community to become party to the agreement. Paragraph 3 describes how the *Parliament* is involved in the process of conclusion. Paragraph 4 makes provision for the delegation by the Council to the Commission of certain powers in relation to the *modification after conclusion* of agreements binding on the Community. Paragraph 5 deals with the case of agreements which necessitate *amendment* of the Treaty. Paragraph 6 sets out the procedure for obtaining the *Court's opinion* on the compatibility of Community agreements with the Treaty. Paragraph 7 restates the rule that agreements concluded by the Community are binding on the Member States and the institutions of the Community. Paragraphs 6 and 7 are considered elsewhere.[47]

Negotiation

The basic rule under the EC Treaty has always been that the Commission negotiates agreements on behalf of the Community. Article 228 (1) provides:

Where this Treaty provides for the conclusion of agreements between the Community and one or more States or international organizations, the Commission shall make recommendations to the Council, which shall authorize the Commission to open the necessary negotiations. The Commission shall conduct these negotiations in consultation with special committees appointed by the Council to assist it in this task and within the framework of such directives as the Council may issue to it.

In exercising the powers conferred on it by this paragraph, the Council shall act by a qualified majority, except in the cases provided for in the second sentence of paragraph 2, for which it shall act unanimously.

'*Where this Treaty provides for*' The EC Treaty provides expressly for the conclusion of agreements by the Community in Articles 109, 113, 130m, 130r, 130y, and 238. With the exception of Article 109,[48] all these Articles refer to the procedures set out in Article 228 as the procedures to be followed in the conclusion of agreements by the Community. But the Community's external competence is not limited to those areas in respect of which the Treaty expressly confers powers to conclude agreements: Articles 126(3), 127(3), 128(3) and 129(3) provide for the Community to foster co-operation with international organizations and third States, and the Community has implied powers to enter into international agreements in many areas in which it has internal legislative

---

[47] Para. 6 is discussed at 111ff. below. The rule in para. 7 is considered in more detail in Ch. 5.
[48] On the procedure for conclusion of agreements under Art. 109 EC, see n. 43 above.

competence.[49] The procedures described in Article 228 also apply in respect of agreements concluded by virtue of these powers. In other words, leaving aside the special provisions of Article 109 EC, the provisions of Article 228 are of general application in all cases where the European Community exercises its competence to enter into international agreements.

'*agreements between the Community and one or more States or international organizations*' The scope of Article 228 is wide: it establishes the procedures by which the Community may enter into all kinds of agreements within the areas of its competence, and is thus the basis for the conclusion of bilateral and multilateral agreements and of agreements involving the Community in membership of international organizations.[50]

'*agreements*' This term includes any undertaking entered into by entities subject to international law which has binding force, whatever its formal designation.[51]

'*the Community*' The procedures set out in Article 228 apply in the case of the European Community properly so called, that is to say, the Community established by the Treaty of Rome, formerly known as the European Economic Community. The procedures which apply where agreements are to be concluded by the ECSC or Euratom are set out in the ECSC Treaty and the Euratom Treaty respectively, and are considered below. The amendments made by the TEU do not remove the need for each Community to follow its own procedures when an agreement to be concluded by the European Community is also to be concluded by the ECSC or Euratom.[52]

'*the Commission shall make recommendations*' In this area, as elsewhere in the Treaty, the right to initiate proposals for Community action rests with the Commission. In the first instance, therefore, it is for the Commission[53] to consider whether it would be appropriate for the Community to enter into agreements in a particular area or with a particular State, and to make the necessary recommendations to the Council. In practice, such 'recommendations' take the form of a communication from the Commission to the Council, explaining why it is thought that conclusion of an agreement would be desirable, and proposing that the Council should authorize the Commission to negotiate such an agreement

---

[49] See further Ch. 3.

[50] Although Arts. 229, 230, and 231 EC allow for other forms of co-operation between the Community and international organizations, it is doubtful whether these Arts. permit the conclusion of agreements which bind the Community in international law. See further below, p. 96 and Ch. 7.

[51] *Opinion 1/75*, n. 5 above, at para. 2; Case C–327/91, n. 6 above, para. 27.

[52] But the approval of an agreement concluded by all three Communities may be given in a single act: for example, see Decision 93/742 [1993] OJ L347/1.

[53] Although the right to initiate proposals rests with the Commission, Art. 152 EC provides that the Council may request the Commission to undertake any studies the Council considers desirable for the attainment of the common objectives and to submit to it any proposals.

in accordance with a set of negotiating directives suggested by the Commission, and annexed to the recommendation.[54]

'*the Council . . . shall authorize the Commission to open the necessary negotiations*' While the Commission has the sole right to make recommendations, the Council alone decides whether such negotiations should begin and, if so, on what terms. The Council has a discretion in this regard: the words 'shall authorize' do not in this context mean that the Council is obliged to accept whatever the Commission offers to it. It is for the Council to assess the proposal of the Commission and to decide whether it is expedient for the Community to enter into the proposed agreement.[55] The Council may modify or reject the Commission's recommendation.[56] When the Commission's recommendation is acceptable to the Council, the Council will authorize the opening of negotiations, usually in a decision recorded in its minutes. Exceptionally, a more structured form of decision may be adopted.[57] To protect the Community's position during the negotiations, decisions granting negotiating mandates and directives are not published.

'*The Commission shall conduct these negotiations*' All agreements relating to areas within the competence of the Community are, in principle, to be negotiated by the Commission, as the representative of the interests of the Community.[58] Article 228 does not preclude the possibility of involvement of experts from the Member States in such negotiations if the Commission is agreeable, but the 'conduct' of the negotiations is the responsibility of the Commission. If the agreement relates to matters within the competences of the Community and the Member States, in theory a choice is open to the Member States within the Council: they may authorize the Commission to negotiate the entire agreement, without prejudice to the eventual decisions about where competence lies and who should become parties. Or they may authorize the Commission to negotiate that part of the agreement which relates to the competence of the Community, leaving it to the Member States to negotiate in their own right in respect of areas within their competence (subject, of course, to the duty to co-operate with the Community and to proceed by common action). In practice, if the Community's competence is likely to be at all extensive in an agreement which is to involve the Community and the Member States, the Commission is usually authorized to negotiate the agreement.[59] The Member States' interests are safeguarded by co-ordination meetings at which the line to be taken by the Commission in the negotiations is decided.

---

[54] These authorizations and directives are commonly known as the 'negotiating mandate'. Strictly, the Commission is not 'mandated' by the Council, but 'authorized'.

[55] Case 22/70 *Commission v. Council* [1971] ECR 263 at para. 70.

[56] Because not 'proposals', recommendations are not subject to the rule in Art. 189a(1): unanimity in the Council is not needed for their amendment.

[57] 'Decision' in this context means 'decision *sui generis*': see n. 26.

[58] But see Art. 109 EC, and n. 43 above.

[59] e.g., the Commission negotiated for the Community and the 12 during the Uruguay Round.

'*in consultation with special committees appointed by the Council to assist it in this task*' Article 113 of the Treaty of Rome as it stood before the entry into force of the TEU established a committee[60] to assist the Commission in the negotiation of agreements within the sphere of the common commercial policy. This committee developed a general monitoring role across the whole field of the common commercial policy, but there was no similar arrangement in the original Treaty for the systematic scrutiny of the conduct of negotiations in other areas. In practice, this caused no great problem: the Commission's progress in negotiation of agreements for the Community was kept under review in the Council's regular working groups and in COREPER or, where appropriate, in the Community's *sur place* co-ordination at conferences or in international organizations. Article 228 codifies the existing arrangements, and develops them. The Council is now specifically given a right to establish special committees and the Commission is required to negotiate 'in consultation with' these committees. It is not clear whether the intention was that committees should be set up in respect of each negotiation, or whether the provision is simply a consolidation of the Council's existing powers to establish such committees as it sees fit. The latter—more flexible—interpretation would seem sensible, and reflects current practice.

The Commission is to negotiate '*in consultation with*'[61] committees appointed by the Council. This phrase underlines the pre-eminent role of the Commission in any negotiation: the committee does not give the Commission direct instructions, and the Treaty does not imply that the committee, or its representatives, may be present during the face to face negotiations, at least when the agreement relates only to matters within the competence of the Community under the Treaty. But the Commission is under an obligation to consult the committee. It would be unlikely to ignore its views: the results of any negotiation have to be acceptable to the Council, so there would be little point in the Commission side-stepping any committee set up to assist in the negotiations.

Article 228(1) does not offer guidance on the composition of the committees to be appointed by the Council. It is open to the Council to appoint any experts it chooses to such committees. In practice, the committees are working groups of the Council which all the Member States attend.

'*within the framework of such directives as the Council may issue*' The Commission does not have unfettered discretion regarding its conduct of negotiations. In the first place, as has been noted, the Treaty imposes on the Commission a duty to negotiate 'in consultation with' any committees established for the purpose by the Council. Secondly, the Treaty requires the Commission to have regard to the Council's instructions regarding the conduct of the negotiations, as such instructions may from to time be given in directives of the Council.

---

[60] It became known (unsurprisingly) as the Art. 113 Committee.

[61] The reference to 'consultation' has no connection at all with the procedure whereby the Council consults the Parliament before adopting measures (e.g., under Art. 228(3) 1st subpara.).

'*directives*' In this context they should be distinguished from legislative 'directives' of the kind described in Article 189. In the context of Article 228(1), a negotiating directive constitutes an instruction to the Commission on the conduct of the negotiation. Negotiating directives are usually incorporated in the 'authorization' or 'mandate' given to the Commission by the Council at the beginning of the negotiation,[62] but the Council may issue further directives unilaterally, without a Commission proposal, during the negotiations.[63] Such instructions could, it would seem, relate to any aspect of the negotiations covered by the mandate agreed originally by the Council, but they could not authorize—or require—the Commission to begin a completely new set of negotiations with other parties. Such a change of tack would require a new Commission recommendation. On the other hand, it would seem to be possible for the Council to call a halt to negotiations by a directive under Article 228.[64]

'*within the framework of*' Although the Commission's negotiating discretion is limited by the directives of the Council, the Commission's basic discretion as negotiator remains: the Council may issue 'directives', but it may not seek to regulate the conduct of the negotiations on a line-by-line basis.

'*the Council may issue*' Once the original negotiating authorization has been agreed by the Council, that is sufficient for the conduct of the negotiation: further directives are not absolutely necessary. It is for the Council to decide whether further directives are necessary: it does not need a Commission proposal before acting.

'*In exercising the powers . . . unanimously*' The second part of paragraph 1 of Article 228 spells out what had before the TEU been assumed to be the legal position underlying the opening of the negotiating process: namely, that the procedures required for Council action at the stage of negotiating an agreement were determined by the legal basis which would apply for conclusion of the agreement being proposed.[65] This was always the position when the agreement to be negotiated related to the common commercial policy: in such cases the provisions of what was formerly Article 113(3) applied.[66]

In practice, however, matters were less clear, at least in other areas of Community activity. It was not always possible to decide what the correct legal basis for conclusion of the agreement to be negotiated should be. The content of the agreement could not be known for certain until after the negotiation, and (a more common problem) there was argument within the Council, or between

---

[62] See above, at p. 87.   [63] This is rare in practice.

[64] If such were the Council's wish, there would be little point in the Commission continuing with the negotiations anyway.

[65] So, e.g., if the agreement related to an area of policy where internal rules were made by unanimity, decisions about the opening of negotiations should be taken by unanimity.

[66] Art. 113(3) provided that 'In exercising the powers conferred upon it by this Article, the Council shall act by a qualified majority.'

the Council and the Commission, as to the correct legal basis for Community action.[67] The solution to this dilemma was the practice that the Council did not come to a view on the legal basis for conclusion of an agreement until after the agreement had been negotiated. The Council's decision to authorize the Commission to open negotiations accordingly would not usually cite a legal basis, and would be agreed within the Council by consensus.

Since the TEU, Article 228(1), read with the second sentence of Article 228(2), makes it clear that the Council may decide any issue relating to the opening of negotiations by qualified majority, unless (a) the agreement covers a field for which unanimity is required for the adoption of internal rules;[68] or (b) the agreement is one of those referred to in Article 238 (commonly known as 'association agreements'[69]). Put in simpler terms, the crucial issue in determining the basis on which the Council may act in deciding whether to open negotiations is the probable legal basis for the conclusion of the agreement envisaged.[70] Although logical, this rule, if applied strictly, would force the Council into debates on the legal basis of an agreement whose substance was not yet known. As in the past, therefore, negotiating authorizations are in most cases agreed by consensus. It should be noted that a decision by the Council to issue directives to the Commission on the conduct of the negotiations may also be adopted according to the voting requirement of the probable legal basis of the agreement being negotiated.

General and specific mandates The Commission usually brings forward a recommendation for the negotiation of an agreement with a particular third country. But it can also seek a general authorization to negotiate agreements about a particular matter with several countries: an important example of such an authorization was the Hague Resolution of 1 July 1976,[71] which formed the basis for the negotiation of fisheries agreements between the Community and several coastal States in the late 1970s and early 1980s. More recent examples in another area are the authorizations contained in decisions establishing specific research programmes.[72]

Initialling and Other Methods of Establishing the Text
The establishment of the negotiated text as definitive marks the end of the process of negotiation, and accordingly lies within the power of the negotiator, under his original mandate. So far as the Community is concerned, therefore, the Commission may take steps to establish a text—by initialling or otherwise—

---

[67] Or indeed whether Community action was at all appropriate in the area in question.
[68] The difficulties inherent in the expression 'covers a field' have been considered above. Examples of agreements which might fall into this category are given below, at p. 97.
[69] On the meaning of 'association agreements' see further Ch. 20.
[70] On choice of legal basis, see above at pp. 81–3.   [71] See Ch. 10 (Fisheries).
[72] See Ch. 16 (Research and Technological Development).

on the basis of the negotiating authorization it originally received from the Council: further authority from the Council is not necessary.

Signature Subject to Approval

The negotiating authorization will not, however, usually permit the Commission to take steps going beyond the establishment of the text at the end of the negotiations. So if the agreement provides that it is to be signed by intending parties subject to subsequent approval or ratification, the Council will have to decide on signature on behalf of the Community. The decision to sign takes the form of a decision *sui generis* which is usually recorded in the Council's minutes but does not usually cite the legal basis on which the Council is acting.[73] If it were necessary to vote on a decision to sign, the majority necessary for adoption of such a decision by the Council would be that required by the probable legal basis of the agreement being signed.[74] The opinion or assent of the Parliament is not sought before signature subject to approval. The signed text is transmitted to the Parliament for its consideration while the Council examines the proposal to conclude the agreement.

Provisional Application

Some Community agreements[75] provide for 'provisional application' by the intending parties in the period before consent to be bound has been expressed. As has been noted, 'provisional application' is probably closer in legal effect to signature 'subject to approval' than to 'conclusion' of an agreement, in that it involves the voluntary implementation of some or all of the provisions of an agreement, not a consent to be bound by it. Provisional application is often of great practical significance, however; and in the Community's practice, decisions to apply agreements provisionally sometimes cite the legal basis which would be required for their conclusion. The Council's decision will be adopted by the majority required by that legal basis. The opinion or assent of the Parliament is not sought before adoption of a decision on provisional application.[76]

Conclusion of Agreements

The final stage of the process of approval of an agreement within the Community legal order is referred to in Article 228 as 'conclusion' of the agreement. This marks its acceptance by the institutions of the Community and constitutes authority for a Community representative to take the steps required under the agreement to express to the third party or parties the Community's

---

[73] See above, pp. 82–3.
[74] In practice, the legal basis is not always determined by the Council at the stage of signature: in such circumstances, the decision to sign would be taken by consensus.
[75] Agreements on fisheries and commodities are the commonest examples.
[76] Council Dec. 94/998 ([1994] OJ L380/1) on the signature and provisional application of the European Energy Charter Treaty was an exception.

definitive consent to be bound. In the EC Treaty, the general principle is that it is for the Council to 'conclude' agreements binding on the Community. The rule is in Article 228 (2), which provides that:

Subject to the powers vested in the Commission in this field, the agreements shall be concluded by the Council, acting by a qualified majority on a proposal from the Commission. The Council shall act unanimously when the agreement covers a field for which unanimity is required for the adoption of internal rules and for the agreements referred to in Article 238.

'concluded' It is important to recall the distinction between two uses of 'conclude' and 'conclusion'. On the one hand, the term signifies the internal Community process by which the institutions, each exercising its own role, together decide that a particular agreement should be accepted by the Community. On the other, it signifies the international act[77] by which the Community expresses its definitive consent to be bound. Without the first step, the expression of Community consent to be bound would be invalid in Community law.[78] Without the second, the third party would not know whether the Community had decided to enter into the agreement in question. The distinction appears clearly in decisions of the Council 'concluding' agreements. These usually state that the agreement in question is approved by the Community, and then go on to provide for the means by which the Community's approval of the agreement is to be expressed to the third party or parties.[79]

The word 'conclude' in Article 228(2) refers to the last step of the internal Community process, and the emphasis is on the role of the Council in that process in relation to the other institutions. In particular, Article 228(2) does not deal with the expression of the Community's consent to be bound on the international level. Although it is common for the Council to authorize its President to take the necessary steps to express the Community's consent to be bound (for example, by signature of the agreement), nothing in the Treaty prevents the Council from deciding that a Commissioner, or a Commission or Council official, should sign on behalf of the Community.[80]

'Simplified' and 'solemn' procedure Within the Community, the stage of conclusion follows one of two procedures, depending on whether the agreement becomes binding on signature or is signed subject to approval.

---

[77] Whether by signature, deposit of an instrument of approval, exchange of letters, etc.

[78] Though probably not in international law: see Ch. 9, n. 36.

[79] See, e.g., Arts. 1 and 2 of Council Dec. 92/509 on the conclusion of the Framework Co-operation Agreement with Paraguay ([1992] OJ L313/71); Arts. 1 and 2 of Council Dec. 92/384 concerning the Conclusion of an Agreement on Civil Aviation with Norway and Sweden ([1992] OJ L200/20); and Arts. 1 and 3 of Council Dec. 93/743 on the Conclusion of the Europe Agreement with Poland ([1993] OJ L348/1). The pattern is repeated in all Council acts authorizing the conclusion of agreements.

[80] It is common for Commissioners to sign beside the President of the Council.

Simplified Procedure When signature of an agreement also constitutes the act by which the Community expresses its consent to be bound towards the other contracting party or parties, the so-called '*simplified*' procedure is used. This procedure involves the following steps. If required by the legal basis for conclusion of the agreement, the opinion or assent of the Parliament is sought in accordance with the relevant provisions of the Treaty. This is usually undertaken on the basis of an initialled text of the agreement. Once the necessary parliamentary procedures have been completed, the Council approves the conclusion of the agreement by the Community. The Council's act thus authorizes the Presidency, or the Commission, to sign the agreement on behalf of the Community.

Solemn procedure Where the agreement in question provides for signature followed by approval or ratification, and only becomes binding on such approval or ratification, the so-called '***solemn***' procedure is used. This procedure authorizes signature as well as conclusion of the agreement, and involves the following stages:

(i) First, the agreement is signed subject to approval. Such signature does not bind the Community, but nevertheless requires a decision of the Council on the basis of a proposal from the Commission. The Council acts by the majority required by the legal basis for the conclusion of the agreement; if that is disputed, or not yet determined, the Council can still authorize signature, but takes its decision by consensus. The decision authorizes the President, or some other person,[81] to sign on behalf of the Community. Decisions authorizing signature subject to approval are usually recorded in the Council's minutes.

(ii) The text of the agreement is then submitted to the Parliament for its opinion or assent, as required by the legal basis for conclusion of the agreement.

(iii) As in the case of the 'simplified' procedure, once the necessary parliamentary procedures have been completed, the Council authorizes the conclusion of the agreement by the Community. The Council's act authorizes the Presidency, or the Commission, to take the necessary steps to express the Community's consent to be bound.

In practice, the solemn procedure is used whenever the Parliament has to be consulted or its assent sought. The simplified procedure could be used in these cases, but it is more appropriate, and more commonly used, in the case of agreements to be concluded under Article 113 (which require no formal involvement of the Parliament in the process of conclusion).

---

[81] e.g., a representative of the Commission. The decision may confer the task of signature on more than one person.

'*agreements shall be concluded by the Council*' The institutional balance created in the EC Treaty contrasts with that in the ECSC and Euratom Treaties, where the task of concluding agreements is usually the Commission's.

'*Subject to the powers vested in the Commission in this field*' The meaning of this phrase is not easy to determine. It may simply refer to the Commission's role in the process of concluding agreements under the EC Treaty; that is to say, its role as the initiator of proposals for the negotiation and conclusion of agreements, and its role as negotiator. Or it could be intended to safeguard the Commission's pre-eminent role in the process of concluding agreements under the other Treaties, by making clear that the Council's role under the EC Treaty does not remove the need for Commission involvement in the process of con-clusion of agreements by the other Communities. Or it could refer to Article 228(4), which provides for the delegation to the Commission, in strictly defined circumstances, of the power to conclude agreements. However, the words 'in this field' suggest that the phrase is intended to safeguard an inherent *Commission* power to conclude agreements binding on the Community, and the question of the existence and scope of such a power accordingly arises.[82]

The leading case on this point is Case C–327/91 *France* v. *Commission*.[83] France, supported by the Netherlands and Spain, challenged the Commission's 'conclusion'[84] of an Agreement between 'the Communities' and the US Government regarding the application of competition laws.[85] The purpose of the Agreement was to promote co-operation and co-ordination and lessen the possibility or impact of differences between the parties in the application of their competition laws. To that end the Agreement provided, among other things, for an exchange of information relating to various matters, co-ordination of enforcement activities, and reciprocal consultation. The principal ground of challenge advanced by France was that the Commission was not competent to conclude such an agreement, because that power was reserved to the Council. The Commission argued that (i) the Agreement was an administrative agree-ment which it was competent to conclude; (ii) it could derive powers to con-clude agreements from sources other than the Treaty, in particular from the practice of the institutions; (iii) an analogy could be drawn from its more exten-sive powers under the Euratom Treaty; and (iv) its pre-eminent role in compe-tition matters within the Community legal order gave it a power to conclude agreements with third countries relating to competition. The Court dismissed all the Commission's arguments, and held that the Agreement with the US Government had, as a matter of Community law, been improperly concluded.[86]

---

[82] On the Commission's power to conclude agreements under the Lomé Convention, see Ch. 20.
[83] [1994] ECR I–3641 .   [84] By a Commissioner's signature.
[85] An account of the Agreement is in 'EC–US Co-operation in Antitrust Matters' (1992) 86 *AJIL* 119.
[86] The Court clearly regarded the Agreement as continuing to bind the Community in interna-tional law: see para. 25. On the legal effects of agreements concluded in breach of the Community's

The judgment clarifies several important points. First, it is the Community alone which has capacity to bind itself by concluding agreements at the international level: the Commission does not have that capacity.[87] Secondly, under Article 228 EC, it is in principle for the Council to conclude agreements binding the European Community.[88] Thirdly, the words 'subject to the powers vested in the Commission in this field' in Article 228 are a derogation from the general rule[89] (which implies that they are to be narrowly interpreted). Further, the powers of the Commission under the EC Treaty are circumscribed by Article 228, and no analogy can be drawn from the powers conferred on the Commission under the other Treaties, if such an analogy would undermine or conflict with the meaning of Article 228.[90] Fifthly, the practice of the Commission in concluding agreements and arrangements (even if acquiesced in by the other institutions) cannot override the provisions of the Treaty.[91] Finally, the Commission's internal powers to apply competition rules cannot alter the allocation of powers between the institutions with regard to the conclusion of agreements.[92]

The judgment nevertheless leaves unclear the extent to which the Commission may conclude agreements binding on the European Community. There are three main areas of uncertainty.

Agreements about the privileges and immunities of Commission delegations. Article 7(1) of the Protocol on the Privileges and Immunities of the European Communities provides that the Commission may conclude agreements for *laissez passer* to be recognized as valid travel documents within the territory of third countries. The Commission has, however, also concluded several dozen 'agreements' or 'arrangements' with third countries conferring on Commission delegations in these countries privileges and immunities analogous to those granted under the Vienna Convention on Diplomatic Relations.[93] Many of these 'agreements' are in the form of binding international commitments, and in Case C–327/91,[94] the Commission relied on this practice in support of its claim that agreements relating to the status of its delegations overseas were within its power to conclude. The opinion of the Advocate General and the judgment of the Court offer little support for that argument, and it may be best to regard agreements or arrangements of that kind as, in essence, unilateral concessions by the host State. It seems clear that, to the extent that any such agreement or arrangement imposed obligations or conferred rights on the European Community, it would require conclusion by the Council.

internal rules, see Ch. 5 below. On the eventual conclusion of the Competition Agreement which was the subject of Case C–327/91, see Dec. 95/145 of 10 Apr. 1995 concerning the conclusion of the Agreement between the European Communities and the US regarding the application of their competition laws ([1995] OJ L95/45).

[87] Case C–327/91, n. 6 above, at para. 16. Nor, presumably, do the other institutions.
[88] *Ibid.*, para. 28.   [89] *Ibid.*, para. 33.   [90] *Ibid.*, paras. 37–39.
[91] *Ibid.*, para. 36.   [92] *Ibid.*, paras. 41 and 42 .   [93] See, generally, Ch. 8.
[94] *France* v. *Commission* [1994] ECR I–3641.

Commission powers under Articles 229, 230, and 231 EC. The scope of these Articles and the practice under them are considered further in Chapter 7. Although Case C–327/91 leaves open the question of the Commission's powers under these Articles, the better view in the light of the Court's comments is that they do not confer on the Commission any power to enter into agreements binding the Community in international law.[95] They are no doubt a basis for administrative co-operation, perhaps in the form of non-binding arrangements between the Commission and the organization concerned.

Administrative arrangements generally. In Case C–327/91, the Commission argued[96] that its Competition Agreement with the US Government was no more than an administrative arrangement between two executive authorities, and that it was accordingly within the Commission's power to conclude it. In support of this, the Commission pointed out that the Agreement required no change in Community law, and could not be interpreted by either party in a manner inconsistent with its laws. The Court, however, found that the Agreement produced legal effects, and that it was accordingly an agreement binding on the European Communities: the scope of the Commission's power to enter into administrative arrangements was not discussed. Given the range of the Commission's responsibilities internally, there are sound practical reasons for recognizing that the Commission has power to enter into informal, non-binding commitments in matters within these areas of responsibility. Provided the commitments do not give rise to legal effects in international law, are consistent with the Commission's powers and with existing Community law, and do not purport to commit the Community as such, there seems no reason to regard them as unlawful, or outside the powers of the Commission. Where, however, such commitments are to be given in the name or on behalf of the Community, the authorization of the Council would seem necessary,[97] before they may be negotiated or concluded.

'on a proposal from the Commission' No matter how desirable the Council finds the outcome of negotiations opened under Article 228(1), it cannot conclude any agreement until the Commission has made a proposal to that effect. The proposal will take the form of a communication from the Commission to the Council, explaining the background to the proposed agreement, justifying the legal basis chosen, and proposing that the Council should adopt the act[98] necessary to authorize the expression at the international level of the Community's consent to be bound.

'acting by a qualified majority' The general rule is that, in deciding whether to conclude an agreement, the Council acts by a qualified majority. Adoption of a

---

[95] See also Mégret, n. 24 above, at 66 ff.   [96] Judgment, paras. 21 ff.

[97] See below, *Informal Arrangements.*

[98] The form of such an act has been considered above: the choice is usually between a dec. *sui generis* and a reg.

decision to conclude thus requires sixty-two votes in favour.[99] Because the Council acts on a Commission proposal, an amendment of the Commission's proposal requires unanimity in the Council.[100]

'*The Council shall act unanimously . . . Article 238*' In derogation from the general rule, there are two categories of agreement in respect of which the Council must act unanimously.[101]

when the agreement covers a field for which unanimity is required for the adoption of internal rules The phrase 'covers a field' is ambiguous. It may mean that the Council is to act unanimously if the agreement relates mainly to an area in which internal rules are adopted by unanimity. Such a reading would correspond with the 'principal aim and content' test applied by the Court in assessing the correct legal basis for adoption of a measure. It could also mean, however, that the Council is to act unanimously if any elements of the agreement relate to an area where internal rules are adopted by unanimity. In such a case, it would still be true that the agreement 'covered' a field in which rules were adopted by unanimity. The latter seems the better interpretation of the language of Article 228, but the practice of the Council appears to follow the law on choice of legal basis. Thus, the Council only acts by unanimity if the main aim and content, or a significant part of the aim and content, of the agreement relates to areas of Community activity in which internal rules are adopted by unanimity.

Examples of 'fields for which unanimity is required for the adoption of internal rules' include: the rights and duties of 'citizens of the Union';[102] the harmonization of legislation concerning certain forms of taxation;[103] the harmonization of certain other laws, regulations, or administrative provisions;[104] culture;[105] some aspects of Community policy on research and development[106] and on the environment;[107] and legislation adopted under Article 235 (for example, legislation on some intellectual property matters).

agreements referred to in Article 238 These are 'association agreements'; that is to say, 'agreements with one or more States or international organizations establishing an association involving reciprocal rights and obligations, common action and special procedures'. The meaning of this provision is considered in Chapter 20.

---

[99] Art. 148(2) EC.
[100] The rule in Art. 189a(1) EC applies. Contrast the position under Art. 228(1), where the Council acts on a Commission recommendation, and has power to amend the recommendation by a qualified majority. The same point applies in respect of agreements referred to in Art. 109 EC (n. 43 above). See also Wyatt and Dashwood, n. 34 above, at 49.
[101] Unanimity may exist even if Members of the Council abstain: see Art. 148(3) EC.
[102] Arts. 8–8e EC.   [103] Art. 99 EC.   [104] Art. 100 EC.   [105] Art. 128 EC.
[106] Art. 130o.   [107] Art. 130s.

Role of the Parliament

The Parliament's involvement in the process of conclusion of agreements by the European Community takes two forms. On the one hand, several political commitments on the part of the Council and the Commission ensure that the Parliament is kept informed and given an opportunity to influence the negotiation and conclusion of agreements by the Community. On the other, the Treaty provides that the opinion, or in some cases, assent, of the Parliament must, as a matter of law, be obtained before an agreement may be concluded.[108]

Informal involvement of the Parliament The original Treaty of Rome gave the Parliament a very limited role in the conclusion of agreements: its opinion had to be sought only before conclusion of association agreements under Article 238. In response to demands from the Parliament for more information and a greater say in the process of concluding agreements, informal procedures were put in place by the Commission and the Council for certain kinds of agreements.[109]

The first such procedure, the so-called 'Luns Procedure', was established for association agreements. The Council decided in February 1964 that a debate could take place in the Parliament before negotiations with a view to the association of a third country with the Community were started. During the negotiations, close contacts would be maintained between the Commission and the appropriate committees of the Parliament. When the negotiations were concluded, but before the agreement was signed, the President of the Council or his representative would inform the appropriate committees, confidentially and unofficially, of the substance of the agreement.

Next, in November 1973, the Council adopted arrangements to give the Parliament fuller participation in the field of trade agreements. Under these arrangements, which became known as the 'Westerwerp[110] Procedure', it was provided that prior to the opening of the negotiations concerning a trade agreement with a third country and in the light of information supplied by the Council to the competent committees of the Parliament, a debate could be held in the Parliament. The Commission undertook to keep the Parliament informed of the progress of the negotiations. When the negotiations were completed, but before the signing of the agreement, the President of the Council or his representative would confidentially and unofficially acquaint the competent committees of the Parliament with the substance of the agreement. Finally, the Council would acquaint the Parliament with the content of the agreement, after signature but before conclusion. It was also agreed that the Council would supply the

---

[108] For an extensive discussion of the role of the Parliament in the external relations of the Community, and of its involvement in the process of conclusion of agreements, see R. Gosalbo Bono, 'The International Powers of the European Parliament, the Democratic Deficit and the Treaty on European Union' [1992] *YBEL* 85.

[109] See Mégret, n. 24 above, 40–4.   [110] Also known as the 'Luns II' Procedure.

relevant committees with memoranda and information so that more significant exchanges of views could take place.

These two procedures, which came to be referred to as the 'Luns-Westerterp Procedure', were enhanced in 1982 following the *Commission's communication on the role of the Parliament in the preparation and conclusion of international agreements and accession treaties.*[111] This communication was intended to meet demands from the Parliament for greater influence on the conclusion process. So far as the stage of preparation and negotiation of agreements was concerned, the Commission agreed to inform the Parliament through the appropriate committee of planned negotiations once the stage of preparing a draft negotiating brief for submission to the Council was reached. The Luns-Westerterp Procedure would be extended to all agreements which the Community proposed to conclude and which were important for the formulation or application of Community policies. At the stage of conclusion, the Council would, except in emergencies, consult the Parliament after signing an agreement, not only where consultation was required by the Treaty, but also where it was not bound to do so, in relation to all treaties and agreements of importance for the formulation and application of Community policies. This would chiefly concern major agreements under Article 113, but would also cover agreements based on other Treaty Articles which did not require the Parliament to be consulted. Further, the Council agreed that if the Parliament voted by a large majority against the conclusion of an agreement on which it had been consulted, there would be a political debate between the three institutions before the agreement was concluded.

The Parliament's informal involvement was extended further by the *Solemn Declaration on European Union*[112] signed by the Heads of State and Government at Stuttgart on 19 June 1981. Paragraph 2.3.7 of that Declaration states that in addition to the consultations provided for in the Treaties with respect to certain international agreements, the opinion of the Parliament will be sought before the conclusion of other significant agreements by the Community. Furthermore, the existing procedures for providing the Parliament with confidential and unofficial information on progress in negotiations were extended, taking into account the requirements of urgency, to all significant international agreements concluded by the Communities.

In April 1995 a Code of Conduct was agreed between the Commission and the Parliament covering several aspects of their institutional relationship. In relation to international agreements, including trade agreements, it was agreed that the Commission would inform the relevant Parliamentary committee, where necessary on a confidential basis, of the draft recommendations relating to the negotiating instructions. The Commission agreed to keep the Parliament fully informed of the progress of negotiations, and also agreed to facilitate the inclusion of Members of the European Parliament as observers in Community

---

[111] Bull. EC 5/1982, 2.4.2 to 2.4.7.   [112] Bull. EC 6/1983, 2.3.7 .

negotiating delegations for multilateral agreements, on the understanding that the Members could not themselves take part in the negotiating sessions where the Commission alone should represent the Community.

The practical effect of these various procedures and declarations should not be underestimated. They are observed closely in the day-to-day conduct of the business of the Council and the Commission in external relations. Their legal effect is, however, limited. The consultation of the Parliament which takes place under these procedures is, for the Council, a unilateral, voluntary act. Failure by the Council or Commission to observe the procedures, or to await the opinion of the Parliament, is not actionable under Article 173 EC as a breach of an essential procedural requirement.[113]

The Parliament's formal powers under the Treaty The TEU changed the whole basis of the Parliament's involvement in the process of concluding agreements, and the informal procedures outlined above have (at least as regards the stage of conclusion of agreements) been to a large extent superseded, or rendered obsolete, by the rights given to the Parliament under Article 228. The relevant provision is Article 228(3), which provides as follows:

> The Council shall conclude agreements after consulting the European Parliament, except for the agreements referred to in Article 113(3), including cases where the agreement covers a field for which the procedure referred to in Article 189b or that referred to in Article 189c is required for the adoption of internal rules. The European Parliament shall deliver its opinion within a time limit which the Council may lay down according to the urgency of the matter. In the absence of an opinion within that time limit, the Council may act.

> By way of derogation from the previous subparagraph, agreements referred to in Article 238, other agreements establishing a specific procedural framework by organizing co-operation procedures, agreements having important budgetary implications for the Community and agreements entailing amendment of an act adopted under the procedure referred to in Article 189b shall be concluded after the assent of the European Parliament has been obtained.

> The Council and the European Parliament may, in an urgent situation, agree upon a time limit for the assent.

'*the Council shall conclude agreements after consulting the European Parliament*' The consultation procedure is the usual form of Parliamentary involvement in the process of conclusion of agreements by the Community.

'*including cases where the agreement . . . for the adoption of internal rules*' This wording makes clear what is implicit in the rest of the paragraph: a decision or other act concluding an agreement on behalf of the Community can never involve the co-operation or co-decision procedures.[114]

---

[113] For a discussion of the distinction between obligatory and optional consultation of the Parliament, see the Opinion of Jacobs A.G. in Case C–316/91 *Parliament* v. *Council* [1994] ECR I–625 at paras. 26 ff.

[114] Before the entry into force of the TEU, the legal basis for the conclusion of some agreements did require the co-operation procedure. See the agreement referred to in n. 42 above.

'*except for the agreements referred to in Article 113(3)*' The EEC Treaty, as it was before the entry into force of the TEU, did not provide for consultation of the Parliament in relation to the conclusion of agreements relating to the common commercial policy under Article 113. The wording of Article 228(3), first sub-paragraph, continues to exempt agreements under Article 113 from the consultation procedure. However, the effect of the opening words of Article 228(3), second sub-paragraph, is less clear. If the opening phrase ('By way of derogation from the previous sub-paragraph') is read as a derogation from the *whole* of the preceding sub-paragraph, it could have the effect of bringing Article 113 agreements within the scope of the second sub-paragraph, if they fulfil any of the criteria listed there. And, indeed, it is arguable that an agreement which, for example, 'entails the amendment of an act adopted on the basis of the procedure set out in Article 189b' should not be exempt from the Parliament's assent simply because the legal basis for its conclusion is Article 113. On the other hand, such a construction would be a radical departure from earlier practice, and there is little doubt that the intention of the drafters was to exempt agreements under Article 113 from any obligatory parliamentary procedure.

'*after consulting the European Parliament*' The Court has made clear that the Parliament's prerogatives include participation in the legislative process.[115] Consultation allows the Parliament to play a part in the process and gives it a power which represents an essential factor in the institutional balance intended by the Treaty. Failure to consult the Parliament, when consultation is provided for in the Treaty, constitutes a breach of an essential procedural requirement.[116] Where consultation is compulsory, the Council must consider the opinion of the Parliament with a receptive mind and pay due regard to the recommendations contained therein. It must give the Parliament the time which is necessary for it to study the Commission's proposal and express an informed view. In principle, a fresh consultation is required whenever the text finally adopted departs in its very essence from the text which the Parliament has seen.[117] The Parliament is also under certain legal duties in the consultation process: it is to look carefully at the Commission's proposal, pay due regard to the issues involved,[118] and 'co-operate sincerely' with the Council.[119]

'*The European Parliament shall deliver its opinion within a time limit which the Council may lay down according to the urgency of the matter.*' Under the consultation procedure as it applies in relation to internal legislation, the Council, though not obliged to act in accordance with the Parliament's opinion, cannot as a rule adopt an act without receiving the Parliament's opinion. It is, however, not clear whether in

---

[115] Case 70/88 *Parliament* v. *Council* [1990] ECR I–2041 at para. 28.
[116] Case 138/79 *Roquette Frères* v. *Council* [1980] ECR 3333.
[117] Case C–316/91, n. 113 above, Opinion of Jacobs A.G. at paras. 24 ff.
[118] *Ibid.*, at para. 28.
[119] Case C–65/93 *Parliament* v. *Council*, judgment of 30 Mar. 1995, not yet reported, paras. 21–3.

exceptional circumstances the Council is entitled to go ahead in the absence of the Parliament's opinion, where the Council has to act urgently and has taken reasonable steps to obtain the Parliament's opinion.[120] If the Parliament failed to co-operate sincerely with the Council and refused without good cause to take steps to render its opinion within an appropriate time, the Parliament would not be entitled to claim that the Council's adoption of the measure without the opinion involved breach of an essential procedural requirement.[121]

The provisions of Article 228(3) allow the Council to lay down a time limit for the delivery of the Parliament's opinion 'according to the urgency of the matter'. Where such a time limit has been laid down, and where, at the expiry of the time limit, the Parliament has not acted, the Treaty provides that the Council may act. It is for the Council to fix the time limit for the Parliament's opinion. Any time limit fixed by the Council would have to be reasonable in all the circumstances; but the Treaty does not say that the Council may only lay down time limits in urgent cases. Time limits may be laid down 'according to the urgency of the matter'. It would seem to be open to the Council to lay down time limits in all cases, provided that in non-urgent cases the Parliament is given an appropriate time for the preparation of its opinion.

'By way of derogation from the previous sub-paragraph . . .' This sub-paragraph creates exceptions which are 'by way of derogation from' the general rule that the Parliament should be consulted. Derogations should be strictly construed: the provisions of Article 228(3), second sub-paragraph, should accordingly not receive an extensive interpretation.[122] The cases in which the Parliament's assent is required are:

(a)   *'agreements referred to in Article 238'*: 'association agreements'; that is to say, 'agreements with one or more States or international organizations establishing an association involving reciprocal rights and obligations, common action and special procedures';[123]

(b)   *'other agreements establishing a specific institutional framework by organizing co-operation procedures'* The meaning of this phrase is obscure: it is potentially very wide, and could cover agreements providing for Community membership of international organizations. It seems more likely that the drafters had in mind agreements which, although not 'association agreements' in the accepted sense of that term, nevertheless establish close co-operation, involving institutional structures between the Community and the Member States on the one hand and the third party on the other;

(c)   *'agreements having important budgetary implications for the Community'* Again, it is not possible to state the scope of this category with certainty. It probably

---

[120] See Wyatt and Dashwood, n. 34 above, at 38.
[121] Case C–65/93, n. 119 above, at paras. 27 and 28.
[122] For discussion of these provisions, see Gosalbo Bono, n. 108 above, at 121.
[123] On the meaning of 'association agreements' see Ch. 20.

refs to agreements which involve not merely large amounts of money, but which, because of the size of the sums involved, or because of the terms on which the money is to be committed, or for some other reason, are out of the ordinary, or exceptional;[124]

(d) '*agreements entailing amendment of an act adopted under the procedure referred to in Article 189b*' Agreements concluded by the Community under Article 228 become part of Community law and can amend or supersede existing internal legislation.[125] The purpose of this exception seems to be to prevent the Council by-passing the Parliament in the legislative process by amending, by means of an international agreement, internal legislation the amendment of which would otherwise require the co-decision procedure. The phrase should be read as applying to any measure, whenever adopted, the amendment of which would now require the co-decision procedure, not just to measures which have in fact been adopted by that procedure. It probably also applies to agreements which alter the substance of an internal measure, even where the text of the measure is not in fact amended.

'*The Council and the European Parliament may, in an urgent situation, agree upon a time limit for the assent*' Time limits may be imposed in cases where the Parliament's assent to conclusion is required. But (in contrast with cases where the consultation procedure applies), a time limit may only be imposed in an 'urgent situation', and the Council and the Parliament must agree together on the time limit. The Treaty makes no provision for the case where the Parliament fails to give its assent within the agreed time limit. The Council could not proceed to conclude an agreement requiring the Parliament's assent without receiving that assent.

'*the assent of the European Parliament*' Before the entry into force of the TEU, the assent of the Parliament was required only for the conclusion of association agreements, and in such cases the Parliament acted by an absolute majority of its component members.[126] As a result of the amendments made by the TEU, the assent procedure applies to a wider category of agreements, but the assent of the Parliament can now be obtained by an absolute majority of votes cast.[127]

Delegation of Powers to the Commission

Article 228 (4) provides that:

When concluding an agreement, the Council may, by way of derogation from paragraph 2, authorize the Commission to approve modifications on behalf of the Community

---

[124] There is some support for this interpretation in the French text of Art. 228(3), which refers to 'des implications notables' (i.e. 'noteworthy' or 'out of the ordinary') rather than 'importantes' ('great' or 'sizeable').

[125] See Ch. 5.   [126] Art. 238(2) EEC, as amended by the SEA.

[127] Art. 141 EC.

where the agreement provides for them to be adopted by a simplified procedure or by a body set up by the agreement; it may attach specific conditions to such authorization.

'*by way of derogation from paragraph 2*' The general rule is that the Council concludes agreements on behalf of the Community. It follows that all amendments to agreements concluded by the Community also require the approval of the Council in accordance with the appropriate procedures, in principle those applying for conclusion of the agreement.[128] Paragraph 4 mitigates the rigour of the general rule, by providing a simplified procedure for the adoption of amendments to certain agreements on certain conditions. It will be noted that paragraph 4 is a derogation from the normal rule and thus to be strictly interpreted:[129] it is not a warrant for conferring on the Commission general powers to amend or modify the text of agreements entered into by the Community.

'*When concluding an agreement*' Article 228(4) does not create a free-standing power to make agreements, but can be exercised only in the context of the conclusion of another agreement, and with specific reference to that agreement. The Council must decide whether to avail itself of the mechanism provided in Article 228(4) at the moment of concluding the underlying agreement. There seems to be no possibility of applying the Article 228(4) procedure retrospectively to agreements which have already been concluded.

'*the Council may*' The Council is not obliged to confer amending powers on the Commission. Nor, it would seem, does the Council require a Commission proposal that such powers should be granted before deciding to grant them.

'*where the agreement provides for [modifications] to be adopted*' This is a further condition on the exercise of the power given in Article 228(4): amending powers can be conferred on the Commission only where the agreement to be amended makes express provision for adoption of amendments by special procedures set up by the agreement. Specifically, in order for the power in Article 228 (4) to be available, the agreement to be concluded should make provision for its amendment by:

(i)   '*a simplified procedure*' Whether any special procedure is indeed 'simplified' would have to be judged in the light of the provisions of the agreement dealing with its amendment. A procedure which allowed certain amendments to be adopted by signature only (without subsequent approval or ratification), or which allowed amendments to be adopted by a limited number of the contracting parties, could probably be regarded as 'simplified' for these purposes;

(ii)   '*a body set up by the agreement*' The drafters may have had in mind agreements such as association agreements which establish Councils and

---

[128] See below, *Amendment and Termination*, pp. 119–20.
[129] There is judicial authority for adopting a narrow interpretation of Art. 228(4): see the Opinion of Tesauro A.G. in Case C–327/91, n. 6 above, at para. 24.

Committees charged with the task of monitoring the application of the agreements and often given legislative powers. If so, it is doubtful whether Article 228(4) is sufficiently wide to authorize every act of such bodies. Strictly speaking, the Article 228(4) procedure only facilitates adoption of 'modifications' to the original agreement: it does not authorize the making of delegated legislation as such.

'*the Council . . . may authorize the Commission to approve modifications on behalf of the Community*' The aim is to avoid the need for the Community institutions to have to follow every step of the Article 228 procedures to approve any modification to the parent agreement, however slight. Modifications approved by the Commission on behalf of the Community under Article 228(4) of course bind the Community in international law, and bind the institutions of the Community and the Member States under Article 228(7).[130]

'*[the Council] may attach specific conditions to such authorization*' These would no doubt be set out in the Council act concluding the agreement, and would be legally binding.

Agreements Requiring Amendment of the Treaty

Article 228 (5) provides that:

When the Council envisages concluding an agreement which calls for amendments to this Treaty, the amendments must first be adopted in accordance with the procedure laid down in Article N of the Treaty on European Union.

If a proposed agreement is outside the competence of the Community, or if, for some other reason, its conclusion by the Community would require amendment of the Treaty, the Community must be given the necessary powers, or the Treaty must otherwise be amended, before the agreement can be concluded. In practice, if it became clear that a proposed agreement was incompatible with the Treaty, and if that problem could not be cured by Member State participation in the agreement alongside the Community, the Community would probably seek amendment of the proposed agreement (or abandon it altogether).[131]

---

[130] On the meaning of Art. 228(7) EC, see Ch. 5.

[131] The draft Agreement on a Laying Up Fund for the Rhine, which was the subject of the request which led to *Opinion 1/76* ([1977] ECR 741), was found by the Court to be incompatible with the Treaty, and it never came into force. The first draft of what became the EEA Agreement, on the other hand, was amended as a result of a negative opinion from the ECJ (*Opinion 1/91 (Re the EEA Agreement)* [1991] ECR 6079) and eventually came into force in 1994.

ECSC

Legal Basis

The ECSC Treaty provides that the institutions of the Community shall, in the common interest, promote the growth of international trade and ensure that equitable limits are observed in export pricing.[132] In addition, the ECSC is to enjoy, in international relations, the legal capacity it requires to perform its functions and attain its objectives.[133] These provisions probably entitle the Community to enter into agreements, but no Article of the ECSC Treaty in terms contains such a power.[134] Perhaps because of the vagueness of the powers conferred on the Community by the Treaty, practice under the ECSC Treaty is far from uniform. Some early agreements were concluded 'by the High Authority' (the Commission). Then, for a time, agreements were entered into on behalf of the ECSC by the Representatives of the Member States meeting within the Council, sometimes with the ECSC itself, sometimes without. More recently, however, the ECSC has tended to conclude agreements in its own name, citing either the ECSC Treaty generally,[135] or Article 95 ECSC.[136]

Procedures for Conclusion of Agreements Binding the ECSC

The ECSC Treaty does not establish procedures to be followed in the negotiation and conclusion of agreements by the Community. Except for agreements concluded under Article 95 ECSC, in respect of which the procedure in that Article would have to be followed, conclusion of agreements on behalf of the ECSC would follow the general legislative scheme of the Treaty. The main difference between the EC Treaty procedures and those applied under the ECSC Treaty is that the Commission has a much wider role in the latter than in the former. Nevertheless, it is the Community, not the Commission, which enters into commitments at the international level.

Negotiation

In principle, it is for the Commission to decide whether an agreement should be negotiated on behalf of the ECSC. The Commission is entitled to undertake such a negotiation on its own authority: the authorization of the Council is not required as it is under the EC Treaty.

---

[132] Art. 3(f) ECSC. [133] Art. 6 ECSC.
[134] Arts. 93 and 94 provide for the maintenance of relations with certain international organizations, and the extent of these powers is considered in Ch. 7.
[135] See Council and Commission Dec. 93/742/Euratom, ECSC, EC of 13 Dec. 1993 on the conclusion of the Europe Agreement with Hungary ([1993] OJ L347/1).
[136] See Commission Dec. 94/51/ECSC of 20 Dec. 1993 concerning the conclusion of the Additional Protocol to the Interim Agreement on trade and trade related matters between the EEC and the ECSC and Hungary ([1994] OJ L25/33).

Signature Subject to Approval and Provisional Application

These steps too fall within the powers conferred on the Commission by the Treaty.

Conclusion

Where the conclusion of an agreement takes place on the basis of the ECSC Treaty generally, without citation of a specific legal basis, authorization of conclusion is, it seems, entirely within the power of the Commission. The Council is not consulted formally under the procedures of the ECSC Treaty, and it is for the Commission to take the necessary steps to express the Community's consent to be bound to the other parties to the agreement.[137]

Where conclusion of an agreement by the Community takes place on the basis of Article 95 ECSC, the Commission must obtain the assent of the Council, and must consult the Consultative Committee.[138] The Commission accordingly submits to the Council the draft of a Commission decision concluding the agreement on behalf of the Community. The Council is required to assent unanimously to the conclusion of the agreement. Unanimity for the purposes of Article 95 ECSC requires all the members of the Council to vote in favour.[139] At the same time, the opinion of the Consultative Committee is sought. If the Commission considers it necessary, it may set the Committee a time limit for the submission of its opinion. In principle, however, the Commission may not adopt a decision under Article 95(1) without receiving the opinion of the Committee. Once the assent of the Council and the opinion of the Consultative Committee have been obtained, the Commission may adopt a decision under Article 95 concluding the agreement on behalf of the Community and making provision for the expression of the Community's consent to be bound.

Euratom

Legal Basis

Article 101 Euratom provides that Euratom may 'within the limits of its powers and jurisdiction' enter into obligations in relation to third States, international organizations, or nationals of third States.[140] In addition to this general

---

[137] It is not easy to square practice under the ECSC Treaty with the case law of the Court on the need to cite a precise legal basis (or, indeed, to detect any rational basis for the procedures apparently adopted for conclusion of agreements involving the ECSC). Perhaps it does not matter much: most ECSC agreements also involve the participation of the Member States, or of the other Communities, so the substance of the agreement is approved by the Member States individually and fully considered by the Council. It does not, however, make for legal certainty.

[138] Art. 95(1) ECSC.   [139] Art. 28(3) ECSC. Contrast Arts. 148(3) EC and 118(3) Euratom.

[140] See J. Raux, 'La procédure de conclusion des accords externes de la Communauté européenne de l'énergie atomique' [1965] *RGDIP* 1019.

power, several Articles of the Euratom Treaty confer on the Community specific powers to act externally in certain areas,[141] but in practice, the great majority of agreements are concluded by Euratom on the basis of Article 101 Euratom.

As in the case of the EC Treaty, association agreements ('agreements with one or more third States or international organizations establishing an association involving reciprocal rights and obligations, common action and special procedures') are concluded under a special procedure. In the Euratom Treaty, the procedure for conclusion of these agreements is set out in Article 206 Euratom.

Negotiation and Conclusion of Agreements falling within Article 101

A distinction is made in the Treaty between agreements the implementation of which does not require action by the Council, and those which do require such action. The structure of Article 101 perhaps suggests that agreements[142] which do _not_ require Council action would be the exception, and accordingly that Council involvement in the process of concluding agreements should be the norm.

Into which category an agreement falls depends, it would seem, entirely on the content of the agreement. Although the Treaty gives the Commission a wide role in the implementation of the Community's tasks under the Treaty, there are no areas of activity which can be said to fall _a priori_ to the Commission and in respect of which the Council will necessarily be completely excluded. 'Action by the Council' no doubt includes the adoption of further internal legislation, or the authorization of exceptional payments or other changes to budgetary provisions. Most significant agreements will probably require action by the Council.

---

[141] See, further, Ch. 3.

[142] The Euratom Treaty also envisages the making of 'contracts' with third States and international organizations. The reference to 'contracts' in this context is confusing. The better interpretation is probably that relations with States and international organizations intended to be governed by international law should be regarded as 'agreements' in line with the meaning given to that term under the EC Treaty in _Opinion 1/75_, n. 5 above, whereas legal relations between the Community and companies and nationals of third States which are to be governed by domestic law are 'contracts'. Art. 10 Euratom appears to envisage 'contracts' between the Community and other international legal persons, but the explanation may be that, because of their subject matter (the carrying out of certain parts of the Community's research programme) the 'contracts' referred to in Art. 10 Euratom are intended to be governed by national, not international, law. But an element of uncertainty remains about the precise meaning of 'contract' in this context. Ultimately, terminology is less important than substance; and if a commitment described as a 'contract' is in reality a commitment governed by a system of domestic law, the rules of private international law will apply to determine questions such as the Community's capacity to enter into it, the formalities necessary for its proper conclusion, its interpretation, and so on. If, however, the commitment is in substance an agreement governed by international law, its validity and interpretation will be determined by the law of treaties, and the procedures to be applied within the Community legal order will be the rules of Community law governing the making of international agreements.

Agreements requiring Council Action

Such agreements are to be negotiated by the Commission in accordance with the directives of the Council. In practice, the Commission will recommend to the Council that the Commission be authorized to enter into negotiations. As under the EC Treaty, the authorization and negotiating directives will be discussed in the working groups of the Council and in COREPER, and eventually approved by the Council. The Commission will usually conduct the negotiations in close consultation with the Member States. The Commission is entitled to initial and sign agreements under Article 101 on its own authority. Once the agreement has been negotiated and, if necessary, signed, the Commission will propose to the Council adoption of a decision approving the conclusion of the agreement by the Commission. The Council gives its approval by qualified majority.[143] Once the Council has approved conclusion, the Commission can adopt a decision to conclude the agreement, and take the steps necessary to express the Community's consent to be bound. A decision to apply an agreement provisionally should, it seems, be treated like a decision to conclude the agreement.[144]

Agreements requiring no Council Action

When the implementation of an agreement requires no action by the Council, and can be effected within the relevant budget, negotiation, signature, provisional application, and conclusion are for the Commission. The Council is kept informed, but its approval is not required at any stage.

Role of the Parliament

The Parliament has no formal role in the procedure under Article 101, and failure to consult it about an agreement to be concluded under that Article would not be actionable for breach of an essential procedural requirement. The Parliament is, however, made aware of the content of proposed agreements, and of the progress of negotiations, by the informal arrangements described in relation to the European Community.[145]

Association Agreements

The first sentence of Article 206 is identical to Article 238 EC, and the meaning of these Articles, and the agreements to which they apply, are considered elsewhere in this work. The procedures in Article 206 Euratom differ fundamentally from those in Article 101. Article 206 provides that agreements within its scope 'shall be concluded by the Council, acting unanimously after consulting the European Parliament'. Thus, first, the role of the *Council* under this

---

[143] On qualified majority voting under the Euratom Treaty, see Art. 118(2).
[144] See the discussion above, at p. 91   [145] See above, pp. 98–100.

Article is closer to its role in concluding agreements under the EC Treaty than to its role in concluding other agreements binding Euratom. Secondly, the *Parliament* is given a role in the process of conclusion which it does not have under Article 101. Agreements under Article 206 can only be concluded after the opinion of the Parliament has been obtained. The Parliament adopts its opinion by an absolute majority of its members.[146] The principles developed by the Court in the context of the consultation procedure under the EC Treaty would no doubt apply in the Euratom context also.[147] Finally, although Article 206 makes no specific provision for the role of the *Commission*, it seems clear that it would be for the Commission to recommend the opening of negotiations; to conduct the negotiations on the basis of the Council's authorization and directives; and in due course to propose to the Council that the agreement should be concluded.

Practice in relation to the conclusion of agreements falling within the scope of Article 206 Euratom is sparse, and apparently inconsistent with practice under the EC Treaty. For example, it seems clear that the Europe Agreements with Hungary and Poland are, so far as the EC is concerned, association agreements.[148] Euratom is also a party to the Europe Agreements with these countries, and one might have expected that the legal basis for conclusion of the Europe Agreements on behalf of the Euratom Community would have been Article 206 Euratom. Instead, Article 101(2) was chosen by the Commission (and apparently accepted by the Council). As has been seen, the choice of Article 101 rather than Article 206 is not without consequence for the roles and prerogatives of the institutions.

Article 29 Euratom

Mention should be made, for completeness, of Article 29 Euratom. This provides that where an agreement or contract for the exchange of scientific or industrial information in the nuclear field between a Member State, a person, or an undertaking on the one hand, and a third State, an international organization, or a national of a third State on the other, requires, on either part, the signature of a State acting in its sovereign capacity, such agreement or contract is to be concluded by the Commission. The Commission may, on such conditions as it thinks appropriate, authorize a Member State, a person or an undertaking to conclude such agreements.

---

[146] Art. 111 Euratom.   [147] See above, at p. 101.
[148] Or at least agreements falling within Art. 238 EC.

Judicial Scrutiny of Proposed Agreements

European Community

Article 228(6) EC[149] provides that the Council, the Commission, or a Member State[150] may obtain the opinion of the Court whether an agreement envisaged is compatible with the EC Treaty. If the opinion of the Court is adverse, the agreement may only enter into force in accordance with Article N TEU.[151]

Task of the Court

The exceptional procedure in Article 228(6) was established for the purpose of elucidating, before the conclusion of an agreement, whether it is compatible with the Treaty. The purpose of the Article 228(6) procedure is thus to forestall complications which may result from legal disputes concerning the compatibility with the Treaty of agreements binding on the Community.[152] The compatibility of an agreement with the provisions of the Treaty must be assessed in the light of all the rules of the Treaty, that is to say, both those rules which determine the extent of the powers of the institutions of the Community and the substantive rules.[153] It is therefore possible under this procedure to consider all questions concerning the compatibility with the provisions of the Treaty of an agreement envisaged, in particular whether the Community, or any Community institution,[154] has power to enter into that agreement,[155] and whether that power has been exercised in accordance with the provisions of the Treaty.[156] A judgment on the compatibility of an agreement with the Treaty may depend not only on provisions of substantive law, but also on those provisions

---

[149] On the procedure in Art. 228(2) EEC (now in Art. 228(6) EC), see J. Boulouis, 'La Jurisprudence de la Cour de Justice des Communautés Européennes relative aux relations extérieures des Communautés' *Hague Recueil* (1992 IV), 9; Rideau, 'Les accords internationaaux dans la jurisprudence de la Cour de Justice des Communautés européennes' [1990] *RGDIP* 289 at 300 ff.; Boulouis, 235 *Hague Recueil* (1992 IV) 9 at 65–74; H. G. Schermers and M. Waelbroek, *Judicial Protection in the European Communities* (4th edn., Kluwer, 1987), at paras. 658 ff. The Court's jurisdiction in relation to the interpretation and scrutiny of agreements *after* conclusion is considered in Ch. 5.

[150] The Parliament has no formal right to seek the opinion of the Court, nor to intervene in such a request. It was, however, given leave by the Court to 'submit observations' in *Opinion 1/92 (Re EEA Agreement)* [1992] ECR I–2821 and *Opinion 1/94* [1994] ECR I–5267.

[151] That is to say, after the EC Treaty has been amended by the Member States.

[152] *Opinion 1/75*, n. 5 above, at para. 10.   [153] *Ibid.*, 1360.

[154] It would appear, therefore, that the request could seek the Court's opinion about whether the agreement was properly for the Council or Commission to conclude.

[155] *Opinion 2/91 (Re ILO Convention 170)* [1993] ECR I–1061 at para. 3. See also Art. 107(2) of the Court's Rules of Procedure, which states that 'The Opinion may deal not only with the question whether the envisaged agreement is compatible with the provisions of the EC Treaty, but also with the question whether the Community or any Community institution has the power to enter into that agreement.'

[156] *Opinion 1/75*, n. 5 above, at para. 13.

concerning the powers, procedure, or organization of the institutions of the Community.[157]

The jurisdiction of the Court under Article 228(6) is accordingly very wide.[158] Most of the opinions delivered by the Court have concerned the compatibility of a proposed agreement with the EC Treaty. The Court has, however, also given its opinion on the correct legal basis for the Community's conclusion of an agreement, in a case where the competences of the Community and the Member States to conclude the agreement were not in doubt.[159] And it has even declared admissible an application in respect of an agreement to which the Community could not in law become party. According to the Court, the application in that case related not to the Community's capacity on the international plane to enter into the agreement in question, but to the scope, judged solely by reference to the rules of Community law, of the competence of the Community and the Member States within the area covered by the agreement. It was not for the Court to assess the obstacles which the Community might encounter at the international level; if necessary, the Community could exercise its competence through the Member States.[160] These comments suggest that, provided it can be shown that an agreement covering an area within the competence of the Community exists,[161] any questions about the division of powers between the Community and the Member States may be submitted for the opinion of the Court under Article 228(6).

The fact that certain questions may be dealt with by means of other remedies, in particular by bringing an action for annulment under Article 173 EC, does not preclude the Court from being asked for an opinion on those questions beforehand under Article 228(6).[162] However, it is not the task of the Court, in an application under Article 228, to provide a final interpretation of the terms of the proposed agreement,[163] but to consider whether the agreement is compatible with the Treaty.

Time Limits for Submission of an Application under Article 228(6)

The procedure in Article 228(6) is non-contentious, so no time-limits are laid down for the submission of an application for the Court's opinion.[164] The Court may be asked to state its opinion at any time before the Community's consent to be bound has been finally expressed.[165] Applications have accordingly been declared admissible after the end of the process of negotiation, but before the

[157] *Opinion 1/78 (Re Draft Agreement on Natural Rubber)* [1979] ECR 2871 at para. 30.

[158] Rideau, n. 149 above, at 302 comments: 'La procédure, conçue comme un moyen d'empêcher la Communauté de dépasser le champ de sa compétence en empiétant sur le domaine réservé des Etats Membres, est devenue un véritable contrôle de constitutionnalité, à l'occasion duquel la Cour a pu adopter des interprétations constructives des compétences communautaires.'

[159] *Opinion 2/92 (Re OECD National Treatment Instrument)*, 24 Mar. 1995, not yet reported.

[160] *Opinion 2/91*, n. 155 above, at paras. 4 and 5.

[161] And has not yet been concluded: see below on *Time limits*.

[162] *Opinion 2/92*, n. 159 above, at para. 14.   [163] *Opinion 1/76*, n. 131 above, at para. 20.

[164] *Opinion 1/75*, n. 5 above, at 1361.   [165] Opinion 1/94, n. 150 above, at para. 12.

Community began the process of conclusion;[166] while the negotiations were still in progress;[167] and after signature of the Final Act of the conference at which the texts of the envisaged agreement were authenticated.[168]

It is unclear whether a request for the opinion of the Court precludes the Council and the Member States from concluding the agreement until the Court has given its opinion.[169] Article 228 is silent on the point, and although in many cases institutional comity will lead the Council and the Commission to await the Court's opinion, practical considerations may mean that the Community concludes the agreement before the Court has given its view.[170] If the Court finds that the agreement is indeed incompatible with the Treaty, the Commission, the Council, and the Member States have the options of amending the Treaty of Rome, amending the agreement under consideration, or abandoning the agreement.[171]

Procedure

Any Member State, the Commission, or the Council may request the opinion of the Court under the Article 228(6) procedure.[172] A request by the Council must be served on the Commission. A request by the Commission must be served on the Council and the Member States. A request by a Member State must be served on the Council, the Commission, and the other Member States.[173] Neither the provisions of Article 228(6) nor the Rules of Procedure of the Court allow the Parliament to make a request, but the Court has allowed the Parliament to submit written observations[174] and to be represented at oral hearings.[175]

As soon as the request has been lodged, the President of the Court appoints a judge to act as Judge Rapporteur,[176] and prescribes a period within which the institutions and the Member States must submit written observations. It is for the Court to decide whether to hold an oral hearing: the Member States and

---

[166] *Opinion 1/75*, n. 5 above.

[167] *Opinion 1/78*, n. 157 above. The Court pointed out that the subject matter of the 'agreement envisaged' was already known when the application was made, so it was able to form a sufficiently certain judgment on the question put to it: see paras. 32–35 of the Opinion.

[168] *Opinion 1/94*, n. 164 above, at paras. 10 and 12.

[169] The general rule that actions before the Court do not have suspensory effect seems inapplicable to requests under Art. 228(6): no act is being challenged (so there is no 'effect' to suspend). Moreover, that rule appears in the context of contentious causes, and the Court has highlighted the non-contentious character of the Art. 228(6) procedure: n. 164 above.

[170] See also *Opinion 1/75*, n. 5 above, at para. 2 on 1361: 'for the purpose of elucidating, *before the conclusion of the agreement*, whether'. The WTO Agreement was, however, concluded by the Community while a dispute about part of the Agreement was still before the Court: see *Opinion 3/94*, still before the Court.

[171] Clearly, some or all of these options might present greater difficulties if the agreement has already been concluded by the Community and *a fortiori* if it is already in force.

[172] Art. 228(6) EC.

[173] Art. 107(1) of the Court's Rules of Procedure.

[174] *Opinions 1/92*, and *1/94*, n. 150 above.

[175] *Opinion 1/94*, n. 150 above.　　　　　　　　　　　　　　[176] *Ibid.*, Art. 108(1).

the institutions cannot insist on being heard orally.[177] To assist it in its deliberations, the Member States and the institutions have sometimes been asked to provide answers to supplementary questions posed by the Court.[178]

All the Advocates-General deliver opinions,[179] but these are not published. The Court delivers its reasoned Opinion in closed session.[180] The Opinion is then served on the Council, the Commission, and the Member States.[181] In urgent cases, the Court has delivered its Opinion within a matter of weeks of the request being made.[182]

ECSC

No procedure exists under the ECSC Treaty whereby the compatibility with the Treaty of a proposed agreement can be tested before conclusion of the agreement.

Euratom

Article 103 Euratom provides that Member States must communicate to the Commission draft agreements with third States or international organizations to the extent that such agreements concern matters within the purview of the Euratom Treaty. If, in the opinion of the Commission, the agreement contains clauses which may impede the application of the Euratom Treaty, the Commission must make its comments to the Member State concerned within one month of receipt of the communication. Thereupon, the Member State may not conclude the agreement until it has satisfied the Commission's concerns. If that proves impossible, the Member State must, if it wishes to conclude the agreement, submit an application to the Court under Article 103 seeking the Court's ruling on the compatibility of the 'proposed clauses' with the provisions of the Treaty. An application may be made at any time after receiving the comments of the Commission. If a Member State attempted to conclude an agreement against the advice of the Commission without seeking the ruling of the Court, it would doubtless be open to Commission action under Article 141 Euratom.

---

[177] In all but one of the requests in which an opinion has been issued to date, the Court has called for an oral hearing. The exception was *Opinion 1/92*, n. 150 above.

[178] See, e.g., *Opinion 1/91* [1991] ECR 6079, Sect. II 'Procedure'; and *Opinion 1/94*, n. 150 above, Pt. XVII.

[179] *Ibid.*, Art. 108(2).   [180] *Ibid.*, Art. 108(2).   [181] *Ibid.*, Art. 108(3).

[182] In *Opinion 1/91*, n. 178 above, the request was made on 14 Aug. 1991; an oral hearing took place on 26 Nov., and the opinion was delivered on 14 Dec. 1991. In *Opinion 1/92*, n. 150 above, the request was made on 27 Feb. 1992; there was no oral hearing, and the Court gave its opinion on 10 Apr. 1992. In *Opinion 1/94*, n. 150 above, the request was made on 6 Apr. 1994; an oral hearing took place on 11 Oct.; the opinion was delivered on 15 Nov. 1994.

Task of the Court

The procedure established by Article 103 Euratom is, on the face of the Treaty, much narrower in scope than that established under Article 228(6) EC. The Council and the Commission do not have a right to request the ruling of the Court. That right is only open to the Member State which intends to become party to the agreement in question, and only after the Commission has examined the agreement. Furthermore, the terms of Article 103(3) arguably limit the jurisdiction of the Court to consideration of those clauses of the agreement in respect of which the Member State has been unable to satisfy the concerns of the Commission.

The Court has, however, taken a much wider view of its powers, and appears to have equated its jurisdiction under Article 103 with its jurisdiction under Article 228(6) EC.[183] It has said that its task is to examine all questions[184] which concern the compatibility of the proposed agreement with the Treaty, taking into account all the relevant rules of the Treaty, whether they concern questions of substance, of jurisdiction, or of procedure.[185] It may be, therefore, that the apparent procedural limitations in Article 103 would not in practice be applied literally.

Procedure

The procedure for making such an application under Article 103(3) Euratom is set out in Article 108 of the Court's Rules of Procedure, and differs in several respects from the procedure for requests under Article 228(6) EC.

Four certified copies of the application must be lodged at the Court. A copy must be served on the Commission.[186] The application must be accompanied by the draft of the agreement in question, by the observations of the Commission, and by all other supporting documents. The Commission must submit its observations to the Court 'within 10 days'. This period may be extended by the President of the Court after the State concerned has been heard. The Commission's observations must be served on the State.[187] A Judge Rapporteur and a single Advocate-General are appointed.[188] The Court's ruling is given in closed session after the Advocate-General has been heard. The Member State concerned and the Commission have a right to present oral argument to the Court if they so request.[189]

---

[183] *Opinion 1/78*, n. 157 above, at para. 32 and *Opinion 2/91*, n. 155 above, at para. 3.
[184] *Opinion 1/78*, n. 157 above, at para. 30.
[185] *Ruling 1/78 (Re the Draft Convention on the Physical Protection of Nuclear Materials)* [1978] ECR 2151 at para. 5
[186] Court's Rules of Procedure, Art. 105(1).   [187] *Ibid.*, Art. 105(2).
[188] *Ibid.*, Art. 105(3).   [189] *Ibid.*, Art. 105(4).

Expression of Consent to be Bound

Once all the internal procedures necessary for approval of an agreement by the Community institutions have been completed, the Community is in a position to signify to the other party or parties to the agreement that it consents to be bound by its terms. This step is described in the Vienna Conventions[190] as the 'expression of consent to be bound' by the agreement and takes place on the international plane. Thus, before an agreement can be regarded as validly 'concluded' in Community and international law, and thus as duly binding on the Community, all the relevant internal procedures must have been followed, and—then—the appropriate gesture must be made with respect to the other party or parties. Three possible questions thus arise at this stage: how is the Community representative to be authorized to express the Community's consent to be bound; how is that representative to prove that authorization to the other party or parties; and by what means is the Community's consent to be bound expressed?

The first question is easily answered: the Council or Commission decision[191] approving conclusion of the agreement on behalf of the Community will provide the necessary authority in Community law for carrying out the act required at the international level to express the Community's consent to be bound.

The answer to the second is more complicated. The general rule is that a person claiming to represent a State for the purposes of the conclusion[192] of an agreement must demonstrate that he has been duly authorized. In principle, and in classical international legal practice, this requires the production of a document containing evidence of formal authorization, commonly called the 'Full Powers'. Nowadays, production of Full Powers is of less importance,[193] and certain individuals are taken as authorized by virtue of their office to undertake formal acts in connection with the conclusion of international agreements.[194] But Full Powers are not yet obsolete, and the consequences of unauthorized action in this area can be drastic.[195]

---

[190] VCLT, VCLTIO, Arts. 11–17.

[191] As the case may be, depending on the Community involved.

[192] It should be noted that signature subject to approval, or acceptance of an obligation to apply an agreement provisionally, may also require the production of Full Powers by the Community representative. In such cases, the principles described above would apply: the signatory would require to be authorized by a decision of the Council or the Commission, as appropriate; and he would have to be furnished with the necessary Full Powers to enable him to carry out his functions.

[193] Oppenheim, n. 13 above, Vol. I, Pt. 4, ch. 14, para. 597 comments 'An instrument of Full Powers is necessarily a formal instrument and will often be unsuitable for the many less formal kinds of international agreement; in such cases they are frequently dispensed with, although even then some kind of written authority to the representative is still usual.'

[194] VCLT, Art. 7.

[195] *Ibid.* Art. 8 VCLT provides that an act relating to the conclusion of a treaty performed by a person who cannot be considered under Art. 7 as authorized to represent a State for that purpose is without legal effect unless afterwards confirmed by that State. Art. 8 VCLTIO is in similar terms.

Where, as in the case of the Communities, an international organization has power to enter into agreements, it is necessary to examine its constitution to determine who is authorized to act for it in a given matter, and how that authority is to be attested. The representatives of the organization would usually have to be furnished with the appropriate Full Powers (or similar authorization) in accordance with the constitutional arrangements of the organization in question. Where the Community's consent to be bound is to be expressed by signature, the Community representative may be required to present evidence of his authorization in the form of Full Powers before being allowed to sign. Accordingly, when a representative of the Commission concludes an agreement on behalf of the Community, the signatory is furnished with Full Powers by the Commission Secretariat General, on the basis of the Commission or Council decision[196] authorizing conclusion of the agreement. When the agreement is to be concluded by a representative of the Council, the Council's decision to that effect will be warrant for the issue of Full Powers to the designated signatories by the General Secretariat of the Council.[197]

The third question (the expression of the Communities' consent to be bound) must be answered by reference to the agreement to be concluded. Some agreements become binding on signature, so the signature of a duly authorized representative of the Community suffices to express the Community's consent to be bound. In other cases, an exchange of letters or other instrument is required, indicating that each side has completed all necessary internal procedures. In the case of the Community, it is for the Council or the Commission to authorize the issue of such a note or letter from the Community side; such authorization is usually given in the act concluding the agreement.

Reservations and Declarations

The Communities are in the same position as other international persons as regards the making of reservations and declarations on acceptance of agreements. Subject to the rules of international law and the terms of the agreement in question,[198] it is open to the Communities to make reservations or declarations in respect of an agreement, including reservations restricting the application of an agreement to certain parts of the territories to which the Community

[196] On cases where a Commission decision will suffice, see Art. 101(3) Euratom, discussed at pp. 108–9 above. Where the agreement falls within Art. 101(2) Euratom, a Council decision is also needed before the Commission's representative may sign.

[197] It will be noted that the signatory signs on behalf of the Community on the authority of the Council. Thus Full Powers or similar authorization from the Council are always required for acts associated with the conclusion of an agreement by one of the Communities, even if the signatory enjoys Full Powers or is otherwise authorized to sign agreements in another capacity, e.g. as a representative of the Commission or as the Minister of Foreign Affairs or duly accredited ambassador of the Presidency.

[198] On which, see VCLT, VCLTIO, Arts. 19–23, and Sinclair, n. 7 above, ch. 3; Brownlie, n. 13 above, ch. XXV.3; Oppenheim, n. 13 above, paras. 614–19.

Treaties apply.[199] Because reservations qualify commitments undertaken in an agreement, reservations to be entered by the Community require the approval of the institutions in the same way as the obligations in the agreement. In practice, therefore, the text of any reservations will be included in the act authorizing the conclusion of the agreement. The same will be the case for declarations.

Publication of Community Agreements

Agreements concluded by the Communities are usually annexed to the act of the institution which authorizes conclusion of the agreement on behalf of the Community. When that act takes the form of a decision[200] of the Council, publication of that decision and thus of the agreement must be approved by the Council, acting unanimously.[201] When the act takes the form of a Commission decision, publication takes place in accordance with the Commission's internal procedures. When the act takes the form of a regulation, it must be published in the Official Journal before the Community's approval of the agreement is notified to the other party or parties to the agreement.[202] In practice, most Community agreements are published in the Official Journal.

Where an agreement concluded between the Communities and one or more States or international organizations sets up a body vested with powers of decision, the Council must decide, when such an agreement is concluded, whether decisions to be taken by that body should be published in the Official Journal.[203] It was agreed in 1994 that in future all decisions of such bodies should in principle be published,[204] and it was also agreed that past practice would be reviewed in order to determine whether it would be feasible to publish decisions of bodies already in existence.[205]

Language Versions

Publication in the Official Journal makes an official text of the agreement available throughout the Community in all the Community languages. No difficulties arise in the case of agreements which have been drawn up in all the Community languages (as will usually be the case for association agreements,

---

[199] e.g., see the Community's acceptance of the *Convention on the conservation of European Wildlife and Natural Habitats* (Dec. 82/72 [1982] OJ L38/1) which applied the Convention throughout the EC except Greenland.

[200] i.e. a dec. *sui generis.*

[201] Art. 19(3) of the Council's Rules of Procedure ([1993] OJ L304/1).

[202] Arts. 191(2) EC, 163 Euratom.   [203] Art. 18(6) of the Council's Rules of Procedure.

[204] Some third States have insisted that the deliberations of committees set up under their agreements with the Community should remain confidential. The Community clearly could not unilaterally publish details of such deliberations. On the effect of decisions of bodies established under Community agreements, see Ch. 5.

[205] Collections of decisions of Association Councils have been published by the Council from time to time.

trade and co-operation agreements, fisheries agreements, and bilateral agreements between the Communities and third parties). Many multilateral agreements (such as those drawn up in the UN framework) are not, however, drawn up in all the Community languages; and in such cases the Community institutions have to decide, when concluding the agreement, whether it should be translated into all Community languages as part of the act authorizing conclusion. If the agreement is likely to have direct effect within the Community legal order, or is otherwise of general importance, it is clearly highly desirable that its provisions should be available in all the Community languages even if the authoritative text is available in only some. Disputes about the accuracy of such translations, or queries as to the precise terms of the agreement, would of course have to be resolved by reference to the authoritative texts.

Registration of Community Agreements at the United Nations

Since 1978, the Council Secretariat have registered with the United Nations Secretariat General all agreements concluded by any of the Communities. Where these agreements are mixed (that is, where the Member States are also parties) this practice ensures that the Member States comply fully with their obligations under the United Nations Charter.[206] It has the additional advantage of placing on public record the international practice of the Communities.[207]

Amendment and Termination of Agreements

Whether an agreement may be amended or terminated depends on its terms and on general rules of international law.[208] The means by which amendment or termination is to be given effect are likewise governed by international law.

Within the Community legal order, amendment or termination of a Community agreement raises in principle the same issues as are raised by conclusion of the agreement, and the rules and procedures which govern the

---

[206] Art. 102(1) of the UN Charter provides that 'Every treaty and every international agreement entered into by any Member of the United Nations after the present Charter enters into force shall as soon as possible be registered with the Secretariat and published by it.' Art. 102(2) provides that 'No party to any such treaty or international agreement which has not been registered in accordance with the provisions of para. 1 of this Art. may invoke that treaty or agreement before any organ of the United Nations.' Strictly speaking, only Members of the UN are required to (and may) register agreements under Art. 102; treaties involving only non-Members are 'filed and recorded'. On this see [1971] *UNJY*, 222–3; Schermers, *International Institutional Law* (2nd edn.) paras. 1672–3; Oppenheim, n. 13 above, para. 663; D. N. Hutchinson, 'The Significance of the Registration or Non-Registration of an International Agreement in Determining whether or not it is a Treaty' (1993) 46 *CLP* II, 257.

[207] See Mégret, n. 24 above, 46 and 47.

[208] See VCLT, VCLTIO, Arts. 39–41 ('amendment and modification of treaties') and Arts. 42–68 (invalidity, termination, and suspension). See also Sinclair, n. 7 above, chs. IV and VI; Brownlie, n. 13 above, ch. XXV; Oppenheim, n. 13 above, para. 624.

conclusion of an agreement also govern its amendment or termination. However, the legal basis for the Community act approving amendment or termination will not necessarily be the same as the legal basis for conclusion of the original agreement. The legal basis of an act of the Community institutions must be determined by reference to the aim and content of that act, not by reference to the legal basis of an act or acts which it amends.[209]

UNILATERAL OBLIGATIONS

In international law, declarations made by way of unilateral acts concerning legal or factual situations may have the effect of creating legal obligations binding on States. An undertaking made with the intention that the maker should become bound according to its terms, if given publicly and with an intent to be bound, even if not made within the context of international negotiations, is binding; and nothing in the nature of a *quid pro quo* nor any subsequent acceptance of the declaration, nor even any reply or reaction, is required for the declaration to take legal effect.[210] Although developed in the context of a dispute between States, it seems reasonable that these principles should apply to declarations made by, or on behalf of, legal entities such as the Communities.

As a matter of Community law, the provisions of the Treaties dealing with the assumption of international obligations by the Communities relate only to 'agreements'. On a strict reading of the Communities' powers, therefore, the making of unilateral obligations is outside the competence of the Communities. The Court has, however, said[211] that the Community 'enjoys the capacity to enter into *international commitments* over the whole field of [its] objectives . . .' (emphasis added). There is no reason to limit these 'commitments' to bilateral or multilateral agreements, and the better view is therefore that the Communities have competence to enter into international obligations unilaterally, as well as through agreements.

The difficulties in any given case will be to show, first, that the intention was indeed to commit the Community to binding obligations, and secondly, that the giver of the commitment was authorized to bind the Community in that way. Everything will depend on the circumstances of a particular case. The submission of a declaration or other unilateral act to the procedures laid down for the making of agreements would be strong evidence of an intention on the part of the Community to be bound by the terms of the declaration. By contrast, the

---

[209] Case C-187/93 *Parliament* v. *Council* [1994] ECR I-2857 at para. 28.

[210] *Australia* v. *France; New Zealand* v. *France* [1974] ICJ Rep. 253 at para. 43. See generally Brownlie, n. 13 above, ch. XXVI; Oppenheim, n. 13 above, para. 577; J.-D. Sicault, 'Du caractère obligatoire des engagements unilatéraux en droit international public' (1979) 83 *RGDIP* 633; for a critical analysis, see A. P. Rubin, 'The International Legal Effects of Unilateral Declarations' (1977) 71 *AJIL* 114.

[211] See Joined Cases 3, 4, and 6/76 *Kramer* [1976] ECR 1279 at para. 17/18.

failure to submit the declaration to such procedures would be evidence that it
was not intended to have a solemn and binding character. The context in which
a declaration was made might also be significant.[212]

INFORMAL OR NON-BINDING ARRANGEMENTS

Agreements binding in international law are not the only means by which States
and other international actors carry out their business. In sensitive or confidential matters, or where legally binding agreements would for other reasons be
inappropriate or undesirable, non-binding instruments are frequently used to
embody arrangements or understandings.[213] Such instruments are not 'treaties'
in international law, and fall outside the scope of the term 'agreement' as
employed in Community law. The Treaties make no provision for the conclusion of such arrangements by the Communities,[214] but there is no reason in
principle why the Communities could not make such commitments, and the
practice bears this out.[215]

Procedure

The 'conclusion' of such arrangements does not have to follow the procedures
laid down in the Treaties for the conclusion of agreements. An act of the
Council or Commission accepting a non-binding arrangement could not usually be regarded as intended to have legal consequences and would therefore
not be capable of challenge before the Court. Nor could a non-binding arrangement have the consequences attributed by the Court to agreements intended to
be binding in international law.

The institutional balance of the EC Treaty in external matters[216] suggests
that non-binding arrangements involving the EC should receive the approval of
the Council before the Community can be regarded as in any way committed.
Indeed, it can be argued that the negotiation of such arrangements by the
Commission also requires the authorization of the Council.[217] In deciding
whether to authorize negotiation of such an arrangement, or to accept it on
behalf of the Community, the Council acts by common accord.[218]

---

[212] In an Association Council, for example.

[213] For discussion of non-binding arrangements, see Eiseman, 'Le Gentleman's Agreement
comme source du droit international' (1979) 106 *JDI* 326; and A. I. Aust, 'The Theory and Practice
of Informal International Instruments' [1986] *ICLQ* 787.

[214] Except to the extent that administrative arrangements may be made under Arts. 229, 230,
and 231 EC (and their counterparts in the other Treaties).

[215] Non-binding measures are frequently adopted in Association Councils, for example. Other
important non-binding instruments include the Transatlantic Declaration (EC–US) and the
EC–Japan Declaration.

[216] In particular Art. 228.

[217] Except, perhaps, when the Commission acts under Arts. 229 and 230 EC.

[218] These are political, not legal, acts, so the rule in Art. 148(1) EC does not apply.

5

Legal Effects of Community Agreements

The legal effects of international agreements concluded[1] by the Communities[2] can be summarized by two principles. Such agreements are binding in international law and must be performed in good faith: *pacta sunt servanda*. And within the Community legal order, agreements form an integral part of Community law.[3]

COMMUNITY AGREEMENTS IN INTERNATIONAL LAW:
PACTA SUNT SERVANDA

'Every treaty is binding on the parties to it and must be performed by them in good faith.' This principle, expressed in identical terms in the 1969 and 1986 Vienna Conventions on the Law of Treaties,[4] is a fundamental rule of custom-

---

[1] On the procedures for conclusion of agreements, see Ch. 4. The principles described in this Chapter also apply to agreements to which the Communities become party by 'succeeding' to the Member States' rights and obligations under them. To date, the only examples of such 'succession' recognized by the ECJ have been the 1947 GATT, the Convention of 15 Dec. 1950 on Nomenclature for the Classification of Goods in Customs Tariffs and the Convention of the same date establishing a Customs Co-operation Council. On Community succession to the Member States, see Ch. 9.

[2] This Chapter deals with agreements to which one or more of the Communities are parties, without the Member States. The general principles outlined here also apply to mixed agreements, but these give rise to certain other difficulties, and are therefore examined in Ch. 6.

[3] See, e.g., Case 142/88 *Hoesch* v. *Bergrohr* [1989] ECR 3413 at para. 30.

[4] Art. 26 of the 1969 Vienna Convention on the Law of Treaties between States ('VCLT') and Art. 26 of the 1986 Vienna Convention on the Law of Treaties between States and International Organizations or between International Organizations ('VCLTIO'). A preliminary difficulty in considering the consequences in international law of agreements concluded by the Communities is in determining the rules of international law which apply. Although the VCLT has been widely ratified or approved by States, the Communities are not parties to that Convention, and cannot become parties to it in its present form. The VCLTIO, which closely follows the provisions of the VCLT, is not yet in force. The Commission apparently considers the provisions of that Convention defective in several respects and unsuited to the special characteristics of the Community: see P. Manin, 'The European Communities and the Vienna Convention on the Law of Treaties between States and International Organizations or between International Organizations' (1987), 24 *CMLRev.* 457. An early proposal that the Communities should accede to it therefore seems unlikely. Accordingly, the rules of customary law must be applied to determine questions relating to the validity, interpretation, and application in international law of agreements concluded by the Communities. For a detailed account of customary law as it applies to treaties involving international organizations, the reader is referred to the standard works on the law of treaties. However, the VCLT and VCLTIO are, on many of the main points of law, regarded as codifications of the law of treaties, and they will accordingly be referred to as representing general principles of international law. It will be noted that the Court has drawn on the Vienna Conventions as a source of legal rules in

ary international law,[5] as applicable to the Communities in their international relations as it is to States. It is the most basic tenet of the law of treaties.[6] Its practical consequences, though obvious, bear restating.

The provisions of agreements entered into by the Communities must be carried out according to the real intention of the parties at the time the agreement was concluded, that is to say, according to the spirit of the agreement, not its mere literal meaning. The Communities may not, except in accordance with the agreement or in the limited circumstances permitted by international law,[7] free themselves from the commitments undertaken in an agreement, or decide to modify its terms, without the consent of the other party or parties to the agreement. In accordance with general principles of law, failure on the part of the Communities to fulfil the terms of an agreement involves a duty to make reparation, however short the breach may be in duration, and however relative it may be in importance.[8]

An agreement is binding whether or not it can be the subject of adjudication before an international tribunal: the legally binding nature of an international commitment does not depend on, nor does it imply, the existence of a court or other tribunal to hold the parties to their obligations.[9]

States may not invoke the provisions of their internal law as a justification for failure to perform an agreement.[10] The same principle undoubtedly applies to international organizations.[11] Thus, in considering whether the Communities should become parties to an agreement, the institutions must ensure that the Communities are in a position to give full effect to their obligations at the moment these obligations come into force.[12]

---

several cases: see Case C–327/91 *France* v. *Commission* [1994] ECR I–3641 at para. 25, (referring to Art. 2 of the VCLTIO), Case C–312/91 *Metalsa Srl* [1992] ECR I–3751 at para. 12 and Case C–432/92 *R.* v. *Ministry of Agriculture, Fisheries and Food, ex parte Anastasiou* [1992] ECR I–3087 at para. 43 (both referring to Art. 31 VCLT).

[5] See Case 104/81 *Hauptzollamt Mainz* v. *Kupferberg* [1982] ECR 3641 at para. 18.

[6] And indeed, since the Communities are created by treaties, of Community law itself. See further, B. Cheng, *General Principles of Law as applied by International Courts and Tribunals* (Grotius, 1987), Ch. 3, especially 112 ff.; Sinclair, *The Vienna Convention on the Law of Treaties* (2nd edn., Manchester University Press, 1984), at 83 ff.

[7] e.g. fundamental change of circumstances: Art. 62 VCLT.

[8] See *Chorzow Factory Case (Merits)* [1928] *PCIJ*, Series A, no. 17, 29.

[9] As will be seen below, the ECJ has a wide-ranging jurisdiction to interpret and apply agreements concluded by the Communities. The rulings of the Court are, of course, only binding in the Community legal order, on the Member States and the institutions of the Communities. They have no effect on third parties (except to the extent to which such parties may have consented to be bound by the Court's jurisdiction).

[10] See Art. 27 VCLT.   [11] Cf. Art. 27 VCLTIO.

[12] Not necessarily at the moment of conclusion of the agreement: there is no legal objection to the conclusion of an agreement by a party which is not at that stage ready to give the agreement effect, provided that effect can be given to the agreement when the obligations it contains come into force.

Community Agreements bind the Community Institutions and the Member States

The capacity of an international organization to enter into agreements and to conduct other relations at the international level is governed by international law.[13] That the Communities each have such capacity can be deduced from the terms of the Community Treaties, from the principles established by the International Court of Justice in the *Reparations* case,[14] from the wide range of agreements into which the Communities have entered, and generally from the participation of the Communities in the day-to-day conduct of international relations.[15] At the international level, therefore, the Communities, as international persons, are bound by the obligations, and benefit from the rights, in the agreements they conclude. Each of the Communities contracts international obligations in its own right: an agreement in the name of one of the Communities binds that Community only.

Thus, in Case C–327/91, *France* v. *Commission*, the Court said:[16]

. . . it is the Community alone, having legal personality pursuant to Article 210 of the Treaty, which has the capacity to bind itself by concluding agreements with a non-member country or an international organization.

(25) There is no doubt therefore that the Agreement is binding on the European Communities.[17] It falls squarely within the definition of an international agreement concluded between an international organization and a State, within the meaning of Article 2(1)(a)(i) of the Vienna Convention of 21 March 1986 on the Law of Treaties between States and International Organizations or between International Organizations. In the event of non-performance of the Agreement by the Commission, therefore, the Community could incur liability at international level.

Although it is the Community which is bound at the international level, the conclusion of an agreement has certain consequences for the Community institutions and the Member States. Article 228(7) EC[18] provides that 'Agreements concluded under these conditions[19] are binding on the institutions of the Community and the Member States.' The ECSC and Euratom Treaties contain no such rule, but it seems certain that the same principle applies.[20]

---

[13] On the personality and powers of international organizations in international law, see Ch. 2 and the sources cited there especially at n. 3.

[14] *Reparations for Injuries Suffered in the Service of the UN*, Advisory Opinion, [1949] ICJ Rep., 174.

[15] See Ch. 2.　　　　　[16] Case C–327/91, n. 4 above, at para. 24.

[17] Because the agreement was between 'the European Communities' and the US.

[18] Formerly Art. 228(2) EEC.

[19] i.e. in accordance with the procedures laid down in the Treaties, in particular the provisions of the first three paras. of that Art.

[20] In *Halsbury's Laws* at para. 4.08, the learned author comments in relation to the rule in Art. 228(2) EEC that: '[t]he importance of this rule is such that were it not explicit it would have to be inferred; accordingly such an inference is made in relation to the ECSC Treaty and the Euratom Treaty.' Similarly D. Lasok and J. W. Bridge, *Law and Institutions of the European Union* (6th edn., Butterworth, 1994) at 73: '[t]hough no such provision [*i.e. Art. 228 (7)EC*] can be found in either

Community Agreements 'are binding on the Institutions of the Community'

The institutions of the Community have no international legal personality. As a matter of international law, it is the Community, not the institutions, which has rights and obligations under the Community's agreements. Article 228(7) EC must therefore be understood as a rule of Community law; an expression of the duty of loyal[21] co-operation which binds all the institutions to assist the Community to achieve its objectives. The extent of this duty will depend on the circumstances, but it applies at the stage of giving effect to an agreement and in its day-to-day application. Thus, before deciding to conclude an agreement, the institutions are under a duty to ensure that the Community is in a position to give effect to the agreement according to its terms from the moment the obligations in it become binding on the Community. While the agreement is in force, it is the duty of each institution to act in accordance with the terms of the agreement in carrying out its functions or exercising its prerogatives under the Treaties.

Community Agreements 'are binding on . . . the Member States'

The Member States, unlike the institutions, are subjects of international law, capable of having rights and obligations in relation to other States and international organizations. The question arises whether an agreement concluded by the Community alone is also binding on the Member States of the Community as a matter of international law. In the draft Articles which formed the basis of the 1986 Vienna Convention on the Law of Treaties between States and International Organizations or between International Organizations, the International Law Commission proposed that the conclusion of an agreement by an international organization could give rise to rights and obligations for the Member States of the organization if the parties to the agreement so intended and provided accordingly in the agreement; if the Member States of the organization were all willing to be bound by the agreement; and if that willingness was brought to the attention of the other participants in the negotiation of the agreement.[22] But the final text of the 1986 Convention made no provision on the matter, reflecting the acute difficulty of the issues involved and the very different situations which such a rule would have to cover.

the Euratom or the ECSC Treaties it is assumed that the EEC formula has a universal application within the Community legal order.'

[21] Or 'sincere' co-operation: see Case C–65/93 *Parliament* v. *Council*, judgment of 30 Mar. 1995, not yet reported, at paras. 22 ff.

[22] Draft Art. 36*bis*: see the ILC's Report on the work of its 34th Session, at 87.

As a matter of international law, the general rule is that international agreements do not create rights or obligations for third States or organizations.[23] The Communities are each international legal persons in their own right, separate from their component Member States, and capable in law of bearing rights and duties towards third parties; and in practice each Community frequently concludes agreements in its own name, without the participation of the Member States.[24] Thus conclusion of an agreement by one of the Communities[25] should not of itself mean that the Member States become parties to the agreement as a matter of international law, nor should it have the effect of binding the Member States directly at the international level *vis-à-vis* the other parties to the agreement. When the Member States participate in an agreement to which one of the Communities is party, they participate by virtue of their own powers, and in respect of their own interests, not as guarantors of the Community interest. This analysis is consistent with the underlying legal theory: as a matter of law, competence in certain matters has been transferred completely to the Communities from the Member States, and, accordingly, the responsibility for the conduct of international relations in such matters can rest only with the Communities, not with the Member States.

Thus, where the proper implementation of an agreement by the Community requires action at the level of the Member States, it is for the Community institutions to ensure that any necessary action is taken, and it is the Community alone which must answer at the international level for any failure on its part, or on the part of its Member States, to fulfil the terms of the agreement.

The principal judicial consideration of the effect on the Member States of an agreement entered into by the Community is in the *Kupferberg* case.[26] There the Court said that the words 'binding on . . . the Member States' in Article 228 meant that the agreements are binding on the Member States '*in the same way as* [on] the institutions' and that the Member States, as well as the Community institutions, are responsible for ensuring that the obligations arising from such agreements are fulfilled. Accordingly, by securing performance of these obligations Member States fulfil a duty not only to the non-Member State concerned, but also, and above all, to the Community which has assumed responsibility for due performance of the agreement.

The Court's comments are not entirely clear, but it is doubtful that the Court meant that the Member States were under an obligation in international law. The meaning to be given to this dictum is probably that the duty owed by the Member States to other parties to an agreement concluded by the Community is a duty in Community law to ensure—in their capacity as Members of the Council—that the Community complies with its international obligations (by,

---

[23] Arts. 34 of the VCLT and VCLTIO.
[24] On the position of the ECSC, see Ch. 23.
[25] For the position in relation to mixed agreements see Ch. 6.
[26] See Case 104/81, n. 5 above, at paras. 11–13.

for example, taking steps to enact any necessary internal legislation). This interpretation fits with the rest of Article 228(7),[27] and with the words of the Court later in the *Kupferberg* judgment, where it stressed that the obligation on the Member States is '*above all* to the Community which has assumed responsibility for the due performance of the agreement'. The Court was thus simply pointing to an application of the general duty of loyal co-operation set out in Article 5 EC.

In summary, the better view is that neither international law nor Community law makes the Member States jointly liable to third States for the performance of the obligations of the Community under an agreement concluded by the Community alone.[28] The Community is solely responsible in international law for the performance of its obligations:[29] the role of the Member States is limited to securing, by their action as members of the Community, that the Community fulfils its obligations.[30]

---

[27] In particular the juxtaposition in that Art. of the Member States and the institutions: the institutions cannot be under obligations in international law.

[28] For the liabilities of the Community and the Member States under a mixed agreement, see Ch. 6.

[29] Mégret, *Le droit de la Communauté Européenne* (Brussels, 1980), vol. 12, at 62 comments 'il faut noter que les auteurs ont choisi le terme "lient" et non pas "engagent" ou un verbe équivalent. En effet, cette disposition ne signifie pas que les Etats membres sont véritables parties aux accords conclus avec les tiers. C'est la Communauté en tant que telle, et elle seule, qui est engagée par ses accords vis-à-vis des tiers co-contractantes.'

[30] The commentators are not all agreed on the effect of Art. 228(7) EC. P. Lachmann, 'International Legal Personality of the EC: Capacity and Competence' [1984] 1 *LIEI* 3; Mégret, n. 29 above; K. M. Meessen, 'The Application of the Rules of Public International Law within Community Law' (1976) 13 *CMLRev.* 497. W. J. Ganshof van der Meersch, 'L'ordre juridique des Communautés Européennes et le droit international', 148 *Hague Recueil* (1975 V) 1 comments: 'Les Etats Membres sont aussi liés par les accords communautaires. C'est là une disposition exceptionelle dans le droit des organizations internationales. Les accords communautaires, au delà du droit applicable à la Communauté et à ses institutions, engagent les Etats en leur qualité de membres de cette Communauté . . . Bien que les Etats Membres ne soient pas parties aux accords externes de la Communauté, puisqu'il n'interviennent plus comme tels dans cette attribution transférée, ils sont tenus en raison des engagements qu'ils ont pris dans le traité constitutif.' H. G. Schermers seems willing to go further: commenting on Art. 228(1) EEC: 'Whenever States have transferred powers to an organization, they ought to be bound by the agreements which the organization concludes within the scope of these powers . . . Apart from the transfer of powers, the obligation of loyalty to the organization offers another ground for accepting such a provision, even when not expressly incorporated in the constitution . . . Freedom of Members to violate agreements of the organization would also lead to unacceptable uncertainty for third States' (*International Institutional Law* (2nd edn., A. W. Sijthoff, 1980), para. 1592). Groux and Manin, 145 suggest that Art. 228(7) EC may amount to a *jus tertio* of the kind envisaged in Arts. 35 VCLT and VCLTIO. Commenting on the *Kupferberg* case, they state: 'On this view, Art. 228(2) [now Art. 228(7)] constitutes a stipulation for others which third parties can invoke in their case. Having failed in their action against the Community, the other contracting party would be entitled to use this Art., in addition to the terms of the Community agreement, as grounds for an action against the Member States. However this situation is very unlikely to arise because it is not easy to see what advantage the Community could gain by hiding behind its Member States in such a manner.' There are at least three reasons for doubting this analysis: (i) it is not clear that this was the intention of Art. 228(7) EC (or its predecessor); (ii) the institutions are also bound by the obligation in that Art., and it is clear that their commitment is not one which exists at the level of international law; (iii) the extent to which treaties

Accordingly, action by a Member State in breach of the terms of an agreement entered into by the Community, or which had the effect of placing the Community in breach of such an agreement, would be a breach of the Member State's obligations under the Treaties.[31] It would therefore be open to the Commission to bring infringement proceedings[32] to secure performance of the Community's agreement, and (at least in theory) open to another Member State to bring an action against the Member State in breach under Articles 170 EC and 142 Euratom.

Implementation of Community Agreements

It is for each party to an international agreement to ensure that it is in a position to give effect to it according to its terms from its entry into force until its expiry or termination.[33] In respect of agreements concluded by the Community, the primary responsibility for securing that the Community complies with its agreements lies with the Commission.

Adoption of Legislation to give Effect to the Agreement

Not all agreements require the adoption of legislation in order to have effect: some involve political commitments, and others may have effect directly in the Community legal order without the need for legislation.[34] If an agreement can be given effect without the adoption of legislation, there is no need to reiterate its terms in a separate measure of Community legislation: the Community act which authorizes its conclusion and the expression of the Community's consent to be bound will have the effect of incorporating the agreement into Community law.

If, however, the agreement envisages or requires measures for its implementation, these will have to be adopted by the appropriate institution before, or at the same time as,[35] the Community's obligations enter into force. It will be for the Commission to assess whether legislation is required to give effect to the

---

can give rise to rights for third States or organizations is, notwithstanding the terms of the VCLT and VCLTIO, controversial. See further, Sinclair, *The Vienna Convention on the Law of Treaties* (2nd edn., Manchester University Press, 1984) 98–106; I. Brownlie, *Principles of Public International Law* (4th edn., Clarendon Press, 1990), 622–4.

[31] Case 104/81, n. 5 above, at para. 13.

[32] Under Arts. 169 EC, 141 Euratom, and 88 ECSC. For examples, see Joined Cases 194 and 241/85 *Commission* v. *Greece* [1988] ECR 1037 at para. 32 (breach of Art. 3(1) of the Lomé Convention) and Case C–228/91 *Commission* v. *Italy* [1993] ECR I–2701 at paras. 45–52 (breach of the EEC–Norway Trade Agreement). See also *Opinion 1/91 (Re EEA Agreement)* [1991] ECR 6079 at para. 38.

[33] The entry into force of an agreement is to be determined primarily by reference to the intention of the parties as expressed in the agreement.

[34] On direct effect of Community agreements, see pp. 135–7.

[35] So that the Community can give effect to the obligations when they come into effect.

agreement, and, if appropriate, to make the necessary proposals to the Council in good time. In considering the Commission's proposals, the Parliament, the Council, and the other organs of the Community would have to keep in mind the need to ensure that the Community was able to fulfil its international obligations.

Where legislation is required to give effect to an agreement concluded by the Community, it might be appropriate, and consistent with the principle of subsidiarity, for that legislation to be adopted by the Member States, rather than the Community. The Community institutions would have to be satisfied that full and timely effect would be given to the agreement throughout the Community.

Day to day Application of the Provisions of the Agreement

The Commission is required to ensure that measures taken by the institutions pursuant to the EC and Euratom Treaties are applied,[36] and that the objectives set out in the ECSC Treaty are attained in accordance with the provisions of that Treaty.[37] Thus, it is the duty of the Commission to take any necessary action to secure that the institutions and Member States do not obstruct the implementation of an agreement by the Community,[38] if necessary by bringing infringement proceedings under the relevant Treaty Article. It is the duty of the Member States and the Council (and indeed the Parliament and, where relevant, the other institutions and bodies established by the Treaties) to act in a manner which enables the Community to give effect to its obligations according to their terms.

Agreements Concluded in Violation of Community Law

The authority of an international organization to enter into a particular agreement, and the procedures which it is required to follow before it can express its consent to be bound, are governed by the powers conferred on the organization and the procedures laid down in its constituent treaty.[39] Whether agreements which exceed the powers conferred on an organization, or which are concluded in violation of its internal procedures, nevertheless bind the organization is, however, a question of international law to be determined by the rules of the law of treaties. Thus, although the internal legal competence of the

---

[36] Arts. 155 EC and 124 Euratom.   [37] Art. 8 ECSC.

[38] e.g. by failing to give effect to any relevant dirs. in their national law.

[39] See Art. 6 VCLTIO. H. G. Schermers, n. 30 above, para. 1553 comments: '[t]he existence of some treaty-making power does not mean however that any international organization may conclude any agreement. In this respect, international organizations differ fundamentally from States . . . As a rule, the power of a State to conclude treaties in any field may be presumed. This presumption does not exist for international organizations. In each individual case, their competence must be demonstrated.'

Communities, and the Communities' procedures for conclusion of agreements, are matters of Community law, the validity and effects *in relation to third parties* of agreements concluded in breach of any rules of Community law must be assessed in terms, not of Community law, but of international law.

The rules of customary law on this question are not easy to state with certainty.[40] Some argue that international law leaves it to the internal rules of the international organization to determine the procedures by which its consent to be bound is to be expressed. Thus it follows that a violation of the internal rules of the organization vitiates the expression of such consent, and renders the agreement which has been 'concluded' void or voidable. Others hold that the acts of a representative of an organization acting within his ostensible authority bind the organization in international law, even if the internal rules of the organization have not been complied with. The principles outlined in Article 46 of the 1986 VCLTIO, which follow closely those of the 1969 Convention, fall somewhere between the two schools, and probably represent the views of the majority of jurists. They provide a convenient reference point for present purposes.

Article 46 provides that:

1. A State may not invoke the fact that its consent to be bound by a treaty has been expressed in violation of a provision of its internal law regarding competence to conclude treaties as invalidating its consent unless that violation was manifest and concerned a rule of its internal law of fundamental importance.

2. An international organization may not invoke the fact that its consent to be bound by a treaty has been expressed in violation of the rules of the organization regarding competence to conclude treaties as invalidating its consent unless that violation was manifest and concerned a rule of fundamental importance.

3. A violation is manifest if it would be objectively evident to any State or any international organization conducting itself in the matter in accordance with the normal practice of States and, where appropriate, of international organizations, and in good faith.

It will be noted, first, that agreements concluded in breach of an organization's internal rules are not *ipso facto* void or non-existent: the rule in Article 46 applies in principle in favour of the State or international organization which has acted in violation of its own internal rules, and amounts to a defence against a claim for performance of the agreement by the 'innocent' party. Thus, it would not be open to a State or organization which has concluded an agreement with the Community to claim, in response to the Community's call for performance of the agreement, that the agreement was void because it had been concluded in violation of a rule of the Community's internal order.

This presumption in favour of the validity of agreements which on their face have been duly concluded is reinforced by the rest of Article 46. In order to revoke an expression of consent to be bound by an agreement, a party must

---

[40] See Brownlie, n. 30 above, ch. XXX; D. W. Bowett, *The Law of International Institutions* (4th edn., Stevens, 1982), 341 ff.

show that the violation of its internal rules was 'manifest'. The test for determining whether a violation is 'manifest' is set out in paragraph 3 of Article 46: the violation must have been 'objectively evident' to a party acting in accordance with normal practice and in good faith. Furthermore, the internal rule involved must have been 'of fundamental importance'.

It will probably be difficult to show that these tests have been fulfilled in respect of an agreement apparently concluded by one of the Communities.[41] It is not always easy to determine the extent of the powers of the Communities in relation to a given agreement, or to say whether these powers are exclusive or shared with the Member States. And although the broad outlines of the correct internal procedures may be evident, the particular roles and competences of each of the Community institutions in the process of concluding agreements may be less obvious. Irregularities in the conclusion of an agreement which are, in terms of Community law, gross may not be 'manifest' to third parties.

This view is supported by the approach taken by the Court in Case C–327/91 *France* v. *Commission*.[42] The issue in that case was whether the Commission had power to conclude an agreement between the Community and the United States relating to competition. The Court found that the Commission had no such power, but that finding did not affect the validity of the agreement in international law: '[t]here is no doubt . . . that the [Competition] Agreement is binding on the European Communities . . . In the event of non-performance of the Agreement by the Commission, therefore, the Community could incur liability at international level.'[43] The conclusion, therefore, must be that an agreement apparently concluded by, or in the name of, one of the Communities will almost always be binding on that Community as a matter of international law.[44]

The status in Community law of agreements concluded in breach of substantive or procedural rules of the Treaties is however uncertain. It seems unlikely that they become an integral part of Community law by virtue of the principle in Article 228(7) EC: that principle only applies to agreement which have been concluded in accordance with the appropriate procedures. Similarly, it is difficult to see how the institutions and the Member States could be obliged as a matter of Community law to give effect to an agreement which was

---

[41] See J. Temple Lang, 'The ERTA Judgment and the Court's Case Law on Competence and Conflict' [1986] *YBEL* 183 at 213.

[42] N. 4 above.   [43] *Ibid.*, at para. 25.

[44] See Mégret, n. 29 above, vol. 12, 63. H. G. Schermers, 'The Internal Effect of Community Treaty Making' in O'Keeffe and Schermers (eds.), *Essays on European Law and Integration* (Kluwer, 1982), 167–78 at 173 comments: '[Foreign States] cannot be expected to know the extent of the competence of the Community. Whenever the Community concludes a treaty, foreign States may presume that it has power to do so. If the Community acted beyond its powers, it will nonetheless be bound unless it or its Member States can prove both its lack of competence and its manifest character. The latter will be especially complicated because of the complicated nature of Community law.'

outside the Community's powers, or which had been concluded in breach of fundamental constitutional principles of Community law.

On the other hand, if, as seems likely, agreements concluded in violation of internal rules of Community law usually remain valid in international law and binding on the Community *vis-à-vis* third States, the institutions and the Member States must ensure that the rights of the third State or international organization under the agreement are respected. The Community institutions and the Member States would therefore have to take steps to align the internal and external effects of the agreement, by withdrawing from the agreement (if that were possible), by rectifying the defect of Community law or practice which had rendered the agreement invalid,[45] or, perhaps, by securing the participation of the Member States in the agreement along with the Community.

Geographical Application of Community Agreements

Not all agreements require action or implementation with respect to a particular geographical area.[46] Some bind the parties as to their political action anywhere. Others govern the treatment, or sometimes conduct, of individuals or companies which are nationals of the parties to the agreement in question wherever that conduct or treatment takes place. In the case of such agreements, the position of the Communities is the same as that of any other subject of international law: the provisions of the agreement must be given effect in the conduct of the Communities, in the exercise of their legislative jurisdiction, their executive powers, or their enforcement jurisdiction, as the case may be.

For agreements in which territorial application is a directly relevant consideration, Article 29 of the 1969 Convention probably represents the accepted rule of customary law. It provides (in relation to agreements between States) that '[u]nless a different intention appears from the treaty or is otherwise established, a treaty is binding on each party in respect of its entire territory.' The application of this rule to States is not straightforward.[47] There is an added difficulty in applying the rule to agreements concluded by international organizations,[48] because the latter cannot be said to have legal control over 'territory' in the sense that States have.

Nevertheless, the rule which emerges from the Communities' practice is that

---

[45] See the Commission's proposal for a Council decision concluding the Competition Agreement with the US which was the subject of annulment proceedings in Case C–327/91, n. 4 above. See Dec. 95/145 ([1995] OJ L95/45).

[46] Lachmann, n. 30 above; J. Groux, ' "Territorialité" et droit communautaire' [1987] *RTDE* 1 at 18 ff. notes that a territorial application clause is not always appropriate (e.g. where the agreement deals with matters outside the territory of the Community—as is the case for, say, fisheries agreements).

[47] See Sinclair, n. 30 above, at 87 ff.

[48] A difficulty recognized in the corresponding provision of the VCLTIO (Art. 29), which provides 'a treaty between one or more States and one or more international organizations is binding *on each State party in respect of its entire territory*' (emphasis added).

agreements entered into by the Communities are binding in respect of the entire territory over which the Communities' competence is exercised,[49] to the extent of that competence, unless a different intention appears from the agreement or is otherwise established.[50] Thus, Community agreements generally include a provision stating that they apply 'to the territories in which the Treaty establishing the Community is applied and under the conditions laid down in that Treaty'.[51] In Community practice internally and in external relations it is common to refer to the 'territory of the Community' as shorthand for 'the territories of the Member States to which the provisions of the Treaties establishing the Communities apply'. Provided the underlying reality is kept in view, this seems an acceptable, even if not entirely accurate, formulation.

COMMUNITY AGREEMENTS ARE AN INTEGRAL PART OF COMMUNITY LAW

The fundamental principle governing the effects in Community law of agreements concluded by the European Community was enunciated in *Haegeman* v. *Belgium*.[52] The Court said that:

The Athens Agreement[53] was concluded by the Council under Articles 228 and 238 of the Treaty . . .

(4) This Agreement is, in so far as concerns the Community, an act of one of the institutions of the Community within the meaning of Article 177(1)(b).

(5) The provisions of the Agreement, from the coming into force thereof, form an integral part of Community law.

The legal consequences of agreements[54] concluded by the Communities have been considered and developed by the Court mainly in the context of

---

[49] On the geographical extent of the Communities' competence, see Ch. 3.

[50] By, e.g., a reservation or declaration made by the Community on acceptance of the agreement. For examples of territorial reservations entered by the Community, see the decision authorizing conclusion of the Convention on the Conservation of European Wildlife and Natural Habitats ([1982] OJ L38/1).

[51] Examples (out of many which could be cited) include Art. 7 1985 EEC–Yemen Agreement ([1985] OJ L126/1); Art. 357, Fourth Lomé Convention; Art. 126 EEA Agreement; Art. 121 Europe Agreement with Hungary ([1993] OJ L347/1); and Art. 27 1994 EC–India Co-operation Agreement ([1994] OJ L223/23).

[52] Case 181/73 [1974] ECR 449 at para. 3. This principle has been reiterated on numerous occasions: see, e.g., Case 12/86 *Demirel* v. *Stadt Schwäbisch Gmünd* [1987] ECR 3719 at para. 7.

[53] i.e. the 1970 Association Agreement between the EEC and Greece.

[54] On the meaning of 'agreement' and the procedures for conclusion of agreements, see Ch. 4. It will be noted that the principle in the *Haegeman* case will not apply to non-binding arrangements or mere political statements made by the Community. The case law has so far arisen almost exclusively in connection with trade and co-operation agreements and association agreements. Whether the ECJ would apply the same criteria to other kinds of agreement concluded by the Community may be an open question: J. Groux, 'L'invocabilité en droit des accords liant la CEE' [1983] *RTDE* 203 at 231.

agreements concluded by the European Community.[55] There has been almost no judicial consideration of the effects of agreements concluded by the other Communities, but it seems certain that the same principle applies to such agreements. That would be consistent with the 'requirement of unity' which the Court has identified as fundamental to the international representation of the Communities,[56] and which it has also applied in the context of the implementation of Community agreements.[57] In commenting on the implementation of an agreement to be concluded by Euratom, the Court expressly attributed to the agreement the effects already accorded to agreements involving the European Community.[58]

It may therefore be said that an international agreement duly[59] concluded by one of the Communities becomes an integral part[60] of Community law as from

[55] The literature is voluminous. See H. Smit and P. Herzog, *The Law of the European Community* (New York, 1976) vol. 6, 248 ff; Groux and Manin, *The European Communities in the International Order* (European Perspectives, 1985) 112–22; T. C. Hartley, *The Foundations of European Community Law* (3rd edn., Clarendon Press, 1994), ch. 6 especially 182–7; Mégret, n. 29 above, *passim*, but especially 181–96; H. G. Schermers, 'Community Law and International Law' (1975) 12 *CMLRev.* 77; Pietri, 'La valeur juridique des accords liant la Communauté économique européenne' [1976] *RTDE* 51; K. M. Meessen, n. 30 above; Imbrechts, 'Les Effets Internes des Accords Internationaux des Communautés Européennes' (1986) *Revue d'Intégration Européenne* 59; Schermers, 'The Direct Application of Treaties with Third States: *Pabst* and *Polydor*' (1982) 19 *CMLRev.* 563; Volker, 'The Direct Effect of International Agreements in the Community's Legal Order' [1983] 1 *LIEI* 131; G. Bebr, 'Agreements concluded by the Community and their Possible Direct Effect: from International Fruit Company to Kupferberg', (1983) 20 *CMLRev.* 35; T. C. Hartley, 'International Agreements and the Community Legal System' (1983) 8 *ELR* 383; J. Groux, 'L'invocabilité en justice des accords internationaux des Communautés Européennes' [1983] *RTDE* 203; Ehlermann, *Application of GATT Rules in the EEC* in *The European Community and the GATT*: M. Hilf, F. G. Jacobs, E.-U. Petersmann (eds.) (Kluwer, 1986); Rideau, 'Les accords internationaux dans la jurisprudence de la Cour de Justice des Communautés européennes' [1990] *RGDIP* 289; J. Boulouis, 'Le droit des Communautés européennes dans ses rapports avec le droit international général', 235 *Hague Recueil* (1992 IV) 74.

[56] *Opinion 2/91 (Re ILO Convention 170)* [1993] ECR I–1061 at para. 36.

[57] See also *Ruling 1/78 (Re Draft Convention on the Physical Protection of Nuclear Materials)* [1978] ECR 2151 at para. 35 ff.

[58] 'The . . . convention . . . , which, once it has been concluded by the Community will form an integral part of Community law', *Ruling 1/78* n. 57 above, at para. 35.

[59] i.e. in accordance with the procedure required by the Treaty in respect of the agreement and the Community in question. See Mégret, n. 29 above, at 63: 'Cette disposition (i.e. Art. 228(2) EEC) précise que ce sont les accords "conclus dans les conditions fixées ci-dessus" à savoir en respectant les règles de procédure prévues au paragraphe 1, qui lient les institutions et les Etats membres. Un accord conclu en violation de ces règles pourrait être non-applicable sur le plan interne mais reste valide sur le plan externe du droit international.'

[60] The status of such an agreement within the Community legal order has not yet been addressed directly by the Court. The generally accepted view is that an agreement duly concluded by the Community ranks below the Treaties constituting the Communities, but above measures adopted by the institutions. Thus, an agreement would not prevail against a conflicting provision of the Treaties, but would supersede a conflicting act of the institutions. Thus, Mayras A.G. in Joined Cases 21–24/72 *International Fruit Company NV v. Produktschap voor Groenten en Fruit* [1972] ECR 1219 at 1233–4: 'There is no doubt that just as the Court has constantly asserted the precedence of Community law over the national laws of Member States it cannot but recognize the superiority of the Community's international agreements over the measures adopted by its institutions.' See also Hartley, n. 55 above, 187–8; Ehlermann, n. 55 above, at 131–2.

the date of its entry into force.[61] This has three principal consequences: such an agreement can give rise to rights and duties which have direct effect in Community law; decisions of bodies created by the agreement likewise form part of Community law; and the Court of Justice has an extensive jurisdiction in the interpretation and application of the agreement.

Agreements can give Rise to Rights and Duties which have Direct Effect in Community Law

Because the provisions of an agreement form part of Community law, they may give rise to rights and duties which individuals can invoke directly before national courts. A provision in an agreement concluded by the Community with a third country must be regarded as being 'directly applicable'[62] (that is to say, capable of conferring rights and duties on individuals) when, regard being had to its wording and the purpose and nature of the agreement itself, the provision contains a clear and precise obligation which is not subject in its implementation or effects to the adoption of any subsequent measure.[63] In considering whether the provisions of an agreement confer such rights on citizens, the Court said that the purpose, spirit, the general scheme, and the terms of the agreement must be considered.[64] If the agreement expressly provides for its effect in the legal orders of the Community and the other party or parties, such provisions will determine the matter.[65]

An agreement containing no such provision has to be considered on its own terms, in the light of its aim and content, in order to determine whether its provisions are capable of having direct effect or not.[66] It is not possible to lay down

---

[61] Case 181/73, n. 52 above, at para. 5; *Opinion 1/91*, n. 32 above, at para. 37. It would no doubt be possible to provide in the Council or Commission act concluding an agreement that its terms should apply within the Community as from an earlier date than its entry into force. In such a case, the agreement itself would not be part of Community law; the Community would be giving effect to the agreement's terms by a unilateral legislative act. But a provision in such an act postponing the date of entry into force of an agreement until after its date of entry into force in international law would risk placing the Community in breach of its international obligations, and would infringe the principle in the *Haegeman* case.

[62] The Court appears to use the terms 'direct effect' and 'directly applicable' interchangeably in the context of agreements. On whether the tests for the existence of direct effect are the same in relation to international agreements as in relation to internal Community legislation, see P. Pescatore, 'The Doctrine of Direct Effect—An Infant Disease of Community Law' (1983) 8 *ELRev.* 153 at 171–4; G. Bebr, n. 55 above.

[63] Case 12/86, n. 52 above, para. 14.   [64] Joined Cases 21–24/72, n. 60 above, at para. 20.

[65] Case 104/81, n. 5 above, at para. 17.

[66] Examples of provisions which were found to have *no* direct effect are: Art. XI GATT (Joined Cases 21–24/72, n. 60 above); Art. II GATT (Case 9/73 *Schlüter* v. *Hauptzollamt Lörrach* [1973] ECR 1135); the GATT generally (Case C–280/93 *Germany* v. *Council* [1994] ECR I–4973); Art. 12 EEC–Turkey Association Agreement and Art. 36 of the Additional Protocol thereto (Case 12/86, n. 52 above); Lomé Convention provisions on right of establishment (Case 65/77 *Razanatsimba* [1977] ECR 2229); Art. V GATT (Case 266/81 *SIOT* v. *Ministero delle Finanze* [1983] ECR 731); GATT Tariff Protocols (Joined Cases 267–269/81 *Amministrazione delle Finanze dello Stato* v. *SPI and SAMI* [1983] ECR 801). Provisions which were found to have direct effect include: Art. 2(1)

detailed rules which will answer that question in every case. But it can be said that, as a general rule, agreements which merely establish a framework for negotiation[67] or for the adoption of legislation, or which rely for the achievement of their objectives on action in the laws of the contracting parties, will be unlikely to have direct effect within the Community legal order.[68] On the other hand, the closer an agreement comes to regulating the conduct of individuals, or to conferring rights on them, the more likely it is that its provisions will have direct effect within the Community. The fact that the agreement contains safeguard clauses which can be invoked by the parties[69] or establishes special institutional structures for its implementation will not preclude its provisions from having direct effect if they satisfy the relevant conditions. Nor will the Court be deterred from finding that the agreement has direct effect by the fact that such a finding will place the nationals of the other party to the agreement in a better position so far as protection of their rights is concerned than Community nationals.[70]

Horizontal and Vertical Direct Effect

All the cases in which the Court has so far had to consider the question of direct effect have concerned the rights and duties of individuals or companies against the State or emanations of the State, such as fiscal authorities ('vertical direct effect'). The question also arises whether agreements entered into by the Community are capable of conferring on individuals rights which they can invoke in proceedings against other individuals ('horizontal direct effect').

Horizontal direct effect is likely to arise very rarely: few international agreements are concluded with the intention of conferring rights and duties directly on individuals or companies in the laws of the contracting parties. Unsurprisingly, therefore, there is no judicial authority on whether agreements concluded by the Community should be regarded as having horizontal direct

---

Yaoundé Convention 1963 (Case 87/75 *Conceria Daniele Bresciani v. Amministrazione delle Finanze dello Stato* [1976] ECR 129); Art. 21(1) EEC–Portugal Free Trade Agreement (Case 104/81, n. 5 above); Art. 6 EEC–Sweden Agreement (Case C–163/90 *Administration des Douanes et Droits Indirects v. Legros* [1992] ECR I–4625; Art. 18(1) EEC–Austria Free Trade Agreement (Case C–312/91 *Metalsa Srl v. Italy* [1993] ECR 3751); Art. 41(1) EEC–Morocco Co-operation Agreement (Case C–18/90 *Office National de l'Emploi v. Kziber* [1991] ECR I–199 and Case C–58/93 *Yousfi v. Belgium* [1994] ECR I–1353); Art. 39(1) EEC–Algeria Co-operation Agreement (Case C–113/94 *Krid*, judgment of 5 Apr. 1995, not yet reported).

[67] e.g. the GATT: see Joined Cases 21–24/72; n. 60 above, at para. 21 ff.; Joined Cases 267–269/81, n. 66 above. On the effect of the GATT, see M. Maresceau, 'The GATT in the Case Law of the European Court of Justice' and C.-D. Ehlermann, *in The European Community and the GATT* Hilf, Jacobs and Petersmann, n. 55 above.

[68] Many agreements adopted in the UN framework will fall into this category.

[69] Case C–192/89 *Sevince v. Staatssecretaris van Justitie* [1990] ECR I–3461; Case 104/81, n. 5 above.

[70] Case 104/81, n. 5 above.

effect.[71] Two views are possible. On the one hand, it could be argued that, in principle, an agreement concluded by the Community is an integral part of Community law; and its effect should depend on its terms. Such an agreement should therefore be regarded as capable of being invoked in proceedings between individuals as well as between the individual and the State, if, on a true construction of its provisions, that can be said to have been the intention of the parties or the effect of what they agreed.[72] On the other hand, it could be argued that a distinction should be made between the provisions of the Treaties and the provisions of international agreements concluded by the Communities. The underlying justification for the principle that certain provisions of the Treaties have direct effect is based on the nature of the Community order: a Community pursuing economic and social objectives and comprising not only the Member States but also their nationals. Those considerations do not apply to agreements with third countries and there is therefore no reason to construe the provisions of such agreements, in the absence of express provision, in such a way as to impose obligations on persons other than the parties to them.[73]

Decisions of Bodies created by Community Agreements form Part of Community Law

Many agreements entered into by the Community establish bodies to monitor the application of the agreement and to take decisions to facilitate their implementation.[74] If an agreement to which the Community is a party establishes a judicial organ to settle disputes between the Community and other parties to the agreement, the decisions of that organ will bind the Court of Justice if the latter is required to rule on the meaning of the agreement as part of the Community legal order.[75] The Court is, however, jealous of its own role as the

[71] The question arose, but was not answered, in Case 270/80 *Polydor Ltd.* v. *Harlequin Record Shops* [1982] ECR 329.

[72] In other words, international agreements should be treated—for the purposes of vertical and horizontal direct effect—like the Community Treaties, not like directives. On the horizontal direct effect of directives, see Case C–91/92 *Faccini Dori* v. *Recreb Srl* [1994] ECR I–3325. See also D. Wyatt and A. Dashwood, *European Community Law* (3rd edn., Sweet & Maxwell, 1993) at 69–76.

[73] The HL Select Committee on the European Communities (Session 1984–5), 16th Rep., *External Competence of the European Communities* (HL 236), had reservations about the direct effect of agreements concluded by the Community, and saw 'certain dangers in further development of the notion of the direct application of terms of the Community's treaties'. The doctrine 'introduces an element of uncertainty into the law of the Member States which could produce unjust results.' It would be preferable if obligations were always 'translated into specific Community or national law . . . [The] position would be markedly less satisfactory if the European Court were to hold provisions to be of direct application where they create rights and obligations between one citizen and another' (i.e. where provisions have horizontal direct effect) (16th Rep., at para. 42).

[74] On the extent to which the Community institutions can confer powers on bodies set up by international agreements, see *Opinion 1/76 (Re the Draft Agreement for a Laying Up Fund for the Rhine)* [1977] ECR 741, *Opinion 1/91 (Re the EEA Agreement)* [1991] ECR 6079 and *Opinion 1/92 (Re the EEA Agreement)* [1992] ECR I–2821.

[75] *Opinion 1/91*, n. 74 above, at paras. 39 and 40.

ultimate arbiter on Community law: in establishing a judicial organ under an international agreement, the Member States and the Community institutions would have to ensure that the pre-eminent role of the Court of Justice under the Treaties was not prejudiced.[76]

More commonly, agreements establish 'committees' or 'councils' to facilitate the implementation of the agreement, and to supplement or give effect to its provisions. In some cases the decisions taken by these bodies are stated to be of a legally binding nature; in others they take the form of non-binding recommendations to the contracting parties on how the agreement should be implemented. Where they are directly connected with the agreement to which they give effect, decisions of bodies set up under Community agreements, in the same way as the agreement itself, form an integral part of Community law, as from their entry into force.[77] The Court of Justice thus has power to give preliminary rulings on the interpretation of such decisions. Furthermore, the provisions of such decisions can have direct effect on the same conditions as the agreement itself.[78] Even non-binding decisions of such bodies have legal effects, because they should be taken into account in determining the obligations of the parties under the agreement.[79]

Judicial Review of Agreements

The role of the Court of Justice in scrutinizing agreements before they have been concluded by the Communities has already been considered.[80] The Court is responsible, in the framework of its jurisdiction to interpret the provisions of agreements, for ensuring that agreements entered into by the Community are implemented uniformly throughout the Community.[81] The Court's jurisdiction has several facets.

---

[76] *Opinion 1/91*, n. 74 above, especially at paras. 44–46. See also *Opinion 1/76*, n. 74 above.

[77] Case 30/88 *Greece* v. *Commission* [1989] ECR 3711; Case C–192/89, n. 69 above; Case C–188/91 *Deutsche Shell* v. *Hauptzollamt Hamburg-Harburg* [1993] ECR I–363; Case C–237/91 *Kus* v. *Landeshauptstadt Wiesbaden* [1992] ECR I–6781; Case C–355/93 *Eroglu* v. *Land Baden-Württemberg* [1994] ECR I–5113.

[78] Case 192/89, n. 69 above.

[79] *Deutsche Shell*, n. 77 above. It would seem to follow from this that economic operators and their legal advisers are to be presumed to have access to and to be familiar with the decisions—binding and non-binding—of bodies set up under Community agreements. But practice regarding the publication of such decisions is, at best, uneven. The Council Rules of Procedure permit, but do not require, publication in the Official Journal: see Rule 18(6) ([1993] OJ L340/41). See Ch. 4, p. 118.

[80] i.e. the Court's role under Art. 228(6) EC and Art. 103 Euratom. See Ch. 4.

[81] Case 104/81, n. 5 above, at para. 14.

Conclusion of the Agreement

Exercise of the powers delegated to the Community institutions in international matters cannot escape judicial review of the legality of the acts adopted.[82] It has accordingly been held that the decision or other act of an institution concluding an agreement is an 'act of the institutions' for the purposes of Community law.[83] Such acts can thus be reviewed by the Court on the same basis as other acts of the Community institutions. It is accordingly possible to challenge before the Court the legal basis chosen by the Council or the Commission for the act concluding an agreement,[84] or other alleged irregularities in the procedure which led up to conclusion. Such a challenge could be made either by way of review of the legality of the act,[85] or by introducing a plea of illegality.[86]

Judicial Review of Acts of the Institutions

Because the terms of an agreement concluded by the Community are binding on the Community institutions, the validity of acts of the institutions[87] may be examined for their compatibility with such an agreement. This question may arise in the context of a reference for a preliminary ruling,[88] in an application for judicial review of the legality of an act,[89] and when a plea of illegality is taken in the course of proceedings before the Court.[90]

Before the validity of such acts may be examined in this way, however, it is necessary to show that the Community is bound by the agreement in question,[91] either by having become a party in the usual way or by succession.[92] Moreover, before the invalidity of a Community act by reference to a provision of an

---

[82] *Ibid.*, at para. 16. The Court referred specifically to Art. 173 EC; acts of the Euratom and ECSC institutions could no doubt be reviewed under Arts. 146 Euratom and 33 ECSC. On the possibility of raising issues under the Euratom or ECSC Treaty in an application under Art. 173 EC, see Case C–62/88 *Greece* v. *Council* [1990] ECR I–1527: 'The need for a complete and consistent review of legality requires that [Art. 173 EC] be construed as not depriving the Court of jurisdiction to consider, in proceedings for annulment of a measure based on a provision of the EEC Treaty, a submission concerning the infringment of a rule of the EAEC or ECSC Treaties.'

[83] See Case C–327/91 *France* v. *Commission* [1994] ECR I–3641, at para. 15.

[84] For a recent example, see Case C–268/94 *Portugal* v. *Council*, judgment awaited.

[85] Under Arts. 173 EC, 146 Euratom, or 33 ECSC.

[86] Under Arts. 184 EC, 156 Euratom, or 38 ECSC.

[87] For cases where the validity of an act of the Council was challenged, see Joined Cases 21–24/72, n. 60 above; Case C–69/89 *Nakajima All Precision* v. *Council* [1991] ECR I–2069; Case C–280/93 *Germany* v. *Council* [1994] ECR I–4973. A Commission act was challenged in Case 70/87 *Fediol* v. *Commission* [1989] ECR 1781.

[88] Under Art. 177 EC: Joined Cases 21-24/72, n. 60 above. On preliminary references generally, see Anderson, *References to the European Court* (Sweet & Maxwell, 1995).

[89] Under Art. 173 EC: Case 70/87, n. 87 above; Case C–280/93 *Germany* v. *Council*, n. 87 above.

[90] Under Art. 184 EC: Case C–69/89, n. 87 above.

[91] Joined Cases 21-24/72, n. 60 above, at para. 7; Case C–69/89, n. 87 above, at para. 29.

[92] On Community succession to Member States' agreements, see Joined Cases 21-24/72, n. 60 above, at paras. 10–18; Case 38/75 *Douaneagent der NV Nederlandse Spoorwegen* v. *Inspecteur der invoerrechten en accijnzen* [1976] ECR 1439. See also Ch. 9, pp. 235–6.

international agreement can affect the validity of that act in proceedings in a national court, the provision of the agreement must be capable of conferring rights on individuals which they can invoke before the national courts.[93] Where, however, the proceedings have arisen before the Court of Justice, it is not necessary to show that the provision of the agreement has direct effect: it suffices to show that the institutions have adopted the act in question to comply with the international obligations of the Community or that the act expressly refers to specific provisions of the agreement.[94]

Interpretation of Community Agreements

The Court's jurisdiction to interpret an agreement will usually derive from the preliminary reference procedures in Article 177 EC[95] and Article 150 Euratom. The procedures for such a reference will apply in the case of the interpretation of an agreement as they apply for the interpretation of any other act of the institutions. The Court may also be called on to interpret an agreement in cases arising under other procedures, such as the procedure for judicial review of acts of the institutions,[96] or where a plea of illegality is taken under Article 184 EC[97] and its equivalents in the other Treaties. The rationale for the Court's interpretative jurisdiction is that the provisions of the agreement in question must be interpreted uniformly throughout the Community and the Member States. The Court can therefore interpret those parts of the agreement the implementation of which is within the responsibility of the Member States.[98]

Many agreements entered into by the Community, particularly association agreements and trade and co-operation agreements, contain Articles similar in terms to Articles of the Community Treaties. It does not follow, however, that the Court will give the same interpretation to provisions in an agreement as it will give to similarly worded Articles of the Treaties. The Court has on several

---

[93] Joined Cases 21–24/72, n. 60 above, at paras. 7 and 8

[94] Case C–69/89, n. 87 above; Case 70/87, n. 87 above; Case C–280/93, n. 87 above. The Court's pronouncements, taken at face value, could have some odd results. e.g. a Council or Commission measure revoking legislation intended to implement an agreement binding on the Community could hardly be described as 'intended to implement' the international obligation. Similarly it is not clear what remedy would be open to a Member State which believed that a measure adopted by the institutions was—in effect if not intentionally—in breach of the Community's obligations under an agreement. In the light of the Court's comments in *Nakajima* and *Germany* v. *Council*, it is not easy to see how the Member State could have the legality of such a measure assessed by the Court. And if the underlying agreement was a mixed agreement, the Member State would have to choose between what it saw as its international obligations under the agreement, and its obligations under Community law. For a comment on Case C–69/89, see (1993) 4 *EJIL* at 430: the writer describes the Court's approach as 'a new development whose consequences cannot yet be fully assessed'.

[95] Examples include Case 181/73, n. 52 above; Case 17/81 *Pabst & Richarz KG* v. *Hauptzollamt Oldenburg* [1982] ECR 1331; Case 87/75, n. 66 above; Case 270/80, n. 71 above; Case 12/86, n. 52 above; Joined Cases 21–24/72, n. 60 above.

[96] Under Art. 173 EC: Case 70/87, n. 87 above.   [97] Case C–69/89, n. 87 above.

[98] On the Court's jurisdiction to interpret mixed agreements, see Ch. 6.

occasions said that it will interpret international agreements entered into by the Community in accordance with the ordinary meaning to be given to their terms in their context and in the light of their object and purpose; and has frequently contrasted the long-term political aims of the Community Treaties with the more limited objectives of agreements entered into by the Community with third countries.[99]

[99] On the Court's general approach, see *Opinion 1/91*, n. 32 above, at paras. 13–29. For examples of similar wording receiving different interpretations, see Case 270/80, n. 71 above; Case C–312/91, n. 4 above. See also Case 17/81, n. 95 above; Case C–163/90 *Legros* [1992] ECR I–4625.

6

Mixed Agreements

Mixed agreements are one of the most distinctive features of the external relations law and practice of the Communities, as well as one of the most difficult.[1] This Chapter considers what is meant by a 'mixed agreement'; then outlines the legal principle which underlies the rules in this area (the 'duty of close cooperation'); and finally describes the practical operation of that principle in the negotiation, conclusion, and implementation of mixed agreements.

THE CONCEPT OF THE 'MIXED AGREEMENT'

Competence for matters covered by an international agreement may be exclusively with the Community, or shared between the Community and the Member States, or exclusively with the Member States. When an agreement relates solely to matters within the competence of the Member States, it is open to a Member State to participate in it if it wishes to do so.[2]

Where the Community is alone competent for matters covered by an agreement, and the agreement allows for Community participation, the Community alone should become party. In some cases, even where the substance of an agreement relates to matters exclusively within the competence of the Community,[3] Member State participation may also be necessary. Although in strict theory, there is in such cases no room for Member State participation alongside the Community in the agreement,[4] in practice, the terms of the agreement may require the Member States to participate in the agreement so that the Community can exercise its competences. For example, an agreement establishing organization X may provide for membership by other non-State entities (e.g. organization Y) and provide that the votes to be attributed to a member like organization Y are to be calculated by reference to the number of mem-

---

[1] See generally, D. O'Keeffe and H. G. Schermers (eds.) *Mixed Agreements* (Kluwer, 1983); E. L. M. Volker, C. W. A. Timmermans *et al.*, *The Division of Powers between the Communities and their Member States in the Field of External Relations* (Kluwer, 1981); J. Groux and P. Manin, *The European Communities in the International Order* (European Perspectives, 1985) 58 to 69; N. Neuwahl, 'Joint Participation in International Treaties and the Exercise of Powers by the EEC and its Member States: Mixed Agreements' (1991) 28 *CMLRev.* 717.

[2] Subject, of course, to the terms of the agreement or to any constraints imposed by Council action under Title V TEU.

[3] On Community competence generally, see Ch. 3.

[4] Because the Member States have transferred their competence to the Communities.

bers of organization Y which are also members of organization X.[5] In such cases, it might be necessary for the Member States to participate alongside the Community in order to enable the Community to participate effectively. Agreements which fall entirely within the competence of the Community, but in which, for whatever reason, the Member States are called on to participate, are probably better seen as exercises of the Community's competence through the Member States.[6]

Agreements also cover areas in which the Member States and the Community share competence. As has been seen,[7] competence may be shared in several ways. Some of the obligations in the agreement may relate to matters in respect of which the Community is exclusively competent, while others relate to matters for which the Member States are exclusively competent. Or it may be that the agreement relates to an area in which the Community and the Member States share competence to act by virtue of the provisions of the Treaty or otherwise. Or the agreement may relate to matters where the powers of the Member States and the Community run in parallel, so that each has a separate and independent interest in participating in it. Or the Community may be potentially competent for the entire subject matter of the agreement, although for the present the Member States retain residual competence to act. Where competence for the subject matter of an agreement is shared between the Community and the Member States, the full implementation of the obligations in the agreement will usually require the participation in the agreement of the Communities and the Member States together, each in respect of their powers and interests.

Any agreement to which the Community and the Member States are parties is, formally speaking, a 'mixed agreement'.[8] But it is arguable that only those agreements which contain provisions relating to matters within the competence of the Community and also provisions relating to matters within the competence of the Member States may be said to be 'truly' mixed. For the purposes of this Chapter, a 'mixed agreement' is an agreement to which one or more of the Communities and the Member States are, or may become, parties, and which contains provisions some elements of which fall within Community competence, and some of which fall within the competence of the Member States.

There has been argument about whether the concept of the mixed agreement is one which should be recognized in Community law, and whether such a concept is compatible with the scheme of the Treaties. There can, however, be little doubt about the existence and legal validity of the concept. A form of mixed agreement is recognized in Article 102 of the Euratom Treaty, which makes

---

[5] For examples, see Ch. 7.
[6] See *Opinion 2/91 (Re ILO Convention 170)* [1993] ECR I-1061 at para. 5. See also pp. 236–7 below.
[7] Ch. 3, pp. 63 ff.
[8] On this, see further Schermers, *A Typology of Mixed Agreements*, in O'Keeffe and Schermers, n. 1 above, 23–33.

explicit provision for treaties which are to be concluded by the Community and one or more of the Member States, and the Court of Justice has on several occasions expressly recognized that some agreements require the participation of the Member States and the Community.[9] In Case 12/86, *Demirel* v. *Stadt Schwäbisch Gmünd*[10] the Court used the term 'mixed agreement' to describe the Association Agreement between the Community and the Member States on the one hand and Turkey on the other. The day-to-day practice of the Community institutions confirms that the concept of the mixed agreement is a well-established part of Community law.

Mixed agreements raise many difficult and interesting legal and political issues about the nature of the Communities and the role of the Communities and the Member States in the international order. The fact that these issues have been more discussed in the learned writings than in the case law of the Court suggests that the problems are greater in theory than in practice. On many points of interest and importance, it is not possible to state the law with certainty. The most that can be done is to identify the principles which, applied to the terms of a particular agreement in the light of the facts of the case, would probably guide the Court's thinking. In any event, too much should not be made of the theoretical difficulties: despite the legal uncertainties, the Community and the Member States in practice participate together effectively and successfully in a wide range of international agreements.

The 'Community' and the 'Member States'

Throughout this Chapter, reference is made to the Community in the singular. There is, however, nothing to prevent more than one of the Communities participating in the same agreement, if the agreement covers matters within the competences of these Communities. In such a case, each Community would have to follow its own procedures for negotiation, conclusion, and implementation of the agreement. Although most mixed agreements involve the EC alone (with the Member States), agreements involving the EC and the ECSC are not uncommon.[11] Agreements involving all three Communities are, however, rare.[12]

If an agreement is mixed, it is usual for all Member States to participate. But it is not always essential that they all do: if an agreement relates to a particular matter concerning only some of the Member States,[13] or within the legal com-

---

[9] *Ruling 1/78 (Re Draft Convention on the Physical Protection of Nuclear Materials)* [1978] ECR 2151; *Opinion 1/78 (Re Draft International Agreement on Natural Rubber)* [1979] ECR 2871; *Opinion 2/91*, n. 6 above; and *Opinion 1/94 (Re WTO Agreement)* [1995] 1 CMLR 205.

[10] [1987] ECR 3719.

[11] Many association agreements are of this type.

[12] The Europe Agreements are an important recent example.

[13] e.g. some of the regional environmental agreements: see Ch. 17.

petence of only some of the Member States,[14] it may be that only these Member States will participate. Participation by fewer than all the Member States usually arises because the substance of the agreement is linked in some way to a geographical area, or is of particular relevance only in that area.

THE 'DUTY OF CLOSE CO-OPERATION' IN THE EXTERNAL RELATIONS OF THE COMMUNITIES

The essence of a mixed agreement is that, to a greater or lesser extent, some of its provisions fall within the competence of the Community, while others fall within the competence of the Member States. In the nature of things, an exact division of powers between the Member States and the Communities within an agreement is usually hard to make. Although responsibility for the negotiation, conclusion, and implementation of the provisions of a proposed agreement could in theory be determined by an analysis of the provisions of the Treaties, in practice the Member States, the Council, and the Commission have always been reluctant to attempt this.[15]

The Court of Justice, for its part, has expressly discouraged attempts to allocate competence between the Member States and the Community.[16] Instead, in considering issues arising under mixed agreements, the Court has emphasized the need for common action, or close co-operation, by the Community and its Member States, 'in close association' with each other in the negotiation and implementation of such agreements. This duty of close co-operation, which follows from what the Court has called the 'requirement of unity in the international representation of the Community',[17] is one of the fundamental principles of the external relations of the Communities.

The origins of the duty of close co-operation may be traced back to the Treaties themselves, and in particular to the duty of loyal co-operation derived by the Court from Articles 86 ECSC, 192 Euratom, and 5 EC.[18] The Court also emphasized the need for Community solidarity in asserting the Community's exclusive competence in relation to the common commercial policy[19] and in its analysis of the draft Agreement on a Laying Up Fund for the Rhine.[20]

A similar duty is contained in Article C TEU: the Council and the Commission are responsible for ensuring the consistency of the external

---

[14] e.g. dependent territory interests: the Indian Ocean Tuna Convention (UK Indian Ocean territories); North Atlantic fisheries (Danish interests in the Faeroes).

[15] See further below, under *Implementation* of mixed agreements.

[16] See *Ruling 1/78*, n. 9 above, at para. 35 (in relation to third parties).

[17] *Ruling 1/78*, n. 9 above, at paras. 34–36 and *Opinion 2/91*, n. 6 above, at para. 36.

[18] For a discussion of the duty of loyal co-operation see P. J. G. Kapteyn and P. VerLoren van Themaat, *Introduction to the Law of the European Communities* (2nd edn., Kluwer, 1989), ch. III, 5.2.

[19] *Opinion 1/75 (Re OECD Local Costs Understanding)* [1975] ECR 1355.

[20] *Opinion 1/76 (Re Draft Agreement on a Laying Up Fund for the Rhine)* [1977] ECR 741.

activities of the Union as a whole in the context of its external relations, security, economic and development policies. The duty in Article C appears to apply
as much to mixed agreements as to any other area of the Union's activity. The
provisions of Title V, which establishes a common foreign and security policy,
are relevant to the outworking of the general duty in Article C, and could apply
to mixed agreements. Title V is considered later in this work.[21]

In the specific context of mixed agreements, the duty of close co-operation
emerged first in *Ruling 1/78 (Re the Draft Convention on the Physical Protection of
Nuclear Materials)*.[22] In that case, the Court was asked to adjudicate on the division of powers between Euratom and the Member States with regard to a draft
Convention on the Physical Protection of Nuclear Materials. Drawing on the
general undertaking in Article 192 Euratom, the Court said that 'the draft convention . . . can be implemented as regards the Community only by means of
a close association between the institutions of the Community and the Member
States both in the process of negotiation and conclusion and in the fulfilment of
the obligations entered into'.[23] With regard to implementation of the convention, the Court said that the Community would implement measures falling
within its competence, the Member States would implement measures falling
within their competence, and the Council would arrange for co-ordination of
the actions of each.[24]

Next, in *Opinion 2/91 (Re ILO Convention 170)*,[25] the Court was faced with an
agreement which covered matters falling within the exclusive competence of the
Community, matters in which the Community and the Member States shared
competence, and matters within the competence of the Member States. The
Court said:[26]

At paragraphs 34 to 36 in *Ruling 1/78*, the Court pointed out that when it appears that
the subject matter of an agreement falls in part within the competence of the Community
and in part within the competence of the Member States, it is important to ensure that
there is a close association between the institutions of the Community and the Member
States both in the process of negotiation and conclusion and in the fulfilment of the
obligations entered into. This duty of co-operation, to which attention was drawn in the
context of the EAEC Treaty, must also apply in the context of the EEC Treaty since it
results from the requirement of unity in the international representation of the
Community.

(37) In this case, co-operation between the Community and the Member States is all
the more necessary in view of the fact that the former cannot, as international law stands
at present, itself conclude an ILO Convention and must do so through the medium of
the Member States.

(38) It is therefore for the Community institutions and the Member States to take all
the measures necessary so as best to ensure such co-operation both in the procedure of

---

[21] Ch. 24.   [22] [1978] ECR 2151.   [23] Ibid., at para. 34.
[24] *Ibid.*, at para. 36.   [25] N. 6 above.   [26] *Ibid.*, at paras. 36 ff.

submission to the competent authority[27] and ratification of Convention 170 and in the implementation of commitments resulting from that Convention.

The agreement under consideration in *Opinion 2/91* was not, strictly speaking, a mixed agreement: the Community as such could not formally become a party to it.[28] The agreement did, however, involve matters within the competence of the Community and of the Member States, and the Court in effect treated it as a mixed agreement. The Court's comments are therefore clearly relevant in the present context.

Most recently, in *Opinion 1/94 (Re the WTO Agreement)*,[29] the issue of co-operation between the Member States and the Community institutions was raised even more acutely. The Commission drew attention to the problems which it said would arise as regards the administration of the various agreements which were part of the WTO package, if the Community and the Member States were recognized as sharing competence to participate in the conclusion of the GATS and TRIPS agreements. The Community's unity of action *vis-à-vis* the rest of the world would, according to the Commission, be undermined and its negotiating power greatly weakened if the Member States were allowed to express their own views in the WTO, or if the 'Community' position had always to be adopted by consensus. The conclusion of the agreement should thus be exclusively for the Community.

In response to the Commission's 'quite legitimate' concern, the Court stressed:[30]

first, that any problems which may arise in implementation of the WTO Agreement and its annexes as regards the co-ordination necessary to ensure unity of action where the Community and the Member States participate jointly cannot modify the answer to the question of competence, that being a prior issue . . .

(108) Next, where it is apparent that the subject matter of an agreement or convention falls in part within the competence of the Community and in part within that of the Member States, it is essential to ensure close co-operation between the Member States and the Community institutions, both in the process of negotiation and conclusion and in the fulfilment of the commitments entered into. That obligation flows from the requirement of unity in the international representation of the Community . . .

(109) The duty to co-operate is all the more imperative in the case of agreements such as those annexed to the WTO Agreement, which are inextricably interlinked, and in view of the cross retaliation measures established by the Dispute Settlement Understanding.[31]

The basic principle is therefore clear: in all aspects of the negotiation, conclusion, and implementation of a mixed agreement, the Member States and the Community are required to co-operate closely and to act in close association.

---

[27] i.e. in the ILO.   [28] N. 6 above, at para. 1.   [29] N. 9 above.
[30] *Ibid.*, at para. 107.   [31] One of the agreements which make up the WTO package.

This duty applies to agreements involving any of the Communities, and is binding on the institutions of the Community as well as the Member States.

Community Co-ordination

The practical consequences of the duty of close co-operation are not easy to describe in detail. As a minimum, the Member States and the institutions are obliged to inform each other of their positions, to seek to reach a common view on matters which fall within the scope of a mixed agreement, and to proceed by common action within the framework of international bodies and conferences. As a practical matter, this involves meetings between the representatives of the Member States and the Community institutions (usually the Commission) at which intended courses of action can be discussed. These meetings—known as 'Community co-ordination'—take place within the framework of the Council, either in Brussels or at the scene of the international forum in which the Community and the Member States are participants.[32]

Community co-ordination in the negotiation of international agreements is well established in practice. Where such negotiations take place under the auspices of an international organization or standing conference, procedures for co-ordination have often become established and have been set down in informal understandings between the Commission and the Council.[33] The precise terms of such co-ordination vary: the aim will be to agree a common statement for delivery by a single spokesman, to which other representatives of the Community and the Member States can rally in support. If there are general rules, they are that the common statement is agreed by consensus; that the Commission expresses the agreed position on matters within exclusive Community competence; and that the Presidency expresses the agreed position on matters in which competence is shared.

'Close Co-operation' and 'Unity'

Within a mixed agreement, the Member States and the Community will only rarely have exactly the same interests and concerns. Inevitably, therefore, the process of agreeing a common position will raise points of difficulty and disagreement, and these may arise at any stage of the life of the agreement. One Member State may wish to take a position divergent from that of the Community and its partners during the negotiation of an agreement; another Member State may prefer not to sign or ratify the agreement, or may wish to denounce the agreement before the Community is ready or willing to do so. The agreement may not be of equal relevance to all the Member States; one

[32] Known as *sur place* co-ordination.
[33] See Ch. 7 for details of co-ordination arrangements in international organizations, in particular the FAO, the UN, and international commodity agreements.

Member State may wish to enter a reservation or make a declaration which is at odds with the position of the other Member States or the Community. The question therefore arises whether the duty of close co-operation requires all the Member States to reach a common position on matters under discussion, or merely to use their best efforts to reach such a position, it being understood that in the end it will be for each Member State to defend its own interests as seems best to it.

There is no judicial authority on this question so conclusions must be tentative, but the position is probably as follows. A distinction should be made between failure to agree a position on matters falling within the exclusive competence of the Community, and failure to agree a common position on matters in respect of which the Community and the Member States share competence.[34] If it proves impossible to reach agreement in the Council on matters within the exclusive competence of the Community, it is difficult to see any room for independent action on such matters by the Member States: by definition no Community position exists, and none can be expressed.[35]

In respect of matters in which competence is shared, on the other hand, the position seems to be that the duty of close co-operation does not amount to an obligation to reach a common position, but only to an obligation to use best endeavours to do so. Thus, if it proves impossible to agree a common position to which the Community and all the Member States can rally, the Member States will be free in the last resort to express national views on matters within national competence, and to exercise their national powers. Some support for this proposition may be derived from the practice of the Council.[36] The informal co-ordination arrangements agreed for Community and Member State participation in bodies such as the FAO suggest that the Member States envisaged a residual right to express national positions if a common position could not be agreed. Similarly, in respect of Member States' dependent territories interests, Declaration (25) in the Final Act of the TEU[37] states that if the interests of the Union and the dependent territories cannot be reconciled, 'the Member States concerned may act separately in the interests of the said [territories], without

---

[34] For examples of 'shared competence', see pp. 63–6 above. In respect of matters exclusively within Member State competence, the Community Treaties have in principle nothing to say (although the provisions of Titles V and VI TEU may of course be relevant).

[35] This is subject to Member States' power (or perhaps duty) to take action in cases of necessity to protect the essential interests of the Community: see Ch. 3 above, at nn. 139–41. As is explained above, this power derives from the Community Treaties: it is not an exercise of the Member States' powers.

[36] And—perhaps—from the Court's comment at para. 109 of *Opinion 1/94*, n. 9 above, that 'the duty to co-operate *is all the more imperative* in the case of agreements such as those annexed to the WTO Agreement' (emphasis added). Arguably, a duty to *reach* a common position is always equally imperative; only a duty to strive to reach a common position can be more imperative in some cases than in others.

[37] Declaration (No. 25) on the representation of the interests of the overseas countries and territories referred to in Art. 227(3) and (5)(a) and (b) of the Treaty establishing the European Community (included in the Final Act of the TEU).

this affecting the Community's interests'. It seems reasonable to apply this by analogy to other areas of Member State competence.

The view that the duty of close co-operation is a duty of best endeavours also fits with the underlying legal position that a mixed agreement involves matters which remain within the sovereign powers of the Member States. It is not difficult to imagine cases in which a Member State might claim that its participation in an agreement was contrary to its national interests or for some other reason undesirable or even impossible. If the agreement was limited to a certain geographical area or a particular regional difficulty, or affected only some of the Member States, there would seem to be no necessity for all the Member States to participate.[38] Similarly, the interests of a Member State in respect of its dependent territories,[39] or its national security interests,[40] might be such as to justify refusal to join a common position. Or a national legislature might reject ratification of a mixed agreement presented to it for approval. In such circumstances, to require a Member State to ratify that agreement as a matter of Community law would risk provoking a constitutional crisis within the Member State and within the Community.

Much would depend on the extent of the Community's competence in the subject matter of the agreement.[41] If the agreement in question related in large measure to areas of extensive or exclusive Community competence, or if Member State competence was of a residual or ancillary character,[42] the Court might place greater emphasis on the need for a common Community front. The same might apply if the participation of most or all of the Member States was necessary to enable the Community to participate fully or effectively[43] in the agreement.

---

[38] e.g., agreements dealing with regional environmental problems. See Ch. 17, n. 13.

[39] On the position in Community law of the dependent territories of a Member State, see *Opinion 1/78*, n. 9 above, at paras. 61 ff. and *Opinion 2/91*, n. 6 above, at para. 35. See also pp. 68 ff above.

[40] Arts. 36, 223, and 224 EC apply in external relations as well as within the Community.

[41] The requirement of unity is arguably stronger in mixed agreements which are in substance bilateral (such as association agreements or co-operation agreements), than in multilateral agreements such as those adopted within the framework of an organization such as the UN. Such bilateral mixed agreements in any event largely concern matters within the competence of the Community.

[42] *Opinion 1/78*, n. 9 above, at para. 56.

[43] If Community votes or financial contributions were linked to the participation of the Member States, for example.

NEGOTIATION, CONCLUSION, AND IMPLEMENTATION OF MIXED
AGREEMENTS

Negotiation

The Authorization

The negotiation of a mixed agreement[44] follows, from the Community's point of view, the same course as the negotiation of any other agreement to which the Community is to be party. The participation of a Community representative in the negotiation of the agreement must be based on an authorization ('mandate') obtained by the Commission in accordance with the appropriate procedure under the relevant Treaty basis. The form of the authorization will depend on the normal practice in the area which the agreement is to cover.[45]

In some cases, it will be clear from an early stage that the bulk of the agreement relates to matters which are within the competence of the Member States, but that certain incidental or accessory aspects involve the competence of the Community.[46] In respect of these parts of the negotiations the Commission usually seeks authority to participate to safeguard the interests of the Community. More often, it is clear that the bulk of the proposed agreement relates to matters within the competence of the Community. Indeed, in some cases, depending on the subject matter of the proposed agreement, it may not be obvious at the stage of agreeing the negotiating authorization that the eventual agreement will require the participation of the Member States. Thus, for example, the authorization granted by the Council may state that the Commission should negotiate the agreement in consultation with the Member States, but all on condition that the question of whether the Member States should eventually be parties to the agreement is held over until the final text of the agreement has been negotiated, and the substance of its provisions is known.[47] This is not as unusual

---

[44] For a discussion of the problems of negotiating a mixed agreement, see Groux, 'Mixed Negotiations' in O'Keeffe and Schermers, n. 1 above, 87.

[45] On negotiating authorizations see Ch. 4, pp. 87 ff above.

[46] e.g. the 1988 Vienna Convention on Illicit Trafficking in Drugs related for the most part to matters which were for the Member States: the penalizing of certain conduct, arrangements for extradition, and so on. But one part of what became Art. 12 of the Convention related to trade in precursors, and the Commission sought and obtained from the Council an authorization to participate in the negotiations in respect of that Art. ([1990] OJ L326/56).

[47] The other side in the negotiations may therefore not know who are to be the parties to the agreement until its final text has been settled. This rather odd situation tends to arise in relation to agreements: (1) which are in substance bilateral rather than multilateral (that is to say, where the 'Community' in the wider political sense intends to negotiate with another country or closely associated group of countries); or (2) which relate to areas where Community competence predominates, e.g. in association agreements and certain trade and co-operation agreements. An example of the former is the negotiation of the Agreement on the European Economic Area in 1991 and 1992 which was conducted by the Commission on the basis that the question whether it should be mixed or not was left until the end: only at a late stage of the negotiation was it agreed that the Member States would be parties along with the Community. An example of the latter is the Agreement

in the Council's practice as at first sight one might suppose it ought to be. As has been noted above,[48] it is usual to leave the question of the appropriate legal basis for conclusion of an agreement until the agreement has been negotiated. The decision on whether the Member States should participate may sometimes be left until the final text and content of the agreement are known.

Content of the Authorization

The authorization will require that the agreement should contain a clause allowing for the participation of the Community in its own name. It will also be important for Community negotiators to consider whether special provision needs to be made for the terms on which the Community should participate[49] (for example the financial contribution to be made by the Community); for the voting rights (if any) of the Community and the Member States, and whether the Community's rights to vote are to be linked to the number of its Member States who are parties to the agreement; for a declaration of competence, where required;[50] and for the means by which the Community should express its consent to be bound.

Co-ordination

The authorization will also make provision for co-ordination of the Community's position during the negotiations. Although in theory the Member States and the Community could each negotiate independently in respect of the areas of the proposed agreement falling to their respective competences, in practice it is rare for the Community and the Member States to negotiate independently, and co-ordination, or at least consultation, among the Member States and the Commission generally takes place as a matter of course in all negotiations in which the Community and the Member States are involved.

Conduct of the Negotiations

In principle negotiations in respect of matters involving an element of Community competence should be conducted by the Commission,[51] and this

establishing the WTO which was signed in 1994. The arguments over competence in relation to that agreement were so acute throughout that no negotiating directives were ever agreed and the whole question of Member State participation was eventually referred to the ECJ for an opinion under Art. 228(6) EC (*Opinion 1/94*, n. 9 above).

[48] Ch. 4, pp. 82–3.

[49] The importance of clauses allowing for Community participation is considered at length in O'Keeffe and Schermers, n. 1 above. See, in particular, the contributions from Ehlermann (3–21), Simmonds (199–206) (focussing on the text of UNCLOS III), and especially Feenstra (207–48). On clauses which make Community participation in an agreement conditional on Member State participation, see G. Close, 'Subordination Clauses in Mixed Agreements' (1985) 34 *ICLQ* 382.

[50] On declarations of competence, see p. 161 below.   [51] Arts. 228(1) EC and Art. 101 Euratom.

accords with the Community's practice. Where the constitutional arrangements of the forum in which an agreement is being negotiated do not allow for the formal participation of a representative of the Community, the Presidency may speak for the Community, or a Commission representative may speak from behind the nameplate of the current Presidency. Exceptionally, where the substance of what is being negotiated falls mainly within the competence of the Member States, but contains elements within Community competence, the negotiations may be conducted by the Presidency.

Initialling, Signature, and Provisional Application

The establishment of the text of an agreement after the conclusion of negotiations is within the authority conferred by the negotiating authorization. Accordingly, where the Commission has negotiated an agreement, it is entitled to adopt the final text, usually by initialling, even when the agreement is one in which the Member States and the Community will participate. If the Member States have also participated in the negotiations, they, too, are of course entitled to initial the text.

Whether an agreement requires the signature[52] of intending parties before the definitive expression of their consent to be bound depends in the first place on its terms. If the Community is required to sign, the necessary authority must be obtained in accordance with the procedures applicable under the Treaties.[53] The Member States will sign in their own right in accordance with their respective constitutional procedures. If necessary, Full Powers or similar authority will have to be obtained by the Community representative, and by the representatives of the Member States.

Where an agreement is subject to subsequent approval or ratification, there seems to be no rule of practice or law that the Member States and the Community should sign at the same time. If the agreement is negotiated at a conference, or in the framework of an organization, the signature stage may take place at the conclusion of the conference or meeting, and in such circumstances the Community and the Member States would no doubt all sign at the same time.

Some agreements provide that the intending parties may provisionally apply some or all of the agreement pending its definitive entry into force. The procedures to be followed within the Community for the provisional application of a mixed agreement would in principle be the same as those followed for the provisional application of an agreement to which the Community alone was a party.[54] The timing of notifications of provisional application by the Community and the Member States, and the possibility of provisional application by

---

[52] Where signature has the effect of expressing final consent to be bound, the considerations outlined below in relation to 'conclusion' of agreements apply.
[53] See further Ch. 4   [54] Ch. 4.

fewer than all the Member States would have to resolved in the light of the duty of close co-operation described above. No doubt similar considerations would apply as apply in respect of conclusion of a mixed agreement.[55]

Conclusion

The procedures by which the Community and the Member States approve or ratify agreements depend on their respective constitutional requirements. For the Community, conclusion of an agreement will require the adoption of an act in accordance with the appropriate legal basis[56] approving or authorizing the conclusion of the agreement on behalf of the Community, and authorizing the Commission or the Presidency, or both, or some other representative of the Community, to communicate the fact of the Community's approval to the other party or parties to the agreement by arranging for deposit of the instrument of approval with the depositary, or otherwise as provided in the agreement. Each of the Member States would likewise have to arrange for formal approval of the agreement in accordance with its own constitutional procedures.

Simultaneous Ratification or Approval

Article 102 Euratom provides that agreements concluded with a third State or international organization to which, in addition to the Community, one or more Member States are parties shall not enter into force until the Commission has been notified by all the Member States concerned that those agreements have become applicable in accordance with the provisions of their national laws. This is usually taken to mean that the Member States and the Community must co-ordinate the deposit of their instruments of ratification or approval so that deposit takes place simultaneously.

No such provision exists in the EC or ECSC Treaty, but there is a strong rule of practice that the Community's instrument of approval is not deposited until all the Member States have deposited theirs. The Commission has frequently proposed that the Member States should not deposit their instruments of ratification or accession or otherwise become parties to an agreement until all the Member States and the Community are in a position to do so together, and some Council decisions authorizing Community participation in certain agreements contain a provision[57] to that effect. Simultaneous ratification or

---

[55] Examples of mixed agreements provisionally applied by fewer than all the Member States include the Agreement amending Pt. XI of UNCLOS III ([1994] OJ L215/10) and the 1994 International Cocoa Agreement ([1994] OJ L52/25).

[56] See the discussion of choice of legal basis in Ch. 4.

[57] Art. 3 of Dec. 88/540 concerning the conclusion of the Vienna Convention for the Protection of the ozone layer and the Montreal Protocol on substances that deplete the ozone layer ([1988] OJ L297/8) requires the Member States to take the necessary steps, by 31 Oct. 1988 at the latest,

approval is obviously a way of giving effect to the duty of close co-operation identified by the Court, and also has several practical advantages. The obligations under a mixed agreement are usually partly for the Member States to perform, and partly for the Community: a coherent legal position on the part of the Community and its Member States thus requires—in theory—that all become parties at the same time. Similarly, the exercise of Community rights under the agreement (such as voting rights) may be directly linked to the number of Member States which are parties.

Member States have often been reluctant to accept a legal obligation to deposit their instruments of ratification or approval at a particular time or in a certain manner. For some Member States, a requirement to ratify an agreement, or to ratify it within a certain time, may cause constitutional difficulties.[58] These sensitivities have meant that the Community's practice in this matter is not uniform.

Implementation

International agreements are binding on the parties to them and must be performed in good faith.[59] The Community and the Member States therefore have to ensure full and timely implementation of mixed agreements. If part of the agreement relates to matters within the competence of the Member States and part to matters within Community competence, implementation can evidently be ensured only by co-operation between the Member States and the Community institutions, at all stages. In considering the issues which arise in implementing mixed agreements, it is convenient to distinguish between the adoption of legislative measures necessary to give effect to an agreement, and the day-to-day application of the provisions of the agreement.

Adoption of Legislation to give Effect to a Mixed Agreement

Some agreements may have effect within the legal orders of the Community or the Member States without the adoption of implementing legislation.[60] Where, however, adoption of legislation is required to give effect to a mixed agreement, the measures necessary to give effect to the agreement will sometimes depend

to permit the deposit as far as possible simultaneously of the Member States' and the EEC's instruments of ratification, acceptance, or approval of the Vienna Convention and the Montreal Protocol.

[58] In the UK, e.g., the Ponsonby Rule (a constitutional practice) requires the Government to lay before Parliament for 21 sitting days the text of any agreement which has been signed subject to ratification.

[59] *Pacta sunt servanda*: see Ch. 5, pp. 122 ff.

[60] e.g., if the provisions relate to matters which do not require adoption of legislation for their implementation (such as commitments to engage in political dialogue), or if the provisions of the agreement are clear, precise, and unconditional and thus capable of conferring rights and imposing duties directly without implementing legislation .

on the Community institutions and sometimes on the Member States according to the substance of the provisions and the state of Community law at the
time.[61] Implementation will require close co-operation between the Member
States and the Community institutions, on the basis of the principles which governed the division of powers with regard to negotiation and conclusion of the
agreement.[62] The relevant provisions of the Community Treaties, together with
the provisions of the agreement to be implemented, which, once it has been
concluded by the Community, forms an integral part of Community law, will
provide an appropriate legal basis for the necessary implementing measures on
the part of the Community.[63] For the rest it will be for the Member States to
adopt appropriate measures, each in its own jurisdiction.

In the context of the Euratom Treaty, it will be for the Council to arrange
for co-ordination of the actions of the Member States and the Community.[64]
More generally, the Council and the Commission are responsible for ensuring
the consistency of the external activities of the Union as a whole in the context
of its external relations, economic and development policies.[65]

Day-to-day Application of the Provisions of a Mixed Agreement

Mixed Agreements are Part of the Community Legal Order

The general principle is clear: agreements concluded by the Community are an
integral part of Community law, binding on the institutions of the Community
and the Member States. There can be no doubt that 'agreements concluded by
the Community' in this context includes mixed agreements: the Court's *dicta* on
this subject are capable of general application, and many of the cases which
have come before the Court have concerned mixed agreements.[66]

It follows that the consequences attributed by the Court to agreements concluded by the Community alone are in principle equally applicable to mixed
agreements, at least in respect of those provisions of such agreements which are
within the competence of the Community. The Court has said[67] that it follows
from the Community nature of the provisions of agreements concluded by the
Community that their effects cannot be allowed to vary in the Community
according to whether their implementation in practice is the responsibility of
the Community institutions or the Member States, and in the latter case,
according to the attitude taken by the law of each Member State regarding the
effects produced by international agreements in its internal legal system. Thus

---

[61] Case 104/81 *Hauptzollamt Mainz* v. *Kupferberg* [1982] ECR 3641 at para. 12.
[62] In the case of the Euratom Community, Art. 115 provides a basis for co-ordination of the
actions of the Community and the Member States in the implementation.
[63] *Ruling 1/78*, n. 9 above, at para. 36.   [64] Art. 115 Euratom.
[65] Art. C TEU.
[66] e.g. Case 12/86, n. 10 above, the case most frequently cited by the Court as the source of the
basic principle.
[67] Case 104/81, n. 61 above, at para. 14.

it is the responsibility of the Court, in the framework of its jurisdiction to interpret agreements, to ensure that they are interpreted uniformly throughout the Community. The Court accordingly has, in principle, jurisdiction to interpret the provisions of such an agreement. The agreement may thus, on the usual conditions, have direct effect; and its provisions may be a basis for the challenge of Community or national legislation which contravenes it. And the implementation of the agreement may be the subject of infringement action by the Commission.[68]

The difficulty is to know whether these consequences always apply to every provision of a mixed agreement, or only to those provisions which fall within matters within the competence of the Community. In principle, the jurisdiction of the Court of Justice and the enforcement powers of the Commission should be exercised only in respect of those parts of an agreement which fall within the competence of the Community. Much will, no doubt, depend on the agreement in question. The Court has described its role in the interpretation and application of mixed agreements in terms which are wide enough to encompass all the provisions of such agreements, but the case law to date has mainly concerned association agreements, and it is arguable that these are special. Their substance tends to relate to matters in which Community competence predominates, and their purpose is to associate the third State with the activities of the Community by applying the rights and freedoms in the Treaties in relations with that State, for the benefit of Community nationals and the nationals of that State. An extensive jurisdiction for the Court might be more appropriate in respect of such agreements than in respect of other mixed agreements. However, even in association agreements, certain provisions may, by reason of their inherent nature or an express reserve contained in the agreement, lie outside the jurisdiction of the Court.[69] Examples might be provisions which related entirely to an area excluded from the Court's jurisdiction under the Treaties,[70] or which were excluded from judicial scrutiny by a provision of the agreement itself, or which were in substance obligations on the Member States acting jointly within areas of their competence,[71] rather than on the institutions of the Community. There seems no reason why the Court should be entitled to interpret and apply such provisions.[72]

---

[68] On these consequences, see further Ch. 5.

[69] See Darmon A.G. in Case 12/86, n. 10 above, at para. 12.

[70] See Art. L of the TEU.

[71] Joined Cases C–181 and C–248/91 *Parliament* v. *Council and Commission* [1993] ECR I–3685 where joint acts of the Member States were immune from review under Art. 173 EC.

[72] See D. Anderson, *References to the European Court* (Sweet & Maxwell, 1995), at para. 3–038: 'Even the Commission considered in *Demirel* that it would be illogical to refer for review by the European Court provisions over which the Member States have exclusive jurisdiction. Certainly, neither logic nor necessity requires the Court to accept jurisdiction over a severable provision of a mixed agreement, lying outside the ambit of Community law and intended to bind only one or more Member States.'

Similarly, it is doubtful whether the Commission can investigate and bring before the Court by way of infringement proceedings the application by Member States of provisions which are wholly within the competence of the Member States. It would first seem necessary to show that the Member State's action or omission—in an area within its own competence—amounted also to a breach of its obligations under the Treaties.

Participation of the Community and the Member States in Bodies set up by an Agreement

Where a mixed agreement establishes an international organization, or other decision-making body, arrangements have to be made for the presentation of the position of the Community and the Member States within such organization or body. Matters to be addressed will include the status of the Community in such a forum; the Community's rights to speak and vote; the number of votes to be attributed to it; the co-ordination and presentation of the views of the Community and the Member States, and so on. The basic principle has been mentioned above: the Member States and the Community institutions are under a duty of close co-operation in the presentation of their views in such fora. The outworking of this principle is considered further in the Chapters on International Organizations and on Association Agreements.

Liabilities of the Community and the Member States to Third States

Within the Community legal order, the Community and the Member States are responsible for the implementation of those parts of a mixed agreement which fall within their respective competences.[73] At the international level, the position is probably more complicated. The only authoritative discussion of the liability of the Community and the Member States under a mixed agreement is in the opinion of Advocate-General Jacobs in Case C–316/91, where he said:[74]

The [Lomé] Convention was concluded as a mixed agreement (i.e. by the Community and its Member States jointly) and has essentially a bilateral character. This is made clear in Article 1 which states that the Convention is concluded between the Community and its Member States of the one part, and the ACP States of the other part. *Under a mixed agreement the Community and the Member States are jointly liable unless the provisions of the agreement point to the opposite conclusion.* (Emphasis added)

This statement is capable of two interpretations. On a narrow reading, it could mean that a mixed agreement which is of an essentially bilateral character entails the joint liability of the Member States and the Community. This would include most association agreements and trade and co-operation agreements, where the essence of the agreement is that an arrangement has been entered into between the 'Community side' on the one hand and a third State or group

---

[73] On this see C. Tomuschat, 'Liability for Mixed Agreements', in O'Keeffe and Schermers, n. 1 above, 125–32, and G. Gaja, 'The European Community's Rights and Obligations under Mixed Agreements', in the same vol. at 133–40.

[74] 1994 ECR I–625, at para. 69.

of States on the other. The bilateral character of such agreements, and the joint nature of liability on the Community side, are underlined by the fact that the Community side will usually speak with one voice in bodies set up to monitor and apply the terms of the agreements.

The wider interpretation of the Advocate-General's comment is that all mixed agreements entered into by the Community and the Member States in principle entail joint liability of the Community and the Member States. Although in general each party to an international agreement is responsible for performance of its own obligations, and joint liability under an agreement is not usually to be presumed, the special circumstances of the Community and the Member States may amount to an exception to this rule. The Community and the Member States generally act together in pursuit of a common policy. In many areas, the legal power to fulfil the obligations in an agreement is shared between them: neither can offer complete performance. As has been seen, it is frequently very difficult to determine where, as between the Community and the Member States, legal powers lie. For the third party, therefore, the most convenient conclusion is that the Community and the Member States assume joint obligations, the performance of which all are required to assure. This view is consistent with the Court's emphasis on the 'requirement of unity' in the external representation of the Community, and it has support also in dicta of the Court in cases such as *Ruling 1/78*[75] and *Kupferberg*.[76]

What exactly the consequences of 'joint liability' are is harder to say. It is unlikely that the Community and the Member States can be held to be jointly and severally liable for all the obligations in the agreement, so that an aggrieved third party would be entitled to seek full satisfaction from any of the Member States or the Community. But it seems that in some sense the performance of obligations under a mixed agreement is (unless the agreement provides to the contrary) a matter for the Member States and the Community together, not for each separately.

The problem of the respective liabilities of the Community and the Member States will arise acutely in agreements where the rights and obligations of the Community and the Member States are inter-linked, so that the possibility of 'cross-retaliation' arises: that is to say, where the nature of the agreement is such that a third party is entitled to respond to Community or Member State action in one area covered by the agreement by retaliation in another area.[77] If the action and retaliation take place in respect of matters entirely within the competence of the Community or entirely within the competence of the Member States, the problems are less intractable. If, however, the third party responds to action in an area of Member State competence by retaliation in an area

---

[75] N. 9 above, at para. 35.   [76] N. 61 above, at paras. 13 and 14.

[77] The most important example is the WTO Agreement and the agreements associated with it, but in principle, the issue could arise in any international agreement to which the Community and the Member States were parties.

within the competence of the Community, the need for close co-operation between the Community and the Member States is evident.

Rights of the Community and the Member States under Mixed Agreements

The enforcement by the Community side of its rights under a mixed agreement gives rise to problems similar to those identified in the preceding section. Again, a close association between the Community and the Member States is necessary to ensure that the agreement operates effectively. In principle, if the right to be enforced falls within an area of exclusive Community competence, the exercise of that right is primarily a matter for the Community. If the matter falls within the competence of the Member States, in principle it is for the Member State or States concerned to decide whether to enforce their rights or not. But, in each case, the duty of close co-operation means that the enforcement of such rights must be undertaken against the background of the wider common interest of the Community and the Member States, and after appropriate co-ordination.

Allocation of Competences between the Community and the Member States in Mixed Agreements

The Community and the Member States have been reluctant to allocate their respective competences publicly, for several reasons.[78] It is rarely easy to reach agreement within the Community on the exact extent of Community competence in a given area. And, because of the difficulty of determining in most areas where the Community's competence begins and ends, any statement of the Community's competence would have to drawn in ambiguous or vague terms,[79] and would probably be of little assistance in answering questions about the precise allocation between the Community and the Member States of responsibilities under the agreement. In addition, the boundaries of Community competence change constantly and a statement made at the time of conclusion of an agreement will quickly become outdated as Community law develops and expands.

Furthermore, the Court has declared that as a matter of Community law, there can be no obligation on the Community and the Member States to provide such a division of competences:[80]

It is not necessary to set out and determine as regards the other parties to the convention, the division of powers in this respect between the Community and the Member States, particularly as it may change in the course of time. It is sufficient to state to other contracting parties that the matter gives rise to a division of powers within the Community, it being understood that the exact nature of that division is a domestic question in which third parties have no need to intervene.

---

[78] See J. Temple Lang, 'The Ozone Layer Convention: A New Solution to the Question of EC Participation in "Mixed" Agreements' (1986) 23 *CMLRev.* 157.

[79] See pp. 17–19 above.   [80] *Ruling 1/78*, n. 9 above.

For these reasons, there is usually no disposition on the part of the Community (either of the Commission or the Member States) to indicate for the benefit of the outside world where, as between the Community and the Member States, competence for a particular matter rests.

Third parties to mixed agreements have, however, frequently insisted on a demarcation of the respective responsibilities of the Community and the Member States, particularly in multilateral mixed agreements such as those adopted within the framework of the United Nations. A statement of the respective competences of the Community and the Member States has often been made a condition of Community participation in such agreements.[81] Where they are required, these statements, commonly known as 'declarations of competence', take the form of a public statement made on behalf of the Community, usually at the time of deposit of the Community instrument of approval or accession. Such a statement describes the Community's competence in general terms, sometimes by reference to Articles of the Community Treaties, sometimes by listing the measures adopted within the Community on the subject matter in respect of which Community competence is claimed. The declaration usually points out that the Community's competence is liable to change over time and that the Community therefore reserves to itself the right to make further declarations of competence as its powers develop.[82] It also states that the declaration is made without prejudice to the allocation of responsibilities of the Community and the Member States under the Treaties.

The legal effect of such declarations is uncertain. From the point of view of international law, a declaration of competence is probably best regarded as an instrument made by one of the parties in connection with the conclusion of a treaty and accepted by the other parties as an instrument related to the treaty within the meaning of Article 31(2)(b) of the Vienna Convention on the Law of Treaties.[83] As such, it forms part of the context of the treaty for the purposes of its interpretation. In some cases, however, the agreement being concluded by the Community and the Member States has appeared to define the obligations of the Community by reference to the declaration of competence, and the wording of the declaration arguably expresses the extent of the Community's

---

[81] e.g., declarations of competence have been demanded as a condition of Community participation in the following agreements: the 3rd UN Convention on the Law of the Sea (Annex IX) (Misc 11 (1983); Cmnd. 8941; (1982) 21 ILM 1261); the Vienna Convention on Illicit Trafficking in Narcotic Drugs and Psychotropic Substances (Art. 27(2)) ((1992) UKTS 26, Cm1923); the Vienna Convention for the Protection of the Ozone Layer (Art. 13 (3) ([1988] OJ L297/8); the Convention on Biological Diversity (Art. 34(3)) ([1993] OJ L309/1); the Framework Convention on Climate Change (Art. 22(3) ([1994] OJ L33/1). See further Ch. 17, p. 331.

[82] e.g., the Community has submitted two supplementary declarations of competence to the FAO: in 1992 (to take account of the adoption of a common organization of the market in bananas) and in 1994 (to take account of amendments in the TEU).

[83] The fact that the Communities are not parties to the VCLT or the VCLTIO would not in most cases be material: the provisions of Art. 31 probably represent customary international law; and in any event declarations are usually made by the Community and the Member States jointly.

obligation. The principal effect of the declaration of competence is probably to put the third parties on notice of those areas covered by the agreement in which Community competence may exist.

As a matter of Community law, a mere declaration of competence by the Council and the Commission cannot override the legal position under the Treaties,[84] and, in the case of a dispute, it is ultimately for the Court to decide where competence on a given matter lies. The terms of a declaration of competence will be a helpful indication, but not decisive. In practical terms, where a matter is included within the scope of Community competence in a declaration of competence, it will be harder for the Member States to deny the Community a *locus* in such matters, or to claim that the matter is exclusively for them.[85]

Where the division of responsibilities is not clear from the terms of the agreement or from any accompanying declarations, it may be possible to infer where competence lies from the conduct of the Community and its Member States during the implementation of the agreement, or from their conduct in other areas. But in the end, the relative responsibilities of the Community and its Member States can only be determined by an analysis of the Treaties and any legislation made under them.

Amendment

Amendments of a mixed agreement may, at least in theory, relate to provisions of the agreement which fall within Member State competence, or to provisions within Community competence, or to provisions in respect of which competence is shared between the Community and the Member States. In law, amendments to an international agreement, like the agreement itself, only bind States and organizations which have accepted them. In principle, therefore, if the Community and the Member States all accepted the original agreement, amendments to that agreement would also have to be accepted by the Community and the Member States. If the proposed amendment related entirely to matters within Community competence, or to matters within Member State competence, it would be theoretically possible that only the Community or the Member States, as the case may be, would need to accept

---

[84] Compare *Opinion 1/94*, n. 9 above, at paras. 52, 60, and 61.

[85] It has been argued that a declaration of competence can have the effect of conferring on the Community powers which were uncertain or non-existent before the declaration was made. It is certainly difficult to deny that such a declaration carries the implication that the Community has competence for the matters described in the declaration. But (a) while there is no doubt that the existence of an international obligation binding the Community in respect of a particular matter can imply internal competence to legislate in respect of that matter, to deduce such an obligation from the terms of a declaration of competence is probably to go too far; (b) the argument leads to the conclusion that no international agreement can ever be *ultra vires* the Community; and (c) it ignores the fact that the measure of the powers of any organization is its constitution—in the case of the Communities, the Treaties. The Court has frequently pointed out that a mere practice cannot alter the legal position as it arises from the Treaties.

the amendment.[86] But such an amendment would not bind those parties which had not accepted it. In practice, therefore, amendments to mixed agreements usually have to be accepted by the Community and the Member States which were parties to the original agreement.

The amendment has to be accepted or approved by the Community and the Member States in accordance with their respective constitutional requirements. So far as the Community is concerned, the legal basis for approval of an amendment is not necessarily the same as the legal basis for conclusion of the original agreement: the legal basis of each act of the Council or Commission must be determined in the light of the aim and content of that act.[87] Once the necessary internal procedures have been completed by the Community and the Member States, each will have to express its consent to be bound in the manner prescribed by the original agreement or by the amending instrument. The same considerations as apply at the stage of conclusion apply in resolving questions such as simultaneous deposit of instruments of acceptance; acceptance by fewer than all the Member States; and so on.[88]

Termination

The right of parties to an agreement to terminate their involvement in it depends on the terms of the agreement. If the agreement is silent on the point, it is necessary to refer to general rules of international law.[89]

Where the Community and the Member States are agreed on the need for termination of a mixed agreement, each has to terminate its commitment in accordance with the agreement and the rules of international law. The Community, for its part, must adopt an internal act[90] authorizing formal withdrawal from the agreement. The legal basis for such an act will be assessed on the usual criteria.[91] The legal basis for termination of an agreement is not necessarily the same as that[92] for the original decision to become a party. In addition, each of the Member States will have to denounce the agreement in respect of its interest in it. These acts of denunciation will, of course, be for each Member State to adopt in accordance with its constitutional requirements.[93]

---

[86] If, e.g., a Protocol or Supplementary Agreement related entirely to matters within the scope of the common commercial policy, the Community alone should become party.

[87] See, further, Ch. 4. [88] See pp. 154–5 above.

[89] Contained in the VCLT between States for those States party thereto, and in customary international law for those States not party to it, and for the Community. See I. Brownlie, *Principles of Public International Law* (4th edn., Clarendon, 1990) 616–26; I. Sinclair, *The Vienna Convention on the Law of Treaties* (2nd edn., Manchester University Press, 1984), ch. VI.

[90] Decision or regulation as appropriate: see above p. 81.

[91] On choice of legal basis, see pp. 81 ff above.

[92] e.g., the legal basis for conclusion might no longer be appropriate because of amendments to the Treaties.

[93] Such practice as there is bears out this analysis: see the discussion of the Association Agreement between the Community and Yugoslavia in Ch. 19.

If a Member State wished unilaterally to terminate its involvement in a mixed agreement, its proper course would no doubt be to advise the other Member States and the Commission of its decision and the reasons for it. If there were no objections to the proposed course of action, it is difficult to see what could prevent the Member State from implementing its decision in accordance with the agreement. If there were objections,[94] the difficult and unresolved question of the Member State's powers of independent action in the framework of a mixed agreement would arise.[95]

---

[94] A Member State's absence could conceivably affect the Community's ability to participate in the agreement if Community voting rights depended on the number of its Member States who were parties.

[95] On this, see further above at pp. 156 ff.

7

The Communities and International Organizations

This Chapter is principally about the Communities'[1] relations with and participation in multilateral[2] international organizations[3] established among States under public international law.[4] The Communities' participation in international conferences will be touched on briefly.

THE COMMUNITIES' RELATIONS WITH INTERNATIONAL ORGANIZATIONS

That the Communities have power to conduct legal relations with international organizations as well as with States is clearly established in the practice of the Community institutions. Such relations broadly take three forms: the conclusion of agreements; arrangements for administrative co-operation; and the establishment of diplomatic or similar relations.

---

[1] In most cases, the European Community. On the Communities' participation in international organizations, see J. P. Jacqué 'La participation de la Communauté économique européenne aux organisations internationales universelles' [1975] *AFDI* 923; J. Groux and P. Manin, *The European Communities in the International Order* (European Perspectives, 1985), Pt. 1, ch. III, 41–54.

[2] Association agreements, and other agreements entered into by the Community and the Member States, establish councils and committees to monitor the application and implementation of the agreement. On these, see Ch. 20.

[3] On international organizations generally, see Bowett, *The Law of International Institutions* (Stevens, 1987); Brownlie, *Principles of Public International Law* (4th edn., Clarendon Press, 1990), ch. XXX; Satow, *Guide to Diplomatic Practice* (5th edn., Longman, 1979), chs. 34–42; Schermers, *International Institutional Law* (2nd edn., A. W. Sijthoff, 1980).

[4] The Communities also participate in bodies which have international aims or objectives but are established within a domestic legal system (a recent example is the International Association for the Promotion of Co-operation with Scientists from the Independent States of the Former Soviet Union, established under Belgian law), and in what may be called 'private international organizations' (such as the International Chamber of Commerce or the International Commission on Civil Status: see, further, *Relations between the European Community and International Organizations* (Commission, 1989), 366–76). The legal problems raised in such cases differ from those arising from the Community's participation in organizations established under international law, and consist principally in determining whether the Community has power to enter into the necessary arrangements within the applicable domestic legal system, and whether that legal system recognizes the power of the Community so to participate, and permits it to do so. The representation of the Community interest in such bodies is usually undertaken by the Commission: cf. Art. 211 EC.

Conclusion of Agreements between the Communities and International Organizations

The Communities' powers to conclude agreements[5] extend to agreements with international organizations as well as with States. Article 228 EC refers to 'agreements between the Community and one or more States or international organizations'; and Article 101 Euratom similarly provides that the Community may conclude agreements with 'a third State, [or] an international organization'. There is no analogous provision in the ECSC Treaty, but it is reasonable to infer that the general power to conclude international agreements derived by implication from the ECSC Treaty encompasses a power to conclude agreements with international organizations, within the areas of the ECSC's competence.[6] The Treaties also contain express powers enabling the Communities to conclude agreements with international organizations in particular fields.[7] For each Community, such agreements would have to be concluded in accordance with the procedural requirements which apply to the conclusion of agreements with States.

Administrative Co-operation between the Communities and International Organizations

The general rule under the EC and Euratom Treaties is that it is for the Commission to 'maintain such relations as are appropriate with all international organizations'.[8] In particular, it is for the Commission to ensure the maintenance of all appropriate relations with the organs of the United Nations, of its specialized agencies and of the GATT.[9] There is no analogous power in the ECSC Treaty, but such a role is consistent with the Commission's functions in the scheme of that Treaty.[10]

The Commission's exercise of these powers is subject to no formal control by the Council,[11] but the apparently wide scope for action afforded by the Treaty

---

[5] On the meaning of 'agreement' see Ch. 4.   [6] On the powers of the ECSC, see Ch. 23.
[7] In the EC Treaty: Art. 109(3) (agreements concerning monetary or foreign exchange regime matters); Art. 113(3) (the common commercial policy); Art. 130m(2) (co-operation in Community research, technological development, and demonstration in implementation of the multi-annual framework programme); Art. 130r(4) (the environment); and Art. 130y (development policy). In the Euratom Treaty: Art. 10 (research programme); Art. 64 (framework agreements for the supply of ores, source materials, or special fissile materials from outside the Community); Art. 73 (agreements for the delivery of products within the province of the Agency); and Art. 77 (safeguards).
[8] Arts. 229(2) EC and 199(2) Euratom. See Mégret, *Le droit de la Communauté Européenne* (Brussels, 1980), vol. 12, *Relations Extérieures*, 64 ff.
[9] Arts. 229(1) EC and 199(1) Euratom.   [10] See Ch. 23.
[11] The Luxembourg Accords of 28 and 29 Jan. 1966 state (sect. (a), para. 5) that 'Within the scope of the application of Art. 162 EEC, the Council and the Commission will consult together on the advisability of, and the procedure for, and the nature of any links which the Commission might establish with international organizations pursuant to Art. 229 of the Treaty'. This is, however, a unilateral statement of the Council and has not been accepted by the Commission as

provisions in question is misleading. The Commission's powers relate to general co-operation of an administrative nature only, and are not a basis for the conclusion of agreements binding the Communities as regards their policies or action in any particular area, nor for Community membership in an international organization. The numerous understandings and arrangements entered into by the Commission with international organizations[12] on the basis of these general powers include commitments between the Commission and the organizations concerned to consult on matters of common interest; to exchange information and documents on such matters; to encourage participation in each others' affairs by exchange of representatives; to consult about possible joint undertakings in fields of common interest; and to establish joint working groups. Some provide that the Communities should have observer status. It seems accepted that the Commission may not, under these powers, commit the other institutions or the Communities to action or expenditure going beyond what may be necessary to maintain administrative links and co-operation between the Community and the organization with which the arrangement is made.[13]

The effect of such arrangements in international law is uncertain. Some are concluded in the name of the Community, rather than the Commission, and employ forms and language usually associated with agreements intended to be legally binding.[14] However, the better view is that 'administrative agreements' concluded by the Commission under the powers conferred on it in Articles 229 EC and 199 Euratom should be regarded as informal arrangements between the executive authorities of one organization and the executive authorities of another, committing the Commission as one of the Community institutions and the Secretariat of the other organization involved in its capacity as Secretariat or other similar organ, rather than the organizations themselves as subjects of international law.[15]

This general power to co-operate with international organizations is supplemented in two ways. First, no doubt because the authors of the Treaties envisaged particularly close co-operation between the Communities and other regional bodies, special provision is made in the Treaties for co-operation with the Council of Europe and the OECD. Thus, it is provided that the European

---

binding on it. For the text of the Luxembourg Accords, see 1966 Bull. CE No. 3, 8; Mégret, n. 8 above, vol. 9, *Le Conseil, etc.*, Annexe, 46; *Encyclopædia of European Community Law* (Sweet & Maxwell, looseleaf), Pt. B–13.001. See also Mégret, n. 8 above, vol. 12, 65.

[12] These instruments have been collected and published in *Relations*, n. 4 above.

[13] See Mégret, n. 8 above, 67, commenting on the scope of Art. 229 EC. Mégret, 64, suggests that if the commitments undertaken by the Commission remained within the constraints of what was necessary to maintain administrative co-operation, they might bind the other Community institutions.

[14] See Mégret, n. 8 above, 64.

[15] Compare the position of the UN Secretariat, which cannot conclude a 'formal agreement of co-operation' with an international organization in the absence of an express authorization from the UN General Assembly: Memorandum of the UN Legal Counsel of 27 Apr. 1981 ([1981] UNJY 149, ST/LEG SER.C/19).

Community and the Euratom Community 'shall establish all appropriate forms of co-operation with the Council of Europe'.[16] In the case of the ECSC, 'relations are to be maintained between the institutions of the Community and the Council of Europe as provided in a Protocol annexed to [the ECSC] Treaty'.[17] Further, the European Community and the Euratom Community are required 'to establish close co-operation with the OECD, the details of which are to be established by common accord'.[18] Under the ECSC Treaty, the Commission is required 'to maintain all appropriate relations with . . . the Organization for European Economic Co-operation'[19] and to keep that organization regularly informed of the activities of the Community.

The form which co-operation with the OECD and the Council of Europe has taken in practice is considered further below. It will be noted that, in contrast to Article 229 EC and Article 199 Euratom, these powers refer to co-operation between the 'Community' and the organization concerned. This does not preclude administrative co-operation between the Commission and the Secretariats of the Council of Europe or the OECD; but co-operation going beyond mere administrative co-operation would require the procedures for the conclusion of agreements by the Communities. The reference to the 'Community' in these Articles may also point to the possibility of co-operation between these bodies and the other Community institutions.[20]

Secondly, the Treaties require the Community institutions and the Member States to establish relations with the competent international organizations in order to foster progress in the peaceful uses of nuclear energy;[21] and to foster co-operation in the field of education,[22] and the spheres of vocational training,[23] culture,[24] and public health.[25] The 'competent organizations' include organizations within the United Nations framework, as well as regional bodies. It seems clear that the power to foster co-operation includes a power to conclude agreements binding in international law.[26]

Diplomatic Relations between the Communities and International Organizations

The *jus legationis* of the Communities is considered in more detail in Chapter 8. For present purposes, it may be noted that Commission delegations have been

---

[16] Arts. 230 EC and 200 Euratom. [17] Art. 94 ECSC.
[18] Arts. 231 EC and 201 Euratom.
[19] Art. 93 ECSC. This Art. was not amended by the TEU, but this was almost certainly an oversight: contrast Art. G(82) TEU (amending Art. 231 EC) and Art. I(27) TEU (amending Art. 201 Euratom).
[20] e.g. the Parliament. See Mégret, n. 8 above, 72, para. 6. [21] Art. 3(h) Euratom.
[22] Art. 126(3) EC: in particular with the Council of Europe. [23] Art. 127(3) EC.
[24] Art. 128(3) EC: in particular with the Council of Europe. [25] Art. 129(3) EC.
[26] See Ch. 3.

established at the United Nations,[27] the FAO,[28] and the OECD,[29] and that these delegations, like the Member States' missions to the organizations in question, enjoy privileges and immunities in the host State. Several organizations have established *bureaux de liaison* in Brussels,[30] but to date no international organization has formally accredited diplomatic representatives to the Communities.

THE COMMUNITIES' PARTICIPATION IN INTERNATIONAL
ORGANIZATIONS

The Establishment of International Organizations

In *Opinion 1/76 (Re Draft Agreement for a Laying Up Fund for Inland Waterway Vessels)*, the Court expressly recognized that the powers conferred on the Community by the Treaty included the power, within the scope of the Community's competence, to participate in the establishment of international organizations, and to be a member of such organizations:[31]

The Community is . . . not only entitled to enter into contractual relations with a third country . . . but also has the power, while observing the provisions of the Treaty, to co-operate with that country in setting up an appropriate organism such as the public international institution which it is proposed to establish under the name of the European Laying Up Fund for Inland Waterway Vessels. The Community may also in this connection, co-operate with a third country for the purpose of giving the organs of such an institution appropriate powers of decision and for the purpose of defining, in a manner appropriate to the objectives pursued, the nature, elaboration, implementation and effects of the provisions to be adopted within such a framework.

There seems no reason to confine this dictum to the European Community alone, and it may thus be assumed that the Communities' powers to enter into international agreements[32] include a power to enter into agreements establishing international organizations.

In deciding whether one of the Communities may become party to such an agreement, the extent of that Community's competence in the matters to be treated in the organization[33] must be considered, and the procedures[34] under the relevant Treaty for the conclusion of agreements must be followed. Furthermore, even where the matters to be dealt with in an organization fall

---

[27] In New York, Geneva, and Vienna.   [28] In Rome.   [29] In Paris.

[30] e.g. the League of Arab States, EFTA, the Council of Europe, the UN, the UN Population Fund, the UN High Commission for Refugees, the ILO, the WHO, the Organization of African Unity, and the International Organization for Migration. For a full list, see further, Ch. 8.

[31] [1977] ECR 741 at para. 5.

[32] This seems implicit in Art. 228(3) EC, which envisages the conclusion by the European Community of 'agreements establishing a specific institutional framework by organizing co-operation procedures'.

[33] Ch. 3.   [34] Ch. 4.

within the competence of the Community, the Community's powers to participate in the creation of that organization are not unconstrained. It is clear from
Opinion 1/76[35] and the two *EEA Opinions*[36] that Community participation in
certain organizations may be precluded because of the structures of such organizations and the effect the operation of such structures may have on the
Community legal order. Particular care would have to be taken in deciding on
Community participation in an organization on which judicial powers had been
conferred: the Court has laid stress on its supreme and unique role as the inter-
preter of the rules of Community law.[37]

Membership and Observer Status

In the present state of international law and practice, membership of international organizations is in general open only to States; the status usually available to international organizations relative to each other is observer status.[38]
Thus Community membership of international organizations is much less common than Community participation as observer. The rights and conditions
attaching to the status of observer or member depend on the constitution of the
organization in question, and the label 'member' or 'observer' in one organization does not necessarily carry exactly the same consequences in another. As a
rule, the status of member allows participation of the fullest kind, placing the
Community on the same footing as States which are members of the organization in question, with the right to vote, to propose motions in its own right, to
speak as of right, and so on. Observer status usually implies a more limited right
to participate, usually without a right to vote. The constitution and procedures
of each organization must, however, be examined to determine the rights and
obligations of the Community within that organization.

  The fact that the Community is a member or observer in an organization
does not necessarily mean that the Member States cease to have a role there.
In some cases, that has been the consequence of Community participation,
because of the extent of the Community's competence in the matters dealt with
in the organization.[39] In most cases, however, Community competence in
respect of the matters covered by the organization is not so extensive as to
exclude Member State participation, and the Member States accordingly
remain members in their own right. The Treaties specifically reserve the

---

[35] N. 31 above.

[36] *Opinion 1/91 (Re Draft EEA Agreement)* [1991] ECR 6079 and *Opinion 1/92 (Re Draft EEA Agreement)* [1992] ECR I–2821.

[37] See, further M. Hardy 'Opinion 1/76 of the Court of Justice' (1977) 14 *CMLRev.* 561; T. C. Hartley, 'The European Court and the EEA' [1992] *ICLQ* 841.

[38] On observer status generally, see E. Suy, 'The Status of Observers in International Organizations' 160 *Hague Recueil* (1978 II) 75. On the EEC and international organizations see Jacqué, n. 1 above, 934–40.

[39] This is the case for many fisheries organizations: see p. 186, and Ch. 10.

Member States' powers to negotiate in the framework of certain organizations alongside the Community.[40]

Presentation of the Community Position in International Organizations

Where a matter falls within the *exclusive competence*[41] of the Community, it is for the Community alone to act in respect of that matter on the international level. Thus it is for the Community, not the Member States, to express a position, vote, or speak on such matters in an international organization. Where competence for a matter which is the subject of consideration in an international organization is *shared* between the Community and the Member States,[42] the Member States and the Community are obliged to seek to present a common position. The Court has said that the 'requirement of unity' in the international representation of the Communities[43] means that it is essential to ensure close co-operation, or a close association,[44] between the Member States and the Community institutions, in the process of negotiation and conclusion and in the fulfilment of the commitments entered into at the international level.[45] This duty to co-operate is more imperative in certain contexts than in others, for example where the Community itself cannot formally participate in an organization,[46] and (it seems) where the rights and obligations of the Community and the Member States under an agreement are inextricably linked.[47]

It is an open question whether 'the requirement of unity' is a requirement on the Member States to reach a common position in negotiations or discussions within the organization, or merely to strive to reach one.[48] In relation to matters within the exclusive competence of the Community, failure to agree means that no position can be expressed on behalf of the Community, because by definition no Community position exists. In relation to matters where the Community and the Member States share competence, it is strongly arguable that the obligation on the Member States is simply to endeavour to reach a common position, and that if no such position can be agreed, the Member States remain free to put their national point of view on matters within their own competence. This interpretation seems implicit in the Court's assertion that the obligation of co-operation is more stringent in some circumstances than in

---

[40] See, e.g., Arts. 109(5), 130r(4) and 130y(2) EC.
[41] On 'exclusive Community competence' see Ch. 3.
[42] On 'shared competence' see Ch. 3. [43] See Ch. 3.
[44] *Opinion 2/91 (Re ILO Convention 170)* [1993] ECR I–1061, at para. 36.
[45] *Ibid. Opinion 1/94 (Re WTO Agreement)* [1995] 1 CMLR 205 at para. 108. A similar duty appears in Art. J.2 TEU in relation to matters falling within the scope of the common foreign and security policy and in Art. K.5 in relation to common positions in international organizations and at international conferences in fields covered by Title VI of the TEU.
[46] *Opinion 2/91*, n. 44 above, at paras. 36–38.
[47] See *Opinion 1/94*, n. 45 above, at paras. 109 ff.
[48] See also the discussion in Ch. 6.

others:[49] if the Member States were always obliged to reach a common position, the obligation would always be equally imperative. The practice of the
institutions in relation to the dependent territories of the Member States outside
the scope of the Treaties also supports this view: it is recognized that in certain
circumstances the Member States concerned may act separately in the interests
of these territories.[50]

Community Co-ordination in Practice

Applying these principles in practice is less easy, not least because it is not
always obvious when a matter is within the Community's exclusive competence.
Where the Community is a member of an international organization in its own
right, or is able to present its own position in the organization, the Community's
position on matters within the Community's exclusive competence will be
expressed through the Community delegation.[51] Where the Community is not
a member, or is not able to express its own view, the Community's competence
may be exercised through the medium of the Member States acting jointly in
the Community's interest.[52] Thus, the Presidency of the Council for the time
being may express the position of the Community.

   Where discussions within an international organization cover matters within
the competence of the Community and the Member States, the Commission
and the Member States meet in advance of the discussions, to try to reach a
common view on the matters to be discussed. This process will determine what
will be said on behalf of the Community and its Member States, or on behalf
of the Community, and by whom. Co-ordination among the Member States is
in practice well established in all international fora in which the Member States
participate, whether the Community participates as a member or observer or
not. The precise terms of such co-ordination vary from forum to forum, and
owe as much to habit and history as to law or logic.[53] If there are generally
applicable rules, they are that:

>   (a) on matters within the Community's exclusive competence, the
>   Community's spokesman is usually the Commission, whereas on matters
>   within the competence of the Member States (and often also on matters

---

[49] *Opinion 1/94*, n. 45 above, at para. 109.

[50] Declaration (No. 25) (on the representation of the interests of the overseas countries and territories referred to in Art. 227(3) and (5)(a) and (b) of the Treaty establishing the EC) annexed to
the Final Act of the TEU.

[51] On the forms which such a delegation may take, see below.

[52] *Opinion 2/91*, n. 44 above, at para. 5.

[53] A series of informal politically binding arrangements have developed between the Council and
the Commission in respect of activities within certain bodies. These are usually recorded in the minutes of the Council, and are therefore not made public. Nevertheless, the details of the more important arrangements have, over the years, found their way into the public domain, and those
governing the Community's participation in Commodities agreements, the FAO, and the UN are
summarized later in this Ch.

where competence is shared between the Community and the Member States), the common position is expressed by the Presidency;

(b) the position to be adopted, whether on matters within Community competence, or on matters in which the Community and the Member States share competence, is in practice determined by consensus. As a last resort, however, the position on matters within the competence of the Community can in theory be decided on the basis of the provisions of the Treaties which confer competence on the Communities in respect of the matters under discussion.[54] A common position on matters within the competence of the Member States can only be agreed by consensus;[55]

(c) if a common position cannot be agreed on matters falling within the competence of the Member States, each Member State is in the end free to present its own position.[56]

Community co-ordination takes place in Brussels, at meetings of Council working groups or in COREPER, or in meetings of the delegations of the Member States and the Commission at the organization itself.[57]

The Division of Competence between the Communities and the Member States

The division of competences between the Community and the Member States is one of the most difficult issues raised by Community participation in international organizations,[58] and a regular source of discussion in Community co-ordination. It is important because the allocation of competence for a particular matter or in respect of an agenda item will usually determine whether the Community or the Member States are entitled to speak or vote on the matter.

[54] Thus, e.g., the Community's position on matters within the scope of the common commercial policy could be decided by a qualified majority of the Member States (see Art. 113 EC); but the position on matters falling within the Community's competence under Art. 130s(2) EC would be decided by unanimity.

[55] Art. 116 EEC (repealed by Art. G(31) TEU) provided a mechanism for co-ordinating the positions of the Member States on matters of particular interest to the common market arising within the framework of international organizations of an economic character. The Member States were obliged, in respect of such matters, to proceed only by common action. To that end, the Commission was empowered to submit to the Council proposals concerning the scope and implementation of such common action. The Council was to act by qualified majority on such proposals. The scope of this Art. was controversial. Not all Member States accepted that it could be used to compel them to adopt particular positions on matters within their national competences: they argued that its purpose was to co-ordinate a position on matters within Community competence in bodies in which, for whatever reason, the Community was not formally a party. The alternative view was that the Art. could be so used, but that it could not require the Member States to adopt binding commitments: see Mégret, n. 8 above Vol 12, 52 and 58. Judicial dicta were ambiguous: see *Opinion 1/78 (Re the Draft International Agreement on Natural Rubber)* [1979] ECR 2871, para. 50.

[56] For an example of this principle in operation, see Declaration (No. 25) , n. 50 above.

[57] So called *sur place* co-ordination.

[58] It is not, of course, unique to Community participation in international organizations: the same problem arises—at least in theory—in any mixed agreement. See, further, Ch. 6.

'Declarations of competence'[59] help in deciding whether a particular matter falls to the Community or to its Member States, but an exact division is usually exceedingly hard to make. Problems are in practice resolved pragmatically, on the basis of consensus between the Council and the Commission; but it has sometimes been necessary to resort to the Court.[60]

Attribution of Votes

Voting rights are attributed to members of an organization, not to observers. Where the Community is a member in its own right, and entitled to vote, the number of votes to which it is entitled will depend on the terms of membership negotiated for the Community and on the constitution of the organization concerned. In practice, there are three models:

(a) the Community entirely replaces the Member States, and exercises one vote in its own name, like other members of the organization;[61]

(b) the Community and the Member States participate in the organization together, each in respect of its own area of competence. When the Community votes on matters within its competence, it exercises the votes of the Member States which are also members of the organization, but has, in strict law, no vote of its own. When the Community exercises the votes of the Member States, they cannot exercise theirs, and *vice versa*. This is the principle of '*alternative voting*' or '*alternative exercise of rights*';[62]

(c) the Community and the Member States participate together in the organization, but their separate and distinct competences and interests are recognized, and the Community is accorded a vote in addition to those held and exercised by the Member States.[63]

Where the Community is not a member of an organization, or is otherwise precluded from voting,[64] the Member States' votes will have to be cast in a way which reflects the respective competences of the Community and the Member States. Decisions about how this should be done will be reached in Community co-ordination.

---

[59] See Ch. 6, p. 161.

[60] See, e.g., *Opinion 1/78*, n. 55 above; *Ruling 1/78 (Re Draft Convention for the Physical Protection of Nuclear Materials)* [1978] ECR 2151; *Opinion 1/94*, n. 45 above.

[61] This is the case for several fisheries organizations: see below.

[62] This is the case in the FAO, the WTO, and commodities organizations: see below.

[63] This is rare: the only examples are the EBRD (a highly specialized case) and the Protocol relating to the Madrid Arrangement concerning the International Registration of Marks.

[64] In a few cases, the Community is entitled to become a member of an organization, but is accorded no vote. Examples include: the Common Fund for Commodities, Art. 4(b) ([1990] OJ L182/2); the International Convention on the Simplification and Harmonization of Customs Procedures (the Kyoto Convention), Art. 11(7) ([1975] OJ L100/2); Customs Convention on the International Transport of Goods under cover of TIR carnets (the TIR Convention), Art. 52(3) ([1978] OJ L252/2).

Composition of the Community's Delegation

The composition of the delegation which represents the Community in an international organization varies depending on several factors, including the extent of the Community's competence in the matters dealt with by the organization, the practice of the Community and the Member States in the organization in question, or in similar organizations, and the attitude of third States. Three kinds of delegation are usually identified (others are possible):[65]

(a) *the 'bicephalous' delegation.* The Community delegation consists of representatives of the Commission, the Council Secretariat, and the Presidency in office, and is usually led by the representative of the Presidency. Sometimes, representatives of all the Member States have participated in the Community delegation. The existence of a Community delegation is without prejudice to the continued presence in the organization of delegations of the Member States;

(b) a *'single' delegation*, composed of representatives of the Commission and the Member States, *replacing* the delegations of the Commission and the Member States;[66]

(c) a *Community delegation* composed of representatives of the Commission.[67] Depending on the circumstances and the extent of Community competence in relation to the work of the organization, the Member States' delegations would also participate in that work.

The position to be expressed by the Community delegation would be determined in accordance with the principles outlined above, or in accordance with the arrangements agreed for the organization in question.

Decision-making within International Organizations

Some organizations establish bodies or mechanisms whose decisions are binding on the parties to the agreement. Within the Community legal system, decisions of such bodies may have legal effects comparable to those of the agreement itself.[68] The difficult question then arises how such decisions should be authorized within the Community legal order. If (for example) a decision relates to an agricultural question, is it necessary for the Parliament to be consulted before the Community side commits itself to a position within the decision-making

---

[65] See Mégret, n. 8 above, vol. 12, 138 ff; Groux, 'Mixed Negotiations', in O'Keeffe and Schermers (eds.), *Mixed Agreements* (Kluwer, 1983), 87 at 92 ff.; House of Lords Select Committee on the European Communities, *External Competence of the European Communities* (HL 236, 1984–5), Evidence at 108 ff.; Jacqué, n. 1 above, 940–3.

[66] An example of this is the arrangement employed in commodities organizations (the PROBA 20 Arrangement); see further below, under *Commodities Organizations*.

[67] Examples include fisheries organizations.

[68] See Ch. 5, pp. 137 ff.

body, and should the Council act by qualified majority, as would be necessary if internal legislation under Article 43 EC were being adopted?

The practice so far appears to be that the Community's position is established in co-ordination and expressed within the decision-making body in accordance with arrangements agreed between the Council and the Commission within the organization in question: the full procedure laid down in the Treaties for the adoption of internal legislation is not usually followed. In some cases, a simplified decision-making procedure is set out in the Council act concluding the agreement.[69] This enables the Community's position to be established and put forward in a relatively efficient and speedy manner.

THE COMMUNITIES AND INTERNATIONAL ORGANIZATIONS: PRACTICE

Organizations of which the Community is a Member

The Food and Agriculture Organization

Aim

The aim of the members of the FAO[70] is to promote the common welfare by furthering separate and collective action for the purposes of raising levels of nutrition and standards of living of the peoples under their respective jurisdictions; securing improvements in the efficiency of the production and distribution of all food and agricultural products; bettering the condition of rural populations; and contributing to an expanding world economy and ensuring humanity's freedom from hunger. The activities of the FAO thus touch on several areas of Community competence, in particular, agriculture and development policy.

Constitutional Provisions

Membership of the FAO is open to regional economic integration organizations constituted by sovereign States, a majority of which are members of the Organization, to which the Member States have transferred competence over a range of matters within the purview of the FAO, including power to make decisions binding on its members in respect of those matters.[71] Such a regional economic integration organization must undertake to accept the obligations of the FAO Constitution as in force at the time of admission, and must submit a declaration of competence specifying the matters in respect of which competence has been transferred to it by the Member States.[72] Member States are presumed

---

[69] Recent examples include Art. 3 of Reg. 3955/92 concerning the conclusion of an Agreement establishing an International Scientific and Technology Centre ([1992] OJ L409/1) and Art. 2 of Dec. 93/743 on the conclusion of a Europe Agreement with Poland ([1993] OJ L348/1).

[70] See Art. I of the Constitution of the FAO in UKTS 47 (1946), Cmd. 6955.

[71] *Ibid.*, Art. II(4).   [72] *Ibid.*, Art. II(5).

to retain competence over all matters in respect of which transfers have not been specifically declared or notified to the FAO.[73]

The Community's Status

Until 1991, the EEC had observer status at the FAO. On 22 October 1990, the Council decided to initiate negotiations with a view to the Community's accession to the FAO, and negotiations formally began on 1 February 1991. The FAO Conference decided to admit the EEC as a member Organization on 26 November 1991,[74] after adopting the amendments to its Constitution necessary to allow an international organization to become a member.

Legal Basis of Community Membership

The Council decision approving Community accession to the FAO was based on Articles 43, 113, and 235 EEC.[75]

Terms of Membership

The European Community is now a 'member Organization' of the FAO.[76] The Member States are also members. Article II(8) of the FAO Constitution provides that a member Organization must exercise membership rights on an alternative basis with those of its Member States that are members of the FAO in the areas of their respective competences and in accordance with rules set down by the FAO Conference. Thus, before any meeting of the Organization, the member Organization or its Member States must indicate which, as between the member Organization and its Member States, has competence in respect of any specific question to be considered in the meeting and which, as between the member Organization and its Member States, will exercise the right to vote in respect of each particular agenda item.[77] Where no specific declaration is made, the Member States are presumed to have competence.[78] Where an agenda item covers matters in respect of which competence has been transferred to the member Organization and matters which lie within the competence of the Member States, both the member Organization and its Member States may participate

---

[73] *Ibid.*, Art. II(6).

[74] The Council (of the EEC) approved the Community's application for membership on 25 Nov. 1991. The Council's decision is unpublished: the Commission's proposal is at [1991] OJ C292/8. The text of the decision adopted by the Council follows the Commission's proposal closely: the Annexes were amended in several respects by the Council.

[75] Art. 235 was then the legal basis for the Community's development policy. On the legal basis now, see Ch. 18.

[76] See, further, Schwob, 'L'amendement à l'acte constitutif de la FAO visant à permettre l'admission en qualité de membre d'organizations d'intégration économique régionale et la Communauté économique européenne', (1993) 29 *RTDE* 1; R. Frid, 'The European Economic Community—A Member of a Specialised Agency of the United Nations' (1993) 4 *EJIL* 239–55; A. Tavares de Pinho, 'L'Admission de la Communauté économique européenne comme membre de l'Organization des Nations Unies pour l'Alimentation et l'Agriculture (FAO)' [1993] *RMC* 656.

[77] General Rules of the FAO, Art. XLI(2).   [78] FAO Constitution, Art. II(6).

in the discussions. In such cases, the meeting, in arriving at its decisions, may take into account only the intervention of the party entitled to vote.[79]

The Community contributes to the administrative expenses of the FAO.

As a member Organization of the FAO, the Community is entitled to participate in matters within its competence, in any meeting of the FAO, including any meeting of the FAO Council or other body, other than bodies of restricted membership in which any of its Member States are entitled to participate.[80]

Voting

Except as otherwise provided in the Constitution, or in rules set down by the FAO Conference, a member Organization of the FAO may exercise on matters within its competence, in any meeting of the FAO in which it is entitled to participate, a number of votes equal to the number of its Member States which are entitled to vote in such meeting. Whenever the Organization exercises its right to vote, the Member States shall not exercise theirs, and conversely.[81]

Declaration of Competence

On accession, the Community deposited a declaration of competence listing those areas of FAO work in which it had competence.[82] The Community and the Member States notify the FAO Secretariat before each FAO meeting, in respect of each item on the meeting's agenda, whether the Community or the Member States are to be regarded as competent. On the basis of this notification the right to speak and vote on each agenda item is determined.

Community Co-ordination

Co-ordination between the Community and the Member States on all aspects of the Community's participation in the FAO takes place on the basis of an unpublished informal arrangement agreed between the Commission and the Council at the time of Community accession to the FAO in 1991.[83] The 'Guidelines' set out in that arrangement provide for circulation of agendas and other papers relevant to forthcoming FAO meetings; for discussion of the allocation of competences between the Community and the Member States; for decisions about who, as between the Community and the Member States, is to speak or vote; and for the position of the non-EC dependent territories of the Member States. The allocation of competences in respect of each agenda item

---

[79] General Rules of the FAO, Art. XLI(3).   [80] FAO Constitution, Art. II(10).

[81] *Ibid.*, Art. II(10).

[82] The Declaration of Competence submitted to the FAO in 1991 follows substantially that proposed by the Commission: see [1991] OJ C292/8. A further Declaration of Competence was made in Oct. 1994 to take account of the TEU, in particular, the Community's change of name ('EEC' to 'EC') and its new powers (Arts. 127, 129, 129a, 130u–130y, 130f–130p, and 130r–130t).

[83] Modified slightly in 1992 to clarify some problems relating to preparation for FAO meetings, and to voting rights on approval of reports.

is, as might be expected, far from easy.[84] The 1991 Guidelines provide that the Member States should speak and vote on matters within their own competence; that the Community should speak and vote for matters within the exclusive competence of the Community; and that in matters within the competences of the Community and the Member States, speaking and voting rights will be decided on the basis of a determination of where 'the thrust of the issue' lies.

The GATT and the WTO

Aims

The General Agreement on Tariffs and Trade (GATT)[85] established a common code of conduct for international trade and provided machinery for reducing and binding tariffs and a forum for regular consultations on international trade. The functions of the World Trade Organization (WTO)[86] are to facilitate the implementation, administration, and operation, and to further the objectives, of the WTO Agreement and of the Multilateral Trade Agreements, and to provide a framework for the implementation, administration, and operation of the Plurilateral Trade Agreements. The WTO is also to provide the forum for negotiations among its Members concerning their multilateral trade relations, and to administer various mechanisms agreed in the Uruguay Round. The Community has competence, in particular under the common commercial policy, and rules adopted within the framework of the Single Market, for a wide range of matters covered by the WTO Agreement.

The Community's Status

As a matter of Community law, the EEC succeeded the Member States as a participant in the GATT.[87] Formally, however, in relation to other GATT Contracting Parties, the Community was not a party to the GATT in its own right; the Member States remained Contracting Parties, responsible for the fulfilment of the obligations under the Agreement. The Agreement establishing the WTO, concluded as part of the Uruguay Round negotiations, is open to acceptance by the 'European Communities' and the Member States.[88] The Final Act

---

[84] In Case C–25/94 *Commission* v. *Council*, not yet reported, the Commission challenged the legality of a decision that a draft Convention on the Flagging of Fishing Vessels related more to the competence of the Member States than the Community and that therefore voting and speaking rights were for the Member States.

[85] The constitution of the GATT is in 55 UNTS 194; Cmd. 7258. On the GATT, see Dam, *The GATT: Law and International Economic Integration* (University of Chicago Press, 1970); Jackson, *World Trade Law and the Law of GATT* (Bobbs-Merrill Co., 1969); Jackson, *The World Trading System* (MIT Press, 1989); Petersmann, *The European Community and the GATT* [1984] 1 *LIEI* 37; Hilf, Jacobs, Petersmann, *The European Community and GATT* (1986).

[86] The Agreement establishing the WTO is in [1994] OJ L336/1.

[87] See, e.g., Joined Cases 24–27/72 *International Fruit Company NV* v. *Produktschap voor Groenten en Fruit* [1972] ECR 1219, and pp. 235–6 below.

[88] Art. XIV of the Agreement establishing the WTO.

embodying the results of the Uruguay Round of multilateral trade negotiations was signed by the Member States and by the Presidency and the Commission on behalf of the Communities in Marrakech on 15 April 1994. The Agreement establishing the World Trade Organization was signed (subject to conclusion) on the same day. On 22 December 1994, the Council adopted a decision concerning the conclusion on behalf of the European Community, as regards matters within its competence, of the agreements reached in the Uruguay Round multilateral negotiations (1986–94).[89] The Member States are also parties to the Agreement establishing the WTO.

Legal Basis for Community Membership

The Council decision approving membership on behalf of the European Community[90] was based on Articles 43, 54, 57, 66, 75, 84 (2), 99, 100, 100a, 113, and 235, in conjunction with the second subparagraph of Article 228(3) EC.[91] The ECSC and Euratom are not parties to the WTO Agreement.

Terms of Membership

As a member of the WTO, the Community has the right to vote and speak at the Ministerial Conference and the General Council. When the Community exercises its right to vote, it has a number of votes equal to the number of Member States which are members of the WTO.[92] The number of votes of the Community and the Member States may in no case exceed the number of the Member States which are members of the WTO.

Community co-ordination of the positions of the Member States and the Community on questions relating to services takes place on the basis of an internal arrangement (a 'code of conduct') agreed in 1994. No comparable arrangements exist for other matters, but in practice co-ordination takes place within the Article 113 Committee.

Commodities Agreements

Several international organizations or bodies have been established within the framework of UNCTAD's Integrated Programme for Commodities. These include the Common Fund for Commodities; commodities organizations established under international commodity agreements; and several 'study groups'. The underlying aim of all these bodies is to improve international co-operation

---

[89] Council Dec. 94/800 concerning the conclusion on behalf of the EC as regards matters within its competence of the agreements reached in the Uruguay Round of multilateral trade negotiations (1986–94) ([1994] OJ L336/1).

[90] The competence of the Community and the Member States in respect of the matters covered by the WTO Agreement and the related agreements was the subject of a request for an opinion of the ECJ under Art. 228(6) EC (*Opinion 1/94*, n. 45 above). See, further, pp. 269 ff.

[91] i.e., a unanimous Council decision following the assent of the Parliament.

[92] Art. IX(1), WTO Agreement.

in trade in commodities, but development policy considerations are also important. The Community's competence in this area derives primarily from its powers to establish a common commercial policy.[93]

The Common Fund for Commodities

Aims and Functions

The Agreement establishing the Common Fund was opened for signature on 1 October 1980.[94] The objectives of the Common Fund are to attain the objectives of the integrated programme for commodities and to facilitate the conclusion and functioning of international commodity agreements.[95] The Fund is to contribute to the financing of international buffer stocks and internationally co-ordinated national stocks within the framework of international commodity agreements; to finance measures in the field of commodities other than stocking; and to promote co-ordination and consultation with regard to measures in the field of commodities.[96]

Community's Status

Membership in the Common Fund is open to any intergovernmental organization of regional economic integration which exercises competence in fields of activity of the Fund. The Council adopted a decision on the conclusion of the Common Fund Agreement by the EEC on 29 May 1990.[97] All the Member States are parties to the Common Fund Agreement.

Legal Basis for Community Membership

The legal basis for Community participation in the Common Fund was Article 113 EEC.

Terms of Membership

The Community is not obliged to undertake any financial obligations to the Fund, nor does it have a vote.[98] It is, however, entitled to exercise the other rights of a Member of the Fund, including the right to appoint a governor and an alternate to the Governing Council.

Community Co-ordination

No informal or formal arrangements are in place governing the presentation of the positions of the Community and the Member States in the Common Fund.[99]

---

[93] See in particular *Opinion 1/78*, n. 55 above. On issues raised by the Community's early participation in commodity conferences, see [1968] UNJY 210, ST/LEG/SER.C/6. See also Ch. 12.

[94] For the text of the Agreement establishing the Common Fund for Commodities, see [1990] OJ L182/2, UKTS 5 (1992), Cm 1797.

[95] Common Fund Agreement, Art. 2.   [96] *Ibid.*, Art. 3.

[97] Council Dec. 90/373 EEC ([1990] OJ L182/1).   [98] Common Fund Agreement, Art. 4.

[99] The PROBA 20 Arrangement (see below) does not apply to the Common Fund.

International Commodities Agreements

For present purposes, the commodities agreements to which the Community is a party[100] can be divided into two broad categories: those which relate to commodities in respect of which a common market has been established within the Community (such as olive oil, sugar, and wheat); and those relating to other commodities (such as coffee, cocoa, rubber, tropical timber, and jute). From the point of view of the Community's external relations,[101] the essential difference between these two categories is that the Member States contribute to the budgets of organizations established under agreements in the latter category, and are on that basis[102] parties to the agreements along with the Community, whereas the Community itself contributes to the budgets of agreements in the former category:[103] the Member States are not parties to these agreements.

Agreements relating to Commodities subject to the Community's Common Agricultural Policy
Three agreements fall into this category: the International Wheat Agreement 1986;[104] the International Agreement on Olive Oil and Table Olives 1986;[105] and the International Sugar Agreement 1992.[106]

---

[100] For a brief historical account of early Community participation in commodity agreements, see E. Wellenstein, 'Participation of the Community in International Commodity Agreements', in T. St John Bates and others (eds.) in *In Memoriam J. D. B. Mitchell*, (Sweet & Maxwell, 1983) at 65. R. Barents, 'The European Communities and the Commodity Organizations' [1984] 1 *LIEI* 77 is somewhat dated.

[101] In terms of international economics, however, the key distinction is between commodities agreements which establish a buffer stock, or other financing mechanism (so called 'economic provisions'), and those which contain no such mechanisms. Of the commodities agreements currently in existence, only the 1987 International Natural Rubber Agreement falls into the former category. On the Community's competence for an earlier version of the 1987 Agreement, see *Opinion 1/78*, n. 55 above.

[102] See, however, *Opinion 1/94*, n. 45 above, para. 21: 'Given that the WTO is an international organization which will have only an operating budget and not a financial policy instrument, the fact that the Member States will bear some of its expenses cannot, on any view, of itself justify participation of the Member States in the conclusion of the WTO Agreement.'

[103] i.e., olive oil, sugar, and wheat.

[104] The International Wheat Agreement 1986 is constituted by the Wheat Trade Convention 1986 and the Food Aid Convention 1986. It maintains in being (Art. 9(1)) the International Wheat Council (established in 1949), a body with legal personality. For the text of the Agreement, see [1986] OJ L195/2. The 1986 Agreement replaces earlier wheat agreements, most recently the 1971 Agreement (to which the Member States were parties). The 1986 Agreement has been renegotiated and will be replaced in due course by the International Cereals Agreement 1995. The latter comprises the Cereals Trade Convention and the Food Aid Convention. A proposal for Community participation in the 1995 Agreement is likely to come to the Council in the summer of 1995.

[105] The International Olive Oil Agreement establishes (Art. 3(1)) the International Olive Oil Council, a body with legal personality. For the text of the Agreement, see [1987] OJ L214/2. The 1986 Agreement replaces earlier agreements on the same matter, most recently the 1979 Agreement (and earlier Agreements). The 1986 Agreement was itself amended and extended by a Protocol in 1993.

[106] The International Sugar Agreement maintains in being (Art. 3(1)) the International Sugar Organization, a body with legal personality. For the text of the Agreement, see [1992] OJ L23/16. The 1992 Agreement replaces the 1987 Sugar Agreement (and its predecessors).

Community's Status

The Community is entitled to become a party to these agreements in its own right, without the Member States.[107] It is a party to the Olive Oil Agreement (and the amending Protocol)[108] and to the Sugar Agreement,[109] and has agreed to apply provisionally the Wheat Agreement.[110] As a party to these Agreements, the Community enjoys the rights and obligations of membership in the organizations established by the Agreements. The votes and shares attributable to the Community,[111] and the contribution to be made by the Community to the budgets, are calculated on the basis of formulae set out in each agreement.[112]

Legal Basis for Community Membership

The legal basis for Community participation is the common commercial policy and the existence of a common organization of the market in the product in question. Decisions on the signature, provisional application, and conclusion of these agreements have been based on Article 113 EEC.[113]

Community Co-ordination

No special procedures exist in respect of Community co-ordination in these bodies.[114]

Other Commodities Agreements

The Community and the Member States have become parties to the International Coffee Agreement 1994[115] and the International Natural Rubber

---

[107] Olive Oil Agreement, Art. 5; Sugar Agreement, Art. 5; and Wheat Agreement, Art. 2(2), all of which provide that 'Any reference . . . to a "Government" or "Governments" shall be construed as including the European Economic Community.'

[108] Council Dec. 87/401/EEC concerning the conclusion of the International Agreement on Olive Oil and Table Olives ([1987] OJ L214/1) and Council Dec. 93/622/EC on the conclusion of the Protocol of 1993 amending and extending the International Agreement on Olive Oil and Table Olives ([1993] OJ L298/36).

[109] Council Dec. 92/580/EEC on the signing and conclusion of the International Sugar Agreement 1992 ([1992] OJ L379/15).

[110] Council Dec. 86/304/EEC on the signing of the Wheat Trade Convention and the Food Aid Convention and the deposit of a declaration of provisional application of these Conventions ([1986] OJ L195/1).

[111] Olive Oil Agreement, Art. 10; Sugar Agreement, Arts. 11, 25, and Annex; Wheat Agreement, Arts. 11, 12, and Annex.

[112] Olive Oil Agreement, Pt. II, and Annexes A and B; Sugar Agreement, ch. VII; Wheat Agreement, Art. 21. These contributions are paid from the Community's budget.

[113] Now, there would also have to be a reference to Art. 228 EC: see n. 123 below.

[114] PROBA 20 does not apply. But, when necessary, discussion of the Community position in these bodies takes place in the same Council working group (the 'PROBA Group') as considers commodities agreements to which the PROBA 20 arrangements apply ('PROBA' is derived from the French 'PROduits de BAse').

[115] Council Dec. 94/570/EC concerning the conclusion by the Community of the International Coffee Agreement 1994 ([1994] OJ L222/1).

Agreement 1987.[116] They have signed the International Agreement on Jute and Jute Products.[117] The Community and a majority of Member States have signed and are provisionally applying the International Cocoa Agreement 1993.[118] The Community is applying the International Agreement on Tropical Timber 1983,[119] and the Member States are parties to that Agreement.

Community's Status

The Community is entitled to become a party to these commodities agreements in its own right, but the Member States are also entitled to participate. In each agreement, references to a 'Government' or 'Governments' are to be construed as including the EEC. In the case of voting on matters within its competence, the Community casts a number of votes equal to the total number of votes attributable to the Member States under the agreement in question. When the Community votes, the Member States cannot exercise their individual voting rights.[120] The Member States contribute to the budget of the bodies established by these agreements, and to any financing arrangements.

Legal Basis of Community Membership

Commodities agreements fall within the scope of the common commercial policy, and the principal legal basis for the Council's decisions to sign, provisionally apply, and conclude these agreements is Article 113 EC.[121] Since the entry into force of the TEU, it is necessary to identify the procedure to be followed in the process of conclusion of the agreements.[122] Article 228(2) EC is therefore also cited, along with Article 113.[123]

---

[116] Council Dec. 92/396/EEC concerning the conclusion of the International Natural Rubber Agreement 1987. The text of the Agreement is at [1988] OJ L58/18. The Agreement was renegotiated in 1994, but a proposal for Community participation had not been made at the time of writing.

[117] Council Dec. 91/51/EEC on the signing of the International Agreement on Jute and Jute Products, 1989 ([1991] OJ L29/1).

[118] Council Dec. 94/109/EC concerning the signing and provisional application of the International Cocoa Agreement 1993 ([1994] OJ L52/25).

[119] Council Dec. 85/424/EEC ([1985] OJ L236/8) on the application of the International Agreement on Tropical Timber 1983. The Tropical Timber Agreement was renegotiated in 1995, but at the time of writing, no proposal for Community participation in the renegotiated agreement had been made.

[120] Cocoa Agreement 1993, Art. 4; Coffee Agreement, Art. 4; Jute Agreement, Art. 5; Natural Rubber Agreement, Art. 5; Tropical Timber Agreement, Art. 5.

[121] Before the entry into force of the TEU, Art. 116 EEC was also cited if the decision envisaged simultaneous action by the Member States: see, e.g., the Decs. on the signing and conclusion of the Natural Rubber Agreement ([1988] OJ L58/18; [1992] OJ L219/56); the signing of the Jute Agreement ([1991] OJ L29/1); and the provisional application of the 1983 Timber Agreement ([1983] OJ L236/8) and the 1986 Cocoa Agreement ([1987] OJ L69/24). The meaning and application of Art. 116 EEC was controversial. It has been deleted by Art. G(31) TEU.

[122] See Ch. 4.

[123] Council Dec. 94/109/EC concerning the signing and provisional application of the International Cocoa Agreement 1993 ([1994] OJ L52/25).

Community Co-ordination

In all commodities agreements covered by the UNCTAD's integrated programme except those under a common organization of the agricultural market,
Community co-ordination takes place in accordance with an informal arrangement, known as 'PROBA 20', agreed between the Commission and the
Member States in 1981.[124] This arrangement, which is intended to improve the
Community's external image and to strengthen its internal cohesion and solidarity, is based on the understanding that all legal and institutional considerations which refer to the respective competences of the Community and the
Member States are set aside. Instead, the Community and the Member States
participate jointly in all agreements covered by the arrangement, through a joint
delegation expressing the joint position of the Community and the Member
States with a single voice. Within the joint delegation, the Member States are
individually identified, but in conference rooms they are grouped around the
Community nameplate. National and Community delegates are included in a
single list of delegations. The joint position is established by consensus in co-
ordination meetings, at the conference or organization concerned, or in
Brussels, and will in principle be delivered by the Commission representative.
The PROBA 20 Arrangement applies to the signing and conclusion of agreements and to participation in negotiations, preparatory work, and administrative bodies of the commodities agreements.

Commodities Study Groups

The commodities Study Groups are each established by 'terms of reference'
which are accepted by intending participants.[125] The Groups have international
legal personality.[126]

Objectives

The objective of the Study Groups is to ensure enhanced international co-operation on issues concerning the commodity in question, by improving the information available on the international economy in that commodity and by
providing a forum for intergovernmental consultations.[127] The functions of each
Group are to monitor the world economy in the commodity under study, to
conduct consultations and exchange information about production, consumption, and trade in that commodity, and to undertake studies on important
issues.[128]

---

[124] PROBA 20 does not, strictly speaking, apply to Commodities Study Groups nor to the
Agreement on the Common Fund for Commodities: see Barents, n. 100 above.

[125] For the text of the Terms of Reference of the Tin and Copper Study Groups, see [1991] OJ
L89/34 and 40 and for the text of the Terms of Reference of the Nickel Study Group see [1991]
OJ L293/24.

[126] Art. 14(a) of the Terms of Reference of the Tin and Copper Study Groups; Art. 13(a) of the
Nickel Study Group Terms of Reference.

[127] Terms of Reference of each Group, Art. 2.   [128] *Ibid.*, Art. 4.

Community's Status
Membership of the Study Groups is open to all States which are interested in the production or consumption of, or international trade in, the commodity concerned, and to any intergovernmental organization having responsibilities in respect of the negotiation, conclusion, and application of international agreements, in particular commodity agreements.[129] The Community and the Member States currently participate in the work of Study Groups on tin,[130] copper,[131] and nickel.[132]

Legal Basis of Community Membership
The Council Decisions accepting the Terms of Reference of the Tin, Copper, and Nickel Study Groups were based on Articles 113 and 116 EEC.[133]

Community Co-ordination
Community co-ordination in the Study Groups is generally along the lines agreed in PROBA 20,[134] but the Member States may decide whether or not to join the Study Groups, and may speak for themselves on matters within their own competence.

Fisheries Organizations

The European Community has exclusive competence to enter into international commitments for the conservation of the living resources of the sea.[135] The Community is thus a party to several multilateral fisheries agreements, and a member of the international organizations set up to oversee the implementation of these agreements. The organizations are:

   (a) the North-West Atlantic Fisheries Organization (NAFO);[136]
   (b) the North-East Atlantic Fisheries Commission (NEAFC);[137]
   (c) the North Atlantic Salmon Conservation Organization (NASCO);[138]

---

[129] *Ibid.*, Art. 5.
[130] Council Dec. 91/178/EEC on acceptance of the Terms of Reference of the International Tin Study Group ([1991] OJ L89/33).
[131] Council Dec. 91/179/EEC on the acceptance of the Terms of Reference of the International Copper Study Group ([1991] OJ L89/39).
[132] Council Dec. 91/537/EEC on the acceptance of the Terms of Reference of the International Nickel Study Group ([1991] OJ L293/23).
[133] See the Decs. cited in the preceding 3 nn. Art. 116 EEC has been repealed.
[134] Although, strictly speaking, PROBA 20 does not apply to commodities study groups.
[135] Joined Cases 3, 4, and 6/76 *Officier van Justitie* v. *Kramer* [1976] ECR 1279 at para. 14. See, further, Ch. 10.
[136] Established by Art. II of the Convention on Future Multilateral Co-operation in the North-West Atlantic Fisheries ([1978] OJ L378/2).
[137] Established by Art. 3 of the Convention on Future Multilateral Co-operation in North-East Atlantic Fisheries ([1981] OJ L227/22).
[138] Established by Art. 3 of the Convention for the Conservation of Salmon in the North Atlantic Ocean ([1982] OJ L378/25).

(d) the International Baltic Sea Fishery Commission;[139]

(e) the International Commission for the Conservation of Atlantic Tunas;[140]

(f) the Commission for the Conservation of Antarctic Marine Living Resources.[141]

In all except one of these bodies, the Community participates alone: the Member States participate only in respect of the interests of those of their dependent territories not covered by the EC Treaty.[142] The exception is the Commission for the Conservation of Antarctic Marine Living Resources in which Belgium, Greece, Italy, France, Germany, Spain, and the United Kingdom all participate in their own right.

Legal Basis of Community Membership

The legal basis for Community conclusion of these agreements was Article 43 EEC.

Terms of Membership

As a member of these organizations, the Community has the same rights and duties as other members.[143] Thus, in all except one case, it is entitled to vote and is required to contribute to the budget. The exception is the Commission for the Conservation of Antarctic Marine Living Resources, in which the Community is a member, but has no vote.

European Bank for Reconstruction and Development (EBRD)

Aims

The European Bank for Reconstruction and Development was set up in 1990 as part of the effort to facilitate the transition towards a market economy in the countries of Central and Eastern Europe.[144] In contributing to economic

---

[139] Established by Art. V of the Convention on Fishing and Conservation of the Living Resources of the Baltic Sea and the Belts ([1983] OJ L237/5), as amended by the Prot. to the Conference of the representatives of the States Parties to that Convention ([1983] OJ L237/9).

[140] Established by Art. III of the International Convention for the Conservation of Atlantic Tunas ([1986] OJ L162/34), as amended by the Prot. attached to the Final Act of the Conference of the Plenipotentiaries of the States Parties to the Convention ([1986] OJ L162/41). This amending prot. is not yet in force: see Ch. 10.

[141] Established by Art. VII of the Convention on the Conservation of Antarctic Marine Living Resources ([1981] OJ L252/27).

[142] Thus Denmark participates in NAFO, NEAFC, and NASCO in respect of the Faeroe Islands.

[143] For examples of the Community replacing the Member States in an organization, see the Prot. to the International Convention for the Conservation of Atlantic Tunas (n. 140 above); and the Prot. to the Convention on Fishing and Conservation of the Living Resources of the Baltic Sea and the Belts (n. 139 above).

[144] The text of the Agreement establishing the European Bank for Reconstruction and Development is at [1990] OJ L372/4, UKTS 70 (1991), Cm 1670, 29 ILM 1083.

progress and reconstruction, the purpose of the Bank is to foster the transition to open market-oriented economies and to promote private and entrepreneurial initiative in the Central and Eastern European countries committed to applying the principles of multiparty democracy, pluralism, and market economics.[145] The Bank is to assist the recipient countries in implementing structural and sectoral economic reforms, including demonopolization, decentralization, and privatization, to help their economies become fully integrated into the international economy by a range of measures, such as the promotion of the establishment of private sector activity, mobilizing domestic and foreign capital, fostering productive investment, provision of technical assistance, and so on.[146]

Legal Basis of Community Membership

The Council Decision approving Community membership of the EBRD was based on Article 235 EEC.[147]

Terms of Membership

The EEC, the European Investment Bank, and all the Member States are members of the EBRD.[148] The Community's voting power is calculated by reference to the number of its subscribed shares in the capital stock of the Bank.[149] The Community is entitled to appoint a governor and an alternate governor,[150] and to participate in the election of the eleven directors allocated to the Community and its Member States.[151] The Community subscribes shares in addition to those of the Member States.[152]

Community Co-ordination

The Commission represents the interests of the Community in the EBRD. It appoints the Community's governor and alternate[153] and designates, on behalf of the Community, the institution to act as depository under Article 34(1) of the Agreement.[154] The Commission is the 'official entity' with which the EBRD communicates under Article 34(2) of the Agreement.[155] Informal consultations take place regularly between the representatives of the Community and the Member States on all matters under discussion in the EBRD, in particular on important political or financial matters.[156] Where there is consensus on an issue,

---

[145] EBRD Agreement, Art. 1.　　　　　　　　[146] EBRD Agreement, Art. 2(1).

[147] On the use of Art. 235 EC as a basis for measures relating to the countries of Eastern Europe, see Ch. 18.

[148] EBRD Agreement, Art. 3(1). For approval of the Agreement on behalf of the EEC, see Council Dec. 90/674/EEC on the conclusion of the Agreement establishing the European Bank for Reconstruction and Development ([1990] OJ L372/1).

[149] EBRD Agreement, Art. 29.　　　　　　　　[150] EBRD Agreement, Art. 23.

[151] EBRD Agreement, Art. 26 and Annex B Sect. A.　　　　[152] EBRD Agreement, Art. 5.

[153] Dec. 90/647/EEC, Art. 2. Before making the Commission's nomination, the President of the Commission has informal contacts with the Presidents of the Council and the Parliament.

[154] *Ibid.*, Art. 3(1).　　　　　　　　[155] *Ibid.*, Art. 3(2).

[156] Such as those listed in Art. 24 of the EBRD Agreement.

the Community and the Member States vote and act in accordance with the consensus. If consensus cannot be reached, the Community representative either follows the line taken by the majority of the Member States, or abstains.

Organizations in which the Community participates as an Observer

The Communities have observer status, or a status approximating to observer status, in many organizations.[157] Observers are not entitled to vote and, as a rule, may only intervene in discussions with the permission of the chairman of the meeting. The detailed rights and duties deriving from the status of observer have to be determined by reference to the constitution of the organization in question, and the rules of procedure governing the conduct of its meetings.

The United Nations

All three Treaties envisage links between the Communities and the United Nations.[158] The Commission is to maintain 'all appropriate relations' with the United Nations, and keep that organization regularly informed of the work of the ECSC.[159] In respect of the EC and Euratom, the Commission is also to ensure the maintenance of all appropriate relations with the organs of the United Nations and of its specialized agencies.[160] There are Commission delegations at the United Nations Headquarters in New York and Geneva.[161]

The General Assembly

Resolution 3208 (XXIX) of 1 October 1984[162] instructed the Secretary General to invite the EEC[163] to participate in the sessions and work of the General Assembly in the capacity of observer. The Community accordingly attends sessions of the General Assembly, its subsidiary bodies,[164] and its Committees and is entitled to speak with permission of the Chairman of the meeting. The

[157] This sect. describes Community participation in some of the more important organizations: the Tables in the Annex provide a fuller list.

[158] See P. Bruckner, 'The European Community and the United Nations' (1990) 1 *EJIL* 174; I. J. Thijn, 'The European Political Co-operation in the General Assembly of the United Nations: A Case Study of the Netherlands' [1991] 1 *LIEI* 101; R. Frid, 'The European Economic Community: A Member of a Specialised Agency of the United Nations' (1993) 4 *EJIL* 239.

[159] Art. 93 ECSC.

[160] Arts. 229 EC and 199 Euratom. The Commission entered into a co-operation and liaison agreement with the UN Secretariat in November 1958. This deals with exchange of documentation, consultation between the staff of the Secretariat and the staff of the Community institutions and the possible participation of Community representatives at certain meetings of the UN.

[161] See, further, Ch. 8.   [162] 1971 UNYB 498.

[163] The title of the Community observer at the UN is now the 'European Community'. See Art. G(1) TEU.

[164] Tables summarizing the Community's participation in the UN system are in Annex I to this Ch.

Community may not vote: the Member States vote in their own right, usually after co-ordination in New York or in Brussels. The Community delegation is made up of representatives of the Commission delegation and representatives of the Presidency, assisted by the Council Secretariat.[165] On many issues, statements are delivered in the name of the European Union, usually by the Presidency. The Member States often deliver national statements to support or supplement statements by the Community, or on behalf of the Union.

The Security Council

The Communities have no formal status, as members or observers, in the Security Council, but France and the United Kingdom are permanent members of the Security Council, and other Member States are elected from time to time. Article J.5(4) TEU provides that Member States which are also members of the United Nations Security Council will concert and keep the other Member States fully informed. Member States which are permanent members of the Security Council will, in the exercise of their functions, ensure the defence of the positions and interests of the Union, without prejudice to their responsibilities under the provisions of the United Nations Charter.

The Trusteeship Council

The Communities do not participate in the work of the Trusteeship Council, as members or observers.

The International Court of Justice

The Communities have no *locus standi* before the ICJ.[166]

The Economic and Social Council (ECOSOC)

At its 1,769th meeting on 20 May 1971,[167] ECOSOC approved a recommendation from the United Nations Secretary General that it should extend a standing invitation to certain intergovernmental organizations to be represented as observers at future sessions of the Council. These organizations included the EEC. The Community has since then participated as observer, without the right to vote, in the work of ECOSOC. The Community also participates as observer

---

[165] The UN Diplomatic List ('the Blue Book') (issued annually) lists the 'EC' as one of the Observer missions to the UN, and states that the EC is 'represented by the Presidency of the Council of the EU and by the European Commission'. Under the heading 'Presidency of the EU' there are listed the representatives of the Member States which will hold the Presidency during the period in question, and the names of the Council Secretariat staff present in New York or Geneva. Under the heading 'European Commission', there are listed the members of the Commission delegation.

[166] Art. 34(1) of the Statute of the ICJ. On the possible involvement of 'public international organizations' in cases before the ICJ, see Arts. 34(2) and (3).

[167] 1971 UNYB 496. On the recognition of the right of the Community to speak as an observer in ECOSOC working groups, see the Memorandum of the UN Legal Counsel of 4 Feb. 1980 ((1980) UNJY 192 ST/LEG/SER.C/18).

in ECOSOC's Regional Commissions,[168] in its Functional Commissions,[169] and in other bodies established under its auspices.

The United Nations Conference on Trade and Development (UNCTAD)

In UNCTAD itself, the EC has the status of observer, without the right to vote.[170] The views of the Community are delivered by the Commission if the subject matter is within the competence of the Community, and by the Presidency on other matters on which a common position has been reached. The Member States are usually permitted to speak in amplification of the Community or common position.

The International Labour Organization (ILO)

Although only States may be members of the ILO, its constitution provides for the participation of representatives of employers, employees, and government in the General Conference and the Governing Body. The Community has the status of non-voting observer.

During the annual sessions of the ILO Conference and meetings of the Governing Body, Member States meet to co-ordinate views on an informal basis, and the Presidency will often express any consensus reached among the Member States and the Commission on matters under discussion within the ILO. Member States remain free to express national positions. More formal co-ordination takes place for the negotiation of proposed conventions relating to matters within Community competence. It has not always been easy to reach agreement:[171] attempts to establish co-ordination arrangements for the participation of the Member States and the Community in ILO Convention 170 on safety in the use of chemicals at work led to the Commission seeking an opinion from the Court of Justice under Article 228. That *Opinion* stressed the importance of close co-operation between the Community and the Member States in the negotiation and implementation of conventions drawn up within the ILO framework.[172]

Each of the Communities has concluded co-operation agreements with the

---

[168] The Economic Commission for Europe; the Economic and Social Commission for Asia and the Pacific; the Economic Commission for Latin America and the Caribbean; the Economic Commission for Africa; the Economic and Social Commission for Western Asia.

[169] The Commission for Narcotic Drugs, the Commission on the Status of Women, the Commission for Human Rights, the Commission for Social Development, the Statistical Commission, the Commission for Sustainable Development, and the Population Commission.

[170] The Community is a member of the Common Fund for Commodities and the various commodities agreements established under the auspices of UNCTAD: see above. The Community also has non-voting member status in the Intergovernmental Group of Experts on Restrictive Business Practices.

[171] For a history, see *Opinion 2/91*, Report for the Hearing, n. 44 above, at paras. 13–20.

[172] *Ibid.*, at paras. 36–38.

ILO.[173] These deal with consultation on matters of common interest; co-operation to ensure effective use of information; exchange of information and documents; technical assistance; and administrative co-operation generally.

The Council of Europe

All three Treaties envisage co-operation between the Communities and the Council of Europe.[174]

Article 94 ECSC states that relations between the institutions of the Community and the Council of Europe are to be maintained in accordance with the Protocol annexed to the ECSC Treaty. This provides, *inter alia*, that the European Parliament is to report each year to the Consultative Assembly of the Council of Europe on its activities.[175] The High Authority[176] is likewise to communicate each year to the Committee of Ministers of the Council of Europe the general report provided for in Article 17 ECSC.[177] The Commission is to inform the Council of Europe of the action it has been able to take on any recommendations that may have been sent to it by the Committee of Ministers of the Council of Europe.[178] Agreements between the Community and the Council of Europe may, among other things, provide for any type of mutual assistance and co-operation between the two organizations and indicate the appropriate forms thereof.[179]

Article 230 EC and Article 200 Euratom provide that 'the Community' is to 'establish all appropriate forms of co-operation with the Council of Europe'. The intention of these Articles seems to have been to provide for more extensive co-operation than the administrative co-operation between the Commission and the Council of Europe provided for under Article 229 EC and Article 199 Euratom.[180] Co-operation under Articles 230 EC and 200 Euratom could include Community accession to agreements negotiated under the auspices of the Council of Europe,[181] or some other form of common action. The European Community and the Member States are to foster co-operation with the Council of Europe in the field of education[182] and the sphere of culture.[183]

In 1989 the Council of Europe and the Commission, building on earlier exchanges of letters in 1959 and 1987,[184] established a series of regular meetings at senior ministerial level to strengthen dialogue between the Community

---

[173] Co-operation agreement between the ILO and the ECSC ([1953] JO 11/167); Co-operation agreement between the ILO and the EEC ([1958] JO 521); Co-operation agreement between the ILO and Euratom ([1961] JO 18/473).

[174] See H. Smit and P. Herzog, *The Law of the European Community* (New York, 1976), vol. 6, para. 279 ff.; Ouchterlony, 'The European Communities and the Council of Europe' [1984] 1 *LIEI* 59.

[175] Prot. on relations with the Council of Europe, Art. 2.   [176] i.e. the Commission.

[177] Prot., Art. 3.   [178] Prot., Art. 4.   [179] Prot., Art. 6.   [180] See above pp. 167 ff.

[181] In accordance with the procedures envisaged in the relevant Treaty.

[182] Art. 126(3) EC.   [183] Art. 128(3) EC.

[184] [1987] OJ L273/35; Bull. EC 6–1987, 2.2.56.

and the Council of Europe. These are attended by the Foreign Minister of the Member State holding the Presidency and by the Secretary General of the Commission.[185] In practice, there are close contacts between the Council of Europe and the Communities across many areas of common interest.[186] A report on the activities of the European Communities, and the Commission's General Report, are sent to the Committee of Ministers of the Council of Europe annually. The President of the Commission sometimes attends the Committee's meetings. Officials from the Commission and the Council Secretariat frequently attend Council of Europe meetings of experts, and representatives of the Council of Europe Secretariat are invited to attend as observers at meetings of the Commission services. Co-operation focuses on areas such as education, culture, youth, public health, and legal matters.

The Council of Europe has established a *bureau de liaison* in Brussels,[187] but there is no Community delegation to the Council of Europe, and none of the Communities has formal observer status at the Council of Europe. The Commission is invited to attend the sessions of the Parliamentary Assembly as observer, and Council and Commission observers regularly attend experts' meetings at the Council of Europe. Representatives of the Council of Europe Secretariat attend meetings within the Commission on various subjects, at the invitation of the Directorate General concerned.[188]

The Organization for Economic Co-operation and Development (OECD)

All three Communities are given express powers to co-operate with the OECD.[189] Under the ECSC Treaty, the Commission is to maintain all appropriate relations with the 'Organization for European Economic Co-operation' and to keep that organization regularly informed of the work of the Community.[190] The EC and Euratom are required to establish close co-operation with the OECD, the details of which are to be determined by common accord.[191] In addition, the Commission is to maintain administrative links.[192]

Article 13 of the OECD Convention provides that the Communities' representation in the OECD is defined in an Additional Protocol to the Convention

---

[185] Text of conclusions at Bull. EC 3–1989, 2.2.51.

[186] For examples of areas of co-operation in recent years, see 26th General Report (1992), paras. 1030–3 and 27th General Report (1993), paras. 916–9.

[187] Committee of Ministers Resolution (74) 13 of 6 May 1974. The purpose of the bureau is to report continuously to the Council of Europe Secretariat on developments in the Communities.

[188] See Mégret, n. 8 above, vol. 12, 70.

[189] See, generally, C. Schricke 'La CEE et l'OCDE à l'heure de l'acte unique' (1989) 93 *RGDIP* 801, who comments that relations between the EC and the OECD are 'à sens unique': despite the extensive rights of participation which the EC has in the work of the OECD, the OECD has no comparable rights to participate in the work of the institutions of the EC.

[190] Art. 93 ECSC.   [191] Arts. 231 EC and 201 Euratom.

[192] Arts. 229 EC and 199 Euratom.

signed on 14 December 1960.[193] That Protocol provides for Commission participation in the work of the OECD. The Commission's rights of participation are set out in the Rules of Procedure of the OECD,[194] and in a Resolution of the OECD Council on relations between the OECD Secretariat and the Commission services. In practice the Commission participates in all the OECD committees (except the budgetary committee) on a basis superior to that of observer, but falling just short of full membership. The Commission may participate in the elaboration of texts and make proposals. It is entitled to speak without having to be formally invited to do so, but it has no vote, and thus cannot block a consensus. The Commission may be elected a member of the bureaux of subsidiary bodies of the OECD. A Commission delegation to the OECD was established in 1961.

Community co-ordination takes place systematically on matters within Community competence under the chairmanship of the Presidency in office.

The International Energy Agency

The Statute of the International Energy Agency, adopted within the framework of the OECD, provides expressly that the Community may become a party, but to date the Community has not done so.[195]

INTERNATIONAL CONFERENCES

If the matters to be discussed at an international conference fall within Community competence, the Community (or Communities) should in principle participate to present and defend the Community interest. The Community will usually be represented by the Commission, or by the Commission and the Presidency. If the rules of the conference preclude or limit formal Community involvement, the Community position will usually be presented by the Presidency, supported by the Member States. The position to be expressed on matters within Community competence will be determined after consultation among the Member States and the Commission in Community co-ordination, on the basis of the principles outlined above.[196]

Conferences held under the auspices of an international organization will often confer on the Community delegation to the conference a status similar to that which the Community enjoys within the parent organization. Even where

---

[193] The texts of the OECD Convention and the Additional Prot. are at 888 UNTS 179, UKTS 20 (1962), Cmnd. 1646.

[194] Art. 7 of the OECD Rules of Procedure.

[195] Statutes of the IEA, Art. 72 (for the text, see UKTS 111 (1976), Cmnd. 6697, 14 ILM 1). In 1990, the Commission presented proposals for the Community's accession, but after some discussion in the Council, these proposals were withdrawn in 1993.

[196] See pp. 172–3.

the Community's status at a conference is limited, it is usually possible to ensure that agreements drawn up at the conference allow the Community to become a party to the extent of its competences.[197]

ANNEX

A. Organizations in the UN Family

1. Principal Organs of the UN

Organ	Area of Activity	Member State participation	Status of the Community
General Assembly (Arts. 9–22 of the Charter)	Any questions within the scope of the Charter	All	Observer
Security Council (Arts. 23–32 of the Charter)	Maintenance of international peace and security	France and the UK as permanent members; others as elected	None
International Court of Justice	Peaceful settlement of international disputes (Statute of the International Court of Justice)	Judges are elected	None
ECOSOC	Activities listed in Art. 62 of the Charter	All	Observer
Trusteeship Council	Chs. XII and XIII of the Charter	France and the UK	None
Secretariat	Arts. 97–100 of the Charter		

[197] Thus the Community is an observer at the UN, and enjoys that status at UN conferences. But it is usually entitled to become a party to agreements negotiated at conferences held under the auspices of the UN (e.g. on the environment).

2. Functional Commissions of ECOSOC

Body	Function	Member State participation	Status of the Community
Statistical Commission	Overall guidance for the statistical activities of the UN	Election	Observer
Population Commission	To study and advise on population changes, including migration, and their effect on economic and social conditions	Election	Observer
Commission for Social Development	To advise on social policies of a general character, in particular on all matters in the social field not covered by the specialized inter-governmental agencies	Election	Observer
Commission on Human Rights	To prepare recommendations and reports on matters concerning human rights	Election	Observer
Commission for Narcotic Drugs	To advise and prepare draft international agreements on all matters relating to the control of narcotic drugs	Election	Observer
Commission on the Status of Women	Promotion of women's rights in the political, economic, social, and educational fields	Election	Observer

Body	Function	Member State participation	Status of the Community
Commission for Sustainable Development	Monitoring progress in the implementation of Agenda 21 agreed at the UN Conference on the Environment and Development	Election	Observer
Commission for Transnational Corporations	Comprehensive and in-depth consideration of issues relating to transnational corporations	Election	Observer

3. Regional Commissions of ECOSOC

Name	Purpose	Member State participation	Community Status
Economic Commission for Europe	To generate and improve economic relations among its members and with other countries of the world and to strengthen inter-governmental co-operation particularly in environment, transport, statistics, trade facilitation and economic analysis	All	Observer

3. cont.

Name	Purpose	Member State participation	Community Status
Economic and Social Commission for Asia and the Pacific	'Clearing house' for technological information; provision of advice; research into economic and social problems	France, the Netherlands and the UK	Observer
Economic Commission for Western Asia	Facilitating concerted action for the economic reconstruction and development of Western Asia, for raising the level of economic activity in Western Asia and for maintaining and strengthening the economic ties between the countries of the region	None	Observer
Economic Commission for Latin America and and the Caribbean	To initiate and participate in measures for facilitating concerted action for dealing with urgent economic problems arising out of the war and for raising the level of economic activity in Latin America and the Caribbean and for maintaining and strengthening the economic relations of the Latin American and	France, the Netherlands, Portugal, Spain and the UK	Observer

Name	Purpose	Member State participation	Community Status
	Caribbean countries both among themselves and with other countries of the world		
Economic Commission for Africa	To initiate and participate in measures for facilitating concerted action for the economic development of Africa, including its social aspects, with a view to raising the level of economic activity and levels of living in Africa, and for maintaining and strengthening the economic relations of countries and territories of Africa both among themselves and with other countries of the world	None	Observer

4. Specialized Agencies of the UN

Name	Purpose	Member States involved	Community
International Labour Organization	To improve working and living conditions through the adoption of international labour conventions and recommendations setting minimum standards in fields such as wages, working hours etc.	All	Observer

4. cont.

Name	Purpose	Member States involved	Community
Food and Agriculture Organization	To promote the common welfare by furthering separate and collective action for the purposes of raising levels of nutrition and standards of living of the peoples under their respective jurisdictions; securing improvements in the efficiency of the production and distribution of all food and agricultural products; bettering the condition of rural populations; and thus contributing toward an expanding world economy and ensuring humanity's freedom from hunger	All	Member Organization
UN Educational Scientific and Cultural Organization	Promoting collaboration among the nations through education, science and culture in order to further universal respect for justice, for the rule of law and for human rights and fundamental freedoms	All except the UK	Observer

Name	*Purpose*	*Member States involved*	*Community*
World Health Organization	Attainment by all peoples of the highest standards of health	All	Observer
International Civil Aviation Organization	Developing the principles and techniques of international air navigation and fostering the planning and development of international air transport so as to ensure the safe and orderly growth of international civil aviation throughout the world	All	Observer
Universal Postal Union	To secure the organization and improvement of postal services and to promote in this sphere the development of international collaboration and undertake as far as possible technical assistance in postal matters requested by member countries	All	Observer
International Telecommunications Union	To maintain and extend co-operation on tele-communications matters	All	Observer

4. cont.

Name	Purpose	Member States involved	Community
World Meteorological Organization	To facilitate the establishment of weather stations and related services	All	Observer
International Maritime Organization	To facilitate co-operation among governments on technical matters affecting international shipping in order to achieve the highest practicable standards of maritime safety and efficiency in navigation. IMO has special responsibility for the safety of lives at sea and for the protection of the marine environment	All	Observer
World Intellectual Property Organization	To promote the protection of intellectual property throughout the world through international co-operation between states and organizations	All	Observer
International Union for the Protection of New Varieties of Plants (UPOV)	To oblige members to recognize and secure to breeders of new plant varieties an industrial property right to harmonize such rights and encourage co-operation in the administration of such rights	All except Austria, Luxembourg, Greece and Portugal	Observer

Name	Purpose	Member States involved	Community
International Fund for Agricultural Development	To mobilize additional financial resources from donors to be made available on concessional terms for agricultural development in developing countries	All	Observer
International Atomic Energy Agency	To seek to accelerate and enlarge the contribution of atomic energy to peace, health and prosperity throughout the world	All	Observer
United Nations Industrial Development Organization	To encourage and extend assistance to the developing countries for the development, expansion, and modernization of their industries; and related purposes	All	Observer
International Monetary Fund	To promote international monetary co-operation; exchange rate stability etc	All	None
World Tourism Organization	To promote and develop tourism with a view to contributing to economic development, international understanding, peace, prosperity and respect for human rights	All	Observer

B. Regional and Other Organizations

Body	Function	Status of the Community	Member State participation
Council of Europe	To work for wider European unity; to defend human rights; and to improve standards of living in Europe	Close institutional links: no formal status	All
International Committee for Migration	To organize migratory movements responding to the specific needs of countries of emigration and immigration	Invited by the Secretariat	Members: Austria, Belgium, Denmark, Greece, Netherlands, and Portugal Observers: France, Spain, Sweden, and the UK
Central Office for International Carriage by Rail	To facilitate and ensure the application of international transport agreements	Observer	All
European Conference of Ministers of Transport	Best and most rational use and development of internal European transport systems and co-ordination of the work of international organizations interested in such matters	Observer	All
Central Commission for the Navigation on the Rhine	To ensure respect for the principles of freedom of navigation and	Observer	France, Germany, Luxembourg,

Body	Function	Status of the Community	Member State participation
	equal treatment for all countries		Belgium, Netherlands, and the UK
European Organization for the Safety of Air Navigation	To reinforce co-operation between members and provide a common organization of aerial traffic at over 9000m	Participates at meetings and conferences	All except Denmark, Spain, and Italy
European Civil Aviation Conference	To improve the co-ordination, better utilization and development of European air traffic	Observer	All
International Centre for Advanced Mediterranean Agronomic Studies	Technical and economic information to develop agriculture in Mediterranean countries	No formal status: institutional links	France, Greece, Spain, Italy, and Portugal
Association of South East Asian Nations	Accelerate development, promote peace and stability, and co-operation among the countries of SE Asia	Institutional links: no formal status	None
Organization of American States	Peace, stability, economic, cultural and social development in the American Continent	Observer	Permanent Observers: Austria, Finland, Germany, Belgium, Spain, France, Greece, Italy, Netherlands, and Portugal

B. *cont.*

Body	Function	Status of the Community	Member State participation
European Space Agency	To develop co-operation among European countries into the peaceful uses of space	Observer	All except Greece, Luxembourg, and Portugal
Council of Arab Economic Unity	Flexible framework for economic integration of its members	Institutional links: no formal status	None
North Atlantic Treaty Organization	Peace and security in the North Atlantic area	At the invitation of the Secretariat, Community attends as observer	All except Austria, Ireland, Finland, and Sweden
Western European Union	To promote unity and encourage progressive integration in Europe	Observer at the Parliamentary Assembly	All except Austria, Denmark, Greece, Finland, Ireland, and Sweden
European Bank for Reconstruction and Development	To assist in the economic reconstruction of Europe	Member	All
Organization for Economic Co-operation and Development	Economic expansion, raising of the standard of living, contribute to expansion of global trade	Participates in accordance with Prot. 1 to the OECD Convention	All
Customs Co-operation Council	Study all matters relating to customs co-operation	Observer	All

Body	Function	Status of the Community	Member State participation
International Standardization Organization	Development of standards to promote trade in goods and services	Commission attends certain meetings at the invitation of the Secretariat. No institutional links	All except Luxembourg
International Council for the Exploration of the Sea	To encourage research and exploration for the study of the sea	Observer	All except Austria, Greece, Luxembourg, and Italy
International Office of Epizootics	Study and research into diseases of cattle	Observer	All
International Organization for Legal Metrology	Documentation and information centre for national offices concerned with measuring instruments	Observer	All except Luxembourg
Organization for Security and Co-operation in Europe	Preventive diplomacy, peacekeeping and conflict management	Observer	All

8

The Diplomatic Relations of the Communities

Over 150 States have established diplomatic missions to the Communities in Brussels, and the Communities are members of several organizations and have observer status in many more. Over a hundred Commission delegations have been set up in third countries, and there are Commission delegations to several organizations. Diplomatic relations between the Communities and other subjects of international law are therefore common and extensive. For these reasons, it has sometimes been asserted that the Communities possess an active and passive right of legation: that is to say, they have the right to send and receive diplomatic representatives in the way that States do.[1]

It is doubtful, however, whether such an assertion is sound in law. In the conduct of diplomatic relations, as in other areas, the Communities possess the powers which have been attributed to them, expressly or by implication, by the Treaties; and they may exercise these powers only in respect of the objectives set out in the Treaties. The question, therefore, is whether powers amounting to a 'right of legation'[2] have been expressly attributed to the Communities, or whether it can be shown, on the basis of practice, that such powers arise by implication from the Treaties.[3]

Article 17 of the Protocol on the Privileges and Immunities of the European

[1] For historical accounts of the early representations of the ECSC, see E. Sauvignon, 'Les Communautés européennes et le droit de légation actif' [1978] *RMC* 176, and J. Groux and P. Manin, *The European Communities in the International Order* (European Perspectives, 1985), Pt. 1, Ch. II, 34–6. International law governing the conduct of diplomatic relations between States is based on practice of very long standing, and is now largely codified in the Vienna Convention on Diplomatic Relations (500 UNTS 95; UKTS 19 (1965); Cmnd. 2565). The rules in respect of international organizations and their representatives are not so developed. International organizations have emerged as active international legal persons relatively recently (see the *Reparations Case*, [1949] ICJ Reports 174; and Ch. 2. See also H. G. Schermers, *International Institutional Law* (2nd edn., A. W. Sijthoff, 1980), paras. 1607 to 1645, especially 1607–24. On diplomatic law and practice generally, see I. Brownlie, *Principles of Public International Law* (4th edn., Clarendon Press, 1990), ch. XVI; Oppenheim, *International Law* (9th edn., Longman, 1992), i, ch. 10; Denza, *Diplomatic Law* (Oceana Publications, 1976); Satow: *A Guide to Diplomatic Practice* (5th edn., Longman, 1979), especially Bk. II, chs. 9–25. The Communities' relations with international organizations are discussed in Ch. 7. The extent of the Communities' immunity from the jurisdiction of the Member States is described in Ch. 2

[2] The term 'right of legation' is probably a misnomer. Oppenheim, n. 1 above, at para. 464 states: 'it is controversial whether the sending and receiving of diplomats involves a right in the strict legal sense, or whether it is rather a matter of competence.'

[3] Oppenheim, n. 1 above, para. 464, at n. 2: 'International organizations may possess a degree of international personality, and this may, in particular cases, involve the possession of the right of legation. It will depend on the constitution of each organization whether it possesses the right of legation, and if so to what extent.'

Communities envisages the accreditation to the Communities of missions of third countries. From this it may be inferred that the Communities enjoy a passive right of legation.[4] But nothing in the Treaties expressly or implicitly confers a power to send diplomatic representatives on behalf of the Communities,[5] and in practice there exists no diplomatic corps which represents the Communities as such. It is true that the Council is involved to an extent in the process of creating Commission delegations and in the appointment of the Head of Delegation.[6] It is also true that 'there is . . . tacit approval by the budgetary authorities (Council and the Parliament) which can be inferred from the adoption of the appropriations necessary for [the Commission's delegations] to function'.[7] But the delegations which have been established in third States by the Commission nevertheless remain delegations of the Commission, not diplomatic representations of the Communities. They are appointed by the Commission, act in its name, receive instructions from it, and report to it. The better analysis, therefore, is that these delegations are established, not under a Community right of legation, but by virtue of the Commission's right as an institution to organize its own resources as it sees fit.

Thus the conduct of the Communities' 'diplomatic relations' with third States and international organizations is more complicated than might at first appear. There is no single representative of the Communities. Instead, the views and interests of the Communities in third States and in international organizations are represented by the combined activities of Commission delegations and the diplomatic missions of the Member States. These channels also combine to present the position of the Union on matters falling within the scope of the common foreign and security policy. The boundary between Community affairs and matters within the common foreign and security policy is not always easy to draw, but this Chapter focuses on the representation of the Communities in the strict sense. The representation of the position of the Union on matters within the scope of the common foreign and security policy is dealt with later in this work.[8] Before considering the Communities' relations with third States and organizations, it may be worth noting briefly how the Communities conduct their formal relations with the Member States.

---

[4] P. Pescatore, 'Les relations extérieures de la Communauté européenne' 103 *Hague Recueil* (1961 II) at 193: 'L'éventualité de l'envoi de missions représentatives d'états tiers auprès des Communautés a été envisagée par les auteurs des traités: on en trouve la preuve dans une disposition du protocole sur les privilèges et immunités de la CEE'.

[5] *Ibid.* p 195: 'Le seul moyen de créer des organes communs pour les relations extérieures [i.e. diplomatic missions of the Communities] sans recourir a une révision formelle des traités, semble être encore une fois l'utilisation du pouvoir général prévu par les Articles 235 CEE et 203 Euratom'.

[6] See further below at p. 216.

[7] Opinion of Tesauro A.G. in Case C–327/91 *France* v. *Commission* [1994] ECR I–3641 at para. 28.

[8] Ch. 24.

THE COMMUNITIES AND THE MEMBER STATES

Member States' Representations to the Communities

Each Member State maintains in Brussels a diplomatic post whose task is to liaise with the institutions of the Communities and the other Member States on behalf of the sending Member State on all matters connected with the activities of the Communities.[9] This post is known as the 'Permanent Representation' of the Member State to the Communities,[10] and is headed in each case by a senior ambassador or civil servant, formally entitled the 'Permanent Representative' of the Member State concerned. He is assisted by a Deputy Permanent Representative and officials drawn from departments of the national (and sometimes regional) government of the Member State.[11]

Privileges and Immunities

The Protocol on the Privileges and Immunities of the European Communities provides that representatives of Member States taking part in the work of the institutions of the Communities, their advisers, and technical experts, enjoy, in the performance of their duties and during their travel to and from the place of meeting, the customary privileges, immunities, and facilities.[12] The Protocol is part of Community law, and can be relied on before national courts in any Member State on the same conditions as any other part of the Treaties. There is therefore no reason to limit the enjoyment of the privileges, immunities, and facilities conferred by the Protocol to meetings and Community activities in Brussels. They could be equally relevant and necessary in respect of business carried out in Luxembourg[13] or Strasbourg,[14] or at other meetings held under the auspices of the Council outside Brussels.

[9] And, increasingly, on matters falling within the scope of the common foreign and security policy (see Ch. 24) and the co-operation in the fields of justice and home affairs established by Title VI of the TEU.

[10] For an account of the activities of the Permanent Representations, see Hayes-Renshaw *et al.*, 'The Permanent Representations of the Member States to the European Communities' [1989] XXVIII *JCMS* 119. (The work of the Committee of Permanent Representatives ('COREPER') is discussed in Noel, 'The Committee of Permanent Representatives', (1966) V *JCMS* 219—an account which, though dated, contains much of interest.) All the Permanent Representations now style themselves the 'Permanent Representation of . . . to the *European Union*.' But as a matter of law, they remain accredited to the Communities. The European Union does not possess international legal personality, and does not accept accreditations from the Member States, or from third States. For the Commission's view, see n. 35 below. For the UK view, see Hansard, HL Debs., vol. 546, cols. 710–11, 8 June 1993; HL Debs., vol. 549, WA2, 11 Oct. 1993.

[11] A full list is given in *Guide to the Council of the European Union*, published annually by the Council Secretariat.

[12] Art. 11 of the Prot. on Privileges and Immunities of the European Communities (hereafter 'Prot.').

[13] At the Court, or at Council or Commission meetings.   [14] At the Parliament.

The Permanent Representations of the Member States in Brussels are full diplomatic missions. Accordingly, so far as the Representations are concerned, the 'customary privileges, immunities, and facilities' referred to in the Protocol are those in the Vienna Convention on Diplomatic Relations, which apply to the staff of the Permanent Representations and to the premises, communications, and archives of the Representations.[15] The extent of the privileges and immunities conferred by the Protocol on other representatives of the Member States (for example, officials from capitals attending meetings of the Council in Brussels) is less clear. It is reasonable to expect that they are immune from suit and legal process in respect of acts done in the course of their official duties, and that their persons and papers are inviolable during the course of their visit. It is very unlikely that they are entitled to the customs or fiscal benefits enjoyed by the staff of the Representations.

Representation of the Communities in the Member States

The institutions of the Communities conduct their relations with a Member State primarily through its Permanent Representation: the Communities as such have no formal representation in the capitals of the Member States. The Commission and the Parliament have offices in each of the Member States, but the function of these offices is to provide information to the public rather than to represent formally the views of the Communities or the parent institution.

Privileges and Immunities

In the territory of each Member State and whatever their nationality,[16] officials and other servants of the Communities enjoy the privileges, immunities, and facilities set out in Articles 12 to 15 of the Protocol. They have immunity from legal proceedings in respect of acts performed and words spoken or written by them in their official capacity.[17] This immunity continues after they have ceased to hold office.[18] Neither they nor their spouses or dependent members of their families may be subject to immigration restrictions.[19] In respect of currency or exchange regulations, they are to be accorded the same facilities as are customarily accorded to officials of international organizations.[20] They are also entitled to certain customs and excise duty benefits.[21] The Protocol provides for the imposition of a special income tax, and deals with the application of other

---

[15] There is no Headquarters Agreement between the Communities and the Belgian authorities: diplomatic privileges and immunities are accorded by Belgium. See J. Mégret, *Le droit de la Communauté Européenne* (Brussels, 1980), vol. 12, 13.

[16] This is unusual: the nationals of a State do not as a rule enjoy privileges and immunities within their own State.

[17] Prot., Art. 12(1)(a).   [18] *Ibid.*, Art. 12(1)(a).   [19] *Ibid.*, Art. 12(1)(b).

[20] *Ibid.*, Art. 12(1)(c).   [21] *Ibid.*, Art. 12(1)(d) and (e).

taxes and duties.[22] The Council is required to lay down a scheme of social security benefits for officials and other servants of the Communities.[23]

These privileges, immunities, and facilities are accorded solely in the interests of the Community,[24] and each institution of the Communities is required to waive the immunity accorded to an official or servant whenever that institution considers that the waiver of immunity is not contrary to the interests of the Communities.[25]

The privileges, immunities, and facilities accorded to officials and servants of the Communities by the Protocol also apply to the members of the Commission;[26] to the Judges, the Advocates-General, the Registrar, and the Assistant Rapporteurs of the Court of Justice,[27] and to the Members of the Court of Auditors.[28]

The Protocol also applies in respect of the European Investment Bank.[29] Provision is made for according privileges and immunities to the European Monetary Institute and the European Central Bank.[30]

The position of the Members of the European Parliament is governed by Articles 8, 9, and 10 of the Protocol.

THE COMMUNITIES AND THIRD STATES

Third States' Missions to the Communities

The Communities' growing international importance has led many third States to establish a permanent diplomatic presence at the seat of the Communities in Brussels to conduct relations with the Communities.[31] Although these States continue to conduct relations with the Member States of the Communities bilaterally on matters of mutual interest and importance, and also on matters arising in the work of the Communities, the principal contact between the outside world and the Communities is through the permanent missions[32] accredited to the Communities.[33] The establishment by a third State of a mission to the

---

[22] Prot., Arts. 13 and 14.   [23] *Ibid.*, Art. 15.   [24] *Ibid.*, Art. 18(1).

[25] *Ibid.*, Art. 18(2): i.e. there is a presumption in favour of waiver.

[26] *Ibid.*, Art. 20.

[27] *Ibid.*, Art. 21. This is without prejudice to the provisions of Art. 3 of the Protocols on the Statute of the Court of Justice concerning immunity from legal proceedings of Judges and Advocates General.

[28] Art. 188b(9) EC.   [29] Prot., Art. 22.

[30] *Ibid*, Art. 23, added by the Prot. amending the Prot. on the Privileges and Immunities of the European Communities, annexed to the TEU.

[31] Sometimes called the Communities' 'passive right of legation'. See generally, Mégret, n. 15 above, vol. 12, 6–13.

[32] The differences in title of these missions ('mission', 'delegation', or 'representation') are commented on by Mégret, n. 15 above, 10, n. 29.

[33] Some third countries' missions to the Communities are also accredited to one or more of the Member States.

Communities does not depend on that State having diplomatic relations with all the Member States.[34]

Establishment of Third States' Missions to the Communities

The basic principle in the establishment of diplomatic relations between the Communities[35] and third States is the same as that applying between States: consent is required on each side.[36] The process by which the Communities' consent is established is as follows:

(a) the State concerned approaches the Community informally, usually through the Commission, seeking agreement in principle to the establishment of diplomatic relations;

(b) the Commission and the Council consult[37] with a view to reaching a decision by common accord[38] on the response to be given to the third State's approach. The Council and the Member States are usually given a period of about thirty days in which to make known any comments or objections;

(c) if the reaction of the Council and the Commission is positive, the Commission informs the third State accordingly. The next step is to agree on the Head of Mission: again the Council and the Commission decide their response by common accord;

(d) the process is completed by the transmission of letters of accreditation from the third State. In relation to the ECSC, the credentials of the third State's Head of Mission are formally presented to the President of the Commission. In relation to the EC and Euratom, identical letters of

---

[34] e.g., Indonesia has established a mission to the Communities, even though it has no diplomatic relations with Portugal. The Commission has established a delegation (or 'representation') there : see n. 49 below.

[35] Following the practice of the Member States themselves (n. 10 above), some third States now designate their missions 'the mission of X to the European Union'. This, no doubt, reflects the fact that these missions are interested in the work of the Union as a whole, not just in the areas within the strictly legal competence of the Communities. The legal and diplomatic reality, however, is that the missions of third States to the Communities are accredited to the Communities, not to the EU. A Commission *Note Verbale*, circulated in Aug. 1994 noted that a number of missions had decided to adopt the title 'Mission to the EU', but reminded missions that under Community law, legal personality was expressly conferred only on the European Communities. Changes to the title of Missions should thus not in any way affect references to the European Communities in legal acts. For the position of the UK Government, see the Hansard references in n. 10 above. For the position in German law, see the judgment of the Federal Constitutional Court of 12 October 1993 [1994] 1 CMLR 57.

[36] Cf. Art. 2 of the Vienna Convention on Diplomatic Relations.

[37] Matters of this delicacy are of course treated in the strictest confidence within the institutions concerned.

[38] Schermers, *The Communities' Relations under Public International Law* in *Thirty Years of Community Law* (European Perspectives Series, Commission, 1991), 221: 'Both for the establishment of diplomatic relations and for the acceptance of a diplomat as *persona non grata*, the Council's decision must be unanimous. Each Member State has, accordingly a right of veto regarding every mission and every ambassador of a third State.'

accreditation are submitted simultaneously without ceremonial to the President of the Commission and the President of the Council. It is usual for the Head of Mission to pay a courtesy visit to the President of the Council.[39]

A list of the staff of missions accredited to the Communities is published annually by the Commission.[40] Heads of Mission rank in seniority according to the date of their letters of accreditation.

Tasks of such Missions

Missions to international organizations perform in relation to the organizations to which they are accredited tasks similar to those performed in their host country by diplomatic missions of States. Such tasks typically include ensuring the representation of the sending State to the organization; maintaining liaison between the sending State and the organization; negotiating with the organization; reporting on activities within the organization, and so on.

Rights and Privileges of such Missions

The 'Member State in whose territory the Communities have their seat'[41] is obliged to accord 'the customary diplomatic immunities and privileges' to missions of third countries accredited to the Communities.[42] As in the case of the Representations of the Member States, the phrase 'customary diplomatic immunities and privileges' may be taken to be a reference to the diplomatic privileges and immunities which are generally recognized in international law, and set out in the Vienna Convention on Diplomatic Relations.[43]

---

[39] See para. (a)3 of the Luxembourg Accords of Jan. 1966 (reproduced in 1966 Bull. CE–3, 8; *Encyclopædia of Community Law* (Sweet & Maxwell, loose-leaf), Pt. 13.001). See also WQ 78 in [1966] JO 4049.

[40] The latest list, comprising 172 countries or territories, is in *Corps Diplomatique accrédité auprès des Communautés européennes et représentations auprès de la Commission*, (Brussels, Oct. 1994).

[41] The Parliament has its seat in Strasbourg. The Council and the Commission have their seats in Brussels. The ECJ and the Court of Auditors have their seats in Luxembourg. There is thus no single Member State in which the institutions of the Communities have their seat. A purposive interpretation of the Prot. would suggest that representatives of third States should be accorded privileges and immunities in all Member States where one of the institutions of the Communities has its seat.

[42] Prot., Art. 17.

[43] It is not, however, always easy to transpose the rules applicable to diplomats and embassies to the staff and premises of international organizations. For example, it is a fundamental principle of diplomatic law and practice that the receiving State is entitled to declare any diplomat accredited to it *persona non grata* at any time without giving reasons (Art. 9, Vienna Convention on Diplomatic Relations). It is less clear how this principle can apply in the case of international organizations such as the Communities, which have no territory of their own from which to exclude the offending diplomat. Nor is it clear by what procedure the Community institutions would act in such a case. Expulsion of a third country representative would seem to require common accord of the Council

Representation of the Communities in Third States

The representatives of third States accredited to the Communities are accredited to the Communities as such and not to the Member States or to the institutions. The Communities themselves, on the other hand, have no diplomatic representatives in third States. Instead, as has been noted, the interests of the Communities and the Member States in third countries are promoted and protected by Commission delegations,[44] and by the diplomatic missions of the Member States. The Presidency for the time being of the Council plays a particular role in this process.[45] These forms of representation have traditionally combined to ensure that the interests of the Communities are safeguarded and promoted, and their views heard;[46] together they constitute the diplomatic representation of the Communities overseas.

Commission Delegations in Third States

There are 116 Commission delegations[47] in third States and territories outside the Communities. These delegations are staffed by Commission officials selected by the Commission from among its services.[48] In certain third countries where the Commission does not have a delegation, a press and information office has been established. Delegations have been established in States which do not have diplomatic relations with all the Member States.[49]

and Commission. A counter argument, deriving from the principle that diplomatic relations are maintained by mutual consent, would be that the objection of either institution to the continued accreditation of an individual would be enough to lead to his expulsion. The accreditation is to the Communities, not to the host State: so the views of the host State, though doubtless taken carefully into account, would not appear to be decisive. (But see Mégret, n. 15 above, 13; and n. 38.)

[44] Sometimes loosely called the Communities' 'active right of legation'. For a description of the functions of Commission delegations, and of the procedures for their establishment, see L. J. Brinkhorst, 'Permanent Missions of the EC in Third Countries: European Diplomacy in the Making' [1984]1 *LIEI* 23. A more up-to-date and extensive account is given by J. M. Sobrino Heredia, 'La Actividad Diplomatica de Las Delagaciones de la Comision en el Exterior de la Comunidad Europea' (1993) 20, *Revista de Instituciones Europeas* 485

[45] On the role of the Presidency in presenting the Union's position in matters within the common foreign and security policy, see Art. J.5 TEU, and Ch. 24.

[46] For a full, if now somewhat dated, account of how the Commission's delegations and the missions of the Member States co-operate in ensuring the representation of the Communities, see Sauvignon, n. 1 above.

[47] Strictly speaking, there are 104 delegations, 2 representations, and 10 'offices'. An updated list of delegations is given in the Annex to this Ch.. The differences in title seems to be based mainly on the size of the mission.

[48] Delegations and representations are usually staffed by officials drawn from DGI, DGIa, and DGVIII. The Commission's overseas offices are often staffed locally.

[49] A Commission delegation has been established in Indonesia, even though that State has no diplomatic relations with Portugal. The delegation is known as a 'representation'. See also n. 34 above.

Tasks of Commission Delegations

With the missions of the Member States, the Commission's delegations play a part in communicating the views and representing the interests of the Communities as a whole.[50] In formal terms, however, and in day-to-day reality, they receive instructions from, and report to, the Commission alone.[51] Most delegations have press and information sections. In the ACP States, they play an important role in the implementation of the Lomé Convention.[52]

Procedure for Appointment of Commission Delegations

The appointment of its overseas delegations is an administrative matter for the Commission,[53] but in practice the Council[54] has a role in the decision to establish a delegation and in the appointment of the Heads of Commission Delegations. In 1989,[55] the Commission placed its procedures on a more formal footing, and agreed to inform the Council unofficially[56] of any intention to open a new delegation or to change the status or level of accreditation of an existing delegation. The Commission also declared itself willing to discuss both the timing and principle of such decisions if the Member States so requested. Similarly, the Commission has undertaken to inform the Council[57] of its choice of its Heads of Delegation and of their courtesy titles, and to give the Council a brief period in which to comment on the choice. Formal nomination of a Head of Delegation is, however, for the Commission, and the credentials of the Head of Delegation are signed jointly by the President of the Commission and the Commissioner responsible for external relations.

Accreditation and Precedence in the Host State

Once the Head of Delegation has been accepted by the third State, his appointment is confirmed by the presentation of a letter of introduction from the President of the Commission to the host government. The Commission's former practice was to seek accreditation at the level of the Ministry of Foreign Affairs of the host State. Recent practice since 1989 is to seek accreditation at

---

[50] See Brinkhorst, n. 44 above; Sauvignon, n. 1 above; Sobrino Heredia, n. 44 above. Also WQ 842/85 (Rogalla) [1985] OJ C87/34.

[51] Commission delegations are sometimes described as 'embassies of the Community'. This is inaccurate. On their status, the correct term is 'delegation', and the entity represented is the Commission.

[52] Below, *The ACP States.*

[53] That is to say, establishment of Commission delegations is not an exercise of a Community right of legation but an expression of the Commission's powers to organize its own resources. See p. 209 above, and also Mégret, n. 15 above, 8; Sauvignon, n. 1 above, 180.

[54] Apart from its role in the budgetary process, the Parliament has no role in the process, though it has sought one: see Res. A3–0322/92 on the establishment of the Communities' foreign and security policy. For a discussion, see R. Gosalbo Bono, 'The International Powers of the European Parliament, the Democratic Deficit and the Treaty on European Union' (1992) 12 *YBEL* 85 at 128.

[55] Even before 1989, the practice was to inform the Council (through COREPER) of the intended nominee: see Brinkhorst, n. 44 above, and Sauvignon, n. 1 above.

[56] Through COREPER.   [57] By the same channels.

the level of Head of State; and if this is not possible for constitutional reasons in the host State, at the level of Head of Government. In diplomatic precedence, representatives of the Commission rank after the diplomatic representatives of States (including the Member States), but before the representatives of other international organizations. The Head of Delegation is generally entitled 'ambassador—head of delegation'. The delegation itself will usually be entitled the 'delegation of the European Commission'.[58] By analogy with normal diplomatic practice, the seniority of a Commission delegation and of its staff is determined on the basis of reciprocity, by reference to the level of accreditation of the State in question to the Communities in Brussels.

Privileges and Immunities of Commission Delegations

The privileges and immunities of Commission delegations do not derive directly from the Vienna Convention on Diplomatic Relations,[59] but from agreements[60] between host States and the Commission, or (less commonly) from unilateral legislative acts on the part of host States.[61] The legal status accorded to Commission delegations varies: in some States, privileges and immunities are expressly accorded to the extent necessary for the performance of the functions of the delegation.[62] More commonly, host States accord the Commission delegation the rights and immunities contained in the Vienna Convention on Diplomatic Relations.

The Commission may conclude agreements for the *laissez-passer* of the Community institutions[63] to be recognized as valid travel documents within the territory of third States.[64]

---

[58] The Commission is for legal purposes the 'Commission of the European Communities', although it decided shortly after the entry into force of the Maastricht Treaty to re-title itself, for more general purposes, 'the European Commission'. Its delegations are now known as delegations of the 'European Commission'.

[59] It is also very doubtful whether customary law confers on international organizations all the rights and privileges accorded to representatives of States in the Vienna Convention on Diplomatic Relations.

[60] There are several dozen such agreements in existence, but their legal status is uncertain. In Case C–327/91, n. 7 above, the A.G. appeared to accept that they were legally valid (Opinion, n. 43), but the judgment of the Court suggests that the Commission has no power to conclude international agreements which purport to bind the European Community. See further, Ch. 4.

[61] For an example, the US Exec. Ord. 5–12–72; Fed. Rep. vol. 37, 7.12.72, relating to the Commission delegation in Washington.

[62] The 'functional need' test. This is the normal standard applied in deciding on the privileges and immunities to be conferred on international organizations: see the Council of Europe Report on *the Privileges and Immunities of International Organizations* (annexed to Resolution (69) 29 of the Committee of Ministers of the Council of European 26 September 1969 on the privileges and immunities of international organisations) (1969). It is a measure of the political importance of the Communities that the Commission's delegations usually benefit from a more extensive range of legal rights and privileges than do other international organizations.

[63] On the Community institutions' *laissez-passer*, see the Prot. on the Privileges and Immunities of the European Communities, Art. 7(1).

[64] Prot., Art. 7(1).

The ACP States

Article 316 of the Fourth Lomé Convention[65] provides that the Commission shall be represented in each ACP State, or in each regional grouping which so requests, by a delegate approved by the ACP State or States concerned.[66] The delegate is to have the necessary instructions and delegated powers to facilitate and expedite the preparation, appraisal, and execution of projects and programmes and to that end several tasks are given to him.[67] A Protocol on privileges and immunities[68] annexed to the Fourth Lomé Convention provides certain exemptions for Commission delegations to the ACP States.[69] The Protocol also deals with the position of other persons taking part in the work of the Convention (including the representatives of the institutions of the European Communities);[70] with the status of property, funds, and assets of the Council of ACP Ministers;[71] and with the position of the staff of the secretariat of the ACP States.[72] The official communications of the Communities, the institutions of the Convention, and the co-ordinating bodies are also protected.[73]

Diplomatic Missions of the Member States

The accreditation and grant of privileges and immunities to diplomatic missions of the Member States in third States are dealt with on a bilateral basis between the sending State and the host State, in accordance with the usual international rules and practices. The Member States are under a general duty to work to further the interests of the Communities, and the activities of their missions in

---

[65] On the 4th ACP–EEC Convention (Lomé IV) ([1991] OJ L229/1), see Ch. 20.

[66] Where a delegate is appointed to a group of ACP States, appropriate steps shall be taken to ensure that the delegate is represented by a deputy resident in each of the States in which the delegate is not resident: Lomé IV, Art. 316(2).

[67] Lomé IV, Art. 317. These tasks are primarily concerned with the Community's control over financing decisions for projects funded in accordance with the Convention. On this, see, further, Ch. 20.

[68] Prot. 3. See also the declarations relating to Prot. 3 in Annexes LXXI, LXXII, and LXXIII to the Convention. The declaration in Annex LXXIII states that 'Within the context of their respective regulations, the ACP States shall grant Commission delegations privileges and immunities similar to those granted to diplomatic missions so that they are able to carry out the functions incumbent on them under the Convention in a satisfactory and effective manner.'

[69] Art. 10 of Prot. 3. Commission representatives apparently do not benefit from Art. 1 as 'representatives of the institutions of the Communities'. The Commission has, however, been able to obtain a more privileged position for some of its delegations in ACP countries on the basis of bilateral agreements with the States concerned.

[70] Representatives of the governments of the Member States and of the ACP States, their advisers and experts taking part, in the territory of the Member States or of the ACP States, in the work either of the institutions of the Convention, or of the co-ordinating bodies, or in work connected with the application of the Convention, are to enjoy 'the customary privileges, immunities, and facilities' while carrying out their duties and travelling to or from the place at which they are required to carry out their duties.

[71] Lomé IV, Prot. 3, Arts. 3–5.

[72] *Ibid.*, Art. 7–9.   [73] *Ibid.*, Art. 6.

third States reflect this commitment:[74] there is close day-to-day co-operation among the missions of the Member States in third countries on all matters of interest to the Communities.[75] Joint démarches to host States by the Member States, and joint reports to capitals on local issues, are made frequently.[76]

Article 8c EC[77] provides that a citizen of the Union is entitled, in the territory of a third country in which the Member State of which he is a national is not represented, to protection by the diplomatic and consular authorities of any Member State, on the same conditions as the nationals of that State. The Member States are to establish[78] the 'necessary rules' among themselves and start the international negotiations required to secure that protection.[79] Even before the entry into force of Article 8c EC, work was already in progress in the EPC framework on 'Guidelines for the Protection of unrepresented EC nationals by EC missions in third countries'. These Guidelines were adopted by the Political Committee in March 1993, and have been applied by the Member States since 1 July 1993.[80] Agreement has also been reached among the Member States on a common format emergency travel document.

Presidency Representation of the Communities in Third States

The Presidency has a particular role in presenting the joint views of the Member States and the Commission on matters where competence is shared between the Community and the Member States, and will frequently be called on to present the agreed position of the Communities and the Member States,

---

[74] For a comprehensive account of co-operation among the Member States within the framework of EPC (i.e. before the TEU), see B. R. Bot, 'Co-operation of the Missions of the EC in Third countries: European Diplomacy in the making' [1984] 1 *LIEI* 149.

[75] In some countries, the Member States share premises: e.g. Abuja, in Nigeria.

[76] The same is true in respect of matters falling within the scope of the common foreign and security policy. On co-operation on these matters, see Art. J.6 TEU and Ch. 24.

[77] Added to the EC Treaty by Art. G(9) TEU.

[78] This was to have taken place before 31 Dec. 1993.

[79] The scope of Art. 8c is unclear. The most obvious, and probably the intended, meaning is that the Member States are to afford consular protection to each others' nationals: that is to say, the Member States are to protect and safeguard the interests of individuals and companies, by assisting them in their relations with foreign authorities. Another possible interpretation, however, would include within the scope of Art. 8c the bringing of international claims in respect of expropriation and the like: what is sometimes called 'diplomatic' protection. It is very unlikely that this broader meaning was intended. The Art. deals with protection of Member States' nationals *within* third countries: the bringing of international claims takes place at the level of inter-State relations, and not within the territories of the alleged offending State. Secondly, international claims are not rights exercised by individuals, but are claims made by the State of which the individual is a national. Indeed, in law, the individual has no right to have his claim asserted at all—the bringing of a claim is entirely within the discretion of his State of nationality. It is unlikely that the Member States had in mind that they would enter into agreements about the conditions in which they would consider bringing claims in respect of their own nationals, still less that they intended to delegate to other Member States the right to decide whether such a claim should be made. No agreements under Art. 8c have yet been made.

[80] The Guidelines were made public through press statements issued by the Member States' Ministries of Foreign Affairs. Work is continuing on the extension of the guidelines to a wider range of consular activities.

or to negotiate on their behalf.[81] If necessary, the Presidency may be assisted in these tasks by the Commission and by the previous and next Member States to hold the Presidency.[82] Where, for whatever reason, no member of the 'troika' is represented in a country, representation is decided on the basis of an unpublished arrangement agreed in the Council, and updated annually.[83] The representatives of the Presidency on such occasions will usually be members of the staff of the Presidency's mission in the third State concerned. The normal rules, of course, govern the appointment of the members of such missions, the conditions on which they act, and the privileges and immunities accorded to them.

THE COMMUNITIES AND INTERNATIONAL ORGANIZATIONS

Representation of International Organizations to the Communities

No international organizations[84] are formally accredited to the Communities, and no procedure yet exists by which such accreditation could take place. Several organizations and international entities have, however, established *bureaux de liaison* in Brussels through which they conduct business with the Communities.[85] The privileges and immunities accorded to those *bureaux* and their staff are matters of Belgian law.[86]

The Communities' Representation at International Organizations

As in relation to third States, there is no single representation of the Communities to international organizations. The Communities and the Member States are represented by the combined activities of Commission delegations to the organization in question and the missions of the Member States.

---

[81] On the role of the Presidency in matters within the common foreign and security policy, see Art. J.5 TEU, and Ch. 24 below.

[82] This triumvirate is known as 'the troika'.

[83] The guiding principle of this arrangement is that, in countries where not all Member States are represented, the functions of the Presidency for the time being pass to the (represented) Member State next due to hold the Presidency.

[84] The general question of the Communities' relations with international organizations is examined in Ch. 7.

[85] *Bureaux de liaison* have been established by EFTA, the IBRD, the International Committee of the Red Cross, the Gulf Co-operation Council, the Council of Europe, the UN Population Fund, the UN High Commission for Refugees, the League of Arab States, the Latin American Parliament, the Organization of African Unity, the UN, the ILO, the International Organization for Migration, the WHO, Hong Kong, Macao, the Sovereign Order of Malta, and the Federal Republic of Yugoslavia (Serbia and Montenegro).

[86] The provisions of Art. 17 of the Prot. on the Privileges and Immunities of the European Communities would not seem to be applicable.

Commission Delegations

Commission delegations have been established at the UN, the FAO, the IAEA, UNIDO, UNESCO, and the OECD. Like Commission delegations in third States, these delegations are staffed by Commission officials. They receive instructions from, and are answerable to, the Commission and its services.

Tasks of Commission Delegations

With the missions of the Member States, the Commission's delegations play a part in communicating the views and representing the interests of the Communities as a whole in matters under consideration within the international organization or body concerned. They may be part of the Community delegation in negotiations or discussions, or they may themselves form the Community delegation, depending on how the Community delegation to the organization is constituted.[87]

Procedure for Appointment of Commission Delegations

The appointment of a Commission delegation to an international organization is in principle an administrative matter for the Commission. The Council is advised informally of the creation of new delegations, of any change of status of existing delegations, and of the Commission's nominee for the post of Head of its Delegation.

Accreditation to the Organization

The Head of the Commission's Delegation to an organization is notified to the organization by means of a letter of introduction from the President of the Commission, or from the Director General in charge of external relations, addressed to the Secretary General of the organization.

Privileges and Immunities of Commission Delegations

The privileges and immunities to be afforded to the delegation of the Commission will depend in the first place on the constitution of the organization to which the delegation is accredited, and in the second place on the law of the Host State of the organization.[88] The position for each organization has to be considered separately .

Diplomatic Missions of the Member States

The procedures for the establishment of missions of Member States to international organizations are, in principle determined by the constitution, rules, and

[87] On the composition of the Communities' delegations, see Ch. 7.

[88] For the privileges and immunities of the Commission delegation to the UN in New York, see Exec. Ord. 12581 of 8 Sept. 1988. On the scope of the privileges and immunities of a permanent observer mission to the UN, see [1982] UNJY (ST/LEG/SER.C/20) at pages 205 to 209.

practices of the organization, as are the privileges and immunities to be accorded to such missions. Member States' missions to international organizations work closely together, and with Commission delegations, to promote and defend the interests of the Member States and the Communities in discussion within international organizations of matters of concern to the Communities.[89] This will include defending the Community position in negotiations, speaking in support of the Community delegation, and seeking to maximize the Community's opportunity to participate in the work of the organization.

Presidency Representation of the Communities in International Organizations

The Presidency delegation to an international organization may in particular be required to represent the views and interests of the Communities and the Member States in the organization.[90] In some organizations, the Presidency in office is part of the Community delegation, along with the representatives of the Commission, and will be the Community spokesman.[91] Even in bodies where the Presidency is not part of the Community delegation as such, the Presidency may take the lead in presenting the agreed position of the Communities and the Member States on matters where competence is shared between the Community and the Member States.

[89] Special provisions apply in relation to matters within the scope of the common foreign and security policy: see Arts. J.2 and J.5 TEU. On international organizations generally, see Ch. 7. On the common foreign and security policy, see Ch. 24.

[90] The Presidency's role in representing the Communities is reflected in the fact that the Presidency mission is often listed along with the Commission delegation in the diplomatic lists of the organization under the entry for the Community. See the UN Diplomatic Lists for New York and Geneva. On the role of the Presidency in matters within the common foreign and security policy, see Art. J.5, and Ch. 24.

[91] For the composition of Community delegations, and the presentation of the Community's position within international organizations, see Ch. 7.

[92] As at Oct. 1994.

ANNEX

I. List of third States with Missions accredited to the Communities[92]

Afghanistan	Czech Republic	Lebanon	St Lucia
Albania	Djibouti	Lesotho	St Vincent and
Algeria	Dominican	Liberia	the Grenadines
Angola	Republic	Libya	San Marino
Antigua and	Dominica	Liechtenstein	Saudi Arabia
Barbuda	Egypt	Lithuania	Sierra Leone
Argentina	El Salvador	Madagascar	Singapore
Armenia	Ecuador	Malaysia	Slovakia
Australia	Eritrea	Malawi	Slovenia
Azerbadjan	Estonia	Maldives	Somalia
Bahamas	Ethiopia	Mali	South Africa
Bangladesh	Fiji	Malta	South Korea
Barbados	Gabon	Mauritania	Sri Lanka
Belarus	Gambia	Mauritius	Sudan
Belize	Georgia	Mexico	Surinam
Benin	Ghana	Moldova	Swaziland
Bhutan	Grenada	Mongolia	Switzerland
Bolivia	Guatemala	Morocco	Syria
Bosnia-	Guinea	Mozambique	Tanzania
Herzegovina	Guinea-Bissau	Myanmar	Thailand
Botswana	Equatorial Guinea	Namibia	Togo
Brazil	Guyana	Nepal	Tonga
Brunei	Haiti	Nicaragua	Trinidad and
Bulgaria	Honduras	Niger	Tobago
Burkina Faso	Hungary	Nigeria	Tunisia
Burundi	India	Norway	Turkey
Cambodia	Indonesia	New Zealand	Turkmenistan
Cameroon	Iraq	Oman	Uganda
Canada	Iran	Pakistan	Ukraine
Cape Verde	Iceland	Panama	United Arab
Central African	Israel	Papua New	Emirates
Republic	Ivory Coast	Guinea	Uruguay
Chad	Jamaica	Paraguay	USA
Chile	Japan	Peru	Uzbekhistan
China	Jordan	Philippines	Venezuela
Colombia	Khazakhstan	Poland	Vietnam
Comoros	Kenya	Qatar	Western Samoa
Congo	Kirghistan	Romania	Yemen
Costa Rica	Kuwait	Russia	Zaïre
Croatia	Laos	Rwanda	Zambia
Cuba	Latvia	St Kitts Nevis	Zimbabwe
Cyprus			

II. List of Commission delegations and offices in third States

(a) Commission delegations in non-ACP States

Albania	Czech Republic	Mexico	Switzerland
Algeria	Egypt	Morocco	Syria
Argentina	Estonia, Latvia and	Norway	Thailand
Australia	Lithuania	Pakistan	Tunisia
Bangladesh	Georgia	Peru	Turkey
Belize	Hungary	Philippines	Ukraine
Bolivia	India	Poland	Uruguay
Brazil	Indonesia	Romania	USA
Bulgaria	Israel	Russia	(Washington,
Canada	Japan	Saudi Arabia	Los Angeles,
Chile	Jordan	Slovakia	and San
China	Kazakhstan	Slovenia	Francisco)
Colombia	Lebanon	South Africa	Venezuela
Costa Rica	Malta	South Korea	Vietnam
Cyprus			

1. Commission delegations are also accredited (on a non-residential basis) to Bhutan, Bolivia, Brunei, Cambodia, Cuba, Ecuador, El Salvador, Guatemala, Honduras, Iceland, Laos, Malaysia, the Maldives, Mongolia, Myanmar, New Zealand, Nepal, Nicaragua, Panama, Paraguay, Singapore, Sri Lanka, Vietnam, and the Yemen.

2. In addition to those listed above, the Commission has an office in Hong Kong and a delegation in Belgrade. There is also a bureau in East Jerusalem.

3. The Commission's office in Indonesia is known as a 'representation' rather than a delegation because Portugal does not have diplomatic relations with Indonesia.

(b) Commission delegations in ACP States

Angola	Eritrea	Liberia	Senegal
Barbados[1]	Ethiopia	Madagascar	Sierra Leone
Benin	Fiji[2]	Malawi	Solomon Islands
Botswana	Gabon[3]	Mali	Somalia
Burkina Faso	Gambia	Mauritania	Sudan
Burundi	Ghana	Mauritius[5]	Surinam
Cameroon	Guinea	Mozambique	Swaziland
Cape Verde	Guinea Bissau	Namibia	Tanzania
Central African	Equatorial Guinea	Netherlands	Togo
Republic	Guyana	Antilles	Trinidad and
Chad	Haiti	Niger	Tobago[6]
Comoros	Ivory Coast	Nigeria	Uganda
Congo	Jamaica[4]	Papua New	Zaïre
Djibouti	Kenya	Guinea	Zambia
Dominican	Lesotho	Rwanda	Zimbabwe
Republic			

1. Responsible for Antigua and Barbuda, Dominica, St Lucia, St Vincent and the Grenadines, St Kitts and Nevis, Anguilla, Montserrat, and the British Virgin Islands.
2. Responsible for Western Samoa, Tonga, Vanuatu, Tuvalu, Pitcairn, Kiribati, New Caledonia and dependencies, and Tahiti.
3. Responsible for Sao Tomé and Principe.
4. Responsible for Belize, the Cayman Islands, the Bahamas, and the Turks and Caicos Islands.
5. Responsible for Réunion, Mayotte, and the Seychelles.
6. Responsible for Grenada, Martinique, Guadeloupe, French Guiana, St Pierre and Miquelon, St Helena, the Falklands, and the Antarctic Territories.

III. Commission delegations to international organizations[93]

The Food and Agriculture Organization (FAO) (Rome)
The United Nations (New York and Geneva)[94]
The Organization for Economic Co-operation and Development (OECD) (Paris)
The United Nations Educational, Scientific, and Cultural Organization (UNESCO) (Paris)
The International Atomic Energy Agency (IAEA)
The United Nations Industrial Development Organization (UNIDO) (Vienna)

---

[93] Lists of organizations in which the Communities are members or observers are in Ch. 7.
[94] A Council Secretariat delegation has also been established at the UN. As regards the conferment of privileges and immunities, the delegation forms part of the Commission delegation.

9

Accession, Pre-existing Agreements and the Member States

This Chapter brings together several issues, some of which have already been mentioned or alluded to. The overall theme is the interaction of the powers of the Communities and the powers of the Member States. The issues considered are the effect of accession on agreements concluded by the Communities and the new Member States; the effect of Community competence on the pre-existing agreements of the Member States; the tension between the exercise of Community and Member State competence in areas of shared competence, or at the boundaries of Community competence; the possibility of Community succession to agreements concluded by the Member States; and the exercise of Community competence through the medium of the Member States.

ACCESSION

Accession to the European Union, and therefore to the European Communities, takes place in accordance with Article O TEU.[1] The procedure for accession involves the Community institutions at several points, but the acceptance of new Member States is not an exercise of Community competence. The international agreement which provides for membership is ratified by the existing and new Member States as sovereign States, in accordance with their constitutional procedures.[2]

The principal effect of accession is that the applicant Member States become members of the European Union and of the Communities.[3] From the date of accession, the provisions of the 'original Treaties' and the acts adopted by the

---

[1] See Ch. 1. Formerly, each of the Community Treaties contained provisions dealing with the admission of new Member States.

[2] Between the creation of the Communities and the entry into force of the TEU, 6 States acceded to the Communities: Denmark, Ireland, and the UK in 1973; Greece in 1981; and Spain and Portugal in 1986. Since the entry into force of the TEU, 3 have acceded to the European Union and the Communities: Austria, Finland, and Sweden, in 1995. In what follows, the Denmark/Ireland/UK Treaty and Act of Accession are referred to as the '1972 Treaty/Act'; the Greek Treaty and Act are the '1979 Treaty/Act'; the Spanish/Portuguese Treaty and Act are the '1985 Treaty/Act'; and the Austria/Finland/Sweden Treaty and Act are the '1994 Treaty/Act'. Before the TEU, accession to the ECSC Treaty was effected by a unanimous decision of the Council, rather than a Treaty of Accession: for the procedure, see what was Art. 98 ECSC.

[3] Art. 1 of each of the Treaties of Accession. There are, of course, other effects. The geographical extent of the Communities' competence is increased (see Ch. 3); the composition of the Communities as international persons changes; and so on. On the consequences for third States, see p. 229 below.

Community institutions before accession bind the new Member States and apply in those States under the conditions laid down in those Treaties and in the Act of Accession.[4]

The basic principles underlying each accession have been the same: the existing body of Community law and practice applies to the new Member States, subject to temporary transitional exemptions and special arrangements to accommodate their concerns. The structure of the legal instruments giving effect to accession has also remained the same. A short Treaty of Accession provides that the new Member States are to become members of the Union and Communities, on the conditions set out in an annexed Act of Accession. Provision is made for amendment of the conditions of accession should one of the applicant States fail to ratify on time.[5] The Act of Accession, which, with its accompanying annexes and protocols, is an integral part of the Treaty of Accession, sets out in detail the conditions on which accession is to take place. Provision is made for amendment of the institutional provisions of the Community Treaties; for adjustments to existing Community legislation; and for implementation of transitional and other provisions negotiated by the new Member States.

A detailed analysis of the content and effects of the Treaties and Acts of Accession is beyond the scope of this work.[6] Mention should, however, be made of the effect of accession on agreements entered into before accession by the Communities, and by the new Member States.

The Communities' Agreements with Third Countries

Agreements entered into before the date of accession by any of the Communities with one or more third States or international organizations are binding on the new Member States under the conditions laid down in the original Treaties[7] and in the relevant Act of Accession.[8]

As regards mixed agreements, the new Member States undertake to accede, under the conditions laid down in the relevant Act of Accession, to agreements concluded by the existing Member States and any of the Communities, acting

---

[4] Art. 2 of each Act of Accession.

[5] Art. 2(1) of each Treaty of Accession. See also Council Dec. 95/1 of 1 Jan. 1995, adjusting the 1994 Act of Accession to take account of the Norwegian decision not to become a member of the Union: ([1995] OJ L1/1).

[6] See, for a discussion of the 1972 Treaty/Act, J. P. Puissochet, *L'élargissement des Communautés européennes* (A. W. Sijthoff, 1974). On the 1994 accession, see D. Booss and J. Forman, 'Enlargement: Legal and Procedural Aspects' (1995) 32 *CMLRev.* 95. For a discussion of the problems posed by the EEA Agreement, see Tichy and Dedichen, 'Securing a Smooth Shift between the Two EEA Pillars' (1995) 32 *CMLRev.* 131.

[7] The 'original Treaties' are the ECSC Treaty, the Euratom Treaty, the EC Treaty as supplemented or amended by treaties or other acts which entered into force before accession, and the TEU.

[8] Art. 4(1) of the 1972 Act, the 1979 Act, and the 1985 Act; and Art. 5(1) of the 1994 Act.

jointly,[9] and to the agreements concluded by the existing Member States which are related to those agreements. The Communities and the existing Member States, in the framework of the Union, are to assist the new Member States in fulfilling this obligation.[10] The new Member States become parties, by virtue of accession, to internal agreements concluded by the existing Member States in order to implement mixed agreements.[11]

The new Member States are required to 'adjust their positions' in relation to international organizations and to those international agreements to which one of the Communities or the other Member States are also parties to take account of their rights and obligations arising from their accession to the Union.[12]

These general principles are given detailed effect in each Act of Accession in the light of the circumstances of the acceding Member States. The transitional arrangements relating to external relations deal specifically with fisheries agreements;[13] the common commercial policy of the Community,[14] including quantitative restrictions on goods,[15] and the generalized system of preferences;[16] association and trade and co-operation agreements;[17] and relations with particular regions and groupings of third States.[18] Provision is made for the negotiation of amendments to the Communities' agreements with third countries, and, in the meantime, for the application by the Member States of the existing agreements.[19]

New Member States' Existing Agreements with Third Countries

Each Act of Accession provides that Article 234 EC and Articles 105 and 106 Euratom are to apply for the new Member States to agreements concluded before accession.[20] The meaning of these Articles is considered below: their aim is to secure that the rights of third States under agreements concluded in good

---

[9] The significance of this phrase is uncertain. It may be intended to limit the obligation to accede to mixed agreements to those mixed agreements to which all the existing Member States are parties.

[10] Art. 4(2) of the 1972 Act, the 1979 Act, and the 1985 Act; Art. 5(2) of the 1994 Act.

[11] Art. 4(3) of the 1972 Act, the 1979 Act, and the 1985 Act; Art. 5(3) of the 1994 Act.

[12] Art. 4(4) of the 1972 Act, the 1979 Act, and the 1985 Act; Art. 5(4) of the 1994 Act.

[13] 1979 Act, Arts. 167 and 354; 1994 Act, Arts. 96 and 124.

[14] 1979 Act, Title V, Ch. 1; 1985 Act, Title II, Ch. 5, Sect. 1 and Title III, Ch. 5, Sect. 1; 1994 Act, Title III, Ch. 4, Title IV, Ch. 4, and Title V, Ch. 4.

[15] 1979 Act, Art. 115; 1985 Act, Arts. 177 and 364; 1994 Act, Arts. 73–75, 97–101, 126–127.

[16] 1979 Act, Art. 117; 1985 Act, Arts. 178 and 365.

[17] 1972 Act, Art. 108; 1979 Act, Arts. 118 to 120; 1985 Act, Arts. 179–182 and 366–369; 1994 Act, Arts. 76–78, 102–105, 128–131.

[18] e.g., the British Commonwealth (1972 Act, Arts. 109–116); the OCTs (1972 Act, Arts. 117–119); the ACP countries (1979 Act, Arts. 121 and 122); the EFTA States (1994 Act, Arts. 78, 104, and 130).

[19] 1972 Act, Art. 108; 1979 Act, Arts. 118 and 119; 1985 Act, Arts. 179, 180, 366, and 367; 1994 Act, Arts. 75 and 76, 100 and 101, and 127 and 128.

[20] Art. 5 of the 1972 Act, the 1979 Act, and the 1985 Act; Art. 6 of the 1994 Act.

faith by the new Member States before accession are not prejudiced by accession.

RIGHTS OF THIRD STATES UNDER PRE-EXISTING AGREEMENTS OF THE MEMBER STATES

It is a basic principle of international law that an agreement creates neither rights nor obligations for States which are not parties to it. It follows that the Community Treaties cannot affect the rights of a third State under an agreement which that State entered into with one of the Member States before the entry into force of the Community Treaties.[21] The rights of third States under such agreements have been recognized by the Court of Justice, and are expressly protected in the EC and Euratom Treaties. The ECSC Treaty makes no special provision in this regard, but, should the need arise, the Court would no doubt apply the general principle for the benefit of the third State's rights.

Article 234 of the EC Treaty

The effect of the EC Treaty on agreements entered into by a Member State with third countries before the provisions of that Treaty became binding on the Member State is dealt with in Article 234, which provides that:

> The rights and obligations arising from agreements concluded before the entry into force of this Treaty between one or more Member States on the one hand, and one or more third countries on the other, shall not be affected by the provisions of this Treaty.
>
> To the extent that such agreements are not compatible with this Treaty, the Member State or States concerned shall take all appropriate steps to eliminate the incompatibilities established. Member States shall, where necessary, assist each other to this end, and where appropriate, adopt a common attitude.
>
> In applying the agreements referred to in the first paragraph, Member States shall take into account the fact that the advantages accorded under this Treaty by each Member State form an integral part of the establishment of the Community and are thereby inseparably linked with the creation of common institutions, the conferring of powers upon them and the granting of the same advantages by all the other Member States.[22]

Article 234 is of general scope: it applies to any international agreement, irrespective of subject matter, which is capable of affecting the application of the EC Treaty.[23] Agreements to which the Article applies do not, however, become

---

[21] For these purposes, the Community Treaties entered into force (i) for the original 6 Member States, on the date of entry into force of the original Treaties of Rome and Paris, and (ii) for Member States acceding subsequently, on the date of their accession.

[22] For a discussion of a recent problem which gave rise to issues under Art. 234 EC, see J. M. Grimes, 'Conflicts between EC Law and International Treaty Obligations: A Case Study of the German Telecommunications Dispute' (1994) 35 *Harv.ILJ* 535.

[23] Case 812/79 *Attorney General* v. *Burgoa* [1980] ECR 2787 at para. 6.

part of Community law, and no new rights are created under them for individuals or economic operators. If a national of a Member State could not claim rights under the agreement before the EC Treaty entered into force for his Member State, he will not derive any such rights by virtue of Article 234. Nor does Article 234 adversely affect rights which such a national held under the agreement with the third State.[24]

The 'rights and obligations' referred to in the first paragraph of the Article are, respectively, the rights of the third parties and the obligations of the Member States.[25] The aim of Article 234 is to enable the Member States, so far as possible, to respect the rights of non-member countries under agreements concluded before entry into force of the Treaty, or accession, as the case may be. Thus although the Article may justify a Member State taking action which would otherwise be contrary to the EC Treaty in order to perform obligations to a third State, it does not allow a Member State to assert its rights under such an agreement, if to do so would violate the Member State's obligations under Community law. Thus, agreements concluded prior to the entry into force of the EC Treaty may not be relied upon in relations between Member States to justify restrictions on trade within the Community.[26] When such an agreement merely allows, but does not require, a Member State to adopt a measure which appears to be contrary to Community law, the Member State must refrain from adopting such a measure.[27]

Article 234 preserves the obligations of the Member States to third States.[28] It places no obligations on the Community itself towards these States as a matter of international law. But as a matter of Community law, the institutions of the Community are under a duty not to impede the performance of the obligations of Member States under the pre-existing agreement. This duty extends to permitting the Member State to fulfil its obligations,[29] if necessary by allowing it to maintain in place legislation which would otherwise be contrary to its Community obligations.[30]

---

[24] Case 812/79 *Attorney General* v. *Burgoa* [1980] ECR 2787 at para. 10.

[25] Case 10/61 *Commission* v. *Italy* [1962] ECR 1, at para. II, B, 3; Case 812/79, n. 23 above, at para. 8.

[26] Case 121/85 *Conegate* v. *HM Customs and Excise* [1986] ECR 1007 at 1024. See also Case 286/86 *Ministère Public* v. *Deserbais* [1988] ECR 4907; Case 34/79 *R.* v. *Henn and Darby* [1979] ECR 3795.

[27] Case C–324/93 *R.* v. *Secretary of State for the Home Department, ex parte Evans Medical Ltd.*, 28 Mar. 1995, not yet reported, at para. 22.

[28] But for cases where the nationals of a third State could not invoke the provisions of a pre-existing agreement between that State and a Member State, see Case 181/80 *Procureur Général* v. *Arbelais-Emazabel* [1981] ECR 2961; Joined Cases 180 and 266/80 *Crujeiros Tome* v. *Procureur de la République*; *Procureur de la République* v. *Yurrita* [1981] ECR 2997; Joined Cases 138 and 139/81 *Directeur des Affaires Maritimes* v. *Marticorena-Otazo et al* [1982] ECR 3819; Joined Cases 13 to 28/82 *Arantzamendi-Osa* v. *Procureur de la République* [1982] ECR 3927; Joined Cases 50–58/82 *Administrateur des Affaires Maritimes, Bayonne* v. *Dorca Marina* [1982] ECR 3949.

[29] N. 23 above, at para. 9.

[30] Case C–158/91 *Ministère Public* v. *Levy* [1993] ECR I–4287; Case C–13/93 *Office National de l'Emploi* v. *Minne* [1994] ECR I–371.

Article 234(2) implies that the Member States should continually monitor the agreements to which that Article applies, so that these agreements are amended, or even denounced, as soon as possible to minimize the conflict between a Member State's obligations under the Treaty and its obligations under the agreements.

Articles 105 and 106 of the Euratom Treaty

Article 105 of the Euratom Treaty states that the provisions of the Euratom Treaty are not to be invoked so as to prevent the implementation of agreements entered into before its entry into force by a Member State with a third State or an international organization, provided such agreements have been notified to the Commission not more than thirty days after entry into force of the Treaty. However, such pre-existing agreements may not be invoked as grounds for failure to implement the Euratom Treaty, if, in the opinion of the Court of Justice, one of the decisive reasons on the part of either of the parties in concluding the agreement was an intention to evade the provisions of the Euratom Treaty.[31]

Article 106 Euratom provides that Member States which, before the entry into force of the Euratom Treaty, have concluded agreements with third States providing for co-operation in the field of nuclear energy shall be required to undertake jointly with the Commission the necessary negotiations with these third States in order to ensure that the rights and obligations arising out of such agreements are, as far as possible, assumed by the Community.

COMMUNITY COMPETENCE AND THE MEMBER STATES

The principle of the attribution of powers—that the Community can only act when it has been given power to do so—implies that national powers are the rule and Community powers the exception.[32] It also implies that, in areas where competence is uncertain, residual competence is with the Member States. Where the Community has no powers to act, Member States are in principle free to act as they wish, subject to any international legal obligations binding on them, such as obligations or commitments undertaken in the framework of the common foreign and security policy,[33] or under the provisions of the Treaty on European Union dealing with co-operation in the fields of justice and home affairs.[34]

Where Community competence has been created, the powers of the Member States are, to varying degrees, limited. The effects of the existence of exclusive

---

[31] This remarkable provision, which allows the Court to enter into an examination of a State's reasons of policy for concluding an international agreement, has not so far been invoked.
[32] European Council, Edinburgh, 11–12 Dec. 1992: Conclusions of the Presidency, 14.
[33] Title V TEU: see Ch. 24.   [34] Title VI TEU.

Community competence have already been noted:[35] where the Communities' competence is exclusive, it is in principle[36] unlawful for the Member States to take any unilateral action, internally or externally. In these areas it is for the Community to become party to any agreement, and to become a member of any international organization, in accordance with the provisions of the relevant Community Treaty.

In areas where the Communities and the Member States share competence, the Member States retain a greater measure of freedom to act unilaterally.[37] However, that freedom is also constrained by certain duties derived from the Treaties: in particular, the Member States are under a duty to ensure that their views and that of the Community are co-ordinated and coherent, and that, so far as possible, a common Community front is presented to the outside world in the negotiation and expression of views in international fora.[38]

Protecting the Competence of the Communities

Several provisions of the Treaties and of subordinate legislation protect the competences of the Communities from encroachment by the Member States, by requiring the Member States to advise the Commission of agreements which they propose to conclude.

The Euratom Treaty

Article 103(1) Euratom provides that the Member States are to communicate to the Commission draft agreements with a third State or international organization which concern matters within the purview of the Euratom Treaty. The Commission is obliged to comment on the draft if in its opinion it contains clauses which might impede the operation of the Euratom Treaty. If the Member State disagrees with the Commission's assessment, it has the option of seeking the ruling of the Court on the disputed points.[39] Article 103 is in very

---

[35] See Ch. 3.

[36] On exceptional cases in which Member States may be called on to act, see below and Ch. 3. The status of an agreement concluded by a Member State in contravention of the powers of the Community is uncertain. As a matter of Community law, the Member State concerned would be in breach of its Treaty obligations. As a matter of international law, there is probably a strong presumption in favour of the validity of such an agreement: it is unreasonable to expect a third State to scrutinize Community law to determine whether the Community Member State with which it is about to enter into an agreement is or is not competent to conclude such an agreement. See Art. 46 of the Vienna Convention on the Law of Treaties, and the discussion in Sinclair, *Vienna Convention on the Law of Treaties* (2nd edn., Manchester University Press, 1984), 169 ff. See also the discussion at pp. 129–30.

[37] See Ch. 3.

[38] The informal co-ordination arrangements developed by the Council and the Commission in the context of the FAO, the UN, and the commodities agreements ('PROBA 20') are practical out-workings of this duty. See, further, Ch. 7.

[39] See, further, Ch. 4.

wide terms: it applies not just to agreements whose main content concerns nuclear matters, but to any agreements which contain provisions which might concern matters within the 'purview' of the Euratom Treaty.[40]

The EC Treaty

The EC Treaty contains no provision exactly mirroring Article 103 Euratom. However, Article 113 gives the Commission the task of submitting to the Council 'proposals for implementing the common commercial policy', and two decisions adopted under that Article establish controls on Member State action in areas which touch on the common commercial policy.

Council Decision 69/494

This Decision[41] adopted on 16 December 1969, laid down the general rule that, as from 1 January 1970, all negotiations with a view to the conclusion of new trade and commercial treaties, agreements, or arrangements, or to the amendment of those in existence, should be conducted in accordance with a Community procedure. The negotiation of such agreements was henceforth to be the responsibility of the Commission, in consultation with the committee (the Article 113 Committee) appointed by the Council to assist the Commission in that task. Secondly, Decision 69/494 provided for the progressive standardization of existing treaties, agreements, and arrangements concerning trade and commercial relations between Member States and third countries. The aim was not the total replacement of all such agreements, but the gradual elimination of any which might hinder the implementation of the common commercial policy. Provision was made for the extension or renewal of those treaties, agreements, or arrangements which fell within the scope of the common commercial policy. Member States were obliged to notify the Commission of all such bilateral treaties, agreements, and arrangements, and a consultation and information process was established the purpose of which was to determine whether the proposed extension or renewal might constitute an obstacle to the common commercial policy. Extension or renewal could last for up to a year, but could itself be renewed. Until December 1993, the Council authorized renewal of agreements on a quarterly basis. Since Council Decision 93/679[42] of 6 December 1993, renewal is granted annually.[43]

Council Decision 74/393

This Decision[44] of 2 July 1974, adopted under Articles 113 and 235, established a consultation procedure for co-operation agreements between Member States

---

[40] The scope of the external competence of the Euratom Community is considered in Ch. 22.
[41] [1969] JO L326/39. [42] [1993] OJ L317/61.
[43] See Council Dec. 95/133 ([1995] OJ L89/30). [44] [1974] OJ L208/23.

and third countries. The aim of the procedure set up by this Decision is to ensure that agreements to be concluded by the Member States which relate to economic and industrial co-operation, or commitments and measures proposed by the authorities of Member States as part of co-operation agreements, are examined before conclusion for their compatibility with the common policies of the Communities. The Decision establishes a procedure whereby other Member States may be consulted in order to determine their views.

Preserving the Member States' Legitimate Freedom to Act

The concept of shared competence[45] means that the Member States retain powers in respect of certain matters in which the Community is also competent. In some matters, Member State competence is transitional and will gradually be replaced as Community powers are exercised. In others, in particular where the elaboration of harmonization measures is less likely to be a feature of Community action,[46] Member States' powers will, in principle, continue to co-exist with those of the Communities.[47] The Treaties and the practice of the institutions safeguard the Member States' continuing powers.

Treaties

In several areas where the Treaties provide for Community co-operation with third countries and organizations, and for the making of agreements, it is also provided that these powers are to be without prejudice to the Member States' competence to negotiate in international bodies and to conclude agreements.[48]

Community Practice

When the Community concludes agreements in certain areas where competence is shared between the Community and the Member States, the Member States have sometimes insisted on a public statement that the Community's competence to enter into commitments on such matters does not prejudice the Member States' powers to enter into similar agreements. Such a statement, usually known as a 'Canada Clause',[49] has appeared in numerous economic co-operation agreements, either as an Article in the body of the agreement, as a preambular paragraph, or as part of the negotiating record. More recently, it has also appeared in agreements on research and scientific co-operation.[50]

---

[45] See Ch. 3.   [46] Such as development policy or economic co-operation.
[47] See Chs. 3 and 17.
[48] In the EC Treaty: see Art. 109(5) (economic and monetary matters); Art. 130r(4) (environment); Art. 130y (development policy). In the Euratom Treaty: Arts. 102 and 103.
[49] Because it originated in the EEC–Canada Agreement of 1976 ([1976] OJ L260/1).
[50] See p. 314.

A 'Canada clause' cannot affect the distribution of competences under the Treaties,[51] but, from the point of view of the Member States, it has political and legal significance. The *political* importance lies in the fact that the continuing competence of the Member States in particular areas is recognized, and brought to the attention of third States. The *legal* significance lies in the fact that the third States are thus put on notice that a continuing Member State competence exists in these areas.[52]

The Community as the Successor to the Member States

Not all international agreements are drafted in terms which allow the Community to become a party. Nevertheless, it appears that some agreements may, at least for the purposes of Community law, bind the Community directly by succession. The leading case is the *International Fruit Company*[53] case.

In that case, the Court had to consider whether the Community could be regarded as a party to the GATT, despite the fact that the Community had never deposited an instrument of approval or acceptance in respect of the GATT.[54] The Court concluded that, in so far as under the EEC Treaty the Community had assumed the powers previously exercised by the Member States in the area governed by the GATT, the provisions of that agreement had the effect of binding the Community. The Court's conclusion was based on (i) the fact that the Member States were bound by the GATT when they concluded the Treaty establishing the EEC;[55] (ii) the provisions of the EEC Treaty (in particular Articles 110 and 234), which, according to the Court, evidenced the Member States' desire to observe the undertakings in the GATT;[56] (iii) the Community's assumption of the functions inherent in its tariff and trade policy, which, according to the Court, showed that the Member States intended to bind the Community by the obligations in the General Agreement;[57] and (iv) by the fact that the Community, acting through its own institutions, had appeared as a partner in tariff negotiations and agreements concluded within the framework of the GATT.[58]

The *International Fruit Company* case is cited as authority for the view that, in certain circumstances, the Community can succeed to the obligations of its Member States under an international agreement. According to Advocate-General Capotorti,[59] the Community may become bound by an agreement

---

[51] Cf. *Opinion 1/94 (Re WTO Agreement)* [1995] 1 CMLR 205 at para. 52.

[52] This could have importance in the context of Art. 46 of the Vienna Convention on the Law of Treaties.

[53] Joined Cases 21 to 24/72 *International Fruit Company et al* v. *Produktschap voor Groenten en Fruit* [1972] ECR 1219.

[54] On the legal status of the GATT, see Dam, *The GATT: Law and International Economic Integration* (University of Chicago Press, Chicago, 1970) 341–344; Jackson: *The World Trading System* (MIT Press, 1989), ch. 2.

[55] Joined Cases 21 to 24/72, n. 53 above, at para. 10.   [56] *Ibid.*, paras. 12 and 13.

[57] *Ibid.*, para. 14.   [58] *Ibid.*, paras. 16 and 17.   [59] Case 181/80, n. 28 above.

entered into by the Member States if the agreement in question was concluded prior to the EEC Treaty and all Member States were parties to it when the EEC Treaty was concluded; if the Member States intended that the Community should observe the agreement; if action was taken by the Community institutions within the framework of the agreement; and if the other parties to the agreement have recognized that powers have been transferred to the Community with regard to the subject matter of the agreement.

But it is doubtful whether matters are quite that straightforward. If Advocate-General Capotorti's summary of the Court's reasoning is correct, it would lead to the conclusion that the Community had not even succeeded to the GATT: there is evidence that the other GATT contracting parties have not accepted that the Community has taken the place of the Member States when it comes to assessing responsibility for alleged failure to comply with GATT obligations. Furthermore, there is very little international practice on questions of succession even between States, and a general doctrine of international succession for the benefit of international organizations, along the lines suggested by the Court in the *International Fruit Company* case, has probably not yet emerged.[60] The Court's conclusion is perhaps better seen as a rule of Community law, applicable in the special circumstances of the GATT and similar agreements,[61] to the effect that, for the purposes of applying such agreements within the Community legal order, the Community should be treated as if it had succeeded to the obligations in them.[62] In subsequent cases where the question of succession arose, the Court refused to accept that the Community had succeeded to the European Convention on Human Rights[63] or to certain international conventions on pollution.[64]

The Member States acting for the Communities

In certain exceptional circumstances, the Member States may be required to act on behalf of the Community as custodians or guardians of the Community interest. As such, they may be required to enact national legislation, even in

---

[60] On this, see H. G. Schermers, *International Institutional Law* (2nd edn.), para. 1406, where it is suggested that the Vienna Convention on the Succession of States in respect of Treaties (1978) 17 ILM 1488 could be 'analogously applied' to succession by an organization. See also Schermers, 'Succession of States and International Organizations' [1975] *Neth. YBIL* 103.

[61] For the only other agreements to which the doctrine of succession has so far been applied, see Case 38/75 *Douaneagent der NV Nederlandse Spoorwegen* v. *Inspecteur der Invoerrechten en Accijzen* [1975] ECR 1439 at para. 21: 'Just as in the case of commitments arising from GATT, the Community has replaced the Member States in commitments arising from the Convention of 15 December 1950 on Nomenclature for the Classification of Goods in Customs Tariffs and from the Convention of the same date establishing a Customs Co-operation Council, and is bound by the same commitments.'

[62] Thus, the GATT (and other agreements to which the doctrine of succession applies) should be treated like agreements concluded by the Community in accordance with the prescribed procedures. See Ch. 5, n. 1.

[63] Cases 50–58/82, n. 28 above. 　　　　　　[64] Case C–379/92 *Peralta* [1994] ECR I-3453.

areas within the exclusive competence of the Community, in order to fill a legislative vacuum arising because of the inability or unwillingness of the Community institutions to act. Such legislation would have to be limited to what was strictly necessary, and would have to be adopted in close consultation with the Community institutions.[65]

When matters within Community competence are included in an agreement to which the Community cannot become a party, or arise in an organization of which the Community is not a member, the Community will be unable to exercise its own competences directly. The Court has recognized that the Community's external competence may, if necessary, be exercised through the medium of the Member States acting jointly in the Community's interest.[66] This technique has been employed by the Council in relation to the conduct of negotiations and the conclusion of agreements.[67]

In areas within Community competence, the Community institutions may also delegate powers to the Member States, setting conditions on the exercise of such powers.[68]

---

[65] Joined Cases 3, 4, and 6/76 *Kramer* [1976] ECR 1279; Case 61/77 *Commission* v. *Ireland* [1978] ECR 417; Joined Cases 185–204/78 *Van Dam et al.* [1979] ECR 2345; Case 804/79 *Commission* v. *UK* [1981] ECR 1045. See also Ch. 3.

[66] *Opinion 2/91 (Re ILO Convention 170)* [1993] ECR I–1061 at para. 5. Close co-operation between the Community and the Member States is all the more necessary in such cases (*ibid.*, at para. 37).

[67] For examples, see Ch. 11, and examples cited there.

[68] See Arts. 19(2) and 21(2) of Council Reg. 259/93 on the supervision and control of shipments of waste within, into, and out of the European Community ([1993] OJ L30/1). The Member States are conditionally authorized by the Council to conclude bilateral agreements for the disposal and recovery of waste.

PART II

The Communities' Powers in Practice

The purpose of this Part is to describe the main external powers of the Communities, and to summarize the external activities of the Communities to date by reference to these powers. Each Chapter falls into roughly two parts. It begins with a description of the powers currently conferred on the Community (or Communities) in a given area, indicating the extent of Community competence (that is to say, the matters which fall within the Communities' powers), and the nature of the Communities' powers (in particular whether the Communities' competence is exclusive or shared with the Member States). In most cases, the procedures for the exercise of these powers are also outlined briefly.

Each Chapter then summarizes the Communities' practice to date in the area of activity corresponding to the power in question. An attempt has been made to refer to multilateral and bilateral agreements and arrangements concluded by the Communities; to outline the Communities' participation in relevant international organizations; and to describe internal Community acts which may have a bearing on the conduct of external relations in each area.

For the purposes of this Part, the European Community's activities have been selected by reference to the main powers which have been conferred expressly or by implication in the EC Treaty, as amended by the TEU. Thus, each of the express powers conferred by the EC Treaty is dealt with in a separate Chapter, with the exception of the powers to make agreements relating to monetary matters (Article 109 EC) and to co-operate with third countries for the purposes of Title XII EC (Trans-European networks). These have been omitted because there has so far been no practice in the areas covered by them. The Community's powers to act in relation to fisheries and transport are the most soundly established and well used of the Community's implied powers, and they accordingly have been given a chapter each. Finally, a chapter on non-nuclear energy has been included because of the historical and continuing importance of that area of Community policy. The order of the chapters follows the order in which the powers appear in the EC Treaty. Separate chapters are devoted to the activities of Euratom and the ECSC.

This analysis clearly carries certain risks. The absence of a full account of the historical development of practice and law in each area may disguise the link between current powers and the legal basis for action in the past (or imply that such a link exists when it does not). And the allocation of each power or area of activity to a separate Chapter may suggest—wrongly—that it is always obvious into which category a proposed measure falls, and that there is never any overlap between one power and another. To remove all these risks would have meant writing a completely different book. The aim of the following Part is to say simply what the Communities can now do in the main areas of their external activities, and to summarize what they have done so far.

10

Fisheries

The external competence of the European Community under the common fisheries policy dates from 1976. The legal basis for the development of external competence in this area was laid by the judgment of the Court of Justice in Joined Cases 3, 4, and 6/76 (the *Kramer* case);[1] the political framework was provided on 3 November 1976, in the Council's 'Resolution on certain external aspects of the creation of a 200 mile fishing zone'. The 'Hague Resolution',[2] as it has become known, envisaged, among other things, the negotiation by the Commission of a series of agreements designed to secure and enhance the Community's access to fishing resources under the jurisdiction of third States.[3]

LEGAL BASIS OF THE COMMUNITY'S EXTERNAL COMPETENCE

The central issue in the *Kramer* case[4] was whether the Community had exclusive competence to enter into international fishery conservation commitments, or whether the Member States also had authority to adopt their own national regulations. The Court said that it was clear from Article 210 EEC that, in its external relations, the Community had the capacity to enter into international commitments over the whole field of its objectives as defined in the EEC Treaty. The Court then examined the Treaty's provisions relating to fisheries. Fish was a commodity within the scope of the common agricultural policy established by Articles 39 to 46 of the EEC Treaty. Furthermore, Council Regulation

---

[1] *Kramer* [1976] ECR 1279.
[2] [1981] OJ C105/1. The full text of the Hague Resolution has not been published, but its terms can be pieced together from various sources: see n. 29 below.
[3] For a fuller treatment of the development and practice of the Community's external competence in relation to fisheries agreements with third countries, and discussion of the internal aspects of the Common Fisheries Policy, see P. J. G. Kapteyn and P. Verloren van Themaat, *Introduction to the Law of the European Communities* (2nd edn., Kluwer, 1989), ch. X.2.7 and sources there cited; R. R. Churchill, *EEC Fisheries Law* (Martinus Nijhoff, 1987), especially ch. 5. For an account of the history of the Common Fisheries Policy in its external aspects, see A. W. Koers, 'The External Authority of the EEC in regard to Marine Fisheries' (1977) 14 *CMLRev.* 269; R. R. Churchill, 'The EEC's Fisheries Management System: a Review of the First Five Years' (1988) 25 *CMLRev.* 369; Yann-Huei Song, 'The EC's Common Fisheries Policy in the 1990s' (1995) 26 *Ocean Development and International Law* 31. For an account of the Common Fisheries Policy as it applies within the Community, see Churchill, *op cit.*, especially chs. 4 and 7. For an account of the international rules on fisheries, see W. T. Burke, *The New International Law of Fisheries UNCLOS 1982 and Beyond* (Clarendon Press, 1995), and the standard works on the Law of the Sea.
[4] N. 1 above.

2142/70[5] made specific provision for conservation measures to be adopted by the Community in relation to the internal waters of the Member States. Finally, Article 102 of the 1972 Act of Accession[6] provided that, at the end of the transitional period, the Council was to determine conditions for fishing with a view to ensuring the protection of the fishing grounds and conservation of the biological resources of the sea.

Extent of the Community's Competence

According to the Court of Justice,[7] it followed from the provisions of the Act of Accession, the Treaties, and the various measures adopted by the Council, taken as a whole, that the Community had at its disposal, on the internal level, the power to take any measure for the conservation of the biological resources of the sea. It also followed that the rule-making authority of the Community extended—in so far as the Member States had similar authority under international law—to control of fishing on the high seas.[8] According to the Court, the only way to ensure the conservation of the resources of the sea both effectively and equitably was through a system of rules binding on all the States concerned, including non-Member countries. It thus followed from the powers and duties established on the internal level that the Community had authority to enter into international commitments for the conservation of the resources of the sea.

However, not every element of the conduct and control of fishing and fisheries is within the Community's internal or external competence. For example, the Member States in principle retain the power to determine which vessels may fly their flag,[9] to set national maritime boundaries[10] and to fix and enforce penalties for non-compliance with legislation on fisheries.

Nature of the Community's Competence

In the *Kramer* case, the Court found that the Community's competence for external fisheries matters was provisional during the transitional phase fixed by the Act of Accession.[11] This meant that, subject to certain duties elaborated by the Court,[12] the Member States were during that period free to enter into international obligations in relation to the matters under consideration.

---

[5] [1970] (III) OJ Spec.Ed. 707.   [6] [1972] JO L73/14.

[7] Joined Cases 3, 4, and 6/76, n. 1 above, paras. 11–14.

[8] See also Case C–258/89 *Commission* v. *Spain* [1991] ECR 3977.

[9] Subject to the rules of Community law on rights of establishment: Case C–221/89 *R.* v. *Secretary of State for Transport, ex parte Factortame* [1991] ECR I–3905; Case C–246/89 *Commission* v. *UK* [1991] ECR I–4587.

[10] Subject to duties incumbent on the Member States in Community law: Case C–146/89 *Re Territorial Sea: Commission* v. *UK* [1991] ECR I–3533.

[11] i.e., during a period of 6 years from the date of accession.

[12] Joined Cases 3, 4, and 6/76, n. 1 above, paras. 40–45. See also Ch. 3 above.

The extent of the Member States' powers after the transitional period had ended was considered in a series of cases culminating in Case 804/79, *Commission* v. *United Kingdom*.[13] In that case, the Court stressed that since the expiry of the transitional period, the power to adopt, as part of the common fisheries policy, measures relating to the conservation of the resources of the sea belonged fully and definitively to the Community.[14] The Member States were therefore no longer entitled to exercise any power of their own in the matter of conservation measures in the waters under their jurisdiction.[15] The transfer of powers to the Community was total and definitive:[16] the Community's competence was exclusive.

The Court recognized that the Member States might be required to legislate at national level to conserve fish stocks in order to protect the Community interest until the Community itself had acted. It was made clear, however, that the Member States' powers to act only continued until the Council had acted, that Member State action should be limited to what was strictly necessary for the conservation and exploitation of the sea's resources in the common interest of the Community as a whole, and that any national action had to be undertaken in close association with the Commission.[17]

Legal Basis

The legal basis for conclusion of agreements on fisheries conservation is Article 43 EC. In the *Kramer* case, a Commission argument that Article 113 was the correct legal basis was not accepted by the Court, but this does not mean that Article 113 is never of relevance to the conclusion of fisheries agreements. The correct legal basis for all Council action depends on the aim and content of the act to be adopted, and where an agreement involves matters falling within the common commercial policy, recourse to Article 113 may be necessary. Accordingly, some agreements relating to fisheries have been concluded on the basis of Article 43 together with Article 113.[18] Since the entry into force of the TEU, the legal basis of acts concluding agreements must cite the relevant provisions of Article 228 in order to make clear which procedure was followed in adopting the act. In the case of fisheries agreements, the usual legal basis will be Article 43 in conjunction with Article 228(2), first sentence, and (3), first subparagraph.[19]

---

[13] [1981] ECR 1045. See also Joined Cases 185–204/78 *Firma J. van Dam en Zonen* [1979] ECR 2345; Case 141/78 *France* v. *UK* [1979] ECR 2923; Case 32/79 *Commission* v. *UK* [1980] ECR 2403.
[14] Case 804/79 at para. 17.   [15] *Ibid.*, at para. 18.   [16] *Ibid.*, at para. 20.
[17] *Ibid.*, paras. 22–27. For a case in which national conservation measures were found to be acceptable in Community law, see Case 287/81 *Anklagemyndigheden* v. *Noble Kerr* [1982] ECR 4053.
[18] See, e.g., Council Reg. 3954/92 of 19 Dec. 1992 on the conclusion of an Agreement on relations in the sea fisheries sector between the EEC and Morocco ([1992] OJ L407/1).
[19] In other words, the act in question may be adopted by qualified majority in the Council, after consulting the Parliament.

Procedures for Conclusion of Fisheries Agreements

The procedures for the negotiation on behalf of the Community of bilateral or multilateral agreements relating to fisheries follow the pattern for other agreements to be entered into by the European Community.[20] The Commission[21] proposes to the Council that negotiations should be formally authorized, and makes recommendations for the directives which should guide the negotiation. If the Council approves these recommendations, the Commission conducts the negotiations on behalf of the Community in consultation with a committee appointed by the Council to assist it in this task. When acceptable terms have been negotiated, the Commission will make a proposal to the Council for a decision authorizing the conclusion of the agreement by the Community.[22]

International Organizations

It is clear from the *Kramer* case[23] that the Community's competence in relation to conservation of fisheries includes a power to participate in fisheries conservation organizations, as well as a power to enter into bilateral agreements with third countries.[24] The Court of Justice stressed that Member States were under a duty to use all political and legal means at their disposal to ensure the participation of the Community in such organizations. Until such participation could be secured, the Member States were under a duty to proceed by common action within the framework of such bodies.

In practice, the Community's position in international organizations and conferences will be agreed in co-ordination, either in Brussels or *sur place*. In those organizations in which the Community participates alone, the Commission will present the Community position and negotiate on its behalf. In organizations in which the Member States also participate, it has become usual for the

---

[20] On which, see Ch. 4.

[21] In the case of bilateral agreements, usually after informal exploratory talks with the third country concerned.

[22] Fisheries agreements are usually entered into for a fixed period, and it may not always be possible to conclude the negotiations for a renewal or modification of the old arrangements before the date of their expiry. Or, where negotiations are ended in time, it may not be possible to arrange for formal approval of the new agreement by the Council. In order to avoid disruption to the conduct of fisheries in the meantime, it is frequently necessary to provide for provisional application of the new agreement (by the Community and the third State) before all the Community procedures have been completed, and it has been formally approved by the Council. Agreements about provisional application usually take the form of an exchange of letters, and their conclusion is authorized by a Council decision *sui generis* (which does not cite a legal basis). The agreement is formally concluded later by a Reg. citing the appropriate legal basis—usually Arts. 43 EC and 228. For an example, contrast Council Dec. 94/646 ([1994] OJ L251/21) on the provisional application of the 1994–6 Financial Prot. with Angola with Council Reg. 3020/94 ([1994] OJ L324/1) on the conclusion of the same Prot.

[23] At paras. 44–45.

[24] A. W. Koers, 'The European Economic Community and International Fisheries Organizations' [1984] 1 *LIEI* 113

Commission to present the Community position on fisheries matters (again after consultation with the Member States). On some occasions, the joint position of the Community and the Member States may be presented by the Presidency.[25]

Dependent Territories

The Community is exclusively competent in respect of the territories of the Member States to which the Treaty of Rome applies. It is also competent to exercise any rights which the Member States could have exercised over the high seas or over other maritime zones.[26] In respect of those dependent territories to which the EC Treaty does not apply, the Member States concerned remain competent to negotiate for their dependent territories in international organizations[27] and to conclude agreements on behalf of these territories.[28]

PRACTICE IN RELATION TO FISHERIES AGREEMENTS

The single most important development in the Community's practice in this area has been the Hague Resolution of 3 November 1976.[29] That Resolution was a reaction by the Community to the then emerging practice of coastal States around the world of declaring exclusive 200-mile fishing zones.[30] The obvious consequence of such increased coastal jurisdiction was a reduction in the area of high seas fishing available to Community vessels. The aims of the Resolution were to recover the Community's lost fishing opportunities by the negotiation of a series of bilateral agreements with those coastal States whose waters were important to the Community's fishing fleet; to maintain traditional fishing activities in certain waters within newly extended fishing zones of third States; and, if possible, to enhance the Community's fishing opportunities in third country waters.

In the Resolution, the Council considered that the 'unilateral steps taken or about to be taken by certain third countries' warranted immediate steps by the

[25] e.g. in the FAO, if Community co-ordination procedures determine that the 'thrust of the issue' in the discussion falls within areas of Member-State competence. For co-ordination in the FAO, see Ch. 7.

[26] Joined Case 3, 4, and 6/76, n. 1 above, para. 14; Case C-258/89, n. 8 above.

[27] Such as the UK's and France's participation in the FAO's Indian Ocean Tuna Commission; and Denmark's participation in NAFO and NEAFO on behalf of the Faeroes.

[28] Including agreements with the Community: see agreements between the Community and Denmark on behalf of Greenland and the Faeroes: [1980] OJ L226/12; [1985] OJ L122/2; [1989] OJ L389/83; [1991] OJ L371/2 (Faeroes) and [1985] OJ L29/9; [1989] OJ L389/80; and [1990] OJ L252/2 (Greenland). The Agreement with Greenland was amended and extended in December 1994: see [1994] OJ L351/1.

[29] The history of the deliberations which led up to the Hague Resolution is recorded in the 24th Review (General Secretariat of the Council, 1976) of the Council's Work at 138–42.

[30] On this, see R. R. Churchill and A. V. Lowe, *The Law of the Sea* (Manchester University Press, 1988), ch. 14; Churchill, n. 3 above, chs. 1 and 5.

Community to protect its legitimate interests in those maritime regions most affected. Accordingly, it was agreed that the Member States would, by concerted action and as from 1 January 1977, extend the limits of their fishing zones to 200 miles from their North Sea and Atlantic coastlines, without prejudice to action being taken in relation to other fishing zones under their jurisdiction, such as the Mediterranean. From the same date, the exploitation of fishery resources in these zones by fishing vessels of third countries would be governed by agreements between the Community and the third countries concerned. There was a need to ensure, by means of appropriate Community agreements, that Community fishermen obtained rights in the waters of third countries and that existing rights should be retained.

To that end, the Commission was instructed to initiate negotiations with the non-member countries concerned with a view to concluding framework agreements covering the general conditions which might be applicable in the future.[31] In effect, the Member States agreed to transfer day to day responsibility for external fisheries relations to the Community. Since then, many multilateral and bilateral agreements have been negotiated.

Multilateral Agreements

The Hague Resolution provides that the Commission, acting under negotiating directives from the Council and assisted by Member States, may enter into negotiations for the establishment of international conventions with the purpose of promoting the conservation and rational exploitation of fish resources beyond the 200-mile zones of coastal States. Where new conventions have been negotiated since 1976, the Member States have withdrawn and allowed the Community to become party alone in its own right. Where old conventions have remained in force after the extension of fishing zones, the practice has been that participating Member States have withdrawn in favour of the Community. This has usually required amendment of the convention in question to allow Community participation.

Many of the international agreements drawn up to promote the conservation of the living resources of the sea have established international bodies or organizations to monitor the implementation of the agreements or to promulgate measures to assist in the achievement of their objectives.[32] The Community's participation in these agreements raises some of the problems which are associated with its participation in international organizations generally.[33]

---

[31] The countries with which negotiations were to begin immediately were the US, Canada, the USSR, Poland, the former GDR, Spain, the Faeroes, Norway, Iceland, Sweden, and Finland.

[32] For a discussion of Community participation in conservation organizations, see Churchill, n. 3 above, ch. 5, 184–91; A. W. Koers, n. 24 above.

[33] Such as the right to vote, and the question of the role of the Member States. On these, see Ch. 7. In fact the Community's participation in fisheries organizations seems to take place with less difficulty than does its participation in other organizations. This may be due to the Community's

The Community is a party to the following agreements and a member of the organizations thereby established.

Convention for the Conservation of Salmon in the North Atlantic Area. The Community played a large part in the negotiation of this Convention, which was opened for signature on 2 March 1982 and entered into force on 1 October 1983. The Community approved the Convention on 14 December 1982.[34] The Convention established the North Atlantic Salmon Conservation Organization, in which the Community participates, exercising one vote. It represents the interests of 'originating States'—such as the United Kingdom and Ireland, and until the withdrawal of Greenland from the EEC in 1985, it also represented the interests of Greenland as 'intercepting State'.

Convention on Future Multilateral Co-operation in Fisheries in the North West Atlantic. This Convention, opened for signature on 24 October 1978, entered into force on 1 January 1979. It established the Northwest Atlantic Fisheries Organization (NAFO). The Community is a full member of NAFO,[35] contributes to its budget and exercises one vote. Denmark is also a member on behalf of the Faeroes and Greenland, but no other Member States are members.

Convention on Future Multilateral Co-operation in North East Atlantic Fisheries.[36] The North East Atlantic Fisheries Commission (NEAFC) was established in 1959. Provision was made for Community participation in the organization by an amending Convention, which was opened for signature on 18 November 1980, and entered into force on 17 March 1982. The Community is a full member, has one vote and contributes to the budget of the organization. Denmark represents the Faeroes and Greenland. No other Member States are parties to this Convention.

Convention on the Conservation of Antarctic Marine Living Resources.[37] This Convention was opened for signature on 20 May 1980 and entered into force on 7 April 1982. Among other things, it established the Commission for the Conservation of Antarctic Marine Living Resources. The Community is a party to the Convention, along with Belgium, Greece, Italy, France, Germany, Spain, and the United Kingdom.

Convention on Fishing and Conservation of the Living Resources in the Baltic Sea and the Belts.[38] This Convention, which established the International Baltic Sea Fishery Commission, was signed on 13 September 1973 by the States bordering the Baltic Sea. A Protocol amending the Convention to allow for Community participation was opened for signature in 1982. The Community became a party

well established and recognized competence in relation to fisheries conservation, and perhaps also to the fact that many of these organizations have relatively few participants.

[34] [1982] OJ L378/24.   [35] [1978] OJ L378/1.   [36] [1981] OJ L227/21.
[37] [1981] OJ L252/26 .   [38] [1983] OJ L237/4.

to this Convention in 1984, replacing[39] Denmark and Germany.[40] The
Community exercises one vote.[41]

Steps have been taken to secure Community participation in the following
agreements.

International Convention for the Conservation of Atlantic Tunas. This Convention was
signed on 14 May 1966, and entered into force on 21 March 1969. In 1979
France, then the only Member State party to this Convention, requested the
necessary amendments to be made to allow Community accession. These were
agreed in 1984, and an amending Protocol was opened for signature. The
Community approved the Protocol but it is not yet in force.[42]

International Convention for South East Atlantic Fisheries.[43] France, Germany, Italy,
Spain and Portugal are contracting parties to this Convention, which entered
into force on 24 October 1971. Procedures were set in motion in 1980 to enable
the Community to become a party.[44]

International Convention for the Regulation of Whaling (1946).[45] The Community participates as an observer. The possibility of amending the Convention to allow
its accession has been discussed, but has not proceeded far. Denmark, France,
the Netherlands, and the United Kingdom are contracting parties.

Fisheries questions also arise in the course of the work of other international
bodies.

FAO Regional Bodies.[46] The Community is now a 'member organization' of the
FAO. Within the FAO system, there are several bodies dealing with aspects of
fisheries: the Commission for the Eastern Central Atlantic Fisheries (CECAF);
the Indian Ocean Fisheries Commission (IOFC); the Indian Ocean Tuna
Commission (IOTC); the Western Central Atlantic Fishery Commission
(WCAFC); and the General Fisheries Council for the Mediterranean (GFCM).
The Community is a member[47] of the Indian Ocean Tuna Commission and
enjoys observer status in the other Commissions.

United Nations Convention on the Law of the Sea.[48] The Community and all the
Member States except Germany and the United Kingdom have signed this

---

[39] Prot., Art. 7(a).
[40] See Fitzmaurice, 'Common Market Participation in the Legal Regime of the Baltic Sea
Fisheries' (1990) 33 *Germ.YBIL* 214.
[41] Prot., Art. 7(b).
[42] [1986] OJ L162/33. Amending Prot. [1986] OJ L162/41.   [43] 801 UNTS 101.
[44] A prot. terminating the Convention was agreed in 1990 but is not yet in force.
[45] 673 UNTS 63; 6 ILM 293.
[46] On Community membership of the FAO, see Ch. 7.   [47] As are the UK and France.
[48] On the terms of Community participation in UNCLOS III, see in particular Koers, 'The
Participation of the European Economic Community in a new Law of the Sea Convention' (1979)

Convention, and the procedures for ratification, accession, and formal approval are under way. Several parts of the Convention are relevant to the regulation of fisheries. The Community is currently involved in the negotiation at the United Nations Conference on Straddling Fish Stocks and Highly Migratory Fish Stocks of an agreement on the implementation of the provisions of UNCLOS on straddling fish stocks and highly migratory fish stocks.

Bilateral Agreements

The bilateral fisheries agreements negotiated and concluded by the Community with individual third countries fall into three broad categories.[49] *Reciprocal agreements* provide for access by each party's vessels to the other party's fisheries zones and stocks. *Surplus agreements* have been made with coastal States which cannot with their own fleets fully exploit the resources of their adjacent waters, and are accordingly prepared to allocate the surplus to third countries in exchange for trade co-operation or financial compensation. Finally, *commercial agreements* provide for access to fish stocks in exchange for commercial benefits such as trade concessions to facilitate the coastal State's exports of its fish products.

Reciprocal Agreements

The basic aim of these agreements is to give each side similar access to the waters of the other. In general, they set out a framework for the conduct of fisheries relations; the detail is filled in later by subsequent Protocols, exchanges of letters, and unilateral measures adopted by each side after discussions. Access is granted by each side to the other's waters and each side is allowed to fish against an allocation set and monitored by the other. Each side's vessels are subject to the jurisdiction of the other while fishing in its waters and disputes about the application of the agreements are to be settled by consultation. Typically, agreements last for ten years and are renewable. Often there is provision for schemes for joint management of shared stocks. Annual bilateral consultations, given effect by unilateral legislation, will make provision for the allocations to each side; the licensing of vessels; conservation measures; and enforcement.

---

73 *AJIL* 426; K. R. Simmonds, 'The Community's participation in the Law of the Sea Convention, in Essays in European Law and Integration' O'Keeffe and Schermers (eds.), (Kluwer, 1982) at page 179; Simmonds, *The UN Convention on the Law of the Sea 1982 and the Community's Mixed Agreements Practice*, in O'Keeffe and Schermers (eds.) *Mixed Agreements* (Kluwer, 1983), 199; K. R. Simmonds,'The Community's Declaration upon Signature of UNCLOS' (1986) 23 *CMLRev.* 521. On the Community's signature and provisional application of the Agreement implementing Part XI of UNCLOS see [1994] OJ L215/9.

[49] See, further, Churchill, n. 3 above, ch. 5.

The Community's agreements with Norway,[50] the Faeroes,[51] Iceland,[52] Dominica,[53] Latvia,[54] Lithuania,[55] and Estonia[56] are usually regarded as reciprocal agreements.

Surplus Agreements

Community Waters

There are no agreements allowing third States to fish for surplus resources in Community waters; all the available catch can be allocated among the Member States.[57]

Waters of Third Countries

The agreements with the United States,[58] Canada,[59] and Greenland[60] are sometimes regarded as 'surplus' agreements. In reality, only the United States agreement (which has now lapsed) fell into that category. The agreement with Greenland was negotiated as part of the terms on which Greenland left the Community, and its aim was to give the Community the access to Greenland waters which it would have had if Greenland had remained. The 1981 agreement with Canada (now also lapsed) gave the Community's fleet access to Canadian waters in return for duty free access to the Community market for certain Canadian produce.[61]

---

[50] [1980] OJ L226/47.

[51] [1980] OJ L226/12; [1985] OJ L122/2; [1989] OJ L389/83; [1991] OJ L371/2; [1995] OJ L54/25.

[52] [1993] OJ L161/1.　　　　　[53] [1993] OJ L299/1.　　　　　[54] [1993] OJ L56/6.
[55] [1993] OJ L56/10.　　　　　[56] [1993] OJ L56/1.

[57] See Council Reg. 3929/92 of 19 Dec. 1992 laying down for 1993 certain measures for the conservation and management of fishery resources applicable to vessels flying the flag of certain non-member countries in the 200 nautical mile zone off the coast of the French department of Guyana.

[58] For the text of the original Agreement with the US see [1977] OJ L141/1. The 1984 Agreement is at [1984] OJ L272/1.

[59] [1981] OJ L379/53.

[60] [1985] OJ L29/9; [1989] OJ L389/80; [1990] OJ L252/2; and [1994] OJ L351/1.

[61] A fisheries agreement was reached with Canada in 1993 which, when ratified by Canada, will supersede the 1981 Agreement. This agreement is unusual in that it does not provide for any substantial fishing opportunities. Instead, the Community and Canada agree to co-operate in NAFO. Canada accepts that certain cod stocks should be managed by NAFO, allocates a share of that NAFO stock to the Community, and reopens her ports and surplus fisheries resources to Community vessels on the same terms as are offered to other NAFO parties. For the text of the 1993 Agreement, see [1993] OJ L340/1. An agreement was reached between Canada and the EC on 15 Apr. 1995 in settlement of a dispute about rights to fish for Greenland halibut in the high seas adjacent to the Canadian EFZ off Newfoundland. The agreement set total allowable catches from 1995 onwards and tightened fisheries inspection and control arrangements.

Commercial Agreements

These agreements, which are mainly with the ACP countries, can be seen as complementary to the Community's aid programme to these countries.[62] The Community is given access to the fisheries of a third country in return for financial and other contributions. In form, these agreements consist of a basic agreement text, supplemented by a financial protocol which sets out the detailed terms and arrangements for co-operation and the amount of the Community's contribution. The financial protocols are of limited duration but renewable.

In substance, the main features of the agreements are as follows. Community vessels are given access to the waters of the country concerned in return for payment by the Community of a global financial compensation package. This package consists of three elements: (a) financial compensation in return for fishing opportunities; (b) a smaller amount for training, scientific research, and education; and (c) financing for the fisheries sector of the third State. The amount of the package will be calculated on the basis of the fishing opportunities afforded to the Community's fleet; the commercial value of these opportunities and of the product; the technical assistance offered to the coastal State, and any related development policy benefits. In addition, the agreements require the Community shipowners to pay to obtain licences to fish, and catches (or part of them) may have to be landed at the ports of the coastal country. It is sometimes a condition that local fishermen have to be employed on the Community's vessels. Community vessels are also required to lodge statements of their catches; to submit to local monitoring; to respect local fishing zones; and comply with local laws and practices.

The agreements with Angola,[63] the Comoros,[64] Ivory Coast,[65] Gambia,[66] Guinea-Bissau,[67] Guinea,[68] Equatorial Guinea,[69] Mauritius,[70] Mauritania,[71] Madagascar,[72] Mozambique,[73] Sao Tome e Principe,[74] Senegal,[75] Seychelles,[76] and Cape Verde[77] fall into this category.[78] An agreement was concluded with

---

[62] On which see Ch. 17.
[63] [1987] OJ L341/1; Financial Prot. (1994–6) [1994] OJ L324/1.
[64] [1988] OJ L137/18; Financial Prot. (1994–7) provisionally applied [1994] OJ L297/35.
[65] [1990] OJ L379/1; Financial Prot. (1994–6) [1994] OJ L297/37 .
[66] [1987] OJ L146/1; Financial Prot. (1993–6) [1994] OJ L79/1.
[67] [1980] OJ L226/33; Financial Prot. (1993–5) [1994] OJ L60/1.
[68] [1983] OJ L111/1 amended by [1987] OJ L29/9; Financial Prot. (1994–5) provisionally applied [1994] OJ L188/3.
[69] [1984] OJ L188/1; Financial Prot. (1994–7) provisionally applied [1994] OJ L297/31.
[70] [1989] OJ L159/1; Financial Prot. (1993–6) [1994] OJ L187/3.
[71] [1987] OJ L388/1; Financial Prot. (1993–6) [1994] OJ L149/1.
[72] [1986] OJ L73/26; Financial Prot. (1992–5) [1993] OJ L106/1.
[73] [1987] OJ L201/1.
[74] [1984] OJ L54/1, amended [1987] OJ L337/1; Financial Prot. (1993–6) [1994] OJ L292/1.
[75] [1980] OJ L226/17.
[76] [1987] OJ L160/1; Financial Prot. (1993–6) [1993] OJ L246/6.
[77] [1990] OJ L212/1; Financial Prot. (1994–7) provisionally applied [1994] OJ L297/33.
[78] As does an agreement with Tanzania which has not yet been ratified: see [1990] OJ L379/24.

Morocco in 1988.[79] This was replaced by an agreement concluded in 1992[80] which provided for financial compensation for Morocco; duty-free access for certain products; training; use of local infrastructures; establishment of joint ventures; and scientific co-operation. An agreement with Argentina, concluded in 1993,[81] which also offered compensation for access to fisheries, involved a more sophisticated balancing of joint ventures and customs benefits than has been the case in other similar agreements, and marked a new stage in the evolution of the Community's practice in this area.[82]

Other Agreements

Provisions on co-operation on fisheries matters appear in other Community agreements, in particular general trade and co-operation and association agreements.[83] The Interim Agreements[84] and the Europe Agreements[85] also contain provisions on fisheries, as do the Lomé Convention[86] and the OCT Decision[87]. The EEA Agreement provides for trade in fish;[88] agreements concluded subsequently with Iceland and Norway make limited provision for co-operation on fisheries and the marine environment.[89]

---

[79] [1988] OJ L181/1.   [80] [1992] OJ L407/1.

[81] [1993] OJ L318/1: in force from 24 May 1994 ([1994] OJ L137/61).

[82] The 1993 Argentina Agreement is commonly referred to as a 'Second Generation' agreement.

[83] Agreements with Syria, Art. 4 ([1978] OJ L269/1); Lebanon, Art. 4 ([1978] OJ L261/1); Jordan, Art. 4, ([1978] OJ L268/1); Tunisia, Art. 4 ([1978] OJ L265/1); Egypt, Art. 4 ([1978] OJ L266/1); Morocco, Art. 4 ([1978] OJ L264/1); Algeria, Art. 4 ([1978] OJ L263/1); Yemen, Art. 3(2) ([1985] OJ L26/1); Pakistan, Art. 3(1)(e) ([1986] OJ L108/1); Chile, Art. 2(2)(b) ([1991] OJ L79/1); Mexico Arts. 2(2)(e) and 24 ([1991] OJ L340/1); Uruguay, Art. 3 (2)(b) ([1992] OJ L94/1); Brazil, Art. 26 ([1992] OJ C163/1); Albania, Art. 15(2) ([1992] OJ L343/1); Macao Art. 4 ([1992] OJ L404/26); Estonia (1992), Art. 15(2) ([1992] OJ L403/1); and (1994), Arts. 15 and 16 ([1994] OJ L373/1); Latvia (1992), Art. 15(2) ([1992] OJ L403/10) and (1994), Arts. 16 and 17 ([1994] OJ L374/5); Lithuania (1992), Art. 15(2) ([1992] OJ L403/19) and (1994), Arts. 16 and 17 ([1994] OJ L375/1).

[84] Interim Agreements with Romania, Arts. 17 and 18 ([1993] OJ L81/1); Bulgaria, Arts. 17 and 18 ([1993] OJ L323/1); Hungary, Arts. 16 and 17 ([1992] OJ L116/1); Poland, Arts. 16 and 17 ([1992] OJ L114/1).

[85] Europe Agreements with Hungary, Arts. 22 and 23 ([1993] OJ L347/1); Poland, Arts. 22 and 23 ([1993] OJ L348/1); Romania, Arts. 23 and 24 ([1994] OJ L357/1); Bulgaria, Arts. 23 and 24 ([1994] OJ L358/1); the Slovak Republic, Arts. 23 and 24 ([1994] OJ L359/1); and the Czech Republic, Arts. 23 and 24 ([1994] OJ L360/1).

[86] Fourth ACP–EEC Convention ([1991] OJ L229/1), Pt. 2, Title III.

[87] OCT Decision ([1991] OJ L263/1), Pt. 2, Title III.

[88] EEA Agreement ([1994] L1/1), Art. 20 and Prot. 9.

[89] Agreements in the form of an exchange of letters with Iceland ([1993] OJ L346/19) and Norway ([1993] OJ L346/25).

11

Transport

Both the ECSC and the EC Treaties envisage Community action on transport, but the latter offers far more scope for such action and is in practice the more important. Transport policy, whether at Community or national level, raises complex and sensitive issues, and it is perhaps not surprising that the development of Community policy in this area has been contentious.[1] For example, the European Economic Community's power to act externally was not put beyond doubt until the *Rhine Navigation* case in 1976, and the precise scope of the Community's power remains a matter of dispute between the Council, the Commission and the Parliament.[2]

THE ECSC

Extent of the Community's Competence

The ECSC Treaty and the Convention on Transitional Provisions both provide for limited Community action on transport to ensure that charges and tariffs are applied in a non-discriminatory fashion. Article 70 of the ECSC Treaty provides that the establishment of the common market necessitates the application of such rates and conditions for the transport of coal and steel as will afford comparable price conditions to comparably placed consumers. Any discrimination in rates and conditions of carriage of every kind which is based on the country of origin or destination of products is prohibited in traffic between Member States, and various more detailed provisions are made to that end. In order to attain the objectives of Article 70, Article 10 of the Convention on Transitional Provisions provided for the setting up of a Committee of Experts to study the arrangements proposed by the Governments of the Member States for the carriage of coal and steel.[3] The negotiations to obtain the agreement of the Governments on the various measures proposed were to be initiated by the High Authority, as were any necessary negotiations with third countries. Article

---

[1] On common transport policy of the EC, see P. J. G. Kapteyn and P. Verloren van Themaat, *Introduction to the Law of the European Communities* (2nd edn., Kluwer, 1989), ch. X.3; and *Halsbury's Laws*, ch. 11; D. Lasok and J. W. Bridge, *Law and Institutions of the European Union* (6th edn., Butterworths, 1994), ch. 25.

[2] For a recent example see *Opinion 1/94 (Re WTO Agreement)* [1995] 1 CMLR 205.

[3] On the transport policy of the ECSC and Art. 10 of the Convention on Transitional Provisions, see Case 9/61 *Netherlands* v. *High Authority* [1962] ECR 213.

10 also set out in more detail the tasks of the Committee of Experts and the timetable within which they were to work.

The last paragraph of Article 70 provides that, subject to the provisions of that Article and the other provisions of the Treaty, transport policy, including the fixing and altering of rates and conditions of carriage of every kind and the making of rates on a basis calculated to secure for the transport undertakings concerned a balanced financial position, is to continue to be governed by the laws and regulations of the individual Member States, as are measures relating to co-ordination or competition between different modes of transport or different routes. Negotiations under Article 10 of the Convention on Transitional Provisions were to be initiated by the High Authority without prejudice to the last paragraph of Article 70.

Practice of the ECSC

Two agreements specifically relating to the transport of coal and steel have been concluded, the Agreement of 28 July 1956 with Switzerland[4] and the Agreement of 26 July 1957 with Austria.[5] The parties to the Agreements are, on the one hand, Switzerland and Austria respectively, and on the other, the Governments of the Member States of the ECSC and the High Authority of the ECSC. Each of these agreements has been amended several times.[6]

The European Community

The EC Treaty provides that the activities of the Community shall include a common policy in the sphere of transport.[7] Title IV provides in more detail for the development of such a policy. In particular, Article 74 provides that the objectives of the Treaty shall, in the matters covered by Title IV, be pursued by the Member States within the framework of a common transport policy. Article 75 provides that for the purpose of implementing Article 74, and taking into account the distinctive features of transport, the Council shall lay down common rules applicable to international transport to or from the territory of a Member State or passing across the territory of one or more Member States, and 'any other appropriate provisions'. Title IV applies to transport by rail,

---

[4] Agreement on the introduction of through railway tariffs for the carriage of coal and steel through Swiss territory ([1957] JO 17/223).

[5] Agreement between the Austrian Federal Government of the one part, and the Governments of the Member States of the ECSC and the High Authority of the ECSC of the other part, on the introduction of through international railway tariffs for the carriage of coal and steel through the territory of the Republic of Austria ([1958] JO 6/78).

[6] The Swiss Agreement by a Supp. Prot. ([1979] OJ L12/15); a 2nd Supp. Prot. ([1981] OJ L227/11); and a 3rd Supp. Prot. ([1987] OJ L397/7). The Austrian Agreement by a Supp. Prot. ([1979] OJ L12/27); a 2nd Supp. Prot. ([1981] OJ L227/1); and a 3rd Supp. Prot. ([1989] OJ L75/1).

[7] Art. 3(f) EC, as amended by the TEU.

road, and inland waterway.[8] The Council may, acting by qualified majority, decide whether, to what extent and by what procedure appropriate provisions may be laid down for sea and air transport.[9]

Extent of the Community's External Competence

The Treaty contains no express power enabling the Community to conclude agreements on transport matters. The Community's external competence on transport therefore arises by implication from Title IV of the EC Treaty and from measures adopted thereunder.[10] The extent of the Community's competence is difficult to determine precisely, but may be summarized as follows.

Where measures have been adopted by the Community institutions, the Community will have competence to enter into agreements on matters covered by these measures. Internal measures can in principle be adopted on any issue relating to the establishment and operation of the common transport policy.

In addition, it appears from *Opinion 1/76*[11] (the *Rhine Navigation* case) that an external Community competence may also arise even in the absence of internal rules. This case concerned rationalization of the economic situation in the inland waterways sector in the Rhine and Moselle basins by elimination of short-term over-capacity. That objective could not be achieved by the establishment of common internal rules, because Swiss vessels traditionally participated in navigation in the waterways in question. It was necessary, therefore, to bring Switzerland into the scheme envisaged. That could only be done by an international agreement. In these circumstances, the Court held that wherever Community law had created for the institutions of the Community powers within its internal system for the purpose of attaining a specific objective, the Community had authority to enter into the international commitments necessary for the attainment of these objectives. This was particularly so in cases where the internal power had been exercised and measures had been adopted. But it was not limited to such cases. The power to bind the Community flowed by implication from the provisions of the Treaty creating the internal power, in so far as participation in the agreement was necessary for the attainment of one of the Community's objectives.

The external competence based on the Community's internal powers may thus be exercised and may become exclusive without any internal legislation having been adopted. But this relates only to a situation where the conclusion of an international agreement is necessary to achieve Treaty objectives which cannot be attained by the adoption of autonomous rules.[12]

---

[8] Art. 84(1) EC.   [9] Art. 84(2) EC.
[10] Not, e.g., from Art. 113: see *Opinion 1/94*, n. 2 above, at para. 48; *Opinion 2/92 (Re the OECD National Treatment Instrument)*, 24 Mar. 1995, not yet reported. On Community competence arising by implication, see Ch. 3.
[11] *Draft Agreement establishing a European laying-up fund for Inland Waterway Vessels* [1977] ECR 741.
[12] *Opinion 1/94*, n. 2 above, at para. 85; *Opinion 2/92*, n. 10 above, at para. 32.

Nature of the Community's Competence

Where common rules have been adopted internally in the area of transport, the Community has exclusive competence in relation to the conclusion of any agreement which might affect these rules, or alter their scope.[13] Common internal rules have been adopted on many aspects of the regulation of transport services, and transport matters generally. The Community's external competence in relation to transport is therefore exclusive across the areas covered by these rules.

The mere power to adopt measures does not, however, automatically lead to the existence of exclusive competence. The Member States only lose the right to assume obligations with non-member countries as and when common rules which could be affected by those obligations come into being. Not all transport matters are covered by common rules, and the Member States remain entitled, in areas not covered by common rules, to continue to conduct relations with third countries.[14] Furthermore, if a measure adopted by the Community only establishes minimum standards, the external Community competence deriving from the measure is shared with the Member States, and is not exclusive.[15]

The Member States' continuing powers to act are subject to certain limitations. First, it is open to the institutions to arrange, in the common rules laid down by them, concerted action in relation to non-member countries or to prescribe the approach to be taken by the Member States in their external dealings.[16] Secondly, although the Member States retain competence in areas in which no internal measures have been adopted, the Community may in certain circumstances have an exclusive competence to enter into agreements in these areas. It appears from *Opinion 1/94* that if internal powers can only effectively be exercised at the same time as external powers, internal competence can give rise to exclusive external competence without the adoption of internal rules. Thus, where, because of the need to involve third countries, a Community objective cannot be achieved by the adoption of internal legislative measures or common rules, external powers may be exercised by the Community, and may become exclusive, without any internal legislation having first been adopted.[17]

Community Practice in Relation to International Transport

Legal Basis

The principal legal bases in the EC Treaty for external action in the area of transport are in Title IV, and the Article which should be cited in a particular

---

[13] Case 22/70, *Commission* v. *Council* [1971] ECR 263 (the *AETR* case) .

[14] *Opinion 1/94*, n. 2 above, at para. 77.

[15] By analogy with *Opinion 2/91 (Re ILO Convention 170)* [1993] ECR I–1061: see also Ch. 3.

[16] *Opinion 1/94*, n. 2 above, at para. 79.

[17] *Opinion 1/76*, n. 11 above, as applied in *Opinion 1/94*, n. 2 above, at para. 85. See also *Opinion 2/92*, n. 10 above, at para. 32.

measure depends on the kind of transport covered by the agreement or measure in question. The legal basis for action relating to transport by road, rail, or inland waterway is Article 75; the legal basis for action on sea or air transport is Article 84.[18] Council acts relating to the conclusion of agreements should of course also cite the relevant procedural provisions of Article 228: paragraph 2, first sentence,[19] and paragraph 3, first sub-paragraph,[20] would usually be the appropriate provisions.[21]

Provisions on transport also appear in agreements adopted under other powers in the Treaty, such as association agreements adopted under Article 238 or agreements on trade and co-operation adopted under Articles 113 and 235 or under Articles 113 and 130y.

Co-ordination of Member-State Action

An interesting feature of the Community's practice in this area is the use of Council recommendations, and occasionally even regulations, to co-ordinate Member State action in relation to the conclusion of international agreements, and the conduct of international relations generally.[22]

Transport Provisions in Community Agreements

General

Multilateral Agreements

The Community is a party to the WTO Agreement,[23] which covers the provision of services including transport services. The Lomé Convention[24] and the EEA Agreement[25] all include provisions on transport, or the provision of transport services.

Bilateral Agreements

Those of the Community's bilateral agreements which deal exclusively with transport are mentioned below. Provisions on co-operation on transport matters also appear in the Europe Agreements (which, as well as providing for

---

[18] See Art. 84(1) and (2) EC.
[19] Requiring adoption by a qualified majority in the Council.
[20] Requiring consultation of the Parliament.
[21] On this, and on the procedure for conclusion of Community agreements, see further Ch. 4.
[22] See G. Close, 'Self-restraint by the EEC in the Exercise of its External Powers'. [1981] *YBEL* 45.
[23] [1994] OJ L336/1.
[24] Fourth ACP–EEC Convention, Arts. 115 and 123 ff. ([1991] OJ L229/1).
[25] [1994] OJ L1/1. Arts. 48–52 EEA apply to road, rail, and inland waterway transport; Annex XIII contains specific provisions on all forms of transport: Art. 47 EEA.

co-operation on transport matters generally,[26] also provide extensively for the provision of transport services,[27] as well as for co-operation on transport matters generally); in association agreements[28] (where the extent of the relevant provisions varies from agreement to agreement); and in trade and economic co-operation agreements (some of which mention co-operation on transport as an aspect of general economic co-operation,[29] while others devote specific Articles to the matter[30]).

Maritime Transport

Multilateral Agreements

Attention has already been drawn to the practice of achieving a Community position by co-ordination of Member State action. This is particularly striking in the area of maritime transport,[31] where it has been employed by the Council on several occasions.

Council Decision 77/587[32] set up a consultation procedure on relations between Member States and third countries on shipping matters and on action relating to such matters in international organizations. Member States and the Commission are to consult each other on questions concerning shipping dealt with in the international organizations, on developments in relations between the Member States and third countries in shipping matters and on the functioning of bilateral and multilateral shipping agreements. The aim of the consultation is to consider whether the questions raise problems of common interest which should be addressed jointly.

The Council has on several occasions recommended that the Member States should become parties to international shipping conventions by a given date. Council Recommendation 78/584[33] of 26 June 1978 on the ratification of conventions concerning safety in shipping recommended that the Member States should sign and ratify or accede to the 1974 International Convention on the

---

[26] See the Europe Agreements with Hungary, Art. 81 ([1993] OJ L347/1); Poland, Art. 81 ([1993] OJ L348/1); Romania, Art. 83 ([1994] OJ L357/1); Bulgaria, Art. 82 ([1994] OJ L358/1); the Slovak Republic, Art. 82 ([1994] OJ L359/1); and the Czech Republic, Art. 82 ([1994] OJ L360/1).

[27] See the Europe Agreements with Hungary, Art. 55; Poland, Art. 55; Romania, Art. 57; Bulgaria, Art. 57; the Slovak Republic, Art. 57; and the Czech Republic, Art. 57.

[28] With Turkey, the 1970 Additional Prot., Art. 41 ([1972] JO L293/68).

[29] See the agreements with Argentina, Art. 4(2)(a) ([1990] OJ L295/66); Brazil, Art. 15 ([1992] OJ C163/11); Chile, Art. 2(2)(i) ([1991] OJ L79/1); Mexico, Art. 2(2)(i) ([1991] OJ L340/1); Paraguay, Art. 2(2)(a) ([1992] OJ L313/71); Uruguay, Art. 3(1)(g) ([1992] OJ L94/2); the countries party to the General Treaty on Central American Economic Integration, Art. 3(2) ([1986] OJ L172/1); Slovenia, Art. 7 ([1993] OJ L189/1, and see the separate agreement with Slovenia on transport, n. 67 below); Albania, Art. 15(2) ([1992] OJ L343/12); Macao, Art. 4 ([1992] OJ L404/26); Estonia, Art. 15(2) ([1992] OJ L403/1); Latvia, Art. 15(2) ([1992] OJ L403/10); Lithuania, Art. 15(2) ([1992] OJ L403/19).

[30] e.g. the agreements (listed in n. 29 above) with Mexico, Art. 27; and Brazil, Art. 15.

[31] See, generally, V. Power, *EC Shipping Law* (Lloyd's of London Press, 1992).

[32] [1977] OJ L239/23.   [33] [1978] OJ L194/13.

Safety of Life at Sea by 1 January 1979; the Protocol thereto by 30 June 1979; the 1973 International Convention for the Prevention of Pollution by Ships, as amended in 1978, by 1 June 1980; and the ILO Convention No. 147 concerning Minimum Standards in Merchant Ships by 1 April 1979. Council Recommendation 79/114[34] on the ratification of the 1978 International Convention on Standards of Training, Certification and Watchkeeping for Seafarers recommended that Member States should sign the Convention by 1 April 1979 and ratify it as soon as possible, but no later than 31 December 1980. Council Recommendation 79/487[35] on the ratification of the International Convention for Safe Containers recommended that Member States should ratify or accede to the Convention before 1 July 1980. Council Recommendation 80/907[36] recommended that the Member States should ratify the Torremolinos International Convention on Safety of Fishing Vessels (1977) by 31 July 1982. Council Recommendation 83/419[37] recommended that the Member States should ratify or accede to the 1979 International Convention on Maritime Search and Rescue as soon as possible. Most of these Recommendations also asked the Member States to advise the relevant treaty depository that the Member States' signature, ratification or accession had taken place pursuant to the Council's recommendation.

Of particular interest is Council Regulation 79/954[38] which provided in detail for the Member States' ratification of or accession to the United Nations Convention on a Code of Conduct for Liner Conferences.[39] That Convention made no provision for the participation of the Community in its own right, so it was necessary to secure that the Member States ratified in accordance with agreed arrangements. Regulation 79/954 obliges Member States to inform the United Nations Secretary General that they are ratifying the United Nations Code in accordance with Council Regulation 79/954,[40] and to enter certain reservations in the form prescribed in Annex I to the Regulation.[41] The Regulation also contains provisions about the operation of existing liner conferences. Member States are to consult the Commission before adopting the provisions necessary to give effect to the Regulation.[42]

[34] [1979] OJ L33/31.   [35] [1979] OJ L125/18.   [36] [1980] OJ L259/29.
[37] [1983] OJ L237/74.   [38] [1979] OJ L121/1.
[39] (1974) 13 ILM 910; UKTS 45 (1987); Cmnd 213.
[40] See Case 355/87 *Commission* v. *Council* [1989] ECR 1517: Reg. 954/79 does not however oblige the Member States to ratify or accede, but merely regulates the conditions for accession. For an analysis of the Reg. and the Code, and comments on the difficulties inherent in the Reg., see P. J. Kuyper, 'The European Communities and the Code of Conduct for Liner Conferences: Some Problems' (1981) XII *Neth.YBIL* 73.
[41] The implementation of aspects of the UN Code has also been the subject of several reg.: see Regs. 4055/86, 4056/86, 4057/86, and 4058/86. All these can be found in [1986] OJ L378.
[42] The Commission has given opinions about the legislation proposed by the Federal Republic of Germany (Opinion 82/24 of 17 Dec. 1981 [1982] OJ L10/29); Denmark (Opinion 82/154 of 22 Feb. 1982 [1982] OJ L65/28); Belgium (Opinion 82/210 of 16 Mar. 1982 [1982] OJ L99/39); the UK (Opinion 82/508 of 13 July 1982 [1982] OJ L229/28); and France (Opinion 85/185 of 28 Feb. 1985 [1985] OJ L71/18).

On 19 December 1978, the Council decided on the adoption by the Member States which are contracting parties to the Convention for the Navigation of the Rhine of an Additional Protocol to the Convention. A common position, to be determined by the Council under Article 75 EEC, was to be adopted within the Central Commission for the Navigation of the Rhine by the Member States concerned.[43] Regulation 2919/85[44] makes provision for conditions of access to the arrangements under the Revised Convention for the Navigation of the Rhine.

Bilateral Agreements

No bilateral agreements exist dealing principally with transport by sea.[45]

Air Transport

The formulation of a Community policy in the area of air transport has been politically controversial, and there is correspondingly little practice in this area.[46] The principal act of the Community in the area of external relations is Decision 80/50[47] which set up a consultative procedure on relations between the Member States and third countries in the field of air transport and on action on such matters within international organizations. The aims of the procedure, and its operation, are similar to those adopted in 1978 in relation to maritime transport.[48]

An agreement on air services was concluded between the Community and Sweden and Norway in 1991,[49] and amended in 1992.[50] It provides that all Community legislation on air transport should apply in Sweden and Norway. Discussion has begun with the countries of Central and Eastern Europe[51] about air services, and the regulation of air services figures in the negotiations with Switzerland about a general transport agreement.[52]

---

[43] See *12th General Report on the Activities of the European Communities* (1978), point 358.
[44] [1985] OJ L280/4.
[45] Short Agreements on Maritime Transport were concluded in 1994 with Estonia ([1994] OJ L373/163); Latvia ([1994] OJ L374/216); and Lithuania ([1994] OJ L375/204) as part of the negotiations for free trade agreements with these countries.
[46] On the Community's external air transport relations generally, see J. Balfour, *European Community Air Law* (Butterworth, 1995). See also J. Balfour, 'Air Transport—A Community Success Story?' (1994) 31 *CMLRev.* 1025. The author observes that air transport is an area where the principle of subsidiarity points toward action at Member State level.
[47] [1980] OJ L18/24.   [48] See above, Council Decision 77/587, n. 32.
[49] [1992] OJ L200/20.   [50] [1993] OJ L212/17.
[51] *27th General Report on the Activities of the European Communities* (1993), point 336.
[52] *Ibid.*, point 334.

Land Transport

Multilateral agreements

The Community applies the European Road Traffic Agreement by virtue of Regulation 2829/77.[53] The aim of this agreement is to regulate the conditions of work of drivers and those involved in the supply of road transport services within the Community and between the Community and certain third States. The Member States are parties to the Agreement, and were obliged to act jointly in ratifying or acceding to it.[54] In particular, they were required to enter reservations in an agreed form.

The Community is a party to the Customs Convention on the International Transport of Goods under cover of TIR Carnets.[55] It has also concluded the Agreement on International Carriage of Passengers by Road by means of Occasional Coach and Bus Services.[56] The purpose of this agreement is to liberalize transport services between the contracting parties,[57] and to make provision for related procedural matters. The Agreement was given effect in the Community by a Council decision adopted in 1982.[58]

By a Council decision in 1979, it was agreed that the Member States would act in common in the negotiation of revisions to the International Convention on the Carriage of Passengers and Luggage by Rail and the International Convention on the Carriage of Goods by Rail.[59]

Bilateral Agreements

The Community has concluded agreements on transit by land[60] with Hungary[61] and on carriage of goods by road and rail with Switzerland.[62] Agreements on land transport infrastructure have been concluded[63] with Hungary[64] and with the Czech and Slovak Republics.[65] A similar agreement has been initialled with Romania.[66] A wide ranging agreement with Slovenia[67] was

---

[53] [1977] OJ L334/11 (the text of the agreement) and [1978] OJ L95/1.

[54] See Art. 2 of Reg. 2829/77: 'In ratifying or acceding to the AETR, the Member States . . . shall act on behalf of the Community.'

[55] [1978] OJ L252/2.   [56] [1982] OJ L230/39.

[57] Currently (after the 1994 accessions) the Community (as enlarged) Norway, Switzerland, and Turkey.

[58] Council Dec. 82/505 [1982] OJ L230/8.   [59] *13th General Report* (1979), point 732.

[60] An agreement was concluded with Austria in 1993 (*27th General Report*, n. 51 above. See now the 1994 Act of Accession, Prot. 9).

[61] [1992] OJ L407/47.

[62] [1992] OJ L373/28. The Council's conclusion of the agreement with Hungary was the subject of a challenge by the Commission under Art. 173 EC: Joined Cases C–73/93 and C–74/93 *Commission* v. *Council* . The Commission had contended that the agreement should have been concluded on the basis of Art. 113 EC (rather than Art. 75, the Art. chosen by the Council). Following *Opinions 1/94*, n. 2 above, and *2/92*, n. 10 above, the Commission withdrew these actions.

[63] An agreement with Yugoslavia was signed in 1992, but never ratified (*25th General Report* (1991), point 732).

[64] [1992] OJ L407/47.   [65] [1992] OJ L407/59.

[66] *26th General Report* (1992), point 681.   [67] [1993] OJ L189/161.

concluded in 1993 covering road, rail, and combined transport infrastructure; market access; supporting legal and administrative measures; environmental matters; and the development of transport policies, with particular regard to transport infrastructure.

Unilateral Community Measures

The OCT Decision[68] provides for action on transport. The TACIS Programme[69] provides for technical assistance in a range of areas including transport infrastructures.

In an area such as transport, internal Community legislation has an impact on the transport operations of third country nationals as well as on those of Community operators. The relevant rules mostly involve the exercise of the Community's internal competence, and therefore fall outside the scope of this work. Some are, however, of direct relevance to the conduct of the Community's external relations.[70]

As regards safety and the environment, Directive 79/116[71] sets down the minimum requirements for tankers entering Community ports, and Directive 93/75[72] deals with vessels carrying dangerous or polluting goods. Directive 80/51[73] imposes limits on the noise emissions from subsonic aircraft operating into the Community.[74] Directive 92/14[75] also deals with noise levels from certain aircraft, and purports to implement Annex 16 to the Convention on International Civil Aviation.

The trade practices of third country shipping operators are regulated by Decision 78/774[76] (dealing with the activities of certain third countries) and Decision 83/573[77] (on counter-measures in the field of international merchant shipping). An important package of maritime transport measures was adopted in December 1986. Regulation 4055/86[78] applied the principle of freedom to provide services to maritime transport between Member States and between Member States and third countries. It required the phasing out or adjustment of existing cargo-sharing arrangements and made cargo-sharing arrangements in any future agreements subject to a Community authorization procedure.[79] This liberalization measure was designed to benefit third country carriers as well as Community carriers. Regulation 4057/86,[80] adopted as part of the same

[68] OCT Dec., Arts. 74 and 75–80 ([1991] OJ L263/1).

[69] Reg. 2053/93 ([1993] OJ L187/1).

[70] e.g., see the account of Community action after the oil spillages at La Corunna and Shetland in 1993: *27th General Report*, n. 51 above, point 322 ff.

[71] [1979] OJ L33/33.   [72] [1993] OJ L247/19.   [73] [1980] OJ L18/26.

[74] *Ibid.*, Art. 7.   [75] [1992] OJ L76/21 .   [76] [1978] OJ L258/35.

[77] [1983] OJ L332/37.   [78] [1986] OJ L378/1.

[79] For an example of the application of this Reg., see Case 355/87 *Commission* v. *Council* [1989] ECR 1517. See also D. Charles-Le Bihan and J. Lebullenger 'Common Maritime Transport Policy: Bilateral Agreements and the Freedom to Provide Services' (1989) 9 *YBEL* 209.

[80] [1986] OJ L378/16.

package, dealt with unfair pricing practices in maritime transport and allowed the imposition of a redressive duty where unfair pricing by third country shipowners engaged in international liner shipping caused serious disruption to the freight pattern on routes to, from or within the Community. Finally, Regulation 4058/86[81] dealt with co-ordinated action to safeguard free access to cargoes in ocean trades, in particular where action by a third country shipowner or its agents restricts or threatens to restrict the free access of Member State shipping to the international maritime shipping market. The provisions of this Regulation are stated to be without prejudice to the obligations of the Member States under international law.

Controls at the Community's internal frontiers on means of transport registered in non-Community countries were abolished by Regulation 3912/92.[82]

Community Participation in International Transport Organizations

The European Community is an observer, without right to vote, in several international organizations operating in the area of transport.

The Central Office for International Carriage by Rail. This body was set up in 1893, by the International Convention on the Transport of Goods by Rail. All Member States are members of the Organization. There have been several exchanges of letters[83] between the Community and the Organization on the establishment of closer relations and collaboration.

The European Conference of Ministers of Transport (ECMT). The ECMT was set up in 1953 by a Protocol Concerning the European Conference of Ministers of Transport.[84] The aims of the ECMT are the better utilization and more rational development of internal European transport, and the co-ordination and promotion of the work of international organizations with an interest in internal European transport. All the Member States of the EC participate in the ECMT as members, and the Commission has participated since 1989.[85] There have been exchanges of letters[86] between the Secretariat of the ECMT and the Commission about closer co-operation between the two organizations.

The Central Commission for the Navigation of the Rhine (CCNR). The constituent instrument is the Convention on the Navigation of the Rhine, which dates from

---

[81] [1986] OJ L378/21. [82] [1992] OJ L395/6.

[83] Dated 22 Jan. 1959 and 2 Mar. 1959; and 27 July 1967 and 18 July 1967. These have been published in *Relations between the European Community and International Organizations ('Relations')*, (Commission, 1989) 269–72.

[84] 184 UNTS 41; UKTS 32 (1954), Cmnd. 9142.

[85] *23rd General Report* (1989), point 656.

[86] Dated 8 Nov. 1962 and 21 Nov. 1962; 18 Feb. 1972, 7 Mar. 1972 and 27 June 1972 (inviting a representative of the Commission's services to attend sessions of the Committee of Deputies of the ECMT); and 27 Mar. 1975 and 23 June 1975 (establishing Community participation in the work of the Council and the Committee of Deputies). *Relations*, n. 83 above, 275–80.

the Congress of Vienna in 1815, but was most recently revised in 1963.[87] The objective of the CCNR is to ensure respect for the principles of freedom of navigation and equal treatment of all countries. The members of the CCNR are the states bordering the Rhine and the United Kingdom and Belgium. There have been exchanges of letters[88] between the Commission and the CCNR on closer relations between the two bodies.

The European Organization for the Safety of Air Navigation (EUROCONTROL). This body was set up by the 1960 Convention relating to Co-operation for the Safety of Air Navigation.[89] All the Member States except Austria, Italy, Finland, Spain, Sweden, and Denmark are parties. The objective is to strengthen co-operation between States and to establish a common organization of air traffic above 9,000 metres. There have been exchanges of letters[90] between the Organization and the Commission.

The European Civil Aviation Conference (ECAC). This was set up by an Agreement of 1955 (since amended). Its aim is to follow the development of European air transport, so as to improve co-ordination in, better utilization of, and co-ordinated development of such transport. All the Member States are parties. The Commission and the Secretariat of the ECAC have established inter-institutional relations by exchanges of letters.[91]

The International Civil Aviation Organization (ICAO). The ICAO was set up by the Chicago Convention of 1947.[92] Its functions are developing the principles and techniques of international air navigation and fostering the planning and development of international air transport so as to ensure the safe and orderly growth of international civil aviation throughout the world. All the Member States are parties; and the Commission has established relations with the ICAO by exchanges of letters.[93]

The International Maritime Organization (IMO). The IMO was set up in 1958.[94] Its aim is to facilitate co-operation among governments on technical matters affect-

---

[87] UKTS 66 (1967); Cmnd. 3371.

[88] Dated 6 June 1961 and 24 Mar. 1987, providing for participation of senior Commission officials in the plenary sessions of the CCNR; for participation at other levels in working groups of the CCNR; for exchange of information and so on ([1963] JO 53/1027). *Relations*, n. 83 above, 283–90.

[89] 523 UNTS 117; UKTS 39 (1963), Cmnd. 2114.

[90] Dated 9 July 1980 and 6 Oct. 1980; and 11 Oct. 1982 and 10 Nov. 1982. These provide for exchange of documentation, and expert advice and the establishment of technical meetings. *Relations*, n. 83 above, 292–7.

[91] Dated 14 Jan. 1980 and 22 Jan. 1980, providing for exchanges of information; Commission participation as an observer in plenary sessions of ECAC and meetings of ECAC standing committees; and for participation of ECAC representatives in certain Commission meetings. *Relations*, n. 83 above, 300–2.

[92] 15 UNTS 295; UKTS 8 (1953); Cmnd. 8742.

[93] Dated 21 Nov. 1988 and 28 Feb. 1989, providing for Community participation as observer in appropriate meetings of ICAO. *Relations*, n. 83 above, 138–9.

[94] 289 UNTS 48; UKTS 54 (1958); Cmnd. 589.

ing international shipping in order to achieve the highest standards of maritime safety and efficiency in navigation. All the Member States are parties and the Commission has established institutional links with the IMO.[95]

[95] Exchanges of letters dated 11 Feb. 1974 and 28 June 1974 (providing for consultation, exchanges of information, Commission participation as observer in IMO conferences, etc.), and 5 Jan. 1983 and 2 Feb. 1983 (dealing mainly with arrangements for effective implementation of IMO conventions). *Relations*, n. 83 above, 163–6.

12

Common Commercial Policy

The Treaty provisions governing the common commercial policy are set out in Articles 110 to 115 EC. Article 113 is probably the most frequently used Treaty provision in the exercise of the European Community's powers in the field of external relations. This Chapter considers the legal basis for the European Community's competence in respect of the common commercial policy and the practice of the EC in the implementation of that policy. It focuses on the common commercial policy of the EC under the Treaty of Rome.[1] Since the Euratom Treaty contains no provisions relating to external trade in products covered by that Treaty, there is nothing to prevent agreements concluded pursuant to Article 113 EC from extending to international trade in Euratom products.[2] The ECSC Treaty, however, contains provisions dealing with commercial policy and commercial policy in respect of ECSC products is considered at the end of this Chapter and in Chapter 23.

LEGAL BASIS FOR THE COMMUNITY'S COMPETENCE

Provisions of the Treaty

Article 3(b) of the Treaty of Rome includes among the activities of the Community a common commercial policy.[3] The means of achieving this are set out in Articles 110 to 115. Articles 111, 114, and 116 were repealed by the Treaty on European Union and Articles 113 and 115 were amended.

Article 110 remains in its original form. It underlines that the EC's commercial policy reflects, and is a necessary corollary of, the customs union estab-

---

[1] The common commercial policy could justify a book of its own and this Chapter is intended as only an outline of the subject. In particular, it does not include all the internal Community legislation on the subject, nor does it consider all the international agreements based on Art. 113. As an introduction the reader is referred to the general text books on EC law, e.g. P. J. G. Kapteyn and P. VerLoren van Themaat, *Introduction to the Law of the European Communities*, (2nd edn., Kluwer, 1989) and Vaughan, *Law of the European Communities* (Butterworths, 1994). The reader is also referred to Piet Eeckhout, *The European Internal Market and International Trade: A Legal Analysis* (Clarendon Press, 1994).

[2] *Opinion 1/94* [1995] 1 CMLR 205, para. 24.

[3] Art. 3 was amended by the TEU. The Art. had previously provided for the establishment of a CCT and of a common commercial policy towards third countries.

lished between the Member States. It also emphasizes that the aim of that customs union is 'to contribute, in the common interest, to the harmonious development of world trade, the progressive abolition of restrictions on world trade and the lowering of customs barriers'.

Article 112 provides that Member States shall, before the end of the transitional period, progressively harmonize the systems whereby they grant aid for exports to third countries. The Council is given power to issue any directives needed for this purpose.[4]

Article 113 provides that the common commercial policy is to be based on uniform principles, particularly in regard to changes in tariff rates, the conclusion of tariff and trade agreements, the achievement of uniformity in measures of liberalization, export policy, and measures to protect trade such as those to be taken in the event of dumping or subsidies. The scope of Article 113 is considered in detail below.

Where international agreements need to be negotiated the Commission is to make recommendations to the Council which shall authorize the Commission to open the necessary negotiations. The Commission is required to conduct the negotiations in consultation with a special committee, the Article 113 Committee, and within the framework of such directives as the Council may issue to it. This part of the paragraph corresponds to Article 228(1) and the paragraph goes on to provide that the relevant provisions of Article 228 are to apply.[5]

Paragraph 4 provides that the Council is to act by a qualified majority. Article 113 makes no provision for involving the Parliament.[6]

The provisions of the Article are broad enough to include not only international agreements but also internal rules of Community law, i.e. regulations, directives, and decisions.

Article 115, as amended by the TEU, provides for the Commission to recommend co-operative measures to Member States. The Commission is to do so where this is necessary to ensure that the execution of measures of commercial policy taken in accordance with the Treaty by any Member State is not obstructed by deflections of trade, or where differences between such measures lead to economic difficulties in one or more Member States. Failing this, the Commission 'may' (prior to the TEU, this read 'should') authorize Member States to take 'the necessary protective measures'. The 'protective' nature of the measures derives from the fact that they exclude indirect imports from the principle of free circulation within the Community set out in Articles 9, 10, and 30 EC.

Prior to the amendment of Article 115 effected by the TEU, Member States were permitted in case of urgency to take necessary measures and then to notify

---

[4] Art. 112 and its relationship to Art. 113 was considered in *Opinion 1/75* [1975] ECR 1355.
[5] See Ch. 4.
[6] The Parliament may be consulted pursuant to procedures giving it an informal role. See Ch. 4, 98–100.

them to the Commission and to the other Member States, the former being able to decide that the measure should be amended or abolished. Member States must now request the Commission's authorization to take necessary measures and the Commission must take a decision on the request as soon as possible. Member States must then notify the measure to the other Member States. The Commission may decide at any time that the measure in question must be amended or abolished. In the selection of measures priority must be given to those which cause the least disturbance to the functioning of the common market.[7]

Article 116 deserves mention even though it was deleted by the TEU. It imposed an obligation on the Member States to proceed, within the framework of international organizations of an economic character, only by common action, in respect of all matters of particular interest to the common market. To this end the Commission was to submit to the Council proposals concerning the scope and implementation of such common action. The scope of this provision was far from clear and, consequently, it was, in practice, rarely used.

The Scope of Article 113

General principles

The scope of Article 113 has been the subject of extensive debate between the Member States, the Council, the Commission, and the Parliament. It has also been considered by academic writers.[8] The definition of the common commercial policy in Article 113 is not exhaustive. It clearly covers the matters listed in the Article but the definition is conceived as a non-exhaustive enumeration of the subjects covered by commercial policy which must not close the door to the application in a Community context of other processes to regulate external trade.[9]

In one of the earliest cases on the scope of Article 113 the Court of Justice held that the concept of common commercial policy has the same content whether it is applied in the context of the international action of a State or that

---

[7] For a discussion of Art. 115 and the amendments made by the TEU see Eeckhout, n. 1 above, 170–85.

[8] Many of the articles have been overtaken by the decisions of the ECJ in *Opinion 1/94*, n. 2 above, and *Opinion 2/92*, not yet reported. However, those *Opinions* still leave a number of questions unanswered. In view of this some of the literature is still of interest. See, in particular, Perreau de Pinninck, 'Les compétence communautaires dans les négociations sur le commerce des services' (1991) 27 *CDE* 390; Timmermans 'Common Commercial Policy (Art. 113 EEC) and International Trade in Services' in *Du droit international de L'intégration: liber amoricorum Pierre Pescatore* (Baden-Baden, 1987), 675–89; Vigneron and Smith, 'Le fondement de la compétence communautaire en matière de commerce international de services' (1992) 28 *CDE* 515; Gilsdorf, 'Portée et limitation des compétences communautaires en matière de politique commerciale' (1989) *RMC* 195; and Eeckhout, n. 1 above.

[9] *Opinion 1/94*, n. 2 above, para. 45.

of the Community.[10] In subsequent cases the Court has drawn attention to the
open nature of the common commercial policy[11] and taken into account the
changing nature of world trade, particularly as it affects relations with developing countries where traditional commercial agreements are not suitable and
where more elaborate means need to be devised with a view to furthering the
development of world trade.

In *Opinion 1/78*, on the International Agreement on Natural Rubber,[12] the
Court held that the common commercial policy applied not only to measures
concerned with the liberalization of world trade but also with developing a commercial policy aimed at a regulation of the world market for certain products.
As the Court said in that case: '[f]ollowing the impulse given by UNCTAD to
the development of this type of control it seems that it would no longer be possible to carry on any worthwhile common commercial policy if the Community
were not in a position to avail itself of more elaborate means devised with a
view to furthering the development of international trade.'

Trade in services

In recent years there has been considerable discussion on whether Article 113
applies to trade in services.[13] The issue came to a head at the conclusion of the
GATT Uruguay Round. The outcome of those negotiations was a series of multilateral trade agreements, including a General Agreement on Trade in Services,
the GATS. The Commission maintained that all the agreements giving effect
to the Round, including the GATS, fell within the common commercial policy
and that they should consequently be concluded by the Community alone on
the basis of Article 113. This was not accepted by the Member States or the
Council who, whilst accepting that the Multilateral Agreements on Trade in
Goods for the most part fell within Article 113, argued that in general trade in
services fell outside the common commercial policy and that both the
Community and the Member States had competence to conclude the GATS.

The Court was asked to give a ruling on the matter under Article 228(6). It
did so in *Opinion 1/94*.[14] In determining the extent to which trade in services
fell within Article 113, the Court took into account the definition of services in
the GATS. For the purposes of that Agreement services are defined as comprising four modes of supplying a service. The Court described the four modes
as: (1) cross-frontier supplies not involving any movement of persons; (2) consumption abroad, which entails the movement of the consumer into the territory of the WTO member country in which the supplier is established; (3)
commercial presence, i.e. the presence of a subsidiary or branch in the territory

---

[10] *Opinion 1/75* [1975] ECR 1355 in which the Court held that the OECD agreement on a Local
Cost Standard was within the scope of Art. 113.
[11] *Opinion 1/94*, n. 2 above, para. 41.   [12] [1979] ECR 2871.
[13] See the literature referred to in n. 8 above.   [14] [1994] ECR I-5267.

of the WTO member country in which the service is to be rendered; (4) the presence of natural persons from a WTO member country, enabling a supplier from one member country to supply services within the territory of any other member country.[15]

The Court decided that as regards the first mode of supply, cross-frontier supplies, the situation is not unlike trade in goods, which is covered by the common commercial policy, and that therefore there was no particular reason why a supply by this mode should not fall within the concept of the common commercial policy. However, as regards the three other modes of supply, set out in the GATS, the Court decided that these methods of providing a service were not covered by the common commercial policy. The Court referred to the fact that Article 3 EC distinguishes between a common commercial policy in paragraph (b) and measures concerning the entry and movement of persons in paragraph (d). Consequently, the treatment of nationals of non-member countries on crossing the external frontiers of Member States cannot be regarded as falling within the common commercial policy. More generally, the Court said that the existence in the Treaty of specific chapters on the free movement of natural and legal persons shows that those matters do not fall within the common commercial policy.

The Court treated transport services, which were also covered by the GATS, somewhat differently. The Commission had argued in two other cases that were pending before the Court[16] that transport services were within the scope of Article 113. In *Opinion 1/94* the Court rejected this argument on the basis that transport was the subject of a specific title of the Treaty, Title IV, distinct from Title VII on the common commercial policy, and referred to its judgment in the *AETR* case.[17] It concluded that all international agreements in the field of transport are excluded from Article 113.

In *Opinion 1/94* the Court settled the debate of principle whether Article 113 applies to services. It is too early to see how the distinction made by the Court between the cross-border supply of services, which is within Article 113, and other cases, which are not, will work when applied to specific factual situations. In some of these cases the Community will have exclusive competence as a result of the AETR principle or because the internal Community rule has given the Community such competence. In other areas the Member States will retain competence or share it with the Community.

---

[15] This is not an entirely accurate summary of the provisions of Art. 1.2 GATS. There trade in services is defined as the supply of a service: (a) from the territory of one member country into the territory of any other member; (b) in the territory of one member to the service consumer of any other member; (c) by a service supplier of one member, through commercial presence in the territory of any other member; (d) by a service supplier of one member, through the presence of natural persons of a member in the territory of any other member.

[16] Cases C-74 and 75/93 *Commission* v. *Council*. These cases have been withdrawn by the Commission.

[17] Case 22/70 *Commission* v. *Council* [1971] ECR 263.

Intellectual Property

In *Opinion 1/94* the Court considered how Article 113 applies to intellectual property. One of the agreements annexed to the WTO Agreement was the Agreement on Trade-Related Aspects of Intellectual Property, the TRIPS Agreement. Despite its title, the primary purpose of the TRIPS is to strengthen and harmonize the protection of intellectual property world-wide. It is concerned with the rights themselves, not merely with regulating trade in goods which may have infringed intellectual property rights. The Court held that those parts of the TRIPS dealing with intellectual property rights were outside Article 113. The TRIPS also contained provisions on the release into free circulation of counterfeit goods. This aspect of the Agreement was, however, within the scope of Article 113.

In excluding from Article 113 those aspects of the TRIPS dealing with intellectual property rights themselves, the Court appears to have been influenced by the fact that the Community is competent, in the field of intellectual property, to harmonize national laws pursuant to Articles 100[18] and 100a and may use Article 235 as the basis for creating new intellectual property rights superimposed on national rights. Those measures are subject to voting rules (unanimity in the case of Articles 100 and 235) or rules of procedure (consultation of the Parliament in the case of Articles 100 and 235 and co-decision in the case of Article 100a) which are different from those in Article 113. The Court was concerned that these important aspects of the Community's legislative process should not be avoided by the Community entering into an international agreement which would have the same effect as adopting internal rules.

A number of agreements adopted on the basis of Article 113 contain provisions relating to intellectual property.[19] However, these provisions are ancillary to an agreement whose main purpose is trade in goods and which impose obligations relating to intellectual property rights only on the other party to the agreement.

Competition

There have been disagreements between the Commission, on the one hand, and the Council and the Member States, on the other, on whether competition policy is within the common commercial policy. A number of agreements adopted on the basis of Article 113 include provisions relating to competition, but these provisions are ancillary to the main purpose of the agreement. Where an agreement has been concerned with competition only the practice of the Council has been to oppose the use of Article 113 and to use Article 87 instead.[20]

---

[18] It is not clear in what circumstances this Art. would be used rather than Art. 100a.

[19] e.g., the Interim Agreements with Central and Eastern Europe. See 285–6 below.

[20] See,e.g., the decision authorizing the Community to conclude the EC/US competition agreement (not yet published).

There has been no direct case law on the question whether competition is within Article 113. However in *Opinion 1/92* the Court said that the Community's power to enter into international agreements in the competition field arose from the competition rules in the EC Treaty.[21]

Trade and Other Policies

Instruments of commercial policy often pursue another aim, for example development policy. Furthermore, increasingly a number of States have sought to link issues, such as the protection of the environment, social rights, employment policies, immigration policies, and tax policies, to negotiations on trade. The question arises whether an agreement which is in some way connected with trade and some other policy is within the scope of Article 113.

Much will depend upon the facts of the case and in particular the aim and content of the particular agreement or instrument in question. In the *GSP* case, *Commission* v. *Council*,[22] the Court was concerned with the correct legal basis for the Community's regulation granting preferential tariff rates to certain products from certain developing countries. The Council disputed the use of Article 113 on the basis that the regulation pursued a development policy aim. The Court rejected this argument. It pointed out that tariff preferences were changes in tariff rates within the meaning of Article 113 and that a link between trade and development had become progressively stronger in modern international relations. It referred to the recognition of this in the United Nations Conference on Trade and Development and said that the Community's system of tariff preferences reflects a new concept of international trade in which development aims play a major role. This does not mean that development policy is itself within Article 113. The decisive factor in the case was that the Community had used an instrument of commercial policy, i.e. changes in tariff rates.

The Court referred to its *Opinion 1/78*[23] which had also raised the question of the relationship between trade and development policy. The agreement in that case had also contained a number of factors of a secondary nature, i.e. a commitment to ensure fair labour standards in the rubber industry, a commitment to consider favourably any requests for technological assistance, the co-ordination of research programmes and consultations on national tax policies. The Court said that the inclusion of these matters could not modify the description of the agreement, which must be assessed having regard to its essential objective rather than in terms of individual clauses of an altogether subsidiary nature. The position would be different if such matters had not been purely secondary. In that case a separate legal base would be necessary or, depending

---

[21] [1992] ECR 2821 at para. 40.
[22] Case 45/86 [1987] ECR 1493. The case was concerned with the Community's generalized system of preferences which is described at 275–6.
[23] N. 12 above.

upon the subject matter, the Member States would need to be parties as well.[24]

Nature of the Community's Competence

The case law of the Court of Justice has established that the Community has exclusive competence in the field of the common commercial policy.[25] In consequence, the Member States are no longer competent to act on their own as far as commercial policy measures are concerned. In *Opinion 1/75*[26] the Court founded this exclusivity primarily on the basis that the commercial policy was conceived in the context of the common market and for the defence of the common interests of the Community, within which the particular interests of the Member States must adapt to each other. The Court confirmed this concept to be incompatible with the freedom to which the Member States could lay claim by invoking a concurrent power, in such a way as to ensure that their own interests were separately satisfied in external relations, at the risk of compromising the effective defence of the common interests of the Community. The Court concluded that it could not be accepted that the Member States could exercise powers which were concurrent with those of the Community in this sphere. It follows as a logical consequence that national commercial policy measures are only permissible by virtue of specific authorization by the Community.[27] The exclusive nature of the Community's competence has most recently been confirmed in *Opinion 1/94*.[28]

---

[24] For a consideration of the choice of legal base generally, see Wyatt and Dashwood, *European Community Law* (3rd edn., Sweet & Maxwell, 1993), 369, and Ch. 3 above.

[25] The concept of exclusive competence and its consequences are considered in detail in Ch. 3.

[26] N. 10 above, at 1363–4.

[27] See Case 41/76, *Criel, née Donckerwolke et al.* v. *Procureur de la République au Tribunal de Grande Instance, Lille et al.*, [1976] ECR 1921 at 1937. Dec. 69/494/EEC ([1969] JO L326/39) contains provisions relating to agreements within Art. 113. Title I provides for the notification of bilateral agreements then in existence. The Commission may propose to the Council that a Member State which is a party to such an agreement may be authorized to extend for a period not exceeding one year the provisions of the agreement within Art. 113. (There are still a number of agreements on friendship and trade which are subject to this procedure.) Titles II and III set out a procedure to be applied if a Member State considers that a bilateral agreement should be negotiated with a third State on matters within Art. 113.

[28] N. 2 above, paras. 22–34. Gilsdorf, n. 8 above, has put forward the argument that the Community may not have exclusive competence in respect of all aspects of the common commercial policy. That argument is difficult to sustain following *Opinion 1/94*, n. 2 above. However, it highlights the difficult issue of the scope for action by one or more Member States in the area of trade in goods, particularly where there are no Community rules, where they consider it necessary for the protection of such matters as public security and public health. See Eeckhout, n. 1 above, 256–8. See also Cases C–70/94 and C–83/94 *Werner* and *Leifer*, in which judgment has not yet been given, on Germany's export controls on strategic goods and Case C–120/94 *Commission* v. *Greece*, in which judgment has not yet been given, concerning restrictions by Greece on trade with Macedonia.

PRACTICE IN THE IMPLEMENTATION OF THE COMMERCIAL POLICY

General

The commercial policy comprises internal rules of Community law (often referred to as autonomous measures) and bilateral and multilateral agreements concluded with third countries (referred to as contractual or conventional[29] arrangements).

Internal community rules relating to commercial policy

The internal Community rules relating to the commercial policy can be divided into two aspects: the common customs tariff ('the CCT') and other measures of the common commercial policy, namely the Community's export regime, its import regime and the commercial defence instruments. This distinction reflects that found at the basis of the multilateral (i.e. the GATT, and now the WTO) system of international trade regulation, that is the distinction between tariff and non-tariff measures. These internal rules are adopted on a unilateral basis by the Community under powers afforded under Community law (either by the Treaties or secondary legislation). However, in spite of their unilateral nature, they are not divorced from international rules: on the contrary, they are for the most part based on the multilateral rules which regulate most aspects of the commercial policy.

The Common Customs Tariff ('The CCT')

The CCT was established even before the date provided for in the Treaty (1 January 1970), namely on 1 July 1968.[30] This was due to two 'speed-up' decisions; one in 1960 and the other in 1962.[31] The tariff appears in a nomenclature (the 'combined nomenclature') which is based on the Harmonized Commodity Description and Coding system.[32] The nomenclature is reviewed annually.[33] The common customs tariff in fact comprises two tariffs: an autonomous tariff and a conventional one. As regards the level of duties, their upper limit is basically defined by the tariff 'bindings' negotiated in the context

---

[29] In this context 'conventional' is derived from the French 'convention' meaning agreement, not from the English 'conventional' meaning usual or traditional.

[30] Council Reg. 950/68 [1968] I OJ Spec. Ed. 275.

[31] These measures were Acts of the Representatives of the Governments of the Member States meeting in the Council [1960] JO 1217 and [1962] JO 1284.

[32] This system was developed in the framework of the Customs Co-operation Council which is a UN body based in Brussels. See Council Reg. 2658/87 on the tariff and statistical nomenclature of the EC and on the CCT, [1987] OJ L256/1.

[33] Council Reg. 2658/87, n. 32 above, was amended most recently by Commission Reg. 3115/94, [1994] OJ L345/1.

of the GATT or of preferential bilateral agreements.[34] However, a considerable number of duties may be suspended or reduced at any one time. In addition, products from many different countries enjoy preferential tariff treatment. Conversely, certain products may be subject to protective measures in the form of tariff quotas.

The origin of the goods is, of course, a decisive factor in determining the appropriate tariff treatment. For the purposes of the application of the common customs tariff, the rules for determining the origin of a particular product as it enters the territory of a Member State are set out in the Community Customs Code.[35] The definitions are those which apply in respect of non-preferential trade and are without prejudice to the more stringent rules of origin which all preferential agreements have. Once the appropriate tariff classification and origin have been established, the customs duty must be calculated on a uniform basis regardless of the product's point of entry into the Community. The majority of the common customs tariff charges are *ad valorem* duties. The substantive rules for customs valuation, which are laid down in the Community Customs Code, follow the rules laid down by international agreements, namely Article VII of the GATT 1994 and the Agreement on Customs Valuation annexed to the WTO Agreement.

Under the generalized system of preferences ('GSP'), tariff preferences are accorded to developing countries with a view to raising their export revenue. The system has its origins in a decision taken in the framework of the United Nations Committee for Trade and Development (UNCTAD). Preferences were to be adopted unilaterally by all industrialized countries on a non-reciprocal and non-discriminatory basis. The system is the subject of a special derogation from the GATT. It was first adopted by the Community in 1971. The system is currently laid down in Council Regulations 3281/94[36] and 3282/94.[37] The former deals with industrial products including textiles. It applies a four year scheme (1995–8) and introduces a number of innovations to the GSP. The latter applies to agricultural products and extends the existing measures with some modifications until 31 December 1995. The new arrangements aim to be more development-oriented. An innovation is the 'special incentive arrangement' whereby, as from 1 January 1998, additional preferences may be granted to countries which can demonstrate that they apply certain International Labour Organization (ILO) Conventions and certain environmental standards. To that end the Council is to carry out a review in 1997 and, in the light of that review and on the basis of internationally accepted, objective, and operational criteria, the Commission is to submit a proposal for a Council decision.[38] In addition,

---

[34] At the time of writing the CCT is contained in Commission Reg. 3115/94, n. 33 above.
[35] Council Reg. 2913/92, [1992] OJ L302/1, as implemented by Commission Reg. 2454/93 [1993] OJ L253/1, as amended most recently by Commission Reg. 3254/94 [1994] L346/1 setting out, in particular, rules of origin for the Generalized System of Preferences.
[36] [1994] OJ L348/1.   [37] [1994] OJ L348/57.   [38] *Ibid.*, Arts. 7 and 8.

preferences may be withdrawn for countries who practise forced labour, fail to control the export of drugs, or indulge in unfair trading practices.[39]

Export Regime

Regulation 2603/69[40] establishes common rules for exports. It was amended by Council Regulation 3918/91[41] to take account of the Single Market. The basic rule is that exports from the Community to third countries are unrestricted. A small number of products to which the basic principle does not apply are listed in the annex to the Regulation and in certain circumstances Member States can restrict exports.[42]

The export and import of certain dangerous chemicals, together with export of certain chemical products used in the manufacture of chemical weapons, are subject to an additional regime.[43] A system of export controls at the Community level in respect of dual-use goods has also been established.[44] A separate regime also applies for export of cultural goods.[45]

Import Regime

Council Regulation 3285/94[46] establishes common rules for imports and includes products covered by the ECSC Treaty. It also covers textile products listed in Annex II of the Regulation which originate in a WTO member (these products are to be integrated into GATT 1994 in conformity with Article 2 of the WTO Agreement on Textiles and Clothing). However, it does not apply to other textile products covered by Council Regulation 517/94.[47] Nor does it apply to the products originating in certain third countries listed in Council Regulation 519/94 (see below). The basic rule is that goods are to be freely

---

[39] [1994] OJ L348/57 Art. 9. [40] [1969] JO L324/25.

[41] [1991] OJ L372/31.

[42] See, in particular, Art. 11. It is not clear to what extent Member States can take unilateral action to control exports on the basis of this Art. or more generally. See Eeckhout, n. 1 above, ch. 7 and Cases C–70 and C–83/94, n. 28 above. See also Case C–120/94 *Commission* v. *Greece* on the power of the Member States to take action based on Art. 224.

[43] Council Reg. 2455/92 ([1992] OJ L251/13) establishes a common system of notification of imports from and exports to third countries of certain chemicals. Council Reg. 428/89 [1989] OJ L50/1 provides for prior export authorizations for the chemicals which appear in a list prepared within the framework of European Political Co-operation (now CFSP).

[44] Council Reg. 3381/94 ([1994] OJ L367/1). The list of goods to which the Reg. applies is established by a joint action of the Member States acting under Art. J.3 of Title V of the TEU; Council Dec. 94/942 [1994] OJ L367/8.

[45] Council Reg. 3911/92 [1992] OJ L395/1, as implemented by Commission Reg. 752/93 [1993] OJ L77/24, provides that the export of certain cultural goods is subject to authorization.

[46] [1994] OJ L349/53. This Reg. replaced Reg. 518/94 [1994] OJ L67/77, which established a new common import regime taking account of the Single Market and reformed it in depth. The further replacement by Reg. 3285/94 was necessary to take account of the Safeguards Agreement annexed to the WTO. The basic structure of the Reg. has not been fundamentally altered.

[47] [1994] OJ L67/1. This Reg. applies to countries which are not WTO members and with which the Community does not have bilateral agreements or a specific import regime.

imported into the Community and are not to be subject to any quantitative restrictions (Article 1(2) of the Regulation) unless restricted by special rules or measures. This is consistent with Article XI of the GATT, which imposes a general prohibition on quantitative restrictions in respect of imports and exports. Exceptions to this rule would have to be justified on the basis of other specific GATT provisions. The Regulation contains a provision allowing for national measures which parallels the terms of Article 36 EC;[48] it also permits special formalities concerning foreign exchange and formalities introduced pursuant to international agreements in accordance with the EC Treaty.

Council Regulation 519/94 establishes common rules for imports from certain third countries.[49] The Regulation applies to the imports of products originating in the countries listed in Annex 1, with the exception of textile products covered by Regulation 517/94 and ECSC products. The countries listed comprise the remaining State-trading countries and countries whose economies are in transition towards a market economy, except where the Community has entered into an Association Agreement or a free trade agreement with the country concerned.[50] The basic rule is that trade shall be liberalized,[51] save for protective measures taken under the Regulation and for the quantitative Community quotas referred to in Annex II. Import into the Community of certain products listed in Annex III is subject to Community surveillance.[52] At the request of a Member State or at the Commission's initiative, Annexes II and III may be the subject of consultations.[53] After such consultations, the Commission may propose, in accordance with the procedure laid down in Article 16, the measures required to adapt Annexes I and II.

Council Regulation 520/94 establishes procedures for administering Community quantitative quotas and it applies in respect of quotas established under Annex II of Council Regulation 519/94.[54] It includes a simplification and standardization of the import formalities to be fulfilled by importers when surveillance or safeguard measures are applied.

Measures to prohibit the putting into free circulation of counterfeit goods have been established.[55] In addition, a potential restriction applies in respect of the introduction into the Community of pelts originating from animals caught in leg-hold traps although it is at present suspended.[56]

---

[48] Art. 24.   [49] [1994] OJ L67/89.

[50] The countries listed in Annex 1 are now Albania, Armenia, Azerbaijan, Belarus, People's Republic of China, Georgia, Kazakhstan, North Korea, Kyrgyzstan, Moldova, Mongolia, Russia, Tajikistan, Turkmenistan, Ukraine, Uzbekistan, and Vietnam. Estonia, Latvia, and Lithuania were removed from the list in Annex I with effect from the entry into force of the Free Trade Agreements with those States by Council Reg. 839/95 ([1995] OJ L85/9). These countries are not members of the WTO.

[51] This contrasts with the previous regime which was based on the principle that imports from these countries were subject to restrictions, unless they were included in the 'liberalization list' annexed to the relevant Regs.

[52] Reg. 519/94, n. 49 above Art. 1(3).   [53] *Ibid.*, Art. 1(4).

[54] [1994] OJ L66/1.   [55] Council Reg. 3295/94 [1994] OJ L341/8.

[56] Council Reg. 3254/91 [1991] OJ L308/1.

The Commercial Defence Instruments

The commercial defence instruments are amongst the most important commercial measures the Community can take in respect of imports and exports. The aim of most of these instruments is protection of the Community market from imports, either because of sudden disruptions caused by such imports ('safeguard' measures) or because the imports are unfairly traded (anti-dumping and countervailing duty measures). Measures can also be taken, however, to react against trade barriers established by third countries or to assert the Community's international rights not only to protect the domestic market, but also (and perhaps primarily) to defend the Community's exporting interests.

Safeguard measures are dealt with in the framework of the basic regulations mentioned above for establishing the Community's import regime.[57] The basic regulations provide for information and consultation procedures whereby trends in the import of products can be patrolled. The Commission is informed by Member States should trends in imports appear to call for surveillance or safeguard measures.[58] Consultation takes place within an advisory committee and covers terms and conditions of importation, import trends, and the various aspects of the economic and commercial situation as regards the product in question together with the measures, if any, to be taken. After consultation, where the Commission considers there is sufficient evidence, an investigation may be initiated.[59] The relevant procedures provide for the collection of the necessary factual information, as well as for various opportunities for parties involved (inside or outside the Community) to make their views known. Within nine months of the commencement of the investigation, it must either be terminated or a decision taken to impose surveillance or safeguard measures.[60]

Whereas surveillance measures have no actual impact on trade flows, the effect of safeguard measures can be substantial. They are subject, therefore, to a number of conditions. The basic requirement is that safeguard measures may be taken if the interests of the Community so require when a product is being imported into the Community in such increased quantities and/or[61] under such conditions that Community producers of similar or directly competing products are seriously injured or such serious injury threatens to occur.[62] In addition, the Council may adopt protective measures to allow the rights and obligations of the Community or of all its Member States to be exercised and fulfilled at the international level, particularly those relating to trade in commodities.[63]

In these cases, the Council may adopt appropriate measures by a qualified majority on a proposal from the Commission: the measures may include the re-

[57] Regs. 3285/94, n. 46 above, 517/94, n. 47 above and 519/94, n. 49 above.
[58] Art. 2 of Reg. 3285/94, n. 46 above.   [59] *Ibid.*, Art. 6.
[60] *Ibid.*, Art. 7.
[61] For the purposes of action in respect of countries which are WTO members the criterion is 'and', for non-WTO countries, the criterion is 'or'.
[62] Art. 16 of Reg. 3285/94, n. 46 above.   [63] *Ibid.*, Art. 23.

introduction of quantitative restrictions. Where immediate action is required, the Commission may then take the necessary action, subject to review by the Council: the measures may be referred to the Council by a Member State within one month of their adoption and the Council must substitute its decision (confirming, amending, or revoking) the decision of the Commission.[64]

Member States may take safeguard measures against imports in certain cases. Member States are required to inform the Commission[65] of the action they intend to take or, in the event of extreme urgency, have taken.

In the field of anti-dumping,[66] the basic EC Regulation[67] provides that the remedy against dumped or subsidised imports is the imposition of anti-dumping duties. These may only be imposed when a formal investigation has shown that dumping has been taking place, the dumped imports are causing or threatening to cause material injury to a Community industry producing products 'like' the imported ones, and the imposition of such duties would be in the Community interest.

Dumping means selling abroad below what is termed 'normal value': that is the comparable price actually paid or payable in the exporting country for the product 'like' the one which is imported into the Community. A comparison between the normal value and the export price to the Community gives the dumping margin. If the prices in the exporting country do not provide a reliable basis for this comparison, the normal price can be established on the basis of alternative methods: the foreign supplier's costs of production or his prices to other export markets.[68]

The material injury to a Community industry which can justify anti-dumping measures must be suffered by the industry as a whole or a major part of it. A determination of injury is to be based on positive evidence and involve an objective examination of both the volume of dumped imports and the effect of the dumped imports on prices in the Community market for like products, and the consequent impact of the imports on the Community industry. Known factors other than the dumped imports, which at the same time are injuring the Community industry are also to be examined to ensure that injury caused by other factors is not attributed to the dumped imports. Where action is aimed at

---

[64] Art. 16 of Reg. 3285/94, n. 46 above.   [65] *Ibid.*, Art. 24.

[66] This is an area of the common commercial policy which is particularly specialized and in which there is a good deal of ECJ case law: this section is not intended to provide a comprehensive guide to the subject but simply to set out a basic framework. Readers are referred to general textbooks such as Van Bael and Bellis, *Anti-dumping and Other Trade Protection Laws of the EEC* (2nd edn., CCH, 1986).

[67] Reg. 3283/94 [1994] OJ L349/1. This Reg. replaces Reg. 2423/88 [1988] OJ L209/1, as amended by Regs. 521/94 and 522/94 [1994] OJ L66/10. The new anti-dumping Regulation follows very closely and in most instances reproduces literally the text of the WTO Agreement on the implementation of Art. VI of the GATT 1994 (the 'Anti-dumping Agreement'). ECSC products continue to be dealt with by Commission Dec. 2424/88 [1988] OJ L209/18. The Commission is expected to propose a new decision to take into account the Anti-dumping Agreement.

[68] Reg. 3283/93, n. 67 above, Art. 2.

countering the threat of injury, rather than actual injury, the change in circumstances which would cause the injury must be clearly foreseen and imminent.[69]

The Community industry is defined as the producers of products which are identical or 'like' (i.e. identical to, or closely resembling) those alleged to be dumped.[70] The Community industry is generally taken to be either all the manufacturers of the product in question or those who account for a major part of the Community's production of the product.[71] This may mean that where a major portion of producers are situated in only one Member State, or one region of the Community, it will be possible to take action on their behalf. The Community interest may cover a wide range of considerations including the interests of consumers and users and the interests of domestic industry and the need to maintain competition on the Community market.[72]

Applications for action against dumped imports may be made by representatives of the Community industry which considers itself to be injured by the imports. The application will normally require the support of a major part of the industry and must include evidence of dumping and of relevant material injury.[73] The Commission is responsible for the opening and the conduct of the investigation. Before making its decision the Commission consults an Advisory Committee consisting of representatives of the Member States with the Commission as chairman. An announcement of the opening is published in the Official Journal. Thus all interested parties are given an opportunity to express their views. During the full investigation the Commission obtains information from the Community industry as well as from the importers, exporters, and, where necessary, from the Member States.[74]

To prevent material injury being caused to an industry while the full investigation of a complaint is being made, the Commission may take provisional action against allegedly dumped imports into the Community. Provisional duties will only be imposed when a preliminary investigation shows that dumping has occurred, that there is sufficient evidence of injury, and where immediate action is in the Community interest. Importers are then required to lodge security for the amount of the provisional duty with the relevant customs authorities. Provisional duties may only be imposed for a limited period.[75]

Where the conditions for the imposition of duties are satisfied a definitive anti-dumping duty is imposed by the Council by a simple majority following a proposal from the Commission, after consulting the Advisory Committee. The Regulation provides not only that dumping and resultant injury must be established but also that the interests of the Community call for intervention.[76] The conclusion of the investigation and the consequent imposition of definitive anti-dumping duties are now subject to an overall time limit of fifteen months, which

---

[69] Reg. 3283/94, n. 67 above, Art. 3.   [70] *Ibid.*, Art. 1(4).   [71] *Ibid.*, Art. 4.

[72] *Ibid.*, Art. 21.   [73] *Ibid.*, Art. 5.   [74] *Ibid.*, Arts. 5 and 6.

[75] *Ibid.*, Art. 7.   [76] *Ibid.*, Art. 9.

is legally binding on the Community institutions (even though investigations should 'normally' be concluded within twelve months).[77]

If, at the conclusion of the investigation, the foreign importer undertakes to raise his prices or cease exports to the Community to the extent that the margin of dumping or its injurious effects are eliminated, then such an undertaking may be accepted as an alternative to the imposition of a definitive duty.[78] Undertakings are accepted by means of a formal Commission decision and they are published in the Official Journal. Where no dumping is established or where no material injury has been caused to the Community industry then the applicants are informed of this and the investigation closed; a formal Commission decision to this effect is published in the Official Journal.[79]

A definitive duty or an undertaking may be reviewed by the Commission on its own initiative or at the request of a Member State. Interested parties may also request a review provided that evidence is submitted that circumstances have changed, and at least one year has elapsed since the remedies were imposed.[80] Duties and undertakings will normally last for a period of five years from the date of their entry into force or latest review (the 'sunset provision'). If evidence is submitted that injury is likely to recur if the remedies lapse, the Commission can conduct a review and the validity of the measures is extended in the meantime.[81]

Countervailing measures are taken to offset the effects of subsidization by a foreign government which benefit, *inter alia*, the exports of the subsidized firms. Subsidies consist of a variety of forms of direct or indirect assistance which a government gives to its exports ('export subsidies') or, more generally, to its producers ('domestic subsidies'). The notion of 'subsidy' in the context of the common commercial policy has followed the definition in GATT.[82] The current Community Regulation on countervailing measures,[83] follows closely the WTO Agreement on Subsidies and Countervailing Measures, and provides for the imposition of duties when subsidized imports cause or threaten to cause material injury to the Community industry producing goods 'like' the imported ones and the imposition of such duties would be in the Community interest.

Notions such as 'like product',[84] 'Community industry',[85] 'material injury',[86]

---

[77] These time limits were introduced by Reg. 521/94, n. 67 above. They have now been incorporated into Reg. 3283/94, n. 67 above, but their application has been delayed. See Art. 24.
[78] *Ibid.*, Art. 8.   [79] *Ibid.*, Art. 14.   [80] *Ibid.*, Art. 11.   [81] *Ibid.*, Art. 11.
[82] The 1979 Subsidies Code contains an illustrative list of export subsidies, which was reproduced in Reg. 2423/88, n. 67 above. A slightly different list is attached to the Subsidies Code attached to the WTO Agreement and is reproduced in the new basic Countervailing Measures Regulation.
[83] Council Reg. 3284/94 [1994] OJ L348/22. Community rules on the imposition of countervailing duties were previously included with the rules on anti-dumping in Council Reg. 2423/88, n. 67 above. Rules on countervailing duties in respect of ECSC products are contained in Commission Dec. 2424/88, n. 67 above. The Commission is expected to propose a new decision to take account of the WTO Agreements.
[84] Compare Art. 1(5) of Reg. 3284/94, n. 83 above, with Art. 1(4) of Reg. 3283/94.
[85] Compare Art. 6 of Reg. 3284/94, n. 83 above, with Art. 4 of Regualtion 3283/94.
[86] Compare Art. 5 of Reg. 3284/94, n. 83 above, with Art. 3 of Reg. 3283/94.

etc., are identical to those in the anti-dumping field and the procedures for investigations, imposition of duties, etc., are also practically identical.

The final measure which forms part of the commerical defence instruments is concerned with obstacles to trade and protecting the exercise of the Community's international rights. In 1984 the Council adopted Regulation 2641/84[87] on the strengthening of the common commercial policy with regard to protection against illicit commercial practices (the so-called 'new commercial policy instrument'). The instrument was adopted with a view to giving the Community a means of defending its legitimate trade interests on a wider scale than is involved in the protection of the Community's domestic market against unfair trade practices, such as dumping and subsidization. The Regulation was designed to deal with commercial practices by third countries which were incompatible with international law or with generally accepted rules, as well as to allow the full exercise of the international trade rights of the Community and of its Member States. This Regulation was amended by Regulation 522/94.[88]

Regulation 2641/84 has now been replaced by Regulation 3286/94[89] on the exercise of the Community's rights under international trade rules (known as the Trade Barriers Regulation). This Regulation emphasizes the exercise by the Community of its rights under international trade rules and provides a proce-dural mechanism to request the Community institutions to take action to defend and enforce those rights. The Regulation is aimed at 'obstacles to trade', which are defined as practices which are prohibited by international trade rules or in respect of which a right to seek elimination of the effect of the practice exists under international trade rules. The concept of 'international trade rules' refers primarily to rules established under WTO auspices but can include rules laid down in other agreements to which the Community is a party.[90] If, following examination, it is found that action is necessary in the interests of the Community, measures must be adopted by the Council by qualified majority, on a proposal by the Commission, within thirty days of the proposal.[91] Any international obligations for consultation or dispute-settlement procedures must be complied with before any appropriate action is taken.[92] Any measures adopted must be consistent with international legal obligations. This principally refers to the WTO and now covers almost all aspects of international trade. The Regulation does not apply in cases covered by other existing rules in the com-mon commercial policy field and is without prejudice to other measures which may be taken pursuant to Article 113 EC.[93] In addition the measure comple-

---

[87] [1984] OJ L252/1. See Bougeois and Laurent, 'Le nouvel instrument de la politique com-mercial: un pas en avant vers l'élimination des obstacles aux échanges internationaux' [1985] *RTDE* 41; Steenbergen, 'The New Commercial Policy Instrument' (1985) *CMLRev.* 421; Denton, 'The New Commercial Policy Instrument and *AKZO* v. *DuPont*' [1988] *ELRev.* 3; and Schoneveld, 'The European Community's Reaction to the 'Illicit' Commercial Trade Practices of Other Countries' [1992] *JWTL* 17.

[88] N. 67 above.
[90] Reg. 3286/94 [1994] OJ L349/79, Art. 2.
[92] *Ibid.*, Art. 12(2).

[89] [1994] OJ L349/71.
[91] *Ibid.*, Arts. 12 and 13.
[93] *Ibid.*, Art. 15.

ments rules set out in the provisions of Community law governing the common organization of agricultural markets. The Regulation thus applies where normal safeguard or anti-dumping measures or countervailing duties cannot be applied.

The Regulation provides for two types of proceedings. A Community industry which considers that it has suffered injury as a result of obstacles to trade that have an effect on the market of the Community may lodge a complaint.[94] In addition, Community enterprises which consider that they have suffered adverse trade effects that have an effect on the markets of a third country may also lodge a complaint.[95] Member States may lodge complaints (described as 'referrals') in both situations mentioned above.[96] This does not, however, derogate from the Member States' more general right to raise similar or identical questions and request action on the part of the Community at the international level through other existing Community procedures, and in particular in the Committee established by Article 113 ('the Article 113 Committee').

As for decision-making procedures, almost all decisions (initiation of an investigation or rejection of a complaint, resort to international dispute settlement proceedings and conduct and termination thereof, suspension or termination of proceedings) are taken by the Commission in accordance with a procedure which resembles that of a management committee.[97] In contrast, where the Community has to take a decision on the common commercial policy measures to be adopted, the Council acts in accordance with Article 113 of the Treaty by a qualified majority.[98]

Contractual Commercial Policy

Introduction

The contractual commercial policy comprises agreements concluded between the European Community and third countries and the European Community's participation in multilateral agreements. After the end of the transitional period,[99] the Community acquired exclusive competence to conclude such trade

---

[94] *Ibid.*, Art. 3.
[95] *Ibid.*, Art. 4. There are differences between the types of complaint set out in Arts. 3 and 4. In particular, complaints on behalf of Community industry may be lodged in respect of all kinds of international agreements to which the Community is a party, i.e. bilateral, plurilateral, or multilateral. In the case of complaints on behalf of Community enterprises, the trade obstacle complained of must be the subject of plurilateral or multilateral rules. In both cases the complaint is to be submitted to the Commisson which is required to take a decision on the opening of a Community examination procedure (Art. 5).
[96] *Ibid.*, Art. 6.
[97] The procedure by which the Council supervises the implementing powers of the Commission is known as comitology. The management committee is procedure 2 in the Comitology Dec.: Council Dec. 87/373 [1987] OJ L197/33. For a description of comitogy generally, see Kapteyn and Verloren van Themaat, n. 1 above, 240–7.
[98] Reg. 3286/94 Arts. 13 and 14.
[99] Art. 113 provided for a transitional period which expired on 31 Dec. 1969.

agreements. During the transitional period, a number of measures were taken to facilitate the replacement for the purposes of the common commercial policy of Member States' bilateral treaties with Community treaties. These measures comprised a progressive replacement of existing Member-State bilateral agreements in the field of commercial policy[100] by Community agreements, consistently with the EC's exclusive competence in this field, although Member States maintain agreements dealing with the wider field of economic co-operation.[101]

Article 113 mentions 'tariff and trade agreements'. In practice this covers a spectrum of different types of agreements which is set out below.[102]

Tariff Agreements

The GATT provides for the negotiation of reductions in tariff levels at the bilateral and multilateral level. Following the establishment of the CCT, the Community has, in addition to .the multilateral negotiating rounds under the GATT to reduce tariffs, negotiated a large number of bilateral agreements within the framework of Article XXVIII of the GATT relating to tariff concessions which have been concluded on the basis of Article 113.

Free Trade Agreements

This Chapter deals only with Free Trade Agreements concluded on the basis of Article 113. Free trade areas have also been created within the framework of association agreements, for example as part of the Europe Agreements. These Agreements are described in Chapter 20.

When the United Kingdom, Ireland, and Denmark joined the Community in 1972, each of the EFTA countries concluded a free trade agreement with the Community. These agreements were based on Article 113. The only agreement still in force is that with Switzerland which continues to apply following that State's decision not to participate in the EEA.[103]

In 1975, an agreement with Israel was concluded providing for the progressive establishment of a free trade area and economic co-operation to enhance trade.[104] The agreement was based on Article 113 EC. It has been extended by way of Additional Protocols which are based on Article 238. The first such Protocol extended the agreement to cover other areas of co-operation similar to

---

[100] See Council Dec. 69/494 [1969] JO 326/39.

[101] Such agreements are subject to a prior consultation procedure, see Council Dec. 74/393 [1974] OJ L208/23. Council Dec.s 69/494 and 74/393 are considered in Ch. 9.

[102] All the agreements adopted under Art. 113 have not been mentioned. The reader is referred to the current *Directory of Community Legislation in Force* and other acts of the Community institutions.

[103] [1972] OJ L300/189. The Agreement is subject to a number of amendments and derogations.

[104] [1975] OJ L136/2.

those contained in the association agreements with the Maghreb and Mashreq countries.[105] A new association agreement based on Article 238, which will eventually replace the 1975 agreement, is currently being negotiated. A free trade agreement has been under discussion with the Gulf Co-operation Council [106] since 1989.

In 1994, free trade area agreements were negotiated and signed with the Baltic States, Lithuania, Latvia, and Estonia.[107] These agreements are modelled on the interim agreements with the Central and Eastern European countries.[108] They entered into force on 1 January 1995. In 1994 the Commission began negotiations for Europe Agreements with the Baltic States which will replace these free trade area agreements.

Customs Union Agreements

As will be seen from Chapter 20 below, the association agreements with Turkey, Malta, and Cyprus provide for the establishment of a customs union between those countries and the Community. A customs union is also foreseen in the agreement between the Community and Andorra.[109] That Agreement is based on Articles 99 and 113 and establishes a customs union for certain products and exempts from import duties other products with Andorran origin. Special provisions preserve duty free allowances for goods imported by travellers from Andorra to the Community.

A customs union is also established by the Community's agreement with San Marino in respect of products covered by Chapters 1–97 of the CCT. The agreement, which is a mixed agreement and based on Articles 113 and 235, also provides for wide-ranging co-operation including provisions on social policy.[110]

'Interim' Agreements

A practice has been established whereby the trade provisions of some association and trade and co-operation agreements have been brought into force in advance of their other provisions by way of 'interim' agreements. The trade provisions are incorporated into a separate agreement which is concluded on the basis of Article 113 EC. This practice has generally been followed for mixed agreements, which require separate ratification by Member States and therefore can result in a significant lapse of time between signature and entry into force.

---

[105] [1978] OJ L270/2.
[106] The State of the United Arab Emirates, the State of Bahrain, the Kingdom of Saudi Arabia, the Sultanate of Oman, the State of Qatar, and the State of Kuwait.
[107] Lithuania [1994] OJ L375/1; Latvia [1994] OJ L374/1; and Estonia [1994] OJ L373/1.
[108] See Ch. 20.   [109] [1990] OJ L374/16.
[110] Certain provisions, including that relating to the customs union, have been brought into force by an interim agreement. [1992] OJ L359/13.

The trade provisions of the association agreements with the Mediterranean countries[111] and the Europe Agreements[112] were implemented by way of interim agreements, as was the customs union provided for in the agreement with San Marino of 1992.[113]

Commercial and Economic Co-operation Agreements

Following the Council's decision that Member States' trade agreements with Eastern European countries should expire by 1 January 1975, Member States concluded a number of 'economic co-operation' agreements with these countries. This provided the impetus for the Community itself to begin to conclude such agreements with other trading partners.

The line between commercial co-operation and economic co-operation is a fine one. However, economic co-operation is not a classical means for developing trade. The main purpose of such co-operation is the development of industry and agriculture with a view to raising standards of living or developing the respective economies of the parties. The economic co-operation provisions found in Community commercial and economic co-operation agreements often extend to industrial co-operation, scientific and technological co-operation, and co-operation on energy, transport, and the environment. The means for this is provided by way of increased links, joint ventures, and joint research programmes. Such provisions go beyond the Community's powers under Article 113 EC and for this reason these agreements have been concluded on the basis of Articles 113 and 235.

One of the first agreements of this kind was that with Canada, which dates from 1976[114] and became for some years the classical model. The legal basis for this agreement was Articles 113 and 235. Similar agreements were concluded with Sri Lanka (1975),[115] the Association of Southeast Asian Nations (ASEAN)[116] (1980),[117] Romania (1980),[118] India (1981),[119] Brazil (1982),[120] the 'Andean Pact' countries[121] (1984),[122] Yemen (1985),[123] China (1985),[124] Central American countries[125] (1986),[126] Pakistan (1986)[127] and the countries of the

[111] Morocco [1976] OJ L141/97; Algeria [1976] OJ L141/1; Tunisia [1976] OJ L141/194.
[112] Poland [1992] OJ 114/1; Czech Republic [1992] OJ L115/2; Slovak Republic [1992] OJ L115/2; Hungary [1992] OJ L116/1; Romania [1993] OJ L81/1; Bulgaria [1993] OJ L323/1. On the Europe Agreements generally, see Ch. 20.
[113] [1992] OJ L359/13.
[114] A number of co-operation agreements were concluded prior to this date, e.g. with Argentina, Uruguay, Mexico and Brazil, but these were very limited in scope and content. The Canada Agreement is at [1976] OJ L260/2.
[115] [1975] OJ L247/1.
[116] Indonesia, Malaysia, Philippines, Singapore, Thailand, and Brunei.
[117] [1980] OJ L144/1.   [118] [1980] OJ L352/5.   [119] [1981] OJ L328/5.
[120] [1982] OJ L281/2.   [121] Bolivia, Colombia, Ecuador, Peru, and Venezuela.
[122] [1984] OJ L153/1.   [123] [1985] OJ L26/1.   [124] [1985] OJ L250/1.
[125] The Republics of Costa Rica, El Salvador, Guatemala, Honduras, Nicaragua, and Panama.
[126] [1986] OJ L172/1.   [127] [1986] OJ L108/1.

Gulf Co-operation Council (1987).[128] Agreements of this type[129] usually confer most favoured nation treatment in respect of goods and provide for commercial co-operation to solve commercial problems and for more general economic co-operation, perhaps with an enumeration of specific sectors. Economic co-operation is normally to be encouraged or fostered by the parties in all suitable fields including industry, technology and science, opening new markets, creation of employment, reduction of regional disparities, and co-operation in the field of the environment. They are mixed agreements and, in order to make clear that economic co-operation is not an area of exclusive Community competence, they also contain the 'Canada' clause,[130] albeit with slight textual variations.

Trade and economic co-operation agreements have also been concluded between late 1988 and 1993 with the Central and Eastern European countries. Agreements were concluded with Hungary (1988),[131] Poland (1989),[132] Czechoslovakia (1990),[133] Bulgaria (1990),[134] the Soviet Union (1990),[135] and Romania (1991).[136] Similar agreements have been concluded with Albania (1992),[137] the Baltic States (1992),[138] and Slovenia (1993).[139] These agreements established a framework for negotiations on agricultural trade, a commitment to commercial co-operation and a timetable for the elimination of quantitative restrictions on industrial products. The rapid disintegration of the Soviet Union meant that the agreement with that country was outdated by the time of its entry into force.

The agreements with Central and Eastern Europe have been, or will be, replaced by Europe Agreements.[140] In October 1992, Foreign Ministers agreed that Partnership and Co-operation Agreements (PCAs) which would be mixed agreements to be based on Articles 113 and 235, should be concluded with the newly independent States of the former Soviet Union. This was confirmed in an exchange of letters under which all these States agreed to fulfil obligations under the Agreement with the Soviet Union until the new PCAs were concluded.[141] PCAs have been signed with Russia, Ukraine, Kazakhstan, and Kyrgyzstan. The three Communities are parties to the PCAs. They include provisions on political dialogue. They cover trade in goods, the treatment of workers legally employed in a Member State, establishment and cross border provision of services, intellectual property protection, industrial and commercial co-operation, as well as co-operation in the harmonization of legislative provisions, cultural co-operation, and provisions on financial assistance. A Co-operation Council, a Co-operation Commission, and a Joint Parliamentary Committee are set up under each of the Agreements. The Agreements are designed to open the way for possible free trade areas. These Agreements clearly

---

[128] [1989] OJ L54/3.
[129] Sometimes described as 'first generation' agreements.
[130] See further on this, Ch. 9.
[131] [1988] OJ L327/1.
[132] [1989] OJ L339/1.
[133] [1990] OJ L291/28.
[134] [1990] OJ L291/8.
[135] [1990] OJ L68/1.
[136] [1991] OJ L79/12.
[137] [1992] OJ L343/2.
[138] Estonia [1992] OJ L430/2; Latvia [1992] OJ L403/10; Lithuania [1992] OJ L403/20.
[139] [L1993] OJ L287/1.
[140] See Ch. 20.
[141] 27th General Report 243.

go beyond Articles 113 and 235.[142] The trade provisions of the PCAs have been brought into force by way of interim agreements.

A further generation of trade and economic co-operation agreements has been negotiated with Asian and Latin American countries.[143] Prior to the entry into force of the TEU these agreements were based on Articles 113 and 235 EC. They contain provisions conferring most favoured nation treatment in respect of goods. The agreements also aim to encourage economic co-operation, including investment. Areas for co-operation are identified which include, for example, energy and mining, agriculture, fisheries, forestry, industry, financial services, transport, telecommunications, tourism, culture, and in certain cases regional integration. The first group of these agreements were negotiated with Argentina (1990)[144] and Chile (1990),[145] Macao (1992)[146] and Mongolia (1992),[147] and these agreements are drawn up in similar terms. The Agreement with Mexico (1991),[148] which is more detailed in terms of the areas for co-operation, clearly served as a model for subsequent agreements with Paraguay (1992),[149] Uruguay (1992),[150] Brazil (1992),[151] the Central American countries (1993),[152] the Andean Pact countries (1993),[153] and those negotiated with Asian countries, namely, India (1993)[154] and Sri Lanka (1994).[155] An agreement with Vietnam is in the course of negotiation. Since that with Brazil, these agreements contain a clause to the effect that protection of human rights and democratic principles are the foundation of co-operation with the countries and an essential element of the agreement.[156] With the entry into force of the TEU, Article 235 EC has been replaced by Article 130y since the co-operation aspects of these agreements are largely aimed at developing the economies of the countries concerned. The use of Article 130y for the agreement with India, the first of these agreements to be concluded on this legal basis, is currently the subject of a challenge before the Court of Justice.[157]

---

[142] At the time of writing the Commission had, in the light of the Court's *Opinion 1/94*, n. 2 above, proposed Arts. 54(2), 57(2), 73c(2), 75, 84(2), 113, and 235, together with Art. 228, (2) and (3), as the legal basis for the PCA with Russia. The interim agreements have been concluded on the basis of Art. 113 EC.

[143] These are often referred to as 'third generation' agreements since for some of these countries this is the 3rd commercial and economic co-operation agreement which they have concluded with the Community.

[144] [1990] OJ L295/66.	[145] [1991] OJ L79/1.	[146] [1992] OJ L404/26.
[147] [1993] OJ L41/46.	[148] [1991] OJ L340/1.	[149] [1992] OJ L313/7.
[150] [1992] OJ L94/1.		

[151] [1992] OJ C163/2. The Agreement has not yet been concluded by the Community.

[152] The Agreement is not yet in force.

[153] The Agreement is not yet in force.   [154] [1994] OJ L223/230.

[155] Signed on 18 July 1994 *General Report* (1994) 30). The agreement is not yet in force.

[156] For the background to the inclusion of such clauses and their effect see: Kuijper, 'Trade Sanctions, Security and Human Rights' in Maresceau (ed.), *The European Community's Commercial Policy after 1992: The Legal Dimension* (Kluwer Academic Publishers, 1993).

[157] Case C–268/94 *Portugal* v. *Council*. The scope of application of Art. 130y is discussed in Ch. 18 below.

The General Agreement on Tariffs and Trade (GATT)

The Member States were all parties to the GATT of 1947 by virtue of their participation in the Protocols of Provisional Application or Protocols of Accession. The Community never formally became a party to the GATT but the Court of Justice held that the Community was bound by the provisions of GATT in so far as it had assumed powers previously exercised by the Member States in the areas covered by the Agreement.[158] Since 1961, the Community has signed the accession agreements of new members. In the Tokyo Round of Negotiations, the Community alone became party to the majority of agreements concluded;[159] the Member States, however, participated in two agreements.[160] The Community was party to the First, Second, and Third Geneva Protocols to the GATT concluded under GATT auspices.[161]

The World Trade Organization (WTO)

The Agreement establishing the World Trade Organization with its Annexes represents the conclusion of the Multilateral Trade Negotiations which started with the 'Ministerial Declaration on the Uruguay Round' of 20 September 1986 at Punta del Este (the 'Uruguay Round'). The objective of the negotiations was stated to be the 'further liberalization and expansion of world trade' and an improvement of 'the multilateral trading system based on the principles and rules of the GATT' and 'increasing the responsiveness of the GATT to the evolving international environment'. The Uruguay Round of negotiations lasted until 15 December 1993 and the Final Act embodying the results of the Uruguay Round was signed at the Conference of Marrakech which convened between 12 and 15 April 1994.

The WTO, which is established by Article 1 of the WTO Agreement, provides the common institutional framework for the conduct of trade relations amongst its members in matters related to the agreements and associated legal instruments in the Annexes to the Agreement (Article II(I)). The Agreement has four Annexes. Annex 1 is divided into three parts. Annex 1A contains the 1994 version of the GATT (this is legally distinct from the GATT 1947 which it incorporates by reference) and understandings relating to the interpretation of

---

[158] Joined Cases 21 to 24/72 *International Fruit Company* v. *Produktscap voor Groenten en Fruit* [1972] ECR 1236.

[159] Arrangement regarding Bovine Meat 1979; International Dairy Arrangement 1979; Agreement on Government Procurement 1979; Agreement on the Interpretation and Application of Arts. VI, XVI, and XXIII 1979; Agreement on the implementation of Art. VI; Agreement on Import Licensing Procedures, 1979; Agreement on the implementation of Art. VII, 1979, together with its prot.

[160] Agreement on Technical Barriers to Trade 1979, and the Agreement on Trade in Civil Aircraft.

[161] Generally on the EC and the GATT, see Hilf, Jacobs and Petersmann (eds.), *The European Community and GATT* (Kluwer Law and Taxation, 1986).

the GATT, the GATT Tariff Protocol of 1994, and agreements relating to trade in goods.[162] Annex 1B contains the General Agreement on Trade in Services (GATS)[163] and its Annexes, and Annex 1C contains the Agreement on Trade Related Intellectual Property Rights (TRIPS). Annex 2 is the Understanding on the Rules and Procedures governing the Settlement of Disputes. Annex 3 is the Trade Policy Review Mechanism. Annex 4 contains what are described as 'Plurilateral' Trade Agreements, which are not an integral part of the WTO since they are not binding on all its members.

All these agreements are administered in one institutional framework with a Ministerial Conference which meets at least once every two years. The functions of the Ministerial Conference are assumed by the General Council, which can also meet as the Dispute Settlement Body and the Trade Policy Review Body. There are also three specialized Councils: the Councils for Trade in Goods, Trade in Services, and TRIPS. There are two types of membership of the organization: original and acceding membership. The Community is an original member. Decision-making is to be by consensus, as under GATT 1947, although where consensus cannot be reached decisions may in certain circumstances be taken by vote. The European Communities enjoy the same number of votes as they have Member States which are members of the WTO.

The legal basis for the Community's participation in the WTO Agreement and the multilateral agreements annexed to it was the subject of *Opinion 1/94*. The Court of Justice ruled that the Community had exclusive competence under Article 113 to conclude the multilateral agreements on trade in goods, the GATS, in so far as it related to the cross-border supply of services, and the provisions of the TRIPS which concern the prohibition on the release into free circulation of counterfeit goods. Competence in respect of other aspects of the GATS and TRIPS was shared between the Community and the Member States.[164]

Textiles

In the context of the Multi-Fibre Arrangement (MFA) the Community negotiated bilateral agreements with a number of supplying countries; these were prin-

---

[162] These comprise a number of agreements which were concluded during the Tokyo Round and which have been amended: the Agreement on Technical Barriers to Trade, the Anti-Dumping Agreement, the Agreement on Subsidies and Countervailing Measures, the Agreement on Customs Valuation, and the Agreement on Import Licensing Procedures. Annex 1A also contains 7 new agreements: the Agreement on Agriculture, the Agreement on the Application of Sanitary and Phytosanitary Measures, the Agreement on Textiles and Clothing, the Agreement on Trade Related Investment Measures (TRIMs), the Agreement on Rules of Origin, the Agreement on Pre-Shipment Inspection, and the Agreement on Safeguards.

[163] For an analysis of the GATS, see Kennedy, 'Services join GATT: An Analysis of the General Agreement on Trade in Services' [1995] *ITL&R* 11.

[164] The legal bases for the adoption of the Uruguay Round agreements were Arts. 43, 54, 57, 66, 75, 84(2), 99, 100, 100a, 113, and 235, in conjunction with the 2nd subpara. of Art. 228(3) ([1994] OJ L336/1).

cipally Asian countries but also included State-trading countries. The main rule was that, in the absence of specific rules to the contrary, quantitative restrictions were abolished. However, safeguards were permitted and quantitative restrictions could be imposed under mutually acceptable bilateral agreements: the Community's bilateral agreements were based on this provision, and as at the end of 1994 some fifty-three agreements (both MFN and preferential arrangements) existed. The WTO Agreement on Textiles and Clothing provides for the progressive dismantling over a period of ten years of import restrictions and the eventual integration of the sector into normal GATT disciplines. As from the date of entry into force of the Agreement quantitative restrictions in bilateral agreements are to be notified to the Textiles Monitoring Body.[165] Following such notification, no new restrictions may be introduced except under the provisions of the Agreement or relevant GATT provisions.

Commodities

The GATT recognizes by way of a general exception from its discipline obligations undertaken pursuant to international commodities agreements.[166] Such international commodities agreements as exist are confined to raw materials and either aim at improving trade flows by various methods, such as exchange of information between importers and exporters, or at the regulation of trade flows by way of import and export quotas, supply and purchase arrangements, and buffer stocks. The Community is a party to all the important commodity agreements, but the Member States are also parties, in particular where the agreement in question provides for them to contribute to the financing of the buffer stocks or other financial mechanism. The Community's participation is described further in Chapter 7.

Customs Co-operation Agreements

The nomenclature used for the common customs tariff is based on international rules developed in the framework of the Customs Co-operation Council which, together with the United Nations Economic Commission for Europe, provides the main forum for discussion on international customs matters. The Community enjoys observer status in both these bodies but is not a member since it is ineligible under their founding statutes. The Court of Justice has said that the Community has replaced the Member States in the Convention establishing the Customs Co-operation Council[167] and in the Convention on the Nomenclature for the Classification of Goods in Customs Tariffs. The latter has been replaced by the International Convention on the Harmonized Commodity

---

[165] Set up under Art. 8 of the Agreement to supervise its implementation.
[166] See Art. XX(h).
[167] International Convention establishing a Customs Co-operation Council.

Description and Coding System to be used by parties in their tariff and statistical nomenclatures to which the Community only is a party.[168]

Customs valuation rules are now regulated by the Agreement on the Implementation of Article VII of the GATT which is contained in Annex 1A of the WTO Agreement.[169] A Convention on the Simplification and Harmonization of Customs Procedures[170] was drawn up under the auspices of the Customs Co-operation Council. The Community is a party, with its Member States, to the Convention together with its numerous Annexes.

The Community is also a party to the Customs Convention on the international transport of goods under cover of TIR carnets,[171] negotiated in the framework of the United Nations Economic Commission for Europe, which restricts customs examinations of goods in transit. It is also a party to the International Convention on the Harmonization of Frontier Controls of Goods which encourages harmonization and co-operation.[172] The Community participates in the Convention relating to Temporary Admission[173] and the Customs Conventions on the temporary importation of private road vehicles and of commercial road vehicles.[174] It has also accepted a number of Resolutions adopted by the Economic Commission for Europe and Recommendations of the Customs Co-operation Council.

Organization for Economic Co-operation and Development (OECD)

The Community is not a party to the OECD Convention but its participation in the Organization is defined in an Additional Protocol to the Convention.[175] While the Community can participate actively and not just as an observer, it has no right to vote and as a general rule cannot participate in decisions of the Organization. Indeed many aspects of the work of the OECD are outside the scope of Article 113. The first example of the Community's participation in an OECD instrument is that of the OECD national treatment instrument which

---

[168] The legal base for the Council Dec. concluding this Convention was considered by the ECJ in Case 165/87 *Commission* v. *Council* [1988] ECR 5545. The Commission had proposed only Art. 113 EC as the legal base and challenged the adoption of the dec. by the Council on the basis of Arts. 28, 113, and 235. The Court concluded that the establishment of a tariff nomenclature, although not specifically provided for in Art. 28 or Art. 113, was indispensible for the application of customs duties and that the Council's competence flowed from both those Arts. The purpose of the statistical nomenclature established by the Convention was to permit information to be gathered, in the case of the Community, in respect of external, rather than intra-Community, trade for which Art. 113 alone provided the legal base. Use of Art. 235 was, in the Court's view, unnecessary. The Court ruled that since, at the time of the adoption of the act, Art. 28 also required unanimity in the Council, addition of Art. 235 did not affect the validity of the act in question. Moreover, the fact that the Parliament had been consulted, even though that was not obligatory, should not be considered as rendering the act illegal.

[169] See Council Dec. 87/369 [1987] OJ L198/1.

[170] Known as the 'Kyoto Convention' [1975] OJ L100/2 (amended on a number of occasions).

[171] Known as the 'TIR Convention' [1978] OJ L252/2.

[172] [1984] OJ L126/3.   [173] See Council Dec. 93/329 [1993] OJ L130/1.

[174] See Council Dec. 94/110 [1993] OJ L56/1.   [175] See, further, Ch. 7.

provides expressly for the accession of the Community. In *Opinion 2/92*[176] the Court of Justice rejected the Commission's argument that the Community alone had competence to participate in the instrument on the basis of Article 113. Instead, it decided that both the Community and the Member States had competence, and that the Community's competence was not based on Article 113 alone.

The Community is a participant in the OECD Arrangement on Guidelines for Officially Supported Export Credits (the 'Consensus')[177] which is a non-binding arrangement which establishes rules governing the grant of export credits and tied aid. The Consensus was first given effect in the Community by a Council Decision of 4 April 1978 which is based on Article 113. The Decision was not published and was subject to annual renewal until 1992 when Council Decision 93/112, which is stated to apply for an indefinite period and which approved a revised version of the Consensus, was published.[178]

In 1994, the Community signed the Agreement on the Elimination of Unfair Competitive Practices in the Shipbuilding Sector which was elaborated under OECD auspices.[179] The principal aim is to control aid to the shipbuilding sector and provide a satisfactory mechanism to combat unfair pricing.

EUROPEAN COAL AND STEEL COMMUNITY

Treaty Provisions

The common commercial policy concerning the European Coal and Steel Community differs in a number of important respects from that of the EC. Article 71 ECSC provides that the powers of the Governments of the Member States in matters of commercial policy are not affected by the Treaty. However, in *Opinion 1/94* the Court of Justice ruled that, where an agreement with third countries is of a general nature, i.e. encompasses all types of goods, even where those goods include ECSC products, the EC has sole competence pursuant to Article 113.[180] Although the Court was there concerned with an international agreement, the same principle would apply to internal rules of Community law. This has resulted in a change of practice in some aspects of the common commercial policy in relation to ECSC products.

Article 72 provides that the Council may fix minimum and maximum rates within which Member States may set their customs duties on ECSC products as against third countries. Within those limits each Government is to determine its own tariffs according to its own national procedures.

---

[176] Not yet reported.
[177] Consistently with the Court's ruling in *Opinion 1/75*, n. 10 above, the Community alone participates in the Consensus.
[178] [1993] OJ L44/1.   [179] Bull. EC 12–94, 58.   [180] See Ch. 23.

Under Article 73 the administration of import and export licences for trade with third countries is a matter for each Government. The Commission is empowered to supervise the administration and verification of these licences and may make recommendations to Member States.

Article 74 enables the Commission to take measures in connection with anti-dumping or other practices condemned by the Havana Charter; if a difference in pricing between quotations by undertakings inside and outside the Community is due to conditions of competition contrary to the Treaty; and if an increase in the quantity of imports of ECSC products causes or threatens to cause a serious injury to production within the common market of like or directly competing products.

Article 75 requires Member States to keep the Commission informed of proposed commercial agreements related to ECSC products and the importation of raw materials or equipment needed for the production of coal and steel. The Commission may make recommendations to the Member States.

Practice in Implementation of the Commercial Policy

The practice in relation to agreements concerning ECSC products with third countries and international organizations is considered in Chapter 23. This section considers the internal rules of Community law and follows as closely as possible the section of this Chapter headed 'Internal Community rules relating to commercial policy'.

The EC's common customs tariff does not apply to ECSC products although, in practice, the rates for ECSC products are included for information only. Member States set their own tariffs based on the figure suggested in the common customs tariff.

The generalized system of preferences applies to ECSC products. The current EC Regulation, Council Regulation 3281/94,[181] includes ECSC products in line with the ruling of the Court of Justice in *Opinion 1/94*.[182]

So far as common rules for imports and exports are concerned, there is no ECSC export regime. EC Council Regulation 3285/94 establishing common rules for imports applies to ECSC products. Prior to the coming into force of Regulation 3285/94 the EC's common rules for imports did not apply to ECSC products, and such products were subject to national measures. Article 26 of Regulation 3285/94 requires residual national restrictions relating to ECSC products to be progressively dismantled in accordance with the provisions of the WTO Agreement. Since the Regulation does not apply to products originating

---

[181] [1994] OJ L348/1.
[182] In previous years the suspension of customs duties in respect of ECSC products was effected by means of a Dec. of the representatives of the Governments of the Member States meeting within the Council.

in the States listed in Regulation 519/94 ECSC products from those States continue to be subject to national measures.

Commercial Defence Instruments

As mentioned above EC Council Regulation 3285/94 applies to imports of ECSC products from most States. The safeguard procedure set out in that Regulation therefore applies to ECSC products without prejudice to any possible measures to apply an agreement specifically concerning ECSC products. So far as imports from States which are outwith that Regulation are concerned, Member States take their own safeguard measures consistently with their international law obligations. In appropriate cases the Member States meeting within the Council have adopted a decision imposing an annual quota on imports from certain States.[183] The Community has adopted surveillance licensing recommendations[184] pursuant to Article 74 ECSC.

Anti-dumping and countervailing measures fall within Article 74 ECSC. The Commission has adopted decisions under that Article which provide, as closely as possible, for analogous application to ECSC products of the principles and definitions contained in the EC Regulations.[185]

The Trade Barriers Regulation[186] does not expressly include, nor does it expressly exclude, ECSC products. In an appropriate case it could therefore cover ECSC products where these products were part of a dispute involving other products. But if the dispute concerned ECSC products alone or concerned an agreement specifically relating to ECSC products it is doubtful whether the Regulation would be applicable.

---

[183] See, e.g., Dec. 92/585 imposing a quota on steel products from the former Soviet Union.
[184] Rec. 85/94 [1994] OJ L17/1.
[185] Dec. 2424/88 [1988] OJ L209/18, which followed very closely the provisions of Reg. 2423/88, which has been replaced, see n. 67.
[186] Reg. 3286/94/EC [1994] OJ L349/71.

13

Education, Vocational Training and Youth

The EEC Treaty contained no provisions on education or youth, and the elaboration of a policy on education did not feature formally in the work of the Commission until 1973, when a Directorate for Education and Training was created within the then Directorate General for Research, Science, and Education.[1] The establishment of external relations in research, science, and education has been an aim of the Community's action in this area since 1973, but work has tended to focus on the development of agreements on research and development.[2] The Communities had no specific powers to adopt measures on education until the insertion of new Article 126 by the TEU.[3]

Article 128 EEC did, however, provide that the Council could lay down general principles for implementing a common vocational training policy capable of contributing to the harmonious development both of national economies and of the common market. This was the basis for several internal initiatives, but there was little Community action on the external plane in this field under that Article, or indeed under other powers in the EEC Treaty. Article 128 EEC has been repealed by the TEU and replaced by Article 127 EC.[4]

LEGAL BASIS OF THE COMMUNITY'S EXTERNAL COMPETENCE

The activities of the European Community include 'a contribution to education and training of quality'.[5] Chapter 3 of Title VII of the EC Treaty, consisting of Articles 126 and 127 EC, provides the means by which the Community's contribution is to be made. Articles 126 and 127 EC are similar in structure. Article 126 deals principally with education, and Article 127 with vocational training, but both envisage action on 'youth' matters. The first paragraph of each Article sets out the Community's general objective in the relevant area. Article 126(1) provides that the Community shall contribute to the development of quality education by encouraging co-operation between Member States and, if necessary, by supporting and supplementing their action, while fully respecting the responsibility of the Member States for the content of teaching and the organization of education systems and their cultural and linguistic diversity. Article 127(1) provides that the Community shall implement a vocational training

---

[1] *7th General Report* (1973), point 369.   [2] On which, see Ch. 16.
[3] Art. G(36) TEU.   [4] *Ibid.*
[5] Art. 3(p) EC.

policy which shall support and supplement the action of the Member States, while fully respecting the responsibility of the Member States for the content and organization of vocational training. The second paragraph of each Article lists the particular aims which Community action should seek to pursue. The procedure for the adoption of Community measures is set out in the fourth paragraph of each Article. To contribute to the achievement of the Community's objectives in the field of education, the Council may adopt recommendations; or, acting in accordance with the co-decision procedure, it may adopt 'incentive measures'. To contribute to the objectives of Community action on vocational training, the Council may adopt 'measures'. Both Articles expressly exclude any harmonization of the laws and regulations of the Member States.[6]

Extent of the Community's External Competence

The Community's competence to act externally is defined in the third paragraph of each Article. Article 126(3) provides that the Community and the Member States shall foster co-operation[7] with third countries and the competent international organizations (in particular the Council of Europe) in the field of education. Article 127(3) provides that the Community and the Member States shall foster co-operation with third countries and international organizations in the sphere of vocational training.[8]

Co-operation with international organizations includes Community participation as observer, and the establishment of other inter-institutional links by exchanges of information and informal co-operation arrangements.[9] Although neither Article expressly gives the Community a power to conclude agreements, such a power is implicit in the wording of Articles 126(3) and 127(3).[10] The practice of the institutions bears out this reading: agreements on co-operation on education are being negotiated between the Community and Canada and the United States under Article 126.[11]

The Community's powers to conclude agreements under Articles 126(3) and 127(3) must be read in the light of the other provisions of these Articles. In the first place, the objectives of Community action, and the aims which such action may pursue, are set out in the first and second paragraphs of these Articles. These objectives and aims guide the Community's action externally as well as internally. Similarly, the prohibition on Community harmonization of the laws and regulations of the Member States applies as much to external acts as to

---

[6] Art. 126(4), first indent, and Art. 127(4).

[7] On the meaning of 'foster co-operation' see 46–7 above.

[8] On the meaning of 'vocational training' under Art. 128 EEC (that is, before the TEU), see Case 242/87 *Commission* v. *Council* [1989] ECR 1425 and Joined Cases C–51/89, C–90/89, and C–94/89 *UK* v. *Council* [1991] ECR I–2757.

[9] Arts. 229 and 231 EC are also relevant to this area of Community activity: see Ch. 7.

[10] See Ch. 3.   [11] Bull. EC 1994–9 1.2.188.

Community action taken internally.[12] Thus, the Community cannot conclude an agreement which has the effect of establishing common rules or harmonizing norms in the field of education or the sphere of vocational training. To the extent that an agreement includes such provisions, the participation of the Member States alongside the Community is necessary.

Nature of the Community's External Competence

To the extent that the Community has competence in the areas of education, vocational training, and youth, that competence is shared between the Community and the Member States. Articles 126 and 127 clearly envisage that the Community's policies and powers in these areas are to co-exist with those of the Member States: Community action is to 'support and supplement'[13] that of the Member States, not to replace or supersede what they do.

PRACTICE OF THE COMMUNITY

Legal Basis

Before the entry into force of the TEU, co-operation with third countries on education, vocational training, and youth took place mainly as an aspect of general economic co-operation. This practice continues; and if provisions on co-operation on education, vocational training, or youth are included in a more general agreement, the legal basis for the conclusion of that agreement will be determined in accordance with the usual criteria.[14]

Since the entry into force of Articles 126 and 127 EC, Council decisions relating to the conclusion of agreements dealing principally with education or vocational training have to cite Article 126 or 127 respectively and also have to cite the appropriate provisions of Article 228.[15] In most cases, the relevant provisions of Article 228 will be the first sentence of paragraph (2) (which requires the Council to act by qualified majority), and the first subparagraph of Article 228(3) (which requires consultation of the Parliament). If an agreement relating to education entails amendment of an incentive measure adopted under Article 126(4) first *tiret*, the assent of the Parliament will be required.[16]

---

[12] See Art. 126(4), first indent, Art. 127(4). Although these prohibitions appear in context to apply to internal measures only, they must, in order to have full effect, also apply to external acts such as agreements. This is because international agreements, when duly concluded, form part of Community law, and are thus in principle capable of harmonizing the laws and regulations of the Member States in the areas they cover.

[13] Art. 126(1) and Art. 127(1).   [14] On choice of legal basis, see Ch. 4.

[15] On conclusion of agreements by the Community, see Ch. 4.

[16] Art. 228(3), 2nd subpara.

Multilateral Agreements

The Community is not a party to any multilateral agreements dealing principally with education or vocational training. There are however provisions on these matters in the Lomé Convention[17] and the EEA Agreement.[18]

Bilateral Agreements

Provisions on education and vocational training have been included in several bilateral agreements concluded by the Community.

Agreements under the Comett II Programme

In 1986, the Community adopted a programme on co-operation between universities and enterprises regarding training in the field of technology.[19] The 'Comett' programme, as it became known, was revised in 1989 in order to extend to co-operation with the EFTA States and with international organizations.[20] Agreements were concluded in 1990 associating the EFTA States and Liechtenstein with that programme.[21] The Comett II programme came to an end in December 1994, but co-operation with the EFTA States in the areas covered by the Comett II programme continues under the EEA Agreement.[22]

Agreements under the Erasmus Programme

The Erasmus Programme was set up in 1987[23] in order to provide for co-operation on education and training. Agreements were concluded between the Community and the EFTA States in 1991 applying the programme to them.[24]

Other Bilateral Agreements

Provisions on co-operation in the areas of education and vocational training have been included in the Europe Agreements,[25] and in agreements on trade

---

[17] Lomé IV, Art. 151 [1991] OJ L229/1.
[18] EEA Agreement, Arts. 78–88, and Prot. 31, Art. 4 [1994] OJ L1/1.
[19] [1986] OJ L222/17.   [20] [1989] OJ L13/28.
[21] See Decs. 90/190 (Austria); 90/191 (Finland); 90/192 (Iceland); 90/193 (Norway); 90/194 (Sweden); 90/195 (Switzerland), all in [1990] OJ L102.
[22] EEA Agreement, Art. 81.   [23] [1987] OJ L166/20.
[24] See Decs. 91/611 (Austria); 91/612 (Finland); 91/613 (Iceland); 91/614 (Norway); 91/615 (Sweden); 91/616 (Switzerland); 91/617 (Liechtenstein), all in [1991] OJ L332. Co-operation with the EFTA countries in the areas covered by the Erasmus programme continues under the EEA Agreement. The agreement extending the benefits of the Erasmus programme to Liechtenstein remains in force.
[25] On the Europe Agreements, see Chs. 18 and 20. Provisions on education and vocational training are in the Agreements with Poland, Art. 76 [1993] OJ L348/1; Hungary, Art. 75 [1993] OJ

and economic co-operation with certain countries of Latin America,[26] Yemen,[27] Slovenia,[28] Albania,[29] the USSR,[30] the Baltic States,[31] Macao,[32] and Sri Lanka.[33] The provisions of these agreements have been the basis for scholarships, grants, and exchange schemes.[34]

International Organizations

Education and vocational training are relevant to the work of several international organizations, of which the more important are UNESCO and the Council of Europe.

UNESCO

The Community is an observer in UNESCO, without the right to vote. Exchanges of letters between the Commission and the Secretary General of UNESCO in 1964 and 1972[35] make provision for exchange of information and documentation, the setting up of joint working groups, and other forms of co-operation in areas of common interest, such as higher education, development aid for education, science, and culture.

L347/1; Romania, Art. 77 [1994] OJ L357/1; Bulgaria, Art. 77 [1994] OJ L358/1; the Slovak Republic, Art. 77 [1994] OJ L359/1; and the Czech Republic, Art. 77 [1994] OJ L360/1.

[26] See the agreements with Argentina, Art. 4(2)(f) [1990] OJ L295/66; Brazil, Art. 27 [1991] OJ C-163/20; Chile, Arts. 2(1)(f) and 14 [1991] OJ L79/1; Mexico, Art. 36 [1991] OJ L340/1; Paraguay, Art. 14 [1992] OJ L313/75; Uruguay, Art. 18 [1992] OJ L94/1.

[27] 1985 Agreement with Yemen Arab Republic, Art. 2(2) [1985] OJ L26/1.

[28] 1993 Co-operation Agreement with Slovenia, Art. 12(1) [1993] OJ L189/1.

[29] 1992 Trade and Economic Co-operation Agreement with Albania, Art. 13(4) (vocational training in customs matters), and Art. 15(2) (development of human resources, vocational training, and management training as part of general economic co-operation) [1992] OJ L343/1.

[30] 1989 Co-operation Agreement with the USSR [1990] OJ L68/1, Art. 20(2). This Agreement is being applied by the countries of the former Soviet Union while partnership and co-operation agreements are negotiated with each of them individually.

[31] 1993 Agreements on Trade and Commercial and Economic Co-operation with Estonia, Art. 13(4) (vocational training in customs matters) and Art. 15(2) (development of human resource training) [1993] OJ L403/1; Latvia, Art. 13(4) (vocational training in customs matters) and Art. 15(2) (development of human resource and training) [1993] OJ L403/10; Lithuania, Art. 13(4) (vocational training in customs matters) and Art. 15(2) (development of human resource and training) [1993] OJ L403/20. See also the 1994 Free Trade Agreements with Estonia, Arts. 35 and 36 [1994] OJ L373/1; Latvia, Arts. 35 and 36 [1994] OJ L374/1; and Lithuania, Arts. 36 and 37 [1994] OJ L375/1.

[32] 1992 Trade and Co-operation Agreement with Macao, Art. 10 [1992] OJ L404/26.

[33] [1995] OJ L85/22, Art. 4(3) and (4).

[34] See *27th General Report*, point 272.

[35] See *Relations between the European Community and International Organizations* (Commission, 1989), 132–135.

The Council of Europe

Article 126(3) lays particular emphasis on co-operation between the Community and the Council of Europe. A fuller account of the relations between the Community and the Council of Europe is provided elsewhere.[36]

Unilateral Community Acts

Co-operation under the Comett II and the Erasmus Programmes has already been noted. The *Tempus Programme* ('trans-European mobility scheme for university students) has also been used to further co-operation in the areas of education and training. Tempus was originally set up in 1990 as a trans-European scheme for university studies with the aim of contributing to training assistance for the Countries of Central and Eastern Europe. It was subsequently extended in 1991 and again in 1993.[37] Tempus II (which will run from 1994 to 1998) extends the co-operation programme to certain States of the former Soviet Union and to the Countries of Central and Eastern Europe eligible for PHARE funds.[38]

The *Youth for Europe II Programme*[39] also provides for co-operation in the international sphere. The programme is to be open to the participation of the associated countries of Central and Eastern Europe in accordance with the conditions set out in additional protocols to the association agreements concluded with these countries, and to Malta and Cyprus on the same terms as apply to the EFTA States.[40] The Commission is to ensure that the programme is compatible with and complementary to action undertaken for young people in the Member States. The Commission and the Member States are to promote co-operation to allow complementarity of action with relevant international organizations, especially the Council of Europe.[41]

The *Socrates Programme*[42] is intended to contribute to the development of quality education and training and to the creation of an open European area for co-operation in education. The programme is open to the participation of the Central and Eastern European countries and Malta and Cyprus on the same conditions as apply in the Youth for Europe III Programme.[43]

---

[36] Ch. 7.

[37] Council Dec. 93/246 adopting the second phase of the trans-European co-operation scheme for higher education (Tempus II) (1994–8) [1993] OJ L112/34.

[38] The eligible countries are Albania, Bulgaria, Estonia, Hungary, Latvia, Lithuania, Poland, Slovenia, Romania, the Czech Republic, Slovakia, Russia, Belarus, and the Ukraine. On PHARE, see Ch. 18.

[39] Dec. 818/95 of the Parliament and the Council adopting the 3rd phase of the Youth for Europe Programme ([1995] OJ L87/1).

[40] *Ibid.*, Art. 7.   [41] *Ibid.*, Art. 8.

[42] Dec. 819/95 of the Parliament and the Council establishing the Community action programme 'Socrates' ([1995] OJ L87/10).

[43] *Ibid.*, Art. 7.

The *Leonardo da Vinci Programme (1995–9)*[44] set up an action programme for implementation of a Community vocational training policy to support and supplement those of the Member States. The programme is to be open to the participation of the associated countries of Central and Eastern Europe in accordance with conditions laid down in additional protocols to association agreements to be concluded with these countries. Cyprus and Malta may participate in the programme on the same terms as the EFTA States.

The *TACIS* Regulation provides for technical assistance in the area of training, including manpower training.[45] Projects eligible for aid under the PHARE Regulation include projects or co-operation measures in the area of training.[46]

The objective of the *European Training Foundation*[47] is to contribute to the development of the vocational training systems of the countries of Central and Eastern Europe eligible for aid under the PHARE Programme, and the States of the Former Soviet Union and Mongolia eligible for assistance under TACIS.[48] The Foundation provides technical assistance and information. It is open to the participation of non-Member States which share the commitment of the Community and the Member States to the provision of aid for training. Such participation is to be on the basis of arrangements to be laid down in agreements between the Community and those countries following the procedure in Article 228 EC.[49]

Other, less formal, co-operation in this area includes the setting up of joint expert study groups with the EFTA States; co-operation with the United States in financing educational consortia; and the making available of finance to enable students from third countries to pursue studies at the European University Institute in Florence.[50]

---

[44] Dec. 94/819 [1994] OJ L340/8.   [45] Reg. 2053/93, Art. 4. [1993] OJ L187/1.
[46] Reg. 3906/89, Art. 3 [1989] OJ L375/11.
[47] Established by Reg. 1360/90 [1990] OJ L131/1, amended by Reg. 94/2063 [1994] OJ L216/9.
[48] Reg. 1360/90, n. 47 above, Art. 3.   [49] *Ibid.*, Art. 16.
[50] See, e.g., the *27th General Report*, n. 34 above, point 272; *1994 General Report*, points 318–20.

14

Culture

Until the entry into force of the Treaty on European Union, none of the Community Treaties contained an express power to adopt measures on culture. The first ministerial meeting to consider cultural issues took place in June 1984, and the basis for external Community action on culture was eventually laid in a resolution of the Council and the Ministers meeting within the Council adopted on 27 May 1988. This resolution set up a Committee on Cultural Affairs to co-ordinate cultural activity within the Community or within the framework of intergovernmental co-operation; and it provided scope for cultural co-operation with European countries not members of the Community and with other international organizations at European and world level, especially the Council of Europe and UNESCO.[1] The first steps to extending cultural co-operation beyond the bounds of the Community were taken in 1989, in meetings with Asian, Latin American, and Central and Eastern European countries,[2] and provisions on cultural co-operation have frequently been included in general Community trade and co-operation agreements since then.

LEGAL BASIS OF THE COMMUNITY'S EXTERNAL COMPETENCE

The activities of the European Community include a 'contribution to the flowering of the cultures of the Member States'.[3] The principal legal basis for Community action on culture is Article 128 EC.[4] That Article provides that the Community shall contribute to the flowering of the cultures of the Member States, while respecting their national and regional diversity and at the same time bringing the common cultural heritage to the fore.[5] Action by the Community is to be aimed at encouraging co-operation between Member States and, if necessary, supporting and supplementing their action in the areas listed in paragraph 2 of Article 128.[6] The Community is to take cultural aspects into account in its action under other provisions of the Treaty.[7] In order to contribute to the achievement of the objectives in Article 128, the Council may adopt recommendations, or, acting in accordance with the co-decision procedure, incentive measures. Such incentive measures may not lead to harmonization of the laws and regulations of the Member States.[8]

---

[1] [1988] OJ C197/1.
[2] *23rd General Report* (1989), point 712.
[3] Art. 3(p) EC.
[4] Added by Art. G(38) TEU.
[5] Art. 128(1) EC.
[6] Art. 128(2).
[7] Art. 128(4).
[8] Art. 128(5).

Extent of the Community's Competence

The Community and the Member States are to foster co-operation[9] with third countries and the competent international organizations in the sphere of culture, in particular the Council of Europe. 'Culture' for these purposes must be interpreted in the light of paragraphs 1 and 2 of Article 128: the Community's external action should thus be aimed at the improvement of the knowledge and dissemination of the culture and history of the European people; the conservation and safeguarding of cultural heritage of European significance; non-commercial cultural exchanges; and artistic and literary creation, including in the audio-visual sector.

The Community has power to conclude agreements on culture, and to participate in the work of international organizations to the extent that the constitutions of these bodies allow, provided that these actions contribute to the achievement of the objectives described in Article 128(1) and (2). The Community may not enter into agreements the provisions of which would lead to harmonization of the laws or regulations of the Member States: if such an agreement were to be concluded by the Community, the participation of the Member States alongside the Community would also be required.

Nature of the Community's Competence

To the extent that the Community has competence in relation to culture, that competence is shared with the Member States. The Community's competence in this area is not intended to replace those of the Member States, but to 'supplement and support' these competences, and to encourage co-operation among the Member States.

PRACTICE OF THE COMMUNITY

Legal Basis

Before the entry into force of the TEU, co-operation on culture was usually treated as an aspect of general economic co-operation. If the Community now decided to conclude an agreement the aim and content of which fell within the scope of Article 128, the decision to conclude the agreement would have to cite Article 228[10] along with Article 128: the relevant provisions would normally be Article 228(2), second sentence,[11] and Article 228(3), first subparagraph.[12] If,

---

[9] On the meaning of 'foster co-operation' see 46–7.

[10] On the procedure for conclusion of an agreement, and the need to cite Art. 228, see Ch. 4.

[11] Which means that the Council would have to act unanimously, because the Council must act unanimously in adopting internal measures on culture: see Art. 128(5) taken with Art. 228(2), 2nd sentence.　　　　[12] The Parliament would have to be consulted: see Art. 228(3), 1st subpara.

however, conclusion of an agreement entailed amendment of an incentive measure adopted under Article 128(5), first indent, the assent of the Parliament would be required.[13] If provisions on cultural co-operation were included in a more general agreement (such as an agreement on trade and co-operation), the usual tests would have to be applied to determine the legal basis of the agreement, and whether Article 128 should be cited as part of that legal basis.

Agreements

Multilateral Agreements

The Community is not a party to any multilateral agreements concerned mainly with cultural co-operation. However, the Lomé Convention makes extensive provision for co-operation in the area of culture,[14] and certain provisions of the EEA Agreement have a bearing on cultural matters.[15]

Bilateral Agreements

No bilateral Community agreements dealing mainly with cultural co-operation yet exist. Provisions on co-operation in this field were included in the Europe Agreements;[16] and in trade and economic co-operation agreements with certain Latin American countries,[17] and with Macao,[18] India,[19] and Sri Lanka.[20]

Unilateral Measures

The OCT Decision contains provisions on co-operation in the area of culture along the lines of those in the Lomé Convention.[21]

---

[13] See Art. 228(3), 2nd subpara.

[14] Fourth ACP–EEC Convention, Arts. 142–148 [1991] OJ L229/1.

[15] In particular Art. 78 (co-operation in, *inter alia*, the fields of tourism and the audio-visual sector) and Prot. 31, Arts. 8 and 9 [1994] OJ L1/1.

[16] On the Europe Agreements, see Ch. 20. Provisions on cultural co-operation appear in the Europe Agreements with Poland, Art. 95 ([1993] OJ L348/1); Hungary, Art. 97 ([1993] OJ L347/1); Romania, Art. 99 ([1994] OJ L357/1); Bulgaria, Art. 98 ([1994] OJ L358/1); the Slovak Republic, Art. 97 ([1994] OJ L359/1); and the Czech Republic, Art. 97 ([1994] OJ L360/1).

[17] See the Trade and Co-operation Agreements with Brazil, Art. 25 ([1992] OJ C163/11); Mexico, Art. 35 ([1991] OJ L340/1); Paraguay, Art. 13 ([1992] OJ L313/71); Uruguay, Art. 16 ([1992] OJ L94/1).

[18] 1992 Agreement with Macao, Art. 9 ([1992] OJ L404/27).

[19] 1994 Agreement with India, Art. 15 ([1994] OJ L223/23).

[20] Agreement with Sri Lanka, Arts. 4(3) and 12 ([1995] OJ L85/32).

[21] Dec. 91/482, Arts. 88 and 89 ([1991] OJ L263/1).

International Organizations

The Community has close links with the work of the Council of Europe.[22]
The Community also participates[23] in the work of UNESCO as a non-voting observer. Exchanges of letters in 1964 and 1972 between the Commission and the Secretariat of UNESCO make provision for the exchange of information and documentation, the setting up of joint working groups, and other forms of co-operation.[24]

[22] Co-operation with the Council of Europe is governed by Art. 230 EC: see further, Ch. 7.
[23] On the Community's participation in international organizations generally, see Ch. 7.
[24] See *Relations between the European Community and International Organizations*, 132–5.

15

Public Health

All three Communities are concerned with aspects of public health. The Euratom Treaty provides for the laying down of basic standards for the protection of the health of workers and the general public against the dangers of ionising radiations.[1] The ECSC Treaty provides that the institutions of the Community should, in the common interest, promote improved working conditions and standards of living of the workers in each of the industries for which the ECSC is responsible.[2] The external relations of the Euratom Community are considered elsewhere,[3] and the agreements concluded by the ECSC have related to trade matters, rather than social conditions in the coal and steel industries. The rest of this Chapter is concerned with the powers of the European Community.

LEGAL BASIS OF THE COMMUNITY'S EXTERNAL COMPETENCE

The activities of the European Community include 'a contribution to the attainment of a high level of health protection'.[4] Article 129 EC establishes the legal mechanism through which this contribution is to be made. It provides that the Community is to contribute towards ensuring a high level of human health protection by encouraging co-operation between the Member States and, if necessary, lending support to their action. Community action is to be directed towards the prevention of diseases, in particular the major health scourges, including drug dependence, by promoting research into their causes and their transmission, as well as health information and education. Health protection requirements are to form a constituent part of the Community's other policies.[5] Member States, in liaison with the Commission, are to co-ordinate among themselves their policies and programmes in these areas. The Commission may take any useful initiative to promote such co-ordination.[6] In order to contribute to the achievement of these objectives, the Council, acting under the co-decision procedure, may adopt incentive measures. These incentive measures may not lead to harmonization of the laws and regulations of the Member States. Acting by a qualified majority on a proposal from the Commission, the Council may adopt recommendations.[7]

---

[1] Art. 30 Euratom. [2] Art. 3(e) ECSC.
[3] On the work of the Euratom Community, see Ch. 22. [4] Art. 3(o) EC.
[5] Art. 129(1) EC. [6] Art. 129(2) EC. [7] Art. 129(4) EC.

Extent of the Community's External Competence

The external powers of the Community in relation to public health are contained in Article 129(3) which states that the Community and the Member States are to foster co-operation[8] with third countries and the competent international organisations in the sphere of public health.[9]

Article 129(3) EC must be interpreted in the light of the objectives set out and the powers conferred on the Community in the rest of that Article. Thus Community action externally must remain within the scope of the first paragraph of Article 129. It will be noted that the Community's action is to be in the field of public health, rather than in relation to the provision of health care as such. The Community's action is to be preventive, and focused on 'the major health scourges'.

The Fight against Drugs

Article 129 envisages Community action in relation to the public health aspects of the drugs problem. The Community's action is to be focused on the problem of drug dependence, and on research into the causes and epidemiology of drug abuse.[10] Much of the Community's action in this area has been through projects funded by various aid programmes.[11]

Article 129 enables the Community to enter into agreements and arrangements with third countries and international organizations, and to participate in the work of organizations to the extent that the constitutions of these bodies permit. The Community may not enter into international commitments which would have the effect of harmonizing the laws or regulations of the Member States in the area of health. If provisions of a proposed agreement had that effect, it would be necessary for the Member States to become parties in respect of those provisions.

Nature of the Community's Competence

To the extent that the Community has competence in the area of public health, that competence is shared with the Member States. Article 129 clearly envis-

---

[8] On the meaning of 'foster co-operation' see 46–7.

[9] Action on health has been part of the Community's general development policy and of the economic co-operation established under trade and economic co-operation agreements. See further Chs. 12 and 18.

[10] The intergovernmental co-operation established in the field of justice and home affairs by Title VI of the TEU also extends to the fight against drugs. Combating drug addiction is specified in Art. K.1 TEU as a matter of common interest for the Member States. Action under Title VI has concentrated more on controlling drug trafficking and related crime than on the public health aspects of the drugs problem.

[11] See below, *Unilateral Measures*.

ages the continuation of the public health policies of the Member States, and the continued exercise of their powers at the international level.

Legal Basis and Procedures

Before the entry into force of the TEU, Community co-operation with third countries on public health was treated as part of economic co-operation, or as an aspect of development assistance. The Community's powers in these areas continue to be relevant,[12] but if the main aim and content of a proposed agreement fall within the scope of Article 129, that Article will provide the basis for conclusion of the agreement by the Community. The Council act relating to the conclusion of such an agreement will require to cite the appropriate provisions of Article 228 along with Article 129. These would normally be the first sentence of Article 228(2)[13] and the first subparagraph of Article 228(3).[14] If, however, the agreement entails an amendment to an incentive measure adopted under Article 129(4), first indent, the assent of the Parliament must be sought under Article 228(3).[15] If provisions on public health are included in a more general agreement (such as an agreement on trade and economic co-operation), the usual tests must be applied to determine the legal basis and procedures for conclusion of that agreement.[16]

Agreements

Multilateral Agreements

Health

The Lomé Convention[17] recognizes the importance of the health sector in ensuring sustainable and self-reliant development. The aim of co-operation under the Convention is to facilitate the right of access of the greatest number of people to adequate health care, thus promoting equity and social justice, alleviating suffering, reducing the economic burden of disease and mortality, and promoting the effective participation of the Community in operations to improve health and well being. Co-operation in the area of health is to seek to support functional and sustainable health services which are financially

---

[12] See Ch. 18.
[13] Which provides that the Council is to act by qualified majority: Art. 129(4) read with Art. 228(2).
[14] Which requires consultation of the Parliament: Art. 129(4) read with Art. 228(3) 1st subpara.
[15] See Art. 228(3), 2nd subpara.
[16] See, further, Ch. 4.
[17] 4th ACP–EEC Convention, Art. 154(1) ([1991] OJ L229/1).

affordable, culturally acceptable, geographically accessible, and technically competent. A range of schemes which may be supported under the Convention are described.[18]

The Community is a party to the Council of Europe Convention establishing a European Pharmacopoeia[19] .

The Fight against Drugs

The Community is a party to the Vienna Convention against the Illicit Traffic in Narcotic Drugs and Psychotropic Substances of 19 December 1988,[20] but only to the extent of its competence for questions of commercial policy relating to the substances frequently used in the illicit manufacture of narcotic drugs and psychotropic substances, questions which are dealt with in Article 12 of the Convention.[21]

Bilateral Agreements

The Community has concluded no bilateral agreements dealing principally with public health.[22] However, the Community's trade and economic co-operation agreements with certain Latin American countries contain provisions on co-operation in the areas of public health,[23] and drug abuse control.[24] The agreements with the Baltic States,[25] Albania,[26] and Macao[27] provide for co-operation in the area of health generally. The protection of the health and safety of workers is an aspect of the social co-operation established by the Europe Agreements,[28] and these Agreements also envisage action against the drugs

---

[18] Fourth ACP–EEC Convention, Art. 154(3).
[19] [1994] OJ L158/17 (as amended by a 1989 prot. which allowed the Community to become a party [1994] OJ L158/22).
[20] Council Dec. 90/611 ([1990] OJ L326/56).
[21] See the Declaration of competence submitted at the time of Community accession (attached to Dec. 90/611).
[22] The negotiation of agreements on medical research was envisaged in the 3rd Framework Programme: see Ch. 16, 317–18.
[23] Agreements with Argentina, Art. 4(2)(a) ([1990] OJ L295/66); Chile, Art. 11(2)(f) ([1991] OJ L79/1); Mexico, Art. 28 ([1991] OJ L340/1); Uruguay, Art. 14 ([1992] OJ L94/11); Brazil, Art. 20 ([1992] OJ C163/11); Paraguay, Art. 15 ([1992] OJ L313/71).
[24] Agreements with Chile, Art. 11(2)(e); Mexico, Art. 29; Brazil, Art. 22; Paraguay, Art. 16.
[25] Art. 15(2) of each of the agreements with Estonia ([1992] OJ L403/1); Latvia ([1992] OJ L403/10); Lithuania ([1992] OJ L403/30).
[26] 1992 Albania Agreement, Art. 15(2) ([1992] OJ L343/1).
[27] 1992 Macao Agreement, Art. 13 ([1992] OJ L404/26).
[28] On the Europe Agreements, see Ch. 20. For co-operation on health see the Europe Agreements with Hungary, Art. 88 ([1993] OJ L347/1); Poland, Art. 87 ([1993] OJ L348/1); Romania, Art. 89 ([1994] OJ L357/1); Bulgaria, Art. 89 ([1994] OJ L358/1); the Slovak Republic, Art. 89 ([1994] OJ L359/1); and the Czech Republic, Art. 88 ([1994] OJ L360/1).

problem.[29] Agreements with India[30] and Sri Lanka[31] provide for co-operation on health[32] and on drug abuse control.[33]

Unilateral Measures

Co-operation in the improvement of living conditions and standards of health is part of the co-operation established in the *OCT Decision*.[34] The Articles dealing with rural promotion measures,[35] cultural and social co-operation,[36] and regional co-operation[37] all provide for co-operation in relation to health. Assistance is to be given to help the OCT combat drug trafficking at regional and inter-regional levels.[38] The assistance available under the *TACIS Programme*[39] has been used to assist in the fight against drugs. A *North-South Programme* for combating drug abuse has existed since 1989.[40] Programmes to combat AIDS in the ACP countries have been financed under the EDF since 1987.[41] A further programme for action against AIDS in the developing countries was adopted on 21 November 1989.[42] Assistance schemes have also been established with the countries of Eastern Europe.[43]

International Organizations

The Community has observer status at the ILO, the WHO, the UNDP, and the United Nations Fund for Drug Abuse Control,[44] and has co-operation agreements or arrangements with these organizations.[45] A co-operation agreement exists between the Community and the United Nations International Drug Control Programme.[46]

[29] Europe Agreement with Hungary, Art. 96; Poland, Art. 94; Romania, Art. 97; Bulgaria, Art. 97; the Slovak Republic, Art. 96; and the Czech Republic, Art. 96, all n. 28 above. The provisions on co-operation in the fight against drugs are more extensive in the Europe Agreements than in the other trade and economic co-operation agreements (e.g. the agreements with the Latin American countries, Macao, and India), because the Member States are also parties to the Europe Agreements.

[30] 1994 Agreement with India ([1994] OJ L223/23). The legal basis for conclusion of this agreement is being challenged before the Court: Case C–268/94, *Portugal* v. *Council*, judgment awaited.

[31] Agreement with Sri Lanka ([1995] OJ L85/32).

[32] Art. 4(3) of each agreement.   [33] Art. 19 of each agreement.

[34] Dec. 91/482 ([1991] OJ L263/1).   [35] *Ibid.*, Art. 23.   [36] *Ibid.*, Art. 88.

[37] *Ibid.*, Art. 93(b).   [38] *Ibid.*, Art. 93(j).   [39] See Reg. 2053/93 ([1993] OJ L187/1).

[40] See *23rd General Report* (1989), point 882; *26th General Report* (1992), point 944 ff.; *27th General Report* (1993), point 826 ff.; *1994 General Report*, point 962 ff. Reg. 443/92 EEC on financial and technical assistance to the developing countries in Asia and Latin America provides for special attention to be given to combating drugs problems.

[41] *21st General Report* (1987), point 843; *1994 General Report*, n. 40 above, point 964.

[42] *23rd General Report*, n. 40 above, point 371.

[43] *25th General Report* (1991), point 1008; *26th General Report*, n. 40 above, points 947–9.

[44] For an example of the Community's contribution to the UN Fund, see *23rd General Report*, n. 40 above, point 882.

[45] The texts of the agreements between the ECSC and the ILO; the EC and the ILO; and Euratom and the ILO are at [1953] JO 11/167; [1959] JO 27/521; and [1961] JO 18/473 respectively. An exchange of letters about co-operation between the European Communities and the WHO is at [1982] OJ L300/20.   [46] *27th General Report*, n. 40 above, point 828.

16

Research and Technological Development

All three Communities have express powers[1] to promote and conduct activities in the area of research and development.[2] The powers conferred on the ECSC[3] have not been used in any significant way for the development of a Community research policy externally, and are not considered further. The research activities provided for in the Euratom Treaty,[4] although in many ways closely linked to the non-nuclear research activities carried out by the European Community,[5] find their external expression through the competences conferred on the Euratom Community, and are considered elsewhere.[6]

The original EEC Treaty contained no provisions dealing specifically with research and development. A non-nuclear research policy associated with the Community began to emerge in the early 1970s, with the establishment of the COST programme,[7] and the adoption by the Council in 1974[8] of resolutions on the co-ordination of national policies on research and development; on an initial programme of Community action; on the establishment of the European Science Foundation; and on a programme of action on forecasting, assessment, and methodology. From that basis there grew a wide-ranging non-nuclear research and development policy, but the principal focus of the Community's activities remained internal for over a decade: with the exception of agreements concluded under the auspices of COST, no agreements on non-nuclear research and development were concluded by the Community until 1985.

The Single European Act added into the EEC Treaty eleven Articles devoted to research and development, thus providing a sound legal basis for Community action, in the external and the internal spheres. These provisions were amended by the TEU, and the Community's powers in relation to research and development now appear in Title XV of the EC Treaty.

[1] The ECSC and Euratom Treaties contained such powers from the outset. Specific provisions on research and development were first introduced into the EEC Treaty in 1986.

[2] For a survey of the Community's action on research and development, see Sharp, 'The Community and the New Technologies', in J. Lodge, *The European Community and the Challenge of the Future* (Pinter, 1989). For discussion of the legal aspects, see Elizalde, 'Legal Aspects of Community Policy on Research and Technological Development' (1992) 29 *CMLRev.* 309, at 340–3.

[3] Art. 55 ECSC.   [4] Arts. 2(a) and 4–11 Euratom.

[5] The 2nd and 3rd Framework Programmes were joint Euratom–EEC Programmes: see Dec. 87/516 ([1987] OJ L320/1) establishing the 2nd Framework Programme, and Dec. 90/221 ([1990] OJ L117/28) establishing the 3rd Framework Programme. Close links between the nuclear and non-nuclear aspects of the Communities' research are also ensured by the role played by the Joint Research Centre. On this, see in particular the *22nd General Report* (1988), point 345 and sources there cited.

[6] See Ch. 22.   [7] On which see below.   [8] *8th General Report* (1974), point 309 ff.

LEGAL BASIS OF THE COMMUNITY'S EXTERNAL COMPETENCE

Article 3(m) EC provides that the Community's activities are to include the promotion of research and technological development. Articles 130f to 130p EC set out the Community's powers and tasks in detail, and several provisions are of particular relevance to the Community's external competence. Article 130f states that the Community is to have the objective of strengthening the scientific and technological bases of Community industry and encouraging it to become more competitive at international level, while promoting all the research activities deemed necessary by virtue of the other chapters of the Treaty. In pursuing the objectives in Article 130f, the Community is to carry out certain activities complementing the activities carried out in the Member States, including the promotion of co-operation in the field of Community research, technological development, and demonstration with third countries and international organizations.[9] Article 130m provides that in implementing the multiannual framework programme, the Community may make provision for co-operation in Community research, technological development, and demonstration with third countries or international organizations. The detailed arrangements for such co-operation may be the subject of agreements between the Community and third parties concerned, which are to be negotiated and concluded in accordance with Article 228.

Extent of the Community's Competence

The Community's internal powers in the area of research and development are principally given effect through multiannual framework programmes adopted by the Council under Article 130i. These framework programmes establish the scientific and technological objectives to be achieved by the Community's activities; fix priorities; indicate the broad lines of such activities; and provide for financing.[10] The framework programmes are in turn implemented by specific programmes developed within each activity. In establishing specific programmes, the Council defines the detailed rules for the implementation of the programmes, fixes their duration, and provides for the funding 'deemed necessary' to carry them out.[11] The framework and specific programmes thus establish the parameters of the Community's research effort, internally and externally. Although they are, of course, principally concerned with the development of research within the Community, the specific programmes also frequently provide for the conclusion of agreements associating third States with the Community's research programmes[12] and, over the years, many bilateral agreements have been concluded with that aim.

---

[9] Art. 130g.   [10] Art. 130i(1).   [11] Art. 130i(3).   [12] See below, *Bilateral Agreements*.

The Community's external activities in the area of research are not, however, confined to the conclusion of agreements associating third countries with the Community's framework and specific programmes. The Community has also entered into a range of 'framework agreements' on scientific and technological co-operation which are general in scope and go beyond the compass of current framework and specific programmes. The Fourth Framework Programme[13] appears to sanction the conclusion of such agreements, in providing that the promotion of co-operation with third countries is itself an 'activity' which is to be pursued by the Community; but the conclusion of framework co-operation agreements predates the Fourth Framework Programme, and the legal basis for such agreements is probably not the framework or specific programmes, but the more general objectives of the Community in the area of research and development.

Nature of the Community's Competence

Article 130g refers to the Community's research and development policy 'complementing' the policies of the Member States. Article 130h states that the Community and the Member States are to co-ordinate their research and technological development activities so as to ensure that national policies and Community policy are mutually consistent. It is implicit in these provisions that the policies and competences of the Member States in this area are not superseded or replaced by the Community's policy, but co-exist with it. Research and technological development policy is thus in principle an area in which the Community and the Member States share competence: the conclusion of agreements and the elaboration of a policy by the Community do not have the effect of depriving the Member States of the power to conclude similar agreements or to elaborate their own policies.[14] The practice of the Community supports this conclusion. Every framework agreement on scientific and technological co-operation concluded so far by the Community[15] contains a provision[16] making clear that the agreement and activities under it will not affect the powers of the Member States to undertake bilateral activity with the third country in the field of science, technology, research, and development, or to conclude agreements to that end.

There are two possible exceptions to this general rule. First, in accordance with the principle in Case 22/70 (the *AETR* case),[17] to the extent that common rules governing research have been promulgated by the Community, only the

---

[13] Council Dec. 1110/94 ([1994] OJ L126/1).   [14] On shared competence, see Ch. 3.
[15] See, e.g., the 1st preambular para. of the framework co-operation agreements concluded with Finland, Norway, and Iceland (nn. 58 and 59 below) and the Council and Commission declaration appended to the agreement with Australia (n. 60 below).
[16] The so-called 'Canada clause': see, further, Ch. 9.
[17] Case 22/70 *Commission* v. *Council* [1971] ECR 263. On the *AETR* case, and the meaning of 'common rules', see Ch. 3.

Community will be competent to enter into agreements affecting those rules or altering their scope. But common rules on research and development are likely to be rare. Secondly, according to a *dictum* of the Court in *Opinion 1/94*,[18] whenever the Community, in its internal legislative acts, expressly confers on the institutions powers to negotiate with non-member countries, the Community acquires exclusive competence in the spheres covered by those acts. As has been noted, Council decisions establishing specific programmes frequently provide for the negotiation of agreements associating third countries with the programmes. It is therefore arguable that the Community has exclusive competence for the negotiation and conclusion of such agreements where only the Community and not the Member States, participates in the specific programme concerned.

PRACTICE OF THE COMMUNITY

Agreements

Legal Basis and Procedures

After the entry into force of the amendments in the Single European Act, agreements on research and development were concluded on the basis of Article 130n EEC[19] or Article 130q EEC.[20] Since the entry into force of the TEU, if the principal aim and content of an agreement falls within the scope of Title XV EC, the legal basis for conclusion of the agreement by the Community appears to be Article 130m EC,[21] in conjunction with Article 228(2) first sentence,[22] and Article 228(3), first subparagraph.[23]

If provisions on research and development are included in a more general agreement (such as trade and co-operation agreements, fisheries agreements, or agreements relating to the environment) the usual tests must be applied to determine the legal basis and procedures for conclusion of that agreement.[24]

---

[18] (*Re the WTO Agreement*) [1995] 1 CMLR 205 at para. 85. On this, see, further, Ch. 3.

[19] If they derived from specific programmes adopted under the multiannual framework programme.

[20] If they were free-standing research and development agreements, such as the framework agreements concluded with the EFTA countries.

[21] See Council Dec. 94/457 ([1994] OJ L188/17) concerning the conclusion of an Agreement relating to Scientific and Technical Co-operation between the EC and Australia. There seems no reason to think that the legal basis for conclusion of agreements adopted under the Framework Programme would be different. On the need to cite Art. 228, see Ch. 4.

[22] Which requires a qualified majority in the Council.

[23] Which requires consultation of the Parliament.

[24] See Ch. 4, p. 82.

Multilateral Agreements

The EC, with Euratom, is a party to the Agreement establishing an *International Science and Technology Centre*.[25] The Centre's task is to channel the knowledge and experience of military scientists from the former Soviet Union into non-military work, thus limiting the potential for spread of nuclear weapons technology and know-how, while also contributing to the transition of the states of the former Soviet Union to market-based economies.

Many international agreements (for example those on commodities, the environment, and fisheries) include provisions on research and development which are incidental, but closely related to, the principal objective of the agreement.[26] The Community's participation in such agreements is considered elsewhere.[27]

Bilateral Agreements

Within the Framework Programmes

Multiannual programmes in specific areas of research and development have long been a feature of the Community's activities.[28] The programmes adopted under the Second, Third, and Fourth Framework Programmes have expressly authorized the Commission to negotiate agreements with third countries in order to associate those countries with the relevant Community research programme. Such agreements are typically linked to the length of the project in question, and are of limited duration. A full history of all agreements concluded since 1986 would serve little purpose, but the legal technique is of interest and may be illustrated by reference to the Second Framework Programme, which was established by Decision 87/516[29] for the period from 1987 to 1991. The following specific programmes of non-nuclear research[30] were among those adopted under that Framework Programme:[31]

---

[25] Council Reg. 3955/92 ([1992] OJ L409/1). The Agreement was provisionally applied in 1994: [1994] OJ L64/1.

[26] In relation to commodities, see the 1993 International Cocoa Agreement, Art. 40 ([1994] OJ L52/25). In relation to the environment, see, e.g., Art. 3 of the Vienna Convention on the Protection of the Ozone Layer, and Art. 9 of the Montreal Protocol on Substances that Deplete the Ozone Layer ([1988] OJ L297/8). In relation to fisheries, see Art. XV of the Convention on the Conservation of Antarctic Marine Living Resources ([1981] OJ L252/26).

[27] See Chs. 7 (commodities agreements), 10 (fisheries), and 17 (environment).

[28] See, e.g., the *14th General Report* (1980), points 493 ff., and the *19th General Report* (1988), point 321. Some of these programmes provided for the negotiation of agreements associating other countries (usually countries participating in COST) with the programme: see, e.g., Dec. 86/234 of 10 June 1986 adopting a multiannual framework in the field of the environment ([1986] OJ L159/31).

[29] [1987] OJ L302/1.

[30] The 2nd Framework Programme was a joint EEC–Euratom programme, and provided for nuclear and non-nuclear research.

[31] The list which follows is illustrative. It is not, and is not intended to be, a complete list of all the specific programmes or of agreements adopted under these programmes.

(a) a European Stimulation Plan for Economic Science (1989–92) (SPES) was established by Decision 89/118.[32] Agreements (negotiated under Article 8 of that Decision) were concluded with Austria, Finland, Norway, Sweden, and Switzerland[33] associating them with the programme;

(b) a research and development plan in the field of applied metrology and chemical analysis (1988–92) was set up by Decision 88/418.[34] Agreements (negotiated under Article 4 of that Decision) were concluded with Finland, Sweden, and Switzerland[35] associating them with the plan;

(c) two research and development programmes in the field of the environment (STEP and EPOCH) (1989 to 1992) were established by Decision 89/625.[36] Agreements associating Austria, Finland, and Norway with the STEP programme were negotiated under Article 8 of that Decision and concluded on 3 February 1992,[37] and agreements associating Iceland and Sweden with STEP and EPOCH were also concluded on that date;[38]

(d) a programme to stimulate the international co-operation and interchange needed by European research scientists (1988–92) (Science) was adopted by Decision 88/419.[39] Austria, Finland, Norway, Sweden, and Switzerland were associated with the programme by agreements negotiated under Article 5 of that Decision and concluded on 12 February 1990.[40]

The Third Framework Programme was adopted in 1990[41] for a period of four years, and, so far as non-nuclear[42] research and development was concerned, provided for the development of 'enabling technologies' (information and communications technologies, and industrial and materials technologies); the management of natural resources; and the management of intellectual resources. To implement the Framework Programme, specific programmes were adopted in the following areas: marine science and technology;[43] communication technologies;[44] telematic systems in areas of general interest;[45] the environment;[46] the life sciences and technologies for developing countries;[47] non-nuclear energy;[48] biomedicine and health;[49] industrial and materials technologies;[50] human capital and mobility;[51] biotechnology;[52] and measurements and testing.[53] Each of these programmes envisaged the negotiation of agreements by the Commission to associate certain countries with the Community's

---

[32] [1989] OJ L46/43.　　　　　[33] [1991] OJ L61/1, 7, 13, 19, and 25 respectively.
[34] [1988] OJ L206/29.　　　　[35] [1991] OJ L61/31, 37, and 43 respectively.
[36] [1989] OJ L359/9.　　　　　[37] [1992] OJ L54/21.　　　[38] [1992] OJ L54/40.
[39] [1988] OJ L206/34.　　　　[40] [1990] OJ L50/1, 8, 15, 22, and 29 respectively.
[41] Dec. 90/221 ([1990] OJ L117/28).
[42] The programme also provided for nuclear research.
[43] Dec. 91/351 ([1991] OJ L192/1).　　　[44] Dec. 91/352 ([1991] OJ L192/8).
[45] Dec. 91/353 ([1991] OJ L192/18).　　[46] Dec. 91/354 ([1991] OJ L192/29).
[47] Dec. 91/366 ([1991] OJ L196/31).　　[48] Dec. 91/484 ([1991] OJ L257/37).
[49] Dec. 91/505 ([1991] OJ L267/25).　　[50] Dec. 91/506 ([1991] OJ L269/30).
[51] Dec. 92/217 ([1992] OJ L107/1).　　　[52] Dec. 92/218 ([1992] OJ L107/11).
[53] Dec. 92/247 ([1992] OJ L126/12).

research.[54] Such agreements were to be concluded on the basis of Article 130n EEC.

The Fourth Framework Programme, adopted on the basis of Article 130i(1) EC on 26 April 1994,[55] follows its predecessors in fixing areas of activity and envisaging the adoption of specific programmes in respect of each. Of particular interest in the context of the Community's external competence is the second 'activity' listed in Article 130g and elaborated in Annex II of the Fourth Framework Programme. This activity envisages the promotion of co-operation in the field of Community research, technological development, and demonstration with third countries and international organizations. A specific programme giving effect to this activity was adopted on 23 November 1994.[56] That programme implements the second activity of the framework programme, and is structured to reflect the different nature of co-operation with developing countries and co-operation with other third countries, including the countries of Central and Eastern Europe and the newly independent States of the former Soviet Union. The activity is the vehicle for co-operation on research and technological development with third countries and international organizations. The essential aim of the activity is to add value to Community research and technological development through targeted co-operation and synergy with other external Community activities, to strengthen the Community's scientific and technological base, and to support the implementation of other Community policies. It also aims at improving co-ordination with the Community's other instruments and the Member States' activities so as to avoid duplication. The proposed activities are scientific and technological co-operation in Europe and with international organizations; co-operation with non-European industrialized third countries; and scientific and technological co-operation with the developing countries.

Under Framework Agreements on Science and Technology

Framework agreements for scientific and technological co-operation were concluded with Sweden and Switzerland (in 1985),[57] with Finland, Norway, and Austria (in 1986),[58] with Iceland (in 1989),[59] and with Australia (in 1994).[60] Negotiations have begun on agreements with Canada[61] and Israel.

The agreements with the EFTA States[62] are all similar in structure and con-

---

[54] See Art. 8 of the Dec. establishing each programme. The Commission was authorized to negotiate with a particular group of countries, usually the EFTA countries or the countries participating in the COST programme.

[55] Dec. 1110/94 ([1994] OJ L126/1).   [56] Dec. 94/807 ([1994] OJ L334/109).

[57] [1985] OJ L313/1 and 5 respectively.

[58] [1986] OJ L78/23 and 27 (Finland and Norway) and [1986] OJ L216/7 (Austria).

[59] [1990] OJ L14/18.   [60] [1994] OJ L188/17.

[61] *27th General Report* (1993), point 245.

[62] The agreements with Sweden, Switzerland, Finland, and Norway appear to have been concluded twice: see Dec. 87/177 of 9 Feb. 1987 ([1987] OJ L71/29). The 1987 dec. contains a legal basis (Art. 235 EEC); the earlier decs. do not, but both appear to 'conclude' or 'approve' the

tent. The objective in each case is to establish a framework for the development of scientific and technical co-operation between the Community and the relevant third country in fields of common interest which are the subject of research and development programmes on each side.[63] Co-operation is to take the form of exchanges of views on research policy and on the development of co-operation, the transmission of information, and the participation in joint programmes.[64] The co-operation is to be implemented by meetings, visits, and exchange of documentation[65] or by further specific agreements.[66] A joint committee on research has been set up by each agreement to develop the co-operation and ensure execution of the agreement.[67] Each agreement envisaged the possibility of concluding a protocol dealing with co-operation in the areas covered by the ECSC Treaty.[68]

The agreement with Australia was concluded in 1994[69] with the aim of facilitating co-operation between Australia and the Community in fields of common interest where each side is supporting research and development activities to advance science and/or technology relevant to these fields of interest.[70] Co-operation is to take place through joint participation in research programmes, shared use of research facilities, visits, and exchanges of information, and is to be restricted to activities in the following areas: biotechnology, medical and health research; marine science; environment; and information and communication technologies.[71] A Joint Science and Technology Co-operation Committee has been set up to administer the agreement.[72]

Co-operation within the Framework of Other Bilateral Agreements

The encouragement of scientific and technological progress and co-operation has long been an aspect of the relationship established between the Community and third countries in association agreements and in agreements on trade and economic co-operation. Provisions about co-operation on scientific and technological research and development appear in the agreements with Latin America countries;[73] with the countries parties to the General Treaty on Central

agreements on behalf of the Community. The agreements with Sweden, Finland, and Austria have, of course, been superseded by these countries' accession to the EU on 1 Jan. 1995.

[63] See Art. 1 of each Agreement.   [64] Art. 3 of each Agreement.
[65] Art. 4 of each Agreement.
[66] Arts. 6 and 7 of each Agreement. A co-operation agreement on research in the field of recycling and utilisation of waste was entered into with Sweden in 1988 ([1988] OJ L276/11), and an agreement on research in advanced materials was concluded with Switzerland, also in 1988 ([1988] OJ L195/86).
[67] Art. 10 of each Agreement.   [68] Art. 12 of each Agreement.
[69] EC–Australia Agreement on Scientific and Technological Co-operation ([1994] OJ L188/17).
[70] *Ibid.*, Art. 2.   [71] *Ibid.*, Art. 4.   [72] *Ibid.*, Art. 5.
[73] See the Framework Trade and Co-operation Agreement with Argentina, Art. 4 ([1990] OJ L295/66); and the Co-operation agreements with Brazil, Arts. 10 and 16 ([1992] OJ C163/12); Chile, Art. 6 ([1991] OJ L79/2): Mexico, Arts. 19–22 ([1991] OJ L340/3); Paraguay, Art. 8 ([1992] OJ L313/71); and Uruguay, Art. 8 ([1994] OJ L94/1).

American Economic Integration[74] and Panama;[75] with the Cartagena Agreement and the member countries thereof;[76] with the countries of the Maghreb and the Mashraq;[77] with the countries parties to the Charter of the Co-operation Council of the Gulf;[78] with the Yemen;[79] Pakistan;[80] India;[81] Albania;[82] Macao;[83] Estonia, Latvia, and Lithuania;[84] China;[85] Mongolia;[86] Slovenia;[87] Sri Lanka;[88] and in the Europe Agreements.[89] The practical results of such commitments will no doubt depend on the circumstances of each agreement, but the provision of research scholarships and grants appears to be a common feature.

The EEA Agreement

Articles 78 to 88 of the EEA Agreement provide that the Contracting Parties shall strengthen and broaden co-operation in the framework of the Community's activities in the fields of, *inter alia,* research and technological development. Those EFTA States which are parties to the EEA Agreement will accordingly henceforth be associated with the Community's research programme by virtue of the EEA Agreement. However, the EEA Agreement is without prejudice to bilateral co-operation taking place under the Third Framework Programme, and, in so far as they concern co-operation which is not covered by the EEA Agreement, co-operation under bilateral framework

---

[74] i.e., Costa Rica, El Salvador, Guatemala, Honduras, and Nicaragua.

[75] Agreement between the EEC and Costa Rica, El Salvador, Guatemala, Honduras, Nicaragua, and Panama, Art. 3(1)(b) ([1986] OJ L172/1).

[76] i.e., Bolivia, Colombia, Ecuador, Peru, and Venezuela. See the 1984 Agreement, Art. 1(1)(b) ([1984] OJ L153/1).

[77] See Art. 3 of each of the Prots. on financial and technical co-operation concluded with Cyprus ([1990] OJ L82/33); Egypt ([1992] OJ L94/22); Israel ([1992] OJ L94/45); Jordan ([1992] OJ L94/30); Lebanon ([1992] OJ L94/37); Morocco ([1992] OJ L352/14); Syria ([1992] OJ L352/21); and Tunisia ([1992] OJ L18/35).

[78] i.e., the UAE, Bahrain, Saudi Arabia, Oman, Qatar, and Kuwait. See the 1989 Agreement, Arts. 3(1) and 8 ([1989] OJ L54/1).

[79] Agreement with the Yemen Arab Republic, Art. 3(2) ([1985] OJ L26/1).

[80] 1986 Agreement with Pakistan, Art. 3(1)(c) ([1986] OJ L108/1).

[81] 1994 Agreement with India, Arts. 4(3) and 14 ([1994] OJ L223/23).

[82] 1992 Agreement with Albania, Art. 16(1) and (2) ([1992] OJ L343/1).

[83] 1992 Agreement with Macao, Arts. 4 and 8 ([1992] OJ L404/26).

[84] See Art. 15(2) of the Agreements with Estonia, Latvia, and Lithuania ([1992] OJ L404/1, 10, and 19 respectively).

[85] 1985 Agreement with China, Art. 10 ([1985] OJ L250/1).

[86] 1993 Agreement with Mongolia, Arts. 9 and 10 ([1993] OJ L41/45).

[87] 1993 Agreement with Slovenia, Art. 5 ([1993] OJ L189/1).

[88] Agreement with Sri Lanka, Arts. 4(3) and 15 [([1995] OJ L85/32).

[89] On the Europe Agreements generally, see Ch. 20. For provisions on co-operation in the area of research, see the Europe Agreements with Hungary, Art. 74 ([1993] OJ L347/1); Poland, Art. 75 ([1993] OJ L348/1); Romania, Art. 76 ([1994] OJ L357/1); Bulgaria, Art. 76 ([1994] OJ L358/1); the Slovak Republic, Art. 76 ([1994] OJ L359/1); and the Czech Republic, Art. 76 ([1994] OJ L360/1).

agreements on scientific and technological co-operation between the Community and the EFTA States.[90]

Other Arrangements for Co-operation

Several unpublished non-binding arrangements exist between the Commission and certain third countries.[91]

Unilateral Acts

Scientific and technological co-operation forms part of the assistance provided under the TACIS programme.[92]

International Organizations

Research and development activities form part of the tasks of several organizations in which the Community participates as observer.[93] Among the more important are the Economic Commissions of ECOSOC (in particular the Economic Commission for Europe); UNESCO; the World Meteorological Organization; the International Fund for Agricultural Development; United Nations Industrial Development Organization; the International Standardization Organization; and the European Space Agency.

COST AND EUREKA

Mention should be made of two areas of co-operation which, though not within the Community legal order, involve the Community and its institutions and are of importance in practice.

COST ('Co-opération scientifique et technique')[94] was established in 1971 as a framework for co-operation on research and development involving the Community, the Member States, and certain other European States.[95] The formal (but legally non-binding) basis for this co-operation is an exchange of

---

[90] EEA Agreement, Prot. 31, Art. 1 (4) ([1994] OJ L1/197).

[91] e.g., with China (on biotechnology research); and with the Republic of Korea (on co-operation in science and technology).

[92] See Reg. 2053/93 ([1993] OJ L187/1). Assistance offered under the TACIS programme is described regularly in the Bull. and the annual *General Reports*.

[93] On the Communities' participation in international organizations, see Ch. 7.

[94] The work of COST is reported annually in the Commission's *General Reports*, and monthly in the Bull. of the EC. For a full statement of what COST is and what it does, see *COST Co-operation; Objectives, Structures, Operations* (EC Commission, Brussels 1992). For details of research carried out under agreements (strictly speaking, memoranda of understanding) entered into under COST, see *COST Collected Agreements* (7 vols.), published by the Council Secretariat.

[95] 25 States currently participate: the Member States of the EC, Norway, Switzerland, Iceland, Croatia, the Czech Republic, Hungary, Poland, Slovakia, Slovenia, and Turkey.

letters in 1969 and 1970 between the President of the Council of the European Communities and the Foreign Ministers of the States invited to participate, supplemented by a Resolution of the European Ministers of Research dated 22 and 23 November 1971. This institutional framework has been developed and expanded by several similar instruments since, most notably the Conclusions of the Committee of Senior Officials on the future role of COST adopted on 23 and 24 June 1986,[96] the resolution of the Council of the European Communities concerning COST and the European Communities adopted on 20 June 1989,[97] and the Resolution of the Ministers of States participating in COST signed on 21 November 1991[98] which admitted the Czech and Slovak Republic, Iceland, Hungary, and Poland to the programme.

The essential features of COST co-operation are as follows. All participating States and the Community can propose projects; participation in those projects is voluntary—only those countries which are interested take part; projects are funded nationally; co-operation takes the form of the co-ordination of national research projects. The overall operation of COST is under the guidance of a committee of senior officials from the participant countries; the work of individual projects is controlled by management committees. A huge range of research and development projects in a wide variety of fields has been established.[99] The Commission and the Council Secretariat are involved in the running of the programme.

Eureka[100] was established in 1985[101] at the conclusion of a Ministerial Conference on European Technology, which was attended by representatives of the Community, Spain and Portugal, the EFTA countries, and Turkey. Its aims are to increase the productivity and competitiveness of Europe's industries and national economies by strengthening co-operation between firms and research institutes in the field of advanced technology, and to develop common standards, remove barriers to trade, and open public contracts in the field of high technology to undertakings from other participating countries. The main difference between COST and Eureka is that COST projects are open to all member countries of COST, whereas companies taking part in Eureka projects can restrict co-operation to the partners of their choice. Eureka is designed to favour market-oriented industrial projects; COST projects are more geared to research. The current participants in Eureka are the Member States, Norway, Switzerland, Iceland, and Turkey.

---

[96] [1986] OJ C247/2.   [97] [1989] OJ C171/1.   [98] [1991] OJ C333/1.

[99] Projects are being undertaken in the following areas: informatics, telecommunications, transport, oceanography, materials, environment, meteorology, agriculture and biotechnology, food technology, social sciences, medical research, civil engineering, chemistry, and forestry and forestry products.

[100] On Eureka generally, see Colliard, 'Eureka ou une co-opération technologique européenne' [1988] *RTDE* 1.

[101] Bull-EC 7/8 1985, 2.1.210–2.1.213 and Bull EC 11/1985, 2.1.182

17

Environment

Until the entry into force of the Single European Act, the EEC Treaty contained no provisions conferring on the Community powers to adopt measures, or to enter into agreements, relating specifically to the environment.[1] Although environmental considerations can be traced in some measures adopted before 1970,[2] the creation of a distinct Community policy on the environment dates from a declaration of the Heads of State and Government of the Member States in 1972,[3] and the Environmental Action Programme which followed in 1973.[4] That Programme, and the four which have followed it,[5] though important as political declarations of intent, were not in themselves legal bases for legislative action by the Community.[6] Until 1987, therefore, a legal basis for internal Community measures dealing with the environment had to be found in Article 100 or in Article 235[7] or in a combination of the two.[8] The basis for external

---

[1] Environmental issues of course arise in the work of the ECSC and Euratom, but it is under the EC Treaty that the Communities' environment policy has developed. This Ch. therefore focuses on the provisions of that Treaty and on the practice of the European Community. For an account of the international rules on the environment, see P. W. Birnie and A. E. Boyle, *International Law and the Environment* (Clarendon Press, 1992); P. Sands, *Principles of International Environmental Law* (Manchester University Press, 1995). A convenient collection of the principal environmental agreements is in *Selected Multilateral Treaties in the Field of the Environment* (2 vols.), i (ed. A. C. Kiss) (UNEP, 1983) and ii (eds. I. Rummel-Bulska and S. Osafo) (Grotius, 1991).

[2] e.g., Dir. 67/548 on the approximation of laws, regs. and administrative provisions relating to the classification, packaging, and labelling of dangerous substances ([1967] JO L196/1); Dir. 70/157 on noise levels of motor vehicles ([1970] JO L42/16); Dir. 70/220 on pollutant emissions ([1970] JO L76/1).

[3] *6th General Report* (1972), 8.   [4] See [1973]OJ C112/1.

[5] See [1977] OJ C139/1 (2nd Programme); [1983] OJ C46/1 (3rd Programme); [1987] OJ C328/1 (4th Programme); and [1993] OJ C138/1 (5th Programme).

[6] For accounts of the Community's environment policy see L. Kramer, *EEC Treaty and Environmental Protection* (Sweet & Maxwell, 1990); N. Haigh, *Manual of Environmental Policy: The EC and Britain* (Longman, 1992) (hereinafter 'Haigh, *Manual*'); Sinclair and Corcelle, *The Environmental Policy of the European Communities* (Graham & Trotman, 1989). See also L. Kramer, 'Community Environmental Law—Towards a Systematic Approach' (1991) 11 *YBEL* 151; A. Nollkaemper, 'The EC and International Environmental Protection: Legal Aspects of External Community Powers' [1987] 2 *LIEI* 55; Leenen, 'Participation of the EEC in International Environmental Agreements' [1984] 1 *LIEI* 93; J. Temple Lang, 'The Ozone Layer Convention: A New Solution to the Question of Community Participation in "Mixed" International Agreements' (1986) 23 *CMLRev.* 157; M. Brusasco Mackenzie, 'The Role of the European Communities', in L. Campiglio, L. Pineschi, D. Siniscalco, and T. Treves (Eds.), 'The Environment After Rio: International Law and Economics'.

[7] For a discussion of the use of these legal bases for environment measures, see D. Vandermeersch, 'The Single European Act and the Environmental Policy of the European Economic Community' (1987) 12 *ELRev.* 407.

[8] e.g. Dir. 75/439 on the disposal of waste oils [1975] OJ L194/23.

action was found in the body of internal measures.[9] The Single European Act provided a secure legal framework for the Community's environment policy by inserting into the EEC Treaty a new Title[10] containing three Articles dealing specifically with the environment.[11] These provisions have in turn been amended by the TEU.

LEGAL BASIS OF THE COMMUNITY'S EXTERNAL COMPETENCE

The legal basis for the development of the environmental policy of the Community is now to be found in Article 3(k) and Title XVI of the EC Treaty. Among these provisions, the following are of particular relevance in determining the Community's powers to take action externally in relation to the environment:

(a) Article 3(k), which provides that the activities of the Community include 'a policy in the sphere of the environment', and Article 130r(1) which lists the objectives of that policy. These include preserving, protecting, and improving the quality of the environment; protecting human health; prudent and rational utilization of natural resources; and promoting measures at international level to deal with regional or world-wide environmental problems;

(b) Article 130r(2) which states (among other things) that Community policy on the environment shall be based on the precautionary principle and on the principle that the polluter should pay;

(c) Article 130r(4), which provides that, within their respective spheres of competence, the Community and the Member States shall co-operate with third countries and with the competent international organizations. The arrangements for such co-operation may be the subject of agreements between the Community and the third parties concerned, which shall be negotiated and concluded in accordance with Article 228. This is without prejudice to Member States' competence to negotiate in international bodies and to conclude international agreements;

(d) a Declaration (No. 10) on Articles 109, 130r, and 130y of the EC Treaty, which is annexed to the TEU,[12] and which reads: 'The Conference considers that the provisions of Article 109(5), Article 130r(4), second paragraph, and Article 130y do not affect the principles resulting from the judgment handed down by the Court of Justice in the *AETR* case'; and

[9] On the basis of the principle in Case 22/70 *Commission* v. *Council* [1971] ECR 263 ('the *AETR* case'). See Ch. 3 above, and *The Extent of Community Competence*, below.
[10] Title VII, *Environment*.
[11] Arts. 130r to 130t were not the only bases for Community measures relating to the environment: where a measure had as its principal objective the establishment or functioning of the internal market, Art. 100a (also inserted by the SEA) was the appropriate legal basis.
[12] Which in substance restates a declaration made in the SEA Final Act.

(e) Article 130t, which states that the adoption of protective measures by the Community is not to prevent any Member State from maintaining or introducing more stringent protective measures.

Extent of the Community's Competence

Article 130r(4) provides that the Community and the Member States are to act 'within their respective spheres of competence' in co-operating with third countries and international organizations. Two views are possible of the 'scope' of the Community's 'sphere of competence' in external matters in the area of the environment. On one view, the Community's power to act on the international level is determined by the extent to which legislation has been adopted internally. Thus, if an agreement concerns matters on which Community rules exist, the Community has power to become a party to that agreement to the extent of the internal rules. But if no such rules exist, the Community has no external competence in the matter, and the Member States may act. The historical basis for this analysis is easy to find. Until 1987, the Community had no specific power to adopt measures (let alone conclude agreements) relating to the environment, and the only possible basis for Community participation in environmental agreements was the existence of internal rules which gave rise to external competence on the basis of the principle in the *AETR* case.[13]

The alternative view is that the Community's power to act externally in relation to the environment is to be determined by reference to the provisions of Title XVI, as amended by the TEU. As a result of these amendments, the development of a policy in the sphere of the environment is now one of the Community's tasks,[14] and one of the specified objectives of the Community's environmental policy is the promotion of measures at the international level to deal with environmental problems.[15] An express power to conclude agreements is to be found in Article 130r(4) EC. Together, these provisions amount to an express power to enter into agreements on any matter falling within the scope of the Community's objectives in the area of the environment. In assessing whether the Community may conclude an international agreement, it is thus unnecessary to rely on the *AETR* principle or the doctrines of implied powers. Internal rules may be relevant in determining whether the Community's competence is exclusive or not; but they are not now a prerequisite for the exercise of external competence. Instead, the Community's external competence arises by express conferment in the EC Treaty.

The second view might be regarded as sounder in law, on the basis of the EC Treaty as it now stands. But the practice of the Council to date[16] supports

---

[13] Case 22/70, n. 9 above.   [14] Art. 3(k) EC.   [15] Art. 130r(1) EC.
[16] Under the SEA amendments, and under the TEU.

the former; there have been few occasions[17] when the Community has been allowed to participate in an agreement relating to the environment in the absence of internal rules covering the subject matter of the agreement, or part of it.[18] Indeed, the Council acts approving the conclusion of agreements on the environment almost always describe in detail the internal measures which have given rise to external competence and which thus justify the Community's participation in the agreement. At least one such act, after citing the relevant internal legislation, expressly states that 'it is necessary for the Community *to that extent* to conclude' the agreement in question.[19] Another, again after listing internal measures, notes that the 'conclusion of the convention implies no extension of the exclusive powers of the European Economic Community'.[20] Similarly, declarations of competence[21] submitted by the Community on becoming party to international agreements have described the Community's competence by reference to legislation already adopted within the Community.

Whatever the correct legal analysis, the safe starting point in any assessment of the extent of the Community's competence in the area of the environment is the body of legislation adopted by the Council. Measures adopted under Article 130s EC will be of primary relevance; but measures adopted under other powers in the EC Treaty may also have a bearing on environmental matters and may therefore have to be taken into account in assessing the extent of the Community's competence to enter into a particular agreement.[22]

Nature of the Community's Competence

The plainly expressed intention of Article 130r, in its original and later forms,[23] was to ensure that the Member States could continue to participate in international negotiations and agreements relating to the environment alongside the Community: the mere existence of a power for the Community to act in the

[17] And they are not recent: examples are Community participation in the 1974 Convention for the Prevention of Marine Pollution from Land-based Sources ('the Paris Convention'); the 1976 Convention for the Protection of the Mediterranean ('the Barcelona Convention'). On these, see below, 333.

[18] See Kramer, 'The Single European Act and Environmental Protection: Reflections on Several Provisions in Community Law' (1987) 24 *CMLRev*. 659 at 671 (commenting on the Arts. added by the SEA).

[19] Council Dec. 81/462 ([1981] OJ L171/13) approving the conclusion of the Convention on Long Range Transboundary Air Pollution ('the Geneva Convention'), penultimate preambular para.

[20] Council Dec. 82/461 ([1982] OJ L210/11) approving the conclusion of the Convention on the Conservation of Migratory Species of Wild Animals (the Bonn Convention), penultimate preambular para.

[21] On the legal effect of declarations of competence, see Ch. 6.

[22] e.g., measures adopted under Art. 100a, or measures on research. For examples, see the declarations of competence made by the Community on becoming a party to the Vienna Convention on the Protection of the Ozone Layer ('the Vienna Convention') ([1988] OJ L297/8); the Convention on Biological Diversity ([1993] OJ L309/1; and the Climate Change Convention ([1994] OJ L33/11).

[23] i.e. in the SEA and in the TEU.

area of the environment was not in itself intended to deprive Member States of the power to act. Article 130r(4) thus states that the Community's powers are to be without prejudice to Member States' competence.

It is doubtful, however, whether that provision was intended to have the effect of preserving complete freedom of action by the Member States. In particular, in cases where the Community and the Member States are parties to an agreement, the duty of close co-operation in the external representation of the Community[24] means that an attempt must always be made to reconcile a national position with that being adopted by the Community. Furthermore, Article 130r(4) is not intended to undermine the principle of the primacy of Community law: the Declaration relating to Article 130r(4)[25] states that 'the principles in the judgment handed down in the *AETR* case' are unaffected by the provisions of that Article. In the absence of direct judicial authority, any attempt to summarize a complex and controversial area of the law must necessarily be tentative, but the position is probably as follows:

(a) the Community has power to enter into international agreements on environmental matters, but its competence is not in principle exclusive. Thus it is open to the Community and the Member States to participate together, or separately, in international agreements and negotiations;[26]

(b) however, where the Community has adopted common rules internally to regulate an environmental issue,[27] the Community is alone competent to enter into international agreements which affect such rules or alter their scope. To that extent, Community competence in certain environmental matters is exclusive;[28]

(c) where, however, the internal rules adopted by the Community are in the nature of 'minimum requirements', Article 130t EC has the effect that it remains open to the Member States to participate in agreements relating to the matters covered by such internal rules.[29]

PRACTICE IN RELATION TO THE ENVIRONMENT

Several features of the practice which has developed in this area are worth highlighting. Although they have arisen regularly in agreements on the environment, they are not necessarily unique to such agreements, but are of potentially wider application.

---

[24] See Ch. 6.   [25] See above, 324.

[26] Subject to the duty of close association elaborated by the Court in relation to mixed agreements: see *Opinion 2/91 (Re ILO Convention 170)* [1993] ECR I–1061, and *Ruling 1/78 (Re Draft Convention on the Physical Protection of Nuclear Materials)* [1978] ECR 2151. For a discussion of this duty, see Ch. 6.

[27] Whether on the basis of the powers in Title XVI or on some other Treaty basis (e.g. Art. 100a).

[28] See Case 22/70, n. 9 above.   [29] See *Opinion 2/91*, n. 26 above.

Status of the Community

Some agreements, particularly those relating specifically to Europe or to European issues, provide simply that the European Community may become a party.[30] Others, particularly those adopted under the auspices of the United Nations, do not refer specifically to the Community, but instead provide for participation by States and 'regional economic integration organizations'.[31] A regional economic integration organization ('REIO') is defined in each agreement in similar terms as an organization constituted by sovereign States to which the Member States have transferred competence in respect of matters governed by the agreement, and which has been duly authorized in accordance with its internal procedures to become party to the agreement.[32] This definition clearly encompasses the European Community, which is accordingly entitled to become a party to such agreements. Special conditions attach to the participation of REIOs in environment agreements. The terms of each agreement must, of course, be examined to determine the rights and duties arising under that agreement, but certain common features have emerged.

REIOs are entitled to exercise rights and duties under the agreements 'in matters within their competence'. Where they exercise such rights, the Member States may not exercise their rights, and vice versa.[33] If the agreement envisages decisions by vote, the usual rule is that the REIO may exercise all the votes of its Member States on matters within its competence.[34] On becoming a party, the REIO is required to submit a declaration of its competence in matters covered by the agreement, and to provide further notifications of any significant changes in its competences. Instruments of approval or accession deposited by an REIO do not count separately in calculating whether enough States have become parties to bring the agreement into force.[35] Some agreements provide that an REIO which becomes party to an agreement without its Member States also becoming parties is bound by all the obligations in the agreement.[36]

[30] See, e.g., the Paris Convention, Arts. 22 and 24; the Barcelona Convention, Arts. 24 and 26; the European Wildlife and Natural Habitats Convention, Art. 19(1).

[31] The Convention on the Control of Transboundary Movements of Hazardous Waste and their Disposal ('the Basel Convention') allows for participation by States and 'political and/or economic integration organizations': Arts. 22(1) and 2(20), n. 81.

[32] See Geneva Convention, Art. 14(1); the Vienna Convention on the Protection of the Ozone Layer ('the Vienna Convention'), Art. 1(6); the Basel Convention, Art. 2(20); the Framework Convention on Climate Change ('the Climate Change Convention'), Art. 1(6); the Convention on Biological Diversity, Art. 2; the Bonn Convention, Art. 1(1)(k).

[33] Geneva Convention, Art. 14(2); Vienna Convention, Art. 13(2); Basel Convention, Art. 22(2); Climate Change Convention, Art. 22; Biological Diversity Convention, Art. 34; Bonn Convention, Art. 1(2).

[34] Geneva Convention, Art. 14(2); Vienna Convention, Art. 15; Basel Convention, Art. 24; Climate Change Convention, Art. 18; Biological Diversity Convention, Art. 31.

[35] Vienna Convention, Art. 17(5); Basel Convention, Art. 25(3); Climate Change Convention, Art. 23(2); Biological Diversity Convention, Art. 36(5).

[36] Vienna Convention, Art. 13(2); Basel Convention, Art. 22(2); Climate Change Convention, Art. 22; Biological Diversity Convention, Art. 34.

Mixed Agreements

All the environmental agreements to which the Community is a party are mixed agreements: that is to say, at least one Member State is a party along with the Community. However, many of these agreements, in particular those applying to specific geographical areas within or around Europe, do not provide for the participation of all the Member States, and only those Member States which are specially concerned by the subject matter of the agreement have become parties. Examples include the Barcelona Convention for the Protection of the Mediterranean;[37] the Convention for the Protection of the Rhine;[38] the North Sea Pollution Convention;[39] the Danube Convention;[40] the Elbe Convention;[41] and the North East Atlantic Pollution Convention.[42] The legal effect of those agreements for the Member States which are not parties to them is not easy to determine. In principle, it would seem that to the extent that the agreement related to matters within Community competence, the non-party Member States would in effect be bound as members of the Community. For matters outside Community competence, only those Member States which were parties to the agreement would be bound by its terms. Applying this distinction in practice might not always be straightforward.

For those agreements to which the Community and all the Member States are parties, difficult issues may arise in determining their respective liabilities under the agreement to third States. A few of the agreements[43] which establish dispute settlement mechanisms attempt to deal with this by providing that third States wishing to begin proceedings against one of the Member States of the Community can demand to know whether that Member State, or the Community, or both, are to be regarded as responsible for the performance of the obligations under the agreement. If an answer is not given within a certain time, the third State is entitled to conclude that the Community and the Member State constitute 'one and the same party' for the purposes of applying the dispute settlement provisions. The same applies when the Community and the Member States declare that they are jointly responsible for the performance of obligations under the agreement. Provisions of this kind are not, however, common; the rights and duties of the Community and the Member States towards third States will usually have to be determined on a case-by-case basis in the light of the provisions of the particular agreement.

---

[37] To which the Community is a party along with France, Spain, Italy, and Greece.

[38] The Community is a party along with France, Germany, Luxembourg, and the Netherlands.

[39] The Community is a party along with Germany, Belgium, Denmark, Ireland, the UK, the Netherlands, Sweden and France.

[40] The Community is a party along with Germany and Austria.

[41] The Community is a party along with Germany.

[42] The Community is a party along with Portugal, Spain, and France.

[43] See Rhine Convention, Annex B; Convention on the Conservation of European Wildlife and Natural Habitats, Art. 18.

Dispute Settlement

Many of the agreements in this area establish mechanisms for the settlement of disputes between the parties.[44] The Community, as a party to the agreements, is entitled to make use of these mechanisms on the conditions set out in the particular agreement, and is likewise subject to their jurisdiction. Binding decisions by such mechanisms would, it seems, be part of Community law.[45]

Legal Basis for the Conclusion of Agreements on the Environment

Article 130r(4) EC provides that agreements between the Community and third parties should be negotiated and concluded in accordance with Article 228. Thus, in accordance with the practice in other areas, the Commission will conduct negotiations for Community participation, on the basis of an authorization from the Council, and in consultation with a committee appointed by the Council. In due course, it will be for the Council to authorize the approval of the agreement on behalf of the Community.[46]

Until the SEA, the legal basis for the Community's participation in agreements relating to the environment was Article 235 EEC. From the entry into force of the SEA until the entry into force of the amendments in the TEU, the legal basis for the Community's conclusion of agreements on the environment was Article 130s, and the procedures in that Article were followed. Since the entry into force of the TEU, at least two Articles of the EC Treaty must be cited in the Council act authorizing the conclusion of an agreement by the Community. The appropriate paragraphs of Article 228 have to be cited as the basis for the procedure followed by the Council, and a reference has also to be made to the substantive power which entitled the Community to act. In the acts approving Community conclusion of the Climate Change Convention[47] and acceptance of the Second Amendment to the Montreal Protocol,[48] the legal bases cited were Article 130s(1) and Article 228(3) first subparagraph.[49]

---

[44] See the Barcelona Convention, Arts. 17, 22 and Annex A (n. 17 above); the Vienna Convention, Art. 11 (n. 22 above); the Basel Convention, Art. 20 (n. 31 above); the Climate Change Convention, Art. 14 (n. 22 above); the Wildlife and Natural Habitats Convention, Art. 18; the Biological Diversity Convention, Annex II (n. 22 above).

[45] See Ch. 5.

[46] For a fuller description of the procedure in Art. 228, see Ch. 4.

[47] Dec. 94/69 [1994] OJ L33/11.   [48] Dec. 94/68 [1994] OJ L33/1.

[49] Adoption by qualified majority in the Council after consultation of the Parliament. These decisions are out of line with Council practice in other areas, in not citing the relevant part of Art. 228(2) as the basis for Council action. On this see, further, Ch. 4. It is also arguable that Art. 130r(4) is a more appropriate legal basis than Art. 130s: see above under *Extent of Community competence.* Contrast the practice in the area of development policy, where Art. 130y is cited.

Declarations of Competence

As has been noted, a common condition of Community participation in environmental agreements is that the Community should submit a declaration of competence listing the areas of the agreement in respect of which competence has been transferred to it by the Member States.[50] Where such a declaration of competence is required, the practice is to submit to the depositary of the agreement, when the Community's formal consent to be bound is expressed,[51] a list of Community measures dealing with the matters covered by the agreement. No attempt is made to relate these measures to particular articles of the agreement.

Multilateral Agreements

Agreements on Water Pollution

The Community is a party to the following agreements:

The Paris Convention for the Prevention of Marine Pollution from Land-based Sources. This agreement was opened for signature in June 1974, and the Community became a party in 1975.[52] The Member States are all parties. By a Decision of 22 December 1986, the Council authorized the approval on behalf of the Community of a Protocol amending the Convention so that it covered atmospheric pollution at sea.[53]

The Barcelona Convention for the Protection of the Mediterranean Sea against Pollution. This convention was signed in 1976. The Member States bordering the Mediterranean[54] are parties, as is the Community.[55] The Community has also become a party to the Protocol on dumping from ships and aircraft;[56] the Protocol concerning co-operation in combating pollution caused by hydrocarbons in emergency situations;[57] the Protocol for protection against pollution from land-based sources;[58] and the Protocol for specially protected areas of the Mediterranean.[59]

The Convention on the Protection of the Rhine against Chemical Pollution. The Community is a party[60] to this convention along with the riparian Member States.[61] The Community is also a party to the Additional Agreement,

---

[50] See Ch. 6. See also, Temple Lang, n. 6 above.

[51] i.e. on deposit of the Community's instrument of acceptance or approval. The Declaration of Competence is annexed to the Council act authorizing approval of the agreement. For examples, see n. 22.

[52] Dec. 75/437 ([1975] OJ L194/5).

[53] Dec. 87/57 ([1987] OJ L24/46).

[54] France, Spain, Italy, and Greece.

[55] Dec. 77/585 ([1977] OJ L240/77).

[56] *Ibid.*

[57] Dec. 81/420 ([1981] OJ L162/4).

[58] Dec. 83/101 ([1983] OJ L67/1).

[59] Dec. 84/132 ([1984] OJ L68/38).

[60] Dec. 77/586 ([1977] OJ L240/37).

[61] France, Germany, Luxembourg, and the Netherlands.

signed in Berne on 29 April 1963, concerning the International Commission for the Protection of the Rhine against Pollution.[62]

The Co-operation Agreement on the Management of the Waters of the Danube. This agreement, signed in 1987, provides for co-operation between Germany, Austria, and the Community in the management of the waters of the Danube. The Community became a party in 1990.[63]

Agreement for Co-operation in dealing with Pollution of the North Sea by hydrocarbons and other harmful substances. This agreement, opened for signature in 1983, is the successor to an agreement drawn up in 1969 which dealt with pollution by oil. The 1983 agreement also extends to pollutant or potentially pollutant substances. The Community is a party,[64] along with Germany, Belgium, Denmark, Ireland, the United Kingdom, Norway, Sweden, the Netherlands, and France.

The Convention on the International Commission for the Protection of the Elbe. Germany, the Czech and Slovak Republic and the Community signed this agreement in 1990, and the Community became a party in 1991.[65] This agreement was amended in 1993 to confer international personality on the International Commission for the Protection of the Elbe.

The Co-operation Agreement for the Protection of the Coasts and Waters of the North East Atlantic against Pollution. This agreement was opened for signature in Lisbon in October 1990. The Community,[66] Portugal, Spain, France, and Morocco are parties.

The Helsinki Convention for the Protection of the Baltic Sea. This convention was negotiated in 1974 by the countries bordering the Baltic. It was revised in 1992. Its aim is to limit pollution of the Baltic from land-based sources, dumping and exploitation of the seabed. The Community is a party to the 1974 Convention and the 1992 Convention.[67]

The Community has signed but not become a party to the following agreements:

The Convention for the Protection and Development of the Marine Environment of the Wider Caribbean Region. The Community has signed[68] but not become a party to this convention. The United Kingdom, France, and the Netherlands are parties in respect of their dependent territories' interests in the region.

The Convention for the Protection of the Marine Environment and the Coastal Areas of East Africa. The Community participated in the negotiation of this convention because of its possible effect on Community law applicable in French overseas territories in East Africa. The Council authorized signature of the convention in 1986, but the Community is not yet a party.

---

[62] [1977] OJ L240/48.

[63] Dec. 90/160 ([1990] OJ L90/18).

[64] Dec. 84/358 ([1984] OJ L188/7).

[65] Dec. 91/598 ([1991] OJ L321/25).

[66] [1993] OJ L267/22.

[67] Decs. 94/156 and 94/157 [1994] OJ L73/1 and 19.

[68] COM(83)733 [1984] OJ C5/1.

Agreements on Air Pollution

The Geneva Convention on Long Range Transboundary Air Pollution. This convention was adopted under the auspices of the United Nations Economic Commission for Europe in 1979. It is a framework convention for the development of policies and measures to reduce air pollution. The Community[69] and the Member States are parties to the convention and to a 1984 Protocol[70] on the financing of the programme for monitoring air pollution in Europe. There has so far been no agreement in the Council to Community participation in Protocols on the reduction of sulphur[71] and nitrogen oxide.[72]

The Vienna Convention on the Protection of the Ozone Layer. This convention was opened for signature in Vienna in 1985. The Community and the Member States are parties to the convention and to a Protocol (the Montreal Protocol) on substances that deplete the ozone layer.[73]

The United Nations Framework Convention on Climate Change. This convention was signed at the United Nations Conference on Environment and Development in 1992 in Rio de Janeiro. The objective of the convention is to stabilize the levels of 'greenhouse' gases in the atmosphere. The Community[74] and the Member States are parties.

Agreements for the Protection of Wildlife and Plants

The Community is a party to the following agreements:

The Convention on the Conservation of European Wildlife and Natural Habitats. This convention was drawn up under the auspices of the Council of Europe in 1979. Its aim is the conservation of flora and fauna in their natural habitat. The Community is a party,[75] as are the Member States.

The Convention on the Conservation of Migratory Species of Wild Animals. This convention was negotiated under the auspices of the United Nations Environment Programme in 1979. The Community[76] and the Member States are parties.

The Convention for the Protection of Animals kept for Farming Purposes. This Convention was drawn up under the auspices of the Council of Europe in 1976. It provides for the housing and care of animals kept for farming

---

[69] Dec. 81/462 ([1981] OJ L171/11).   [70] Dec. 86/277 ([1986] OJ L181/1).
[71] The Helsinki Prot.: see the Commission's proposal, COM(87) 67.
[72] The Sofia Prot.: see the Commission's proposal, COM (91) 368.
[73] Dec. 88/540 ([1988] OJ L297/8). See also Dec. 91/690 ([1991] OJ L377/28) on the approval of and amendment of the Montreal Prot. On the difficulties experienced in securing EC participation in the Convention, see Haigh, *Manual*, n. 6 above, at sect. 6.12; and Temple Lang, n. 6 above.
[74] Dec. 94/69 ([1994] OJ L33/11).   [75] Dec. 82/72 ([1982] OJ L38/1).
[76] Dec. 82/461 ([1982] OJ L210/10).

purposes, in particular in intensive stock-farming systems. The Community[77] and the Member States are parties.

The Convention on Biological Diversity. This convention is another product of the 1992 United Nations Conference on Environment and Development. The Community[78] and the Member States are parties.

The Community was not at the time of writing a party to the *Convention on International Trade in Endangered Species of Flora and Fauna* (usually called 'CITES'), although the amendments necessary to allow Community participation have been negotiated, and await the necessary ratifications by other parties to the Convention in order to come into force. The Convention is given effect within the Community by Regulation 3626/82, as amended.[79] The Community has signed, but is not yet a party to the Council of Europe *Convention for the Protection of vertebrate animals for experimental and other scientific purposes.*[80]

Movement of Hazardous Waste

The Basel Convention on the Transboundary Movement of Hazardous Waste. The Community[81] and the Member States are parties to this convention, the purpose of which is to control the movement of certain wastes intended for disposal.[82]

Other Agreements and Arrangements

Provisions on co-operation in relation to the environment are to be found in more general agreements concluded by the Community. Thus, co-operation on the environment is an aspect of the economic co-operation envisaged in the trade and co-operation agreements with Pakistan;[83] the Maghreb countries;[84]

---

[77] Dec. 78/923 ([1978] OJ L323/12). The Convention was amended by a prot. signed in 1992 ([1992] OJ L395/22).

[78] Dec. 93/626 ([1993] OJ L309/1).

[79] Reg. on the implementation in the Community of the Convention on international trade in endangered species of wild flora and fauna ([1982] OJ L384/1), as last amended by Commission Reg. 558/95 ([1995] OJ L57/1). For a discussion of the Reg. and the application of CITES within the Community, see Haigh, *Manual*, n. 6 above, sect. 9.5; Sinclair and Corcelle, n. 6 above, ch. 8.3.

[80] Signed by the EEC in 1987. See also Council Res. dated 24 Nov. 1986 on the signature by the Member States of the European Convention for the Protection of vertebrate animals used for experimental and scientific purposes ([1986] OJ C331/1).

[81] Dec. 93/98 ([1993] OJ L39/1).

[82] See also Council Reg. 259/93 ([1993] OJ L30/1) which provides for the supervision of waste shipments within, into, and out of the Community, and Dec. 90/170 on the acceptance by the Community of the OECD Recommendation on the control of transfrontier movements of hazardous wastes (n. 114).

[83] 1986 Agreement with Pakistan, Art. 3(1)(a) [1986] OJ L108/1.

[84] i.e. Algeria, Morocco, and Tunisia. See the 1978 Agreements with each, Art. 4(1) [1978] OJ L263/1, 264/1, and 265/1 respectively.

the Mashraq countries;[85] Israel;[86] Canada;[87] the countries parties to the General Treaty on Central American Economic Integration;[88] the countries parties to the Charter of the Co-operation Council for the Arab States of the Gulf;[89] the countries parties to the Cartagena Agreement;[90] Argentina;[91] the Baltic States;[92] Albania;[93] China;[94] Macao;[95] Mongolia;[96] India;[97] and Sri Lanka.[98] The agreements with Chile, Mexico, Uruguay, Brazil, and Paraguay[99] also include co-operation on the environment under the general heading of economic co-operation, but they provide in more detail for training programmes, publicity, and information and research.

The Europe Agreements state that co-operation on the environment is 'a priority', and list various fields for action. There is to be co-operation on the transfer of technology, exchange of information, and training, and co-operation within the framework of the European Environment Agency.[100] The EEA Agreement[101] and the Fourth Lomé Convention[102] each contain several articles on the environment, as does the Energy Charter Agreement.[103]

Informal arrangements exist between the Commission and several third

---

[85] i.e. Egypt, Lebanon, Jordan, and Syria. See the 1978 Agreements with each, Art. 4(1) [1978] OJ L266/1, 267/1, 268/1, and 269/1.

[86] 1975 Agreement with Israel, Art. 4(1) [1975] OJ L136/3.

[87] 1976 Agreement with Canada, Art. III(1) [1976] OJ L260/2.

[88] i.e. Costa Rica, El Salvador, Guatemala, Honduras, and Nicaragua: 1986 Agreement, Art. 3(1)(e) [1986] OJ L172/1.

[89] i.e. the United Arab Emirates, Bahrain, Saudi Arabia, Oman, Qatar, and Kuwait: 1986 Agreement, Art. 1(1)(b) [1989] OJ L54/1.

[90] i.e. Bolivia, Colombia, Ecuador, Peru, and Venezuela: 1984 Agreement, Art. 1(2)(c) [1984] OJ L153/1.

[91] 1991 Agreement with Argentina, Art. 4(2)(i) [1990] OJ L295/66.

[92] 1992 Agreement with Estonia, Art. 15(2); 1992 Agreement with Latvia, Art. 15(2); 1992 Agreement with Lithuania, Art. 15(2) [1992] OJ L404/1, 10, and 19 respectively.

[93] 1992 Agreement with Albania, Art. 15(2) [1992] OJ L343/1.

[94] 1985 Agreement with China, Art. 10 [1985] OJ L250/1.

[95] 1992 Agreement with Macao, Arts. 4 and 11 [1992] OJ L404/27.

[96] 1993 Agreement with Mongolia, Art. 9 [1993] OJ L41/45.

[97] 1994 Agreement with India, Arts. 4(3) and 17 [1994] OJ L223/25.

[98] Agreement with Sri Lanka, Arts. 4(3) and 15 ([1995] OJ L85/32).

[99] 1991 Agreement with Chile, Arts. 2(1)(g) and 4 [1991] OJ L79/1; 1991 Agreement with Mexico, Arts. 2(1)(g) and 31 [1991] OJ L340/3; 1992 Agreement with Uruguay, Arts. 3(1)(g) and 6 [1994] OJ L94/1; 1992 Agreement with Brazil, Arts. 3(1)(g) and 18 [1992] OJ L163/12; and 1992 Agreement with Paraguay, Arts. 3(2)(d) and 6 [1992] OJ L313/71.

[100] On the Europe Agreements, see Ch. 20. Provisions on co-operation on the environment are in the Europe Agreements with Hungary, Art. 79 ([1993] OJ L347/1); Poland, Art. 80 ([1993] OJ L348/1); Romania, Art. 81 ([1994] OJ L357/1); Bulgaria, Art. 81 ([1994] OJ L358/1); the Slovak Republic, Art. 81 ([1994] OJ L359/1); and the Czech Republic, Art. 81 ([1994] OJ L360/1). Art. 80 of the Hungary Agreement and Art. 82 of the Romania Agreement provide for co-operation in water management.

[101] EEA Agreement, Arts. 73–75 and Art. 78 ([1994] OJ L1/1).

[102] Fourth ACP–EEC Convention, Arts. 33–41 ([1991] OJ L229/1).

[103] Energy Charter Agreement, Art. 19 ([1994] OJ L380/1). The Energy Charter Agreement is being applied provisionally by the Community and a majority of the Member States.

countries about administrative co-operation in environmental matters. These are unpublished and take the form of exchanges of letters.[104]

Unilateral Acts

The *OCT* Decision[105] provides in detail for co-operation in relation to the environment. Under the *TACIS* Regulation, due account must be taken of environmental considerations in designing and implementing programmes.[106] Projects and co-operation measures under the *PHARE* Regulation should be undertaken in particular in areas such as environmental protection.[107] Environmental considerations figure prominently among the objectives of the financial and technical assistance available to developing countries under the Community's unilateral development policy measures.[108]

Community Participation in International Organizations

As well as in bodies established by some of the agreements listed above,[109] the Community participates in the work of several international organizations and bodies which are concerned with the protection of the environment and with other aspects of the Community's environment policy. Among the more important are the United Nations Economic Commission for Europe, the OECD, the Commission for Sustainable Development, and the United Nations Environment Programme.[110]

An exchange of letters[111] dated 30 September 1958 and 7 October 1958 between the Commission and the *Economic Commission for Europe* provides for exchange of documentation, appropriate representation at meetings of technical bodies on each side, regular joint study of future work programmes, and consultation on questions of common interest. The Community participates in the work of the Economic Commission for Europe as an observer, without a right to vote.

The *OECD* is active in several aspects of environmental law and policy.[112] There are close institutional links between the Community and the OECD.[113]

---

[104] Such arrangements exist with Canada (signed 6 Nov. 1975: SEC(75)2132); Switzerland (signed 12 Dec. 1975: SEC(75)4081); Japan (signed 1 July 1977: SEC(77)645); and Norway (signed 2 Feb. 1981: SEC(81)244).

[105] Dec. 91/482 ([1991] OJ L263/1) Arts. 11–18.

[106] Reg. 2053/93, Art. 4(3) ([1993] OJ L187/1).

[107] Reg. 3906/89, Art. 3(1) ([1989] OJ L375/11).   [108] See Ch. 18.

[109] e.g. the International Commission for the Protection of the Rhine (established by the Rhine Convention) and the International Commission for the Protection of the Elbe (established by the Elbe Convention).

[110] On the Community's status in these bodies, see Ch. 7.

[111] See *Relations between the European Community and International Organizations* (Commission, 1989), 42 and 43.

[112] See Birnie and Boyle, n. 1 above, 71–2.   [113] See Ch. 7, 193–4.

An OECD recommendation on the control of transfrontier movements of hazardous wastes has been accepted by the Community.[114]

The Community also participates in the work of the *Commission on Sustainable Development*.[115]

The Community has non-voting observer status in the *United Nations Environment Programme*. An exchange of letters dated 15 and 21 June 1983 provides for the strengthening of co-operation between the Commission and UNEP. Such co-operation is to take the form of exchanges of documents, Community participation in UNEP meetings on the usual terms, regular contacts and exchange of information between the two institutions, consultation on problems of common interest, and liaison through the Commission delegation in Nairobi.

The Community also participates in the International Conference on the Protection of the North Sea. Belgium, Denmark, France, Germany, the Netherlands, Sweden, and the United Kingdom also participate.

[114] [1990] OJ L92/52.
[115] See *27th General Report*, points 897 and 898; *1994 General Report*, points 495 and 1054.

18

Development and Assistance Policies

Until the entry into force of the TEU, the Community Treaties contained no powers expressly relating to development co-operation, but, in practice, development considerations featured in many measures adopted under other Articles of the EEC Treaty.[1] Thus the generalized system of preferences was adopted under Article 113 as a commercial policy instrument,[2] as were decisions relating to the conclusion by the Community of international commodity agreements.[3] Some fisheries agreements (adopted under Article 43 EEC) were in effect measures of development aid,[4] as were many association agreements and trade and economic co-operation agreements. Assistance to certain dependent territories of the Member States (the 'overseas countries and territories') was based on a Council decision under Part IV of the EEC Treaty which in substance followed the pattern of the assistance to the ACP countries. Where no other legal basis was adequate or appropriate, development or assistance policy measures were adopted on the basis of Article 235 EEC.

Provisions relating expressly to development co-operation policy were inserted in the EC Treaty by the TEU, and these are now the principal legal bases for action in this area. The powers relating to the common commercial policy, fisheries, and association agreements may, as formerly, have to be relied on for the adoption of certain measures which have developmental aims. But, in view of the specific powers conferred on the Community in this area, there is now much less scope for adoption of such measures on the basis of Article 235 EC. That Article is of continuing relevance mainly in respect of assistance

---

[1] For discussion of aspects of the European Community's development co-operation policy, see P. J. G. Kapteyn and P. Verloren van Themaat, *Introduction to the Law of the European Communities* (2nd edn., Kluwer, 1989) ch. XI.3; D. Vignes, 'Communautés européennes et pays en voie de développement' 210 *Hague Recueil* (1988 III) 223–400 (a general survey of development co-operation under Lomé III and the legal and institutional structure of the Community's aid to developing countries); F. Snyder, 'European Community Law and Third World Food Entitlements' (1989) 32 *Germ.YBIL* 87; J. Lebullenger, 'La renovation de la politique communautaire du développement' (1994) *RTDE* 631. For recent surveys, see HL Select Committee on the European Communities, 21st Rep. (1992–3), *EC Development Aid* (HL Paper 86) and *27th Report* (1992–3), *EC Aid and Trade Policy* (HL Paper 123).

[2] On the legal basis for adoption of a generalized system of preferences, see Case 45/86, *Commission* v. *Council* [1987] ECR 1493.

[3] On the legal basis for conclusion of commodity agreements, and the relationship between the common commercial policy and development policy, see *Opinion 1/78 (Re the draft Agreement on Natural Rubber)* [1979] ECR 2871.

[4] See Ch. 10.

to the countries of Central and Eastern Europe and the States of the former Soviet Union.

LEGAL BASIS OF THE COMMUNITY'S EXTERNAL COMPETENCE

Since the entry into force of the TEU, the activities of the Community include 'a policy in the sphere of development co-operation'.[5] Title XVII EC comprises five Articles which provide the legal mechanism for the implementation of that policy. Article 130u sets out the objectives of the Community's development policy, which are to 'foster the sustainable economic and social development of the developing countries, and more particularly the most disadvantaged among them; the smooth and gradual integration of the developing countries into the world economy; and the campaign against poverty in the developing countries'. The Community's policy in this area is to contribute to the general objective of developing and consolidating democracy and the rule of law, of respecting human rights and fundamental freedoms.[6] The Community and the Member States are to comply with commitments and take account of objectives approved in the context of the United Nations and other competent international organizations.

Article 130v provides that the Community must take account of the objectives referred to in Article 130u in the policies that it implements which are likely to affect the developing countries. Article 130w provides a legal mechanism for achieving the Community's objectives in this area, and states that the Council may adopt measures which may take the form of multiannual programmes. The European Investment Bank (EIB) is to contribute, under the terms laid down in its statute, to the implementation of such measures. The provisions of Article 130w are not to 'affect co-operation with the African,

---

[5] Art. 3(q) EC.

[6] See also Art. J.1(2) of Title V TEU, which provides that the development and consolidation of democracy and the rule of law and respect for human rights and fundamental freedoms are among the objectives of the Common Foreign and Security Policy of the EU. Arts. 130u(2) EC and J.1(2) TEU represent the crystallization in legal form of the policy on human rights expressed prior to the TEU in instruments which were not legally binding. The most significant of these was the Res. of the Council and the Member States meeting within the Council on Human Rights, Democracy, and Development of 28 Nov. 1991 (Bull. EC 11-1991, point 1.3.67). That Res. establishes a clear link between human rights and democracy and balanced and sustainable development. The Community and its Member States undertake to give high priority to a 'positive approach' in the form of measures which stimulate respect for human rights and encourage democracy. In the event of grave and persistent human rights violations or the serious interruption of the democratic process, the Community and its Member States will consider appropriate responses in the light of the circumstances, guided by objective and equitable criteria. Since 1992 it is standard practice to include references to human rights in the preamble and in the first substantive Art. of all co-operation or association agreements. The Art. recalls that co-operation between the Community and the third country is founded on respect for human rights, which forms an essential element of the agreement. See, e.g., the Community's Agreement with India ([1994] OJ L223/23) and the Europe Agreement with Bulgaria ([1994] OJ L358/1).

Caribbean and Pacific countries in the framework of the ACP-EEC Convention'.[7]

Article 130x requires the Member States and the Community to co-ordinate their policies on development co-operation and consult each other on their aid programmes, including in international organizations and during international conferences. They may undertake joint action.[8] Member States are to contribute if necessary to the implementation of Community aid programmes. The Commission may take any useful initiative to promote such co-ordination.

Article 130y provides that, within their respective spheres of competence, the Community and the Member States are to co-operate with third countries and international organizations. The arrangements for Community co-operation may be the subject of agreements between the Community and third parties which are to be negotiated and concluded in accordance with Article 228. The Community's powers are without prejudice to Member States' competence to negotiate in international bodies and conclude international agreements. A declaration in the Final Act of the TEU relating to Article 130y states that 'the provisions of Article 130y do not affect the principles resulting from the judgment handed down by the Court in the *AETR* case'.

Extent of Community Competence

The objectives of Article 130u are wide ranging, encompassing political as well as purely humanitarian or economic considerations, and the boundaries of action which is within the scope of Article 130u are hard to draw. For example, an agreement may contain provisions on human rights, the fight against drugs, culture, and intellectual property, all of which, on one view, may be aimed at promoting the economic and social development of one of the parties, and thus fall within Title XVII. On the other hand, however, it may be argued that provisions of that kind either fall within the scope of other provisions of the EC Treaty (such as Article 113 or 128) or else fall outside the powers of the Community altogether. The point is not academic: the scope of the Community's development policy is at the time of writing before the Court in Case C–268/94, in which Portugal is challenging the Council's decision to conclude a partnership and co-operation agreement with India on the basis of Article 130y EC. The Portuguese argument is that the areas covered by the agreement go beyond the scope of application of Article 130y since they extend to matters such as human rights, and co-operation in matters of energy, tourism, culture, intellectual property, and prevention of drug abuse. The Council's

---

[7] That is, the arrangements established under the Fourth Lomé Convention. On Lomé IV, see Ch. 20.

[8] In French 'actions conjointes', and thus, strictly speaking, not 'joint action' ('action commune') in the technical sense of Title V TEU. But the Council could, acting under Title V, co-ordinate the development policies of the Member States by a 'joint action' under Art. J.3 TEU.

defence is based on the argument that the aim of the co-operation in these areas is to contribute to the development of the third country and therefore that they form part of the objectives of the Community's policy in the sphere of development co-operation. The Court's answer will clearly be important in shaping the Community's future development policy.

The Community's development policy is aimed at assisting 'developing countries'. The scope of the powers in Title XVII therefore depends to a great extent on what is meant by 'developing country', but there is no definition of that term in the Treaty, nor have any clear criteria yet emerged in the practice of the Community. Indeed, although certain criteria[9] have been established by UNCTAD, the World Bank, and the OECD, no internationally recognized definition of a developing country exists. While the Community's development policy takes account of the criteria established by other international organizations, the determination of the category of developing countries will rest largely on political considerations and the circumstances of a particular case.[10] A distinction has emerged in the Community's practice between assistance to the countries of Central and Eastern Europe and the States of the former Soviet Union (the so-called 'countries in transition') and development aid generally. As will be seen,[11] Article 235 EC continues to form the basis for assistance to the 'countries in transition', which suggests that they do not fall within the scope of Title XVII.

It is expressly provided that the Community's development assistance under Title XVII is not to affect co-operation with the ACP countries in the framework of the ACP–EEC Convention. The effect of this is to preserve the structures established under the Lomé Convention as the sole mechanism for development assistance to the ACP States. In particular, decisions relating to the Community's aid to these States will continue to be based on Article 238 EC, and funding for such assistance will remain outside the Community budget.[12]

The Community's development policy includes internal measures adopted by the Community institutions (such as regulations on food aid or emergency aid), and agreements concluded between the Community and third countries. The Community is empowered to enter into international agreements on development matters 'within its sphere of competence'. It does not seem from the prac-

---

[9] e.g. the gross domestic product per head of population, share of manufacturing production in the gross domestic product, and literacy rate of the inhabitants.

[10] Some of the Community's agreements expressly recognize that the country concerned is to be regarded as a developing country: see the Agreement with the Yemen Arab Republic, Art. 4 ([1985] OJ L26/1).

[11] See 348 ff. below.

[12] The Final Act to the TEU contained a Declaration on the European Development Fund (the financial mechanism under the Lomé Convention) which stated that 'the European Development Fund will continue to be financed by national contributions in accordance with the current provisions'. On the relationship between the Community budget and funding to the ACP countries under Lomé, see Case C–316/91 *Parliament v. Council* [1994] ECR I–625 (the 'EDF case').

tice of the Council that this 'sphere of competence' is limited to matters on which internal rules or measures have been adopted. It appears that the Community has competence to enter into any agreement the aim and content of which fall within the scope of Article 130u, whether internal rules have been adopted on the matters covered by the agreement or not.[13]

Nature of Community Competence

The wording of Title XVII implies that the Community's powers in relation to development aid are not intended to supersede the powers of the Member States, but to co-exist with them. Thus, Article 130u(1) states that the Community's policy in the sphere of development co-operation is to be 'complementary' to the policies pursued by the Member States. Article 130u(3) envisages that the Community and the Member States will undertake commitments in the context of the United Nations and other competent international organizations. Article 130x indicates that Community and Member States' policies are to continue together: they are to be co-ordinated, and the Community and the Member States are to consult each other on their aid programmes. Finally, Article 130y states that the Community's competence to enter into international agreements is without prejudice to Member States' competence to negotiate in international bodies and to conclude agreements.

Two recent judgments of the Court of Justice have underlined that the Community's competence in relation to development policy is not exclusive. In Joined Cases C–181/91 and C–248/91 *Parliament* v. *Council and Commission*,[14] the Court considered the nature of the Community's competence in the sphere of humanitarian aid and noted that 'the Community's competence is not exclusive, and in consequence, the Member States are not prevented from exercising their competences in this respect collectively, within or outside the Council'.[15] In Case C-316/91 *Parliament* v. *Council*,[16] the Court confirmed that its conclusion about humanitarian aid applies more generally in the field of development aid, stating that 'the Community's competence in that field (development aid) is not exclusive. The Member States are accordingly entitled to enter into commitments themselves *vis-à-vis* non-Member States, either collectively or individually, or even jointly with the Community'.[17] It referred specifically to Title XVII, in particular Article 130x, as corroborating that analysis. The Court held that, according to the terms of the Lomé Convention, the Community and the Member States were jointly responsible to the ACP States, and enjoyed shared competence, for the obligations undertaken, including the financial undertakings. In consequence, the Member States were entitled to finance the objectives set out in the Convention outside the Community bud-

---

[13] Contrast the practice of the Council in relation to the environment: Ch. 17.
[14] [1993] ECR I–3685 (the 'Bangladesh case').   [15] *Ibid.*, paragraph 16.
[16] N. 12 above.   [17] *Ibid.*, at para. 26.

get and in accordance with different procedures, associating the Community institutions as they saw fit.

Thus the Community and the Member States each have competence to enter into international agreements and to adopt measures in relation to development co-operation. This shared competence[18] may be described as parallel or concurrent in nature, in that the exercise of Community competence does not of itself necessarily deprive the Member States of their competence to act in relation to the same matters. In the area of development policy, the Member States may enter into commitments collectively, rather than within the framework of the Community, or they can enter into commitments individually.

There are, however, two qualifications to these principles:

Once the Community enters into an international agreement, the Member States are precluded from doing anything capable of affecting that agreement or altering its scope. The exact limits of the duty imposed on the Member States in that context cannot be laid down in the abstract but depend on the agreement in question . . . [In] the field of development aid to third States, the risk that action undertaken by the Member States may have adverse consequences on action undertaken by the Community is much less than it is in other areas such as that of social policy.[19]

Secondly, as has been noted, Article 130y, which envisages that the Member States should be able to continue to negotiate and conclude international agreements, is not to affect the principle in the *AETR* case.[20] Thus, to the extent that the Community has adopted common rules on matters within the scope of the development policy in Title XVII, the Member States are precluded from entering into agreements which would affect those rules or alter their scope. The likelihood, of course, is that in the area of development policy, 'common rules' in the *AETR* sense will be rare.

PRACTICE OF THE COMMUNITY

This part focuses on those aspects of the Community's practice in the area of development and assistance policy which do not fall within the scope of the Communities' powers in relation to fisheries, the common commercial policy, or association agreements.[21]

---

[18] See, further, Ch. 3.

[19] Case C-316/91, n. 12 above, Opinion of Jacobs A.G., at para. 49.

[20] See Declaration No. 10 to the EC Treaty in the Final Act of the TEU. On the *AETR* case (Case 22/70, *Commission* v. *Council* [1971] ECR 263), and the meaning of 'common rules', see Ch. 3.

[21] On these, see Chs. 10 (Fisheries), 12 (Common commercial policy), and 20 (Association agreements).

Legal Basis and Procedures

The legal basis for the adoption of internal Community measures the aim and content of which fall within the scope of Title XVII EC is Article 130w(1). The Council acts in accordance with the co-operation procedure. The legal basis for the conclusion of agreements falling within the scope of Title XVII is Article 130y, in conjunction with Article 228(2), first sentence, and (in most cases) Article 228(3), first subparagraph. Thus, for most agreements, the Council decides on conclusion by qualified majority, after consulting the Parliament. The assent of the Parliament is required if the agreement falls into one of the categories in Article 228(2), second sentence.[22]

Agreements

Development considerations form an important element of many of the agreements concluded by the Communities. Association agreements and trade and economic co-operation agreements, which can be said to contribute to the Community's development policy in the wider sense, are considered elsewhere,[23] as are international commodity agreements[24] and agreements on fisheries.[25]

The Community is a party to a bilateral convention with the United Nations Relief and Works Agency for Palestinian Refugees (UNRWA) concerning aid to refugees in the countries of the Near East.[26] This provides for aid in the form of contributions in kind or in cash, extending over a three-year period for use under the UNRWA education, health, and feeding programmes.

Unilateral Measures

The Community's Generalized System of Preferences (GSP) for developing countries is described in the context of the common commercial policy. The OCT Decision, which forms the basis of the Community's assistance to certain of the Member States' dependent territories, is considered in Chapter 20.

Food Aid

The Community's food aid policy[27] and food aid management are governed by Regulation 3972/86,[28] and are administered by the Commission. The food aid

---

[22] On this, and the procedures for conclusion of agreements generally, see Ch. 4.

[23] On association agreements, see, further, Ch. 20. On trade and economic co-operation agreements, see Ch. 12.

[24] See Ch. 7.   [25] Especially so-called 'commercial' agreements: see Ch. 10.

[26] Council Dec. 94/13 ([1994] OJ L9/16).

[27] For accounts of the Community's food aid programmes in recent years, see *24th General Report* (1990), points 808–13; *25th General Report* (1991), points 1011–16; *26th General Report* (1992), points 950–5; and *27th General Report* (1993), points 830–4; *1994 General Report*, point 966.

[28] [1986] OJ L370/1. The implementing rules for this Reg. are laid down in Reg. 1420/87

programme relating to cereal products is partly based upon international obligations flowing from the Food Aid Convention.[29] General measures relating to
food aid policy have been based on Article 235, whereas specific measures are
usually based on the relevant measure dealing with the common organization
of the market for the product being supplied.

Humanitarian Aid

The European Community's Office of Humanitarian Aid (ECHO) was established in 1991 as a special department of the Commission.[30] It administers a
programme of emergency aid, which has been used to provide assistance for
refugees; and for relief of suffering caused by natural disasters and civil war.[31]
This programme is covered by lines in the EC budget although it has not yet
been given a specific legal framework. There is close co-operation with the Non-
Governmental Organizations active in the area of development.

Financial Assistance

The Community's financial assistance covers the Mediterranean countries,
Central and Eastern European countries, the States of the former Soviet Union
(FSU), and developing countries in Asia and Latin America. The loans and
guarantees provided to these countries are of three types: (i) Community macro-
financial assistance loans, which are granted in particular to Central and
Eastern European countries to supplement IMF operations; (ii) Community
guarantees for loans granted by the EIB and Euratom for micro-economic projects (Mediterranean countries, Central and Eastern Europe, developing countries in Asia and Latin America) and (iii) Community guarantees for commercial
transactions, which are guarantees for loans granted by private financial institutions to finance the supply of food and medicines (granted to Central and
Eastern European countries and the FSU). A Guarantee Fund has now been
established to cover risks related to loans and guarantees granted to third countries or for projects executed in third countries.[32] The purpose of the Fund is

([1987] OJ L136/1) which lays down the list of countries and organizations eligible for food aid
operations and in Commission Reg. 2200/87 ([1987] OJ L204/1), laying down general rules for
the mobilization of the products to be supplied by the Community as food aid.

[29] The Convention currently in force is the 1986 Convention ([1986] OJ L195 /16) which,
together with the Wheat Trade Convention ([1986] OJ L195/5), constitutes the International
Wheat Agreement. Both Conventions have been accepted by the Community.

[30] *25th General Report*, n. 27 above, point 1017.

[31] For examples of emergency aid disbursed in recent years see the *23rd General Report* (1989)
points 890 and 891; *24th General Report*, n. 27 above, point 814; *25th General Report*, n. 27 above,
points 1017–20; *26th General Report*, n. 27 above, point 962–6; and *27th General Report*, n. 27 above,
points 836–42; *1994 General Report*, n. 27 above, points 971–84.

[32] Council Reg. 2728/94 ([1994] OJ L293/1). A reserve for guarantees has also been entered in
the Financial Perspectives and the budget; the Guarantee Fund draws its resources from this reserve.

to reduce the exposure of the Community budget to financial risk resulting from guarantees covering loans to third countries. The Regulation is based on Articles 235 EC and 203 Euratom. Financial management of the instrument has been entrusted to the EIB.[33]

The EC Investment Partners Facility was developed by the Commission in 1988 as part of its economic co-operation policy with developing countries in Asia, Latin America, and the Mediterranean. It was given a formal legal framework in Regulation 319/92,[34] which provided for the implementation for a three-year trial period of the EC Investment Partners financial instrument (ECIP). Its overall purpose is to promote investment in Mediterranean, Asian, and Latin American countries by private-sector operators, particularly in the form of joint ventures with EC firms. Four kinds of financing facility are offered: grants for the identification of projects and partners; interest-free advances for feasibility studies; capital injections; and interest-free advances for training, technical assistance or management expertise.[35] Projects eligible for financing are to be selected on the basis of the anticipated soundness of the investment and the quality of the promoters, and the contribution to development in terms of criteria identified in the Regulation (including impact on the local economy; creation of local jobs; transfer of technology and know-how; and impact on the environment).[36] Countries eligible for assistance are the developing countries of Latin America, Asia, and the Mediterranean region which have previously benefited from Community development co-operation measures or which have concluded regional or bilateral co-operation or association agreements with the Community.[37] The Commission is to implement the instrument.

Aid to Mediterranean States

The Community's aid to Mediterranean States which are not members of the EC is based on a series of trade and co-operation agreements and financial protocols. Two regulations are of particular interest in the application of the Community's policy towards these States. Implementation of the financial protocols is governed by Regulation 1762/92,[38] which aims at co-ordinating the different types of financing available under the protocols (grants, special loans, contributions to the constitution of risk capital, and loans from the EIB's resources for structural adjustment programmes). Implementation is in the hands of the Commission.

Regulation 1763/92[39] provides for financial co-operation in respect of all Mediterranean non-member countries, in addition to any assistance they receive under the financial protocols. It establishes a programme worth 230m ECU, to run from 1992 to 1996, intended to supplement the measures foreseen in the

---

[33] *Ibid.*, Art. 6.　　　　　[34] [1992] OJ L35/1.　　　　　[35] *Ibid.*, Art. 2
[36] *Ibid.*, Art. 6.　　　　　[37] *Ibid.*, Art. 7.　　　　　[38] [1992] OJ L181/1.
[39] [1992] OJ L181/5.

financial protocols.[40] The aims of the measures under the Regulation are the implementation of operations of regional interest (that is, operations extending beyond a single country); co-operation with regard to the environment; and the encouragement of investment, by means of risk capital on behalf of European operators for the financing of partnership with operators in the region. Co-operation may also concern demographic matters, in particular those relating to population growth. The cultural dimension of development is to be taken into account.[41] Financial co-operation under the Regulation is to be available to all Mediterranean non-member countries with which the Community has concluded association or co-operation agreements,[42] and is to consist of risk capital, loans, and interest rate subsidies on EIB loans.

The Occupied Territories

Council Regulation 1734/94[43] lays down the detailed arrangements and rules for administering financial and technical assistance for the Occupied Territories under a five-year programme running from 1994 to 1998. The aim of the programme is to aid the sustainable economic and social development of the Territories.[44] The priority areas for projects and measures are infrastructure, production, urban and rural development, education, health, the environment, services, foreign trade, the setting up of institutions for public administration, and the advancement of human rights and democracy.[45]

Asia and Latin America

Regulation 443/92[46] provides for financial and technical assistance to, and economic co-operation with, the developing countries in Asia and Latin America which are not signatories to the Lomé Convention and do not benefit from the EC's co-operation policy with the Mediterranean States. Co-operation under the Regulation is to be additional to assistance from the Member States, and is to involve financial and technical development assistance and economic co-operation. The Community attaches the greatest importance to the promotion of human rights, support for the process of democratization, good governance, environmental protection, trade liberalization, and strengthening the cultural dimension, by means of dialogue on political, economic, and social issues conducted in the mutual interest.[47] The aim of Community development and co-operation policies is human development.[48] Increased support is to be given to countries most committed to the principles of human rights and democracy. Fundamental and persistent violations of human rights and democratic

---

[40] *Ibid.*, Art. 1(1). [41] *Ibid.*, Art. 3(1). [42] *Ibid.*, Art. 1(2).
[43] [1994] OJ L182/4. [44] *Ibid.*, Art. 1. [45] *Ibid.*, Art. 2(1).
[46] [1992] OJ L52/1. [47] *Ibid.*, Art. 1. [48] *Ibid.*, Art. 2.

principles may lead to alteration or suspension of co-operation.[49] Assistance under the Regulation is to be administered by the Commission.[50]

Financial and technical assistance under the Regulation is targeted primarily on the poorest sections of the population and the poorest countries in the regions.[51] Priority is afforded to developing the rural sector and improving the level of food security. Protection of the environment and natural resources, and sustainable development, are long-term priorities. Special attention must be given to measures to combat the fight against drugs. The human and cultural dimensions are to be kept in view. The Community's aid is to favour operations which have an impact on the structure of the economy and on the development of sectoral policies and institutions. Regional co-operation is a priority for financial and technical assistance, particularly in fields such as co-operation on the environment, the development of inter-regional trade, research, training, rural development, and energy.[52] Assistance to the more advanced countries is to focus on certain priority areas, including the environment and natural resources, regional co-operation, the spread of democracy, and the fight against drugs.[53]

Economic co-operation is to help the developing countries to build up their institutional capacity so as to create an environment more favourable to investment and development and to enable them to make the most of the opportunities offered by the growth in world trade.[54] Economic co-operation is to include three sectors: the improvement of scientific and technological potential and of the economic, social, and cultural environment in general by training schemes and the transfer of know-how; improvement of the institutional structure; and support for undertakings, by trade promotion, training, and technical assistance schemes.[55] Regional co-operation is to be regarded as an important sector, in particular with respect to industrial ecology, trade, research and training and energy.

ASSISTANCE TO CENTRAL AND EASTERN EUROPE AND THE STATES OF THE FORMER SOVIET UNION

Central and Eastern Europe

The Community's response to the changes in Central and Eastern Europe in the late 1980s included the establishment of trade and commercial co-operation agreements, now being transformed into association agreements,[56] and the granting of economic assistance through unilateral Community measures. These countries have not been regarded by the Community and the Member States as developing countries, but rather as 'countries whose economies are in tran-

---

[49] [1992] OJ L52/1 Art. 2.   [50] *Ibid.*, Art. 15(1).   [51] *Ibid.*, Art. 4.
[52] *Ibid.*, Art. 5.   [53] *Ibid.*, Art. 6.   [54] *Ibid.*, Art. 7.   [55] *Ibid.*, Art. 8.
[56] The 'Europe Agreements'. See further, Ch. 20.

sition'. Title XVII of the EC Treaty has therefore not replaced Article 235 EC[57] as the legal basis for unilateral measures to assist these countries.

Agreements

The trade and economic co-operation agreements and the association agreements between the Communities and the countries of Central and Eastern Europe are described elsewhere.[58]

Unilateral Community Measures

The PHARE (Poland–Hungary Assistance for the Restructuring of the Economy) programme is based on Regulation 3906/89.[59] The programme originally applied only to Hungary and Poland but it has subsequently been extended to other countries.[60] Its purpose is to support the process of economic and social reform under way in these countries, in particular by financing or participating in the financing of projects aimed at economic restructuring.[61] Such projects should be undertaken in particular in the areas of agriculture, industry, investment, energy, training, environmental protection, trade, and services, and should be aimed in particular at the private sector.[62] Aid is in general to be in the form of grants.[63]

The States of the FSU

The Communities' response to the break-up of the Soviet Union initially took the form of technical assistance and food and medical aid.[64] The GSP has been extended to certain countries of the FSU and, pending the entry into force of the Partnership and Co-operation Agreements, trade preferences have been granted under Regulations 848/92[65] and 3917/92.[66]

The TACIS programme, based on Regulation 2053/93,[67] aims to support the newly independent States of the FSU in their efforts to move from centrally planned to market economies. The beneficiary States are Armenia, Azerbaijan, Belarus, Georgia, Kazakhstan, Kyrgyzstan, Moldova, Russian Federation,

---

[57] And in some cases, Art. 203 Euratom.

[58] Chs. 12 (Common commercial policy) and 20 (Association Agreements).

[59] [1989] OJ L375/11.

[60] The Reg. currently applies to 11 countries, namely Poland, Hungary, Bulgaria, the Czech Republic, Slovakia, Albania, Romania, Estonia, Latvia, Lithuania, and Slovenia. See Regs. 2698/90 ([1990] OJ L257/1); 3800/91 ([1991] OJ L357/10); 2334/92 ([1992] OJ L227/1); and 1764/93 ([1993] OJ L162/1).

[61] Reg. 3906/89, n. 59 above, Art. 3(1).   [62] *Ibid.*, Art. 3(2).

[63] *Ibid.*, Art. 5.

[64] For summaries of Community action, see *26th General Report*, n. 27 above, points 771–88; *27th General Report*, n. 27 above, points 671–83; *1994 General Report*, n. 27 above, points 806–14.

[65] [1992] OJ L89/1.   [66] [1992] OJ L396/1.   [67] [1993] OJ L187/1.

Tajikistan, Turkmenistan, Ukraine, Uzbekistan, and Mongolia.[68] These States may benefit from TACIS 'in so far as' they do not benefit from financial and technical assistance under Regulation 443/92.[69] The programme takes 'the form of technical assistance for the economic reform under way in the beneficiary States for measures aimed at bringing about the transition to a market economy and thereby reinforcing democracy'.[70] It may cover the cost of supplies required in support of the technical assistance, and also costs related to the preparation, implementation, monitoring, and evaluation of the projects carried out.[71] Technical assistance is to be concentrated in the following areas: human resources development (including training, restructuring of public administration, and legal assistance); enterprise restructuring and development (including the development of small and medium-sized enterprises, conversion of defence industries, and restructuring and privatization); infrastructures (transport and telecommunications); energy, including nuclear safety; and food production, processing, and distribution.[72] Community assistance is to take the form of grants. Indicative programmes for the period from 1 January 1993 to 31 December 1995 were established for each of the recipient States. Action programmes showing a list of the main projects to be financed are drawn up annually.[73] The programme is implemented by the Commission.[74]

International Organizations

The European Community is a party to the agreement establishing the European Bank for Reconstruction and Development.[75] The Community is a member organization of the FAO, and of several commodities organizations.[76]

The Community is an observer in numerous organizations which are active in the fields of development co-operation and aid policy. Among the more important are the Regional Economic Commissions of ECOSOC, UNCTAD, the UNHCR, International Fund for Agricultural Development (IFAD), and United Nations Industrial Development Organization (UNIDO). Administrative co-operation between the Community and these organizations, in the form of exchanges of information and expertise, is secured by arrangements agreed between the Commission and the organizations.[77] There is an

---

[68] [1993] OJ L187/1 Art. 1 and Annex I.

[69] Ibid., Art. 2. For Reg. 443/92, see n. 46 above.

[70] Reg. 2053/93, n. 67 above, Art. 4(1). [71] Ibid., Art. 4(1) and (2).

[72] Ibid., Art. 4(3) and Annex II. [73] Ibid., Art. 6(1) and (2). [74] Ibid., Art. 7.

[75] See Council Dec. 90/674 [1990] OJ L372/1 on the conclusion of the Agreement establishing the EBRD. For a description of the aims and operation of the EBRD, and the terms of Community participation in its work, see Ch. 7, 187–9.

[76] See Ch. 7, 180 ff.

[77] These arrangements typically provide for regular exchanges of documents and information, and exchanges of views about matters of common interest. See Relations between the European Community and International Organizations (Commission, 1989) for the arrangements with the UNHCR (66–7) and UNIDO (172–4).

agreement between the EEC, the Member States, and the International Development Association.[78]

The Community has links with regional bodies such as the Association of South East Asian Nations, Organization of American States, the League of Arab States, and the Council of Arab Economic Unity.[79]

[78] [1979] OJ L43/13.
[79] The Co-operation agreement between the CAEU and the Communities is reproduced in [1982] OJ L300/23.

19

Sanctions

The nature of sanctions means that the subject matter of this Chapter is different from that of most of the other chapters in this Part. Those chapters are in general concerned with agreements with third countries and international organizations. Sanctions involve the interruption or reduction of relations with a third country and are intended to force or encourage that country to take or desist from a course of action. It is an area where there is an overlap between foreign policy and action in the commercial field; it is an area where the policy reason for action falls outside Community competence but the means of achieving that policy include measures falling within Community competence. The policy reason for action is a matter of foreign or security policy but the means of achieving it will include the interruption or reduction of economic relations.

The TEU amended the EC Treaty to include provisions expressly enabling the European Community to impose sanctions against third countries. Those provisions, Articles 228a and 73g, built on the procedure that had become established over the preceding decade. That procedure sought to reconcile the desire of the Member States to ensure that sanctions were imposed uniformly throughout the Community as quickly as possible while at the same time not encroaching on matters that fell within the competence of the Member States. It also sought to reconcile the desire of the Member States to retain control over matters of traditional foreign and security policy with the exclusive competence of the Community in relation to the common commercial policy.

Before the TEU the procedure that was adopted was for the Community and its Member States meeting within European Political Co-operation to agree to the imposition of sanctions. Political Co-operation was formalized in Article 30 of the Single European Act and proceeded by consensus. Thus at this stage unanimity was preserved. The Council would then adopt a regulation under Article 113 preventing, *inter alia*, the import of goods from and the export of goods to the third country in question. At the same time a Decision of the Representatives of the Governments of the Member States meeting within the Council would sometimes be adopted dealing with coal and steel products on the basis that Article 113 does not cover such products.[1] Member States would adopt their own measures for matters which clearly fell outside the common commercial policy, for example the imposition of an arms embargo, restrictions on the provision of financial services, and freezing the assets of nationals or residents of the country concerned.[2] In practice, the issue would also have been considered in most cases by the United Nations Security Council which has the power to adopt resolutions requiring the imposition of sanctions.[3]

While the procedure had advantages in that it separated the foreign-policy justification for action, which fell outside Community competence, from the means of action for achieving that policy where the means adopted fell within Community competence, the use of Article 113 was not without difficulties. These difficulties centred principally on two arguments: first, whether the action involved could properly be described as being in furtherance of the common commercial policy and, secondly, whether the action proposed fell within the scope of Article 113.

So far as the first difficulty is concerned, it was argued that the interruption of trade relations was not a commercial policy objective; rather it was an objective of foreign or security policy. Although there is force in this argument, the more generally held view is that, where the action taken is interference with trade flows, that action properly falls within the common commercial policy.[4]

The second difficulty arose from doubts about the scope of Article 113. As discussed in Chapter 12, there was a long running dispute about whether Article 113 applied to services, in particular transport services. The Council did not wish to prejudice its position in connection with this, but there needed to be balanced against this consideration the desire of the Member States urgently to adopt the measure in question. The inclusion of other legal bases in addition to Article 113 would lead to delay because of the need to consult the Parliament or comply with the co-operation procedure. This was a serious problem, particularly in the case of Iraq, where the first set of measures needed to be adopted

---

[1] No measures have been adopted under the Euratom Treaty. To the extent that Community measures have included nuclear products they have been included within the measures adopted pursuant to Art. 113 and now Art. 228a. Following the decision of the ECJ in *Opinion 1/94* [1994] ECR I–5267 on the extent to which measures adopted under the EC Treaty can include ECSC products a separate decision dealing with such products is less likely to be necessary. On Decisions of the Representatives of the Governments of the Member States see Ch. 23, 405.

[2] The UK has implemented Security Council resolutions in respect of matters falling within the common commercial policy as well as matters falling outside it, in reliance on Art. 234 EC. In *R. v. Searle, R. v. KCS Products Ltd., R. v. Borjanovic* and *R. v. BYE Ltd.* (*The Times*, 27 Feb. 1995) the English CA held that Art. 234 EC operated to prevent the Community from impeding the UK's performance of its obligations under the UN Charter, that is its obligations to comply with a mandatory resolution of the Security Council.

[3] See n. 19 below on the desirability of such a resolution where there is an international agreement to which the State concerned and the Community are parties.

[4] In *R. v. Searle, R. v. KCS Products Ltd., R. v. Borjanovic* and *R. v. BYE Ltd.*, n. 2 above, the English CA accepted the validity of Regs. 1432/1992 and 990/1993 made under Art. 113 imposing sanctions against Serbia and Montenegro.

in August when the Parliament was not sitting and when the timescale involved meant that there was no time to request a special sitting of the Parliament. Consequently, some sanction regulations adopted under Article 113 included services.[5]

To overcome these difficulties Article 228a was inserted into the Treaty of Rome by the TEU to provide a specific legal base for the imposition of sanctions. However, the position prior to the coming into force of Article 228a is not of academic interest only, since some of the sanction measures in force at present were adopted under the old procedure.[6]

PRESENT BASIS FOR COMMUNITY ACTION

Article 228a EC provides–

Where it is provided, in a common position or in joint action adopted according to the provisions of the Treaty on European Union relating to the common foreign and security policy, for an action by the Community to interrupt or reduce, in part or completely, economic relations with one or more third countries, the Council shall take the necessary urgent measures. The Council shall act by a qualified majority on a proposal from the Commission.

The Article envisages two stages. First, it envisages that a common position or joint action will have been adopted according to the provisions of the Treaty relating to common foreign and security policy, the second pillar of the Treaty on European Union.[7] Therefore as a first stage the Council will adopt, by a CFSP Decision, a common position or joint action providing for action by the Community to interrupt or reduce economic relations with one or more third countries. The second stage is for the Community to take the action provided for by a measure adopted under Article 228a.

The imposition of sanctions will usually also involve restrictions on the movement of capital and on payments. Although Article 228a is broad enough to include such restrictions, a provision has been included in the Treaty Chapter on capital and payments, Article 73g. That Article provides: 'If, in the cases provided for in Article 228a, action by the Community is deemed necessary, the Council may, in accordance with the procedure provided for in Article 228a, take the necessary urgent measures on the movement of capital and on payments as regards the third countries concerned.' Therefore, if the measure includes restrictions on capital movements or payments, the measure will include Article 73g in the Treaty base.[8]

---

[5] In *Opinion 1/94*, n. 1 above, the ECJ rejected the relevance of these precedents in determining whether Art. 113 applies to trade in services.

[6] Although Art. 228a constitutes a *lex specialis*, there may be exceptional cases where the use of another Art. is appropriate. See 357 below.

[7] See Ch. 24.

[8] See, e.g., Reg. 2471/94 [1994] OJ L266/1.

Article 73g is different from Article 228a in that it goes on to provide, in paragraph (2), that Member States may, for serious political reasons and on grounds of urgency, take unilateral measures against a third country with regard to capital movements and payments. The Commission and the other Member States are to be informed of such measures by the date of their entry into force and the Council may, acting by a qualified majority, decide that the Member State concerned should amend or abolish the measures it has taken. The reason for this provision is that it may be necessary for the Member State to take immediate action to prevent the removal of financial assets from its jurisdiction.

Article 73g is expressed to be without prejudice to Article 224. That Article provides that Member States are to consult each other with a view to taking together the steps needed to prevent the functioning of the common market being affected by measures which a Member State may be called upon to take in the event of serious internal disturbances affecting the maintenance of law and order, in the event of war, serious international tension constituting a threat of war, or in order to carry out obligations it has accepted for the purpose of maintaining peace and international security. That Article remains in force and, in appropriate cases, one or more Member States could take action in accordance with it.[9]

Provisions of Article 228a

'*Where it is provided, in a common position or in joint action adopted according to the provisions of the Treaty on European Union relating to the common foreign and security policy, for an action by the Community*'—There is a need for a prior decision in accordance with the pillar of the Treaty dealing with common foreign and security policy. This replaces the former procedure of a decision in European Political Co-operation. The procedure that has been adopted has been for there to be a common position under Article J.2.[10] In practice, the CFSP measure is often adopted on the same day as the Community measure. However, the latter measure recites the former, thereby respecting the logic that the former is adopted first.

'*to interrupt or to reduce, in part or completely, economic relations with one or more third countries*'—This power is clearly wider in scope than Article 113. It is now clear that there is power to impose economic sanctions going beyond restrictions on trade

---

[9] Art. 228a is not expressed to be subject to Art. 224. The power of the Member States to take unilateral action relying on Art. 224 is before the ECJ in Case C–120/94 *Commission* v. *Greece*, which concerns unilateral action taken by Greece prohibiting trade with the former Yugoslav Republic of Macedonia. Although Art. 224 has been used in the past for collective action by the Member States (e.g. under Art. 224 Member States agreed to take national action to implement a ban on the export of all goods except food and medicine to Iran following the seizure of the US embassy in Tehran), the use of the Art. for collective action by the Member States is now less likely in view of the development of CFSP.

[10] See, e.g., 94/672/CFSP [1994] OJ L266/10.

in goods or services directly related to trade in goods. In addition, the question whether sanctions can properly be regarded as part of the common commercial policy does not arise when a sanctions measure is based on Article 228a. The Article covers services, including transport services.[11] The Article is also wide enough to include the termination or suspension of economic agreements between the EC and the third country concerned.[12] Although it does not expressly so provide it can be used to suspend, relax, or lift sanctions.[13] The Article has been used for measures that go beyond the prohibition of imports and exports of goods or the provision of services. The Article has been used to make provision in respect of performance bonds where this has been required by a Security Council Resolution.[14]

It would seem, following the Opinion of the Court of Justice in *Opinion 1/94*, that a separate decision of the Representatives of the Governments of the Member States meeting within the Council will not be required in all cases. In that case the Court of Justice advised that an agreement which included ECSC products could fall within the common commercial policy under Article 113. By parity of reasoning, it would seem that a measure adopted under Article 228a could include ECSC products, but probably not deal exclusively with such products.[15]

Since the Article refers to economic relations it could not be used to impose an arms embargo or to sever amateur sporting or cultural ties. That would need to be done by the Member States themselves or, in appropriate cases, action under other provisions of the EC Treaty. In addition, a common position could be defined under Article J.2 of the CFSP pillar of the Treaty on European Union.

'*the Council shall take the necessary urgent measures*'—The measures in question will usually be regulations since they are directly applicable and therefore can come into effect without the need for implementing measures in the Member States. However, there is no reason why, in an appropriate case, a directive or a decision should not be adopted. Article 73g enables the Council to take the necessary urgent measures on the movement of capital and on payments. When Article 73g is used, the Monetary Committee established under Article 109c is also involved.

---

[11] The Art. would seem to be wide enough to cover areas of economic relations which remain within Member States' competence.

[12] While the Art. could be used in respect of an agreement to which the EC is a party, it could not form the legal basis of action for terminating or suspending an agreement to which the ECSC or Euratom was a party. An instrument under the Treaties governing those Communities would be needed.

[13] See, e.g., Reg. 2543/94 discontinuing sanctions against Haiti: [1994] OJ L271/1.

[14] See 358–9 below.

[15] See Ch. 23, 403. But see n. 12 above for the need for a dec. under the ECSC Treaty where the ECSC is a party to an agreement. Depending on the circumstances, a dec. of the representatives of the Governments of the Member States meeting within the Council may be needed where the Member States of the ECSC are parties to the agreement.

In cases of urgency, the written procedure contained in Article 8.1 of the Council's Rules of Procedure can be used for the adoption of the common position or joint action and/or the Community measure.

'*the Council shall act by a qualified majority on a proposal from the Commission*'— Since the Council acts by qualified majority, it is possible for a Member State to be outvoted. Consensus is preserved by the prior action under the CFSP pillar. There is no requirement to involve the Parliament. The justification for this is that, in practice, there will be no time to do so given the need for urgent action. Under the procedure that applied before the coming into force of the Article the Parliament was not consulted.

There may, in the future, be cases where the Community may want to impose a form of sanctions at a time or in a manner that fell outside the scope of Article 228a but within Community competence.[16] Given the wide scope of Article 228a and the fact that it would seem to constitute a *lex specialis*, that is unlikely to happen in practice but, if it were to do so, it would seem to be possible to use another Treaty Article. However, it is most likely that the Member States would agree that the two stage procedure in Article 228a should apply and that a common position should first be adopted under Article J.2 of the CFSP pillar.

Effect on Existing Agreements

The power in Article 228a must be exercised consistently with international law. This means that the Community must act consistently with its obligations under agreements to which it and the country concerned are parties. The agreements in question can include bilateral agreements between the Community and the country concerned and multilateral agreements to which both are contracting parties, such as the Agreements annexed to the World Trade Organization Agreement, in particular the GATT. As the Community enters into an increasing number of bilateral agreements, and as more countries become parties to multilateral agreements, so this will become an increasingly important and potentially difficult issue. In some cases the Community will want to suspend or terminate bilateral agreements or rely on exceptions in multilateral agreements. It is beyond the scope of this book to consider how international law would apply generally.[17] However, the way the Community has acted in the former Yugoslavia and Haiti illustrates how the Community has dealt with the matter.

---

[16] This would include where the test of urgency is not satisfied. However, the Council has, in practice, taken a fairly relaxed view of urgency, see e.g. Reg. 1733/94 [1994] OJ L182/1 on performance bonds in respect of the embargo against Serbia and Montenegro.

[17] See P. J. Kuyper, 'Trade Sanctions, Security and Human Rights and Commercial Policy' in M. Marescau (ed.), *The European Community's Commercial Policy after 1992: The Legal Dimension*, (Kluwer Academic Publishers, 1993).

RECENT PRACTICE

This section considers the practice of the Community since 1990[18] and looks at the action the Community has taken against Iraq, Libya, Yugoslavia, and Haiti and in respect of Unità. Each case is different, reflecting the different problems each case presented, but running through them is a common thread. The foreign policy issues are considered by the Community and its Member States in political co-operation or under the CFSP pillar of the TEU. The matter is also considered by the United Nations Security Council which adopts resolutions.[19] Where the action is within the scope of Article 228a those are, in practice, implemented in the Community by a Community measure. That includes a ban on imports to and exports from the territory concerned, sometimes of a particular product (e.g. petroleum and petroleum products) and sometimes all products, and a prohibition on the provision of services, in particular air services. After the coming into force of the TEU the measures adopted include a prohibition on financial services and a freeze on assets. Exceptions are usually included for medical supplies and foodstuffs and supplies for humanitarian purposes, subject to controls to prevent diversion.

The Community measure usually contains a provision giving it a wide territorial application. The general practice is for it to apply within the territories to which the Community Treaties apply, including their air space, and in any aircraft or vessel under the jurisdiction of a Member State, and to any person elsewhere who is a national of a Member State and any body elsewhere which is incorporated or constituted under the law of a Member State.[20]

It has become the practice for a regulation to be adopted dealing with performance bonds in order to prevent the State concerned negating the effect of sanctions by claiming under such bonds. It becomes particularly important when sanctions are lifted in whole or in part . While a freeze on payments is in

[18] The Community imposed sanctions against the USSR (Reg. 596/82 [1982] OJ L72/15) in reaction to its interference in the Polish crisis of 1981–2 and Argentina (Reg. 877/82 and ECSC Dec. 82/221 [1982] OJ L1 and 3) during the Falklands War in 1982. For an introduction see Kuyper, 'Community Sanctions against Argentina: Lawfulness under Community and International Law' in O'Keeffe and Schermers (eds.), *Essays in European Law and Integration* (Kluwer, 1982). Sebastian Bohr, 'Sanctions by the United Nations Security Council and the European Community' (1993) 4 *EJIL* 256 and the literature there referred to.

[19] Although it is the practice of the Community and the Member States to act only where there is a resolution of the UN Security Council this is not a requirement of the TEU and in appropriate cases it would be possible for the Community to act in the absence of such a resolution. The advantage of such a resolution is that it can enable the Community to act in a way that is inconsistent with the terms of agreements to which it and the State concerned are parties. This is because Art. 25 of the UN Charter requires its Members to accept and carry out dec.s of the Security Council and, by virtue of Art. 103 of the Charter, the obligations arising under the Charter override those arising under other agreements. The Community is not itself a member of the UN but all the Member States are.

[20] See, e.g., Art. 11 of Reg. 990/93 [1993] OJ L102/14. See Ch. 3 67 ff, on the territorial scope of the EC Treaty.

force the State concerned would not be able to receive payment under a performance bond but there is a real risk that it would be able to do so once the restrictions on payments are relaxed. It has also been the practice to adopt a separate decision dealing with products within the ECSC Treaty on the basis that the EC Treaty does not cover trade in such products. However, following the decision of the Court of Justice in *Opinion 1/94*[21] such a decision will not be needed unless coal and steel products are dealt with specifically.[22]

Iraq

Iraq invaded Kuwait on 2 August 1990. On the same day the United Nations Security Council adopted Resolution 660(1990) condemning the Iraqi invasion and requesting the immediate and unconditional withdrawal by Iraq of its troops from Kuwait. On 4 August the Community and its Member States meeting in political co-operation stated that they would work for, support, and implement a Security Council resolution to introduce mandatory and comprehensive sanctions. On 6 August the United Nations Security Council adopted Resolution 661(1990) imposing an economic, trade, finance, and arms embargo. Two days later, on 8 August, the Council adopted Regulation 2340/90/EEC preventing trade as regards Iraq and Kuwait.[23] That Regulation, adopted under Article 113, prohibited the introduction into the Community of all commodities and products originating in, or coming from, Iraq or Kuwait and the export to those countries of all products originating in, or coming from, the Community. It prohibited all activities or commercial transactions the object or effect of which was to promote the export of products from Iraq or Kuwait, the sale or supply of products to persons in Iraq or Kuwait and any activity the object or effect of which was to promote such sales or supplies. On the same day the representatives of the Governments of the Member States meeting within the Council adopted a decision to the same effect dealing with products covered by the ECSC Treaty.[24] Both the Regulation and the Decision recite the decision of the Community and its Member States which had been taken in Political Co-operation.

Regulation 2340/90 has been amended on four occasions. The first was by Regulation 3155/90[25] which extended the restrictions on trade to include the provision of non-financial services with the object or effect of promoting the economy of Iraq or Kuwait. The prohibition included air services but not postal or telecommunication services nor medical services necessary for the operation of existing hospitals. It also excluded from the sanctions regime the carrying out of commercial transactions and the provision of services to Kuwaiti bodies controlled and recognized by the legitimate Government of Kuwait.

---

[21] N. 1 above.   [22] See Ch. 23.   [23] [1990] L213/1.
[24] 90/414/ECSC [1990] OJ L213/3.   [25] [1990] OJ L304/1.

Following the liberation of Kuwait from Iraq the Council adopted Regulation 542/91[26] lifting the prohibitions contained in Regulations 2340/90 and 3155/90 as regards Kuwait. In 1991 the Security Council adopted two further resolutions which required amendments to the Regulations adopted by the Community. These resolutions were implemented by Regulations 811/91[27] and 1194/91[28] amending Regulations 2340/90 and 3155/90.

On 7 December 1992 the Council adopted Regulation 3541/92, the performance bonds regulation.[29] The Regulation gives effect to paragraph 29 of United Nations Security Council Resolution 687(1991). It seeks to prevent Iraq being able to take advantage of obligations owed to it under performance bonds. On the lifting of restrictions on payments it might, in the absence of specific provision, have been able to claim under those bonds thereby negating to some extent the effect of the sanctions that had been imposed. The aim of the Regulation was to create uniform rules that would apply throughout the Community. The Regulation is based on Article 235. The justification for the use of this Article is set out in the recitals as being to avoid distortion of competition which would flow from different provision in different Member States.

The Community's legislation does not include a prohibition on the provision of financial services or the freezing of assets. This was left to Member States' own legislation.

Libya

On 21 January 1992 the United Nations Security Council adopted Resolution 731(1992) calling upon Libya to remove all support for international terrorism and to deliver up the persons suspected of the Lockerbie bombing. On 31 March the Security Council adopted Resolution 748(1992) imposing a selective trade embargo on arms and services against Libya to take effect if Libya failed to comply with Resolution 731. Libya failed to comply with that Resolution. The Community and its Member States meeting in political co-operation expressed their strong support for the measures decided upon by the Security Council and agreed to have recourse to a Community instrument to ensure uniform implementation throughout the Community of certain of the measures decided upon by the Security Council, that is the measures relating to air transport, but not the arms embargo. The latter was outside Community, competence and was therefore a matter for the Member States' own legislation rther than a Community measure. On 14 April 1992 the Council adopted Regulation 945/92.[30] Unlike the measures adopted against Iraq this measure was primarily concerned with transport. It required Member States to deny permission to any aircraft to take off from, land in, or overfly their territory if the aircraft was destined to land in or had taken off from Libya. There was an exception when

---

[26] [1991] OJ L60/5.   [27] [1991] OJ L82/50.   [28] [1991] OJ L115/37.
[29] [1992] OJ L361/1.   [30] [1992] OJ L101/53.

the particular flight had been approved on grounds of significant humanitarian need by the Committee set up by the United Nations. The activities of all Libyan Arab Airlines offices were prohibited. The Regulation went on to prohibit the supply or provision, directly or indirectly, of any aircraft or aircraft components to Libya, any engineering and maintenance servicing of Libyan aircraft or aircraft components, any certification of air-worthiness for Libyan aircraft, payment of new claims against existing insurance contracts for Libyan aircraft, and any new insurance for Libyan aircraft.

The Regulation was adopted on the basis of Article 113 but, following the Opinion of the Court of Justice in *Opinion 1/94*,[31] it is doubtful whether it was adopted on the correct Treaty basis. In fact the Commission, in its arguments in that case, had referred to the practice of the Council of including measures relating to transport in sanctions instruments as justification for the use of Article 113 for agreements relating to transport services generally.[32] However, the Court said that the practice of the Council was not capable of derogating from the rules of the Treaty and, consequently, could not create a precedent binding on the institutions of the Community concerning the choice of the correct legal basis.

Regulation 945/92 has been replaced by Regulation 3274/93 adopted under Article 228a.[33] That Regulation expands the scope of the Community's sanctions against Libya following a further Security Council Resolution adopted in view of the persistent non-compliance by Libya with the earlier Resolutions. The Regulation goes beyond air services to include a more general prohibition on trade in goods with and the provision of services to Libya.

On the same day the Council adopted Regulation 3275/93[34] prohibiting the satisfying of claims with regard to contracts and transactions the performance of which was affected by the Security Council Resolutions. Its terms are similar to those of Regulation 3541/92 relating to Iraq, but following the coming into force of Article 228a it was adopted under that Article.

Yugoslavia

The sanctions regime that applies to the former Yugoslavia is more complicated than that which applies to Iraq and Libya for three reasons:

(1) the former Yugoslavia was a party to agreements with the Community and was a beneficiary under preferential trading rules;
(2) the former Yugoslavia broke up into a number of separate States and the Community needed to treat them differently; and
(3) there was a particular need to prevent the diversion of goods that would undermine the sanctions regime.

[31] [1995] 1 CMLR 205. [32] See Ch. 12, 269–70, on the issue of Art. 113 and services.
[33] [1993] OJ L295/1. [34] [1993] OJ L295/4.

The Member States and the Community had entered into a Co-operation Agreement with Yugoslavia which came into force on 1 April 1983.[35] It contained provisions relating to economic, technical, and financial co-operation, and trade and social matters. Article 60 provided that it was concluded for an unlimited duration. The Article enabled either Contracting Party to denounce the Agreement by notifying the other and the Agreement would cease to apply six months after the date of such notification. At the same time the Member States of the ECSC had entered into an agreement relating to coal and steel products.[36]

As part of their call for compliance with a cease-fire agreement reached in October 1991, the Community and its Member States meeting in political co-operation announced their decision to terminate the Co-operation Agreement if the cease-fire agreement was not observed. Since it was not, in the event, observed the Community took steps to bring the Agreement to an end and to suspend the benefit Yugoslavia enjoyed under it with immediate effect. This was done by a package of measures adopted on 11 November 1991. By a decision of the Council and the representatives of the Governments of the Member States meeting within the Council[37] the application of the Co-operation Agreement and the Agreement on coal and steel products was suspended with immediate effect. The justification, both political and legal, for this was described in recital 3 of the decision as being that the pursuit of hostilities and their consequences on economic and trade relations constituted a radical change in the conditions under which the Agreements were concluded, calling into question their application. It was considered possible, as a matter of international law, to suspend the Agreements with immediate effect on this basis and thereby avoid the delay involved in relying on denouncing the Agreement under Article 60.

On the same day the representatives of the Governments of the Member States adopted a decision[38] denouncing the Agreement between the Member States of the ECSC and Yugoslavia and on 25 November the Council adopted a similar decision[39] denouncing the Agreement between the EEC and Yugoslavia. The reason for the delay in denouncing the latter Agreement was the need to obtain the assent of the European Parliament. Its assent was required because the legal basis for the decision was Article 238, the legal basis for the adoption of the Agreement.

Also on 11 November the Council adopted a regulation and the representatives of the Governments of the Member States adopted a decision[40] suspending the trade concessions granted by or in pursuance of the Co-operation

---

[35] [1983] OJ L.41/2. [36] [1983] OJ L41/113.

[37] Dec. 91/586/ECSC, EEC [1991] OJ L315/47.

[38] Dec. 91/587/ECSC [1991] OJ L315/48.

[39] Dec. 91/602/EEC [1991] OJ L325/23.

[40] Reg. 3300/91 [1991] OJ L315/1 and Dec. 91/588/ECSC [1991] OJ L315/49.

Agreement and the Agreement on coal and steel products. The political and legal justification for doing so was, as with the suspension of the Agreements, the change in conditions from those applying when the Agreements were entered into brought about by the pursuit of hostilities and their consequences on economic and trade relations.

Special provision needed to be made for the import of textiles from Yugoslavia to prevent Yugoslavia gaining a benefit over other countries which export textiles to the Community but whose exports are subject to restrictions. The Council accordingly adopted Regulation 3301/91[41] establishing arrangements for imports of certain textiles from Yugoslavia.

Yugoslavia was a beneficiary of the Community's scheme of generalized tariff preferences for 1991. By Council Regulation 3302/91 and a decision of the representatives of the Governments of the Member States, 91/589/ECSC,[42] Yugoslavia ceased to benefit from that scheme from the date of publication of the Regulation and the Decision respectively in the Official Journal.

After the break up of Yugoslavia into a number of republics, the Community and the Member States recognized certain of those republics as independent States. In addition, as the conflict developed, it was no longer possible to treat all the parts of the former Yugoslavia in the same way. It was therefore appropriate to maintain normal relations with certain republics whilst imposing sanctions against others.

The process started in December 1991. By Regulation 3567/91/EEC[43] the Council adopted trade provisions, which were equivalent to those contained in the Co-operation Agreement which had been terminated by the 11 November package of measures, applicable to Croatia, Slovenia, Bosnia-Herzegovina, and Macedonia. At the same time the benefits of the 1991 generalized tariff preferences were restored to those States by Regulation 3587/91/EEC.[44] In due course these benefits were extended to Montenegro. In 1992 there was a serious deterioration in the situation, particularly in Bosnia-Herzegovina. The President of the Republic of Bosnia-Herzegovina called on the international community to assist his country against the intervention of Serbia and Montenegro in the internal affairs of the republic. In May 1992 the Community and the Member States agreed in political co-operation that measures needed to be taken to dissuade Serbia and Montenegro from further violating the integrity of Bosnia-Herzegovina and to induce them to co-operate in the restoration of peace and dialogue in the region. At the same time the Security Council adopted Resolution 757(1992) establishing an economic embargo on Serbia and Montenegro. On 1 June the Council adopted Regulation 1432/92[45]

[41] [1991] OJ L315/3.   [42] [1991] OJ L315/46 and 50.
[43] [1991] OJ L342/1.   [44] [1991] OJ L341/1.
[45] [1992] OJ L151/4. See also Dec. 92/285 [1992] OJ L151/20 dealing with ECSC products. Both measures were amended and have been repealed by Reg. 990/93 and Dec. 93/235. See 364 below.

prohibiting trade with those countries. It prohibited imports from and exports to those countries and the provision of non-financial services, subject to certain exceptions relating to medical products and foodstuffs, goods being transhipped through those countries and the activities related to the peace-keeping bodies in the republics.

On the same day Montenegro was removed from the list of countries benefiting from the series of measures that had been adopted to replace the benefits contained in the Co-operation Agreement.[46]

The situation deteriorated further in 1993 and on 26 April the Council adopted Regulation 990/93.[47] This strengthened the embargo against Serbia and Montenegro and repealed Regulation 1432/92 and two Regulations, 2655/92 and 2656/92, which had made provision to prevent goods being diverted in breach of the sanctions regime.

The situation changed in 1994. The Bosnian Serbs refused to accept the settlement accepted by the other Bosnian parties but the authorities of the Federal Republic of Yugoslavia (Serbia and Montenegro) supported it. The Security Council adopted two resolutions. The first, Resolution 942(1994), reinforced and extended the measures imposed with regard to areas of Bosnia-Herzegovina under the control of Bosnian Serb forces; the second, Resolution 943(1994), suspended certain elements of the embargo on Serbia and Montenegro. These measures were implemented under Articles 228a and 73g. First there were decisions under Article J.2. of the CFSP pillar and then regulations under the EC Treaty. Decision 94/672/CFSP[48] was in broad terms and provided: '[e]conomic and financial relations with those parts of the territory of the Republic of Bosnia-Herzegovina under the control of the Bosnian Serb forces will be reduced in accordance with the relevant provisions of Resolution 942(1994) adopted by the United Nations Security Council on 23 September 1994.' The Decision was implemented by the Council by Regulation 2471/94[49] adopted under Articles 228a and 73g. It is much broader than earlier sanctions regulations and, in accordance with the wide scope of the Articles, covers economic and financial activities, including a freeze on assets.

Decision 94/673/CFSP[50] covered Resolution 943(1994) and was implemented by Council Regulation 2472/94[51] which amends Regulation 990/93/EEC by suspending, in part, certain of its provisions relating to air and ferry services.

As had been the case with Iraq and Libya a regulation, Regulation 1733/94,[52] dealing with performance bonds has been adopted in the same terms as the regulations relating to those States.

---

[46] Reg. 1433/92 [1992] OJ L151/7.
[47] [1993] OJ L102/14.   [48] [1994] OJ L266/10.   [49] [1994] OJ L266/1.
[50] [1994] OJ L266/11.   [51] [1994] OJ L266/8.   [52] [1994] OJ L182/1.

Haiti

Following the military take-over of Haiti after the election of Jean-Bertrand Aristide as president, the United Nations Security Council adopted Resolution 841(1993) obliging all States to restrict trade with Haiti. The Resolution expressly provided that the restriction on trade should apply notwithstanding any rights or obligations conferred or imposed by any existing international obligation. This was relevant to the Community since Haiti was a party to the Fourth ACP–EEC Convention[53] and it was necessary for any Community measure to override Haiti's rights under that Convention.

The Community imposed sanctions against Haiti by adopting two measures. The first was Council Regulation 1608/93/EEC[54] adopted on 24 June 1993 under Article 113 which introduced an embargo in respect of petroleum products. It recited the fact that the Security Council had decided that the restrictions on trade should apply notwithstanding any existing agreements. The recital states that 'therefore the fourth ACP–EEC Convention, to which the Community and Haiti are parties, does not pose an obstacle to the implementation of the . . . Security Council decision'. The view was taken that no other action was needed to suspend Haiti's rights under the Convention.

The second measure adopted by the Community was an ECSC decision of the representatives of the Governments of the Member States meeting within the Council of 30 May 1994[55] prohibiting trade with Haiti in products covered by the ECSC Treaty. In addition to the usual exception for products required for essential humanitarian needs the decision contained an exception for products exported to Haiti in response to requests of President Aristide and also to products in transit to other destinations where the product was carried by regularly scheduled maritime shipping lines.

Regulation 1608/93 had a somewhat unstable history. It was suspended on 13 September 1993 when it seemed that progress was being made towards normalization of the political situation in Haiti[56] and reactivated and amended when the process of normalization ran into difficulties[57] a few weeks later.

In order to put further pressure on the military authorities the Security Council extended the sanctions regime to include a prohibition on air services and an embargo on trade with Haiti. The resolution concerned was implemented in the Community by Regulation 1263/94,[58] adopted under Article 228a, and a corresponding decision of the representatives of the Governments of the Member States dealing with coal and steel products.[59] On the same day

---

[53] See Ch. 20, 380–2.
[55] [1994] OJ L139/8.
[57] Reg. 3028/93/EEC [1993] OJ L270/73.
[59] Dec. 94/313/ECSC [1994] OJ L139/8.

[54] [1993] OJ L155/2.
[56] Reg. 2520/93/EEC [1993] OJ L232/3.
[58] [1994] OJ L139/1.

the Council adopted Regulation 1264/94 dealing with performance bonds. It is in essentially the same terms as those for Iraq, Libya, and Yugoslavia.[60]

When agreement had been reached on the return to Haiti of President Aristide the Security Council adopted a resolution bringing to an end the measures concerning Haiti contained in its earlier resolutions. The Council of the EU adopted a common position under Article J.2 providing for the termination of measures for reducing economic relations with Haiti.[61] By Regulation 2543/94,[62] adopted under Article 228a, the Council repealed its regulation imposing an embargo against Haiti and, on the same day, the corresponding decision under the ECSC Treaty was also repealed by a decision of the representatives of the Governments of the Member States.[63] Regulation 1264/94 prohibiting the satisfaction of claims under performance bonds remains in force.

Unità (Angola)

By Regulation 2967/93/EEC[64] the Community prohibited the supply of petroleum and petroleum products to parts of Angola. This was done following the adoption of a resolution by the United Nations Security Council to obtain compliance with previous demands by the Security Council and to encourage the implementation of a peace plan. The Regulation was adopted under Article 113 and following agreement by the Community and its Member States meeting within the framework of political co-operation.

---

[60] [1993] OJ L139/4.
[62] [1994] OJ L271/1.
[64] [1993] OJ L268/1.

[61] 94/681/CFSP [1994] OJ L271/3.
[63] 94/680/ECSC [1994] OJ L271/2.

20

Association Agreements

Article 238 of the EC Treaty provides an express power for the European Community to enter into agreements with a third State or international organization 'establishing an association involving reciprocal rights and obligations, common actions and special procedures'. Such agreements are known as association agreements.[1] This description is far from precise, and it is not easy to draw a clear line between association agreements and other co-operation agreements concluded by the Community. This Chapter will comment on the legal basis for the Community's competence, including a consideration of Article 238, and then describe the practice.

THE LEGAL BASIS FOR THE COMMUNITY'S COMPETENCE

The Treaty Provision

Article 238 provides that 'the Community may conclude with one or more States or international organizations agreements establishing an association involving reciprocal rights and obligations, common action and special procedures'. The component parts of this definition are worth examining in detail.

'One or More States or International Organizations'

The Community has entered into a number of bilateral agreements and a few multilateral agreements with States.[2] It has not yet entered into any association agreements with any international organizations.

'Agreements'

The term 'agreement' has no special meaning in this context; it denotes an undertaking entered into under international law which has binding force. An

---

[1] Art. 206 Euratom provides a similar power, which is worded in identical terms, for the Euratom Community. No corresponding provision is found in the ECSC Treaty. In spite of this, the ECSC is a party to the Europe Agreements with the ECSC Treaty being cited as the legal basis.

[2] In Case C–316/91 *Re the European Development Fund: Parliament* v. *Council* [1994] 3 CMLR 149, Jacobs A.G. described the Lomé Convention as having essentially a bilateral character.

association agreement concluded under Article 238 is, as far as the Community is concerned, an act of one of the institutions of the Community within the meaning of sub-paragraph (b) of Article 177. From the date of its entry into force its provisions form an integral part of Community law. In certain circumstances its provisions may have direct effect.[3]

'Establishing'

This term implies a degree of permanence in the relations created and, in fact, all Article 238 agreements have been concluded for an indefinite period of time, except for the Yaoundé and Lomé Conventions (agreements concluded with respectively African countries and ACP States[4]). However, these Conventions contained a specific provision to the effect that they should be replaced, and there have been successive generations of agreements which have been adapted to fit the development needs of the countries in question. The permanence of association agreements contrasts with commercial and economic co-operation agreements, which are usually concluded for a fixed period. This suggests that one notable feature of Article 238 agreements is that they create a permanent or durable link.

'An Association'

The establishment of an association involves the creation of a special or privileged relationship with the Community. This is reflected in the nature of the links established and the fact that they often span across a range of the Community's activities.

Article 238 does not define the association and does not give particulars of possible contents of an association agreement. An element of political judgement or appreciation by the Council as the Community's legislator is involved; its objective is to create an association with the third country concerned. Advocate-General Mayras[5] said that an association agreement may lead to the establishment of very close institutional co-operation between the Community and the associated country without going as far as the unconditional accession of that country. Conversely, an agreement of this nature may be limited to the grant of non-discriminatory advantages, the establishment of a free trade area, a customs union, or even establishment of a true preferential system. In the *Demirel* case,[6] the Court of Justice appears to have considered the nature of association agreements to be more closely circumscribed than was suggested in the

[3] See Case 181/73 *R & V Haegeman* v. *Belgian State* [1974] ECR 449 at paras. 4–6 (the *Haegeman* case). This has been confirmed in, e.g., Case 12/86 *Meryem Demirel* v. *Stadt Schwäbisch Gmünd* [1987] ECR 3719 at para. 7 (the *Demirel* case) and in Case 30/88 *Greece* v. *Commission* [1989] ECR 3711 at para. 12. This question is considered further in Ch. 5.

[4] See pp. 380–2 below.

[5] Case 96/71 *Haegeman* v. *Commission* [1972] ECR 1005.   [6] See n. 3.

approach of Advocate-General Mayras when it described Article 238 agreements as 'creating special privileged links with a non-member country which must, at least to a certain extent, take part in the Community system'.

Association agreements are founded on trade provisions, but their content usually also extends to other sectors such as social, financial, technical, and cultural co-operation. Although the traditional view is that an interest only in financial or trade agreements is not enough to constitute an association with the Community,[7] some agreements are, however, little more than preferential trade agreements, notably the early agreements with Tunisia, Morocco, Malta, and Cyprus. An association might be founded on an agreement which covers only one sector of Community activity, provided that the nature of the agreement is such as to allow the 'participation' of the third State in that sector of Community activity.

'Involving Reciprocal Rights and Obligations'

The better interpretation of this phrase seems to be that an association agreement establishes mutually beneficial rights and obligations. It does not appear to mean *equivalent* rights and obligations, since the majority of agreements, especially those with developing countries, are characterized by unbalanced commitments.[8]

'Common Action and Special Procedures'

The notion 'common action' implies more than simply joint activities. One of the fundamental characteristics of an association agreement is that the associated State participates in the objectives of the Community.[9] Some authors have echoed this, suggesting that 'association signifies close and continuous co-operation with the Community. Thus, the eligibility of a third country for association should be determined chiefly by its interest in sharing the Community's ideals and efforts'.[10] Others argue that, although this may be true for association agreements intended to lead to eventual accession, it is not necessarily true for other agreements for which the existence of a specific common objective is sufficient.

---

[7] See H. Smit and P. Hertzog (eds.), *The Law of the European Community* (New York), 6–413.

[8] In Case 87/75 *Bresciani* v. *Amministrazione delle Finanze dello Stato* [1976] ECR 129, the Court stated in respect of the Yaoundé Convention, 'The Convention was not concluded in order to ensure equality in the obligations which the Community assumes with regard to the Associated States, but in order to promote their development', see para. 22. The Court underlined that this inequality in the obligations undertaken did not prevent the agreement from having direct effect in the Community legal order.

[9] P. Pescatore, 'Les Relations Exterieurs de la Communauté Européenne', 103 *Hague Recueil* (1961 II), 138.

[10] Smit and Hertzog, n. 7 above.

The 'special procedures' are one of the most important and distinctive features of association agreements. They take the form primarily of joint bodies which have as one of their tasks putting flesh on the bones of the agreement. Usually there is an association council which is responsible for implementing the agreement and taking binding decisions by unanimous vote. Representation in the association council is usually at a high level, often Ministerial level. In many cases provision is also made for the setting up of association committees, and, if necessary, other committees, to assist the association council.

Association councils, or in a few cases joint committees, are often endowed with decision-making powers in respect of the implementation of the agreement.[11] Since they are directly connected with the agreement to which they give effect, such decisions of an association council or of a joint committee form an integral part, as from their entry into force, of the Community legal system and are capable of having direct effect.[12] It may nonetheless be necessary for further measures to be adopted within the Community or by the Member States to give effect to the decisions of the joint body.

It follows that a number of key factors serve to distinguish association agreements from other agreements concluded by the Community. They are:

(a) association implies a close relationship between the parties, extending to a 'participation' of the associated country in certain of the objectives of the EC Treaty;

(b) the content of association agreements usually goes beyond merely commercial matters and covers a number of fields of Community activity;

(c) the institutions created by such agreements are generally highly developed and include organs enjoying decision-making power; and

(d) the links established by an association agreement are permanent in nature and, in consequence, these agreements are generally concluded for indefinite periods or at least for longer periods than other types of agreements.

Procedure for Conclusion

Before the coming into force of the TEU Article 238 contained the procedure for the conclusion of association agreements. It is still the substantive legal basis,

---

[11] The extent of the powers of the bodies set up under agreements varies. E.g. under the agreements with Turkey and Morocco the Association Council has power to take decisions in order to attain the objectives of the agreement in the cases provided in the agreement. Under the Lomé Convention, the ACP–EC Council of Ministers may take decisions relating to the inclusion of products in the Stabex mechanism and may adopt any transitional measures that may be required until a new Convention comes into force.

[12] See Case 30/88, n. 3 above, para. 13; Case C–192/89 *S.Z. Sevince* v. *Staatssecretaris van Justitie* [1990] ECR 3461 at para. 9. Until the Court's ruling in these cases, it was standard practice for specific measures to be adopted to transform these acts into Community law. For an analysis of the implications of the *Sevince* case, see Gilsdorf, 'Les organes institués par des accords communautaires: effets juridiques de leurs decisions' [1992] *RMC* 328.

but the procedure is now set out in Article 228. As with all agreements the Commission conducts the negotiations in accordance with a mandate from the Council. The Council acts by unanimity in agreeing the mandate.[13] At the stage of concluding the agreement, the Council acts by unanimity after the assent of the Parliament has been obtained.[14] The Parliament acts by an absolute majority of the votes cast.

Where the ECSC or the Euratom Community is a party to an association agreement, the procedure applicable to the conclusion of agreements by those Communities will apply. Thus in the case of the ECSC a decision of the Commission is adopted, and in the case of the Euratom Community a decision of the Council is adopted.[15] In practice there is usually one composite decision.[16]

A number of recent decisions by the Council authorizing the conclusion of association agreements have contained a provision setting out how the position to be taken by the Community within the Association Council is to be agreed.[17] It is usually to be laid down by the Council, on a proposal from the Commission, or in the case of ECSC matters by the Commission, in accordance with the corresponding provisions of the EC Treaty, the ECSC Treaty, and the Euratom Treaty.[18] The decision could be a formal Council decision or recorded in the minutes of the Council.

The decision may also set out who is to preside over the Association Council and association committee established by the agreement and who is to present the position of the Community in those bodies.

In the absence of a specific provision dealing with the position to be taken by the Community in the bodies established by an association agreement it would seem that the procedure set out in Article 228 should be applied by analogy where the decision of the association council will be binding in international or EC law.

Member States as Parties to Association Agreements

The Communities have exclusive competence to enter into association agreements in the sense that only a Community may associate a third State with that Community. However, this does not mean that all matters dealt with in an association agreement fall within the exclusive competence of the Community. It depends on the subject matter. On the one hand the subject matter may fall within the exclusive competence of the Community as being part of the

[13] Art. 228(1). [14] Art. 228(2) and (3)
[15] The Europe Agreements recite Art. 101 Euratom. It is not clear why Art. 207 Euratom is not also recited.
[16] See the decs. for the Europe Agreements: p. 375 below.
[17] See, e.g., Reg. 2894/94 concerning arrangements for implementing the Agreement on the European Economic Area [1994] OJ L305/6.
[18] See, e.g., Art. 2 of the decision concluding the Poland Europe Agreement [1993] OJ L345/1.

common commercial policy or because the Community has exclusive competence pursuant to the *AETR* principle.[19] On the other hand the subject matter may be outside the exclusive competence of the Community, for example in the fields of the free movement of workers, establishment, and the supply of services, and co-operation in economic, social, and cultural matters. In addition, the agreement may contain matters which are outwith the competence of the Communities, for example the Europe Agreements provide for a regular political dialogue between the parties.

Where this is the case, the Member States may be parties to the association agreement in question as well as one or more of the Communities. The agreement is therefore mixed; the issues that arise in the context of mixed agreements are considered in Chapter 6.

PRACTICE IN RELATION TO ASSOCIATION AGREEMENTS

The practice is not entirely coherent, since political considerations have served to influence the choice of countries to be afforded what is regarded as the privileged status of being 'associated' with the Community as well as the nature of that association. To date, the Community has only concluded association agreements with third countries, although Article 238 EC enables association agreements to be concluded with international organizations as well. As has been mentioned above, association agreements are usually mixed in character, that is both the Community and the Member States are parties.[20]

The practice is presented in four broad categories:

(a) association as a preliminary to membership (Greece, Turkey, and Central and Eastern European countries);
(b) the European Economic Area (the EEA);
(c) association as a special type of development assistance (Lomé and OCTs); and
(d) association of the countries which form part of the Community's Mediterranean policy (Mashreq and Maghreb countries).

This is not the only method of categorizing the agreements, and it should be stressed that the division has been adopted for ease of presentation and to facilitate comparison of the similarities and differences in the agreements.

---

[19] See Ch. 3.
[20] Some of the early association agreements, e.g., those with Cyprus and Malta, are not mixed agreements.

Association as a Preliminary to Membership

Greece

The first example of an association agreement was that with Greece (known as the 'Athens Agreement'). That agreement provided for a customs union with Greece together with a progressive harmonization of the agricultural policies of the Community and Greece, supplemented by certain aspects of economic policy and the introduction of freedom of movement for workers.[21]

Turkey

The association agreement with Turkey (the 'Ankara Agreement') was confirmed on behalf of the Community on 23 December 1963.[22] One of the primary objectives of the association agreement with Turkey was to establish a customs union in stages. No time limit was set for the transition from the first 'preparatory' stage to the second 'transitional' stage, and eventually a customs union in the third 'definitive' stage. The agreement sets out the aims of the association and lays down guidelines for their attainment: in order to achieve the aims the Association Council is vested with decision-making power. Provision is made for the adjustment of state monopolies to abolish discrimination between the parties' nationals as regards conditions of procurement and marketing of goods. In addition, the agreement provides for Turkey to bring its agricultural policies gradually into line with the Common Agricultural Policy. As regard workers, the provisions state that there should be non-discrimination in respect of conditions of workers and remuneration.[23] More detailed rights have been added by the Association Council relating to job entitlement and social security.[24] The agreement also precludes new restrictions on establishment and freedom to provide services.

The customs union was to be established gradually in the transitional stage and detailed arrangements were to be agreed five years after the entry into force of the agreement or within a four-year period thereafter. The 1972 Protocol to the agreement fixed a timescale of twelve to twenty-two years, depending upon

---

[21] The agreement has been interpreted by the ECJ on a number of occasions. In the *Haegeman* case, n. 3 above, the Court interpreted Art. 2 of Prot. 14. In Case 40/72, *Schröder* v. *Germany* [1973] ECR 125, the Court responded to questions put concerning the application of Art. 41 of the Agreement. In Case 17/81, *Pabst & Richarz KG* v. *Hauptzollamt Oldenburg* [1982] ECR 1331, it ruled that Art. 53 of the Agreement was to be interpreted in the same manner as Art. 95 EC.

[22] Council Dec. 64/732, JO 3687/64.

[23] In the *Demirel* case, n. 3 above, the Court considered Art. 12 of the Agreement dealing with free movement of workers, Art. 36 of the Additional Prot., together with Art. 7 of the Agreement.

[24] In the *Sevince* case, n. 12 above, the Court decided that Arts. 2(I)(b) and 7 of Dec. 2/76 and Arts. 6(1) and 13 of Dec. 1/80 of the Association Council had direct effect. This line of case law has been further confirmed in Case C–237/91 *Kazim Kus* v. *Landeshauptstadt Wiesbaden* [1993] 2 CMLR 887.

the product, for transition towards abolition of customs duties and adoption by Turkey of the common customs tariff in 1995. Free movement of workers was to be achieved within the same period. Reciprocal trade concessions took effect on 1 September 1971 under an interim agreement.

The agreement provided for assistance during the preparatory stage for Turkey to strengthen its economy, and Turkey has received financial assistance in the form of aid, loans, and investment schemes.[25] This assistance has been provided under financial protocols. Turkey has also received funds under the economic aid programme for countries affected by the Gulf Crisis and by way of a direct grant; it can also apply for assistance under the overall package of aid for Mediterranean countries agreed in 1992.

Guidelines intensifying co-operation were agreed at the Lisbon European Council in June 1992 and further developed at the Association Council of 8 November 1993 which adopted a resolution establishing a joint action plan to complete the customs union. At the time of writing agreement has not been reached on the establishment of the customs union.

Malta and Cyprus

These agreements provide for the establishment of a customs union in two stages to be completed over a ten-year period.[26] Both agreements establish Association Councils, comprising members of the EC Council, of the Commission, and of the associated countries, which meet annually. A mutual reduction of customs duties was agreed for Malta in the first stage, and may be extended automatically following a Council Decision of 25 April 1991.[27] Three financial protocols have been agreed for the agreement with Malta, the most recent in 1989.[28] A protocol agreed with Cyprus in 1987 implements the second stage of the customs union, which is to be completed in two phases. Three financial Protocols have been agreed, the most recent in 1990.[29] New financial protocols are currently under discussion for both countries.

---

[25] The legality of the provision of such aid has twice been challenged before the Court, see Cases 204/86 *Greece* v. *Council* [1988] ECR 5323 and 30/88, n. 3 above.

[26] In Case C-432/92, *R.* v. *Minister of Agriculture, Fisheries and Food, ex parte S.P. Anastasiou (Pissouri) Ltd.* [1995] 1 CMLR 569, the ECJ ruled that the 1977 Prot. to the Cyprus Agreement was capable of direct application. The Court was also requested to interpret Art. 5 of the agreement, in particular on whether the stipulation therein that the agreement should be applied without discrimination as between all Cypriots could justify the acceptance of origin certificates and health certificates from the part of the island north of the UN buffer zone. The Court considered that the regime regulating the grant of such certificates was clear: the certificates should be issued only by the Government of the Republic of Cyprus and that therefore the practice of the Commission and certain Member States of the Community, which was based on Art. 5, of accepting certificates issued by authorities of the northern part of the island was precluded.

[27] Council Dec. 91/246 [1991] OJ L116/66.

[28] [1989] OJ L180/46.　　　　　　　　[29] [1990] OJ L82/32.

Agreements with Central and Eastern European Countries (Europe Agreements)

The 'Europe Agreements' replaced the bilateral framework trade and economic co-operation agreements concluded with the countries of central and eastern Europe.[30] The 'Europe Agreements' have their origins in the Commission's Communication to the Council of 27 August 1990, and they reflect the conclusions of the Edinburgh European Council of 11–12 December 1992, based on the Commission's report entitled *Europe and the challenge of enlargement*, which established that any country with a European identity, democratic status, and respect for human rights which was able to adopt and implement the Community 'acquis' would be eligible for membership. They provide the framework for the gradual integration of the central and eastern European countries into the Community and aim to create the conditions for political and economic reform, recognizing that the final objective of the countries in question is to become a member of the Community. Progress under the agreements is conditional upon progress in political and market reform.

Agreements have been concluded with six countries. They were concluded by the EC and the ECSC acting together with the Euratom Community where the participation of that Community was necessary because of provisions on co-operation in the fields of nuclear and energy safety. The first Europe Agreements were signed with Hungary, Poland, and the Czech and Slovak Federal Republic on 16 December 1991.[31] After the split of the Czech and Slovak Republic the original agreement was amended to allow for the conclusion of two separate Europe Agreements which were signed on 4 October 1993.[32] Europe Agreements were signed with Romania on 1 February 1993[33] and Bulgaria on 8 March 1993.[34] The Agreements with Poland[35] and Hungary[36] came into force on 1 February 1994; those with Bulgaria, Romania, the Czech Republic and Slovakia on 1 February 1995. A significant difference between the first round of Europe Agreements and the second is that in the latter a reference to respect for the rule of law and human rights, 'including the rights of persons belonging to minorities', is included in the preamble. In addition, they contain a provision whereby 'respect for the democratic principles and human rights established by the Helsinki Final Act and the Charter of Paris for a New Europe inspires the domestic and external policies of the Parties and

---

[30] See Ch. 12, p. 287.

[31] The content and structure of the Europe Agreements are described by Maresceau, 'Les Accords Européens: Analyse Générale', [1993] *RMC* 507.

[32] For the Slovak Agreement see [1994] OJ L359/1 and for the Czech Agreement see [1994] OJ L360/1. Arts. 123 and 124 of both Agreements deal with their coming into force.

[33] [1994] OJ L357/1. [34] [1994] OJ L358/1.

[35] [1993] OJ L348/1. [36] [1993] OJ L347/1.

constitute essential elements of the association'.[37] It is possible 'in cases of special urgency' unilaterally to suspend the application of the agreement without
prior consultation.[38] Europe Agreements are currently being negotiated with
Slovenia and the Baltic States.

The agreements provide for an association which includes a transitional
period of a maximum duration of ten years, divided into two successive stages,
each in principle lasting five years. The agreements provide for regular political dialogue with the aim of achieving a convergence of positions on international questions. This is the first time that political dialogue provisions have
been included within an association agreement, the more traditional mechanism
being a joint declaration with the third country concerning political dialogue
concluded in parallel with the agreement. The agreement envisages the gradual
implementation of a free trade area, with protection in the most sensitive sectors (such as textiles, steel, agriculture, and fisheries). The third countries have
a longer period in which to remove tariffs and in certain cases they have the
opportunity of introducing certain exceptional derogations of limited duration
to protect infant industries of particular sectors which are being restructured.
ECSC products are dealt with in a separate protocol. The trade provisions of
the Europe Agreements have been implemented by way of 'interim agreements'
based on Article 113 EC and Article 95 ECSC. Additional protocols to the
interim agreements signed on 20 December 1993 implemented the European
Council's decision of June 1993 to grant further trade concessions. These
included increases in quota levels and reductions in some tariff ceilings, levies,
and duties, and improved access to the EC market for textiles and ECSC products. Specific protocols on trade in textile products provide for the abolition of
quantitative restrictions by 1 January 1999, improved market access, and lower
customs duties.

The agreements also contain provisions on movement of workers, freedom of
establishment, provision of services, and payments and movement of capital.
These provisions do little more than state general principles which are based on
the relevant EC Treaty provision and the Article on free movement of workers
encourages the conclusion of further agreements. The principles of competition
found in Articles 85, 86, and 92 EC are applied and the necessary rules relating to their implementation are to be adopted by the Association Council.
There is to be approximation of laws in certain areas and the agreements provide an overall encouragement for the associated countries to adopt EC legislation without providing the obvious framework for doing so. Provision is also
made for economic co-operation in an extensive range of areas. Financial assis-

[37] See Art. 6 of the Europe Agreements with Bulgaria and Romania. Art. 6 of the Europe
Agreements with the Czech Republic and the Slovak Republic include a reference to the principles
of the market economy.
[38] e.g., Art. 117 of the Europe Agreement with the Czech Republic and the Declaration on Art.
117(2) in the Final Act.

tance is to continue in the framework of the PHARE and TACIS programmes, and by way of loans provided by the European Investment Bank. In addition, assistance may be provided for currency stabilization and restructuring efforts. The agreements also provide for political dialogue which is to accompany and consolidate rapprochement between the parties.

The institutional framework of the agreements is identical to that contained in the agreement with Turkey. An Association Council meets at ministerial level once a year. The Association Council has decision-making power in the cases specifically provided for in the agreement; it may also make appropriate recommendations. The Association Council is assisted by an Association Committee which meets at senior civil servant level. An Association Parliamentary Committee is also established.

The Agreement on the European Economic Area

The Agreement on the European Economic Area (EEA) was signed in May 1992[39] by the EEC, the ECSC, their Member States, and what were at the time the seven Member States of the European Free Trade Association (EFTA) (Austria, Finland, Iceland, Liechtenstein, Norway, Sweden, and Switzerland). Following Switzerland's rejection of the agreement by referendum, a protocol[40] was agreed making the necessary adjustments to the Agreement to enable it to enter into force on 1 January 1994[41] following ratification by the other signatories.[42] The Protocol also postponed Liechtenstein's participation until it had redefined its close legal, administrative, and trade links with Switzerland. A corresponding agreement between the EFTA countries, which provides for the establishment of an EFTA Court and an EFTA Surveillance Authority, entered into force at the same time. The application of the EEA for Austria, Finland, and Sweden as members of EFTA was very short lived since their membership of EFTA ended on their accession to the EU on 1 January 1995. The

---

[39] The EEA Agreement was the subject of two ECJ Opinions. In the first, *Opinion 1/91 (First EEA Opinion)* [1991] ECR I-6079, the Court ruled that the system of judicial supervision set up by the agreement was incompatible with the EC Treaty. The Agreement had provided for the establishment of an EEA Court which would include judges from the ECJ. It would deal with, among other matters, disputes between the contracting parties. There was also provision enabling the EFTA States to authorize their courts and tribunals to ask the ECJ for its interpretation of the provisions of the Agreement. Following the ECJ's ruling, the Agreement was amended to alter the system of judicial supervision. The amended provisions were the subject of *Opinion 1/92 (Second EEA Opinion)* [1992] ECR I-2821. The Court ruled that the provisions were compatible with the EC Treaty provided certain conditions were satisfied. The Court's *Opinions* are analysed in Schermers, 'Opinions 1/91 and 1/92' (1992) 29 *CMLRev.* 991.

[40] Prot. adjusting the Agreement on the EEA signed in Brussels on 17 Mar. 1993.

[41] This was 1 year after the original date for the entry into force of the agreement.

[42] The Joint Declaration by the Contracting Parties to the Final Act of the Adjusting Prot. of 17 Mar. 1993 leaves open the opportunity for Switzerland to accede, but new negotiations would be required which would be based on the results laid down in the original EEA Agreement and bilateral agreements together with subsequent changes in those agreements.

agreement continues to apply for Iceland and Norway and, following a referendum, it will apply to Liechtenstein from 1 May 1995.

The core of the Agreement provides for the application, as between the Community and the participating EFTA States, of the EC Treaty provisions and secondary legislation relating to free movement of goods, persons, services, and capital, i.e. the internal market legislation. It also provides for the establishment of a system to ensure that competition is not distorted which is based on Articles 85 and 86 EC and for the application of a prohibition on state aids which is modelled on Articles 92–94 EC. It also provides for the extension of the Community's 'horizontal' policies in areas such as social policy, consumer and environmental protection, and 'flanking' measures, such as participation in research and development programmes, education and training initiatives, and other sectoral projects. The participating EFTA countries contribute to the Community's cohesion funds by way of grants, interest rate subsidies and loans.[43]

The objective of the Agreement is to establish a dynamic and homogeneous European Economic Area, based on common rules and equal conditions of competition and providing for adequate means of enforcement including at the judicial level, and achieved on the basis of reciprocity and of an overall balance of benefits, rights, and obligations for the parties. In addition, the EEA Agreement stipulates that provisions of the Agreement, in so far as they are identical in substance to corresponding provisions of the EC Treaty, are to be interpreted in conformity with the relevant rulings of the Court of Justice given prior to signature of the Agreement on 2 May 1992.[44] The formal legislative process is, however, kept separate and the autonomy of the Community legal order is preserved.[45] Experts from the EFTA countries are consulted prior to the submission of legislation to the EC Council[46] and within the framework of the EEA Joint Committee, while legislation is in the process of adoption, but the EFTA States have no direct input into the decision-making. Following the adoption of legislation, the EEA Joint Committee is then responsible for implementation of corresponding legislation in the EEA.[47]

---

[43] For general descriptions of the matters covered by the EEA see Norberg, 'The Agreement on a EEA' (1992) 29 *CMLRev.* 1171; Toledano-Laredo, 'The EEA Agreement: An Overall View' (1992) 29 *CMLRev.* 1199; Frisch and Meyer, 'Le traité sur l'espace économique européen: cadre juridique d'une "Europe du deuxième cercle"' [1992] *RMC* 596; O'Keeffe, 'The Agreement on the European Economic Area' [1992] 1 *LIEI* 1; Stuyck and Looijetijn-Clearie (eds.), *The European Economic Area EC–EFTA* (Kluwer, 1994); Bright (ed.) *Business Law in the European Economic Area* (Clarendon Press, 1994); Norberg and others, *The European Economic Area EEA Law* (Kluwer, 1993); and Blanchet and others, *The Agreement on the European Economic Area: A Guide to the Free Movement of Goods and Competition Rules* (OUP, 1994).

[44] Art. 6 of the EEA Agreement.

[45] For a discussion of the extent to which it has been possible to achieve these aims see Cremona, 'The 'Dynamic and Homogeneous EEA: Byzantine Structures and Variable Geometry' [1994] *ELRev.* 508.

[46] Art. 99 of the EEA Agreement.

[47] EEA acts and other information from the institutions are published in an EFTA section of the Official Journal and the Nordic EFTA languages appear in an EEA supplement.

An EEA Council, comprising members of the EC Council and Commission together with one member of the government of each EFTA country, meets twice a year and is responsible for the overall political direction of the Agreement.[48] The EEA Joint Committee, in which all the parties to the Agreement are represented, oversees the implementation and operation of the Agreement. It integrates EC acts adopted by the Council or the Commission which are relevant to the EEA through amendments of the Annexes to the EEA Agreement.[49] The Joint Committee is a political organ, but it has a special role to play in the 'homogeneous interpretation of the Agreement' since it must keep under constant review the case law of the Court of Justice and the EFTA Court,[50] although in so doing its decisions must not affect the case law of the Court of Justice.[51] In the event of a disagreement, the Joint Committee may settle the dispute, but once again any decision taken is without prejudice to the case law of the Court of Justice.Disputes concerning the interpretation of provisions identical in objective to EC Treaty rules may also be referred to the Court of Justice for a ruling which will be binding on the parties to the Agreement. Alternatively, a party may take safeguard measures or suspend the affected part of the Agreement. The EEA Joint Parliamentary Committee provides a forum for consultation between members of the European Parliament and EFTA Parliamentarians. The EEA Consultative Committee provides a framework for consultation between the social partners.

An EFTA Surveillance Authority (ESA) and an EFTA Court are responsible for monitoring and enforcing EEA rules in participating EFTA countries. The ESA has functions similar to those of the Commission in respect of EC Member States. For example, in the field of competition it has power to investigate infringements, issue decisions, and authorize necessary measures to bring infringements to an end. In the field of competition policy, the ESA and the EC Commission enjoy parallel powers, but in order to avoid encroachment upon the Community legal order, there is a clear division of powers; and, for example, while the ESA decides upon cases where only trade between the EFTA States is affected, the Community enjoys jurisdiction in cases where trade between Member States is affected appreciably, and even in some cases where trade between one Member State and one or more EFTA States is affected.

The provisions relating to the EFTA Court are modelled on those

---

[48] Arts. 89–91 of the EEA Agreement.

[49] Under Art. 102 of the EEA Agreement the Joint Committee has power to take decisions to amend the Annexes of the Agreement which contain the detailed provisions relating to legislation. Failure of the Joint Committee to amend the Annex to the agreement may result in the suspension of the affected part of the agreement. For an example of the Joint Committee's exercise of its decision-making powers see its dec. of 21 Mar. 1994, when the EEA Joint Committee adopted the first such dec. which integrated some 400 Community acts adopted between the conclusion of the drafting of the EEA Agreement, 31 July 1991, and its entry into force: Bull. EU 3–1994.

[50] See Art. 105 of the EEA Agreement.

[51] See Prot. 48 relating to Art. 105.

establishing the Court of Justice.[52] The EFTA Court is responsible for the implementation of the EEA Agreement in participating EFTA countries. The EFTA Court must interpret provisions in the EEA which are in substance identical to the provisions of EC law in conformity with the relevant rulings of the Court of Justice given prior to the signature of the Agreement.[53] Furthermore, the EFTA Court (and the ESA) must take due account of the principles of Court of Justice rulings made after the date of the entry into force of the Agreement which concern the interpretation of provisions of the EEA Agreement which are identical to those of the EC Treaty.[54] At the time of writing, the EFTA Court had delivered two rulings. The first[55] was an advisory opinion on the compatibility of the Finnish alcohol monopoly with Articles 11 and 16 of the EEA. The EFTA Court ruled that Article 11 of the EEA was identical in substance to Article 30 EC and it applied the case law of the Court of Justice on Article 30 EC in ruling that the grant of exclusive import rights or the obligation to obtain authorization from a state monopoly was a measure having equivalent effect which was prohibited by Article 11. It also ruled that Article 16 was in substance identical to Article 37 EC and that it was sufficiently clear and precise to be capable of being relied upon by individuals before the national court. The second[56] was a challenge to a decision of the EFTA Surveillance Authority declining jurisdiction to investigate a complaint. The EFTA Court annulled the decision in issue.

The EEA Agreement is certainly the most highly developed of the association agreements concluded by the Community, both in terms of the extent to which the associated States participate in the Community's activities and the institutional framework established to control and monitor the system, which reflects closely the system set up under the EC Treaty. Prior to the EEA Agreement, third States had agreed to apply certain aspects of Community rules, but the EFTA States have agreed to apply a whole corpus of legislation which lies at the centre of the Community's activities.

Association as a Special Type of Development Assistance

The ACP–EC Convention (The Lomé Convention)

The original ACP–EC Convention was signed in Lomé on 28 February 1975 and succeeded the Yaoundé Convention which was an agreement between the

---

[52] Agreement between the EFTA States on the establishment of a surveillance authority and a Court of Justice ([1994] OJ L344/1).

[53] Art. 6 of the EEA Agreement.

[54] Art. 13 of the Agreement concerning the ESA and the EFTA Court.

[55] Case E–1/94 [1995] 1 CMLR 161. Two cases, requests from Swedish courts for advisory opinions have been withdrawn. The issue in one of those cases, E–7/94, has been referred to the ECJ for a preliminary ruling on the equivalent provision of the EC Treaty following Sweden's accession to the EU (Case C–43/95).

[56] Case E–2/94 *Scottish Salmon Growers Association Ltd.*v. *EFTA Surveillance Authority*, not yet reported.

six founder members of the EC and many of their former (mostly French) colonies.[57] The accession of the United Kingdom provided the impetus for the creation of a more ambitious framework for developing relations with a wider network of countries of the ACP regions and for the first Lomé Convention in 1975.[58] Since that date a further three Conventions (Lomé II, 1979; Lomé III, 1984, and Lomé IV, 1989) have been concluded.[59]

Successive Lomé Conventions have included provisions relating to trade and development. Under the trade provisions, the Community grants preferential access for ACP products to EC markets on a non-reciprocal basis. EC exports are granted most favoured nation treatment. Financial and technical co-operation is funded by the European Development Fund (EDF).[60] Aid is disbursed on the basis of national and regional indicative programmes. Projects are the subject of financing conventions between the Community and the ACP State which then concludes contracts for the provision of goods and services in connection with the project. Under the Convention the Community is responsible for preparing and adopting financing decisions on projects and programmes, and contracts concluded for works and services remain national contracts which the ACP States alone are responsible for negotiating and concluding.[61] The Convention provides that disputes relating to such contracts shall be subject to arbitration. There are a number of specific instruments created under the Convention which are designed to take account of the special needs of the ACP States. Stabex aims to stabilize export earnings and covers most agricultural products exported by the ACP States, providing compensatory transfers to offset shortfalls in export earnings. Sysmin provides a parallel system for mineral exports and aims to protect mining production. A sugar protocol guarantees

---

[57] The first Yaoundé Convention of Association was signed in July 1963 in the capital of Cameroon. The association established by the Convention lasted until 1969. The Associated African and Malagasy States (AAMS) comprised Burundi, Cameroon, the Central African Republic, Chad, Congo, Brazzaville, Congo, Leopoldville, Dahomey, Gabon, Ivory Coast, Madagascar, Mali, Mauritania, Niger, Rwanda, Senegal, Somalia, Togo, and Upper Volta. Nigeria negotiated an association agreement with the Community in 1966 but the Lagos Convention never came into force because of the war in Biafra. In 1968, the Arusha Convention between the Community and Kenya, Tanzania, and Uganda was signed.

[58] Prot. 22 of the Act of Accession of 1973 extended an invitation to the English-speaking countries in Africa and elsewhere to negotiate association agreements with the Community and an invitation to Asian countries to negotiate trade agreements.

[59] On co-operation under Lomé, see Vignes, 'Communauté Européenne et pays en voie de développement' 210 *Hague Recueil* (1988 III) 224. For a critical account, see Addo, 'A Critical Analysis of the Perennial International Economic Law Problems of the EEC–ACP Relationship' [1990] *Ger.YBIL* 33.

[60] The EDF is not part of the Community budget but is established under an agreement concluded by the Representatives of the Governments of the Member States meeting in the Council, known as the 'Internal Financial Agreement'. Financial contributions are calculated according to a formula based on the GNP of each Member State.

[61] The tasks incumbent on the Community are performed by the Commission. This division of responsibilities and powers between the Community and the ACP States has been confirmed on a number of occasions by the ECJ. See, e.g., Case 33/82 *Murri Frères* v. *Commission* [1985] ECR 2759.

prices for sugar. An ACP–EC Council meets annually and an ACP–EC Joint Assembly twice per year.

The Convention currently in force (Lomé IV) runs for a ten-year period until 29 February 2000, in contrast with previous conventions which were adopted for five-year periods. Aid under the Convention is focused on rural development, road improvement, social and economic infrastructure, and better use of human resources. The Convention improved the conditions for the import of agricultural products, prolonged the Stabex and Sysmin mechanisms, and improved the consultation mechanism prior to the use of safeguard measures. The chapter dealing with economic co-operation was extended to cover services. For the first time direct aid was made available for structural adjustment. Twelve billion ECU was provided for the first five years of the Convention in the form of grants, soft loans, and interest rate subsidies. The Convention provided for a mid-term review to be implemented by 1 March 1995; this was not achieved, principally because of disputes over the financial protocol. Under the mid-term review, the five-year financial protocol is being reviewed, the human rights clause strengthened, provision made for enhanced political dialogue at regional level, and decision-making procedures streamlined.

Association with the Overseas Countries and Territories (OCTs)

The association between the Community and the non-European countries having special relations with certain Member States which are listed in Annex IV of the EC Treaty currently takes the form of a Council Decision adopted unanimously on the basis of Article 136 EC.[62] The association does not, therefore, take place within the framework of an association agreement, but its content and objectives are similar to those found in the context of the Community's relationship with the ACP States. The aim of the association is stated in Article 131 to be to promote the economic and social development of the OCTs and to establish close relations between them and the Community. The most recent OCT decision places particular emphasis on decentralization of co-operation and partnership with the establishment of a three-way partnership between the OCT, the Commission, and the responsible Member State to function as a forum for discussion. Specific areas for co-operation are identified. Free access to the Community market is granted for all products originating in the OCTs although the Community retains the power to take safeguard measures in cer-

---

[62] Between 1957 and 1962, as stipulated in Art. 136, the details and procedures of the association were set out in an implementing convention annexed to the Treaty. This has been followed by series of Council decs. establishing details of co-operation arrangements which have largely mirrored those found in the Lomé Conventions. The current dec. is Dec. 91/482 [1991] OJ L263/1. It has been amended on a number of occasions.

tain circumstances.[63] Funding comes from the European Development Fund. The Decision also contains provisions on establishment.[64]

Association with Mediterranean Countries

Maghreb (Algeria, Morocco, and Tunisia)

These agreements[65] cover trade and economic, technical, and financial co-operation, and contain provisions on freedom of movement of workers. The co-operation is aimed at contributing to the development of the Maghreb countries and strengthening economic links. As far as trade is concerned industrial products enjoy free access to the Community market since all customs duties and quantitative restrictions have been abolished, save for certain ceilings for oil and cork products. Other products are accorded most favoured nation treatment. Agricultural products not subject to the Common Agricultural Policy (CAP) are given unrestricted entry. Those covered by the CAP (meats, fish, vegetables, fresh fruit, fruit juices, prepared fish, wine, and olive oil) are given preferences ranging from 20 to 100 per cent. Sensitive agricultural products are also subject to other protective measures. Maghreb countries grant EC exports most favoured nation treatment. The trade provisions of the agreements were implemented by way of interim agreements based on Article 113. Grants, EIB loans, and loans on special terms are made available under financial protocols. To date, there have been four financial protocols for each of the agreements.

The Articles on co-operation in the field of labour provide that workers of Maghreb origin employed in the territory of the Member States shall be afforded non-discriminatory treatment as regards working conditions or remuneration and the Maghreb countries undertake to give the same treatment to workers who are EC nationals. Non-discriminatory treatment is also granted in

---

[63] Art. 133 EC states that customs duties on imports into the Member States from the OCTs shall be abolished in accordance with the timetable set out in the EC Treaty. Customs duties on imports into the OCTs are also to be progressively abolished save that the OCTs may continue to levy customs duties which meet the needs of their development and industrialization or produce revenue for their budgets. Such duties shall be reduced to the level imposed on countries with whom the OCT enjoys special relations and shall not give rise to any discrimination in law or in fact as between imports from the various Member States. On this see Case 260/90 *Leplat* v. *Polynesia* [1992] ECR 643.

[64] Art. 132 EC contains the basic rule on the right of establishment in relations between Member States and the OCTs. It applies subject to any special provisions laid down in the Dec. On Art. 132 see Cases C–100 and C–101/89 *Kaefer and Procacci* v. *French State* [1990] ECR I–4647.

[65] Co-operation Agreement of 26 Apr. 1976 between the Member States and the EEC and Algeria ([1978] OJ L263/2), Co-operation Agreement of 27 Apr. 1976 between the Member States and the EEC and Morocco ([1978] OJ L264/2), and Co-operation Agreement of 25 Apr. 1976 between the Member States and the EEC and Tunisia ([1978] OJ L265/2). See p. 407 for agreements relating to ECSC products.

respect of social security matters.[66] These provisions were to be implemented by decisions taken by the Co-operation Council.

The agreements provide for Bilateral Co-operation Councils, composed of the EC Council and Commission and of the governments of the Maghreb countries. The Co-operation Councils are empowered to take decisions and to formulate resolutions, recommendations, and opinions. They also have responsibility for resolving disputes relating to the agreement with the opportunity for a party to refer a dispute to arbitration. Co-operation committees exist to assist the Co-operation Councils.

New 'Euro-Mediterranean' Association Agreements are being negotiated with Morocco and Tunisia,. It is envisaged that these will provide for close co-operation in trade matters (possibly the creation of a free trade area in industrial products and progressive liberalization in agricultural products and services), economic co-operation, and financial and technical assistance. The agreements will also include provisions on political dialogue and new areas of co-operation such as social policy, culture, and communications will provide for technical assistance for economic reform, balance of payments support, and investment financing for infrastructure projects.

Mashreq (Egypt, Jordan, Syria, and Lebanon)

The agreements[67] cover trade and economic, technical, and financial co-operation. The trade provisions abolish, or provide for progressive reductions in, customs duties and quantitative restrictions for industrial products, as well as privileged access for certain agricultural products. These aspects of the agreements were implemented by interim agreements. EC exports enjoy most favoured nation treatment. Financial assistance in the form of grants and EIB loans has been provided under four financial protocols. Each agreement establishes a Co-operation Council composed of representatives of the EC and its Member States and of the Mashreq country government.

A Euro-Mediterranean Association Agreement is being negotiated with Egypt. It will be similar to those being negotiated with Morocco and Tunisia. The purpose of the proposed agreement is to strengthen political dialogue based on respect for human rights and democratic principles, gradually create a free-trade area, step up economic and financial co-operation, and encourage regional co-operation.

---

[66] In Case C–18/91 *Office National de l'Emploi* v. *Kziber* [1991] ECR I–199, the ECJ ruled that Art. 41 of the Agreement with Morocco was sufficiently clear, precise, and unconditional to be directly applicable.

[67] Co-operation Agreement of 18 Jan. 1977 between the Member States and the EEC and Egypt ([1978] OJ L266/2), Co-operation Agreement of 18 Jan. 1977 between the Member States and the EEC and Jordan ([1978] OJ L268/2), Co-operation Agreement of 3 May 1977 between the Member States and the EEC and Lebanon ([1978] OJ L267/2). See p. 407 for agreements relating to ECSC products.

Israel

A Euro-Mediterranean Association Agreement is being negotiated with Israel. The agreement will contain a clause on respect for democratic principles and human rights and will govern economic and trade relations between the Community and Israel. It will provide for co-operation in scientific, technical, social, cultural, and regional matters and will include institutional provisions for the establishment of political dialogue.

Yugoslavia

In 1983, the Community concluded an agreement with Yugoslavia which was intended to equate Yugoslavia's status with that of other Mediterranean countries. Under the agreement most Yugoslavian industrial products entered the Community free of customs duties, quantitative restrictions, and measures having equivalent effect, although many were subject to import ceilings. Yugoslavia was obliged to grant the Community most favoured nation treatment in trade and certain tariffs and quotas necessary for its industrialization and development were permitted. The agreement extended to co-operation in the sphere of industrial co-operation, energy, transport, tourism, environment, and fishing. It also contained provisions on co-operation in the field of labour establishing non-discrimination on grounds of nationality as regards working conditions and remuneration, together with rules on social security entitlements. A Co-operation Council was set up with responsibility for operation of the Agreement.

The advent of the civil war in Yugoslavia led to the suspension of the commercial preferences granted under the Agreement as from 15 November 1991 on the basis that there had been a fundamental change in circumstances since the conclusion of the agreement.[68] The Agreement was suspended by a decision of the Council and the Representatives of the Member States meeting in the Council[69] and the denunciation of the Agreement took effect as from 25 November following the European Parliament's assent to a Council Decision to that effect based on Article 238.[70]

A Europe Agreement is being negotiated with Slovenia.[71]

---

[68] Council Reg. 3300/91 [1991] OJ L315/1.   [69] [1991] OJ L315/47.
[70] Dec. 91/602 [1991] OJ L325/23. See Ch. 19, p. 362.   [71] See 376 above.

21

Non-nuclear Energy

All three Communities are concerned, to varying degrees, with energy issues. The principal concern of the Euratom Community is with the development of nuclear energy, and the powers and activities of Euratom are considered in more detail elsewhere.[1] This Chapter focuses on the external powers of the European Community and the ECSC in the energy field.

Although the Treaties establishing the ECSC and the EC do not have energy policy at the heart of their provisions in the way that the Euratom Treaty does, the tasks outlined in the ECSC Treaty[2] include the orderly supply of coal to the common market, ensuring that consumers have equal access to the sources of production, and the maintenance of conditions which will encourage undertakings to promote a policy of using natural resources rationally; and the EC Treaty states that the activities of the Community are to include 'measures in the sphere of energy'.[3]

THE LEGAL BASIS OF THE COMMUNITIES' EXTERNAL COMPETENCE

Neither the ECSC Treaty nor the EC Treaty contains provisions expressly empowering the Communities to adopt internal or external measures on energy generally, such as are to be found in the EC Treaty in relation to, for example, transport[4] or the environment.[5] Instead, the measures on non-nuclear energy[6] have been adopted on the basis of powers which have been conferred on the Communities primarily for other purposes. This is not to say that the adoption of these measures has been an abuse of Treaty powers, or that adoption of further measures in future would be of dubious legality. The point is rather that, in considering whether the Communities may adopt measures or enter into agreements relating to energy, no express general power which may be used to that end will be found in the Treaties. Instead, the aim and content of the measure or agreement in question must be analysed in the light of the other powers conferred on the Communities in order to determine whether it can properly be adopted on the basis of those powers.

In principle, several provisions of the Treaties may provide a legal basis for

---

[1] Ch. 22. [2] Art. 3 ECSC. [3] Art. 3(t) EC.
[4] Title IV of the EC Treaty. [5] Title XVI of the EC Treaty.
[6] See, e.g., the measures listed in the 24th edn. of the *Directory of Community Legislation in Force* (Office for Official Publications of the European Communities), vol. 1, 845 ff.

the adoption of measures[7] relating to energy. Those most likely to be of direct relevance are the following:[8]

(a) the powers to establish a common commercial policy (if the measure relates to trade in raw materials such as coal or oil);[9]

(b) the powers to adopt research and development programmes and agreements;[10]

(c) the powers to adopt measures relating to the environment;[11]

(d) the powers in the area of development co-operation policy,[12] if the measure or agreement is part of the Community's co-operation with less developed countries;

(e) the powers to encourage the establishment and development of trans-European networks, if the measure concerns energy infrastructures;[13]

(f) the powers to conclude association agreements[14] (which have provided for co-operation in energy matters);

(g) Article 100a EC, if a proposed agreement might 'affect' internal common rules adopted under the powers conferred by that Article;[15]

(h) Articles 95 ECSC and 235 EC if no other powers can be found and the proposed measure meets the criteria in these Articles.

Extent and Nature of the Communities' Powers

It will be evident that the extent or scope of the Communities' powers in the sphere of energy must be assessed in the light of its other objectives and powers. Similarly, whether the Communities' competence is exclusive or shared depends on the particular agreement or measure being adopted and the Treaty power being employed.

PRACTICE OF THE COMMUNITIES

Piecing together the practice of the Communities in the sphere of energy is not easy. Measures adopted under provisions of the Treaties dealing with the common commercial policy, the environment, and research and development have all to be taken into account. Practice in these areas has been summarized in other Chapters: this section will list only those provisions in multilateral and

---

[7] Including decs. relating to the conclusion of agreements.

[8] In each case, the aim and content of the proposed measure would have to be examined to determine whether it could properly be based on the power in question.

[9] Art. 113 EC and Arts. 71–74 ECSC. On the common commercial policy, see Ch. 12.

[10] Title XV of the EC Treaty: see Ch. 16.

[11] Title XVI of the EC Treaty: see Ch. 17.

[12] Title XVII of the EC Treaty: see Ch. 18.   [13] Title XII of the EC Treaty.

[14] Art. 238 EC: see Ch. 20.   [15] The 'AETR principle': on which see Ch. 3.

bilateral agreements which deal specifically with energy. It will be noted that most of the relevant activity has taken place under the EC Treaty.

Agreements

Multilateral Agreements

European Energy Charter

In December 1991, representatives from forty-eight States and the European Community agreed to the objectives and principles set out in a 'European Energy Charter', a declaration of political intent which also included a commitment to negotiate an agreement. Negotiations for such an agreement culminated in 1994 with agreement on the European Energy Charter Treaty.[16] The European Community and the Member States may become parties to the Charter Treaty, which establishes a legal framework to promote long term cooperation in the energy field and provides that trade in energy materials and products shall be governed by the provisions of the GATT and its related instruments. The Treaty recognizes State sovereignty over energy resources, but contracting parties commit themselves to facilitate access to resources and to keep national rules on exploration, development, and acquisition of energy resources transparent and non-discriminatory. The Treaty contains provisions on access to markets. Alongside the trade rules, it provides for countries and investors to be able to transit countries in sending their energy to markets. It also contains provisions on the promotion and protection of investments and provides for the negotiation of a supplementary treaty. An institutional framework consisting of a Charter Conference and Secretariat is established. The European Community signed the Charter in December 1994 and is provisionally applying it to the extent that it has competence for matters governed by the Treaty. The legal basis for signature and provisional application was Articles 54(2), 57 (2), last sentence, 66, 73c(2), 87, 99, 100a, 113, 130s(1), and 235 in conjunction with Article 228(2) second sentence, and Article 228(3) first subparagraph.[17]

Lomé IV

The Lomé Convention[18] provides in detail for 'energy development'. Cooperation in this area is to place particular emphasis on energy programming, operations for saving and making efficient use of energy, reconnaissance of energy potential, and the economically and technically appropriate promotion of new and renewable sources of energy. Article 106 sets out the main objectives of energy development, and Article 107 lists matters on which energy cooperation schemes may be targeted.

---

[16] Council Dec. 94/998 ([1994] OJ L380/1).   [17] *Ibid.*
[18] 4th ACP–EEC Convention, Arts. 105–109 ([1991] OJ L229/1).

Bilateral Agreements

Co-operation agreements with Arab countries. A series of co-operation[19] agreements were concluded in the mid-1970s with certain Arab countries. These typically provided for the participation of European Community operators in programmes for the exploration, production, or processing of the natural resources of the third country concerned[20] and also for trade in petroleum and petroleum products.[21] Agreements providing for trade in the products covered by the ECSC Treaty were also concluded with most of the countries with which the EEC concluded co-operation agreements.[22]

The *'Europe' Agreements*[23] provide for co-operation on energy within the framework of the principles of the market economy. Such co-operation is to develop against a background of progressive integration of the energy markets of Europe. Co-operation is to focus in particular on, *inter alia*, modernization of infrastructure; formulation and planning of energy policy; development of energy resources; promotion of energy saving and energy efficiency; and the opening up of the energy market.[24]

Trade and economic co-operation agreements. The trade and economic co-operation agreements concluded in 1990, 1991, and 1992 with certain countries of Latin America each include co-operation in the area of energy as an aspect of the economic co-operation envisaged under the agreement.[25] Provisions establishing co-operation on energy matters have been included in agreements with Macao;[26] Mongolia;[27] the Central American Economic Integration countries[28] and Panama;[29] the Cartagena Agreement and the countries members thereof;[30]

---

[19] Concluded under Art. 238 EEC.

[20] See Art. 4(1) of each of the co-operation agreements with Tunisia ([1978] OJ L265/1); Egypt ([1978] OJ L266/1); Algeria ([1978] OJ L263/1); Syria ([1978] OJ L269/1); Lebanon ([1978] OJ L267/1); and Jordan ([1978] OJ L268/1). See also the 1985 Agreement with the Yemen Arab Republic, Art. 3(2) ([1985] OJ L26/1).

[21] See the Agreements (listed at n. 20 above) with Tunisia, Arts. 12 and 13; Egypt, Arts. 14 and 15; Algeria, Arts. 12 and 13; Syria, Arts. 14 and 15.

[22] See [1978] OJ L263/1 (Algeria); [1978] OJ L264/1 (Morocco); and [1978] OJ L265/1 (Tunisia).

[23] On the Europe Agreements, see Ch. 20.

[24] For the provisions on co-operation in the area of energy, see the Europe Agreements with Hungary, Art. 77 ([1993] OJ L347/1); Poland, Art. 78 ([1993] OJ L348/1); Romania, Art. 79 ([1994] OJ L357/1); Bulgaria, Art. 79 ([1994] OJ L358/1); the Slovak Republic, Art. 79 ([1994] OJ L359/1); and the Czech Republic, Art. 79 ([1994] OJ L360/1).

[25] See the agreements with Argentina, Art. 4(2)(g) ([1990] OJ L295/66); Brazil, Art. 14 ([1990] OJ C163/11); Chile, Arts. 2(2)(a) and 6(2)(d) ([1991] OJ L79/1); Mexico, Arts. 2 (2)(f) and 30 ([1991] OJ L340/1); Paraguay, Art. 3(2)(f) ([1992] OJ L313/71); Uruguay, Art. 3(2)(a) ([1992] OJ L94/1).

[26] 1992 Agreement with Macao, Art. 4 ([1992] OJ L404/26).

[27] 1993 Agreement with Mongolia, Arts. 9 and 10 ([1993] OJ L41/.45).

[28] i.e. Costa Rica, El Salvador, Guatemala, Honduras, and Nicaragua.

[29] 1989 Agreement, Arts. 1(b) and 6 ([1989] OJ L54/1).

[30] i.e. Bolivia, Colombia, Ecuador, Peru, and Venezuela. See the 1984 Agreement, Art. 1(2)(c) ([1984] OJ L153/1).

the Gulf Co-operation Council;[31] Albania;[32] Estonia;[33] Lithuania;[34] Latvia;[35] the USSR;[36] China;[37] Pakistan;[38] and India.[39]

Unilateral Measures

The OCT Decision[40] provides for co-operation on energy development with a view to finding solutions to the energy problems of the overseas countries and territories.[41] Particular emphasis is to be placed on energy programming, operations for saving and making efficient use of energy, reconnaissance of energy potential, and the economically and technically appropriate promotion of new and renewable sources of energy.[42] Co-operation in the field of energy is to promote the development of the OCTs' conventional and non-conventional energy potential and their self-sufficiency.[43] The objectives of the provisions of the OCT Decision dealing with energy may be pursued with finance from the Community.[44]

Under *the PHARE Programme*,[45] the Community provides economic aid to countries of Central and Eastern Europe by financing or participating in the financing of projects aimed at economic restructuring. Such projects are to be undertaken in particular areas, including energy, and should be aimed in particular at the private sector.[46]

The *TACIS Programme*[47] provides technical assistance for economic reform and recovery in the independent States of the former Soviet Union and Mongolia. Technical assistance under the programme is to be concentrated in particular in the indicative areas listed in Annex II to the Regulation establish-

---

[31] i.e. the UAE, Bahrain, Saudi Arabia, Oman, Qatar, and Kuwait. See the 1986 Agreement, Arts. 3(1)(a) and 3(2)(d) ([1986] OJ L172/1).

[32] 1992 Agreement with Albania, Art. 15(2) ([1992] OJ L343/1).

[33] 1992 Agreement with Estonia, Art. 15(2) ([1992] OJ L403/1).

[34] 1992 Euratom Agreement with Lithuania, Art. 15(2) ([1992] OJ L403/19).

[35] 1992 Agreement with Latvia, Art. 15(2) ([1992] OJ L403/10).

[36] On the current status of this agreement, see Ch. 12, p. 287. Provisions on energy co-operation are included in Art. 20(2) ([1990] OJ L68/1).

[37] 1985 Agreement with China, Art. 10 ([1985] OJ L250/1).

[38] Art. 3(1)(d) ([1986] OJ L108/1).

[39] 1994 Agreement with India, Arts. 4(3) and 7 ([1994] OJ L223/23).

[40] Council Dec. 91/482 of 25 July 1991 on the association of the overseas countries and territories with the EEC ([1991] OJ L263/1).

[41] *Ibid.*, Arts. 57 to 60.   [42] *Ibid.*, Art. 57(2).

[43] *Ibid.*, Art. 58(1).   [44] *Ibid.*, Art. 60.

[45] Council Reg. 3906/89 of 18 Dec. 1989 ([1989] OJ L375/11) on economic aid to Hungary and Poland; extended to include Bulgaria, Czechoslovakia, the GDR, Romania, and Yugoslavia by Reg. 2698/90 ([1990] OJ L257/1); to include Albania, Estonia, Latvia, and Lithuania by Reg. 3800/91 ([1991] OJ L357/10); and to include Slovenia by Reg. 2334/92 ([1992] OJ L227/1).

[46] Art. 3(1) of Reg. 3906/89, n. 45 above. On projects under PHARE, see *24th General Report* (1990), point 615; *25th General Report* (1991), point 757; *27th General Report* (1993), point 296.

[47] Reg. 2053/93 (Euratom, EEC) of 19 July 1993 ([1993] OJ L187/1).

ing TACIS.[48] Annex II states that assistance is to give priority to, *inter alia*, energy including nuclear safety.[49]

International Organizations

The Community participates actively as an observer in the International Energy Agency (IEA).[50] The statute of the IEA provides that the Community may become a party, but a proposal for a Council decision to that effect was withdrawn by the Commission in 1993.

The Community also conducts regular dialogue on energy related matters with OPEC and OAPEC,[51] and with the members of the G7 and G24.[52]

---

[48] *Ibid.*, Art. 4(3).
[49] For examples of assistance given under TACIS, see *26th General Report* (1992), points 706 and 710–12 and *27th General Report*, n. 46 above, points 294 and 295.
[50] UKTS 111 (1976); Cmnd 6697; 14 ILM 1.
[51] e.g., *24th General Report*, n. 46 above, point 610; *1994 General Report*, points 359–60.
[52] See, e.g., *25th General Report*, n. 46 above, point 757.

22

Euratom

The Euratom Treaty provided more comprehensively for the conduct of external relations than did either of the other two Community Treaties. The powers conferred on Euratom in that regard, and the procedures to be followed for the conclusion of agreements, have already been described in Chapters 3 and 4. This Chapter considers the extent and nature of these powers and describes the use that has been made of them to date.

LEGAL BASIS OF EURATOM'S EXTERNAL COMPETENCE

The principal legal basis for the exercise of external competence by Euratom is Article 101 Euratom, which provides that: 'The Community may, within the limits of its powers and jurisdiction, enter into obligations by concluding agreements or contracts with a third State [or] an international organisation.'[1] Euratom's external competence is therefore co-extensive with its internal competence: it has power to enter into agreements and arrangements on any matter on which it is entitled to act internally.[2] In addition to this general power to make agreements, the Treaty also confers on the Community a power to enter into association agreements,[3] and expressly envisages the conclusion of agreements by the Community in several areas.[4]

Extent of the Euratom's Competence

The task of Euratom is to contribute to the raising of the standard of living in the Member States and to the development of relations with other countries by

---

[1] On the meaning of 'contracts' in this context, see Ch. 4.

[2] See T. C. Hartley, *The Foundations of European Community Law* (3rd edn., Clarendon Press, 1994), 180 ff. But note that since the Euratom Treaty contains no provisions relating to external trade, there is nothing to prevent agreements concluded pursuant to Art. 113 EC from extending to international trade in Euratom products: *Opinion 1/94 (Re WTO Agreement)* [1995] 1 CMLR 205 at para. 24.

[3] i.e. agreements concluded with 'one or more State or international organizations . . . establishing an association involving reciprocal rights and obligations, common action and special procedures': see Art. 206 Euratom. On the characteristics of association agreements generally, see Ch. 20. In the case of Euratom, the power to conclude association agreements has been used very rarely. E.g. the Europe Agreement with Hungary ([1993] OJ L347/1) is, for the purposes of the EC Treaty, an association agreement (concluded under Art. 238 EC). The legal basis for Euratom participation, however, was Art. 101 Euratom, not Art. 206.

[4] Arts. 10, 29, 46(2), and 52 Euratom.

creating the conditions necessary for the speedy establishment and growth of nuclear industries.[5] To perform that task, the Community is required to act in the areas listed in Article 2. These include promotion of research; promotion of uniform health and safety standards to protect workers and the general public; ensuring that all users in the Community receive a regular and equitable supply of ores and nuclear fuels; making certain that nuclear materials are not diverted to purposes other than those for which they are intended; establishment of a nuclear common market as provided in the Treaty; and establishment with other countries and international organizations of such relations as will foster progress in the peaceful uses of nuclear energy.[6]

The powers of Euratom, although conferred in respect of a relatively narrow sector of activity, are, within that sector, extensive. It has, however, no power or jurisdiction in relation to the use of nuclear fuels or nuclear installations for military purposes,[7] nor does it have powers in respect of the safe design, construction, or operation of the Member States' nuclear facilities and installations.

Nature of the Community's Competence

The Court of Justice has held that Euratom's powers under the Treaty are exclusive in at least three areas.[8] First, it has exclusive jurisdiction with regard to supplies of ores, source materials, and special fissile materials coming from outside the Community, and, in general, with regard to the normal functioning of the nuclear common market.[9] Secondly, in relation to safeguards, Euratom is required to exercise central supervision of the use made of nuclear materials for which it is responsible, and must be able to guarantee to third parties obligations which it has assumed in that regard in agreements concluded with other States or international organizations.[10] Finally, Euratom is the exclusive holder of the rights which form the essential content of the right of property in the nuclear materials to which the Treaty applies.[11] It follows that the power

---

[5] Art. 1 Euratom.   [6] Art. 2 Euratom.

[7] Arts. 84 and 86 Euratom; *Ruling 1/78 (Re the Draft Convention on the Physical Protection of Nuclear Materials)* [1978] ECR 2151 at para. 12.

[8] It should be noted that Chs. VI and VIII of the Euratom Treaty have not been implemented in full and the Community does not have the central role envisaged for it when the Treaty was drafted in the mid-1950s. Commission attempts to revise Ch. VI in 1964, 1970, 1982, and 1984 all foundered due to a lack of political consensus about what should take its place. For further comment, see D. Allen, 'The Euratom Treaty, Ch. VI: New Hope or False Dawn?' (1983) 20 *CMLRev*. 473.

[9] *Ruling 1/78*, n. 7 above, at paras. 13–18. In practice this means that Euratom must satisfy itself that ores, source materials, and special fissile materials are not diverted from their intended use and that safeguards obligations assumed by the Community under agreements concluded with a third State or international organization are complied with.

[10] *Ibid.*, at para. 19 to 23. Notwithstanding this right of property, Euratom has conferred on the Member States an unlimited right to use and consume special fissile materials which have properly come into their possession.

[11] *Ibid.*, at paras. 24 ff.

to enter into agreements which relate to these areas is exclusively that of Euratom.

In other areas of Euratom's activities, the nature of the Community's competence must be determined by reference to the general principles developed in the case law of the Court.[12] Thus, to the extent that the Community has adopted common rules for the attainment of the objectives of the Euratom Treaty, the Member States are precluded from entering into international commitments capable of affecting those rules or altering their scope:[13] such commitments are exclusively for the Community to undertake. On the other hand, there seems no reason to hold that Euratom's competence to enter into agreements relating to research and scientific co-operation has deprived the Member States of all their powers in these areas.[14] Nor should the adoption by the Community of minimum rules on health and safety prevent the Member States from adopting more stringent measures nationally, or in international agreements.[15] However, even in areas where the Member States retain powers, the provisions of Article 103 Euratom place a constraint on their action, and ensure that the Community interest is protected.[16]

Procedure for the Conclusion of Agreements

The distinctive features of the procedures established for the conclusion of agreements by Euratom have been examined elsewhere.[17]

PRACTICE OF EURATOM IN EXTERNAL RELATIONS

Multilateral Agreements

Agreements in Implementation of the Treaty on Non-Proliferation of Nuclear Weapons

An agreement on the implementation of the Non-Proliferation Treaty[18] was concluded by Euratom, Belgium, Denmark, the Federal Republic of Germany,

---

[12] See *Opinion 2/91 (Re ILO Convention 170)* [1993] ECR I–1061 at paras. 9 ff, and Ch. 3.

[13] The *AETR* principle: there seems no need to confine this principle to the EC Treaty: it is a reflection of the general doctrine of the supremacy of Community law: see, further, Ch. 3.

[14] Compare the EC's powers in relation to research and technological development: Ch. 16.

[15] Thus Euratom's duty to set 'uniform standards' (Art. 2(h) Euratom) does not preclude the Member States from applying—at least in certain circumstances—stricter standards than those set by the Community: see Case C–376/90 *Commission* v. *Belgium* [1992] ECR I–6153 at para. 19. See also *Opinion 2/91*, n. 12 above, at para. 18 ff.

[16] Art. 103 Euratom requires Member States to communicate to the Commission draft agreements or contracts with a third State, an international organization, or a national of a third State to the extent that such agreements or contracts concern matters within the purview of this Treaty. The meaning and effect of Art. 103 are examined in Ch. 4: see p. 114.

[17] See Ch. 4.

[18] See T. F. Cusack, 'External Relations of the European Atomic Energy Community in the

Ireland, Italy, Luxembourg, and the Netherlands on the one hand, and the International Atomic Energy Agency (IAEA) on the other, in 1977.[19] This agreement requires these seven Member States to apply the safeguards in the agreement in respect of all source or fissionable material in all peaceful nuclear activities within their territories, or under their jurisdiction or control, for the exclusive purpose of verifying that such material is not diverted to nuclear weapons or other nuclear explosive devices. The IAEA is given the right to ensure that safeguards will be applied and the Community agrees to co-operate with the IAEA to that end. The agreement sets out the safeguards and makes provision for inspection. The United Kingdom, Euratom, and the IAEA concluded a co-operation agreement in relation to non-military materials and equipment in 1978,[20] and France, Euratom, and the IAEA concluded a similar agreement in 1981.[21]

International Convention on the Physical Protection of Nuclear Materials

The aim of this convention[22] is to deal with the risk of theft and misuse of nuclear materials put to civil uses. Parties are required to take all appropriate measures to prevent such occurrences, and precautions are prescribed in respect of the transport, storage, export, and import of nuclear materials. Parties are required to make certain conduct an offence, and extraditable. Euratom and the Member States are parties to this convention.[23]

Agreement Establishing an International Science and Technology Centre

This agreement was concluded between the United States of America, Japan, the Russian Federation, and, acting as one party, the EEC and Euratom.[24] Its purpose was to channel the know-how of military research scientists and technicians of the former Soviet Union into non-military projects. The Member States are not parties to the agreement.

Field of Supply and Safeguards: Developments in 1982 and 1983' [1983] 3 *YEL* 347, at 356; J. Gissels, 'L'Accord entre l'Euratom et l'AIEA pour l'adoption du Traité sur la non-proliferation des armes nucléaires' [1972] *AFDI* 837.

[19] [1978] OJ L51/1.

[20] Agreement between the UK, Euratom, and the IAEA for the Application of Safeguards in the UK in connection with the Treaty on the Non-Proliferation of Nuclear Weapons. See *Collection of Agreements concluded by the European Communities*, viii (II), 3381.

[21] Agreement between France, Euratom, and the IAEA *Collection*, n. 20 above, xi (II), 2497.

[22] Misc. 27 (1980), Cmnd. 8112; 18 ILM 1419.

[23] See M. J. Bowman and D. J. Harris, *Multilateral Treaties*, 10th Cumulative Supplement, p 279 (Entry 773).

[24] See Commission Reg. 3956/92 of 21 Dec. 1992 on the conclusion of the Agreement by the Euratom ([1992] OJ L409/10).

Co-operation on Controlled Thermonuclear Fusion

On 21 July 1992, Euratom, Japan, the United States, and the Russian Federation signed a Co-operation Agreement on engineering design activities for the International Thermonuclear Experimental Reactor. The project is designed to produce a detailed plan for a reactor which would demonstrate the scientific and technological feasibility of using fusion for peaceful purposes.[25]

Euratom, together with the European Community and a majority of Member States, is applying the *European Energy Charter Treaty* on a provisional basis to the extent that it has competence for the matters governed by the Treaty.[26]

In September 1994, the Commission proposed that the Community should become a party to the Nuclear Safety Convention along with the Member States.

Bilateral Agreements

Agreements involving the Transfer of Nuclear Material

Agreements on co-operation on the peaceful uses of nuclear energy have been concluded with the United States, Canada, and Australia.[27] Free Trade Agreements concluded in 1994 with Estonia,[28] Latvia,[29] and Lithuania[30] include provisions on trade in energy matters. Similar provisions are being negotiated with the States of the former Soviet Union.

The United States of America

A short agreement concluded on 29 June 1958 provided that the United States and Euratom would co-operate in programmes for the advancement of peaceful applications of atomic energy.[31] This was soon followed by an agreement concerning peaceful uses of atomic energy,[32] which established a joint programme to bring into operation large-scale power plants, and to initiate a joint research and development programme. This agreement also provided for transfer of nuclear materials, and exchange of information and research. More significant still was the Additional Agreement for Co-operation concerning the peaceful uses of atomic energy[33] which provided for the transfer of nuclear equipment and materials. The Additional Agreement remains in force until 31 December 1995. A successor agreement is being negotiated.

---

[25] [1992] OJ L224/13.　　　　　　　[26] See Council Dec. 94/1067 ([1994] OJ L380/1).
[27] Agreements with Argentina ([1963] JO 2966) and Brazil ([1969] JO L79/7) expired in 1983 and 1985 respectively .
[28] [1994] OJ L373/1 and 166.　　　　[29] [1994] OJ L374/1 and 219.
[30] [1994] OJ L375/1 and 207.　　　　[31] [1959] JO 17.
[32] *Ibid.*, amended in 1962 ([1962] JO 72). This agreement terminated in 1985.
[33] [1961] JO 31; amended in 1962 ([1962] JO 72); 1963 ([1964] JO 163); and 1975 ([1974] OJ L139/24).

Canada

An agreement establishing co-operation on the peaceful uses of atomic energy was concluded in October 1959 between Euratom and Canada. This agreement provided for the supply of information and materials, the procurement of equipment and devices, the protection of intellectual property rights, and the safeguarding of materials and information.[34]

Australia

An agreement on nuclear transfers from Australia to Euratom was signed on 21 September 1981, for a period of thirty years from 15 January 1982. The agreement establishes arrangements for the transfers of nuclear material to the Community, and sets conditions for retransfer, enrichment, reprocessing, and peaceful uses.[35]

Agreements on Scientific Co-operation and Research

Agreements have been concluded in three areas: thermonuclear fusion and plasma physics; radiation protection; and the management of radioactive waste.

Thermonuclear Fusion and Plasma Physics

Agreements have been concluded with Switzerland[36] and Japan[37] on co-operation on thermonuclear fusion and plasma physics. A Memorandum of Understanding was drawn up with Canada on fusion research and development in 1986,[38] and a similar agreement was entered into with the United States in the same year.[39] In December 1994, the Commission was authorized to conclude a co-operation agreement on controlled nuclear fusion with Russia.[40]

Radiation Protection

An agreement was drawn up in 1990 between the Community and Sweden on research and training in the field of radiation protection.[41] The aim was to develop a scientific basis for regular updating of Basic Safety Standards for the protection of the health of the public and workers. Under the Third Framework Programme,[42] agreements on research and education in the field of radiation protection were concluded in 1994 between Euratom and Norway and Switzerland[43] providing for these States' participation in the Community's specific research and education programme in the field of nuclear fission safety.[44]

---

[34] Amended in 1978 ([1978] OJ L65/16); and 1981 ([1982] OJ L27/25).
[35] [1982] OJ L28/8. See Cusack, n. 18 above.
[36] [1978] OJ L242/1; amended [1982] OJ L116/18.   [37] [1989] OJ L57/62.
[38] [1986] OJ L35/9.   [39] [1987] OJ L46/49.
[40] *1994 General Report*, point 353; Bull. EU 12–1994, 1.2.112.
[41] [1990] OJ L228/35.   [42] Dec. 90/221 ([1990] OJ L117/28).
[43] [1994] OJ L219/1. The Agreement with Norway is at 2; that with Switzerland is at 18.
[44] Dec. 91/626 Euratom ([1991] OJ L336/42).

Management of Radioactive Waste

Within the framework of the co-operation established in the 1959 Agreement between the Community and Canada, an Agreement for Co-operation in the field of nuclear waste management research was drawn up in 1980 between Atomic Energy of Canada Limited and the Euratom, and renewed in 1985 and 1990.[45]

Miscellaneous

Some bilateral agreements establishing a more general basis for co-operation between the Community and third countries contain provisions on co-operation in the nuclear field. In December 1994, the Commission was authorized to conclude a co-operation agreement with Russia on nuclear safety.[46] The framework agreements on scientific and technical co-operation concluded with Iceland[47] and Switzerland[48] contain such clauses.

The Europe Agreements provide for co-operation on energy;[49] and on nuclear safety[50] or on the nuclear sector generally.[51]

Unilateral Community Measures

The programme to assist economic recovery and reform established by the TACIS Regulation is to be concentrated in certain indicative areas, including nuclear safety.[52]

Euratom and International Organizations

International Atomic Energy Agency (IAEA)

Euratom has the status of observer at the IAEA. In accordance with a co-operation agreement between the Community and the IAEA,[53] the two organizations agreed to consult regularly and to co-operate on matters of common interest. Arrangements were to be made for each to be represented at the other's meetings; for the exchange of documents and information; and for administrative and technical co-operation.

---

[45] Unpublished: see SEC(90)1986, 24 Oct. 1990.

[46] *1994 General Report*, n. 40 above, point 353; Bull. EU 12–1994, 1.2.112.

[47] [1990] OJ L14 /18.   [48] [1985] OJ L313/5.

[49] On the Europe Agreements, see Ch. 20. For provisions on co-operation in the field of energy, see the Europe Agreements with Hungary, Art. 77 ([1993] OJ L347/1); Poland, Art. 78 ([1993] OJ L348/1); Romania, Art. 79 ([1994] OJ L357/1); Bulgaria, Art. 79 ([1994] OJ L358/1); the Slovak Republic, Art. 79 ([1994] OJ L359/1); and the Czech Republic, Art. 79 ([1994] OJ L360/1).

[50] Europe Agreements with Hungary, Art. 78; Bulgaria, Art. 80; the Slovak Republic, Art. 80; and the Czech Republic, Art. 80.

[51] Europe Agreements with Poland, Art. 79; and Romania, Art. 80.

[52] Art. 4, Reg. (Euratom, EEC) 2053/93 ([1993] OJ L187/1).

[53] [1975] OJ L329/28.

International Labour Organization

The Community has observer status at the ILO. In accordance with an Agreement on co-operation between the ILO and Euratom,[54] the two organizations agree to hold consultations on matters of common interest in order to achieve their objectives in the social area, in particular in relation to health and safety. Provision is made for exchanges of representatives, attendance at each other's meetings, technical consultation, and the optimal use of information.

The OECD

Euratom has observer status at the Nuclear Energy Agency of the OECD.[55]

Council of Arab Economic Unity

A Co-operation agreement between the CAEU and the Euratom provides for each side to keep the other informed on areas of common interest.[56]

---

[54] [1963] JO 18/473.   [55] On the Communities' links with the OECD, see Ch. 7.
[56] [1982] OJ L300/23.

23

The European Coal and Steel Community

This Chapter considers the powers of the ECSC in the conduct of external relations. It is in two parts. Under the heading of legal position it looks first at the capacity of the ECSC to enter into international agreements and then considers the extent of the powers of the ECSC, in particular whether the Community or the Member States should act where the agreement in question includes matters within commercial policy. It considers the legal basis for action by the ECSC and the decision where Member States are parties. Under the heading of practice of the ECSC it describes the use that has been made of the powers to date.

LEGAL POSITION

Capacity of the ECSC to enter into International Agreements

The Treaty of Paris establishing the ECSC (the ECSC Treaty) contains no provisions equivalent to Article 228 EC or Article 101 Euratom providing for the Community to enter into international agreements with non-member countries or international organizations. However, it is clear that the ECSC has the power to enter into international agreements. Article 6 provides that the ECSC is to have legal personality and that, in international relations, the Community is to enjoy the legal capacity it requires to perform its functions and attain its objectives. In addition, Article 3(a) implies an international role for the Community by providing that the institutions of the Community shall in the common interest ensure an orderly supply to the common market, taking into account the needs of third countries. Similarly paragraph (f) of the Article includes the objective of promoting the growth of international trade.

Articles 93 and 94 contain provisions equivalent to Articles 229 and 230 EC. Article 93 provides that the High Authority (now the Commission) is to maintain all appropriate relations with the United Nations and the Organization for European Economic Co-operation (now the Organization for Economic Co-operation and Development[1]) and Article 94 provides for the maintenance of relations between the institutions of the Community and the Council of Europe.

---

[1] This Art. was not amended by the TEU as a result, it appears, of an oversight.

As a matter of practice, the ECSC has entered in a number of agreements with non-member countries and its power to do so has been recognized by the Court of Justice.[2]

Extent of the Community's Powers

Although there is no Court of Justice authority on the point, it would seem, as a matter of principle, that the case law of the Court on the implied powers of the EC should apply by analogy to the ECSC[3] given the absence of express powers in the ECSC Treaty. Therefore, for example, if an agreement extends a provision of the ECSC Treaty and measures adopted under it to a non-member country, the ECSC would have the power to enter into such an agreement.[4] Similarly, the case law on the nature of those powers and whether and in what circumstances they are exclusive would apply by analogy to the ECSC.

The most important limitation on the powers of the ECSC is Article 71 ECSC. Article 71 ECSC provides that the powers of the Governments of the Member States in matters of commercial policy are not affected by the Treaty, save as provided in it. Prior to the decision of the Court of Justice in *Opinion 1/94*[5] the meaning of this provision and its relationship with Article 113 EC was not clear; however, the practice had been for the Member States of the ECSC to take action in the commercial policy field rather than the ECSC or the EC.

Consequently where an agreement covering coal and steel products dealt with such trade matters as customs duties, quantitative restrictions on imports, and competition matters relating to trade with the country concerned the Member States, rather than the ECSC or the EC, were parties. These matters were regarded as falling outside the competence of the ECSC or the EC by virtue of Article 71.

A change in practice occurred in 1991 and 1992 when the Communities concluded a series of protocols on trade and commercial and economic co-operation with certain countries of Central and Eastern Europe. The protocols contained provisions dealing with customs duties, quantitative restrictions, and competition matters. In accordance with the procedure that had previously been adopted, the protocols would have been entered into by the Member States of the ECSC. However, the ECSC was a party to the protocols rather than the Member States. The reason for the change was as follows. Around the same time the Communities and the Member States concluded a series of agreements with the same group of countries, the Europe Agreements, which were

---

[2] Most recently in *Opinion 1/94 (WTO Agreements)* [1995] 1 CMLR 205. See also the opinion of the A.G. in Case C-327/91 *France v. Commission* [1994] ECR I-3641.

[3] See Ch. 3.

[4] See, e.g., Art. 20 of the agreement of 14 May 1973 between the ECSC, its Member States and Norway [1974] OJ L348/17.

[5] N. 2 above.

intended to strengthen and widen the relations previously established with the countries of Central and Eastern Europe.[6] The Europe Agreements were mixed and therefore required ratification by the Member States. The need for ratification delayed their entry into force. The parties, however, wanted to implement the trade and trade-related matters contained in those Agreements as speedily as possible. Consequently interim agreements were entered into covering trade and trade-related matters. Each contained a protocol applying to ECSC products, dealing with customs duties, quantitative restrictions, and competition matters related to trade with the country concerned. If the Member States had been parties on the basis that these matters were within their competence, the agreements would have needed to be ratified by them. Thus, the benefit of adopting interim agreements, at least as far as coal and steel products were concerned, would have been negated.

It was therefore decided to have recourse to Article 95. That Article enables the Council to assent to the adoption of a decision by the Commission where there is no express power in the Treaty but a decision is necessary to achieve one of objectives of the Community set out in Articles 2, 3, and 4. The basis for the use of Article 95 in these circumstances was that the protocols, and later the interim agreements, would attain one of the objectives set out in those Articles, in particular Article 3(f) which provides that the institutions of the Community shall in the common interest promote the growth of international trade. The participation of the ECSC in these agreements did not amount to a concession that the Community had exclusive competence in respect of commercial policy relating to ECSC products as it has under Article 113 EC in respect of other products. On the contrary the Member States, through the Council, agreed in the case of the particular agreements in question that the ECSC should be a party to them. The Council was therefore exercising a discretion that the Community should be a party to the agreements to achieve one of the objectives of the Community as opposed to acknowledging that the Community had the exclusive competence to enter into the agreements concerned.

More broadly, the Commission did not accept that coal and steel products were outside the scope of the common commercial policy under Article 113 EC. Their view was that Article 71 ECSC does not reserve the rights of Member States as regards ECSC products. All that Article does is to provide that the ECSC Treaty does not transfer competence in respect of commercial policy to the *ECSC* and the effect of Article 113 is to transfer competence to the *EC*. This has not been accepted by the Council or most of the Member States.

The issue arose in *Opinion 1/94*.[7] The Multilateral Agreements on Trade in Goods covered ECSC products in the same way as other products: they contained no specific provisions dealing with ECSC products. The Court of Justice

---

[6] See Ch. 20, p. 375.   [7] See n. 2 above.

held that, since none of the Multilateral Agreements related specifically to ECSC products, the European Community had exclusive competence to conclude those Agreements under Article 113 EC. The reasoning of the Court was that, since the ECSC Treaty was drawn up at a time when the European Economic Community was not yet in existence, Article 71 ECSC can only have been intended to refer to coal and steel products. In any event it can only have reserved competence to the Member States as regards agreements relating specifically to ECSC products. The Court said that, on the other hand, the European Community has sole competence to conclude an external agreement of a general nature, that is to say, encompassing all types of goods, even when those goods include ECSC products. Since none of the Multilateral Agreements related specifically to ECSC products it followed that the European Community had exclusive competence to conclude those Agreements.

The effect of the Court's opinion is that, if an agreement covers ECSC products but does not deal with them specifically, the European Community has exclusive competence if the agreement would otherwise fall within the common commercial policy. However, if the agreement deals only with ECSC products or contains provisions dealing specifically with such products, the agreement is not within the common commercial policy and falls within the competence of the Member States or within that of the ECSC. Consequently, the Multilateral Agreements on Trade in Goods forming part of the Uruguay Round fell within the exclusive competence of the European Community although they covered ECSC products. On the other hand, the bilateral agreement negotiated during the round with Australia on coal was concluded by the Member States of the ECSC, since it dealt solely with products within the ECSC Treaty.[8]

It should be borne in mind that not all coal and steel products are within the ECSC Treaty. Article 81 provides that the expression 'coal and steel' as used in the Treaty is defined in Annex 1 to the Treaty. In so far as products not covered by the ECSC Treaty are concerned, the position is governed by the EC Treaty.

Legal Basis for Action by the ECSC

In contrast to the position under the EC and Euratom Treaties, the power to adopt legislative acts is vested in the Commission, although in some areas this is subject to control by the Council, for example by requiring the Council's assent. This means that the decision authorizing the ECSC to enter into an agreement will be a decision of the Commission.[9] Consequently, although the party to the agreement will be the Community, it is a decision of the Commission that authorizes the Community to conclude the agreement

[8] Bull. EU 12–94 point 1.3.98.
[9] See, e.g., the Decision on the conclusion of the Europe Agreement with Poland, Dec. 93/743/Euratom, ECSC, EC ([1993] OJ L348/1).

concerned. If external action can be based on a Treaty Article which enables the Commission to act without any formal control by the Council, in particular obtaining its assent, there is no formal control of the Commission by the Member States, either directly or through the Council. The Council has therefore been reluctant to agree to the use of Treaty Articles which do not require its assent.

The Commission has argued that, where the power of the Community to act is derived from the existence of internal rules that will be affected (that is under the *AETR* principle) the legal basis that should be used is the legal basis of the internal measure. Similarly, where the Community has an implied power because the field is occupied by the Community or because Community rules are being extended to a non-member country, the Treaty Articles giving the Community the power to act internally should be used for the external exercise of the power. The Council has not accepted this on the basis that the power to adopt internal rules does not extend to entering into international agreements. Instead it has argued that Article 95 ECSC should be used. That Article is equivalent to Article 235 of the EC Treaty and provides:

In all cases not provided for in this Treaty where it becomes apparent that a decision or recommendation of the High Authority is necessary to attain, within the common market in coal and steel and in accordance with Article 5, one of the objectives of the Community set out in Articles 2, 3 or 4, the decision may be taken or the recommendation made with the unanimous assent of the Council and after the Consultative Committee has been consulted.

An example of this difference of view was the decision which authorized the Community to conclude the agreement of 21 October 1982 between the ECSC and the United States. That agreement provided for export ceilings relating to steel products; the period for which the restrictions should apply; how the ceilings were to be calculated, revised, and modified; the conditions to be fulfilled for it to enter into effect and to be terminated; and setting out how the export ceilings were to be controlled. The Commission had proposed the use of Articles 58 and 95 but the inclusion of Article 58 was not accepted by the Council.[10] In the end the view of the Council prevailed and the decision to conclude the agreement was based on Article 95 alone.

The issue was considered in Case C–327/91, *France* v. *Commission*[11] which concerned an agreement on competition which had been entered into by the Commission with the United States. The Court held that the Commission had no power to enter into the agreement. The Court did not deal in any detail with ECSC aspects but the Advocate-General advised that the agreement should have been concluded on the basis of Article 95 with the unanimous assent of

---

[10] See Benyon and Bourgeois, 'The European Community–United States Steel Agreement' (1984) 21 *CMLRev.* 305.
[11] N. 2 above.

the Council. Despite this, the legal basis for the decision[12] authorizing the ECSC to conclude the agreement entered into as a result of the Court's decision was Articles 65 and 66 ECSC.

Member States as Parties to Agreements

When the Member States of the ECSC are to be parties to an agreement, a decision of the representatives of the Governments of the Member States meeting within the Council is adopted. The decision in question provides for the approval of the agreement in question on behalf of the Member States of the ECSC.[13]

In contrast to other areas where a matter is outside the competence of the Community it is the practice in the case of the ECSC for there to be a formal decision adopted within the framework of the Council which is published in the Official Journal. The reason for this is not clear. In many cases the agreement on ECSC products will have been negotiated as part of a wider package covering other products which are within the exclusive competence of the EC, but this is not so in all cases. The justification may go back to the Convention on Transitional Provisions, Article 14 of which provides that, once the High Authority was established, Member States were to open negotiations with non-member countries on the whole range of economic and commercial relations concerning coal and steel between the Community and those countries. In these negotiations the High Authority was to act, upon instructions unanimously agreed by the Council, for the Member States jointly.[14] The negotiations were thus brought within the Community framework.

Agreements entered into by the European Community form part of the Community legal order and are subject to the jurisdiction of the Court of Justice. In addition, Community law principles, such as direct effect, can apply to such agreements.[15] There is no reason why the same principles should not apply to agreements to which the ECSC is a party. However, it does not follow that the same principles should apply to those to which the Member States of the ECSC are parties. The better view would be that those agreements operate only in international law and international law concepts apply to them.

This section has dealt with cases where the Member States are parties but act within the Council. There will also be cases where the Member States act independently and without there being a decision of the Governments of the Member States meeting within the Council. Article 75 ECSC imposes an obligation on the Member States to keep the Commission informed of proposed

[12] Not yet published. In many cases no Treaty basis is in fact cited. This would seem to be contrary to the decision of the Court in Case 45/86 *Commission* v. *Council* [1987] ECR 1493.

[13] See, e.g., the dec. relating to coal and steel products concluding the Tokyo Round [1980] OJ L71/179.

[14] Representatives of the Member States may be present at the negotiations.

[15] See Ch. 5, pp. 135–6.

commercial agreements or arrangements having similar effect where these relate to coal and steel or to the importation of other raw materials and specialized equipment needed for the production of coal and steel in Member States.

PRACTICE OF THE ECSC

The ECSC is a party to a number of agreements. This section outlines the most important ones that are still in force. It then briefly considers unilateral measures that have been adopted by the ECSC in the external field.

Multilateral Agreements

Agreement on the European Economic Area

The ECSC and the Member States are parties to this agreement. Protocol 14 deals with trade in coal and steel products and Protocol 25 deals with competition regarding coal and steel.[16]

The Fourth Lomé Convention

The ECSC and the Member States are parties. Protocol 9 contains provisions concerning products within the provisions of the ECSC Treaty.[17]

Bilateral Agreements

International Labour Organization

In 1956 the ECSC concluded an agreement on collaboration with the ILO.[18] The Member States are not parties. It provides for the parties to confer together, to exchange information and to co-operate on administrative matters.

Agreement on Railway Tariffs with Switzerland

In 1956 the Member States and the High Authority of the ECSC entered in an agreement with Switzerland on the introduction of through international railway tariffs for the carriage of coal and steel through Switzerland. It has been amended on a number of occasions.[19]

---

[16] See, further, Ch. 20, pp. 377 ff.   [17] See, further, Ch. 20, pp. 380 ff.
[18] [1953] JO 167.
[19] [1957] JO 223. See also [1979] OJ L12/15 and [1981] OJ L227/11.

Agreements with the EFTA Countries

At the time that the EC entered into free trade agreements with the EFTA countries[20] the Member States entered into agreements dealing with products within the ECSC Treaty. In the case of Norway,[21] the ECSC was a party as well but not in the case of Iceland[22] or Switzerland.[23]

Agreements with Maghreb Countries

The Member States of the ECSC entered into agreements relating to ECSC products at the same time as the EC concluded association agreements[24] with those countries, Algeria,[25] Morocco,[26] and Tunisia.[27]

Agreements with Mashreq Countries

Similarly the Member States of the ECSC entered into agreements with the countries of the Mashreq at the same time as the EC concluded association agreements[28] with those countries, Egypt,[29] Jordan,[30] Lebanon,[31] and Syria.[32]

Israel

The Member States of the ECSC entered into an agreement with Israel on 11 May 1975 at the same time as the conclusion of the agreement between that country and the EC.[33]

Central and Eastern Europe

The ECSC and the Member States are parties to the Europe Agreements with Poland, Hungary, Romania, Bulgaria, the Czech Republic, and the Slovak Republic. These Agreements and the procedure by which the provisions were brought into force are considered in more detail elsewhere.[34]

---

[20] See Ch. 12, p. 284.
[21] N. 4 above.
[22] Agreement of 22 July 1972 [1973] OJ L350/2.
[23] Agreement of 22 July 1972 [1973] OJ L350/13.
[24] See Ch. 20, p. 383.
[25] Agreement of 26 Apr. 1976 [1978] OJ L263/119.
[26] Agreement of 27 Apr. 1976 [1978] OJ L264/119.
[27] Agreement of 25 Apr. 1976 [1978] OJ L265/119.
[28] See Ch. 20, p. 384.
[29] Agreement of 18 Jan. 1977 [1979] OJ L316/2.
[30] Agreement of 18 Jan. 1977 [1979] OJ L316/13.
[31] Agreement of 3 May 1977 [1979] OJ L316/24.
[32] Agreement of 18 Jan. 1977 [1979] OJ L316/35.
[33] [1975] OJ L165/62.
[34] See Ch. 12, p. 286 and p. 402 above.

India

The ECSC is a party to a Protocol dated 23 June 1981 with India.[35]

Slovenia

The ECSC and the Member States are parties to an agreement signed on 5 April 1993[36] concluded in conjunction with the trade and co-operation agreement with that State.[37]

Unilateral Measures

The unilateral measures that are relevant to the subject matter of this Chapter are dealt with elsewhere. In particular, the instruments that are relevant to the commercial policy in respect of coal and steel products are considered in Chapter 20. A number of unilateral measures have been adopted in the context of sanctions. These are considered in Chapter 19.

---

[35] [1981] OJ L352/28.   [36] [1993] OJ L287/1.   [37] See Ch. 12, p. 287.

PART III

The Common Foreign and Security Policy

The common foreign and security policy of the European Union is governed not by the Community Treaties but by a distinct part of the Treaty on European Union. Although it is carried on within a separate legal framework, and involves no Community legal instruments or procedures, the common foreign and security policy is often closely related to the conduct of the external relations of the Communities. This Part outlines the legal framework and procedures established by the Treaty on European Union for the development of the common foreign and security policy.

24

The Common Foreign and Security Policy

The Member States of the European Communities have for many years co-operated in the sphere of foreign policy, beyond and outside the scope of the Community Treaties.[1] In a report by the Foreign Ministers, adopted in Luxembourg on 27 October 1970, the Member States undertook to co-operate in the field of foreign policy by consulting regularly, harmonizing views, concerting attitudes, and, where possible, undertaking joint action. The process, known as political co-operation, was carried out at three levels: Heads of State or Government, Foreign Ministers, and senior officials in a 'Political Committee'. It was a purely intergovernmental process, which took place outside the Community institutions but without affecting their responsibilities. It resulted in agreed declarations of policy, common negotiating positions, and co-ordination at international conferences and organizations, some common action, and co-operation on the ground between the Member States' overseas missions.[2] The purpose was to enhance the influence of the Member States on the international stage.

As political co-operation grew, the insulation from the Community institutions diminished. Foreign Ministers often met for political co-operation, not in capitals, but in Brussels when they were there for Councils. The Commission was increasingly invited to attend political co-operation meetings, and the European Parliament was briefed and informed more regularly. But political co-operation remained an intergovernmental process, not a Community one.

The process was put on a more formal basis in the Single European Act in 1986. Title III, consisting of Article 30, set out a framework for 'European Political Co-operation' (EPC), and for the first time gave the process a Treaty foundation. Foreign policy co-operation was thus thereafter carried out by the Member States subject to the rights and duties, binding in international law, flowing from Title III. The scope of EPC was, according to Article 30(2)(a), 'any foreign policy matters of general interest'. The degree of commitment was not particularly strong in terms of treaty language: for example, 'the determination of common positions shall constitute a point of reference for the policies of the

---

[1] There is much literature on the subject. For a recent historical survey in English, which contains an extensive bibliography, see Nuttall, *European Political Co-operation* (Clarendon Press, 1992). The classic work is de Schoutheete, *La Coopération politique européenne* (2nd edn., Paris, 1986).

[2] Most EPC declarations and public documents from 1970 onwards are contained in the monthly *Bull.* of the EC. The practice has been continued since the CFSP succeeded EPC in November 1993. EPC and CFSP developments have also been reported in the Commission's annual *General Report*.

High Contracting Parties', and 'the High Contracting Parties shall endeavour to avoid any action or position which impairs their effectiveness as a cohesive force in international relations or within international organizations'.[3]

In the structure of the Single European Act, Title III was clearly separated from the provisions of the Act which amended or related to the Community Treaties. EPC, pursuant to Title III, remained an intergovernmental process governed by international law, and not by Community law. While the Commission and the Parliament continued to have a limited role,[4] none of the Community institutions had any powers in the process. The jurisdiction of the European Court of Justice in relation to Title III was expressly excluded.[5] EPC was carried out by and between the High Contracting Parties (the Member States), assisted by a distinct international Secretariat. Meetings continued to be held by Foreign Ministers, often on the occasion of, but in separate format from, meetings of the Council, and they were, as before, prepared by the Political Committee. Decision-making continued to be by consensus.[6] Article 30(5) required the external policies of the European Communities and the policies agreed in EPC to be consistent, and gave the Presidency and the Commission special responsibility for ensuring that such consistency was sought and maintained.

In 1992, the TEU took matters a stage further. Article P(2) of that Treaty repealed Title III of the SEA. It was replaced by Title V of that Treaty, entitled 'Provisions on a common foreign and security policy'. Title V sets out a more developed framework within a wider scope, pursuing defined objectives through specific means, and, according to special procedures, involving some of the Community institutions. But the process remains intergovernmental, subject to international law, not Community law. Its product is instruments governed by international law, not Community legislation. The jurisdiction of the European Court of Justice in relation to Title V is expressly excluded by Article L of the Treaty.

The rest of this Chapter is a brief survey of the common foreign and security policy (CFSP) established by Title V of the TEU.[7]

---

[3] Art. 30(2)(c) and (d).

[4] The Commission was to be 'fully associated with the proceedings' of EPC: Art. 30(3)(b). The Parliament was to be 'closely associated' with EPC and regularly informed by the Presidency: Art. 30(4).

[5] Art. 31.

[6] But Art. 30(3) provided that 'the High Contracting Parties shall, as far as possible, refrain from impeding the formation of a consensus and the joint action which this could produce'.

[7] On the CFSP, see articles by M. R. Eaton ('Common Foreign and Security Policy'), N. Neuwahl ('Foreign and Security Policy and the Implementation of the Requirement of "Consistency" under the Treaty on European Union'), and M. Cremona ('The Common Foreign and Security Policy of the European Union and the External Relations Powers of the European Community'), all in D. O'Keeffe and Twomey (eds.), *Legal Issues of the Maastricht Treaty* (Chancery Law Publishing, 1994); Fink-Hooijer, 'The Common Foreign and Security Policy' (1994) 5 *EJIL* 173.

As explained in Chapter 1, the Treaty establishes a European Union founded on three distinct elements (or 'pillars'): the European Communities, the common foreign and security policy, and co-operation in the fields of justice and home affairs. The Treaty structure reflects this distinction. Titles II, III, and IV set out a series of amendments to the three Community Treaties. Title V deals with CFSP. Title VI deals with justice and home affairs co-operation. Title I (Common provisions) and Title VII (Final provisions) relate both to the Community provisions and to the intergovernmental provisions in Titles V and VI.

One of the Union's objectives, according to Article B, is 'to assert its identity on the international scene, in particular through the implementation of a common foreign and security policy including the eventual framing of a common defence policy, which might in time lead to a common defence'; and 'the objectives of the Union shall be achieved as provided in this Treaty and in accordance with the conditions and the timetable set out therein'.

Article C provides that the Union shall be served by a single institutional framework 'which shall ensure the consistency and the continuity of the activities carried out in order to attain its objectives'. It continues:

The Union shall in particular ensure the consistency of its external activities as a whole in the context of its external relations, security, economic and development policies. The Council and the Commission shall be responsible for ensuring such consistency. They shall ensure the implementation of these policies, each in accordance with its respective powers.

The 'single institutional framework' is explained in Article E. This provides:

The European Parliament, the Council, the Commission and the Court of Justice shall exercise their powers under the conditions and for the purposes provided for, on the one hand, by the provisions of the Treaties establishing the European Communities and of the subsequent Treaties and Acts modifying or supplementing them and, on the other hand, by the other provisions of this Treaty.

This draws a careful and deliberate distinction between the exercise of these institutions' powers according to whether they are acting under the Community Treaties or under 'the other provisions of' the TEU. These 'other provisions' are, principally, Titles V and VI. Under Title V, the Council is the main forum for decision-making. By contrast, the Commission and the European Parliament have a limited role and no decisive powers. None of these three institutions may act on CFSP matters pursuant to the Community Treaties; they can only exercise the powers, according to the special procedures, stipulated in Title V. The Court of Justice has no jurisdiction at all in relation to Title V.

The Treaty deals expressly with the potential overlap between CFSP and the powers and activities of the Communities. Article M provides that, subject to the Treaty's provisions amending the Community Treaties and to its final provisions, 'nothing in this Treaty shall affect the Treaties establishing the European Communities or the subsequent Treaties and Acts modifying or supplementing them'. This preserves the Communities from encroachment by action under CFSP. Action which, according to the Community Treaties and Community law, can only be taken by the Communities may not be carried out under CFSP. The Court of Justice has jurisdiction to determine this boundary, since by virtue of Article L it has jurisdiction in relation to Article M.

THE SCOPE OF THE COMMON FOREIGN AND SECURITY POLICY

Title V of the Treaty consists of twelve Articles, Articles J–J.11. Article J states simply: '[a] common foreign and security policy is hereby established which shall be governed by the following provisions.' So CFSP is a matter for Title V, and not for the Community Treaties. This is emphasized in Article J.1, which begins: '[t]he Union and its Member States shall define and implement a common foreign and security policy, governed by the provisions of this Title and covering all areas of foreign and security policy.'.

The potential scope for CFSP action is therefore extremely wide: 'all areas of foreign and security policy'. It is for the Union and its Member States to define and carry it out, in accordance with the framework established in Title V. Article J.2(2) sets out some broad objectives of CFSP: to safeguard the common values, fundamental interests, and independence of the Union; to strengthen the security of the Union and its Member States in all ways; to preserve peace and strengthen international security, in accordance with the principles of the United Nations Charter and the Helsinki Final Act and the objectives of the Paris Charter; to promote international co-operation; and to develop and consolidate democracy and the rule of law, and respect for human rights and fundamental freedoms. Article J.1(3) requires the Union to pursue these objectives by establishing systematic co-operation between Member States in the conduct of policy, in accordance with Article J.2; and by gradually implementing, in accordance with Article J.3, joint action in the areas in which the Member States have important interests in common.[8]

The CFSP is therefore a dynamic process. It is to be built up and given specific content gradually, in the pursuit of defined objectives through co-operation and joint action, within a potentially broad scope. Its precise scope and content

---

[8] References to 'the Union' implementing CFSP might appear confusing. Since the Union has no legal personality (see Ch. 1) it can only act through its components, the Communities and the Member States. Although agreed political CFSP statements are commonly made in the name of the Union, any international agreements or other acts having legal consequences in pursuit of CFSP (as opposed to the EC Treaties) have to be concluded by the Member States.

are constantly changing, and overall are likely to expand as the Member States achieve agreement in increasing areas of foreign policy. The Treaty imposes a parallel obligation on the Member States to support CFSP as it develops. Article J.1(4) provides:

The Member States shall support the Union's external and security policy actively and unreservedly in a spirit of loyalty and mutual solidarity. They shall refrain from any action which is contrary to the interests of the Union or likely to impair its effectiveness as a cohesive force in international relations. The Council shall ensure that these principles are complied with.

Article J.4 contains special provisions relating to security policy and approaches, in cautious and anticipatory language, the sensitive question of defence policy. Article J.4(1) states: '[t]he common foreign and security policy shall include all questions related to the security of the Union, including the eventual framing of a common defence policy, which might in time lead to a common defence.' The Western European Union (WEU) is requested to elaborate and implement decisions and actions of the Union which have defence implications; and the Council, in agreement with the WEU institutions, is to adopt the necessary practical arrangements.[9] Issues having defence implications dealt with under Article J.4 are excluded from the procedures concerning joint actions in Article J.3. There are two important and express safeguards. First, the CFSP must be compatible with the security and defence policy established within the framework of the NATO Treaty and must respect the obligations of certain Member States under that Treaty.[10] Secondly, closer co-operation between two or more Member States in the framework of the WEU and NATO is not ruled out, provided it does not run counter to or impede the co-operation provided for in Title V.[11] Article J.4 is subject to specific review at the 1996 Intergovernmental Conference provided for in Article N.2.

The potentially wide scope of CFSP has inevitably raised questions about the borderline between Title V and the Community Treaties. This arises most often in the sphere of external economic policy, in respect of which the Communities have extensive, and in some matters exclusive, competence. At first sight it might appear that a CFSP covering 'all areas of foreign and security policy' would be incompatible with that.

[9] In two declarations noted by the Maastricht Intergovernmental Conference and contained in its Final Act, the Member States which were WEU members stated their objective of strengthening the WEU in stages and that it would be developed as the defence component of the EU and as a means to strengthen the European pillar of NATO; and they invited the Member States which were not WEU members—Denmark, Greece, and Ireland—to accede to the WEU or to become observers. Greece was in the process of acceding at the time of writing. Pursuant to the dec. on Denmark agreed at the Edinburgh European Council in Dec. 1992, Denmark does not participate in the elaboration or implementation of Union action in the sphere of defence ([1992] OJ C 348/1).

[10] The reference to 'certain Member States' takes particular account of Member States which are not members of NATO (Ireland and, since their accession, Austria, Finland, and Sweden).

[11] This takes account, e.g., of arrangements such as the European Corps, composed of French, German, and Belgian troops.

There is no express exclusion of economic aspects of foreign policy, or indeed of any matters which fall within the competence of the Communities. Indeed, Article C expressly enjoins the Council and the Commission, within the single institutional framework, to ensure the consistency of the Union's external activities as a whole in the context of its external relations, security, economic and development policies. The object is plainly a consistent and coherent external policy of the Union, whether acting through its Communities component or through its Member States. A comprehensive foreign policy in relation to a non-member country cannot ignore the economic dimension. The Treaty permits this to be done in the context of CFSP, and a common position or joint action under Title V may refer to economic or other elements of an overall policy which would or might require implementation under the Community Treaties.[12] But a Title V instrument may not itself take legislative or executive action which could only lawfully be taken under the Community Treaties; nor can it legally bind the Communities or their institutions acting in accordance with the powers conferred on them by the Community Treaties. This follows from the express preservation of the Community Treaties in Article M.

In one area, economic sanctions, the EC Treaty expressly envisages CFSP action followed by, or in combination with, Community measures.[13] Article 228a provides that, where a CFSP common position or joint action provides 'for an action by the Community to interrupt or to reduce, in part or completely, economic relations with one or more third countries, the Council shall take the necessary urgent measures'. This procedure has been used several times, in particular in response to United Nations Security Council Resolutions, the usual form being a Council Decision on a CFSP common position accompanied by a (separate) Council Regulation containing the necessary Community legislation. Article 73g of the EC Treaty provides a specific legal basis for such action in relation to capital movements and payments.

MEANS OF ACTION

Information, Consultation, and Common Positions

Article J.2 consolidates the form of co-operation, resulting in common positions, which was the traditional work of EPC. But it does so in more mandatory terms. Member States 'shall inform and consult one another within the Council on any matter of foreign and security policy of general interest in order to ensure that their combined influence is exerted as effectively as possible by means of concerted and convergent action'. Article J.2 continues: 'whenever it deems it nec-

---

[12] See, e.g., the common positions in relation to Rwanda (94/697/CFSP: [1994] OJ L283/1) and Ukraine (94/779/CFSP: [1994] OJ L313/1).

[13] See further Ch. 19.

essary, the Council shall define a common position.' Member States are then expressly obliged to ensure that their national policies conform to the common positions; to co-ordinate their action in international organizations and at international conferences; and to uphold the common positions in such fora.

The Member States have continued the EPC practice of adopting agreed statements in the field of foreign policy, usually in the name of the European Union, and most often on the occasion of meetings of the Foreign Affairs Council or of the European Council. These political declarations might loosely be described as 'common positions', and in some circumstances they might trigger the general obligation of support and solidarity in Article J.1(4). But they should be distinguished from the formal type of common position envisaged by Article J.2(2), which in practice has taken the legal form of a Council decision *sui generis* ('Beschluß').[14] Such decisions are adopted, in accordance with Article J.8(2), by unanimity. They are not Community law decisions, for example in the sense of Article 189 of the EC Treaty. But, as a matter of international law, they can impose specific obligations on the Member States and, as noted above, they produce for the Member States the duties of compliance and support set out in Article J.2 itself. Some such decisions have had limited scope, dealing with economic sanctions against a particular State or territory;[15] others have addressed broader policy objectives in relation to a given country.[16]

Joint Action

In a development going beyond traditional EPC practice, Article J.3 sets out in detail the procedure for adopting joint action in matters covered by CFSP. The Council is to decide, on the basis of general guidelines from the European Council, that a matter should be the subject of joint action. This is a rare specific example of the Treaty subjecting action to guidance from the European Council, which therefore sets, at the highest level, the general political framework for CFSP joint action. The decision of the Council that a matter should be the subject of joint action is taken, in accordance with Article J.8(2), by unanimity. Whenever the Council decides on the principle of joint action, it must also, again by unanimity, lay down the specific scope, the Union's general and specific objectives in carrying out such action, if necessary its duration, and the means, procedures, and conditions for its implementation. The Council may,

[14] See Ch. 1 on the Beschluß form. They are given a number followed by the letters 'CFSP', e.g. 94/276/CFSP ([1994] OJ L119/1), and are published in a separate section of the Official Journal, 'L' series.

[15] See e.g. Council Decs. 93/614/CFSP concerning Libya ([1993] OJ L295/7), 94/165/CFSP concerning Sudan ([1994] OJ L75/1), 94/315/CFSP concerning Haiti ([1994] OJ L139/10), and 94//672/CFSP concerning those parts of the territory of the Republic of Bosnia-Herzegovina under the control of the Bosnian Serb forces ([1994] OJ L266/10).

[16] See Council Decs. 94/697/CFSP on Rwanda, and 94/779/CFSP on Ukraine, both n. 12 above.

by unanimity, determine that some or all implementing measures shall be decided by qualified majority voting.[17]

Once a joint action is adopted by the Council, Member States are committed to it in the conduct of their foreign policy. Article J.3(4) provides: '[j]oint actions shall commit the Member States in the positions they adopt and in the conduct of their activity.' Incompatible unilateral action by a Member State is therefore in principle ruled out. But there are important safeguards. Article J.3(6) allows Member States, in cases of imperative need arising from changes in the situation and failing a Council decision, to take the necessary measures as a matter of urgency having regard to the general objectives of the joint action, and provided they inform the Council immediately of any such measures. Article J.3(3) requires the Council to review joint actions if circumstances change. Under Article J.3(7) the Council must seek appropriate solutions for any Member State which has major difficulties in implementing a joint action.

A further safeguard is offered by a Conference declaration included in the Maastricht Final Act concerning certain dependent territories of Member States. The Conference agreed that where divergences arise between the interests of the Union and those of dependent territories, and if the Council fails to reach a solution, the Member State concerned may act separately in the interests of its dependent territory, without this affecting the Community's interests. The declaration applies to the overseas countries and territories referred to in Article 227(3) and (5)(a) and (b) of the EC Treaty, and to Macao and East Timor. Its application is not in terms confined to CFSP, but it might need to be invoked in that context.

As with common positions formally adopted under Article J.2, joint actions agreed pursuant to Article J.3 take the legal form of Council decisions *sui generis*, which are governed by and have effect in international law.[18] Joint actions have been used for a variety of purposes, ranging from support for the Middle East peace process,[19] the transition to democracy in South Africa,[20] election monitoring in Russia,[21] and the convoying of humanitarian aid in Bosnia-Herzegovina,[22] to the preparation of the 1995 Conference of States Party to the Treaty on Non-Proliferation of Nuclear Weapons.[23]

---

[17] For this purpose the votes of the Member States are weighted in accordance with Art. 148(2) EC and, for their adoption, acts of the Council require at least 62 votes in favour, cast by at least 10 members: Art. J.3(2).

[18] See p. 417 above, and n. 14.　　　　　　[19] Council Dec. 94/276/CFSP, n. 14 above.

[20] Council Dec. 93/678/CFSP ([1993] OJ L316/45).

[21] Council Dec. 93/604/CFSP ([1993] OJ L286/3).

[22] Council Decs. 93/603/CFSP ([1993] OJ L286/1), 93/729/CFSP ([1993] OJ L339/3), 94/158/CFSP ([1994] OJ L70/1), 94/308/CFSP ([1994] OJ L134/1), and 94/510/CFSP ([1994] OJ L205/3).

[23] Council Dec. 94/509/CFSP ([1994] OJ L205/1).

Representation

Article J.5(1) continues the EPC rule that the Presidency represents the Union in matters coming within CFSP.[24] According to Article J.5(2) the Presidency is responsible for the implementation of common measures; and 'in that capacity it shall in principle express the position of the Union in international organizations and international conferences'. Article J.5(3) continues that, in performing these tasks, the Presidency 'shall be assisted if need be' by the previous and next Member State to hold the Presidency (the system known as the 'troika'); and that the Commission is to be fully associated with these tasks. Accordingly, by contrast with the Commission's representative role in the Communities' external relations, it is the Presidency which has the pre-eminent responsibility in CFSP. The troika system can add extra weight and authority, and enables experience to be gained from the previous Presidency and by the succeeding one, as well as sharing the burden (which might be especially helpful for smaller Member States). The Commission's role is as an associate.

Article J.5(4) makes special provision for international organizations and conferences where not all Member States participate. Member States which are represented in such fora must keep the others informed of any matter of common interest (and, in accordance with Article J.2(3), they must uphold the common positions adopted by the Council). Member States which are also members of the United Nations Security Council 'will concert and keep the other Member States fully informed'. Member States which are permanent members of the Security Council[25] commit themselves to ensure the defence of the positions and interests of the Union, but 'without prejudice to their responsibilities under the provisions of the United Nations Charter'. These provisions reflect long-standing practice, and the important proviso explicitly recognizes the special position under the Charter of permanent members of the Security Council, which has primary responsibility for the maintenance of international peace and security.[26]

Co-operation on the Ground

Article J.6 requires the diplomatic and consular missions of the Member States and the Commission delegations in third countries and to international conferences, and their representations to international organizations, to co-operate in ensuring that the common positions and common measures adopted by the

---

[24] Representation *vis-à-vis* the outside world could involve the Presidency being legally authorized by the Member States to conclude on their behalf international agreements on CFSP matters.

[25] They are not named. Only the UK and France were permanent members when the TEU was signed, as is the case at the time of writing, but the situation might change.

[26] In any case, if any incompatibility should arise between a Member State's obligations under the Treaty and those under the UN Charter, the latter must prevail by virtue of Art. 103 of the Charter.

Council are complied with and implemented. They are to increase co-operation by exchanging information, carrying out joint assessments, and contributing to the implementation of Article 8c of the EC Treaty (which provides for diplomatic and consular protection by Member States represented in a third country of Union citizens whose State of nationality is unrepresented there). These provisions largely reflect and build on a long-established practice of co-operation on the ground, which is particularly intensive in international organizations and at international conferences. Indeed the Member States have begun to go further by establishing mission-sharing facilities, for example at Ajuba in Nigeria and in some of the Republics of the former Soviet Union.

THE INSTITUTIONAL FRAMEWORK

In accordance with the Union's single institutional framework, as established in Articles C and E of the TEU, some of the Community institutions have a role in CFSP. Their powers and functions in this regard are laid down in Title V. Furthermore the European Council, which is not a Community institution and which is provided for in Article D, is given an explicit and important part to play.

The European Council

Article J.8(1) provides that the European Council shall define the principles of and general guidelines for the common foreign and security policy. Thus the political direction of CFSP is assured at the highest level, and in practice foreign policy forms a substantial part of the agenda of each summit, as it has done for many years. Successive European Councils continue to issue statements and declarations on various foreign policy matters.[27] In accordance with Article J.8(2), the Council is to take the decisions necessary for defining and implementing the CFSP on the basis of the general guidelines adopted by the European Council. Moreover, as noted above in the discussion of joint actions, Article J.3(1) is a specific application of this general rule; it provides that, in deciding whether a matter should be the subject of joint action, the Council must act on the basis of general guidelines from the European Council.

The Council

Subject to the overall direction of the European Council, the leading institutional role in the operation of CFSP is played by the Council. In practice this means the Council composed of Foreign Ministers (the Foreign Affairs Council

---

[27] These can be found in editions of the Bull. EC reporting meetings of the European Council.

or, more correctly, the General Affairs Council), although since the Council is constitutionally indivisible the Council in any of its compositions could in theory do CFSP business. It is the Council which, under Article J.8(2), has the power to take the 'decisions necessary for defining and implementing' CFSP, and the duty to 'ensure the unity, consistency and effectiveness of action by the Union'. It is the Council which has the power, under Article J.2(2), to define common positions and, under Article J.3, to decide on joint action. Article J.8(2) also provides that the Council 'shall act unanimously,[28] except for procedural questions and in the case referred to in Article J.3(2)'. Procedural questions, in accordance with the Council's Rules of Procedure,[29] are decided by simple majority. The case referred to in Article J.3(2) is the possibility of measures implementing a joint action being decided by qualified majority,[30] but the decision providing for resort to that possibility must itself be taken by unanimity.

Article J.8(3) provides that any Member State or the Commission may refer to the Council any question relating to CFSP and may submit proposals to the Council. Accordingly, each of the Member States and the Commission has an equal right of initiative for CFSP action in the Council.

Article J.8(4) acknowledges the possible need for urgency. In cases requiring a rapid decision, the Presidency is to convene an extraordinary Council meeting within forty-eight hours or, in an emergency, within a shorter period. It may do so of its own motion or at the request of the Commission or a Member State. Meetings can therefore be called at short notice between the regular monthly meetings of the Foreign Affairs Council. There is also provision in the Council's Rules of Procedure for decisions to be taken rapidly by a written procedure, using the 'Coreu' telegraphic system which links the Member States, the Council Secretariat and the Commission.[31]

Article J.8(5) deals with the machinery at official level to prepare the work of the Council. It establishes a committee of senior officials, reflecting the former EPC practice. It is called the Political Committee and is composed of Political Directors (senior Foreign Ministry officials). Its function is 'to monitor the international situation in the areas covered by common foreign and security policy and contribute to the definition of policies by delivering opinions to the Council at the request of the Council or on its own initiative'. It must also 'monitor the implementation of agreed policies, without prejudice to the responsibility of the Presidency and the Commission'. All this is stated to be without prejudice to Article 151 EC, the effect of which is to preserve the responsibility of COREPER to prepare the business of the Council and to carry out the tasks assigned to it by the Council.

---

[28] In a declaration contained in the Maastricht Final Act, the Conference agreed that, with regard to Council decisions requiring unanimity, Member States will, to the extent possible, avoid preventing a unanimous decision where a qualified majority exists in favour of that decision.

[29] Council Dec. 93/662/EC ([1993] OJ L304/1).

[30] As defined in Art. J.3(2): see n. 17 above.

[31] Art. 8(4).

In practice the detailed work on CFSP business is done in Council working groups of officials representing the Member States, which report to the Political Committee. The Political Committee meets before and sometimes in the margins of Council meetings. The involvement of COREPER helps the Council to ensure coherence between CFSP and Community action. At all levels the General Secretariat of the Council and its Legal Service are present and available to provide assistance and independent advice.

The Commission

The Commission also attends meetings at all levels. Article J.9 provides that the Commission 'shall be fully associated with the work carried out in the common foreign and security policy field' (as it was with EPC). The Commission is given an explicit but shared right of initiative by Article J.8(3); and it is to be 'fully associated' with the Presidency's representative and implementing tasks by virtue of Article J.5(3). But it is not a participant in the process on the same footing as the Member States. It can have influence but no vote in Council decision-making, and its proposals carry no special weight.[32] With the Council itself, the Commission has a special duty under Article C to ensure consistency between CFSP and Community action. The Commission has in relation to CFSP nothing equivalent to its powers under the Community Treaties to monitor and police compliance with Community law.[33]

The European Parliament

The role of the European Parliament in relation to CFSP is described in Article J.7. The Presidency is to consult the Parliament on 'the main aspects and the basic choices' of CFSP and ensure that the views of the Parliament 'are duly taken into consideration'. The Parliament's views are therefore not binding on the Council, and there is no requirement to consult the Parliament systematically before the Council decides on common positions or joint actions. Article J.7 also requires the Presidency and the Commission to keep the Parliament regularly informed of the development of the Union's foreign and security policy. This is done both by written communications and by regular appearances before the plenary and the responsible committees of the Parliament. Finally, Article J.7 expressly enables the Parliament to ask questions of the Council or make recommendations to it; and the Parliament is to hold an annual debate on progress in implementing CFSP.

---

[32] Contrast the position under the EC Treaty, where unanimity is normally required to amend a Commission proposal: see Art. 189a(1).

[33] See, e.g., Arts. 155 and 169 EC.

Functioning and Financing

Article J.11(1) imports into Title V a number of provisions of the EC Treaty relating to the functioning of the Parliament, the Council, and the Commission. These do not include provisions conferring important powers on these institutions under the EC Treaty.[34]

Article J.11(2) deals with financing of CFSP. Administrative expenditure which the provisions relating to CFSP entail for the institutions are charged to the budget of the European Communities. For operational expenditure occasioned by CFSP action, the Council has a choice. Either it may decide unanimously that such expenditure is to be charged to the budget of the European Communities, in which case the budgetary procedure laid down in the EC Treaty is applicable;[35] or it may determine that such expenditure shall be charged to the Member States, where appropriate in accordance with a scale to be decided. The Council has in practice resorted to both options, and it has usually made specific provision regarding financing in the decision concerning the joint action in question.[36] At the time of writing, the Council had not adopted any general decision regarding the financing of CFSP.

The Court of Auditors and the Court of Justice

Two of the Community institutions listed in Article 4 of the EC Treaty have no express role under Title V. One is the Court of Auditors, but by virtue of its powers under the Community Treaties[37] in relation to Community expenditure, it is involved in so far as CFSP operational expenditure is charged to the Community budget. The other is the Court of Justice, the jurisdiction of which in respect of Title V is excluded by Article L. This is not to say that it cannot take account or notice of CFSP instruments; it may need to do so, for example, in the context of considering Community legislation on sanctions adopted under Article 228a or 73g of the EC Treaty. It might also be called upon to do so in exercising its jurisdiction to determine the bounds of Community competence or, put another way, to ensure the preservation of the Community Treaties pursuant to Article M.

The absence of jurisdiction of the Court of Justice to enforce the CFSP does not of course mean that Title V is any less binding on the Member States as a

---

[34] In particular, among the provisions *not* imported are Arts. 138b (EP powers in the legislative process), 138c (EP committees of inquiry), 138d (petitions to EP), 138e (Ombudsman), 145 (Council powers, including delegation of implementing powers to Commission), 148 (Council decision making), and 155 (Commission powers).

[35] In particular Arts. 199–209 EC.

[36] See, e.g., Council decs. 94/308/CFSP, n. 22 above; 94/510/CFSP, n. 22 above; 93/678/CFSP, n. 20 above; 94/276/CFSP, n. 19 above.

[37] Arts. 188a–188c and 206 EC. The Court of Auditors has also been invited to audit non-Community budget accounts: see e.g. Council Dec. 94/308/CFSP, n. 22 above.

matter of international law. The fundamental rule *pacta sunt servanda*[38] applies irrespective of the availability of an international tribunal to settle disputes to which a treaty may give rise. The same applies to any agreements or decisions reached by the Member States in implementing Title V which may give rise to legal rights and obligations, since these, too, are governed by international law. The International Court of Justice would be available if necessary, to the extent that Member States had reciprocally accepted its jurisdiction; and it would be open to Member States, by agreement, to submit a dispute to arbitration or another form of settlement. It is more likely, however, that the Member States will continue to settle their differences politically by discussion and negotiation within the Council, which is given general responsibility for ensuring compliance by Article J.1(4).

REVIEW

Article N(2) of the Maastricht Treaty provides that an Intergovernmental Conference of the Member States shall be convened in 1996 to examine those provisions of the Treaty for which revision is provided, in accordance with the objectives set out in Articles A and B.

Article J.4(6) provides that the provisions of Article J.4 may be revised as provided for in Article N(2) on the basis of a report to be presented in 1996 by the Council to the European Council, which shall include an evaluation of the progress made and the experience gained hitherto. Article J.10 provides that, on the occasion of any review of the security provisions under Article J.4, the Conference which is convened to that effect shall also examine whether any other amendments need to be made to provisions relating to the common foreign and security policy.

Accordingly, these provisions require the whole of Title V of the Treaty and the operation of CFSP to be reviewed at the Intergovernmental Conference in 1996, but they do not prejudge the outcome.

[38] Codified in the VCLT, Art. 26: 'Every treaty in force is binding upon the parties to it and must be performed by them in good faith'.

Index